# Martin Bronfenbrenner

is Chairman of the Department of Economics in the Graduate School of Industrial Administration of Carnegie-Mellon University. Previously Dr. Bronfenbrenner taught economics at the University of Minnesota, Michigan State University, the University of Wisconsin, and Roosevelt College, as well as in Japan as a visiting scholar. He has served as an economic analyst for the U.S. Treasury, a financial economist for the Federal Reserve Bank of Chicago, a tax economist for SCAP (Tokyo), a consultant for UN-ECAFE (Bangkok), and a visiting fellow at the Center for Advanced Study in Behavioral Sciences. He received his Bachelor of Arts degree from Washington University and his Ph.D. from the University of Chicago. Dr. Bronfenbrenner has also served on the editorial boards of the *American Economic Review* and *Southern Economic Journal,* and has authored or co-authored numerous scholarly papers in both Economics and Japanology.

Thirty-eight social scientists representing fourteen countries have contributed to this discussion of the possible obsolescence of the conventional business cycle. Papers from both capitalist and socialist countries are included. They reflect both qualitative and quantitative methods of research.

The answer to the question "Is the business cycle obsolete?" is, in general, affirmative regarding major depressions, but the case is "not proven" for smaller ones. Several writers suggest that contemporary cycles are "growth cycles," in which economic growth rates oscillate, but seldom fall below zero. Most of the papers deal with the post-1950 experience of individual countries, both capitalist and socialist. An important sub-group of technical papers outlines, compares, and evaluates econometric methods of projecting economic conditions and guiding policy so as to maintain stable full employment conditions.

# Is the Business Cycle Obsolete?

# Is the Business Cycle Obsolete?

*Based on a Conference of the Social Science
Research Council Committee on Economic Stability*

## Martin Bronfenbrenner

*Editor*

Robert Aaron Gordon
Don J. Daly
Miyohei Shinohara
R. C. O. Matthews
J. C. R. Dow
Jørgen H. Gelting
Kurt W. Rothschild
Rudolf R. Rhomberg

Alec Nove
Andrew Bródy
Josef Goldmann
Michael K. Evans and
    Lawrence R. Klein
Bert G. Hickman
Erik Lundberg
P. J. Verdoorn and J. J. Post

Wiley-Interscience A Division of John Wiley & Sons
New York · London · Sydney · Toronto

Library of Congress Catalogue Card Number: 70-82973

SBN 471   10595   3

Printed in the United States of America

# PREFACE

This book is based on a conference on the possible obsolescence of the 10-year business cycle and the various patterns of long-and-short-term fluctuations that have characterized capitalistic economic life. The conference was held at St. Ermin's Hotel, London, on 3–7, April 1967.

The proposal for this conference was made by Professor Lawrence Klein to the Committee on Economic Stability of the Social Science Research Council (SSRC) and much of the preliminary work was done by a subcommittee of that group[1]. The plan was to arrange for a successor to the International Economic Association's Oxford conference of 1952 on the developing postwar business cycle[2]. The subcommittee was most appreciative when Professor Erik Lundberg, who had played a leading role at the 1952 conference, agreed to participate. In London the National Institute of Economic and Social Research, and particularly its director, Mr. G. D. N. Worswick, accepted responsibility for all local arrangements, including mechanical recording and reproduction of the discussion[3]. Additional financial support was provided by the Ford Foundation. Mr. Paul Webbink, Vice-President of the SSRC, provided liaison between the various groups and also handled the financial administration of the conference.

Although the conference itself could not be held until 1967, arrangements were begun in the rather different economic atmosphere of 1964–1965, before the escalation of the Vietnam War. In those complacent days (but in hindsight's eye) the obsolescence of the business cycle in all its forms was a more current, and

---

[1] In addition to Professor Klein, the subcommittee was composed of Professors Robert Aaron Gordon, Bert G. Hickman, and myself.

[2] The papers and proceedings of this Oxford conference were published under the editorship of Professor Lundberg, with the assistance of A. D. Knox, as *The Business Cycle in the Postwar World,* London and New York, 1955.

[3] Messrs. Adam Broadbent and C. H. OHerlihy were selected as conference rapporteurs by Mr. Worswick.

v

less "academic," issue than it became in 1967. To quote one American monetary economist[4]:

> In the gloom of late winter 1968, with the country heavily burdened by an unpopular war, civil disorders, and sagging confidence in the quality of national leadership, it is hard to remember the optimism and pride that ruled America's thinking as recently as two years [before]. The contribution of economics to this modern era of good feeling was the belated achievement of a consensus that the Keynesian New Economics really worked. It was felt that if the policy prescriptions of the New Economics were applied, business cycles as they had been known would be a thing of the past.

Be that as it may, the conference was laid out with a preponderance of "country" papers pertaining to the post-Korean War experience of individual countries or groups of countries. The first group of seven country or regional papers—chapters of the present volume—dealt with North America, Western Europe, and Japan. A single and relatively technical paper considered the problem of transmission of cyclical disturbances between developed and developing countries, primarily *from* the former *to* the latter. The three subsequent papers, on experience under socialist planning, lie at or near the boundary between Eastern European country studies and more general models of fluctuations in an abstract "socialist regime." The conference then proceeded to three econometric papers, which describe dynamic economic models both as subjects of statistical research and as devices for nipping real-world cyclical movements in the bud. One of these papers dealt with the United States, one with the Netherlands, and the third with the international comparison of models from numerous countries and of coefficients derived from them. The final paper, primarily institutional, appraised the general record of anti-cyclical economic policy, which had been treated on a piecemeal basis in all the country papers. Each paper was followed by at least one formal discussion[5] which was thrown open to comments and criticisms from the floor.

From the papers and discussion it became clear that the answer to the basic question, "Is the Business Cycle Obsolete?" would be in the negative except in the sense of strict tidal-type periodicity. At the same time it was suggested that the cycle's character had changed in a number of ways; for example, both the period and amplitude seemed to be decreasing, although neither have yet become clearly smaller than in the 15 to 20 years immediately preceding World War I. Also in many countries the cycle was taking the form of a "growth cycle," meaning that recessions were largely, if not entirely, limited to decelerations in the rates of economic growth; nevertheless, these rates had remained positive

---

[4] Hyman P. Minsky, "The Crunch of 1966 – Model for New Financial Crises"? *Trans-Action* (March 1968), 44 f.
[5] An exception was the paper by Dr. Josef Goldmann. Because of the author's illness, completion was delayed until after the conference had adjourned.

(almost) throughout the years since World War II. A third novelty, discussed in relation to several countries, was the alleged "political cycle," a term introduced into economic literature by Michael Kalecki of Poland[6]. Such a cycle may result when exclusive concern with checking inflation (during booms) produces recessions and when exclusive concern with increasing employment (during recessions) produces inflationary booms. More generally, it arises from the alternation between undue delay in taking appropriate action and undue severity in whatever action is finally taken.

Even in the socialist countries there is some discussion of policy cycles or pseudo-cycles. The conference reacted favorably to the thesis that socialist planning had reduced economic fluctuations to random shocks in the U.S.S.R., if not in the socialist countries as a group. These shocks were sometimes caused by political circumstances (e.g., the death of Stalin) as well as natural ones (e.g., bad weather).[7]

The common theme of the two "dynamic model" papers was that greater reliance by "politicians" on economic "technocrats," particularly on econometric macroeconomists, might soon render the cycle obsolete (even without further development in the models themselves). The "Wharton School" discussion (Professors Evans and Klein) concentrated on the ability of a large-scale dynamic model in tracking, simulation, and policy-suggestion for the relatively free U.S. economy. The "Central Planning Bureau" discussion (Professors Verdoorn and Post) assigned to the economic-planning mechanism of the Netherlands a considerable amount of the credit for that country's postwar stability, when compared with the interwar period. By the reckoning of this discussion, the effect of external shocks on the Dutch economy had, if anything, been more severe in the later period.

In summarizing the oral discussion, we have departed from usual practice in two principal ways.

1. We have included brief summaries of both the main presentations and the critiques as made orally. Our reason for doing this is that the subsequent discussion sometimes owed more to the emphases of these oral presentations than to the full papers.

2. We have preserved the anonymity of individual discussants from the floor. This change has been made reluctantly, at the urging of several nonacademic participants who did not wish their own views to embarrass the agencies with which they were affiliated. Discussants from the floor are therefore identified

---

[6] Kalecki, "Political Aspects of Full Employment," *Political Quarterly* (October 1943). For an assessment see Joan Robinson, "Kalecki and Keynes," *Problems of Economics Dynamics and Planning* (Warsaw, 1964), p. 340.

only as "the first participant," "the next participant," and so on. Of course, "the first participant" in one discussion need not be "the first participant" in any other one.

The main thread of controversy running through the discussion from the floor was not, as anticipated, the issue of capitalism *versus* socialism, nor yet of more *versus* less governmental planning and control. Rather it was one of methodology, between the quantitative econometricians and those with less faith in the stability or usefulness for the future of statistical uniformities observed in the past. (The latter group, however, were not necessarily anti-planning; rather their position was that the quantitative approach was a partial, incomplete, and sometimes misleading basis for planning.)

Certain important threads of agreement ran through the discussion, marking the attenuation of ideological extremism. It was generally agreed that another catastrophe of the 1929–1933 type is, if not impossible, conceivable only by an extraordinary combination of erroneous policies. It was also agreed, at least tacitly, that maintenance of a high degree of stability was entirely compatible with a basically capitalistic economic organization and that the most mature socialist country had succeeded in making itself cycle-free. (One wonders whether an all-Western, or all-socialist, congress of specialists would have achieved equal measures of agreement on both propositions.)

Other important areas of agreement underlying the conference discussion, although common to business-cycle specialists, were discipline-bound in the sense, say, that monetary theorists or welfare economists might register a higher proportion of dissent; for example, no participant suggested that growth and stability might involve unacceptably high costs in price inflation or in direct controls over economic activity. The cases for limiting planning to the economic aggregates, for alternative theoretical frameworks to the Keynesian one, for monetary rather than fiscal policy as the major vehicle of economic stabilization, for monetary or fiscal "rules," as against "authorities," and for sacrificing stability to technical progress were expressed infrequently, gingerly, and sometimes not at all. This does not imply a "packed" conference; these viewpoints are part of the profesional armory of specialists in business-cycles economics or stabilization policy. To quote the Rudyard Kipling of *Just So Stories*, "That is the way python-coloured rock snakes always talk."

One of our participants, Dr. Stanislav Menshikov, published in 1967 his own account of the papers and proceedings and expressed the opinion that (from a Marxist viewpoint) it was our title, rather than the cycle itself, that was obsolete. Menshikov's summary (in Russian) may be found in the August 1967 issue of *Mirovaya Ekonomika i Mezdunarodniya Otnosheniya*. An abridged German translation, entitled "Ist der ökonomische Zyklus überholt?" is also available (*Sowjetwissenschaft, Gesellschaftswissenschaftliche Beiträge*, 1968, no. 3).

There were nearly 40 participants present at the conference sessions. The following list includes those authors and co-authors who were present in spirit but unable to attend either because of other professional commitments or illness.

| | |
|---|---|
| F. T. Blackaby | National Institute of Economic and Social Research, London |
| Adam Broadbent | National Institute of Economic and Social Research, London |
| Andrew Bródy | Hungarian Academy of Sciences, Budapest |
| Martin Bronfenbrenner | Carnegie-Mellon University, Pittsburgh |
| Donald J. Daly | Economic Council of Canada, Ottawa |
| Peter A. de Janosi | Ford Foundation, New York |
| Michael K. Evans | University of Pennsylvania, Philadelphia |
| P. de Wolff | University of Amsterdam |
| J. C. R. Dow | OECD, Paris |
| Karl A. Fox | Iowa State University, Ames |
| Jørgen H. Gelting | University of Aarhus |
| Josef Goldmann | Czechoslovak Academy of Sciences, Prague |
| Robert A. Gordon | University of California, Berkeley |
| Henri Guitton | University of Paris |
| Bert G. Hickman | Stanford University |
| Harry G. Johnson | London School of Economics and University of Chicago |
| Lawrence R. Klein | University of Pennsylvania, Philadelphia |
| Herbert S. Levine | University of Pennsylvania, Philadelphia |
| Erik Lundberg | Stockholm School of Economics |
| Angus Maddison | Twentieth Century Fund, Paris |
| R. C. O. Matthews | Oxford University |
| Stanislav M. Menshikov | Institute of World Economy and International Relations, Moscow |
| F. J. M. Meyer zu Schlochtern | OECD, Paris |
| Geoffrey H. Moore | National Bureau of Economic Research, New York |
| Jürg Niehans | Johns Hopkins University, Baltimore |
| Alec Nove | University of Glasgow |
| C. J. OHerlihy | Cambridge University |
| Richard Portes | Oxford University |
| J. J. Post | Central Planning Bureau, The Hague |
| Paul Nørregaard Rasmussen | University of Copenhagen |
| Rudolf R. Rhomberg | International Monetary Fund, Washington |
| Gideon Rosenbluth | University of British Columbia, Vancouver |

| | |
|---|---|
| Kurt W. Rothschild | Institute of Economics and Politics, Linz |
| Francis Seton | Oxford University |
| Miyohei Shinohara | Hitotsubashi University, Tokyo |
| Luigi Spaventa | University of Perugia |
| Max Steuer | London School of Economics |
| P. J. Verdoorn | Central Planning Bureau, The Hague |
| Paul Webbink | Social Science Research Council, New York |
| G. D. N. Worswick | National Institute of Economic and |
| | Social Research, London |

Miss Dorothy Wescott of Washington, D.C., has introduced a substantial modicum of readability into the English prose of many of the foreign-language participants and of certain others addicted to jargon and higher mathematics. Mrs. Mary Jo McClure, of Carnegie-Mellon University in Pittsburgh risked her eyesight to reduce many illegible interlineations and faded photocopies to a form fit for further processing. Toshihisa Toyoda, also of Carnegie-Mellon University (on leave from Kobe University) assisted in proof-reading and indexing.

*Pittsburgh, Pennsylvania*                                    Martin Bronfenbrenner

# CONTENTS

---

\* Written comments not received for inclusion in this volume.

# Is the Business Cycle Obsolete?

# I  THE EXPERIENCE OF THE WESTERN WORLD AND JAPAN

Chapter One

# THE STABILITY OF THE U.S. ECONOMY

R. A. GORDON
University of California (Berkeley)

In view of the title chosen for this conference, this chapter should perhaps be called "Is the Business Cycle Obsolete in the United States?" The question leads me to counter with two of my own: (a) What is meant by "the business cycle" in this context? (b) What, precisely, are the implications of the word "obsolete"? [1]

## Some Problems of Definition

How should the business cycle be defined for the purposes of this discussion? I believe I reflected a general consensus when I once defined it as consisting of "recurring alternations of expansion and contraction in aggregate economic activity, the alternating movements in each direction being self-reinforcing and pervading virtually all parts of the economy" [2]. This is not very different from the widely cited definition offered by W. C. Mitchell and A. F. Burns in *Measuring Business Cycles*. To the definition may be added the rule of thumb that, to be called a business cycle, an alternation of cumulative expansion and contraction should last from, say, a minimum of 2 years to a maximum of 10 or 11 years (measured from trough to trough or peak to peak).

Postwar European experience and the unprecedented length (in peacetime) of the current expansion in the United States raise the following question with respect to this definition. Can business cycles be said to exist if a country experiences "recurring alternations" of acceleration and retardation in the rate of growth of output and employment rather than alternating expansions and contractions in the absolute level of these and other important variables?

3

I should answer this question in the affirmative. If swings in rates of growth are regular (but not necessarily periodic) and if these swings are of roughly the same duration and are associated with many of the same phenomena (such as cyclical changes in interest rates, the balance of trade, cost-price relations, and unemployment) as was true of past fluctuations that were called business cycles, then I should be inclined to say that these "growth cycles" should be called "business cycles." The issues for policy are the same if retarded growth (rather than an absolute decline in output) leads to a rise in unemployment—or if inflationary pressures resulting from accelerated growth force governments to impose fiscal and monetary restraints that, hopefully, will merely retard the rise in output and employment rather than bring on a decline in absolute levels. I am prepared to include cycles in growth rates in my definition of business cycles as long as they display the cumulative and pervasive features mentioned in my original definition and if their duration falls within the time limits that have customarily been thought of in connection with business cycles.

Now let me ask: How is the word "obsolete" in the title of this conference to be interpreted, particularly with respect to the U. S. economy? As far as the postwar period up until 1961 is concerned, it is clear that the United States did continue to experience business cycles, and the National Bureau of Economic Research (N.B.E.R.) has dated them. It is true that the recessions were mild and brief (although not unprecedentedly so). But up to 1961, these postwar cycles resembled the "minor" business cycles that have characterized U. S. economic development as far back as the N.B.E.R. records go.

What *was* obsolete, most economists believed, was not the business cycle in any form but serious depressions. Not only were a number of reasons adduced for the belief that prolonged periods of severe depression (such as the 1870's, 1890's, or the 1930's) were unlikely or even impossible, but it also was felt that very sharp but brief recessions (such as those of 1907–1908, 1920–1921, and 1937–1938) were extinct phenomena. I need not review all the reasons for believing that "major" depressions were obsolete — reasons that included banking and financial reforms, the increased importance of the automatic stabilizers, the acceptance of the goal of full employment, and so on.

This was the situation in the United States up to 1961. Serious depressions were obsolete, but clearly minor cycles were continuing to occur. What then, has changed since 1961?

In effect, the conjunction of two developments in the United States has reopened the question as to whether the business cycle is obsolete. One is the recognized success of an expansionary fiscal policy, particularly the tax cut in 1964, and the increased acceptance by the Administration, the Congress, and the informed public of the so-called New Economics. Some observers are prepared to believe, apparently, that a wisely applied discretionary fiscal and monetary policy will ensure that cumulative recessions will from now on be nipped in the bud. This optimistic view of the new effectiveness of monetary and fiscal policy is a bit vague as to whether cumulative accelerations in the rise in the price level can also be prevented and, if not, whether the sequel of an eventual decline in real variables can then be avoided.

The other development that has raised the question of the possible obsolescence of the business cycle is simply the unprecedented length (in peacetime) of the current expansion. By February 1967 the upswing had lasted six full years. The longest peacetime expansion before this was during 1933—1937, an upswing that lasted 50 months.

Thus, as far as the United States is concerned, the presumption that the business cycle is obsolete reflects (a) a new belief, acquired largely since the early 1960's, in the omniscience and omnipotence of government in the area of stabilization policy; (b) a willingness to project into the indefinite future the experience of half a decade; and (c) little or no consideration of the possibility that a continued expansion of output at a retarded rate below the rate of growth of potential output can be associated with a relatively high and even increasing level of unemployment. In this connection it should be recalled that after 1957 the unemployment rate on a quarterly basis (seasonally adjusted) did not fall below 5 per cent until the first quarter of 1965 and that unemployment has been at 4 per cent or below only since the beginning of 1966. To say that the business cycle is obsolete in the United States is to generalize from what is indeed a limited period of economic history.

## Possible Sources of Change in Dynamic Properties

To suggest that little or no cyclical instability will be experienced in the future is to imply that significant changes have occurred, or are occurring, in the dynamic characteristics of U. S. economy. Where have such changes taken place—particularly in the last half dozen years? Consider this question from the point of view of the formal properties of a dynamic system. This can be done by posing the following three questions:

1. What important changes have occurred in the character of the relations determining the behavior of the endogenous variables in the system?
2. In what respects may it be assumed that the important variables which must be taken as exogenous will in future follow a time path different from that in the past?
3. Have there been any significant changes in the pattern of random shock to which the economy is continuously subjected?

## CHANGES IN RELATIONSHIPS

The variety of ways in which the relationships determining endogenous variables may change over time should be kept in mind. I think that a fair criticism of most econometric work on the determinants of the important macroeconomic variables in that not enough attention is paid to the possibility of testing for such changes. Regressions fitted to all or most of the data for the postwar period imply, of course, that there has been no change in the way in which the endogenous variables respond to the relevant parts of a changing environment. (Inclusion of calendar time as an additional variable does not carry us very far in testing for significant changes in the relationships with which we may be concerned.)

Let me review here the different ways in which the response mechanism determining the behavior of particular variables may change and thereby influence the stability of the system as a whole.

First, the relative importance of different explanatory variables may change over time. In some cases a variable which apparently had little or no explanatory value in the past may come to exert an important influence on the behavior of the "dependent" variable. In other cases variables which seemed once to be important may cease to have any explanatory value. In the more typical case the regression coefficients attached to particular explanatory variables may change, within narrow or fairly wide limits. If the attempt is being made to assess how much more stable the U. S. economy is today than it was 10 or 20 years ago, then more needs to be known about possible changes in the relative weight to be given to different variables as they interact with each other. Some of these parameter changes may, of course, be the results of policy changes—as when tax rates are changed—but others may result from a variety of types of structural change.

A second possible type of change in relationships has to do with changes in lag structure. Since the war econometricians have become much more sophisticated in their handling of lagged relationships, and a variety of methods are available for determining distributed-lag patterns. But knowledge of this area still does not extend very far. Not much can be said about possible recent changes in the lags applying to particular relationships and how these changes in lag structure have affected the stability of the system as a whole; for example, have there been significant changes in timing in the relation between wage changes and the level of unemployment or the rate of profit, between different types of investment and various monetary variables, between inventory investment and changes in sales or prices?

I shall only mention a third possible change in relationship, namely, a change in functional form. Relationships that were once readily approximated by linear functions may come, gradually or suddenly, to demonstrate various types of nonlinearities—from the appearance of new constraints to the introduction of exponents significantly different from one.

I do want to emphasize one final kind of possible change in the relationships among macrovariables. This is the kind of change that results from the changing composition of aggregates. Thus behavioral relations applying to each of the different components of an aggregate may, while differing among themselves, remain unchanged over time. If, however, the relative importance of the components changes significantly, the parameters of the aggregative relation are also likely to change. The determinants of plant expenditures are, presumably, somewhat different from those of equipment purchases. Has the relative importance of these two types of investment been changing? If so, for this reason alone some change should be expected in the way that total nonresidential capital expenditures respond to a change in total output or to an index of corporate bond yields. The same sort of changes in aggregative relationships may result from changes in the industrial composition of output.

## CHANGES IN BEHAVIOR OF EXOGENOUS VARIABLES

Given a set of dynamic relations determining the stability properties of the economy, the actual behavior of the system will, of course, depend both on the behavior of identifiable variables that are taken to be exogenous and on the time pattern of disturbances that reflect the operation of forces that cannot be identified in detail.

What are the important exogenous variables that have to be considered here? The major ones are of four types: those reflecting government expenditures; demographic variables; those reflecting conditions outside the country; and monetary variables that are directly controlled by the monetary authorities [3]. I discuss some of these important exogenous variables later in this chapter.

## CHANGES IN PATTERN OF DISTURBANCES

The chief point to be mentioned under this heading is whether, in some or all of the behavior equations that summarize our limited understanding of the relevant dynamic relationships, a change over time can be detected in the distribution of the error term. Does the pattern of the residuals (i.e., the part of the variation in the endogenous variables that is not explained by the behavior equations) tend to alter in any readily identifiable way?

The type of change here that may be important in making for greater stability in the system is a decline in the variance of the error term. If we should observe such a decline in variance, and it was not due merely to an improvement in the data being used, then our inference would be that the strength of the disturbances resulting from the totality of unidentified variables was diminishing. If the system is stable to begin with, then a weakening of the effect of outside disturbances, as reflected in the error term, should reduce the amplitude of cyclical movements in, for example, total output and employment.

Of the possible reasons for a decline in the variance of the error terms, on the assumption that the specified functional relationships themselves have not changed, two obvious ones might be mentioned. There may be one or more unidentified explanatory variables which now display less period-to-period fluctuations than in the past or, with the same amplitude of fluctuation, the causal significance of these unidentified variables may have declined.

### HOW TO PROCEED

In the foregoing discussion I have suggested a formal and comprehensive approach to the questions of whether, and in what ways, the U. S. economy has become significantly more stable during the last decade or so. I hope that these suggestions will tempt some of my econometrically inclined friends to ask such questions of the models they have constructed and the new ones they will build. In the remainder of this paper, I shall discuss a few aspects of the behavior of the U. S. economy that I believe are particularly relevant for the topic of this conference, although my treatment will not be as rigorous as some would desire. As far as possible, I shall relate what I have to say to the questions I have raised so far.

## Relation Between Disposable Income and GNP

The emphasis placed on "automatic stabilizers" is one reflection of the significance attached to the relation between the gross national product (GNP) and disposable personal income (i.e., personal income after taxes). The less that disposable income declines when GNP falls—say, in response to a decline in investment—the more stable will be consumers' expenditures and the more quickly, presumably, will investment begin to expand again. During expansion periods, the less that disposable income rises for a given rise in GNP, the greater are the taxes and gross business savings available to finance investment and government expenditures and, other things equal, the more restrained will be the expansion.

How has disposable income (YD), as related to GNP in the current upswing, compared, say, with a similar relationship during the boom of the 1950's? In Figure 1—1 the behavior of YD/GNP during the upswing which began in 1961 is compared with that during the expansion of 1954-1957. Two features of this chart call for comment. First, it is not surprising that the ratio of YD to GNP has fluctuated at a somewhat lower level in the 1960's than in the 1950's. The reasons why the ratio was lower in 1966 than in 1956 are summarized in Table 1—1. The largest increases between 1956 and 1966 in withholdings from GNP were in social insurance contributions and personal income taxes[4]. Substantial increases also occurred in the percentages of GNP going into capital consumption allowances and indirect business taxes. (Neither of these two act

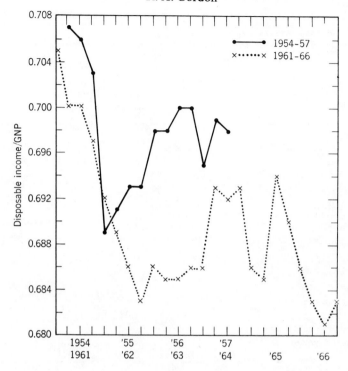

**Figure 1–1.** Ratio of disposable income to GNP, 1954–1957 and 1961–1966.

particularly as automatic stabilizers.) Corporate income taxes, which are very sensitive to changes in GNP, played a relatively less important role in 1966 than in 1956. Another significant change was the large increase in the relative importance of government transfer payments. All of this increase came between 1956 and 1961; government transfer payments were a slightly smaller fraction of GNP in 1966 than in 1961. These payments can be expected to play an important stabilizing role in any future incipient recession.

On net balance it may be said that the relation between YD and GNP probably provides a somewhat stronger buffer against a cyclical decline in YD and consumption than it did in, say, the 1957–1958 recession. (This buffer would have been even stronger had the fiscal stimulus in 1964 taken the form of maintaining tax rates and increasing government expenditures by an equivalent amount, rather than concentrating on tax reductions.)

The second feature of Figure 1–1 which calls for comment is the similarity in the behavior of the ratio in the two upswings. In both expansions the ratio first declined, then recovered part of the loss, and then, late in the expansion, began to decline again. In the earlier period, on net balance, YD fell in relation to GNP

TABLE 1–1　Components of the Difference Between Gross National Product (GNP) and Disposable Income, 1956 and 1966

| | 1956 | | 1966 | |
|---|---|---|---|---|
| | Amount (billion dollars) | Per Cent of GNP | Amount (billion dollars) | Per Cent of GNP |
| **Deductions** | | | | |
| Capital consumption | 34.1 | 8.13 | 63.1 | 8.53 |
| Indirect business taxes | 34.9 | 8.33 | 65.5 | 8.86 |
| Corporate income taxes | 21.7 | 5.18 | 33.7 | 4.56 |
| Undistributed corporate profits* | 13.2 | 3.15 | 25.2 | 3.41 |
| Social insurance contributions | 12.6 | 3.01 | 37.8 | 5.11 |
| Personal taxes | 39.8 | 9.49 | 75.1 | 10.16 |
| Total† | 156.3 | 37.29 | 300.4 | 40.63 |
| **Additions** | | | | |
| Government transfer payments | 17.1 | 4.08 | 41.9 | 5.67 |
| Government and consumer interest payments | 11.2 | 2.67 | 22.8 | 3.08 |
| Other†† | 0.8 | 0.20 | 1.3 | 0.18 |
| Total | 29.1 | 6.95 | 66.0 | 8.93 |
| Net deductions† | 127.2 | 30.34 | 234.4 | 31.70 |

Source: Economic Report of the President, January 1967, pp. 227–229 and 290.
*Includes inventory valuation adjustment.
†Excludes statistical discrepancy of −1.1 billion in 1956 and −0.2 billion in 1966.
††Subsidies less current surplus of government enterprises.

during the last three calendar quarters of the upswing. After 1961 the highest ratio was reached in the third quarter of 1965; since then, there has been a moderately significant decline. Thus despite the dramatic tax reduction of 1964 and other pieces of fiscal legislation during the 1960's, the cyclical behavior of the ratio of YD to GNP was rather similar during 1961–1966 and 1954–1957. There were some shifts in parameters, for example, in the tax functions, but, on the whole, there does not seem to have been any basic change between the 1950's and the 1960's in the way that the ratio of YD to GNP varies during a long and vigorous upswing.

## Behavior of Consumers' Expenditures

Is there any evidence that consumers' expenditures have, in the last decade or so, become a more or less stabilizing factor in the behavior of the U. S. economy? During the long expansion since 1961 annual consumers' expenditures on goods and services have remained a remarkably constant fraction, about 92 per cent, of consumers' income after taxes (Table 1−2). Except for a spurt to 0.927 in 1963, the average propensity to consume disposable income has remained in the narrow range of 0.919 to 0.922 since 1961[5]. The figure was slightly more variable in the 1950's, in part because of the spurt in automobile purchases in 1955.

The rate of personal saving appears to have been considerably lower during the current upswing than during the boom of the 1950's. The percentage of disposable income saved was about 5.5 in the three years 1964-1966, compared with about 6.5 during 1955−1957[6]. It was as high as 7.0 in 1956; it has not been higher than 5.8 since 1959. Further, there has been a tendency for the personal saving rate to decline slightly during the course of the present upswing. This does not contribute to stability when, as in late 1965 and in 1966, demand in pressing against capacity.

The ratio of consumers' expenditures to GNP fell very slightly from 0.635 to 0.629 during 1964−1966, while the decline in YD/GNP offset the modest fall in the rate of personal saving out of disposable income. In 1955−1957 also,

TABLE 1−2  **Components of Consumers' Expenditures and Total Personal Saving as Percentages of Disposable Income, 1954−1957 and 1961−1966**

| | Durable Goods | | | | | Total | |
| Year | Total | Autos | Other | Nondurable Goods | Services | Consumers' Expenditures | Personal Saving* |
| --- | --- | --- | --- | --- | --- | --- | --- |
| 1954 | 12.7 | 5.3 | 7.4 | 46.0 | 33.2 | 91.9 | 6.4 |
| 1955 | 14.4 | 6.7 | 7.7 | 44.8 | 33.2 | 92.4 | 5.7 |
| 1956 | 13.3 | 5.6 | 7.7 | 44.1 | 33.6 | 91.0 | 7.0 |
| 1957 | 13.2 | 5.9 | 7.3 | 44.0 | 34.0 | 91.2 | 6.7 |
| 1961 | 12.1 | 5.0 | 7.1 | 42.8 | 37.1 | 92.0 | 5.8 |
| 1962 | 12.8 | 5.7 | 7.1 | 42.2 | 37.1 | 92.2 | 5.6 |
| 1963 | 13.3 | 6.0 | 7.3 | 41.7 | 37.7 | 92.7 | 4.9 |
| 1964 | 13.6 | 5.9 | 7.7 | 41.0 | 37.4 | 91.9 | 5.6 |
| 1965 | 14.1 | 6.4 | 7.7 | 40.6 | 37.3 | 92.0 | 5.5 |
| 1966 | 13.7 | 5.9 | 7.8 | 40.8 | 37.5 | 92.0 | 5.3 |

**Source:** Based on data in *Economic Report of the President,* January 1967, pp. 224, 229.
*Personal saving is the difference between disposable income and personal outlays. The latter include consumers' expenditures, interest paid by consumers, and personal transfer payments to foreigners.

consumption remained a fairly steady percentage of GNP; but at that time the personal saving rate *rose* and so did YD/GNP. It would appear that, in terms of its moderating effect on the upswing, the behavior of disposable income was more stabilizing in 1964–1966 than in 1955–1957, but that the behavior of personal saving (given disposable income) was more destabilizing.

The way in which the composition of consumers' expenditures has changed since the boom of the 1950's is of interest (Table 1–2). Expenditures on durable goods in the last few years have been about as large a fraction of disposable income as they were in 1954–1957. Indeed, Table 1–2 emphasizes that, relative to disposable income, the boom in automobiles and other consumer durables in 1964–1966 was quite similar to that in the mid–1950's. The big changes were the decline in the fraction of disposable income spent on nondurables and the rise in the percentage spent on services.

When the implications for the stability of the economy of changes in the pattern of consumer spending are considered, attention usually is concentrated on expenditures on durables, because of their inherent instability. In this respect the economy was about as sensitive to destabilizing forces in the mid-1960's as it was in the 1950's—unless forces were at work to make spending on durables, including automobiles, more stable than in the past. Can anything be added regarding the possible implications of the shift from nondurables to services? Econometric research indicates that expenditures on services are less closely related to current changes in disposable income than are expenditures on nondurables[7]. It may be inferred that the continued shift from nondurables to services tends to make total consumer expenditures somewhat more resistent to moderate and brief declines in disposable income. Before much is made of this, however, it is well to remember that, in current prices, expenditures on services were nearly as large a percentage of disposable income in 1929 (36.4 per cent) as they were in 1966 (37.5 per cent). The rapid rise in the relative importance of such expenditures in the postwar period represents largely a recovery from their depressed level, relative to disposable income, during World War II[8].

I have said nothing about possible changes in the determinants of the different types of consumer spending, because there is little that I *can* say. An enormous amount of empirical work has been done on the consumption function, of course, but I am not aware of any research that asks the kind of question being raised here: Have the relevant functions changed in any significant way during the last decade or so?[9]. My rough impression is that, apart from the effects of changes in composition, such structural changes have not been important.

*Behavior of Investment*

COMPOSITION OF INVESTMENT

The instability of private investment is, of course, at the heart of the problem of the business cycle. The kind of brief and mild recession experienced in the United States since the war is particulary a reflection of the volatility of inventory investment. Is there any reason to believe that fixed and inventory investment will play less of a destabilizing role in the future than in the recent past?

Gross investment was an unusually small fraction on GNP during 1960-1964 (under 15 per cent), and even in 1965-1966 this fraction was somewhat smaller than in 1955–1956. But gross capital formation still acounts for between one-sixth and one-seventh of GNP, and its destabilizing potential is still very great. It is fair to say that in the absence of a more expansionary fiscal policy during 1958–1963 private investment must take most of the blame for the high rate of unemployment that persisted during those years[10]. Can it be safely assumed that this will not happen again?

Since different components of gross capital formation behave differently, changes in the composition of investment should first be investigated. When the data in Table 1–3 are examined, the outstanding changes in the three years 1964–1966 are seen to be (a) the sharp decline in the percentage of gross investment accounted for by residential building and (b) the relatively large (and rising) percentage in the form of inventory investment.

The behavior of residential building is, on the whole, reassuring—just as it has been in previous expansion periods since the war. Housing construction has tended to fall off as the expansion of nonhousing investment has accelerated during each boom; it has then begun to expand again before each recession is over. The same pattern is evident in the present boom, but the decline is unusually sharp. Residential building was a considerably smaller fraction of total gross investment in 1964–1966 than in either of the two preceding cyclical expansions. If it is assumed that demographic factors are favorable and that monetary conditions will ease, then there is reason to believe that housing investment would expand to take up a substantial amount of the slack if plant and equipment expenditures should decline or level off[11].

A different picture emerges for inventory investment. The fraction of gross investment in the form of inventory accumulation has been high and rising. In 1966 this fraction exceeded that of any previous postwar year except 1946, 1948, 1950, and 1951. The high rate of inventory accumulation during 1965–1966 occurred in the face of the improvements in inventory management that brought about a downward secular trend in the inventory-sales ratio.

TABLE 1–3  Percentage Composition of Gross Private Domestic Investment, 1955–1957, 1959–1960, and 1964–1966

| | 1955 | 1956 | 1957 | 1959 | 1960 | 1964 | 1965 | 1966 |
|---|---|---|---|---|---|---|---|---|
| Plant and equipment | 42.6 | 50.1 | 54.6 | 43.2 | 47.7 | 48.3 | 48.8 | 52.0 |
| Residential nonfarm construction | 33.7 | 29.9 | 28.8 | 32.9 | 29.7 | 29.0 | 25.5 | 21.7 |
| Farm construction and equipment | 5.8 | 5.3 | 5.9 | 5.8 | 5.2 | 5.5 | 5.2 | 5.5 |
| Other fixed investment* | 9.1 | 8.0 | 8.8 | 11.7 | 12.7 | 12.2 | 12.0 | 11.0 |
| Total fixed investment | 92.1 | 93.3 | 98.1 | 93.6 | 95.3 | 95.0 | 91.5 | 90.2 |
| Inventory investment | 8.9 | 6.7 | 1.9 | 6.4 | 4.8 | 5.1 | 8.5 | 9.8 |

Source: Based on data in *Economic Report of the President*, January 1967, pp. 225, 258.
*This item is a residual.

TABLE 1–4  Percentage Composition of Plant and Equipment Expenditures, 1955–1957, 1959–1960, and 1964–1966

| | 1955 | 1956 | 1957 | 1959 | 1960 | 1964 | 1965 | 1966 |
|---|---|---|---|---|---|---|---|---|
| Manufacturing, total | 39.9 | 42.6 | 43.2 | 37.1 | 40.6 | 41.4 | 43.2 | 44.6 |
| Durable goods | 19.0 | 21.7 | 21.7 | 17.7 | 20.1 | 21.0 | 21.9 | 23.2 |
| Nondurable goods | 20.9 | 20.9 | 21.5 | 19.3 | 20.5 | 20.4 | 21.3 | 21.4 |
| Mining | 3.3 | 3.5 | 3.4 | 3.0 | 2.8 | 2.7 | 2.5 | 2.4 |
| Transportation | | | | | | | | |
| Railroads | 3.2 | 3.5 | 3.8 | 2.8 | 2.9 | 3.1 | 3.3 | 3.2 |
| Other | 5.6 | 4.9 | 4.8 | 6.2 | 5.4 | 5.3 | 5.4 | 5.7 |
| Public utilities | 15.0 | 14.0 | 16.8 | 17.4 | 15.9 | 13.9 | 13.4 | 13.7 |
| Commercial and other | 33.0 | 31.5 | 28.1 | 33.4 | 32.4 | 33.7 | 32.2 | 30.3 |

Source: Based on data in *Economic Report of the President*, January 1967, p. 258

The high rate does give some cause for concern, and can hardly be considered a factor contributing to greater stability of the economy. Some (and probably considerable) reduction from the rate reached in 1966 is inevitable. This is a matter to which I shall return.

For plant and equipment expenditures (Table 1–4) changes that have occurred since the 1950's are not startling. However, public utilities have become relatively less important, and durable manufacturing somewhat more important—changes that hardly contribute to greater stability. The tendency for investment in manufacturing, particularly in durable-goods industries, to account for an increasing fraction of total plant and equipment outlays as a boom progresses is evident in the 1960's as it was in the 1950's. In this respect the economy is just as vulnerable today as it was in 1957.

Also of interest are recent changes in the relative importance of nonresidential construction and producers' durables. In the present boom producers' durables have been a larger fraction of nonresidential, nonfarm fixed investment than they were in the mid-1950's (about 63 per cent in 1964–1966, compared with about 60 per cent in 1954–1956). Does this moderate change make for greater stability? I am skeptical.

TABLE 1–5  Composition of Gross Private Domestic Investment in Recessions of 1957–1958 and 1960–1961* (Amounts in billions of dollars)

| | Amount | | Percentage Change | Amount | | Percentage Change |
|---|---|---|---|---|---|---|
| | II/1957 | I/1958 | | I/1960 | I/1961 | |
| Gross investment | 70.9 | 57.5 | −18.9 | 79.9 | 62.4 | −21.9 |
| Fixed investment | 67.9 | 63.1 | −7.1 | 70.2 | 65.8 | −6.3 |
| Nonresidential | 48.0 | 43.3 | −9.8 | 46.6 | 44.9 | −3.6 |
| Structures | 18.2 | 17.3 | −4.9 | 17.6 | 17.6 | − |
| Producers' durables | 29.8 | 26.0 | −12.8 | 29.0 | 27.3 | 5.9 |
| Presidential construction | 19.9 | 19.8 | −0.5 | 23.7 | 20.9 | −11.8 |
| Charge in inventories | 3.0 | −5.6 | − | 9.6 | −3.4 | − |
| Nonfarm | 2.4 | −6.5 | − | 9.7 | −3.6 | − |
| Farm | 0.6 | 0.9 | − | 0.1 | 0.2 | − |
| Gross National Product | 455.2 | 437.5 | −3.9 | 490.2 | 482.7 | −1.5 |
| Unemployment rate† (per cent) | 4.3 | 6.5 | − | 5.2 | 6.8 | − |

Sources: Based on data in *Survey of Current Business,* August 1965, pp. 26–27, and *Economic Report of the President,* January 1959, p. 159, and January 1962, p. 231.
*Measured between calendar quarters in which real gross national product reached a peak or trough.
†Quarterly average of seasonally adjusted monthly rates.

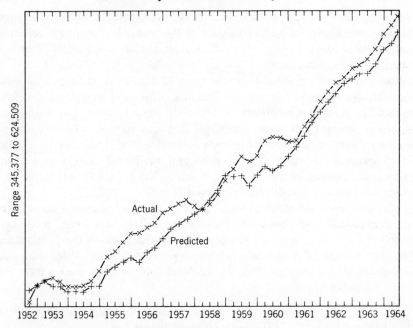

Range 345.377 to 624.509

Actual

Predicted

1952 1953  1954  1955  1956  1957  1958  1959  1960  1961  1962  1963 1964

**Chart 1–1**    Actual and predicted U.S. Gross National Product, annual rates by quarters, 1952.III–1964.II. (In billions of current dollars.)

An examination of private domestic investment in the last two recessions shows that in both downswings total gross investment declined sharply—by about 20 per cent each time (Table 1–5). In 1957–1958 about two-thirds of the decline was accounted for by the sharp swing in inventory investment; in 1960–1961 the fraction was closer to three-fourths. This merely confirms our general impressions regarding the importance of inventory decumulation in "minor" recessions. Also, the declines in fixed investment—notably in producers's durables in 1957–1958—were not insignificant. (As noted in the preceding paragraph, producers' durables have been playing an even more important role in the present boom than in the mid-1950's.) In 1960–1961, in contrast to previous postwar recessions, residential building accounted for more than half the decline in fixed investment. This reflected longer run factors as well as the direct effect of the recession in business activity.

FACTORS INFLUENCING FIXED INVESTMENT

What are some of the factors influencing nonresidential fixed investment? What changes might tend to make such investment more stable in the future than in the past? In this connection attention should be directed not only to the possibility of cumulative, absolute declines in plant and equipment expenditures, but also to the possible recurrence of a retardation in the growth of investment. In such a retardation aggregate demand may fail to rise as rapidly as "potential output," and unemployment may rise and stay at an uncomfortably high level. (This was the situation in 1958–1964.)

What are some of the possible changes in parameters that might have altered over the last decade or so, the way plant and equipment expenditures react to changes in the relevant variables: to output or sales, to particular monetary and financial variables, and to whatever else might be selected for inclusion in the investment function?

In the early postwar years a number of informed observers emphasized that large-scale business was using a longer horizon in its investment planning and that, consequently, business fixed investment was becoming more immune to changes in current business conditions. It is undoubtedly true that business firms are engaging in more long-range planning, but cancellations of orders and deferment of expenditures can still play an important role in generating short-run instability in investment expenditures. This is recognized in recent econometric work that seeks to explain not only the behavior of planned or anticipated investment but also the difference between anticipations and realizations[12]. (Even the equations for investment intentions depend heavily on output or sales in the very recent past.) And whatever the particular investment function fitted, I know of no tests which suggest, for the last decade or more, any significant change in the lags or partial regression coefficients for current or recent output or sales.

Business investment is not insensitive to changes in the tax liabilities of business firms[13]. In the postwar period, the relation between corporate tax liabilities and corporate profits has changed because of (a) changes in the rate of the corporate income tax, (b) the introduction and recent suspension of the investment tax credit, and (c) liberalization (until some recent tightening) in the regulations governing depreciation. Until suspension of the investment tax credit in October 1966, the effect of the relevant changes during the 1960's had been to raise the level of investment for given values of the other relevant variables, but the effect on the *stability* of investment is less clear. The liberalization of depreciation allowances may have some stabilizing effect on investment since it results in the generation of a larger internal cash flow without regard to the level of output or net profits. Also, if tax reductions do raise the level of investment and thus the size of the capital stock, depreciation and replacement rise, and replacement expenditures are presumably more stable than is net investment. In this connection it is worth noting that there has been a long-run tendency for the ratio of capital consumption to gross fixed investment to rise.

The reduction of a proportionate corporate income tax by a given percentage does not reduce the relative amplitude of fluctuations in after-tax profits. It raises the level of net investment, presumably in accordance with some distributed lag pattern; and it raises the level of replacement on a capital stock that is larger than it otherwise would have been. But I do not see that lowering the level of corporate taxes makes business investment more stable. Only the prewar experience needs to be cited.

The most important consideration with respect to the relation between corporate taxes and the stability of business investment has to do with the frequency and timing of tax changes; this is a question that carries over into the broader area of the effectiveness of discretionary fiscal policy in stabilizing aggregate demand. How frequently will, for example, the rate of the corporate income tax be altered in the future, and how often will the investment tax credit be suspended and then reinstated? Can the assumption be made that the appropriate fiscal instruments will be used equally promptly to restrain investment when it is too high and to stimulate investment when it is too low? What are all of the lags involved (it is clear that some of them are fairly long), and how often will action be taken too late? (This is more of a danger when restrictive action is called for than when expansionary measures are needed.) Space and time do not permit me to pursue this range of considerations. I shall simply record a certain skepticism that discretionary corporate tax policy is likely to succeed by itself in completely eliminating cyclical fluctuations in fixed business investment[14].

During the first four years of the present upswing, corporations were able to finance an unusually large fraction of their total investment from internal sources; but this fraction fell rapidly in 1965–1966, leading to a sharp rise in external financing[15]. Corporate bond yields began to rise rapidly from mid-1965, and short-term rates shot upward from the end of 1965 until the closing months of 1966. The latter year saw the highest level of interest rates since the boom following World War I.

These developments again raise the question concerning the sensitivity of investment to changes in the cost and availability of capital funds. Interest rates, it is quite clear, still reveal a cyclical pattern; indeed, the amplitude of the cycle in interest rates has, if anything, widened since the early 1950's. And recent econometric work has tended to confirm that the cost of capital *does* influence investment behavior—with a significant lag[16]. The recent and current monetary tightness has certainly contributed to the retardation in the rise now under way in business investment and some of the effects if monetary restriction are still to be felt. The dynamics of the U. S. economy still generate cycles in the important monetary variables with some consequent effect on the behavior of business investment.

In concluding this brief treatment of fixed investment, I cannot resist mentioning a notion that has gone out of style—the notion of "investment opportunities" and the related concept of "autonomous" investment. The many dimensions associated with growth increases in total output, changes in the composition of output, changes in the size and composition of the capital stock appropriate to a given level and composition of output, demographic changes, changes in the organization of firms and the structure of markets, etc.) lead to changes in the parameters of aggregate investment functions as they are usually formulated for econometric work[17]. The changing pattern of growth can alternately strengthen and weaken the stimuli to private investment, thereby contributing to the recurrence of periods of retarded growth and increased unemployment—and to the continuation of business cycles in the usual sense. A variety of structural changes (financial reforms, the growth of the large corporation and of scientific management, the lessened importance of "dominant innovations" like the railroad, and others) means that the "changing state of investment opportunities" is not likely to bring about a serious depression in the future. But it can, particulary in the absence of appropriate government action, bring on periods of retarded growth, such as the United States experienced in the late 1950's and early 1960's, and also contribute to recessions, such as that of 1957—1958.

### INVENTORY INVESTMENT

Earlier in this chapter it was pointed out that during the current upswing, inventory investment as a fraction of total gross capital formation has been rising, and that in 1966 this fraction was larger than in any year since 1951. There is, however a reassuring side to this story. Through 1961, there had been a tendency for the swings in inventory investment to diminish in importance, in relation to GNP. The decline in inventory investment as a percentage of GNP in the preceding year (both series measured in 1958 prices) was as follows in recessions beginning with that of 1937—1938 (excluding the brief 1945 downturn):

|           |        |
|-----------|--------|
| 1937—1938 | −3.9%  |
| 1948—1949 | −2.6   |
| 1953—1954 | −0.7   |
| 1957—1958 | −0.6   |
| 1960—1961 | −0.3   |

Thus the year-to-year swing in inventory investment in 1960—1961 was only 0.3 per cent of GNP in 1960, compared with 0.6—0.7 per cent in the two preceding recessions, 2.6 per cent in 1948—1949, and 3.9 per cent in 1937—1938[18]. Also, the ratio of the maximum rate of inventory accumulation to current GNP during the 1954—1956 and 1959—1960 upswings was much lower than during the first two postwar cyclical expansions, or during 1933—1937. However, the ratio of inventory investment to GNP in 1966 was a trifle higher than in 1955, although only half 1946 or 1951 ratio and somewhat more than half the 1937 ratio.

Thus fluctuations in inventory investment seem to have become less important sources of cyclical instability. This tendency has been particularly evident since the 1953–1954 recession, and is not wholly explained by the mildness of the last three business recessions. I am, of course, discussing an interdependent system. Any causes—for example, the automatic stabilizers—that tend to reduce the amplitude of downswings in sales will also tend to reduce the relative importance of swings in inventory investment. But other factors have also been at work: these include a continuing downward trend in inventory—sales ratios, other aspects of better inventory management that make for more stable inventories, and a marked decline since the war in the ratio of goods output to GNP (and a corresponding increase in the relative importance of services).

All this is gratifying, but it should be remembered that inventory accumulation *has* been important in the current upswing. The ratio of inventory investment to GNP in 1966 was higher than in any of the years in the period 1955–1957. Also, the proportion of total manufacturers' inventories held by the durable-goods industries was larger than usual. It is possible that a significant decline in inventory investment could occur while the boom continued. In the expansions of 1949–1953 and 1954–1956, the peak in inventory investment came some two years before the peak in total output, with the result that the inventory liquidation during the business recession itself was moderate. There is a fair possibility that this might happen again.

Econemetricians are still attempting to construct a set of equations for inventory investment in which they have confidence: some progress has been made[19]. But this work tells nothing about possible changes that may have been occurring since World War II, or even earlier, in the relevent parameters. The brief discussion in this chapter indicates that some changes in relationships have been occurring, with the result that fluctuations in inventory investment have apparently become less important relative to GNP. Nonetheless, changes in inventory investment can, it seems to me, still play a significant role in generating "minor" business cycles.

## Prices, Costs, and Profits

One of the striking features of the present upswing has been the behavior of prices, costs, and profits. This is an area of business-cycle analysis emphasized by Wesley Mitchell many years ago, but neglected until rather recently in the construction of dynamic aggregative models. Although the recent literature shows a commendable interest in the interrelated behavior of productivity, costs, prices, and profits, relatively little attention has been paid to the possibility of changing relationships during the postwar period[20].

Wholesale prices hardly rose during the first four years of the present upswing; and even the rise during 1965–1966 was moderate, particularly if farm products are excluded. The rise in wholesale nonfarm prices was considerably more rapid in 1955–1956 than in 1965–1966. Unit labor costs in manufacturing showed no rise between 1961 and 1965. As a result, at least in manufacturing, the ratio of price to unit labor costs and the share of profits in total sales and in income behaved in a way not typical of previous upswings.

The ratio of price to unit labor costs in manufacturing usually rises rapidly in the early stages of an upswing, reaches a maximum fairly early, and then declines during the later part. Profits per dollar of sales behave in the same way. A tendency for costs to encroach on profits in the late upswing was an important feature of Mitchell's explanation of the upper turning point, and this sequence apparently continued to operate during the postwar expansions to 1960[21].

In the current upswing, however, in the important manufacturing sector the ratio of price to unit labor costs and profits per dollar of sales rose briefly in 1961, remained remarkably stable through 1964, and then rose further in 1965. Not until after the first quarter of 1966 did a decline in profit margins seem to be getting under way[22]. Curiously, the rise in profit margins in 1965 came just at the time that the rate of utilization of capacity reached its highest point since 1955. The unusual stability of unit labor costs during 1961–1965, compared with 1955–1957 and earlier upswings, reflects both a more rapid increase in labor productivity and a more moderate rate of wage increase in the 1960's than during the boom of the mid-1950's.

The result of these movements was, of course, a rapid rise in total profits and in the rate of profits on stockholders' equity—a rise that continued into early 1966. Because of unutilized capacity, the profit rate in manufacturing remained below the 1955–1956 rate until 1965; but in 1965–1966, the rate was the highest since 1950[23]. In the 1954–1957 and 1959–1960 upswings, the profit rate reached a peak well before business activity finally turned down.

Some reasons for the unusual behavior of costs, prices, and profits during 1961–1966 may be adduced from the data. Wages rose more slowly than in 1954–1956 and, indeed, more slowly than would have been predicted on the basis of the "Phillips-curve"[23-a] type of regressions that have been computed for the earlier postwar period. Some shift in parameters, possibly temporary, seems to have occurred either as a result of the "guideposts" or of other factors. The rise in labor productivity was particularly rapid during 1962–1964, reflecting in part a more effective utilization of capacity. It also reflected, presumably, the more effective use of overhead labor, which leads to a topic that is worth discussing briefly.

Since the end of the war, and particularly *before* 1958, nonproduction (supervisory and white-collar) workers have comprised an increasing percentage of total employment. In manufacturing, the percentage rose from 16.4 in 1947 to 19.9 in 1953, 23.2 in 1957, and 25.1 in 1960. Since 1960, there has been little further rise: indeed, the percentage began to decline as the rise in industrial output accelerated; it dropped from 26.1 in 1963 to 25.6 in 1966[24].

Prior to the 1960's the only years in which the percentage declined were 1950, 1955, and 1959; each of these years was the first one after a business recession when the increase in output was particularly rapid. For other years of each postwar expansion through 1957, however, the percentage continued to rise, which is not what the textbooks describe as happening when output rises rapidly in the short run[25]. Only in the current expansion has the textbook type of behavior emerged: an increase in the relative importance of direct labor during the more vigorous part of the upswing, accompanied by some retardation in the rate of increase in labor productivity[26].

All this suggests a difference between the present expansion and earlier postwar upswings through 1957. In the earlier cycles production (and employment) rose rapidly in the early phase of the upswing, and "normal" rates of capacity operation were reached relatively early. In the 1960's capacity utilization remained relatively low (below 85 per cent, according to the Federal Reserve index) until 1964. Thus only during the last two years or so has there been a move into the rising section of short-period cost functions.

What effect does the growing importance of indirect labor in manufacturing and other sectors have on the stability of the economy? Clearly, it is leading to a change in production functions, such that a given percentage decline in output should result in a smaller percentage decline in total employment (and in payrolls and in disposable income) than formerly, at least during relatively brief and mild declines[27]. On the other hand, larger overhead costs make profits more volatile; this might have some destabilizing effect. On net balance I judge the development to be in a stabilizing direction, particularly if it can be assumed that an active (and not too blundering) monetary and fiscal policy will, in any event, hold business downswings within modest limits[28].

## Exogenous Variables

The past and prospective behavior of some of the important exogenous variables are now considered briefly[29].

### GOVERNMENT SPENDING

The fraction of GNP taken by all levels of government varied only between 20 and 21 per cent during the years 1961–1966. Since the end of the Korean War, the percentage has fluctuated between 18.6 and 21.1, the higher figures occurring during periods when private investment was somewhat depressed. The 1966 percentage of 20.7, inflated by the upsurge in federal defense expenditures, compares with 18.8 per cent in 1956 and 19.5 per cent in 1957.

Important changes have occurred in the composition of total government spending. The shifts in defense spending probably come immediately to mind. But the relative importance of state and local government expenditures has risen rapidly and steadily—from about 5 per cent of GNP in 1946—1947 to 10.3 per cent in 1966. (The federal share in 1966, after the step-up in defense expenditures, was 10.4 per cent.)

This rapid growth has, of course, provided important support for the growth in aggregate demand. Further, state and local spending has shown less erratic changes than have federal expenditures. State and local tax revenues are less sensitive than federal revenues to moderate cyclical swings in GNP, and state and local spending does not have the same potential as federal spending for rapid acceleration during recession. An increasing share of state and local revenues, however, are coming from federal government transfer payments. This will help to support the upward trend in state and local spending, and possibly to provide a stronger countercyclical stimulus in the event of a future rise in unemployment. Uncertainty exists, however, as to how state and local governments will finance the rise in their expenditures projected over the next decade and more. The answers eventually found will help to determine both the rate at which such spending continues to rise and the kind of stabilizing role that state and local revenues and expenditures are likely to play [30].

Where federal government spending is concerned, it has varied between 9.8 and 13 per cent of GNP since the end of the Korean War. It was 10.4 per cent in 1966. Professor Hickman has complained that between 1946 and 1958, federal spending was "the least stable of the major components of domestic expenditure for final goods and services" [31]. This instability, which was by no means always in a contracyclical direction, can be traced primarily to the dominating role of national defense expenditures in the federal budget. These expenditures rose sharply in 1966 to 78 per cent of federal spending on final output, and this rise was the chief source of additional inflationary pressures in that year. Hickman's conclusion that "federal expenditure cannot be counted among the inherently stable components of aggregate demand as long as it consists predominantly of outlays for national defense" [32] can hardly be argued. The situation has become only moderately better than in the mid-1950's, and even this improvement may not last for long. Defense spending accounted for 8.1 per cent of GNP on 1966, compared with an annual average of about 9.8 per cent during 1955—1957. (It was 13.4 per cent in 1953.)

The deflationary consequences of any future large reduction in defense expenditures could be offset by a vigorous use of discretionary fiscal policy—through quickly-enacted tax reductions and, though this is less readily achieved, prompt and substantial increases in spending for nondefense purposes. I think it is safe to conclude that the present level and composition of federal expenditures and their probable behavior in the future still permit, and even make probable, some degree of cyclical instability in the economy.

MONEY

Another important exogenous variable is the supply of money. Although the issue is certainly debatable, I am inclined to believe that monetary policy during the 1960's may have contributed to somewhat greater stability of the economy. Monetary policy does seem to have become more sophisticated. The Federal Reserve authorities permitted the money supply to increase at a moderately accelerating rate through 1965. "Operation Twist" succeeded until the second half of 1965 in holding down long-term interest rates while short-term rates were pushed up rapidly to protect the balance of payments.

Although the Federal Reserve authorities tightened credit markedly in 1966 and permitted long and short rates to reach their highest levels since the beginning of the 1920's, they continued to be sensitive to changes in business conditions, and some easing in the degree of restraint became evident toward the end of 1966 as the pace of the advance in spending began to moderate [33]. It would appear that the Federal Reserve authorities are less likely now and in the future, than they were on some past occasions, to permit monetary tightness to last for too long; and the monetary ease that persisted from 1961 through 1964, in the face of a rapid expansion in spending and output and continued balance of payments difficulties, suggests that the monetary authorities in the United States now take the goal of full employment more seriously than they did in, say, 1959–1960. This is not to suggest, however, that they do not still give heavy emphasis to the need for restraining a rise in prices and for protecting the balance of payments [34].

To say this much is by no means to suggest that monetary policy by itself can prevent either inflationary booms or business recessions. Lack of knowledge is still great in this area. The monetary authorities can err in their evaluation of current and prospective conditions; there is uncertainty as to how particular policy instruments affect the important monetary variables; and there is even greater ignorance of how and to what extent these policy instruments affect spending, output, and prices—and with what lags.

Recent monetary developments in the United States raise three questions, among others, regarding the stability of the economy during the late 1960's. First, what will be the lagged effects of the extreme credit tightness in 1966? Second, to what extent will continuing balance of payments difficulties lead the monetary authorities to take action prejudicial to the continuance of rapid growth and full employment? And third, when will the upward trend in interest rates, which has been going on since the 1951 Accord between the Treasury and the Federal Reserve, be halted?

FOREIGN CONDITIONS AND THE BALANCE OF PAYMENTS

Despite its size and relative self-sufficiency, the U. S. economy is not immune to developments abroad. While the balance of payments does not impose the constraint on domestic expansion in the United States that it seems to impose in such open economies as, e.g. the United Kingdom and the Netherlands, it clearly affects the course of American economic activity.

For the purpose of this chapter two ways in which the balance of payments acts as a restraint on domestic expansion should be distinguished. One is of domestic origin; it results when, under a system of fixed exchange rates, prices and incomes at home rise faster than those abroad. This is the classical case, of which there have been numerous examples in Europe in the last 15 years or so. In this case, because of its effect on exports and imports, domestic expansion will sometimes encounter the balance of payments constraint.

Because of changes in exogenous variables at home or abroad, the balance of payments can create difficulties in another way. Recent U. S. difficulties have been primarily of this latter type, and there is as yet no indication of their end. First, there is U. S. aid to other countries. This source of pressure on the dollar is tending to decline. Second, there is the large volume of private capital exports, which, contrary to some expectations, have not declined rapidly as a result of the accelerated expansion in domestic activity. The high level of capital exports, including direct investment, can be related to various developments abroad which increase both the attractiveness of foreign securities for U. S. investors and the relative profitability of direct foreign investment by U.S. corporations.

It is true that the federal government has acted with considerable skill and circumspection in minimizing the effect of the balance of payments deficit on domestic expansion—using techniques ranging from the Interest Equalization Tax to various forms of voluntary restraint on the outflow of capital. But there is nothing on the positive side to suggest that developments associated with the balance of payments will make the U. S. economy more stable in the future than it has been in the past[35].

### DEMOGRAPHIC FACTORS

To some degree the important population variables not only react on but are affected by economic variables, and to that extent they are not completely exogenous. This is particularly true for longer-run movements[36].

A variety of demographic changes can affect the stability of the economy in the years ahead; for example, a decline in the birth rate has been underway since the late 1950's. The postwar baby boom led, first, to a sharp increase in the school-age population and, more recently, to an acceleration in the growth of the labor force. These will be followed, presumably, by an upsurge in household formation and in the demand for housing. The changing age-sex composition of the labor force is affecting the pattern of employment and unemployment, and affecting employers' expenditures on training and on equipment. Internal migration (among regions and from farm to city) is having a variety of effects on consumption, private investment, public expenditures, and other economic variables.

I do not see that such current and prospective demographic changes necessarily make the economy more stable that in the past. Indeed, they are part of an interacting process that seems to generate the long cycles in the rate of growth that we now call Kuznets cycles. These swings can affect the duration and other characteristics of the shorter movements called business cycles. The retarded growth and high unemployment in the United States in the late 1950's and early 1960's have been explained plausibly in these terms[37]. Although long swings can continue to contribute to shorter-run cyclical instability, appropriate government action can both attenuate these swings in growth and offset undesired effects in the form of shorter run fluctuations[38].

### New role of Discretionary Fiscal Policy

Early in his first Godkin lecture at Harvard University last year, Professor Heller declared,

We at last accept what was accepted in law twenty years ago (in the Employment Act of 1946), namely, that the Federal government has an over-arching responsibility for the nation's economic stability and growth. And we have at last unleashed fiscal and monetary policy for aggressive pursuit of those objectives[39].

Among many economists, particularly those who have served with or been close to the Council of Economic Advisers since 1961, this is thought to be the great change that has occurred since the 1950's, making the economy more stable than it was before. The "unleashing" of fiscal policy in particular, rather than any structural changes in the private economy, is on its way to making the business cycle obsolete.

This position needs to be interpreted carefully. There are at least two aspects to the new use of discretionary fiscal policy in the United States, and I think it is important to distinguish between them.

First, as Heller puts it, policy emphasis has been "redirected from a *corrective* orientation geared to the dynamics of the cycle, to a *propulsive* orientation geared to the dynamics and the promise of growth . . . . The main instrument for dethroning the cyclical model and enthroning the growth model has been the *GNP* or *performance gap* and the associated estimates of the economy's potential and growth rate at 4 per cent unemployment ('full' or 'high' employment)"[40].

What this seems to mean is that the *level* of output and employment has become a more important guide to policy than the direction of change. If there is a significant "gap" and unemployment in above 4 per cent, an expansionary fiscal policy is called for, even though a cyclical expansion is already under way.

Heller certainly speaks too strongly here when he talks of "dethroning the cyclical model." Elsewhere in his Godkin lectures, he speaks of the need to couple with the emphasis on long-run policy a "flexibility in response to short-run fluctuations"[41]. Indeed—and this is the second point to be made about the new role of stabilization policy in the United States—Congress and the Administration are prepared, within limits and with some lag, to use a discretionary fiscal policy more vigorously and more flexibly now than they were before 1961 in order to cope with undesirable changes in the level of spending and employment. To this extent, a contracyclical discretionary fiscal policy plays a more, not a less, important role than it did in the Eisenhower and earlier Administrations. But the contracyclical policy is subject to the constraint that restrictive fiscal measures are not to be taken during an expansion if a significant full employment "gap" exists.

This emphasis on eliminating the "gap," and the associated use of the guide of the potential budgetary surplus at full employment, undoubtedly add to the stability of the economy. Interestingly, this approach puts more emphasis on the "fiscal drag" created by the automatic stabilizers as the economy expands than on the role of the stabilizers in cushioning a recession. Continued growth in potential output requires periodic fiscal stimuli, through tax reductions or increased government expenditures, if aggregate demand is to rise at the appropriate rate. The assumption here is that, except in periods of accelerated defense spending (as during 1966), the increase in tax revenues will significantly exceed the rate at which government expenditures can be expected to increase.

Thus discretionary tax reductions are to be made not merely when business recessions threaten or occur. The continuation of this policy promises that a fiscal stimulus will continue to be applied to the economy, although probably in rather irregular way. The result should be more stable growth than in the past (other things being equal), with longer expansions and possibly milder recessions than before the 1960's. Consistent application of such a policy should preclude future periods of prolonged high unemployment, such as 1958–1963.

One question needs to be asked: How much will such a policy, if long maintained and in the primary form of tax reductions, reduce the effectiveness of the automatic stabilizers in a downward as well as an upward direction? Repeated reductions in progressive tax rates on personal incomes and in the levy on cyclically sensitive corporate profits will reduce the strength of the automatic stabilizers. In the absence of offsetting discretionary fiscal action they will widen the amplitude of fluctuation in disposable income for a given amplitude on movement in GNP. Thus implicit in this discretionary fiscal policy for growth there is a lessened reliance on the automatic stabilizers, and acceptance of a greater need to use discretionary policy to cope with both expansions that are too vigorous and actual or incipient recessions. Indeed, something of a paradox is involved here. Over the long run, growth and stability are to be promoted by making the economy somewhat more unstable in the absence of a vigorous discretionary fiscal policy. This offers an argument for taking a considerable part of the required fiscal action in the form of increased government expenditures and transfer payments, rather than as tax reductions[42].

Under this new approach "not only monetary but fiscal policy has to be put on constant, rather than intermittent, alert"[43]. That does not dispose of the problem of the business cycle. Errors in forecasting will still be made; and the inevitable lags—"inside" ones in recognizing the need for action and "outside" ones in the economy's responses to various kinds of monetary and fiscal action—will still be with us. If deflationary forces begin to operate, whether because of the internal dynamics of the system or because of unpredicted changes in important exogenous variables, monetary ease and vigorous fiscal action when the need is finally recognized will not necessarily prevent enough of a downswing to warrant the N. B. E. R.'s marking off another business cycle in its chronology.

In this connection, it is worth remembering that the stabilizing fiscal policy is intended to work in both directions[44]. Restrictive action when a boom becomes too vigorous and inflation threatens will have effects that cannot always be foreseen; here again, the lags may be long and variable. The debate and uncertainty in the United States during the last year around how much and what kinds of restrictive action shoud be taken, and when, is a case in point.

Thus I agree with Gardner Ackley, Chairman of the Council of Economic Advisers, that "despite the unprecedented duration of our present expansion, we cannot assume that recessions are a thing of the past"[45]. They may not be much, if any, briefer or milder than those that occurred between 1949 and 1961. But there is reason to hope that the acceptance of the "new economics" in Washington will mean that recessions will occur less frequently than they did before the 1960's—and that periods of excessive unemployment will be less prolonged than that from which the economy has just emerged.

## Conclusion

The business cycle, although in a gratifyingly attenuated form, still exists. Some structural changes have occurred in the last decade that tend to make the U. S. economy more stable, and recent developments in the field of stabilization policy have moved the economy further in the same direction. But is is important to remember that the economic system is dynamic and subject to almost continuous shock. Imperfect foresight and mistakes of judgment, the strains and stresses of the political process that so often lead to second-best solutions, and limited knowledge of the internal dynamics of the system all suggest that, even with the improvements in stabilization policy of the last six years, the United States has not seen its last recession.

Knowing that Dr. Moore would be a discussant of this chapter, I turned to the last issue of *Business Cycle Developments,* published by the Bureau of the Census, and examined the business cycle indicators and diffusion indices which Moore and his colleagues have developed[46]. The leading indicators are still leading, and those that lagged in the past are still lagging[47]. On the basis of figures through December 1966 of 30 leading indicators all but three seemed to have reached a peak, at least for the time being, by October 1966. Of 15 coinciding indicators only three had been declining for as much as two months. Virtually all of the diffusion indices were falling, and some had fallen to or below the 50 per cent mark. This evidence alone would not lead me to predict a recession in 1967. It suggests that the same kinds of differential responses to a cyclical expansion in total spending that have occurred in previous cycles are occurring this time also. *Plus ça change, . . . ?*

## Notes

* I acknowledge the assistance of the research program on Unemployment and the American Economy being carried on at the Institute of Industrial Relations at the University of California, Berkeley, under a grant from the Ford Foundation. Thanks are due particularly to Mrs. Barbara Palmer and Mr. David Kotz.

[1] For an earlier consideration of some of the issues raised in this chapter, see papers by John Lintner and Frank Garfield, in American Statistical Association, *Proceedings of the Business and Economic Statistics Section*, 1965, pp. 388–394 and 405–413.

[2] R. A. Gordon, *Business Fluctuations*, 2nd ed., New York, 1961, p. 249.

[3] Perhaps one or more variables representing the course of "technological change," if agreement could be reached on how to define and measure this phenomenon, might be included as a fifth type of exogenous variable.

[4] Social insurance contributions, as a result of new legislation, jumped from 4.2 per cent of GNP in the fourth quarter of 1965 to 5.1 per cent in the first quarter of 1966.

[5] The quarterly data, of course, would show somewhat wider fluctuations. Over the last three years, for example, the quarterly ratios ranged between 0.913 and 0.926 whereas the annual ratios were between 0.919 and 0.920.

[6] Under the revisions in the national income accounts made by the Department of Commerce in 1965, a distinction is now made between "personal outlays" and "consumption expenditures." The former include the latter plus interest paid by consumers and personal transfer payments to foreigners. Personal savings are obtained by subtracting personal outlays—rather than the smaller total, consumtion expenditures—from disposable income. This explains why although consumption has recently been about 92 per cent of disposable income, personal saving has been only about 5.5 per cent.

[7] James S. Duesenberry *et al.*, eds., *The Brookings Quarterly Econometric Model of the United States,* Chicago and Amsterdam, 1965, pp. 208–209, 215–216, and 684; Daniel B. Suits, "Forecasting and Analysis with an Econometric Model," *American*

*Economic Review,* Vol. 52, March 1965 (reprinted on R. A. Gordon and L. R. Klein, ed., *Readings in Business Cycles,* Homewood, Illinois, 1965, p. 606); and the equations in the new model of the Office of Business Economics, Department of Commerce, in *Survey of Current Business,* May 1966, p. 30.

[8] Hickman makes the point that "the very steadiness of service demands can be destabilizing during contractions." If consumers wish to decrease total expenditures by a given amount, then the less service expenditures decline, the greater will be the fall in spending on goods. But a decline in spending on goods brings about also a decline in inventory investment, which is not true of spending on services. See Bert G. Hickman, *Growth and Stability of the Postwar Economy,* Washington, p. 263. Hickman's point leaves unanswered the question whether the resistance of service expenditures to a decline in income would serve to hold up total spending or would be at the expense of spending on goods. If the spending-income relations hold in the short run for each component separately, then the stability of service expenditures would not be at the expense of spending on goods.

[9] Work has been done, however, on comparing the postwar period as a whole (up to 1960 or so) with the prewar period. See, for example, Hickman, *op. cit.*; S. H. Hymans, "The Cyclical Behavior of Consumers' Income and Spending: 1921–61," *Southern Economic Journal,* Vol. 32 (July 1965), pp. 23–34; L. J. Paradiso and Mabel A. Smith, "Consumer Purchasing and Income Patterns," *Survey of Current Business,* March 1959, pp. 18–28; and Daniel B. Suits, "The Determinants of Consumer Expenditure: A Review of Present Knowledge," in Commission on Money and Credit, *Impacts of Monetary Policy,* Englewood Cliffs, New Jersey, 1963, esp. pp. 30, 33–35.

[10] See R. A. Gordon, "The Current Business Expansion in Perspective," in R. A. Gordon and Margaret S. Gordon, eds., *Prosperity and Unemployment,* New York, 1966, pp. 25–28.

[11] Time and space do not permit consideration of the longer run prospects for residential building.

[12] As in the Brookings model. See the chapters by Jorgenson and Eisner in Duesenberry *et al., op. cit.*

[13] Robert Hall and Dale Jorgenson have estimated that the stimulating effects on investment of the tax incentives provided since 1954 have been very substantial. See their "Tax Policy and Investment Behavior" and "The Role of Taxation in Stabilizing Private Investment." The first has appeared in *American Economic Review,* vol. 57 (June, 1967); the second will appear in J. D. Coker and H. B. Schecter, ed., *The Role of Economic Models in Policy Formulation,* (forthcoming).

[14] For some further considerations on this range of issues, see—in addition to the papers by Hall and Jorgenson previously cited—Commission on Money and Credit, *Stabilization Policies,* Englewood Cliffs, New Jersey, 1963, pp. 10–13, 138–141, and (on the relation of the corporate income tax to corporate financial policies) pp. 381–470. On the subject of lags, see Dale W. Jorgenson and James A. Stephenson, "The Time Structure of Investment Behavior in United States Manufacturing, 1947–1960," *Review of Economics and Statistics,* Vol. 49 (February 1967), pp. 16–27.

[15] See the data on sources and uses of funds, *Economic Report of the President,* January 1967, p. 294; also pp. 53–55.

[16] For a useful survey of econometric studies of investment (as of about 1960), see Robert Eisner and Robert H. Strotz, "Determinants of Business Investment," in *Impacts of Monetary Policy, op. cit.*, pp. 138 ff.; more recent work is covered by Michael Evans, *Macro-Economic Activity: An Econometric Approach*, New York, 1969, Chapter 5. For an explicit consideration of the effect of monetary policy on investment, see the study by Kareken and Solow in *Stabilization Polices, op. cit.*, esp. pp. 25-28. See also Robert Ferber, ed., *Determinants of Investment Behavior*, New York, 1967; and Z. Griliches and N. Wallace, "The Determinants of Investment Revisited," *International Economic Review*, Vol. 6 (September 1965). esp. pp. 326–327.

[17] Cf. Hickman, *op. cit.*, Chapter 11, and R. A. Gordon, "Investment Behavior and Business Cycles," *Review of Economics and Statistics*, Vol. 37 (February 1955), pp. 23–34.

[18] Similar results would be obtained if the measurement were in current prices. The percentages would be larger of course, if the changes were measured from peak to trough quarters, but the same trend would be evident. This downward trend is partly but not entirely explained by the tendency toward milder recessions in total output.

[19] See the useful survey by Eisner and Strotz in *Impacts of Monetary Policy, op. cit.*, pp. 192–227; Michael Evans, *op. cit.*, Chapter 8; Joint Economic Committee, *Inventory Fluctuations and Economic Stabilization*, 87th Cong., lst sess., Washington, 1961; two papers by Michael Lovell, one in Conference on Research in Income and Wealth, *Models of Income Determination*, Princeton, New Jersey, 1964, and one in Robert Ferber, ed., *op. cit.*; and the chapter by Paul Darling and Michael Lovell in Duesenberry *et al.*, *op. cit.*

[20] A particularly useful study in this area is Edwin Kuh, *Profits, Profit Markups, and Productivity*, Study Paper No. 15 for Joint Economic Committee, *Study of Employment, Growth, and Price Levels*, 86th Cong., 1st sess., Washington, 1960. See also the contributions by Kuh, Schultze and Tryon on Duesenberry *et al.*, *op. cit.*, and Evans, *op. cit.*, Chapters 10–11.

[21] See Thor Hultgren, *Costs, Prices, and Profits: Their Cyclical Relations*, New York, 1965; also Kuh, *op. cit.*, pp. 75–82.

[22] Based on data through the fourth quarter of 1966.

[23] A peak may have been reached in the second quarter of 1966.

[23-a] A. W. Phillips, "The Relation between Unemployment and the Rate of Change of Money Wages in the United Kingdom, 1861–1957," *Economica*, New Series, Vol. 25 (November 1958), pp. 283–299.

[24] The figures through 1965 are from *Manpower Research of the President*, March 1966, p. 201; those for 1966 are computed from data in *Employment and Earnings and Monthly Report on the Labor Force*, January 1967.

[25] For an interesting discussion of the relation between investment during a cyclical expansion and the rise in overhead labor requirements, see Kuh, *op. cit.*, pp. 86–93.

[26] For other recent studies of the behavior of labor productivity, see Kuh, "Cyclical and Secular Labor Productivity in United States Manufacturing," *Review of Economics and Statistics*, Vol. 47 (February 1965), pp. 1–12 and Thomas A. Wilson and Otto Eckstein, "Short-Run Productivity Behavior in U. S. Manufacturing," *Review of Economics and Statistics*, Vol. 46 (February 1965), pp. 41–54.

[27]  For the Brookings model, Kuh has estimated employment functions for manufacturing separately for production and nonproduction workers. See his paper in
Duesenberry *et al., op. cit.,* pp. 241 ff.

[28]  Another stabilizing change in the relation between total employment and total real
GNP results from the changing industrial composition of nonagricultural employment.
Manufacturing accounted for only 29.9 per cent of such employment in 1966,
compared with 34.9 per cent in 1953 and 32.5 per cent in 1957. The percentage of
total employment accounted for by government and by the service industries has risen
significantly over the postwar period. Employment in both these sectors has
continued to rise in every postwar recession.

[29]  A particular serious omission here is failure to deal with monetary and financial
relationships.

[30]  For some of the issues involved here, see J. A. Maxwell, *Financing State and Local
Governments,* Washington, 1965; G. F. Break, *Intergovernmental Fiscal Relations in
the United States,* Washington, 1967; and *Economic Report of the President,* January
1967, pp. 161–167. Much discussed in this connection is the so-called Heller Plan; see
Walter Heller, *New Dimensions of Political Economy,* Cambridge, Massachusetts,
1966.

[31]  Hickman, *op. cit.,* p. 215.

[32]  *Ibid.,* p. 215.

[33]  The increase in the rediscount rate in December 1965 led to a heated controversy, as
did the rapid tightening of credit that followed in 1966. For some of the reactions to
this episode, see *Recent Federal Reserve Action and Economic Policy Coordination,*
Hearings before the Joint Economic Committee, 89th Cong., 1st sess., Washington,
1966.

[34]  There is, of course, a vast literature on postwar American monetary policy. For a
useful bibliography (as of 1965), see Board of Governers of the Federal Reserve
System, *Monetary Theory and Policy: A Bibliography,* Washington, 1965. Special
mention should be made of *The Report of the Commission on Money and Credit,*
Englewood Cliffs, New Jersey, 1961, and the volumes of study papers that were
subsequently published. For criticism and defense of recent Federal Reserve policy,
see the hearings before, and the reports of, the Joint Economic Committee on the
January 1966 and January 1967 *Economic Report of the President.* A useful critical
appraisal of Federal Reserve policy in the 1950's is in *Staff Report on Employment,
Growth, and Price Levels,* prepared for the Joint Economic Committee, 86th Cong.,
1st sess., Washington, 1959.

[35]  Mention should be made also of short-term capital movements, in a world in which
financial markets are being steadily tied more closely together. Changing interest rates
abroad (and the particular kinds of cooperation that central bankers chose to adopt)
are another set of exogenous variables (from the point of view of the U. S. economy)
that influence U. S. monetary policy and thus the behavior of the domestic economy.

[36]  Thus, in growth models, it is not always wise to take Harrod's "natural rate" as an
exogenously determined constant.

[37]  See Bert G. Hickman, "The Postwar Retardation: Another Long Swing in the Rate of
Growth?" *American Economic Review,* Vol. 53 (May 1963), pp. 490–507; also the
accompanying papers by Burnham Campbell and Jeffrey Williamson and the
comments by a panel of discussants.

[38]  The way demographic factors interact with other variables to generate swings in growth has certainly changed since the 1920's. See Hickman, "The Postwar Retardation . . .", *op. cit.,* and R. A. Easterlin, "Economic-Demographic Interactions and Long Swings in Economic Growth," *American Economic Review,* Vol. 56 (December 1966), pp. 1063–1104.

[39]  Heller, *op. cit.*, pp. 1–2.

[40]  *Ibid.,* p. 62 (italics in the original.)

[41]  *Ibid.,* p. 81.

[42]  Including possibly remitting a share of federal taxes to the states, as under the Heller plan. (*Ibid.* Chapter 3.) To the extent that this might lead to a substitution of cyclically sensitive federal tax revenues for less sensitive state and local receipts, the automatic stabilizers would be strengthened.

[43]  *Ibid.,* p. 69.

[44]  Recent experience in the United States and the experience of other Countries suggest that discretionary fiscal policy is not as symmetrical as it should be, but adds an element of inflationary bias to the economy.

[45]  Statement before the Subcommittee on Fiscal Policy, Joint Economic Committee, July 20, 1965, to which Heller has added, "The 'new economics' provides no money-back guarantee against occasional slowdowns or even recessions." *Op. cit.,* p. 104.

[46]  See Geoffrey H. Moore and Julius Shiskin, *Indicators of Business Expansions and Contractions,* New York, 1967, where references to an earlier work on the indicators will also be found.

[47]  This was written early in 1967.

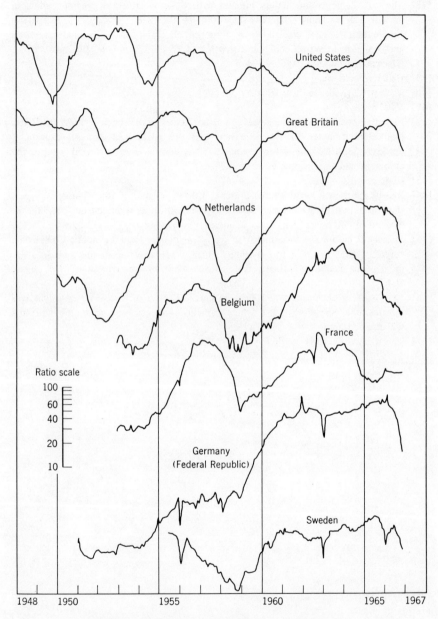

**Figure 1–2.** Ratio of job vacancies to unemployment.

34

# COMMENTS

STANISLAV M. MENSHIKOV
Institute of World Economy
and International Relations, Moscow

I should like to begin with problems of scope and definition and then turn to problems of substance. The subject of Professor Gordon's paper is in my opinion much wider than the problem of the business cycle proper. Gordon's problem might include such aspects of the stability or instability of an economy as the absence or presence, or extent of, chronic inflation, long-term balance of payments difficulties, hard-core unemployment, chronically depressed areas, disproportions created by sharp increases in military expenditure, etc. The stability of an economy could perhaps be assessed mainly, or even exclusively, on the basis of cyclical performance in the nineteenth century or the first third of the twentieth century: at the present time, I do not consider such an approach sufficient. In order to settle the question of the stability or instability of an economy, many other things would have to be bought into the analysis. If the data used were related mainly to the business cycle proper, then adequate conclusions on the stability or the instability of the U. S. economy might not be reached. In other words, the fact that the magnitude of recessions has become smaller when compared with the 1920's and 1930's does not necessarily mean that the economy is more stable than it was at that time.

My second observation is on the problem of definition. I do not feel that the definition used by Gordon ("recurring alterations of expansion and contraction in aggregate economic activity, the alternating movements in each direction being self-reinforcing and pervading virtually all parts of the economy") is fully adequate for the purpose of this discussion. It is correct in two points: the self-reinforcing nature of the cyclical movement and the general character of it for virtually all parts of the economy. It lacks a few points that that I consider crucial.

35

First, the business cycle is contingent on periodic contractions resulting from general overproduction, that is, the temporary inability to sell all the goods that have been produced. Of course, the causes of cyclical business contractions are not so simple, but I am now pointing to their nature and not to their causes. If this contingency is not pointed out, then any business contraction might be considered cyclical, though its nature might be quite different. Take, for example, the postwar reconversion of 1945–1946 in the United States, or the collapse of the economies of Germany and Japan in the early postwar years. These events obviously are not cyclical, although Gordon unfortunately refers to "the brief 1945 recession." With the increase in the role of military expenditure, people favor such thinking, since these phenomena are not caused by the working of the business cycle, although they affect the changing behavior of the business cycle in modern times.

The second point about definition is this: it would be useful to mention the principal physical basis for cyclical movement, that is the periodic waves of renovation of fixed capital in industry (and, it could now be added, the waves of renovation of fixed assets in households).

Gordon recognizes this point when he says the instability of private investment is, of course, "at the heart of the problem of the business cycle." But I believe that this aspect should have been included in his initial definition. It is essential in distinguishing the business cycle from irregular fluctuations caused by different factors, or combinations of factors.

For example, I think there is nothing to justify calling the 1958–1961 period in the United States a separate complete business cycle. Neither time (only three years) nor anything else typical of a complete cycle is present there. If the figures for private capital investment are examined, then the differences between the various postwar downturns in the United States become quite obvious.

The contraction of private capital investment in industry, transport, commerce, utilities, and services (in 1958 prices) from its maximum value of 1947 (the downturn in capital investment began in 1947 and not in 1948) to the minimum value of 1949 was 17.3 per cent. Declines from maximum to minimum values were 5.8 per cent for 1953–1954, 19.8 per cent for 1956–1958, and 4.1 per cent for 1960–1961[1]. These figures, added to certain others, led me in my own studies to consider the 1948–1949 and the 1957–1958 recessions as regular cyclical contractions; 1953–1954 as an "intermediate" recession; and 1960–1961 as an "aftermath" recession, taking place for the reason that the task of the previous cyclical recession had not been

[1] Business expenditures for new plant and equipment divided by the price deflator for nonresidential fixed investment used in statistics on Gross National Product (GNP). (From the *Economic Report of the President,* Washington, D. C., 1966, Tables C-5 and cC-36). These figures do not include inventory investment, which should be dealt with separately.

wholly fulfilled. By the same reasoning, such U. S. recessions as those of 1924 and 1927 would be considered different from the 1920–1921 or 1929–1933 contractions.

With the diminished amplitude of the cyclical swing in many other indicators, it becomes difficult to find the quantitative differences between intermediate and cyclical recessions. The movement of private capital investment still provides a valuable clue; for example, it is a crucially important fact that in the United States the 1956 peak in private capital investment in real terms was not surpassed until 1963, when the real cyclical boom period began. On the other hand, any possible downturn in capital investment beginning in 1967–1968 would surely be one of the principal features of a new cyclical recession, whatever its magnitude in aggregate economic activity or industrial production.

It is essential that the whole analysis of the business cycle be based on cyclical rather than regular fluctuations. For example, if the U. S. average annual growth rate for 1953–1961 is compared with that for 1961–1966, then the great difference might lead to wrong and strange conclusions, to a temptation to look for drastic changes in the business cycle itself where really there are no major changes, as Gordon's paper clearly shows. A more meaningful basis for comparison would be the regular business cycle fluctuation. A comparison of the 1948–1957 and 1957–1966 periods would show that the average annual growth is practically the same in the two periods—about 4.5 per cent for industrial production and about 3.8–4 per cent for gross national product in real terms. Of course, many other factors besides fixed capital renovation are extremely important, but the heart of the cycle is surely there.

I am in agreement with Gordon's main conclusion that nothing very significant has happened in the U. S. economy in the 1960's to make the minor cycle, as he calls it, obsolete. This conclusion has been reached on the basis of rather convincing arguments.

It also seems certain that very deep and long depressions are, at present, unlikely to occur[2]. But let me make one correction. When it is said that "serious" depressions are obsolete, the depressions that are meant are ones like 1920–1921 and 1929–1933. From the time that the regular cyclical movement began (somewhere around 1825) up to the beginning of the 1920's, there was not a single yearly downturn of industrial production in Great Britain of more than 10 per cent. In the history of the cycles in the United States this limit was exceeded only twice: in 1893–1894, when the contraction was 14 per cent and

---

[2] It might be useful to refer to some of my recent publications, where this point is developed at some length, as well as other aspects of the business cycle *The Economy of Contemporary Capitalism and Its Contradictions,* Moscow, 1966 (available in Russian); "On the Mechanism of the Contemporary Cycle," *World Economy and International Relations,"* Nos. 4 and 5, 1966 (in Russian, but available also in German in *Konjunktur und Krise,* Heft 3–4, Berlin, 1966).

in 1907–1908 when it was 17 per cent. The 1948–1949 and 1957–1958 recessions in the United States with downturns of 5.4 per cent and 7 per cent per annum, respectively, are very much in the order of most recessions in the nineteenth century and the beginning of the 20th. Not until the 1920's and the 1930's did depressions become very serious.

The earlier recessions occurred at a time when the structure of the economy was very different from what it is now. Among other things, the predominance of the individual entrepreneur and the practical absence of adequate information on what was really happening in the economy as a whole led to great panics, mass bankruptcies, etc., even though the actual contractions in production were rather small. Although in quantitative economic terms the present-day recessions ary not much milder that they were in the 19th century, there is no point in asserting that the pre-1914 type of cycle is returning, since, in qualitative terms, there are deep changes in the cyclical mechanism.

These changes are dependent on the following principal factors of long-term character: the current revolution in science and technology; the predominance of large corporations (with their new structure and their new planning methods) instead of individual entrepreneurs; the drastically increased role of government in economic activity; the new balance of power between labor and capital; the emergence of numerous newly independent developing countries instead of the few empires formerly constituted which the world economy; and, last but not least, coexistence and competition between capitalist and Socialist systems.

These factors have many ways of influencing the business cycles, both in stabilizing and destabilizing directions: having brought an end to the type of depression of the 1920's and 1930's such factors have gradually led to the emergence of a number of new developments which tend to make recessions reappear at the very moment that the cycle is beginning to be considered obsolete. Having intensified technological change, they have at the same time created a tendency to lessen, relatively speaking, the demand for capital investment goods, bringing stagnation to certain branches of industry and certain areas, and creating new unemployment problems; having decreased the relative amount of overproduction of commodities in recessions, they have increased the excessive accumulation of fixed capital and excess capacity. The long stagnation in private capital investment in the United States during 1958–1962 was a direct result of this excessive accumulation.

Also, having provided the governments with anti–cyclical tools, these factors have given central authorities the power to "plan" recessions and bring them about; and having created an increasing demand on the part of labor for consumer goods, they have made the wage-price-profit relationship one of the most significant factors in current cyclical behavior. The very change in the magnitude of the recessions is one of the main explanations of persistent price inflation. This inflationary tendency is in sharp contradiction to the revolution in science and technology, which should tend to lower the price of products instead of making them more expensive from year to year.

I agree with Gordon when he writes in his conclusion: "it is important to remember that the system is dynamic and subject to almost continuous shock." It is the remaining predominance of private ownership in an economy, whether in the form of individual entrepreneurship or of large corporations, which—despite the changing economic role of government—leaves the capitalist system open to the shocks of the business cycle.

# COMMENTS

GEOFFREY H. MOORE
National Bureau of Economic Research
(U.S. Commissioner of Labor Statistics, 1969–)

When the conference with which this discussion deals was planned, in 1964–1965, the question "Is the Business Cycle Obsolete?" seemed more plausible than it does in the spring of 1967. The United States is now (April 1967) flirting with recession,and lately it has experienced two concomitants of booms—a taste of inflation and a near financial crisis. Great Britain is engineering something like a recession. The Federal Republic of Germany is experiencing its most severe recession since World War II. The question posed by the conference may be obsolete, the problem of booms and recessions is not.

Figure 1–2, on 7-country ratios of job vacancies to unemployment, which was recently constructed at the National Bureau of Economic Research[1], suggests that the conference is not dealing with an "academic" topic. The ratios do not pertain directly to anything in Professor Gordon's paper, but I am sure he will find them of interest, since it was the Gordon Committee on Measuring Employment and Unemployment that recommended—so far, in vain—the compilation of comprehensive statistics on job vacancies in the United States. These ratios are not based on comprehensive job vacancy data, but rather on administrative statistics from employment placement offices; yet they do seem to have indicative value.

The vacancy-unemployment ratio is one of the most sensitive of cyclical indicators, since the numerator tends to move positively with the business cycle, the denominator inversely. Furthermore, it is plausible to suppose, and the statistical evidence suggests, that the ratio has a higher degree of sensitivity at turning points than either of its components alone. For example, when an economy is close to full employment, unemployment will be low and relatively

---

[1] As part of a study of cyclical movements in job vacancies, by Charlotte Boshan.

stable, yet vacancies may well continue to rise sharply for a time and then to fall, so that the ratio undergoes a cyclical rise and fall, imparted largely by vacancies. On the other hand, when depression has reduced vacancies to a low level, the rise or fall in unemployment may be more consequential, and then it will be unemployment that moves the ratio. The ratio, then, should be a better detector of turning points than unemployment at the top of the business cycle, and a better detector than vacancies at the bottom.

It is interesting therefore to observe the postwar swings in this sensitive index of demand–supply pressure in the labor markets of many of the countries represented at this conference. What is especially interesting is the consensus toward recession that has been developing recently. Surely, it lends credence to the view that the business cycle is not yet obsolete.

The principal issue raised in Gordon's paper is whether or not there are observable tendencies toward greater stability in the U. S. economy. The question is not inappropriate for one who has espoused an historical approach to business cycles, even though he couches it in an econometric framework. Moreover, the answer is of some international consequence—if there is any truth in the ancient view that the United States exports its recessions. I might point out, however, that quite recently it has appeared that the United States is now importing its recessions. At least, the current situation in the United States has recently been described as a "Japanese recession."

Indeed, this is the kind of recession that Gordon is willing to embrace in his definition—a retardation, or slower rate of growth, rather than an absolute decline in aggregate activity. I must say, whatever the scientific merits of the Gordon—or Japanese—definition, that at the present time much more excitement is generated in New York and Washington by the prospect of an old-fashioned, absolute decline. In fact, the New Economics, both in the United States and elsewhere, seems to be having enough trouble preventing the old-fashioned kind, without taking on a new breed of recession as well.

There is no need, however, to rely exclusively on a rate-of-growth criterion. Many respectable indicators still undergo up-and-down movements. The vacancy-unemployment ratio, as the chart shows, is one of them. The movements in this ratio came quite close to matching, in the United States, the up-and-down movements in aggregate activity that the National Bureau's business cycle chronology purports to represent. In Germany, the movements in the vacancy-unemployment ratio have corresponded quite closely with periods of rapid growth and slower growth in industrial production and in retail sales. Indeed, it appears, from some studies which Mrs. Ilse Mintz has begun at the National Bureau, that these periods of alternating high and low rates of growth appear quite generally in different economic variables at about the same time. She is examining these relationships for several countries, starting with the Federal Republic of Germany. When her studies are completed, a test of the cycle concept that Gordon has suggested should be available.

From the viewpoint of business-cycle policy, the concept of a rate-of-growth cycle needs to be examined carefully. A mere reduction in the rate of growth of aggregate economic activity may not warrant an anti-recession policy. The slower rate may be more sustainable than the faster one, and more compatible with price-level stability. Moreover, in U. S. experience, shifts from a rapid rate of expansion to a slower one have often occurred shortly after recovery from an absolute decline has begun. This decline in the rate of growth is associated with absorption of idle capacity, re-employment of workers previously laid off, attainment of a full workweek, and so on. Slower growth, in these circumstances, does not call for additional stimulation.

Similarly, when the rate of decline during a contraction in activity gives way to a smaller rate of decline, this should surely not be taken as a signal that anti-recession policies should be relaxed. In short, a cycle defined as an alternation of algebraically higher and lower rates of growth does not have simple implications for policy.

In one respect the task that Gordon sets for himself in his discussion is particularly difficult. Much of it is directed to the question whether there has been a significant change in the business cycle since 1961. It might almost be said that he is dealing with the problem of indentifying or measuring a secular change on the basis of one observation—the expansion from 1961 to 1966. This is the reason, it seems to me, why Gordon's discussion proceeds on a rather speculative plane. Business cycles in the past have differed greatly from one another. It is, therefore, exceedingly difficult to determine what changes are basic, permanent, secular, or systematic. A single observation is not very dependable, though it is, of course, better than none, especially since it is the very latest.

I find it difficult, therefore, either to accept or to reject Gordon's results. Instead of pursuing the matter, I should like to call attention to several changes in American cyclical experience that are of a longer-run nature, and fairly well supported by statistical evidence. This is not a comprehensive survey of the kind that Gordon provides in his discussion. The changes represent results of several recent or ongoing studies at the National Bureau, which point to factors that seem likely to make the business cycles of the future differ from those of the past.

The first change is the greatly increased importance of what may be called consumer capital investment, as compared with business capital investment. It is perhaps not generally known that the annual investment by consumers in durable goods and houses in the United States is now far larger than investment by business enterprises in plant and equipment. According to estimates by F. Thomas Juster[2], household investment was about 9 per cent less than business

[2] *Household Capital Formation and Financing, 1897–1962*, New York, 1966.

investment in 1920, about equal to it in 1929, about 28 per cent larger in 1948, and nearly 90 per cent larger in 1960. The rate of growth in household investment since 1920 has been more than double that of business investment.

Now both types of investment have been cyclically volatile. Juster has measured the volatility of each in terms of deviations from long-term trend, in dollars of constant purchasing power. He finds that from 1897 to 1915 the deviations in the household sector were only 24 per cent as large as in the enterprise sector. In the postwar period, 1947–1962, the household sector variations exceeded those in the business sector by 37 per cent.

Hence the motivations of the consumer, and the economic policies affecting his ability and incentive to invest in automobiles, appliances, furniture, houses, and other durable goods, have become exceedingly important. It is possible that they will operate in a stabilizing direction, partly because consumer income is more stable than business income, and partly because the fluctuations in the different forms of consumer investment do not appear to be highly synchronized with one another or with business investment.

A second secular shift in cyclical behavior concerns the labor force. Professor Jacob Mincer, among others, has been investigating the sensitivity of the labor force to cyclical fluctuations[3]. He finds that labor-force participation rates of the primary working groups—notably married males—are insensitive, but that participation rates of the so-called secondary groups—students, married women, and older persons—are quite sensitive. Moreover, with the exception of the older group, the sensitive groups have been increasing in relation to the total labor force. This, then, has imparted a perceptible tendency for the labor force—employed plus unemployed—to rise during a business expansion and to fall (or rise more slowly) during a contraction. This in turn implies a greater stability in unemployment rates, as well as a somewhat higher average level.

It seems likely, therefore, that the labor force in the United States is taking on one of the characteristics that the labor force in some other countries derive from immigration, namely, a tendency to fluctuate in accordance with the demand for labor. This may have the effect of evening out some of the pressures of the labor market.

A third secular shift has appeared in the cyclical behavior of U. S. exports. Mrs. Mintz's book on this subject demonstrates that the swings in exports during U. S. business cycles have been much wider since the 1920's than before[4]. This shift has persisted in recent cycles, and has pervaded all the major classes of exports. Mrs. Mintz attributes it to the higher degree of synchronization between U. S. business cycles and fluctuations in world demand (as represented by world

[3] See his report, "Research in Labor and in Unemployment," in the 47th Annual Report of the National Bureau, June 1967.
[4] *Cyclical Fluctuations in the Exports of the United States Since 1879*, (NBER, 1967).

imports exclusive of U. S. imports) as well as to the increased instability of world demand. These have been factors tending to destabilize rather than to stabilize U. S. aggregate demand. Their effect on the trade balance has been to make it move more nearly with, rather than against, the U. S. business cycle.

The fourth change in cyclical behavior has been the increasing size of the swings in interest rates. Even before the sharp upsurge in rates in 1965–1966, it had appeared that interest rates were moving much more widely during the mild business cycles of the 1950's than during the equally mild business cycles of the 1920's. Professor Cagan finds that this can be explained, at least in part, by the tendency for the rate of change in the money supply to move more nearly inversely to business activity in recent cycles[5]. That is, a decline in the rate of growth of the money supply tends to lift interest rates in the short run; and if the decline corresponds to an expansion of business, then the rise in interest rates that is due to the expansion of demand is augmented. The situation during the expansion of business that began in 1961 fits in with this explanation. The very rapid increase—indeed, the accelerating increase—in the money supply from 1961 to 1965 helped to keep most interest rates relatively stable despite the expansion of demand. When the money supply was curtailed during 1966, interest rates shot up in a manner very reminiscent of that under similar circumstances in 1956–1957 and in 1959.

My four illustrations of secular changes in cyclical behavior broadly support the main point in Gordon's discussion, namely, that there are progressive shifts in the U. S. economy that tend to alter the character of the business cycle. I am perhaps less optimistic than Gordon in thinking that changes both in the structure of the economy and in economic policy are working in the direction of milder fluctuations. I see a considerable similarity between the monetary policies of 1959 and those of 1966, as well as a similarity in the factors underlying them, namely, an incipient inflation and a balance of payments problem. On the fiscal side, federal tax receipts rose at least as rapidly during 1966 as they did in 1959, but the shift toward a surplus did not get as far as in 1959, because expenditures were not held down as much. The chief difference, as I see it, between the 1959 and 1966 experience is that sharply restrictive policies were applied too early in one expansion and too late in the other. But these are differences in judgment with respect to a very complicated subject. Gordon's discussion will remain a most suggestive guide to further research on the stability of the U. S. economy.

---

[5]   Phillip Cagan, *Changes in the Cyclical Behavior of Interest Rates*, Occasional Paper 100 (NBER, 1966).

Chapter Two

# BUSINESS CYCLES IN CANADA: THEIR POSTWAR PERSISTENCE

DONALD J. DALY
*Economic Council of Canada, Ottawa*

A short answer to the question "Is the business cycle obsolete in Canada?" is easy to give. The answer is "No." And only two pieces of evidence are necessary for such an answer. One is that the unemployment rate for Canada ran in excess of 5 per cent of the labor force for six full years after 1957. This gives Canada the dubious distinction of having had, for an extended period, the highest unemployment level of any of the countries for which performance records are being examined in this book. The second piece of evidence is the material on postwar business cycles, as measured by the methods of the National Bureau of Economic Research (NBER). This material suggests that the business cycle has continued in Canada in a fairly moderate manner compared with earlier experience, but in a clearer fashion than for most of the countries, except the United States, being considered.

Although such a brief answer would not be misleading, it would still not be regarded as complete. In this instance, as in so many others, it is more important to know the reasons for a conclusion than to know the conclusion itself. Two things are regarded as necessary parts of this conclusion: one is a framework of analysis of why business cycles persist; the second is a review of the factual material on the relationships that are regarded as important.

This is recognized as an ambitious undertaking for a short chapter. What makes it feasible is a growing body of published material by academic and government economists who have been working in this area for the last two decades. As the material may not be widely known by many of those attending this conference, this chapter will summarize the main points essential to the themes being developed in this book[1]. Much of the broad framework and detailed methodology follows that which is developed elsewhere, and primarily in the United States [2].

## Some Initial Considerations

Three points would be largely accepted by those who have been working in this area in Canada. First, it is important to have a theoretical framework of what are considered to be the important relationships in the economy, and that it is preferable to have this fairly explicit. Second, it is important to have some orders of magnitude of the key relationships, and of the length of any lags in the system. Third, it is preferable to use a variety of approaches to method rather than to limit the work to any single approach. Examples of these three considerations run through this chapter. I shall not try to defend or justify these points but will leave it to the reader to appraise the results.

To provide some guidance, the topics covered will first be outlined, with special emphasis on some topics which could have broader implications for other countries. As part of this sorting-out process, some initial remarks will be made on the type of cycles being covered and why they occur.

### WHAT CYCLES?

Although the published literature contains a number of classifications of business cycles[3], this paper will deal with only two. One is the long cycle (or Kuznets cycle), which in North America has averaged about 20 years and has been particularly marked in business investment. The second is the National

---

[1] For reference to published material that gives a full presentation of tables, charts, and related analysis, see the list at the end of this chapter.

[2] This chapter is heavily influenced by the business cycle work done in the Economics branch of the Department of Trade and Commerce, and more recently by the Economic Council of Canada (established in the latter part of 1963). The primary emphasis in Trade and Commerce has been on the current economic situation and short-term outlook; the emphasis at the Economic Council has been mainly on longer-term growth and stabilization policy. The Trade and Commerce work included an econometric model initiated by T. M. Brown in 1947, with L. R. Klein as an initial staff member and adviser, and continued by S. J. May until 1965. About 1955, many of the National Bureau business cycle measures were duplicated for Canada by W. A. Beckett and continued by D. A. White. Geoffrey H. Moore and Julius Shiskin have provided advice and encouragement in this area for many years. It will be apparent in later parts of this paper that I have been more impressed by the similarities than the differences of the substantive empirical results of the econometric method and the National Bureau approach to cycles. Special mention should be made of the contribution of Derek White, who has been associated with this work since 1947, and has heavily influenced our joint thinking.

Bureau or inventory cycle, which has averaged about 45 months over the full cycle in North America since the 1850's.

It is recognized that the evidence on and the reasons for the long cycles have been studied less fully than the short cycles in both Canada and the United States. I believe that the distinction between the two is important. One reason is the existence of evidence that the phase of the long cycle influences the duration and amplitude of the short cycle [4]. A second reason is that the distinction between short and long cycles is important for stabilization policy. These points will be amplified at various places later in the discussion.

WHY CYCLES?

Although it would take us too far afield to attempt anything extensive on the reasons for cycles, it might help to point out some key features in current economic thinking and past experience in North America that are relevant. Current business cycle literature of an empirical variety emphasizes two considerations in cycles: the role of lags in a number of key relationships, and the influence of uncertainty and disturbances. Recognition of the importance of both these elements is present in the thinking and studies of both the econometric workers and the National Bureau.

"Frisch's paper (on Propagation Problems and Impulse Problems in Dynamic Economics) charted as early as 1933 the course that was to be followed by future builders of aggregative dynamic models. It combines an internal mechanism which may be cyclical by itself with external shocks which may be either random or autonomous" [5]. Mitchell emphasized the significance of timing lags, as indicated in Friedman's appraisal of Mitchell's work:

> At the very broadest level of generality, persistent, self-generating fluctuations in economic activity can occur only in a world characterized by both uncertainty (in the sense of unpredictable change) and lags in response (in the sense of different timing of response) ... Lags in response are the central elements in theories of this type.... The lags in response must be pervasive, they must operate on a broad range of activities, these activities must be linked with one another and to the remainder of the system, and the whole must display consistent, though not identical, response in successive cycles [6].

---

[3] Alvin Hansen, J. A. Schumpeter, and R. A. Gordon have summarized a number of these. Interest in the Kondratieff swing has tended to wane since World War II. See George Garvy, "Kondratieff's Theory of Long Cycles," *Review of Economic Statistics*, Vol. 25, November 1943, pp. 203–220. See also Arthur F. Burns and Wesley C. Mitchell, *Measuring Business Cycles*, New York, 1946, Chapter II.

[4] Moses Abramovitz, Staff Report in NBER, *Forty-first Annual Report*, May 1961, pp. 27–30; D. J. Daly, "Long Cycles and Recent Canadian Experience," in Royal Commission on Banking and Finance, *Appendix Volume*, Ottawa, 1965, pp. 281–301.

[5] R. A. Gordon and L. R. Klein, *Readings in Business Cycles*, Homewood, Illinois, 1965, p. 153.

[6] Milton Friedman, "The Economic Theorist," in Arthur F. Burns, *Wesley Clair Mitchell: The Economic Scientist*, New York, 1952, pp. 259–260.

This emphasis on the differences in timing of various economic processes is a crucial part of the business cycle work of the National Bureau and underlies the selection of business cycle indicators for the diagnosis of the stage of the business cycle on a current basis. These lagged relationships contribute to both the oscillatory and recurring nature of cycles and to a high degree of damping. Random shocks and major disturbances are also an integral part of past experience.

DISCUSSION OUTLINED

The central parts of this chapter deal with the evidence on, and the interpretation of, the question "Is the business cycle obsolete in Canada?" Much of the material covers Canadian developments in relation to similar material on the United States. Although the emphasis is on developments since World War II, the more recent cyclical pattern is considered in the context of the longer-term evidence on the duration and amplitude of cycles. The chapter also draws on both National Bureau and econometric evidence on particular aspects or relations. The following topics are covered: cycles in the United States and Canada, with a summary of the facts on both long and short cycles, and with special emphasis on timing and amplitude; postwar growth and cycles, and some of the reasons for the mildness of the postwar recessions in Canada; the importance of lags in some of the key relationships; the implications of these lags for stabilization policy; and some implications for the future.

## Cycles in the United States and Canada

As mentioned earlier, this chapter distinguishes between the long or Kuznets cycle and the shorter-term business cycle. In the description and analysis of the long cycle the procedure developed by Abramovitz is followed[7]. This procedure uses the dates selected along the lines developed at the N.B.E.R. for business cycles, develops averages over full business cycles, and then calculates the annual rates of change between adjacent full business cycles[8]. The main result of the averaging over business cycles is to smooth away much of the variation that is so apparent *within* business cycles. However, significant

---

[7] Moses Abramovitz, "The Nature and Significance of Kuznets Cycles," *Economic Development and Cultural Change,* Vol. 9, April 1961 (reprinted in Gordon and Klein, *op. cit.*).

[8] In this discussion, the turning points in long cycles are dated by the share of investment in GNP. This is frequently different from rates of change in the major aggregates. The practice of different workers in this field has not been uniform, partly reflecting differences in their areas of interest.

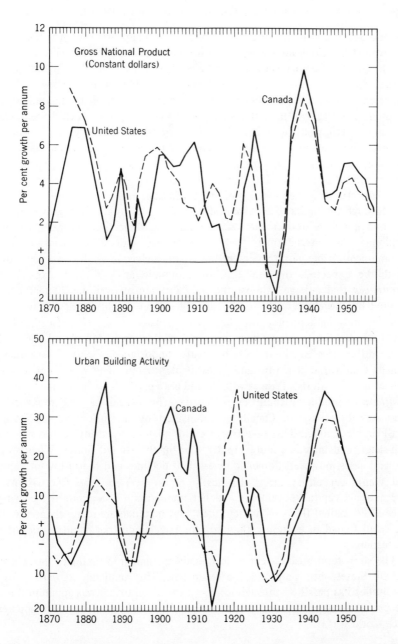

**Fig. 2-1.** Long cycles in gross national product and urban building activity, United States and Canada, 1870's to date. Reproduced from D. J. Daly, *Long Cycles and Recent Canadian Experience*, in Royal Commission on Banking and Finance, *Appendix Volume*, Ottawa, 1965, p. 287.

variations *between* different business cycles are still apparent, such as the impact of severe depressions and the vigor of different business cycle expansions.

The great differences in growth rate over time are illustrated by Figure 2-1. These differences are particularly significant when it is recalled that the variations *within* the short-term business cycles have been eliminated by the method of averaging. This reflects a persistent tendency for growth to take place in surges, followed by reactions and periods of slower growth. Another important feature evident from the chart is the broad similarity in the timing (both in Canada and the United States) of changes in gross national product (GNP) and urban building activity. A third point suggested is that the amplitudes of long cycles are somewhat greater in Canada than in the United States.

Although timing has been essentially similar, the variations in growth rate in the two countries reflect the very strong interconnections between the two economies—in international trade, commodity prices, financial markets, communication media, etc. Similarities in the behavior of the two economies would be expected; the real task of economic analysis is to explain any *differences* that emerge. Almost the only differences over the 90-year period covered by the chart relate to the slightly greater amplitude of the swings in Canada, and the tendency for the long expansion in the first decade of the twentieth century to persist over a somewhat more extended period in Canada. These differences largely reflect the greater importance of natural resources in Canada's industrial structure and investment program. The world demand for industrial raw materials is quite volatile and has a particularly large impact on such raw-material producing countries as Canada. When world markets are favorable, the rate of activity in Canada is intensified by an inflow of capital and considerable immigration. Investment is stimulated, especially in the resource industries, and increases more rapidly than in the United States. When world demand eases, however, domestic investment declines and the inflow of capital and manpower either drops drastically or is reversed. The fluctuations in international capital movements and net immigration accentuate these swings, since international flows of money, men, and materials are relatively greater for the small Canadian economy than for the larger industrial countries providing the resources.

The short-term business cycles in Canada are similar in timing to those in the United States, but amplitudes are smaller. This tendency toward smaller amplitudes has persisted throughout the present century; it was apparent during the period between the two world wars and has become even more apparent since World War II.

## *Postwar Growth and Cycles in Canada*

The growth of over-all output and employment in Canada has been fairly substantial over the last two decades, compared with previous experience. This has contributed to the duration and vigor of the economic expansions from the end of World War II to the first half of 1957 and from 1961 to 1966.

### LONG-TERM SUPPLY FACTORS

Over the long term, the rate of growth of total output reflects the quantity and quality of the main factors of production (labor and capital), and changes in the efficiency with which those resources are combined and used in producing total output. From 1946 to 1966, the labor force grew by 2.1 per cent a year (on a compound rate basis), compared with 1.3 per cent a year from 1926 to 1946. The growth was considerably greater than that in the United States, Western European countries, and Japan. This reflects a higher rate of natural increase (especially the high birth rates over several decades) in Canada, more rapidly rising labor force participation rates for women, and a high rate of net immigration.

The growth in the stock of capital was even more pronounced. From 1946 to 1963, the gross capital stock grew at a rate of 4.9 per cent a year, compared with 1.1 per cent from 1927 to 1946. This is a more rapid rate than that in the United States or in some European countries.

The two groups—women and young people—that have contributed substantially to the growth of the labor force over the last two decades, earn incomes that are only about two-thirds of the incomes received by adult males: thus, they have contributed less to the growth of output than to growth of the labor force. In addition, the level of education of the labor force for most of this period has been improving at a slower rate than in the United States. (However, rapid improvement is expected in the years ahead, as a large number of young people with a high level of education begin to enter the labor force and older workers with less formal education retire.)

The growth in output in relation to total factor inputs has been somewhat less than in the United States since 1950, and more in line with Canadian experience from the late 1920's to the early postwar years. It is in this area that the experience of the European countries and Japan has been exceptional, with rates of growth in output per worker or in relation to total factor inputs that are frequently well above their long-term experience.

### POSTWAR LONG CYCLES

Past experience in a number of countries provides some evidence of longer swings in a number of important economic processes and variables. The evidence for Canada is summarized in K. A. H. Buckley, *Working Paper on Population, Labour Force, and Economic Growth*, Banff, 1963. Long-cycle expansions are marked by low levels of unemployment, high rates of growth in the major aggregates (even after averaging over full business cycles), widespread growth in individual industries (but with considerable diversity between the individual industries), and a high and growing share of investment to total output. On the other hand, the periods of long-cycle decline are marked by high levels of unemployment, slow growth in the major aggregates and a majority of the individual industries, and a low share of investment in total output. During periods of long-cycle decline, severe business cycle depressions have occurred; however, not all periods of long-cycle decline have culminated in severe depressions.

Although the evidence and the discussion of the factors contributing to long cycles are helpful in interpreting both the past and the differences between the various postwar business cycles in North America, there is not yet a consensus among those working in this area on the relative importance of various factors. Three main alternatives can be distinguished: major shocks of accidental events; the construction cycle (with the emphasis on real factors in business cycles); and the monetary cycle. Although the interest and work in this field currently have been greater than several decades ago, the emphasis has been more on *what* happens than *why* long cycles persist. Until there is more work on the mechanism of long cycles and more of a consensus among those working in this field, misgivings about and criticisms of the work are bound to occur. I do not, myself, emphasize periodicity, and shall offer reasons for the exceptional duration of the expansion from the 1930's to the mid-1950's (measured by the share of investment in total output). For these reasons, I do not find objection to the Kuznets cycle hypothesis convincing when based mainly on the duration of that expansion.

In light of the recognized uncertainty about the nature of the mechanism of long cycles, I have taken a fairly pragmatic position. Can the notion of a *recurring* but *not periodic* long cycle help in the interpretation of postwar economic development?

If the notion of a long cycle is applied to postwar Canada, it would suggest two long-cycle expansions and one intervening period of long-cycle decline. The start of the first long-cycle expansion is in the early 1930's, with a terminal peak in 1956–1957. The late 1950's and early 1960's were periods of slow growth and high employment, and by the middle of the 1960's a new expansion was under way.

The long-cycle expansion from the early 1930's to the mid-1950's is one of the longest Kuznets cycle expansions on record. However, a number of widely recognized and accepted factors contributed to the prolonged expansion. The period included World War II and the Korean War, both of which caused substantial increases in the volume of government expenditures on goods and services for defense. In addition, the duration and extent of the depression of the 1930's left a backlog of suppressed demand for consumer durables, housing, and business and social capital at the end of World War II. War finance had left large quantities of liquid assets; both money and government bonds were higher in relation to income and assets in most sectors of the economy in 1945 than at any other time since the 1920's. The money supply increased fairly rapidly for most of the period, although the rates of increase were restrained for several years in the 1950's and interest rates tended to advance in several stages after 1950. Employment and output increased considerably from the depression lows, and the increases were widespread throughout industry. After about 1941 unemployment was low—apart from moderate increases during the mild recessions. Prices rose at a more rapid rate than during any other period from 1920 to date. Investment increased markedly over the period and during 1956 and 1957 business investment reached a higher proportion of GNP than at any time since before World War I. The gross stock of capital increased by 6 per cent or more a year for several consecutive years during the 1950's; this was well in excess of the growth in total output in Canada or the United States during that period.

The general picture from 1957 to 1963–1964 was quite different. The growth in employment and output was more modest in total, and the slower increases were reflected in many industries. There was a definite tendency for the slower growth to be most marked among the industries which had previously been among the most rapidly growing. The unemployment rate, seasonally adjusted, began to increase in the autumn of 1956, and it persisted in excess of 6 per cent continuously from September 1957 until December 1963. During that period unemployment was higher in Canada than in the United States, after having been lower from 1945 to 1952. The change in business investment was particularly marked. After the first half of 1957 the decline in real terms was about 20 per cent, and six years later business investment was still about one-fifth below the 1957 high, even though output had by then increased more than one-third. The capital stock continued to grow, but the rate of increase dropped to about 3½ per cent by 1962—much below the average rate of increase from 1946 to 1957. It was not until early 1965 that investment was as high as it had been eight years earlier. The only symptom of long-cycle decline that did not emerge during this period was a severe business depression. However, actual output in Canada in 1961 was estimated to be about 9 per cent below potential [9] which is quite significant in the light of North American experience from 1900 to date.

[9] B. J. Drabble, *Potential Output to 1970*, Economic Council of Canada, Staff Study No. 2. Ottawa, 1964, p. 39.

The period since the lower turning point of the long cycle has been relatively short, but there is ample evidence that the underlying situation in recent years has been quiet different from the downphase period. The increase in employment the five year period from 1961 was at large absolutely as the  increase from 1929 to 1946 or from 1946 to 1961. Also, the expansion of output was large amounting to more than 5 per cent a year from 1960 to 1966, with the increase being widespread in industry. Although unemployment was high at the start of the 1961 business cycle expansion and continued in excess of 5 per cent until 1964, it was in the neighborhood of 3.5 per cent in late 1965 and early 1966, the lowest level in a decade and slightly below the level then prevailing in the United States. Business investment increased sharply and more rapidly than total output; by 1966 it was close to the share of GNP that it had attained in 1956–1957. Prices had begun to increase at a somewhat more rapid rate in 1965 and 1966 than in the earlier period of slow growth, but the rate of increase was still much below that in many of the European countries or in North America before 1951. The vigor of the expansion after 1962 (more rapid than in the United States) was undoubtedly accentuated by the lower value of the Canadian dollar (which was devalued in 1962).

IMPLICATIONS FOR SHORT CYCLES

One of the advantages of measuring long cycles along the lines introduced by Abramovitz is facilitated study of the interrelationships of duration and amplitude between short and long cycles. His evidence and analysis suggest that during long-cycle expansions the individual cyclical expansions will be prolonged and vigorous and the recessions relatively short and mild. On the other hand, during long-cycle contractions the individual expansions will be short and hesitant and the recessions will be long and pronounced. These periods of extended weakness are associated frequently with severe depression [10].

The Canadian postwar cycles fit this interpretation quite well. The three expansions of 1945–1948, 1949–1953, and 1954–1957 were prolonged and fairly vigorous, and the recessions of 1949 and 1953–1954 were mild. (The 1949 one was so mild that not all observers would regard it as a recession. However, unemployment at that time would suggest that it was a weaker period of activity than 1947 or 1950.)

The 1957–1958 recession, on the other hand, was the most pronounced

<hr>

[10] For a full discussion relating to construction, see Moses Abramovitz, *Evidences of Long Swings in Aggregate Construction Since the Civil War*, N.B.E.R., Occasional Paper No. 90, New York, 1964, pp. 72–88. Although the evidence has not been examined as systematically for more comprehensive aggregates, the generalizations appear valid for them also. A more negative conclusion in Burns and Mitchell, *op. cit.*, Chapter 11, was based on a smaller number of construction series, a shorter period of data, and included wartime periods.

recession of the postwar period. The 1958–1960 expansion was hesitant; even at the peak in January 1960, unemployment was still 6.1 per cent of the labor force. This was higher than during either of the mild recessions prior to 1957. Following the 1960 peak, unemployment increased even further. This extended period of slow growth persisted in spite of significant monetary expansion during parts of the period, and the emergence of a substantial budget deficit on a national accounts basis.

The expansion beginning in 1961 has been the longest in Canada's history, except for the upswing including World War II. The expansion in investment, employment, and output has been marked, and more price increases emerged in 1965 and 1966 than during the early years. No business cycle peak has yet been recognized, although a number of the indicators that usually experience decline in advance of a business cycle peak showed signs of weakness during the latter part of 1966 and early 1967. In light of the large growth of the labor force currently taking place, the working hypothesis of a long-cycle expansion being under way would suggest that any recession would be relatively short and mild. The monthly and quarterly data can be reviewed as they are published, in order to see whether the evidence accumulates in a manner inconsistent with the view that any recession will be short and mild and that a prolonged period of extended growth is still ahead.

If used along these lines, the long-cycle framework can be helpful in interpreting shorter-term developments, even if the mechanism of long cycles is not yet understood as well as the mechanism of short cycles. In addition, if long cycles can help our understanding of current trends, then more study of their characteristics by economic theorists, business analysts, and those interested in broad economic policy would seem to be in order.

### FURTHER FACTORS IN THE MILDNESS OF POSTWAR RECESSIONS

The nature and duration of underlying long cycles have been emphasized in the preceding discussion as contributing to the mildness of the postwar recessions; however, other factors also have been important. A forthcoming study bearing on this point is Derek A. White, *Business Cycles in Canada*, Staff Study 17, Ottawa.

*Increased World Stability.* The mildness of the postwar recessions in other countries is an important background factor for Canada, where the effects of international trade and external conditions have large implications for domestic developments. For one thing the U.S. economy has successfully avoided a deep depression during the postwar period. The average duration of the three postwar recessions in that country was ten months, considerably shorter than the average experience from 1854 to 1939. Furthermore, the average rate of decline per month during contractions was significantly less than it had been earlier. The shortness and mildness of the contractions have been reflected in associated increases during expansions, as the extent of slack at the recession trough influences the rate of expansion, especially in the early stages of recovery. In most of the European economies postwar patterns have been influenced more heavily by high growth rates (with marked price increases for much of the last decade) than by business cycles. These high growth rates, and the mildness of recessions, have contributed to a high world demand for Canadian exports, especially of industrial raw materials.

*Increased Government Expenditures.* Canadian Government expenditures on goods and services which were only 4.6 per cent of GNP in 1870, increased to 8.1 per cent in 1910, 11.1 per cent in 1929, and 16.2 per cent in 1962[11]. The decisions in this area are not influenced by profit considerations or recessions. Transfer payments from the government to persons have also increased in relative importance. At the start of the century they were relatively insignificant and in 1929 they were still only about 2 per cent of personal income. But with the introduction of family allowances, old age pensions, and unemployment insurance, they had increased to 12 per cent early in the 1960's. Most of these payments continue irrespective of the state of the economy, and unemployment insurance payments increase during recessions. The rise in importance of government has contributed to greater stability for the economy as a whole.

*Built-in Revenue Stabilizers.* Short-term variations in demand in relation to potential output are partially offset by variations in tax collections. The degree to which variations in revenues occur can be measured by the share of taxes in relation to GNP and by the short-term elasticity of the tax system. For the Canadian federal level and structure of taxes in recent years, tax collections would change to the extent of about 34 per cent of the change in GNP, a very significant amount. This compares with only 13 per cent in 1929. It indicates that the increased quantitative importance of the built-in stabilizers is a major change in the economic environment relevant to stabilization policy[12].

*Residential Construction.* During the postwar recessions, residential construction expanded, reflecting the essential strength of demand for housing and the

---

[11] O. J. Firestone, *Canada's Economic Development, 1867–1953,* London, 1958, Table 38, p. 127.

[12] D. J. Daly, "Variability in Federal Tax Collections," *Canadian Tax Journal,* September–October 1964, pp. 324–336 (reprinted in *Federal Tax Revenues at Potential Output, 1960 and 1970,* Economic Council of Canada, Staff Study, No.9, Ottawa, 1964). This is higher than most estimates for the U.S., where the tax structure has somewhat less revenue variability, and where most estimates do not adequately isolate the higher elasticity for short-term variability from the lower long-term elasticity.

enlarged supply of mortgage funds which became available when the demands for funds in other areas diminished. The rigidities and imperfections in the mortgage market *reduced* the instability of the economy as a whole by *increasing* the instability of new residential construction.

Recently, steps have been taken to permit the chartered banks to lend on mortgages to a greater extent than before and to permit the maximum lending rate in CMHC loans (insured by the government housing corporation on new homes) to be adjusted each quarter to keep in line with interest rates on long-term bonds. This will contribute to a steadier flow of funds into mortgages than has prevailed during the postwar period to date, improve the allocation of funds between alternative uses, and contribute to greater stability in housing activity. It will, however, reduce the contribution of this sector to over-all economic stability.

*Financial Institutions.* Financial crises were often integral features of earlier depressions. The Canadian banking system, with a few major national banks—each with many branches—is quite different from the more decentralized commercial banking structure of the United States. During the 1930's the Bank of Canada was developed as a central bank, and this has made possible more effective coordination of monetary and public debt policy.

The powers of the central bank and the system of bank inspection have not, however, extended to all of the provincially incorporated and supervised financial institutions—trust and loan companies, etc. The failure of several small-sized institutions in recent years has contributed to renewed public interest in this area: legislation has been introduced for federal deposit insurance; and discussions of further possible measures to strengthen the financial system are planned.

Most of the institutional changes will continue in the future to provide an important element of support during recessions. However, they have not been sufficient to prevent either a number of recessions over the last two decades or many years of slow growth in demand. Furthermore, if housing expenditures in the future are influenced more by underlying demographic and economic demand forces and less by an erratic supply of mortgage funds, then more short-term instability in the economy as a whole could result.

## Role of Lags in Key Areas

Earlier in this chapter it was noted that in empirical work lags are recognized as an important part of the dynamic cyclical process. Some expansion of this point may help to throw light on sensitive areas of business decision-making and thus aid both in explaining the recurrent nature of cycles and in diagnosing current economic developments. The discussion is also relevant to the issue of the timing of stabilization policy, which is discussed later in this chapter.

Lags in the cyclical process in three areas—inventories, business investment in plant and equipment, and the relations between prices, costs and profits—are summarized briefly.

### INVENTORIES

The most volatile of the various demand sectors in both the United States and Canada is the physical change in inventories. Holding inventories is an essential part of carrying on business in manufacturing, mining, and trade. Any unexpected change in demand can be reflected in an unplanned building up or running down of inventories. Inventory investment is thus an integral part of the whole process of production scheduling, ordering, and selling in a wide range of plants, firms, and industries. This should be viewed in the whole context of short-term business decision-making within the firm. This is not attempted here; instead, a brief exposition of one aspect of the lag process will be sketched[13].

Many business firms base their appraisal of current trends in orders, sales, etc., on a comparison of the most recent month (or months) with the same period a year ago. This is an understandable procedure when business operations of so many companies and industries have wide seasonal swings. It shows what has happened over the whole intervening twelve-month period, but *not* what has developed *within* that period—say, the last six months. Changes are recognized only with a lag. During the period inventories may tend to accumulate at a greater rate than planned, and this will eventually lead to a necessary adjustment. Of course, other factors—slow processing of data on orders or the need to wait until trends become clear—also contribute to the lags in recognition.

Delayed recognition of changes in orders and sales will persist as long as business firms continue to use year-to-year comparisons rather than seasonally adjusted data (monthly or quarterly) for analyzing developments in their own companies and industry experience. Although this point has been discussed with a fair number of large business firms in Canada, the proportion using seasonally adjusted data is still in a minority. As long as this is so I am convinced that inventory cycles will persist.

### BUSINESS INVESTMENT

An important theme in recent North American literature on investment decisions is the lag between early consideration of projects and the completion of construction. Part of this lag reflects technical factors: the extended period of planning, drafting, preparing specifications, placing contracts, and the period of

---

[13] For a fuller exposition, see D. J. Daly, "Seasonal Variations and Business Expectations," *Journal of Business,* July 1959, pp. 258–270.

construction. The period of construction is related to the size of the project; large projects typically extend over a long period. Further factors are business confidence and the length of time that a program of expansion may be considered before detailed planning is initiated. This can be illustrated by considering business attitudes after a severe depression. Businessmen then are understandably concerned about low rates of utilization, low profit margins, high rates of business failures, and high unemployment. They are cautious about long-term commitments, and hesitate to expand facilities. Even when production, sales, and unemployment have risen in several periods of expansion, they continue to be cautious. It takes a series of extended expansions with only minor setbacks until they begin to abandon their concerns about low rates of utilization and low profit margins and become enthusiastic about longer-term growth prospects. The lags that arise from this combination of technical factors, and the understandable time taken for major decisions, contribute to lags in the adjustment of the stock of capital to underlying changes in final demand, and eventual readjustments in investment plans and expenditures.

In light of these lags shifts in the vigor of business investment will persist as long as variations in the rate of growth of the remaining components of final demand occur.

### PRICES, COSTS, AND PROFITS

It is fairly clear from past experience that there are important differences in the speed of adjustment of different commodity and factor prices to the changing tempo of the business cycle. This is an important part of W. C. Mitchell's view of the cyclical process. These same lags in the speed of adjustment are of importance in the social and political problems associated with price movements.

Some of the main points about the different timing responses in the main price and income measures can be summarized. The over-all wholesale price index moves broadly in line with changes in general business activity. However, sensitive commodity prices traditionally lead changes in economic activity, and corporate profit margins in the commodity-producing industries reflect changes in demand pressure ahead of changes in production and employment for the economy as a whole. On the other hand, certain other parts of the pricing process undergo changes in a fairly belated fashion, some time after changes in over-all activity have taken place. Labor costs per unit of output, wage rates, and the consumer price index all continue to for a fairly significant period after production and employment have begun to decline. This delayed response in labor costs per unit of output is, in turn, related to the tendency for corporate profits to lead changes in business activity. This interconnection has been summarized by Geoffrey Moore as follows:

These reversals in unit costs, which may be thought of as either lagging behind similar turns in sales or leading opposite turns in sales, tend to produce opposite reversals in profit margins. That is, the cyclical upturn in costs often generates a downturn in margins before sales reach their peak, while the cyclical downturn in costs helps to bring about an upturn in margins before sales reach their trough. Prices usually do not contribute to this tendency. More often than not, they tend to offset it by continuing to rise at least as long as sales do and by declining, if at all, toward the end of the contraction in sales. But these movements in prices are typically not as sharp as those in costs. The upshot is that early reversals in margins are fairly common, particularly during expansions in sales, and they are chiefly attributable to the behavior of costs. This process has important implications for the generation of business cycles because of the importance of profits in motivating economic activity[14].

As long as these different lags in response occur and contribute to marked and widespread changes in profit margins, variations in business spending on inventories and on fixed capital are likely to persist. Thus this discussion of the interaction of prices, costs, and profits is relevant to the earlier discussion on inventories and business investment.

IMPLICATIONS

The existence and timing of these lagged relationships are important. Insofar as current business spending on inventories and fixed capital is based on earlier decisions within the business firm, and on views about sales and the pressure of demand against capacity, there is a risk that subsequent adjustment in spending plans will be necessary. This adjustment under conditions of uncertainty is an integral part of the dynamic process of cycles that is reflected, either explicitly or implicitly, in most recent empirical business cycle research.

These lags are likely to be a factor in the highly damped structure that emerges from economic models. Without the impact of new shocks and disturbances, the econometric model would tend to settle down around the long-term growth in supply (although it should be recognized that the time to reach a situation of complete stability is measured in terms of perhaps a decade). The continuance of cycles of observed magnitude thus seems to require the continuance of "shocks" of the magnitude of historical experience.

I have no basis for suggesting whether future shocks and disturbances will be greater or less than past experience. However, it would seem prudent in a world of uncertainty to recognize that shocks can occur, but very little will be known ahead of time about how large they will be and the direction in which they will operate. As long as the world is like this it seems hard to establish that the business cycle is obsolete.

---

[14] Foreward to Thor Hultgren, *Costs, Prices and Profits: Their Cyclical Relations*, N.E.B.R. Studies in Business Cycles, No. 14. New York, 1965.

## Scope for Discretionary Policy

Effective discretionary stabilization policy requires that changes be initiated in time for their effects to be operative while they are still needed. On the basis of the evidence available, I am rather skeptical that this is possible for the short cycles of the variety experienced in North America over the last two decades.

One area of evidence relates to the three lags in policy: the recognition, the action, and the response lags[15]. The recognition lag reflects the lag in publication of current data behind the period to which they relate and the time taken for an appraisal to be made of the factors contributing to important changes. The action lag reflects the time elapsing between recognition of the need for action and the taking of action, including the time necessary to obtain agreement on the need and type of measures appropriate for a changing situation, especially in a democratic society and system of government. The response lag reflects the slow response by decision makers in the private sector to changed government expenditure and tax decisions, money supply, and credit conditions. The evidence for Canada suggests that these three lags are additive, quite long in extent, and rather variable in duration[16].

These lags are certainly very long in relation to contractions, or even full business cycles in North America. The postwar recessions in Canada have averaged about 10 months, certainly much less than the duration of the lags distinguished in the preceding paragraph.

However, it does not seem that a continuance of these minor recessions is a very serious economic problem. Almost by definition these cycles are largely

---

[15] This terminology follows that initiated by Milton Friedman, "A Monetary and Fiscal Framework for Economic Stability," *American Economic Review,* June 1948, and "The Effects of a Full Employment Policy on Economic Stability: A Formal Analysis," in *Essays in Positive Economics,* Chicago, 1953.

[16] This evidence is summarized in *Conference on Stabilization Policies*, Ottawa, 1966. (In the discussion in this chapter, two questions in this area arose. One was whether the three lags are additive. The primary reason for regarding the lags as additive is that the decisions are made by quite different individuals and economic organizations. A second question was whether the short lags for the automatic stabilizers are consistent with the emphasis on the long lags for discretionary policy. An advantage of the automatic stabilizers is that the recognition lags and outside lags are relatively short for these instruments. The main timing problem in discretionary fiscal-policy changes is the possible lag in recognition and the action lag, neither of which is present for the built-in stabilizers. In Canada during the 1950's and 1960's the major source of the lag has been the lag at the political and administrative level. This is likely to become more serious with the increased size and influence of provincial governments and crown companies. To some degree, this action lag reflects differing priorities on short-cycle stabilization policies and difficulties in selecting the appropriate combinations of policies.)

associated with mild slowdowns in the growth of final demand and a swing in the rate of inventory investment. Such recessions are likely to be fairly quickly self-reversing, with the type of factors discussed earlier limiting the declines.

It is difficult to obtain public support for relatively quick and frequent changes in policy. Experience would suggest that about five changes in direction in a decade would be required, and it is doubtful that support for such a program is politically feasible.

More important is the prevention of severe and extended periods of inflationary pressure or prolonged and extended periods of slack demand. These are associated with the major swings in business investment of the Kuznets cycle variety. They are important in giving rise to severe depressions or extended periods of inflation. An important part of public policy should be to moderate and offset these extreme situations. For the situations that could persist over several shorter term cycles the problem of the timing of policy changes is much less acute. In addition, public support for infrequent changes in policy to cope with major economic problems should be much easier to get that frequent adjustments when the need for changes in policy is not clear and overwhelming.


## Implications for the Future

A number of points, based on the Canadian postwar experience, can be summarized here. In many essential respects, the underlying cyclical mechanism has been in line with the longer-term experience. Close connections with the United States have persisted, and this is expected to continue to be a dominant factor in the period ahead. In addition, the basic role of lags and uncertainty has continued to be reflected in cycles in Canadian inventories and investment, and in the relations between prices, costs, and profits.

The important new element is the increased role of government—in expenditures, taxes, explicit acceptance of responsibility for monetary policy, and greater recognition of the need for government-held goals for price stability, high employment, and growth. The increased size of government expenditures on both transfer payments and goods and services provides a potential source of stability. The considerable extent of short-term elasticity in the federal tax structure and the increased size of federal revenues in relation to GNP contributes a greater degree of built-in stability than existed in the 1920's. These changes contribute to a moderation of cyclical instability in comparison with historical experience.

Mild inventory cycles have continued in the postwar period, and the underlying mechanism is expected to continue in the future. The cyclical swings in profits, inventories, and business investment reflect the persistence of important timing differences in response, in an economic environment where uncertainties about future markets and costs continue to exist. I am not too hopeful that discretionary policies of government can offset the mild and short recessions in the private sector, which are expected to persist.

On the question "Are major depressions a phenomenon of the past, never again to be feared?" I hesitate to be categorical. At some time during the last three decades, international disturbances have had important impacts on the economies of all the countries represented at the conference with which this volume deals, and it seems prudent to recognize that such disturbances could occur again. The Korean and Vietnamese wars are postwar examples. Canada is relatively small, despite the high rate of growth in her labor force during the present century. It is heavily dependent on world markets for minerals, forest products, and grain. Therefore, for Canada, the foregoing question can be answered only in the context of assumptions about economic performance in the major industrial countries. If the United States can and does maintain a fairly steady long-term growth in demand, in line with potential output, then the Canadian economy will also grow. If the United States were to experience another period of slow growth, such as that from 1957 to 1962, then it would be difficult, if not impossible, for Canada to avoid a similar situation. It is possible for Canada to achieve a measure of stability in growth over an extended period only if these same objectives can be attained in the world economy, and especially in the United States.

## Notes

For full discussion of subjects that are considered only briefly in this chapter, see the following publications:

Abramovitz, Moses, *Evidences of Long Swings in Aggregate Construction Since the Civil War,* N.B.E.R., Occasional Paper No. 90, New York, 1964.
———, "The Nature and Significance of Kuznets Cycles," *Economic Development and Cultural Change,* Vol. 9, April 1961 (reprinted in Gordon and Klein, *Readings in Business Cycles*).
Adelman, Irma, and Frank L. Adelman, "The Dynamic Properties of the Klein-Goldberger Model," *Econometrica,* 1959 (reprinted in Gordon and Klein, *op. cit.*).
Ando, A., E. Cary Brown, R. M. Solow, and J. Karekan, "Lags in Fiscal and Monetary Policy," Commission on Money and Credit, *Stabilization Policies,* Englewood Cliffs, New Jersey, 1963.
Buckley, K. A. H., *Working Paper on Population, Labour Force, and Economic Growth,* Banff School of Advanced Management, 1963.
Burns, Arthur F., and Wesley C. Mitchell, *Measuring Business Cycles,* New York, 1947.
Crozier, R. B., "Canada: Short-Term Forecasting in the Federal Service," *Techniques of Economic Forecasting,* Paris, 1965.
Daly, D. J., "Long Cycles and Recent Canadian Experience," Royal Commission on Banking and Finance, *Appendix Volume,* Ottawa, 1965.

– – –, "The Scope for Monetary Policy–A Synthesis," *Conference on Stabilization Policies,* Ottawa, 1966.

– – –, "Seasonal Variations and Business Expectations," *Journal of Business,* July 1959.

– – –, and D. A. White, "Economic Indicators in the 1960's," *Proceedings of the Business and Economics Section of the American Statistical Association,* 1966.

Denison, E. F., *The Sources of Economic Growth in the United States and the Alternatives Before Us,* Committee for Economic Development, Supplementary Paper No. 13, New York, January 1962.

– – –, *Why Growth Rates Differ: Post-War Experience in Nine Western Countries,* Washington, 1967.

Easterlin, R., "Economic-Demographic Interactions and Long Swings in Economic Growth," *American Economic Review,* December 1966.

Economic Council of Canada, *First Annual Review,* Ottawa, 1964, Chapter 3; and *Third Annual Review,* Ottawa, 1966, Chapter 2.

Friedman, Milton, "The Effects of a Full Employment Policy on Economic Stability: A Formal Analysis," *Essays in Positive Economics,* Chicago, 1953.

– – –, "A Monetary and Fiscal Framework for Economic Stability," *American Economic Review,* June 1948 (reprinted in *Essays in Positive Economics*).

– – –, "The Monetary Studies of the National Bureau," N.B.E.R., *Forty-Fourth Annual Report,* New York, 1964.

Garvy, George, "Kondratieff's Theory of Long Cycles," *Review of Economic Statistics,* Vol. 25, November 1943.

Gordon, R. A., and L. R. Klein, *Readings in Business Cycles,* Homewood, Illinois, 1965.

Hickman, Bert G., *Growth and Stability in the Post-War Economy,* Washington, 1960.

– – –, "The Post-War Retardation: Another Long Swing in the Rate of Growth?" *American Economic Review,* May 1963.

Lintner, John, "What is Left of the Business Cycle in the United States?" *American Statistical Association Proceedings, 1965.*

May, S. J., "The Dynamic Multipliers and Their Use for Fiscal Decision-Making," *Conference on Stabilization Policies,* Ottawa, 1961.

Moore, Geoffrey H., "The 1957–58 Business Contraction: New Model or Old?" *American Economic Review,* May 1959.

– – – (ed.), *Business Cycle Indicators,* Princeton, New Jersey, 1961.

O'Leary, P. J., and W. Arthur Lewis, "Secular Swings in Production and Trade, 1870–1913," *The Manchester School,* May 1955 (reprinted in Gordon and Klein, *op. cit.*).

Poapst, J. V., *The Residential Mortgage Market,* Ottawa, 1962.

Rhomberg, R. R., "A Model of the Canadian Economy under Fixed and Fluctuating Exchange Rates," *Journal of Political Economy,* Vol. 72, February 1964.

Rosenbluth, Gideon, "Changes in Canadian Sensitivity to United States Business Fluctuations," *Canadian Journal of Economics and Political Science,* Vol. 23, November 1957.

– – –, "Changing Structural Factors in Canada's Cyclical Sensitivity, 1903–54," *ibid.,* Vol. 24, February 1958.

Shiskin, Julius, "The Current Experience in Historical Perspective," *Business Cycle Developments,* January 1965.

———, *Signals of Recession and Recovery: An Experiment with Monthly Reporting,* N.B.E.R., Occasional Paper No. 77, New York, 1961.

Tinbergen, J., *Business Cycles in the United States of America,* Geneva, 1939.

White, Derek A., *Business Cycles in Canada,* Economic Council of Canada, Staff Study No. 17, Ottawa, 1967.

Will, Robert M., "The Time Lags of Fiscal Policy," *Conference on Stabilization Policies,* Ottawa, 1966.

# COMMENTS

GIDEON ROSENBLUTH,
University of British Columbia

Dr. Daly follows the dominant current trend among students of business cycles in recognizing the National Bureau cycle as averaging about 40 months in length and the Kuznets cycle of about 20 years, neither of which he regards as obsolete for Canada. On the other hand, the major or Juglar cycle discussed by Gordon, Hansen, and Shumpeter, and the 40-year Kondratieff cycle are denied independent existence.

Long cycles are discussed in two places in Dr. Daly's discussion. Near the beginning there is a comparison of long cycles in Canada and the United States, with a chart that shows the latest long-cycle peak occurring in the late 1930's for the rate of growth of gross national product (GNP), and the early 1940's for the rate of growth of urban building activity. A few pages further, there is a discussion of postwar long-cycle developments, and here it is asserted that the start of the first long-cycle expansion is in the early 1930's, with a terminal peak in 1956–1957. The discrepancies in the location of the peak are not explained or discussed in the chapter.

The origin of these discrepancies is the fact that both U.S. and Canadian series measuring *rates of growth* have their peaks in the 1940's or late 1930's, while series representing the *level* of construction activity, and, for Canada, such series as investment as a proportion of GNP, immigration as a proportion of the labor force, and the balance of foreign trade as a proportion of total foreign trade, have their peaks in the late 1950's. Abramovitz, in his well known 1961 paper[1], places the peak in six "rate of change" indicators in the late 1930's or early 1940's. In *Evidences of Long Swings in Aggregate Construction*[2], he

---

[1] "The Nature and Significance of Kuznets Cycles," *Economic Development and Cultural Change,* Vol. IX, April 1961.
[2] National Bureau of Economic Research, Occasional Paper No. 90, New York, 1964, pp. 101–103.

places the peak in various indicators of the *growth rate* in construction in 1944–1948. On the other hand, in the same volume the peak in various series measuring the *level* of construction is placed in 1959[3]. Similar results for Canada are shown in the charts in Daly's "Long Cycles and Recent Canadian Experience"[4].

The fact that turning points in rates of change precede those in levels of the same variables is, of course, to be expected. What is surprising is Daly's descriptive and analytical discussion of the Kuznets cycle peak and trough, which he places in the late 1950's and early 1960's, and which cannot, therefore, be turning points in rates of growth of output or construction. Daly states that long-cycle expansions are marked by high rates of growth in the major aggregates, but his charts show that the rate of growth of GNP (measured Kuznets-cycle fashion) has not been particularly high at any time since World War II, in terms of the historical record, and the same may be said of the rate of growth of urban building activity since 1950. He states that the late 1950's and early 1960's were a period of slow growth, but again his charts show that the difference in growth rates between the late and the early 1950's was slight (in comparison with the historical range of growth rates) for both GNP and urban building activity.

While the lead of rates of change over levels is to be expected, it should be noted that in the case of this most recent Kuznets peak the lead has been exceptionally long. Abramovitz's tabulation of indices of aggregate construction shows a lead of 11 years (1948 and 1959). In his record, going back to the 1870's, such a long lead is approached on only two occasions: by an eight-year gap in 1884 and 1892, and a 10-year gap in 1903 and 1913. The typical time interval is three to four years[5].

According to the theory of Kuznets cycles, as expounded by Abramovitz and others, the level of capital formation follows the rate of change of GNP, with a lag of several years. The typical lag in Abramovitz's record is, however, again of the order of three years, and the postwar lag in this relationship also is exceptionally long[6].

Perhaps the correct conclusion is that the 20-year Kuznets cycle *is* obsolete in the postwar world, because an analysis that relies on the rough coincidence of long swings in the level of construction and the rate of growth of output is no longer applicable when the peaks in the series concerned are 12 to 20 years apart. Perhaps, for a useful framework to explain the puzzling developments since 1956, we should turn back to the discredited Juglar or major cycle based on

---

[3] *Ibid.*, pp. 31–36, 90.
[4] Royal Commission on Banking and Finance, Appendix Volume, 1964, Ottawa, 1965, pp. 284, 286–287.
[5] N.B.E.R., Occasional Paper No..90, 1964.
[6] See the chronology in "The Nature and Significance of Kuznets Cycles."

investment in business plant and equipment. A postwar investment cycle with troughs at the end of the war and in 1962, and peaks in 1956 and perhaps 1966, would seem to fit the data fairly well.

The important feature of Canadian cycles, both long and short, which Daly correctly emphasizes, is their close correspondence to cycles in the United States. In comprehensive indexes of output and prices, a close coincidence is found in both large and small fluctuations, so that no matter what concept of the cycle one adopts, a correspondence of U.S. and Canadian cycles will always be found. In an earlier investigation, I found that, for a U.S. fluctuation of given amplitude in an indicator of total output, the Canadian fluctuation was lower in the 1930's and postwar period that it had been in the 1920's, and probably lower in the 1920's than before World War I. The method used was to fit straight lines to the relation between U.S. and Canadian amplitudes, using the Canadian amplitudes as dependent variables, and to study the trend in the deviations. I interpreted these results as indicating declining Canadian sensitivity to U.S. fluctuations, which in turn could be related to the development of built-in stabilizers, and the declining importance of exports in the economy (compared with the 1920's)[7]. Thus it might be thought that the postwar mildness of Canadian cycles must be related to a double dose of stabilizers—the U.S. *and* the Canadian. I should now like to report further findings that cast doubt on simple interpretations of the previous results.

Three price indicators—wholesale prices, common stock prices, and long-term bond yields—do *not* show this phenomenon of declining sensitivity to U.S. fluctuations, although they too exhibit the very close correspondence of U.S. and Canadian fluctuations. In fact, the wholesale price index exhibits increasing sensitivity. These findings are illustrated and contrasted with those for one of the output indices in Tables 2-1 and 2-2.

These results show that there is much that remains to be explained regarding the transmission of cycles between the United States and Canada. They have some relevance to Daly's remark that "similarities in the behavior of the two economies should be expected; the real task of economic analysis is to explain any *differences* that emerge." I would submit that things are not so simple, and I would add that research workers have not in fact taken adequate account of the close correspondence of cycles in the two countries. I am thinking particularly of the design of econometric models of the Canadian economy. Can one assume that cycles in the United States and Canada coincide because the lag structure of the two economies is the same? This is hardly plausible in view of major

---

[7] "Changes in Canadian Sensitivity to United States Business Fluctuations," *Canadian Journal of Economics and Political Science,* Vol. 23, November 1957, pp. 480–503, and "Changing Structural Factors in Canada's Cyclical Sensitivity, 1903–1954," *Ibid.,* Vol. 24, February 1958, pp. 21–43.

differences, such as the more important role in Canada of primary industries producing industrial materials for export, and the much greater importance of exports and imports to the Canadian economy. Could the coincidence be due to a coincidence of erratic shocks in the sense of "disturbances in the equations?" Again the answer must be "no" because, first, one can think of many erratic factors that must have a different impact in the two countries (for example, a railway strike in Canada would have a negligible impact in the United States). Second, since the equations and lag structure must, as we have said, be different, even a coincidence of disturbances would not produce the same cycles.

One is left with the conclusion that the Canadian economy must be constrained to follow the U.S. economy because of what Daly calls "the very strong interconnections" which must be essentially one-way connections. This surely must mean that the behavior of a plausible model of the Canadian economy must be controlled by a variety of exogenous variable representing different aspects of the U.S. economy.

The econometricians who build models of the Canadian economy have not given due weight to this point. For example, Rhomberg's quarterly model, which focuses on the balance of payments mechanism, uses 18 exogenous variables of which three represent specifically U.S. influences, namely U.S. interest rates and net foreign investment; while three more represent "world" influences, namely the import and export prices facing Canada and world industrial production [8]. The Department of Trade and Commerce annual model, described in a report by Sydney May, uses about 100 exogenous variables of which only two relate to external conditions [9]. Clearly, a great deal of research remains to be done on the inter-connections of the two economies.

Finally, I should like to comment on Daly's views regarding the uses of countercyclical policies. He says that discretionary policies are not likely to be effective against the 40-month cycle, and that this is no tragedy since such fluctuations are no longer of sufficient amplitude to cause serious concern, largely because of the operation of automatic stabilizers. Countercyclical policies should be reserved for the Kuznets cycle.

This position exaggerates the difference between automatic and discretionary countercyclical devices. The fact that automatic devices work shows that the "outside lag" is not too long for countercyclical effectiveness. The action lag can be reduced or eliminated by making policies normally considered discretionary more or less automatic. For example, there may be a countercyclical schedule of *tax rates* for current deductions at the source, automatic countercycle

[8] R. R. Rhomberg, "A Model of the Canadian Economy under Fixed and Fluctuating Exchange Rates." *Journal of Political Economy*, Vol. 72, February 1964, p. 1.
[9] Economic Council of Canada, *Conference on Stabilization Policy*, Ottawa, 1966, pp. 178–187.

TABLE 2-1 Regression Analysis: Amplitude of Matched Fluctuations, United States and Canada*

|  | Contractions | Expansions | All Fluctuations |
|---|---|---|---|
| **Correlation Coefficients** | | | |
| Railway gross revenue | 0.88 | 0.64 | 0.83 |
| Bond yields | 0.79 | 0.78 | 0.74 |
| Common stock prices | 0.99 | 0.94 | 0.97 |
| Wholesale prices | 0.96 | 0.94 | 0.95 |
| **Regression Coefficients** | | | |
| Railway gross revenue | 1.08 | 0.56 | 0.98 |
| Bond yields | 0.56 | 0.93 | 0.72 |
| Common stock prices | 0.85 | 0.92 | 0.88 |
| Wholesale prices | 0.95 | 0.84 | 0.89 |
| **Number of Observations** | | | |
| Railway gross revenue | 12 | 12 | 24 |
| Bond yields | 7 | 9 | 16 |
| Common stock prices | 16 | 16 | 32 |
| Wholesale prices | 13 | 14 | 27 |

**Sources of Data:**

**Railway gross revenue:** see G. Rosenbluth, "Changes in Canadian Sensitivity to United States Business Fluctuations," *Canadian Journal of Economics and Political Science,* Vol. 23, November 1957, pp. 501, 502.

**Bond yields, U.S.: 1900–1915,** Historical Statistics of the United States, 1949 edition, Appendix Table 29, p. 348 (Macaulay railway bonds): **1919–1955,** *Federal Reserve Bulletin* (partially tax exempt bonds to 1943; fully taxable, marketable 2½ per cent bonds, from 1941)

**Canada: 1900–1915, Dominion Bureau of Statistics (DBS),** *Prices and Price Indexes, 1913–1940* (index of Province of Ontario bond yields); **1919–1955. D.B.S.** *Prices and Price Indexes, 1949–1952* and later issues (index of Canadian Government bond yields).

**Common Stock Prices, U.S.:** *Historical Statistics of the U.S.,* 1949 edition, Appendix Table 25, and *Survey of Current Business* (index of common stock prices, Cowles Commission and Standard and Poors').

**Canada, 1900–1913:** Compiled from data in Board of Inquiry into the Cost of Living, Report Vol. 11, 1915, pp. 627–656; **1914–1955 DBS.** *Prices and Price Indexes,* various issues (investor's index of common stock prices).

**Wholesale Prices, U.S.:** *Historical Statistics of the U.S.,* 1949 edition, Appendix Table 23, and *Monthly Labor Review* (Bureau of Labor Statistics wholesale price index).

**Canada:** DBS *Prices and Price Indexes,* various issues.

* Amplitudes are half the difference between values at two successive turning points, as a percentage of their average. Values at turning points are three-month averages. Signs are reversed for contractions. In the regression analysis, Canadian amplitudes are the dependent variable.

TABLE 2–2   **Average Amplitudes, Matched Fluctuations, United States and Canada*** *(In per cent)*

| | Contractions | | | | Expansions | | | | All Fluctuations | | | |
|---|---|---|---|---|---|---|---|---|---|---|---|---|
| | 1904– 1915 | 1919– 1929 | 1929– 1939 | 1946– 1954 | 1904– 1915 | 1919– 1929 | 1929– 1939 | 1946– 1954 | 1904– 1915 | 1919– 1929 | 1929– 1939 | 1946– 1954 |
| **Railway Gross Revenue** | | | | | | | | | | | | |
| United States | 6.3 | 8.5 | 19.3 | 8.6 | 11.0 | 9.6 | 13.5 | 13.5 | 8.2 | 9.1 | 16.4 | 11.0 |
| Canada | 7.0 | 5.2 | 16.4 | 3.9 | 13.2 | 11.4 | 10.9 | 11.6 | 9.5 | 8.8 | 13.6 | 7.7 |
| Ratio | 111 | 62 | 85 | 45 | 120 | 119 | 81 | 86 | 116 | 96 | 83 | 70 |
| Deviation | +3.6 | −0.5 | −1.1 | −2.0 | +2.0 | +1.0 | −1.7 | −1.0 | +2.6 | +1.0 | −1.3 | −2.0 |
| **Bond Yields** | | | | | | | | | | | | |
| United States | 3.3 | 15.1 | 7.6 | 7.7 | 6.9 | 6.1 | 13.1 | 11.8 | 5.4 | 9.7 | 10.4 | 9.8 |
| Canada | 4.1 | 10.1 | 7.7 | 7.5 | 9.6 | 5.6 | 11.6 | 10.6 | 7.4 | 7.4 | 9.6 | 9.1 |
| Ratio | 126 | 67 | 101 | 97 | 139 | 92 | 88 | 90 | 136 | 76 | 93 | 93 |
| Deviation | −0.2 | −0.9 | +0.9 | +0.7 | +2.3 | −1.0 | −1.5 | −1.3 | +1.5 | −1.6 | +0.2 | −0.0 |
| **Common Stock Prices** | | | | | | | | | | | | |
| United States | 12.4 | 8.8 | 24.2 | 7.9 | 14.6 | 25.7 | 18.2 | 19.4 | 13.5 | 17.3 | 21.2 | 13.7 |
| Canada | 9.9 | 4.7 | 18.7 | 6.8 | 14.8 | 22.3 | 12.7 | 18.1 | 12.4 | 13.5 | 15.7 | 12.5 |
| Ratio | 80 | 54 | 77 | 86 | 102 | 87 | 70 | 93 | 92 | 78 | 74 | 91 |
| Deviation | +0.7 | −1.5 | −0.6 | +1.4 | +2.5 | −0.3 | −3.1 | +1.3 | +1.5 | −0.7 | −2.0 | +1.4 |
| **Wholesale Prices** | | | | | | | | | | | | |
| United States | 3.3 | 12.6 | 15.3 | 3.4 | 6.6 | 5.9 | 10.1 | 22.0 | 5.0 | 8.7 | 12.7 | 12.7 |
| Canada | 0.6 | 10.3 | 13.2 | 3.7 | 4.4 | 4.5 | 9.2 | 20.6 | 2.5 | 7.0 | 11.2 | 12.2 |
| Ratio | 17 | 82 | 87 | 110 | 66 | 77 | 91 | 94 | 50 | 80 | 88 | 96 |
| Deviation | −0.9 | +0.1 | +0.4 | +2.1 | −1.0 | −0.2 | +0.9 | +2.3 | −1.0 | +0.2 | +0.9 | +1.8 |

**Sources:** See Table 2-1.

* "Ratio" means the Canadian amplitude as a percentage of the U.S. amplitude, and "deviation" means the average deviation of actual Canadian amplitudes from the values computed by the regression equations.

71

governing depreciation allowances, countercyclical formulae in welfare payments, old age pensions, etc. That leaves only the recognition lag, which is a
technical matter. Surely, if the present automatic stabilizers, which are largely
"accidental", are as effective as Daly finds them, then it is worthwhile to devote
some effort to devising fiscal measures specifically for the purpose of stabilization.

As for truly discretionary policies, a policy of reserving them for the Kuznets
cycle would imply that there are sufficiently good economic indicators to
distinguish the Kuznets from the other cycles. In view of the postwar behavior
of Kuznets cycle indicators discussed earlier, this seems unduly optimistic. I
should think, therefore, that the attempt must be continued to devise policies to
meet any deficiency or excess of demand without waiting to establish whether
or not they are genuine Kuznets fluctuations.

Chapter Three

# POSTWAR BUSINESS CYCLES IN JAPAN

MIYŌHEI SHINOHARA
Hitotsubashi University, Tokyo

Before taking up the problem of "Is the Business Cycle Obsolete?" I shall analyze Japan's postwar experience in detail. This chapter considers three aspects: (a) Inventory Cycles, (b) Fixed Investment Cycles, and (c) Some Policy Observations. Some observations concerning the "obsolescence" of the business cycle will follow (a) and (b).

## Inventory Cycles

After the chaotic postwar years (1946–1951), which included a hyperinflation (1946–1949), Japan has had at least four short cycles (inventory cycles) since the peak of the Korean War boom (Table 3–1).

TABLE 3–1    Economic Planning Agency's Reference Dates for Postwar Business Cycles in Japan

| Cycle | Trough | Peak | Trough | Periods (months) | | |
|-------|--------|------|--------|---------|-----------|-------|
| | | | | Upswing | Downswing | Total |
| I | | June 1951 | Oct. 1951 | | 4 | |
| II | Oct. 1951 | Jan. 1954 | Nov. 1954 | 27 | 10 | 37 |
| III | Nov. 1954 | June 1957 | June 1958 | 31 | 12 | 43 |
| IV | June 1958 | Dec. 1961 | Oct. 1962 | 42 | 10 | 52 |
| V | Oct. 1962 | Oct. 1964 | Oct. 1965 | 24 | 12 | 36 |
| | | Average periods | | 31 | 11 | 42 |

**Source:** Economic Planning Agency, *Keizai Hendō Kansoku Geppō* (Monthly Report of Business Cycle Developments), December 1966, No. 13.

73

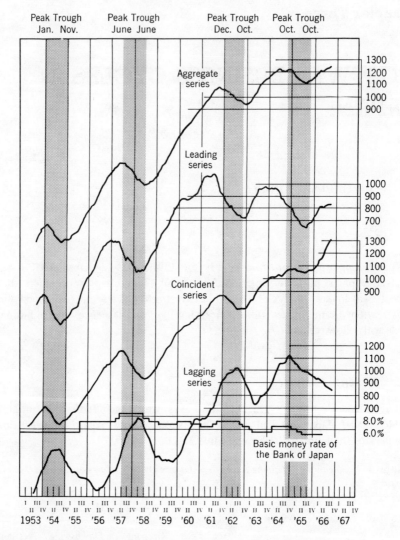

**Fig. 3–1.** Cumulative diffusion index of the Economic Planning Agency of Japan. These are the cumulative totals of the current diffusion indices. Leading, coincident, and lagging series consist of the indicators listed in the Appendix. A cumulative diffusion index is not an index number but a total of (diffusion index minus 50) over time. From Economic Planning Agency, *Keizai Hendō Kansoku Geppō* (Monthly Report of Business Cycle Developments), December 1966, No. 13.

The reference dates determined by the Economic Planning Agency (EPA) almost coincide with the peaks and troughs of that agency's cumulative diffusion index. Since the current diffusion index falls below the 50 per cent line in recession, but rises above 50 per cent in prosperity, the cumulative difference between the diffusion index and 50 per cent seems nearly to coincide with the actual peaks and troughs of the short cycles. This is depicted by Figure 3–1, which shows the aggregate series (25 indicators), the leading series (10 indicators), the coincident series (8 indicators), and the lagging series (7 indicators), together with the basic money rate of the Bank of Japan.

The reference dates as well as the cumulative diffusion index indicate, first, that the four recession periods (excluding the one following the Korean armistice) are nearly equal in length. Each covers a period of 10 to 12 months. On the other hand, the duration of the upswing gradually increases from 27 months (second cycle) to 42 months (fourth cycle), but then decreases to 24 months (fifth cycle). There seems to be some irregularity in the length of the upswing; when the underlying fixed investment cycles are rising, the upswings of the cycle seem longer than when the fixed investment cycles are falling. The opposite seems to be true of the downswings of the inventory cycles.

Another aggregate business cycle indicator was formerly published by the Bank of Japan; formal publication ceased in 1959, but for about a year thereafter, the index was available on an informal basis. According to this indicator, the reference dates are considerably different from those of EPA. As is shown in Table 3–2, the three downswings are of longer duration, and—surprisingly—each one covers 16 months. Since the peaks in the Bank of Japan series differ by only one month from the EPA series, the peak in the fourth cycle may be assumed to have been reached in December 1961. If so, then the period of the upswing in the fourth cycle is 39 months, and the lengths of upswings (17, 23, and 39 months) are all shorter than those of the EPA series (27, 31, and 42 months). Both series show considerable regularity in the duration of the recessions and a lengthening of the upswing period from the second to the fourth cycle.

TABLE 3–2    Bank of Japan's Reference Dates for Postwar Business Cycles in Japan

| Cycle | Trough | Peak | Trough | Periods (months) | | |
|---|---|---|---|---|---|---|
| | | | | Upswing | Downswing | Total |
| I | | May 1951 | Sep. 1952 | | 16 | |
| II | Sep. 1952 | Feb. 1954 | June 1955 | 17 | 16 | 33 |
| III | June 1955 | May 1957 | Sep. 1958 | 23 | 16 | 39 |
| IV | Sep. 1958 | | | | | |

Source: Bank of Japan, *Wagakuni no Keiki Hendō Shihyō* (Japan's Business Cycle Indicator, from 1951 to June 1959), September 1959.

In the Bank of Japan series, each indicator (money, prices, industrial production, employment, wages, consumption, etc.) is first computed in accordance with the following formula: [(basic data minus seasonal fluctuation minus irregular fluctuation minus trend)/trend] × 100. After each series is standardized, the several series are averaged with certain weights, which are computed according to the conformity of each series to business fluctuations. As a trend, a forty-month moving average, or the least squares trend from peak to peak or from trough to trough, is used. Therefore, in such a rapidly growing economy as that of Japan, the recession period computed from the basic data without trend elimination is often shorter than that computed from the data after trend elimination. This is why the peaks and troughs of the Bank of Japan series differ from those of the cumulative diffusion index of EPA. Some series

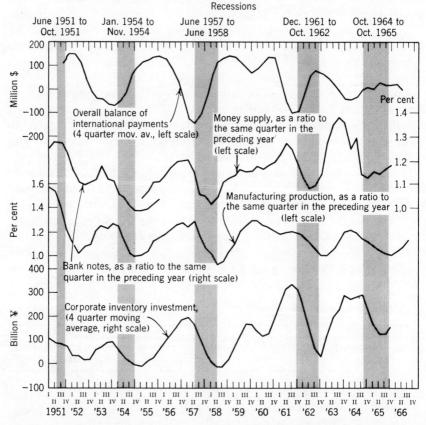

**Fig. 3—2.** Japan's balance of payments, money supply, manufacturing production, and inventory investment. (Corporate inventory investment is gross of inventory valuation adjustment.)

show a mere leveling-off in the recession, because of the high growth potential; therefore determination of the trough is sometimes difficult. For the series from which trend is eliminated, however, locating troughs is generally easy.

It is of interest to check the EPA reference dates against Figure 3–2, which shows the overall balance of payments (including current and capital transactions), money supply, manufacturing production, and corporate inventory investment as a four-quarter moving average or as the ratio to the same quarter in the preceding year. When the reference dates are checked against the rate of change in manufacturing production and against inventory investment, a high degree of coincidence is evident for the recessions of 1954, 1957–1958, and 1962, but some discrepancies appear in the recessions of 1951 and 1964–1965. The overall balance of payments shows an interesting lead over the money supply, while the latter leads manufacturing production and inventory investment. In the 1956 boom, the peak of manufacturing production (1957–II) lags by six quarters the peak of the overall balance of payments (1955–IV). The trough of manufacturing production in 1958 lags that of the balance of payments by one year, and so on.

This suggests that balance of payments constraints exercised a predominant influence upon the growth and cycles of production in Japan during the postwar years. In every recession, a tight money policy came first, in order to overcome an increasing balance of payments deficit. This was reflected in the decline of the growth rate of the money supply as well as that of effective demand; as a result, the rates of increase in manufacturing production and inventory investment fell. In contrast, an increase in the balance of payments surplus seems to have caused an easy money situation and a rise in the growth rates of money supply and effective demand, stimulating increases in production and inventory investment. Liquidity was generally a limiting factor, so that its increase or decrease exerted a strong influence on the fluctuations of production and inventories. There seems to have been no uniform lead or lag period between the changes in manufacturing production and in corporate inventory investment.

The behavior of corporate inventory investment in wholesale trade is of special interest. As Figure 3–3 indicates, it has always led aggregate corporate inventory investment. Since the statistics of wholesale trade inventories are heavily weighted by large international trading companies, the lead of corporate inventory investment in wholesale trade reflects the sensitivity of commodity imports to changes in the balance of payments situation. The degree to which their inventory investment has been responsive is revealed in Figure 3–3. From this relation, the influence of the balance of payments in the inventory cycle is again clear.

In such a highly expansive economy with its excess demand, and with liquidity consequently limited in comparison with that in advanced countries, inventory cycles can differ by degree of liquidity. In Japan, they differ as

78

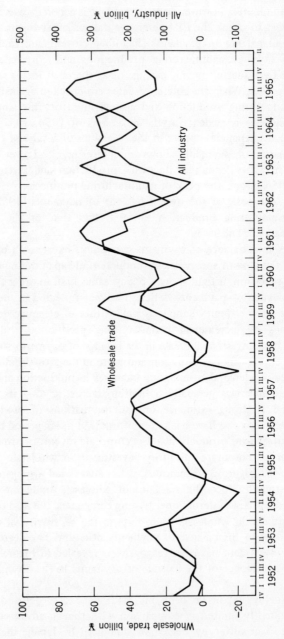

**Fig. 3–3** Corporate inventory investment in Japan (four-quarter moving averages). From Ministry of Finance, *Corporate Enterprise Quarterly Survey.*

between large and small enterprises, because, when a tight money policy is enforced, the banks often cut their lending to small enterprises first. Since there have always been close ties between banks and large enterprises, the pressure of tight money is likely to be shifted to small enterprises in this way. The decline of loans to large enterprises lags. When the balance of payments becomes favorable to a consequence of a tight money policy, easier money may eventually be expected, with bank funds temporarily in surplus. Then the banks seek borrowers even among medium-sized and small enterprises. In the recovery phase of short-term cycles, therefore, an increase of loans to small enterprises may lead those to large enterprises. However, as a boom progresses, the demand for funds by large enterprises becomes more intense, so that the supply of funds to small enterprises will be curtailed. Consequently, loans to medium and small enterprises may decrease before any tight money policy is adopted officially. This explains why large and small enterprises have different credit and inventory cycles, when the economy is short of liquidity and priority in borrowing is given generally to the large enterprises[1].

As a measure of short-term credit of financial institutions, the sum of short-term loans and discounted receivables is used [2]. Changes in short-term borrowings outstanding (four-quarter moving averages) are shown in Figure 3–4. In the 1956–1957 boom, for example, the peaks for the smaller enterprise groups (B) and (C) preceded the peak for the large enterprise group (A) by three of four quarters. Other peak and trough leads and lags among the three enterprise-size groups may be determined from Figure 3–4 by following the same numbers from the (A) to the (C) group. For the (B) and (C) groups. the oscillation of the credit cycles was reversed for 1958–1965, while for the (A) and (B) groups they were reversed in 1956–1961. The competitive relationship in borrowing from financial institutions is thus evident. This may be one of the most important reasons for the difference between the inventory cycles of enterprises of different sizes.

The cycles of corporate inventory investment are depicted in Figure 3–5. If Figure 3–4 is superimposed on Figure 3–5 and the movements of short-term loans and inventory investment are compared, it is found that the peaks and troughs of the (A) and (C) series almost correspond with each other, but those of the (B) series do not. Thus, as far as the (A) and (C) series are concerned, the hypothesis set forth earlier holds true. However, in 1960–1962 there seems to have been a temporary cessation of the lead-lag pattern.

---

[1] In accordance with this hypothesis, I published my first empirical analysis on the duality of inventory cycles in 1959: *Ryūdōsei to Keiki Junkan* (Liquidity and Business Cycles), *Kinyū*, February 1959. See also Chapter 8, "Inventory Cycles and the Dual Structure," in Miyohei Shinohara, *Growth and Cycles in the Japanese Economy*, Tokyo, 1962.

[2] These data are from the Ministry of Finance, *Corporate Enterprise Quarterly Survey*.

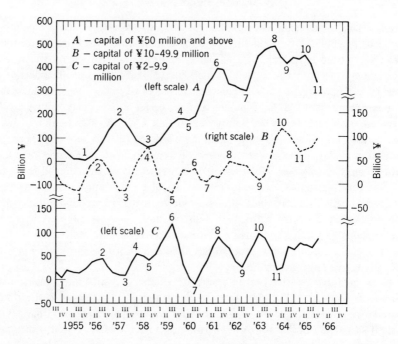

Fig. 3–4.

Fig. 3–4. Short-term borrowings from Japanese financial institutions by corporate enterprises of different sizes (four-quarter moving averages). Short-term borrowings include receivables discounted by financial institutions. From Ministry of Finance, *Corporate Enterprise Quarterly Survey*.

Fig. 3–5. Inventory investment in Japanese corporate enterprises, by size groups. (All series are four-quarter moving averages. Changes in inventories are gross of inventory valuation adjustment.) From Ministry of Finance, *Corporate Enterprise Quarterly Survey*.

Fig. 3–6. Loans outstanding of all Japanese financial institutions relative to loans in the same month of preceding year. Until August 1964, the large enterprises are those with paid-in capital of over 10 million, and the medium and small enterprises are those with less than that amount. After September 1964, the large enterprises are those with paid-in capital of over 5 million, and the medium and small enterprises are those with less than that amount. From Chūshō Kigyō Kinyū Kōko (The Small Business Finance Corporation), *Kinyū Tōkei Geppō* (Monthly Report of Financial Statistics).

80

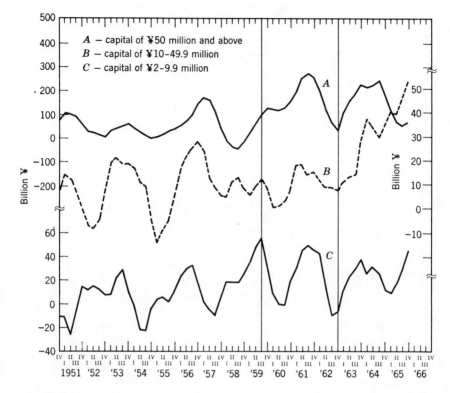

Fig. 3–5.

Fig. 3–6.

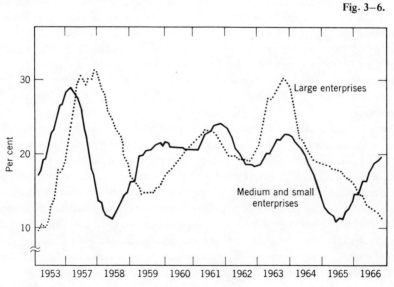

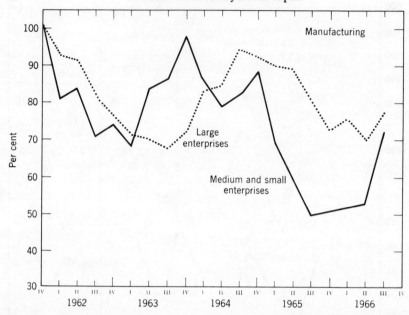

**Fig. 3–7.** Fixed investment in large and small enterprises. From the Bank of Japan, *Shuyō Kigyō Tanki Keizai Kansoku* (Short-term Economic Forecasts for Major Enterprises) and *Chūshō Kigyō Tanki Keizai Kansoku* (Short-term Economic Forecasts for Medium and Small Enterprises.) Note that the latter survey starts only from 1961, IV.

The foregoing analysis is based on a series derived from corporate financial statements. What happens when the analysis is based on aggregate financial statistics? As shown in Figure 3–6, the outstanding loans of medium and small enterprises (relative to loans in the same month of the preceding year) generally lead those of large enterprises. During 1963–1964, the lead disappeared, but it reappeared in 1965. The trough of the loan series for medium and small businesses came in mid-1965, while loan series for big enterprises was still decreasing.

Other data indicate differences between the fixed-investment behavior of large and small enterprises. The Bank of Japan publishes quarterly its *Shuyō Kigyō Tanki Keizai Kansoku* (Short-term Economic Forecasts for Major Enterprises) and its *Chūshō Kigyō Tanki Keizai Kansoku* (Short-term Forecasts for Medium and Small Enterprises). The first publication considers corporations with paid-in capital of more than ¥100 million, usually with stocks listed on the stock exchange; the sample covers about 500 corporations, including about 350 manufacturing corporations. The second publication considers nearly 3,600 manufacturing corporations with the number of employees ranging from 50 to 299. Figure 3–7 indicates that the 1963 trough of the medium and small enterprises series was in the first quarter, two quarters earlier than the trough for large enterprises. For medium and small corporations, (1963–IV) leads by three quarters the peak (1964–III) for large enterprises. The recovery of fixed investment in 1965–1966 also came earlier for the medium and small enterprises than for the large ones.

### Fixed Investment Cycles

After the war every industrial country experienced clearly visible inventory cycles, but not clearly visible fixed investment or Juglar cycles, as measured by the ratio of private fixed investment to Gross National Product (GNP). Japan may have been among the few countries which did experience such a Juglar cycle. Figure 3–8 indicates that for 1946–1954 (or 1946–1955) the ratio of private fixed investment to GNP (the fixed investment ratio) traced out one

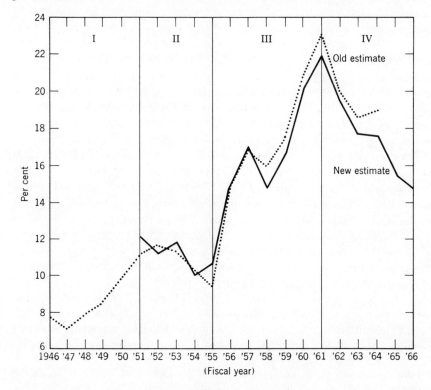

**Fig. 3–8.**    Ratio of Japanese private fixed investment to gross national product. Private fixed investment does not include residential construction. From Economic Planning Agency, National Income Section's new and old estimates.

cycle and for 1955–1965 another such cycle. The two cycles, with durations of
9 to 11 years, are quite different from the shorter cycles discussed earlier.

The proportion of private fixed investment (excluding residential construction) to GNP determines the growth rate of capacity. The fixed investment ratio
was between 10 and 12 per cent for 1951–1955, when the GNP growth
rate was about 7 per cent on the average. For 1955–1961, the ratio averaged
about 16 per cent and the GNP growth rate rose to about 10 per cent. The
marginal private fixed capital-output ratio implied in both periods is about
1.6–1.7. In connection with the increase of the growth rate from 7 per cent
(1951–1955) to 10 per cent (1955–1961), my judgment is that the required
fixed investment ratio rose from about 11 per cent to about 16 per cent; the
fixed investment ratio of 10 per cent for 1955 was too low for the later growth
rate of 10 per cent. The consequence was the sharp increase of the fixed
investment ratio from 10 per cent in 1955 to 21.9 per cent in 1961. The
capacity shortage or excess-demand situation that accompanied the rising fixed
investment ratio ended in 1961 when total capacity and demand seem to have
been temporarily balanced. However, the high fixed-investment ratio (21.9 per
cent in 1961) would probably have brought about too high a capacity growth
rate (about 14 per cent per annum) had it persisted in the years after 1962.

Since the demand growth rate was only about 10 per cent even in the peak
growth period of 1955–1961, it was completely impossible to anticipate a rate
of 14 per cent after 1961. Therefore, the adjustment needed to balance the
growth of capacity and demand would have been a decline of the fixed
investment ratio even below that prevailing with a growth rate of 10 per cent.

What actually happened was a downward adjustment of the fixed investment
ratio from 21.9 per cent in 1961 to 15.3 per cent in 1966. I predicted in 1961 that
the ratio would decline to about 14 per cent in the next few years [3]. In the
fall of 1962, I also predicted in a nonacademic essay that the annual average of
private fixed investment (excluding residential construction) for 1961–1965
would be about four trillion yen, and that private fixed investment would level
off for at least five years [4]. This prediction depended not on a econometric
model but on a simple numerical calculation based on the supposed magnitudes
of the growth rate (10 per cent) and the marginal gross fixed capital-output
ratio. In the computaton, however, I assumed that a capacity shortage had
prevailed in 1955–1961, and that excess capacity would emerge after 1962.
Such equilibrium is the cause of the rise or fall of the fixed investment ratio. I
computed the required fixed investment as a first step, assuming an equilibrium

[3] Miyohei Shinohara, "Keizai Seichō to Setsubitoshi Kyūshin no Hyōka" (Evaluation of
Economic Growth and Galloping Fixed Investment), in Oriental Economist, *Keizai Tōkei
Nenkan (Yearbook of Economic Statistics)*, June 1961.
[4] Miyohei Shinohara, "How Will Fixed Investment Develop?" (in Japanese), in *Nihon
Keizai Shimbun,* October 1962.

growth of 10 per cent for 1961–1965; but I adjusted the numerical results by additional assumptions of excess capacity and of some increase of the marginal gross fixed capital-output ratio. The estimated result was not an absolute decrease of private fixed investment, but a leveling off for five years. The hypothesis I had in mind was along the lines of the capital stock-adjustment theory.

According to the revised national income estimates, private fixed investment for the five years 1961–1965 was ¥4231.7 billion, ¥4105.3 billion, ¥4388.7 billion, ¥5010.6 billion, and ¥4812.1 billion; the five-year average therefore was ¥4509.7 billion. Since my prediction was based on the old national income estimate, and private fixed investment (excluding residential construction) in the new estimate was about 5 per cent higher, my prediction of the private fixed investment for 1961–1965 was overestimated by only 5 per cent.

The excess capacity phase, 1962–1966, was characterized by the following phenomena: (1) an abnormal rise in inventories of finished commodities as a proportion of shipments; (2) an excessive rise of interfirm credit (charge accounts, bills receivable) as a percentage of sales; (3) a sudden rise of the Marshallian $k$; (4) striking increases in dishonored bills and bankruptcies, and (5) a tapering-off of stock prices, as a reflection of the decline of the profit rate after 1962. For instance, in April-September 1961, the rate of increase of corporate sales was 25 per cent; in the period January–June 1964, it was 26.3 per cent. Although the growth rates were almost the same in the two periods, the operating profit rate was 8.7 per cent of total capital in the former period and 7.5 per cent in the latter period. Table 3–3 seems to show very distinctly how the 1961–1965 period differs from the preceding one, and cannot be understood as a purely inventory cycle. The fixed investment cycle must also be taken into account, although I do not know why that cycle lasted 9–11 years, just like the prewar Juglar cycle of advanced countries.

Other questions are of interest: When will the downward adjustment of the fixed-investment ratio cease? When will it turn up again, for 11 years have already passed since the 1955 trough? Sumio Shishido, in a recently published article [5] insisted that, since the fixed investment ratio in the manufacturing sector in 1965 had already dropped to the 1956 figure and in 1966 had fallen to a much lower level, it was then destined to rise. According to the Nomura Institute survey of corporations listed on the Tokyo Stock Exchange, First

[5] *"Tenkeiki wa Owatta"* (The End of the Transition Period), *Ekonomisuto,* January 17, 1967. Shishido was the author of the Economic White Paper of 1962, in which he developed the idea of *Tenkeiki*, meaning that the 1962 recession should also be understood as a medium cycle of fixed investment. He analyzed the transition of the investment-oriented growth pattern of 1955–1961 (and a capacity-shortage phase in the same period) to a government expenditure-oriented growth pattern from 1962 onward (and an excess-capacity phase).

TABLE 3–3    Development of the Excess Capacity Phase (1962–1965) in Japan.

| Calendar Year | Dishonored Bills (billion yen) | Bankruptcies | | Ratio of Inventories of Finished Commodities to Shipments in Mining and Manufacturing (per cent) | Ratio of Interfirm Credit to Sales in Corporate Sector (per cent) | Ratio of Money Supply to Gross National Product (per cent) | Tokyo Stock Exchange Stock Price Average (year) |
|---|---|---|---|---|---|---|---|
| | | Number | Liabilities (billion yen) | | | | |
| 1954 | 1,652 | 845 | 76.9 | 117.6 | 48.3 | 21.5 | 340.8 |
| 1955 | 1,235 | 605 | 44.2 | 107.1 | 49.8 | 21.2 | 374.0 |
| 1956 | 1,152 | 1,123 | 46.4 | 89.5 | 49.8 | 22.4 | 485.3 |
| 1957 | 1,687 | 1,736 | 76.7 | 99.6 | 49.6 | 21.4 | 535.6 |
| 1958 | 1,555 | 1,480 | 58.0 | 128.4 | 51.8 | 22.5 | 572.0 |
| 1959 | 1,546 | 1,166 | 48.4 | 104.7 | 55.8 | 23.0 | 821.5 |
| 1960 | 1,853 | 1,172 | 65.2 | 100.0 | 58.1 | 22.7 | 1,116.6 |
| 1961 | 2,085 | 1,102 | 80.4 | 103.1 | 63.4 | 23.1 | 1,548.9 |
| 1962 | 2,805 | 1,779 | 184.0 | 126.2 | 73.2 | 23.0 | 1,419.4 |
| 1963 | 3,492 | 1,738 | 169.5 | 120.5 | 75.5 | 27.0 | 1,440.6 |
| 1964 | 5,265 | 4,212 | 463.1 | 120.0 | 78.3 | 27.5 | 1,262.9 |
| 1965 | 5,575 | 6,141 | 562.4 | 130.6 | 77.7 | 29.1 | 1,203.2 |

Sources: Dishonored bills, Tokyo Tegata Kōkansho (Tokyo Clearing House), Annual and Monthly Reports of Tokyo Bank Clearings; Bankruptcies, Tokyo Shōkō Kōshinsho (Tokyo Commercial and Industrial Inquiry Agency, National Survey of the Bankruptcy of Companies); Inventory–Shipment ratio, based on the quantity indices of the Ministry of International Trade and Industry; Interfirm credit–sales ratio, the Ministry of Finance, Corporate Enterprise Quarterly Survey; Money supply, Bank of Japan; Stock price average, Tokyo Stock Exchange.

Section, Shishido's computation indicates that the fixed investment-sales ratio was 5.57 per cent in September 1966, which is much lower than the 8.52 per cent of September 1956.

I have tried to check this assertion by constructing the same ratio for corporate enterprises with a paid-in capital of over ¥2 million [6]. Changes in this ratio during the period 1953–1966 are shown in Figure 3–9 for all industry and for manufacturing corporations. Not only in manufacturing but also in all industry, the fixed investment ratio in 1966 returned to the 1955 level. When based upon national income statistics, however, the ratio was higher in 1966 than in 1955 (in fiscal year 1965, it was 15.4 per cent in current prices and 18.3 per cent in 1965 constant prices, compared with 10.7 per cent in current prices and 11.4 per cent in constant prices in fiscal year 1955).

The apparant difference should therefore be traced to the behavior of fixed investment in the noncorporate sectors, particularly the agricultural one. Since the major portion of private fixed investment is in secondary industries, and the increase of income originating in the agricultural sector is very low, it is possible that the return of the fixed investment ratio to the 1955 level in the corporate sector is consistent with the ratio for the national economy as a whole remaining

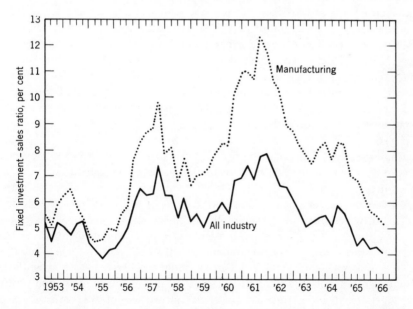

**Fig. 3–9.** Fixed investment-sales ratio of Japanese corporate enterprises with paid in capital of over 2 million yen.

[6] Data from Ministry of Finance, *Corporate Enterprise Quarterly Survey.*

higher than in 1955. As manufacturing is both an important industry and the mainspring of investment activity, any judgment as to whether or not the fixed investment ratio will revive should depend primarily upon the movement in manufacturing. The fact that the fixed investment ratio dropped to the low 1955 figure seems to herald the coming of a new fixed-investment boom. The domestic private orders received for machinery (except for water transport) showed an increase of 59.8 per cent between November–December 1965 and the corresponding months in 1966. For the same periods, the production of pig iron increased by 26.6 per cent, and that of crude steel by 37.8 per cent.

However, one problem remains in the continuation of this fixed investment surge. Japan experienced a very long investment boom in 1956–1961. This corresponds to the growth acceleration from 7 per cent (1951–1955) to 10 per cent (1956–1961). Although the government prediction (March 13, 1967) was for a real GNP growth rate of about 9 per cent in 1967, it is expected that the rate will exceed 10 per cent even in real terms, in view of recent brisk investment activity. Therefore, there is no doubt about the existence of an investment boom in 1967; but if the growth potential over a longer period (the coming five years) were only 8 per cent per annum, the buoyancy of fixed investment would be limited. Since in 1951–1955, when the growth rate of GNP was 7–8 per cent, the increase of private fixed investment was relatively moderate, a fixed investment surge in a period of growth deceleration cannot last long. Moreover, when account is taken of the fact that in other advanced industrial countries no clear Juglar cycle has been discernible in the postwar period, the emergence of the fixed investment cycle in postwar Japan appears to have been due to a chance factor (introduction of foreign high-level technology on an unprecedented scale); and in a growth phase of 8 per cent the fixed investment cycle may be expected to vanish, or to be overwhelmed by short-run oscillations (inventory cycles).

Consequently, by emphasizing the existence of the fixed investment cycle, I am not asserting the mechanical perpetuation of a fairly regular Juglar cycle. On the contrary, my belief is that its existence, with a duration of about 10 years, will probably be temporary. However, I strongly feel that my analysis and judgment, which took into account the fixed investment cycle, were to some extent correct. In other words, after an unprecedented increase in the fixed-investment ratio, I had the opinion that it would start to decline, and this led me to adopt a fairly correct judgment about the five-year path after 1961. This was based not only on observation of the medium-term oscillation of the fixed-investment ratio, but also on some calculations of the required fixed investment, by use of the assumed future growth rate and the marginal gross private fixed capital-output ratio.

## Some Policy Observations

The studies of Japan's postwar cycles, outlined earlier, are merely descriptive. They do not attempt to construct an econometric model; rather, they try to explore some findings with relation to regularities and peculiarities. My impression is that the Bank of Japan and the government have adopted, time and again, certain cyclical policies mostly in "passive" ways in order to deal with difficulties or improvements in the balance of payments, so that business cycles have revealed themselves with considerable clarity. Figure 3–10 indicates on the one hand that, at least for 1953–1963, there was a positive correlation between the rate of increase of GNP and of tax revenues, and also that, in the recessions of 1957–1958 and 1962, the rate of increase of the former surpassed that of the latter, thus contributing to the moderation of the recessions to some extent. On the other hand, in the upswings from 1956-II to 1957-I, and from 1959-III to 1961-II, the rate of increase of tax revenues was higher than that of government expenditure and contributed a mitigating influence to the investment booms. However, this depends upon some lag in government expenditure compared with tax revenues. Therefore, it cannot be stated that the government has intentionally adopted, as yet, a contracyclical policy. Its worst mistake was in the depression of 1964–1965, when growth rate of tax revenues tended to increase while that of government expenditure turned downward. There was criticism of the so-called "policy depression" caused by the stringent attitude of the Sato Cabinet. However, shortly thereafter, the government decided to issue national bonds for the first time since the war. This was reflected in a rate of increase of government expenditure which exceeded that of tax revenues after 1965-II (Figure 3–10). The most effective policy was in 1962, when the government, foreseeing investment stagnation, maintained a high growth rate of government expenditure. However, during the continued investment boom of 1959–1961, government expenditure tended to increase, under the aggressive Ikeda Cabinet's expansionist policy, although tax revenues grew even more rapidly. The expansionist policy naturally played an important role in accelerating growth, but, from the viewpoint of the fixed investment cycle, the medium-term oscillation of the fixed investment ratio is believed to have become more intense. But if high-pitched growth should be considered essentially a disproportionate process, this should be taken as a necessary evil.

If there had not been a tax reform, then changes in tax revenues would have shown a very strong built-in flexibility. In Table 3-4, tax reduction is computed as the difference between the estimated increment of tax revenues with no changes in the tax laws and the actual increment in the general account of the central government. Thus, in 1957, the Ikeda Cabinet attempted a tax reduction amounting to ¥114.9 billion. This must have provided some check to the recession of 1957–1958. Two other tax reductions—in 1962 and 1965—are also

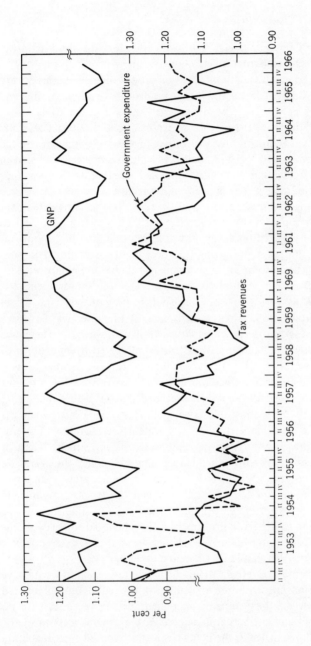

**Fig. 3–10.** Ratios of Japanese government expenditure and tax revenues to expenditure or revenues in same quarter of preceding year. (Government expenditure equals government current purchases of goods and services plus government investment excluding investment of government enterprises. Tax revenues equal personal and corporate taxes.) From the Economic Planning Agency, *Kokuminshotoku Nempō* (Annual Report on National Income Statistics), 1966.

TABLE 3–4  Tax Reduction in Central General Account of Japan (Cols. (a)–(e) in billions of yen; cols. (f) and (g) in per cent).

| Fiscal Year | Tax Revenues in General a/c (a) | Increases in (a) (b) | Tax Revenues under Prior Year Legislation (c) | $(c) - (a)_{-1}$ (d) | Tax Reduction $(d) - (b)$ (e) | Rate of Tax Reduction $(e)/(a)_{-1}$ (f) | Rate of Tax Reduction $(e)/(d)$ (g) |
|---|---|---|---|---|---|---|---|
| 1950 | 456.4 | — | — | — | — | — | — |
| 1951 | 604.0 | 147.6 | 791.4 | 335.0 | 187.4 | 41.1 | 55.9 |
| 1952 | 708.5 | 104.5 | 759.8 | 155.8 | 51.3 | 8.5 | 32.9 |
| 1953 | 782.8 | 74.3 | 892.1 | 183.6 | 109.3 | 15.4 | 59.5 |
| 1954 | 798.4 | 15.6 | 841.2 | 18.4 | 2.8 | negligible | 15.2 |
| 1955 | 796.0 | – 2.4 | 865.1 | 66.7 | 69.1 | 8.7 | 103.6 |
| 1956 | 950.2 | 154.2 | 994.1 | 198.1 | 43.9 | 5.5 | 22.2 |
| 1957 | 1,049.9 | 99.7 | 1,164.8 | 214.6 | 114.9 | 12.1 | 53.5 |
| 1958 | 1,031.8 | – 18.1 | 1,059.6 | 9.7 | 27.8 | 2.6 | 286.6 |
| 1959 | 1,213.4 | 181.6 | 1,253.0 | 221.2 | 39.6 | 3.8 | 17.9 |
| 1960 | 1,618.3 | 404.9 | 1,626.0 | 412.6 | 7.7 | 0.4 | 18.7 |
| 1961 | 2,017.6 | 399.3 | 2,118.1 | 499.8 | 100.5 | 6.2 | 20.1 |
| 1962 | 2,195.9 | 178.3 | 2,358.4 | 340.8 | 162.5 | 8.1 | 47.7 |
| 1963 | 2,530.2 | 334.3 | 2,606.1 | 410.2 | 75.9 | 3.5 | 18.5 |
| 1964 | 2,949.7 | 419.5 | 2,989.0 | 458.8 | 39.3 | 1.6 | 8.6 |
| 1965 | 3,049.6 | 99.9 | 3,213.2 | 263.5 | 163.6 | 5.5 | 62.1 |

Source: Ministry of Finance, *Zeisei Shuyō Sankōshiryō* (Main Reference Data on the Tax System).

conspicuous, because both amounted to more than ¥160 billion. Since the ratio of the accumulated amount of the actual tax increase to the estimated amount, on the assumption of no tax reforms, that is, $\Sigma b/\Sigma d$—was 48.0 per cent for 1951–1958 and 77.6 per cent for 1959–1965, the higher proportion of the potential tax increase, brought about by economic growth, was used for increased government expenditure rather than for tax reductions in the later stages.

Monetary policy has always worked very effectively as a response to, or remedy for, balance of payments difficulties. According to the Economic Planning Agency's business cycle reference dates, the peak of the second cycle was January 1954, but the Bank of Japan had already begun to strengthen its credit rationing on September 6, 1953 as a first step in a tight money policy. In the third cycle, the reference dates indicate that the peak was June 1957, but the Bank of Japan had raised its basic money rate on March 20. In the fourth cycle, the peak was December 1961, but a rise in the basic money rate and an increase of the deposit reserve ratio had preceded it by a few months (July 22 and October 1, respectively). In the fifth cycle, the peak was October 1964, but the Bank of Japan had raised its deposit-reserve ratio on December 16, 1963, and increased its basic money rate on March 18, 1964. Thus, it is evident that in all recessions, balance of payments difficulties and the tight money policies both preceded the peaks of the business cycle.

However, the dates when the basic money rate was reduced have almost always coincided with the troughs of the cycles, as in 1958 and 1962 (June 1958 and October 1962, respectively); in 1965, however, the easy money decision of the Bank of Japan preceded the trough of the cycle. If this is true, it may be speculated that, in the 1958 and 1962 recoveries, downward inventory adjustment had already paved the road to recovery before monetary policy had begun to operate. In other words, monetary policy acted strongly as a brake to the expansion or as a remedy for balance of payments deficits before the recession occurred, but it did not always precede recovery. Probably, as the balance of payments became more favorable and inventory adjustment proceeded, an impetus to the upswing would have been given "automatically" because of increasingly easy money conditions and decreasing inventories rather than because of monetary policy change.

It may be useful to explore the sources of finance for medium and small enterprises from the viewpoint of short-term fluctuations. Figure 3-11 indicates that loans from government financial institutions increased just when loans from banks decreased. Also, when the duality of cycles between big and medium and small enterprises ceased temporarily, loans from private financial institutions for small business showed a very high rate of increase for more than three years (1961–1963). These financial institutions consist of *Sōgō Ginkō* (Mutual Loan and Savings Banks), *Shinyō Kinkō* (Credit Associations), *Shōkō Kumiai Chūō*

*Kinko* (The Central Bank for Commercial and Industrial Cooperatives, etc. But, once the rate of increase of loans from these institutions declined sharply (1965), the dual behavior exhibited itself again.

These are brief considerations about some aspects of policy. They are only preliminary explanations, which are incomplete in that the quantitative repercussions are not explored. However, my belief is that in the postwar business cycle process the cycles themselves have still survived, despite all these policy effects, mainly because most of the monetary and fiscal policies can be thought of as *ex post* adjustments (with some time lags) to the disequilibrium caused by the balance of payments. In that sense, the policies themselves worked like endogenous variables. This may be the reason why the cycle survives persistently in postwar Japan [7]. Most conspicuous is the survival of the Juglar cycle, but this seems to be due to some chance pattern in the enormous injection of foreign technology after about 1955. The expansionist policies (cheap money policy, income-doubling plan, etc.) seem to have worked primarily as accelerators of the Juglar cycle.

[7] Mr. Bronfenbrenner has pointed out that I made no reference to the econometric work in Japan, and emphasized the need of contact between model-building econometricians and ordinary quantitative-cycle theorists and analysts. However, one of my reasons for omitting any reference to them is that in Japan the econometricians have been so eager to forecast the future growth rate that they have provided relatively scanty econometric information about cyclical characteristics and responsiveness to policy changes. However, some hindsight simulation analysis of the cyclical aspects of the economy is given in the following articles:

Kei Mori, "Simulation Analysis of Fluctuations and Growth of the Japanese Economy: 1955–1960", in Ryutaro Komiya, ed., *Postwar Economic Growth in Japan*, Berkeley, 1966, p. 189; and

Chikashi Moriguchi, "Japan's Economic Growth and Business Cycles in Twenty Years: An Econometric Presentation", *KIER Discussion Paper* NS. 001, February 1967.

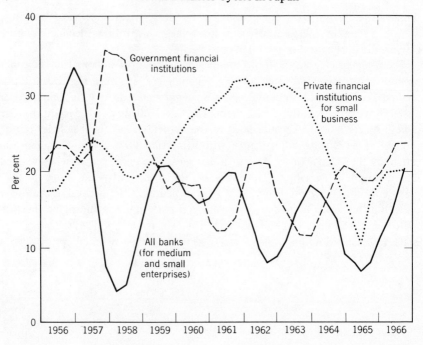

**Fig. 3–11.**　Loans outstanding at Japanese medium and small enterprises relative to loans in same month of preceding year. Source: See the footnote for Figure 3–6. Ministry of Finance, *Kinyū Tōkei Geppō* (Monthly Report of Financial Statistics).

## *APPENDIX  Series Included in EPA Diffusion Indices*

### LEADING SERIES

1. Gold and foreign exchange reserve
2. Tokyo stock exchange stock price average
3. New orders for machinery (private demand, excluding water, transport and electric power)
4. New orders for construction (private)
5. Average hours worked per regular worker, by industry (total)
6. Rate of job accession (manufacturing)
7. Index of raw and finished materials inventories (changes)
8. Outstanding orders for machinery (excluding ships) (changes)
9. Index of producers' inventories of finished goods relative to shipments (mining and manufacturing)
10. Number of bankruptcies of firms (inverted)

COINCIDENT SERIES

1. Index of industrial production (mining and manufacturing)
2. Index of producer's shipments (mining and manufacturing)
3. Index of raw and finished materials consumption (manufacturing)
4. Commodity imports (customs clearance basis)
5. Construction starts (mining and manufacturing)
6. Over-time working hours (manufacturing)
7. Index of wholesale prices (manufacturing products)
8. Freight transportation by national railroad (ton-kilometers)

LAGGING SERIES

1. Outstanding orders for machinery (excluding ships)
2. Index of raw and finished material inventories (manufacturing)
3. Index of producer's inventories of finished goods
   relative to shipments (mining and manufacturing)
4. Interest rate on loans of all banks
5. Loans-deposits ratio of all banks
6. Turnover of deposit currency
7. Wages and salaries as a ratio to shipments (manufacturing)

# COMMENTS

MARTIN BRONFENBRENNER
Carnegie-Mellon University, Pittsburgh

Professor Shinohara is best known internationally as the leading light of Japanese business cycle analysis in its less self-consciously econometric forms, on the basis of quantitative-historical studies of Japanese growth and cycles in the half-century before World War II. More widely discussed in Japan are his frequent and trenchant comments on the current scene, including the economic policy of the Japanese Government. The present paper combines both these aspects of Shinohara's work and thought.

To an American brought up on National Bureau of Economic Research "reference cycles" and "leading series," Shinohara's paper is more than usually easy to follow, since the Japanese Economic Planning Agency (EPA) has taken over so much of the National Bureau apparatus. The Japanese data go further than their U.S. models, and I dare say further than those of most other countries, in distinguishing movements of series relating to big business, on the one hand, and to medium and small business, on the other. This distinction is important for Shinohara's analysis, since the "medium and small" series on, for example, inventories, seem consistently to lead the series for "large" firms. This is what would be expected from the Japanese credit system with its familial (not to mention the wicked word *zaibatsu*) ties between each leading national or regional banking chain and its associated stable of large companies. This makes the medium and small firm the residual claimant for credit. It also makes the medium and small firms immediately vulnerable to the lightest touch of credit stringency and an almost-as-immediate beneficiary of the initial easing of the money supply. This effect would probably be even more pronounced if it were practical to distinguish truly independent medium and small firms from dependencies of the large ones (suppliers, subcontractors, selling agencies, and so on). I should expect the subseries for truly independent companies to lead even more markedly than the series for medium and small firms as a group.

96

Perhaps Shinohara's most interesting substantive finding is the isolation of medium-term or Juglar cycles in fixed investment, along with the shorter inventory cycles—Kitchins, in Schrumpeter's terminology—which are found to persist also in many other countries. Insofar as Shinohara is right, the cycle is even less obsolete in Japan than in most other countries, "economic miracles" to the contrary notwithstanding. Whether he is right or not, however, depends upon a deeper methodological point, namely, his treatment of trends.

For most countries, National Bureau "reference cycles" for the postwar period, computed about the mean of each cycle rather than about any smoothed trend, will not look like the standard ones in National Bureau publications. Instead of the up-and-down movements found in those publications, there will be almost unbroken upward movements, with steeper slopes during boom periods and shallower ones during recessions. It is understandable that these slope alternations are called "growth cycles" (as in Professor Gordon's discussion about the U.S. record) and are regarded as "modernized" business cycles. Some people call them "Japanese" cycles. Shinohara, however, has gone one step further in the quantitative direction. He has computed four-quarter moving averages and has treated deviations from these moving averages as constituting business cycles.

The problem here is sensitivity to the choice of a trend line. Business analysts have obtained widely different results by altering trend lines. For example, I recall the late Roger Babson supporting his quadrature theory—each area above the trend line being balanced by an equal area below—by shifting the U.S. economy from an upward trend to a stagnant constancy at March 1933 (Roosevelt's first inaugural). Shinohara indulges in no such horrors, but until a better theoretical reason than his is given for choosing moving averages in preference to some other trends, any results are in the nature of statistical artifacts—possibly as to the existence of two Juglar cycles, more probably as to their amplitudes and detailed dating. Incidentally, Shinohara's discussion of inventory cycles touches on this same point, since the Bank of Japan and the EPA found different peaks and troughs because the EPA used diffusion indices while the Bank used deviations from a moving average.

Like many other countries strongly dependent upon international sources for raw materials and international markets for finished products, Japan has adopted a primarily monetary version of cycle policy, responsive to balance of payments conditions. (I had thought that this orientation had diminished in the 1960's. with the expansive influence of Dr. Shimomura in the Ikeda Cabinet, but Shinohara finds no break between Ikeda and pre-Ikeda policies.) On the fiscal side, Japan balanced its budget annually until 1965, according to "sound finance" principles as expounded by Joseph Dodge, the Detroit banker, and the U.S. Occupation. Questions may well be raised about the why and wherefore of this apparent anomaly and anachronism, the persistence of a foreign-imposed balanced-budget rule through a dozen years of independence, when that rule was at least obsolscent at the moment of promulgation. Let me interpose three suggestions on this point, as a postscript to Shinohara's factual paper. (1) Monetary policy was itself expansionary most of the time, with the money supply rising approximately half again as fast as the real GNP. The appeal of further expansion from the fiscal side was accordingly less than it might have been under continuous "tight money." (2) Japanese growth permitted substantial tax cuts almost every year after 1950, within the limits of budgetary balance and rising public revenues. (3) An additional "fiscal dividend" of Japanese growth was a steady rise in real public expenditures, although housing and social security lagged behind. (National defense has never reached 2 per cent of Japan's GNP.) What this adds up to is that the usual distressing effects of "sound" fiscal policy have been averted in the period that Shinohara covers, largely because of the conjuncture of an increasing supply of Japanese exports and an increasing world demand for them.

Let me revert in closing to yet another methodological note, applying to several of the other chapters as well as to this: It is the paucity of contact between model-building econometricians and ordinary quantitative-cycle theorists and analysts. (Shinohara falls in the latter category.) It is both noteworthy and fairly typical that he makes no reference to the work being done in the former category. Japan is by now, as many economists know, one of the most thoroughly modelled countries in existence—by both Japanese and foreigners. On my own most recent visit to Japan (September 1966) one econometrician, Father Antonio Sagrista, told me of nearly 25 econometric models in Japan in various stages of development and operation [1]. (One of these, the Osaka model, may be the largest and most elaborate in the world.) Yet, it would appear, Shinohara has found nothing of great value in these models. I do not suggest that the fault is mainly his. Some of the 25 models—and there are probably more—are incomplete. Others deal with longer-term problems exclusively. The models as a group have not been fully compared, tested, or rendered intelligible to the rest of us. I point out the yawning gap, not in criticism of Shinohara, but as evidence of unfinished business to be filled by subsequent work in all our countries.

[1] These models are sampled in Sagrista, *Sophia-I: An Econometric Quarterly Model of the Japanese Economy, 1955–1965* (Tokyo 1967), pp. iii–iv; also items 4, 11, 12, 20, 21, 61, 62, 85, 86, 107, and 118, of the bibliography (pp. 225–231).

Chapter Four

# POSTWAR BUSINESS CYCLES IN THE UNITED KINGDOM

R. C. O. MATTHEWS
Oxford University*

Cyclical movements in the British economy in the postwar period have been at least as clear-cut and regular as in earlier times. Growth has proceeded in a series of four cycles, with peak years 1951, 1955, 1960, and 1964, and trough years 1952, 1958, 1962, and (probably) 1967. Comparison with *the* prewar business cycle is complicated by the fact that this cycle was itself by no means a homogeneous phenomenon. In particular, the two cycles in the British economy in the interwar period differed considerably from each other, and from pre-1914 cycles; and in all periods, British cycles have differed in a number of respects from those in the United States and elsewhere. But on any reckoning, postwar cycles have had some major differences from past ones. They have been shorter and (by most measures) milder. In no postwar year has there been a significant decline in real gross domestic product (GDP)[1]. Fluctuations have taken the form of oscillations in the growth rate. Moreover, the prominent part played by the government has led many, if not most, observers to believe that what has been witnessed is not the old-style business cycle but a new kind of phenomenon known as "stop-go."

The first postwar cycle (peak 1951, trough 1952) was in important respects different from the subsequent ones, which, in contrast, have strong family resemblance with each other. The expansion in the late 1940's was characterized

---

* I am much indebted to Mr. J. Odling-Smee and Mrs. P. Yudkin for assistance in the preparation of this chapter.

---

[1] In years 1952 and 1958, real GDP showed virtually no change from the preceding years, and by some measures it declined fractionally.

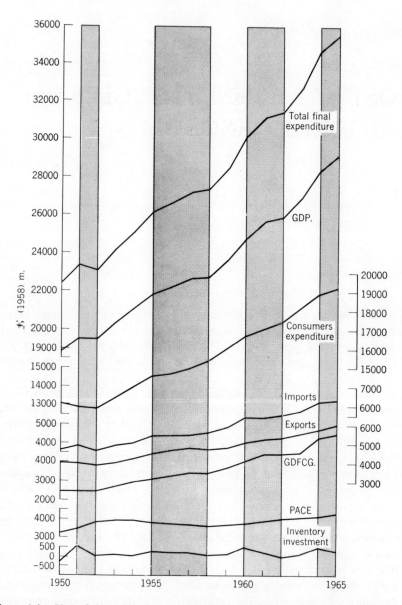

**Chart 4-1**   United Kingdom: gross domestic product (GDP) and components, 1950-1965.

Source of data in charts in Chapter 4: Blue Books on *National Income and Expenditures,* Central Statistical Office, London. (Except where otherwise stated.)

by chronic excess demand, and the peak and downturn were dominated by the repercussions of the Korean War. It is the three subsequent cycles (peaks 1955, 1960, and 1964) that are of main interest, both for diagnosis of the nature of the cyclical movement and for future policy. Discussion will therefore for the most part be confined to them [2].

First, some measures of the duration and amplitude of postwar fluctuations will be considered.

I

The general picture of postwar movements is evident from the annual figures of real GDP and components shown in Chart 4-1, with recession periods shaded. The regularity of the cycles is apparent. Because of the regularity, it is possible to use average measures of cyclical behavior in a way that would not be appropriate with more irregularly fluctuating series [3].

To do this and make comparisons with past cycles, it is necessary to define the end years of each cycle. The concept of a turning point has some conceptual ambiguities when there is no absolute decline in recession years, and in making comparisons with earlier periods it is important to use consistent definitions. But in principle the issue is straightforward. The essence of the concept of the business cycle is that it is a fluctuation of demand relative to productive potential. A cyclical depression year is a year in which output is low relative to potential, a year, that is to say, when there is a more than average amount of idle or underutilized productive resources. The extent of underutilization of resources is difficult to measure directly; therefore, I define a peak as a year in which the rate of growth of GDP passes from being above trend to being below trend, and a trough year vice versa. On this definition, the turning points are placed in the years stated above [4]. The same procedure is used to define turning points in prewar cycles for the purposes of comparisons made below [5].

[2] For an account of the first postwar cycle, see E. A. G. Robinson, "Industrial Fluctuations in the United Kingdom 1946–1952," in E. Lundberg (ed.) *The Business Cycle in the Postwar World*, London, 1955; and J. C. R. Dow, *The Management of the British Economy*, 1945–1960, Cambridge, 1965. My indebtedness to Dow's work is apparent throughout this chapter.

[3] The averages used in this section are based on peak-to-peak cycles rather than the more usual trough-to-trough ones. This is done because, at the time of writing, the British economy is in an uncompleted downswing, so that if trough-to-trough measures were used it would not be possible to take account of any year later than 1962. The three postwar cycles averaged in this section thus include the downswing phase of the "Korean" cycle but not the preceding upswing.

Measures of the duration and amplitude of cycles in GNP in various periods are given in Table 4-1. Because postwar cycles have been shorter than earlier ones, it is important to have a measure of amplitude that takes account of duration. A given difference between the average annual growth rate in the upswing and the average annual growth rate in the downswing will lead to larger deviations from the trend line if the cycle is long than if it is short, and it will also lead to larger deviations from the trend line if the downswing and upswing are of equal duration than if they are of unequal duration. In Table 4-1 (and subsequently), therefore, amplitude is measured by the difference between average annual upswing and downswing growth rates, multiplied by a duration factor, $\dfrac{t_u t_d}{2(t_u + t_d)}$ where $t_u$ and $t_d$ are the duration of upswing and downswing, respectively. The amplitude thus defined measures what would be average percentage short-fall below the peak-to-peak trend if the cycle were a linear one [6]. Other measures of amplitude are, of course, possible, and might be preferable for certain purposes. The present measure has the merit of separating the contributions made by the duration pattern of the cycle on the one hand and the difference between upswing and downswing growth rates on the other. This is of some importance in the present context.

---

[4] Throughout this paper, annual figures will be used, except where otherwise stated. Statements like "stock-building fell in 1961" must therefore be understood to mean that stock-building was lower in 1961 than in 1960, not that it had a downward trend in 1961. The use of quarterly data is essential for forecasting and other purposes, but annual data provide the most convenient framework for the general view attempted in this paper.

[5] Because the definition of turning points used in this chapter takes account of the trend rate of growth, the reference cycle dates differ on some occasions from those of authors who have based their dating mainly on turning points in absolute values. Thus, the dates used here compare as follows with those in Arthur F. Burns and Wesley C. Mitchell, *Measuring Business Cycles,* New York, 1946:
*Peaks*
    My dates: 1856,1860,1865,1872,1883,1889,1900,1907,1913,1920,1929,1937.
    Burns & Mitchell: 1857,1860,1866,1873,1883,1890,1900,1907,1913,1920,1929,1937.
*Troughs*
    My dates:    1858,1862,1868,1879,1886,1893,1904,1908,1921,1932,1938.
    Burns & Mitchell: 1860, 1866, 1873, 1883, 1890, 1900, 1907, 1913, 1920, 1929, 1937.
Burns and Mitchell locate additional turning points:
*Peaks:*          1903,1917,1924,1927.
*Troughs:*        1901,1914,1919,1926,1928.
    I reject the 1901 and 1903 turning points since they are not revealed by either output or employment figures. The turning points in 1914, 1917 and 1919 are omitted because they are affected by war, and those of 1924 through 1928 because they are affected by the coal strike and the general strike and their aftermath.

TABLE 4–1   United Kingdom: Average Duration and Amplitude of Cycles in Gross Domestic Product (GDP) at Market Prices*

| | Average duration (in years) | | Annual growth rates (in per cent) | | | Dura-tion factor | Ampli-tude |
|---|---|---|---|---|---|---|---|
| | Downswing | Upswing | Downswing | Upswing | Difference ((4) − (3)) | | |
| | (1) | (2) | (3) | (4) | (5) | (6) | (7) |
| | | | Constant prices | | | | |
| 1951–1964 | 2.0 | 2.3 | 1.2 | 4.8 | 3.6 | 0.49 | 1.8 |
| 1920–1937 | 2.0 | 6.5 | −6.6 | 3.2 | 9.8 | 0.69 | 5.8 |
| 1872–1914 | 3.8 | 4.4 | −0.4 | 2.7 | 3.1 | 0.91 | 2.5 |
| | | | Current prices | | | | |
| 1951–1964 | 2.0 | 2.3 | 6.9 | 7.8 | 0.9 | 0.49 | 0.5 |
| 1920–1937 | 2.0 | 6.5 | −13.2 | 1.6 | 14.8 | 0.69 | 8.5 |
| 1872–1914 | 3.8 | 4.4 | 1.4 | 3.7 | 5.1 | 0.91 | 4.2 |

**Sources:** 1951–1964, Blue Books on *National Income and Expenditure;* Central Statistical Office, London, pre-1938, C. H. Feinstein, *National Income and Expenditure,* Cambridge, (forthcoming).

* Measures of growth rates, duration factor, and amplitude were calculated separately for each peak-to-peak cycle, and averaged to give the figures in the Table. Column (7) is therefore not exactly equal to the product of columns (5) and (6). Annual downswing and upswing changes within each cycle are measured as percentages of the initial peaks of the cycles in which they occur. The reference cycle dates given in Footnote 5, based on the constant-price series, are used for both constant-price and current-price measures, and do not necessarily correspond in all cases to turning points in current price GDP.

[6] Consider a peak-to-peak cycle. Write $y=$ actual income; $y^*=$ income on linear peak-to-peak trend; subscript $o$ for initial peak year; subscript $T$ for trough year; $u =$ arithmetic mean of annual increases in $y$ as proportion of $y_0$ in upswing; $d =$ arithmetic mean of annual increases in $y$ as proportion of $y_o$ in downswing; $t_d$ and $t_u$ as duration in years of downswing and upswing, respectively. Then

$$y_T = y_0 + t_d \, dy_0$$

$$y_T^* = y_0 + t_d \left( \frac{t_d \, dy_0 + t_u \, uy_0}{t_d + t_u} \right)$$

$$\frac{y_T^* - y_T}{y_0} = \frac{t_u t_d}{t_u + t_d} (u - d)$$

If the cycle is a linear one ($u$ and $d$ constant throughout the upswing and downswing), then the average shortfall of $y$ below $y^*$ over the cycle is half of $(y^*_T - y_T)$. The duration factor by which $(u - d)$ must be multiplied in order to give the average shortfall of $y$ below $y^*$ as a proportion of $y_0$ is therefore (as stated in the text)

$$\frac{t_u t_d}{2(t_u + t_d)}$$

which is equal to a quarter of the harmonic mean of $t_u$ and $t_d$.

103

As expected, Table 4-1 shows that postwar cycles in constant-price GDP have been milder in amplitude than earlier ones, and have been distinguished by the persistence of some positive growth in downswing phases. But the difference in amplitude is mainly by comparison with the exceptionally disturbed interwar period[7]. The difference in amplitude between postwar and pre-1914 years is not very great. The difference between upswing and downswing average annual growth rages is actually larger in 1951–1964 than in 1872–1914, but the shorter duration of the 1951–1964 cycles makes their overall amplitude somewhat less. Therefore, as far as real GDP is concerned, postwar fluctuations have not been so very small by the standards of the past, but they have been much smaller than they were between the wars.

A comparison of cycles in current prices shows a rather different story. In the interwar period and before 1914, the amplitude of cycles in current price GDP is greater than that of cycles in constant price. This is as would be expected; prices as well as output fluctuate over the cycle. In the postwar period, on the other hand, the current-price amplitude is less than the constant-price amplitude, which implies that prices on balance fluctuate *inversely* with the cycle. The current-price amplitude is consequently much lower in the postwar period than it was either between the wars or before 1914. The constant-price amplitude is the more fundamental measure of the severity of the cycle. But the disappearance of the fluctuations in output has no doubt contributed to the impression that cycles have been milder.

Even more important in producing this impression is the fact that fluctuations in *employment* have diminished in amplitude when compared with prewar years, by an extent that is far greater than can be accounted for by the diminution in the amplitude of fluctuations in output. This is discussed later.

So much for the severity of fluctuations in aggregate output in the postwar British economy, compared with earlier times. What about the comparison with the postwar experience of other countries? The popular view of stop-go as the "English disease" has led to a common belief that fluctuations in Britain have been more severe than those elsewhere. This belief is not well founded. Because the trend rate of growth in Britain has been low by international standards, growth has been brought nearer to a complete standstill in recession phases than it has in more rapidly growing countries. But this is not the same thing as having more severe cycles.

This issue has been discussed by Wilson, using several alternative measures of amplitude[8]. The one nearest to the concept used here is the standard

---

[7] The interwar period contained only two complete peak-to-peak cycles, both severe (amplitude measures 6.1 and 5.5). The contraction of 1921 was more severe than that of 1929–1932 and was by far the worst ever recorded in the British economy.

[8] T. Wilson, "Instability and the Rate of Growth," *Lloyds Bank Review,* July 1966.

deviation of annual growth rates[9]. By this measure, the amplitude of the cycle in GDP has been lower in Britain than in Japan, the United States, West Germany, and Sweden (ranked in order of amplitude) and only fractionally higher than in Italy and France.

The comparison with prewar fluctuations can be carried further by examining the fluctuations in the different classes of expenditure that comprise GDP.

Measures of amplitude, calculated in the same way as those already given, are shown in Table 4-2. The first panel shows the average amplitude of fluctuations over reference cycles in each class of expenditure as a proportion of itself; in the second panel, these figures are multiplied by the weight of the component in GDP, to show the amount of fluctuation in GDP that is proximately due to each component; in the third panel, these amounts are shown in percentage form.

The relative contributions of different components of expenditure to fluctuations in GDP were, on the average, fairly similar in the interwar period to what they had been before 1914 (third panel of Table 4-2). Postwar fluctuations, on the other hand, show some marked differences, thus giving *prima facie* support to the hypothesis that they have been a rather different sort of phenomenon.

The most important difference is the diminished role of exports, which previously accounted for about half of the total amplitude. The instability of exports used to be the major source of fluctuations in the British economy. This has ceased to be the case. On the other hand, fluctuations in consumption (especially of durables) have become more important, and have actually been larger than they were before 1914. How far postwar fluctuations in consumption have been due to inherent instability, mainly among durables, and how far to government policy is a matter that needs to be considered. Stockbuilding and (to a less extent) fixed capital formation have also become more important as a source of fluctuations in GDP[10]. On the other hand, the amplitude of cyclical movements in imports has increased relatively, and this has diminished the amplitude of fluctuations in GDP associated with given fluctuations in total final expenditure.

---

[9] This is not identical with my concept, but it is sufficiently near for the present purpose. It does not take account of the duration of the cycle, but in this respect there has not been much difference between countries during the postwar period.

[10] Before 1914, fluctuations in gross domestic fixed capital formation (GDFCF) were large, but on many occasions they were poorly synchronized with reference cycles; the amplitude of fluctuations over reference cycles therefore understates the amplitude of specific cycles in GDFCF before 1914 than it does for the postwar period. For stockbuilding, no usable data are available to years prior to 1914, and the interwar averages are much affected by the single year 1921, when disinvestment in stocks was certainly very large, but there is a wide margin of error in the actual figures. But it is unlikely that more reliable data would alter the conclusion that stockbuilding has been a more important source of fluctuations since the war than it used to be.

TABLE 4–2   United Kingdom: Amplitude of Fluctuations in Components of Gross Domestic Product (GDP) at Constant Market Prices

| | Exports* | GDFCF† | PACE§ | Consumption | | | Stock-building | Imports* | GDP |
|---|---|---|---|---|---|---|---|---|---|
| | | | | Total | Durables | Nondurables | | | |
| | | | | *Amplitude* | | | | | |
| 1951–1964 | 1.8 | 3.4 | -0.9 | 1.6 | 4.2 | 1.0 | 7.0 | 4.2 | 1.8 |
| 1920–1937 | 14.3 | 4.1 | 3.6 | 2.8 | 6.5 | 2.0 | (49.4) | 7.1 | 5.8 |
| 1872–1914 | 5.5 | 4.1 | 1.8 | 1.2 | – | – | – | 3.4 | 2.5 |
| | | | | *Amplitude relative to GDP* | | | | | |
| 1951–1964 | 0.4 | 0.5 | -0.2 | 1.0 | 0.5 | 0.5 | 1.0 | 0.9 | 1.8 |
| 1920–1937 | 2.8 | 0.5 | 0.4 | 2.2 | 0.9 | 1.3 | (1.3) | 1.3 | 5.8 |
| 1872–1914 | 1.3 | 0.3 | 0.1 | 1.0 | – | – | – | 0.8 | 2.5 |
| | | | | *Percentage contribution to amplitude of GDP* | | | | | |
| 1951–1964 | 20 | 27 | -9 | 57 | 28 | 29 | 57 | -52 | 100 |
| 1920–1937 | 48 | 9 | 7 | 38 | 16 | 22 | (22) | -22 | 100 |
| 1872–1914 | 52 | 12 | 4 | 40 | – | – | – | -32 | 100 |

**Sources:** See Table 4-1.
* Exports and Imports include both goods and services.
† GDFCF = Gross Domestic Fixed Capital Formation.
§ PACE = Public Authorities' Current Expenditure on Goods and Services.
‡ Consumer durables include the goods placed in this category in the National Income *Blue Books* (motor cars and cycles, furniture and floor coverings, and radio and electrical goods) together with clothing, footwear, and household textiles.

   In 1872–1914 the constituents in the second and third panels do not add to the total, because GDP has been calculated to include a stockbuilding figure estimated at 40 per cent of annual change in national income.

In the late 1950's, it was still possible to believe that the recession or "pause" phases in the movement of the economy were of the nature of more or less irregular interruptions in the growth process. In the early 1960's, as the events of the 1955–1958 downswing repeated themselves, it became more customary to talk about "the" cycle. The Labour Party uttered brave works in repudiation of the stop-go policy during its election campaign in 1964; but when it proceeded during the next two years to adopt a contractionary policy, indistinguishable in essentials from that of its predecessors, it finally became clear that the forces involved, whatever they are, work themselves out in a very specifically cyclical manner.

Government policy has occupied the front of the stage in the postwar cycle. Each upswing has terminated in balance of payments difficulties, the government has applied restrictive measures; after a while, when the balance of payments has improved, the government has encouraged a resumption of expansion. Hence the view that there has been a government-driven cycle rather than an old-style business cycle. Granting that government action has been important, however, there remains room for considerable variety of opinion about why the results have worked out cyclically. One such divergence of opinion may be illustrated from quotations from two authors who agree about the primacy of the government's role

It is because the recessions followed from acts of policy that I think the term business cycle does not fit. They came about more or less as planned; their results were broadly accepted as desirable . . . and they ended, likewise through acts of policy, when the authorities considered that the economy could safely resume expansion[11].

The major fluctuations in the rate of growth of demand in the years after 1952 were thus chiefly due to government policy. This was not the intended effect; in each phase, it must be supposed, policy went further than intended, as in turn did the correction of these effects[12].

The second of these views would command the more general assent. But numbers of substantially different models of the government role can be, and have been, envisaged. For example, (1) the endogenous elements in the economy are such as to produce a high degree of *stability*, and the economy is dragged around in a cycle by fluctuations in government policy; (2) the government attempts to stabilize the system but its efforts are largely

[11] Milton Gilbert, "The Postwar Business Cycle in Western Europe," *American Economic Review*, May 1962, p. 100. Gilbert was speaking of Western European countries, generally, including the United Kingdom.
[12] Dow, *op. cit.*, p. 384.

unsuccessful and introduce cyclical elements of their own; (3) the system is inherently *unstable in both directions* and bounces between limits set by the government in the form of a balance of payments ceiling and a general election floor; (4) the system is inherently unstable upward, and the government periodically holds it on the leash ("stop-go").

None of these models is tenable in an extreme form. It would be generally agreed that the actions of the government have impinged on a system which contains at least some endogenous elements of instability. The questions that have to be considered are what these elements have been, how they have been related to government action, and why the government has been induced to act in a destabilizing fashion—if it has. In order to do this, the behavior of the different components of total expenditure (Chart 4—1), will now be examined.

### PRIVATE SECTOR FIXED CAPITAL FORMATION

*Manufacturing.* Fluctuations in manufacturing investment have been substantial and regular, much more so than fluctuations in other classes of fixed capital formation (Chart 4-2)[13]. In recession phases, manufacturing investment suffered an actual fall, not merely a retardation of growth. The falls have been increasingly severe; measured from peak year to trough year, they were 7½ per cent in 1951—1953, 10 per cent in 1957—1958, and 18 per cent in 1961—1963. In relation to GNP these movements are not so enormous, since manufacturing accounts for only about one-fifth of total fixed capital formation; nevertheless they are still substantial.

However, the timing of the fluctuations in manufacturing investment prevents them from being assigned their classic role as prime mover in the business cycle. Since 1952, they have regularly lagged behind the general cycle (including the movement of manufacturing production) by two years in the cycle of the mid-1950's and by one year at all other turning points. They have thus not initiated either the upswing or the downswing, but have strengthened them once they have been initiated by other causes.

The concentration on anticipatory data for short-term forecasting purposes has rather distracted attention from the study of the underlying causes of fluctuations in manufacturing investment in the postwar British economy, and not much systematic work on these causes has been published. But the general and probably correct belief among *Konjunktur* commentators has been that the fluctuations in manufacturing investment have been mainly the lagged result of fluctuations in general demand and the degree of capital utilization and have not been directly caused by government action[14]. A simple capital-stock adjustment equation gives reasonably close predictions of the fluctuations[15].

The policy instruments used in periods when the authorities wanted to cut demand have largely been chosen so as *not* to impinge on manufacturing investment, because the authorities have not wished to discourage expenditure that might raise productivity[16]. But manufacturing investment has been

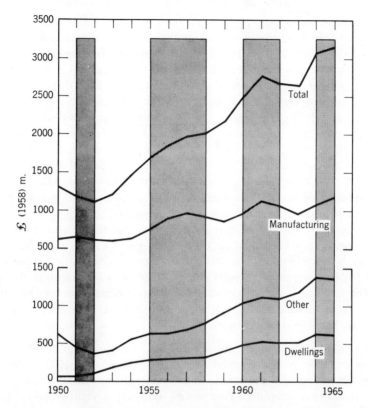

**Chart 4-2**    United Kingdom: private fixed capital formation, 1950–1965.

[13] The series shown in the chart includes a small amount of manufacturing capital formation in the public sector. (Public sector capital formation in the steel industry is excluded, however).

[14] This is the view that has regularly been put forward in the *National Institute Economic Review.* Dow, *op. cit.,* pp. 204–209, gives more weight to the financial consequences of government action.

[15] The amplitude of the different cycles has also been influenced by events in individual industries which an aggregative model cannot take into account. In particular, the apparent feebleness of the 1963–1965 upswing in manufacturing investment, compared with the previous one, was due entirely to the iron and steel industry. Shortages of steel in the mid- and late-1950's led the industry (with government prompting) to undertake a tremendous once-for-all expansion program in 1960–1962. Investment in iron and steel reached a peak in 1961 and continued to decline throughout the expansion of 1963–1965.

[16] An exception was in 1952, when part of the object of policy was to reduce private investment so as to make room for rearmament.

109

exposed to general changes in interest rates and tax rates; in addition, the tax allowances on investments (initial and investment allowances) have been manipulated partly for demand-regulating purposes. Since the changes in tax allowances have usually taken place at about the same time as the level of demand in general has changed, their effects are difficult to distinguish. Survey evidence suggests, though not at all conclusively, that the short-term effects have not been great[17]. The general trend has been for the allowances to become more generous over time: more concessions have been given than have been withdrawn. So it is possible that, if these allowances have had a cyclical role, that role has been asymmetrical: the concessions made in 1953–1954, 1958, and 1963 may have helped to trigger off expansions which presently reversed themselves, not because the concessions were withdrawn but because demand fell or capital expansion programs had been completed.

The cumulative effect of changes in allowances and tax rates has been to reduce greatly the burden of taxation on profits. Whatever the effect of tax changes on *fluctuations* in investment, there seems little doubt that the cumulative effect has been important in sustaining manufacturing investment in the longer run. The trend rate of growth of manufacturing investment has been higher than that of manufacturing production, notwithstanding that the trend of the *pre-tax* profit rate has been steadily downward.

*Other private nonresidential capital formation.* Investment in distribution and services was severely held back by controls on building until 1953; since then it has grown very rapidly and is now somewhat larger than manufacturing investment. It has been subject to fluctuations, but they have been milder than in manufacturing. This may be attributed partly to the large pent-up demand and partly to the smaller amplitude of fluctuations in sales of the final product. Fluctuations in nonmanufacturing investment have shown less tendency than fluctuations in manufacturing investment to lag behind the general cycle. The reasons for this are not entirely clear; a shorter average gestation period is one conjecture; greater sensitivity to monetary policy is another[18]. In 1965 direct controls again became important, and were responsible for a sharp retardation in that year.

*Private capital formation in dwellings.* Private housebuilding, like other nonmanufacturing capital formation, was severely controlled until the early 1950's. Since then it has risen in the usual three cycles. The exact timing, in

---

[17] R. R. Neild, "Replacement Policy," *N.I.E.R.*, November 1964; D. C. Corner and A. Williams, "The Sensitivity of Businesses to Initial and Investment Allowances," *Economica*, February 1965, and earlier literature there cited.

[18] The timing is influenced in part by idiosyncratic movements in shipbuilding, a relatively small but severely fluctuating element in the total.

relation to the general cycle, has been irregular. The customary view is that the cycles have been due to fluctuations in the availability of finance through Building Societies. This attributes them indirectly to official monetary policy, since the relatively inflexible interest rate policy of the Societies makes them lose funds in periods of high interest rates. While this has certainly been a very important factor, the booms in private housebuilding have corresponded very imperfectly, both in timing and magnitude, to the financial indicators. Moreover, in some years of low private housebuilding, like 1958, Building Societies have increased their liquidity, which suggests a shortage of demand for funds rather than a shortage of supply. The exact causes of the fluctuations are in need of further research[19].

The inflexibility of interest rates in the mortgage market and the consequent dependence of mortgage availability on the general level of interest rates are quite like the situation in the United States and elsewhere. But the net effect has been different. In the United States (as pointed out by Professor Gordon in his chapter) the effect has been to make housebuilding a stabilizing factor in the cycle, varying inversely with other classes of expenditure. In Britain, on the other hand, private housebuilding has approximately conformed in timing to the general cycle and so has contributed to its amplitude. The main reason for this—on the assumption that it is correct to regard the availability of finance as the chief cause of fluctuations in private housebuilding—lies in the timing of interest rate movements in Britain. Government policy in the face of balance of payments difficulties (further discussed in Section IV of this chapter) has caused interest rates to lag very substantially behind the cycle, so that they have generally been lower in the upswing than in the downswing.

*Public authorities' expenditure on goods and services.* There has not been any regular relation between public spending and the general cycle (Chart 4-3). There have, however, been some substantial fluctuations in public spending. In a narrow majority of years, its movement contributed to the overall trend of demand, sometimes to an important extent. The main causes of fluctuations in public spending have lain in considerations unconnected with management of demand.

Public expenditure on goods and services may be divided into three parts: public authorities' current expenditure on goods and services (PACE); local authority housebuilding; and other public sector capital formation.

[19] Two curious features of the housing market may be noted. First, private housebuilding has not been visibly affected, either in trend or fluctuations, by the very large movements of public housebuilding discussed later. Second, house *prices* have moved in a way quite unlike other prices: they rose rapidly until 1951, actually fell from 1951 to 1954, and thereafter rose at an accelerating rate, with only small fluctuations. (See M. F. W. Hemming and H. Duffy, "The Price of Accommodation," *N.I.E.R.*, August 1964, and more recent data in the *Occasional Bulletins* of the Cooperative Permanent Building Society.)

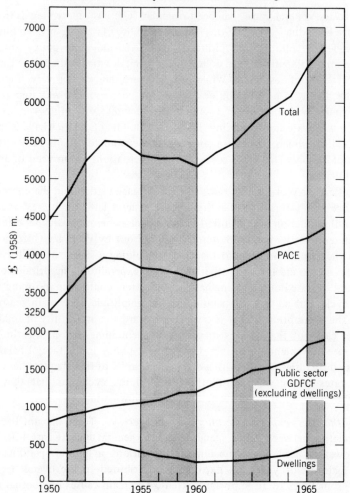

**Chart 4-3**   United Kingdom: public sector government expenditure, 1950-1965.

*PACE*. Movements in the total of this group have been dominated by defense expenditure, which experienced an enormous rise from 1950 to 1953 and an almost equally enormous fall from 1953 to 1958. This class of expenditure thus contributed to the early stages of the 1952–1955 economic upswing, but acted as a restraining factor in later stages and contributed to the weakening of demand in 1955–1958. The end of the decline in defense enabled total PACE to rise substantially in 1959 and so helped to promote overall recovery in that year. Since then, there has been a mild but regular inverse relationship between PACE and the cycle. Oddly enough, this too has been due mainly to defense expenditure. Year-to-year fluctuations in nondefense items in PACE have been very small.

*Local authority housebuilding.* The pattern here is curiously similar to defense expenditure: a rise from 1950 to 1953, a steep fall from 1953 to 1958, and then a resumed rise. The rise was slight until 1961, and accelerated again very markedly in 1964. The resemblance to defense is not entirely a nonsense correlation: both were influenced by the increasingly urgent efforts of the Conservatives in the mid-1950's to cut public expenditure on the grounds of general political principle. The movements in local authority housebuilding have broadly corresponded to the government's intentions. The upswing to 1953 was the Macmillan housing drive; the ensuing decline was the result of the new policy initiated by the White Paper [*Houses – The Next Step* (Cmd. 8996)] published in November 1953, and by subsequent contractionary measures. The recovery brought about in 1959 reflected partly the retreat from the extremes of the Thorneycroft policy, but it was also influenced to some extent by the recognized need for reflation. The further rise in 1964 followed from a new five-year plan introduced in a White Paper of May 1963[20]. The expansion proposed in this plan may have been influenced in part by the need for reflation (and by electoral considerations), but it also reflected the general euphoria about the capabilities of the economy which were beginning to prevail at that time.

*Other public sector capital formation.* The nonresidential capital expenditure of central and local government and of the nationalized industries has influenced the behavior of demand in certain years, but its fluctuations were neither regular nor large until 1964. Frequent attempts have been made by the government to adjust this expenditure in accordance with the short-run state of the economy. The effects were seen in a number of years, particularly in the retardation in 1958 and the recovery in 1959, both of which took place more or less as planned; and the policies leading to the increase in expenditure in 1963 and 1964 were also partly influenced by the existence of a slack in the economy[21]. But to achieve big changes—either upward or downward—at short notice has been found difficult, and the result has often diverged from the intention. The imposition of stop-go policies (the term really *is* applicable in this context) lead to the creation of arrears, either because projects are held in cold storage when restrictions are imposed or because it is physically impossible to carry out all the work that has been sanctioned when expansion is being encouraged. These arrears impede exact planning. Possibly for this reason, the net result between 1956 and 1963 was a peculiar two-year cycle, high in odd years, low in even ones.

---

[20] *Housing*, Cmnd. 2050, May 1963.

[21] *Public Investment in Great Britain, October 1963*, Cmnd. 2177, November 1963, pp. 6–7.

This two-year pattern was broken by the great acceleration in public capital expenditure in 1964, which made a major contribution to the overall increase in demand in that year. It was the result of a new long-run program of capital spending for the public sector, initiated by the Conservatives in 1963[22]. The difficulties of using public investment for stabilization purposes were by now well recognized, and emphasis was placed on the need for long-term planning[23]. The enlarged program was instituted because opinion had moved in favor of a more generous provision of public capital, not for stabilization reasons–although, in planning it, regard was paid to the prospective real resources available. A program of continued rapid expansion was embodied as part of the National Plan after the Labour Party had come into power[24]. The rate of increase of expenditure slackened considerably in 1965, but still remained very high. The slackening was probably due only to a minor extent to the "rephasing" enforced as part of the deflationary measures of that year; a continuation of 1964's exceptional rate of increase had never been intended and would in any case have been impossible for public authorities to carry out.

### EXPORTS

Exports have exhibited a mild but fairly regular cycle, corresponding for the most part to the general cycle. The occasions when exports made their most important contribution to changes in activity were in 1958–1959 and in 1953 (when exports recovered from the ill effects of the reduction of primary producers' purchasing power in the post-Korean War price decline of 1952). The retardation of exports in the recession of 1961–1962 was much milder than in 1958.

The general course of the fluctuations in exports is explained adequately by fluctuations in world demand. It is true that the fall in the British share of world exports has tended to be more than usually sharp in years when world trade has increased most rapidly, and also in years when domestic demand has been high.

---

[22] *Public Expenditure in 1963–1964 and 1967–1968,* Cmnd. 2235, December 1963.

[23] Cf. Dow, *op. cit.,* p. 221, quoting statements by Amory and Selwyn Lloyd in 1960. The most recent statement of policy retains the emphasis on long-term planning, but adds somewhat uneasily: "The question of phasing will recur, for public expenditure is too large an element in the national economy to be treated entirely on a long-term basis independently of the short-run economic situation." *Public Expenditure: Planning and Control,* Cmnd. 2915, February 1966, p. 14.

[24] *The National Plan,* Cmnd. 2754, September 1965, Chapter 5, paragraphs 7–8, and Chapter 18.

[25] R. J. Ball, J. R. Eaton, and M. D. Steuer, "The Relationship between United Kingdom Export Performance in Manufactures and the Internal Pressure of Demand." *Economic Journal.* September 1966. Some of the data are conveniently tabulated in N.I.E.R., February 1967, p. 16.

(The two conditions tend to coincide, so the two effects are difficult to separate[25].) But this, though significant from the point of view of balance of payments policy, is of second-order importance in the present context of explaining fluctuations in total demand.

The reduced role of exports in the cycle, as compared with former times, was commented on earlier in this paper. The main reason is, no doubt, the greater stability of the world economy. Another contributory factor is probably the reduction in the importance of fluctuations in primary producers' purchasing power in determining the course of British exports. The proportion of British exports sold to primary producers is smaller than formerly, and prices of primary products have themselves been less unstable[26].

Despite the reduction in importance, there is one reason why fluctuations in exports may have more impact on demand than fluctuations of equal amount in other classes of expenditure. Because of concern with the balance of payments, the government is unlikely to try to compensate for a contraction in exports by reflation elsewhere in the economy. There is one clear case in point in the period under review: a cautious attitude toward reflation on these grounds was displayed in 1958[27]. Since then, because cycles in the rest of the world have not been well synchronized, there has not been any occasion when the recession in exports has been so large or so clearly foreseeable. But if such an occasion were to occur in the future, the same reaction would be likely. Conversely, in periods when exports are doing very well, the government will tend to feel a less urgent need to restrict demand in the interests of the balance of payments[28].

STOCKBUILDING

Fluctuations in stockbuilding (inventory investment) have been of major importance in the cycle. The short cycle in which inventory investment plays a large part used to be considered, on the basis of prewar experience, a U.S. monopoly. This is no longer true (if it ever was). The increased *relative* importance of stockbuilding in the cycle, compared with former times, has to be viewed in connection with the shorter duration of the cycle: stockbuilding is less prone than fixed investment to prolonged cumulative movements.

---

[26] The large fluctuations in prices of primary product in former times not merely made British exports fluctuate but also tended to *diminish* the amplitude of fluctuations in British real income and consumption, by their effects on the terms of trade. They thus served on both sides to make fluctuations in exports account for a high proportion of fluctuations in Gross National Product (GNP).

[27] Dow, *op. cit.,* pp. 103–104.

[28] This is roughly comparable to the monetary effect of changes in exports that has to be added to the direct income effect in Keynesian analysis of the working of the orthodox gold standard.

Which of the various possible inventory-cycle models best fits the postwar British experience has not been established[29]. It is doubtful whether the pattern of behavior has been sufficiently regular or consistent for a clear-cut answer to be possible. Fluctuations in stockbuilding have conformed closely in timing to those of GDP since 1951. The possibly more relevant comparison with total final sales (total final expenditure minus stockbuilding) is less clear-cut. Until 1952 and (less clearly) from 1953 though 1955, stockbuilding had an inverse relationship to *changes* in total final sales—suggesting that stockbuilding took the strain of short-period movements in sales. Since 1956, on the other hand, stockbuilding has regularly moved in the same direction as changes in total final sales[30].

Certain regularities can be seen however, especially at peak years, the phase of the cycle when stockbuilding has been most important. When output rose rapidly in the recovery phase of the cycle (1953, 1959, 1963), stockbuilding did not at first respond very much, and the immediate effect was a fall in the stock-output ratio. Then, after a delay, stockbuilding rose very rapidly (1955, 1960, 1964). Had it not been for the effect of stockbuilding, the rate of growth of total final expenditure would have suffered a retardation in 1955, and the acceleration in total final expenditure in 1960 and 1964 would have been considerably less than it was. Moreover, in the immediately succeeding years, producers no longer found it necessary to maintain stockbuilding at such an abnormally high level, and substantial decline occurred. The delayed increase in stockbuilding and its reversal thus made a major contribution to the timing and magnitude of the cyclical peaks and downturns.

At the lower turning points of the cycle, fluctuations in stockbuilding, though considerable, have not been so violent as at the upper turning point, and there has not been the same pattern of delayed reaction in adjusting stocks to output[31]. This probably reflects the asymmetrical pattern of the cycle as a whole, noted by Wesley Mitchell[32] as characteristic of business cycles generally and equally valid for postwar British cycles; after the lower turning point, the economy's change of direction is sharp, the rate of growth being fastest

---

[29] The literature on British data is very scanty compared with that on U.S. data. See Dow, *op. cit.,* pp. 377–379; C. H. Feinstein, "Stockbuilding, Expenditure and the Balance of Payments," *London and Cambridge Economic Bulletin* December 1962, and "Stocks, Sales and Stockbuilding," *ibid.,* March 1963; R. J. Ball and P. S. Drake, "Stock Adjustment Inventory Models of the United Kingdom Economy," *Manchester School,* May 1963; "The Relationship of Stocks to Production," *Economic Trends,* No. 133, November 1964.

[30] The separation of data on stockbuilding into materials and fuel, work in progress, and finished goods is, unfortunately, not available before 1956; the inverse relationship between stockbuilding and changes in final sales might suggest that before 1956 fluctuations in stockbuilding in finished goods contributed significantly to the total. Since 1956, however, the other two categories have shown the largest and most regular movements and have mainly accounted for the movements of the total.

in the early stages of the upswing; after the upper turning point, on the other hand, the falling off (relative to trend) is at first mild and only gradually becomes more severe. In the downswing, therefore, producers have less difficulty in keeping stocks in line with output.

It would be going too far to describe the postwar British cycle as an inventory cycle. There have been other causes of instability as well, and without them stockbuilding alone would scarcely have been sufficient to sustain the cycle. But it is at least clear that cyclical reaction patterns in stockbuilding have served to distort and almost certainly amplify the fluctuations that would have come about from other sources[33].

CONSUMPTION

The usual way to analyze the movements of consumption has been in terms of disposable personal income and the personal sector saving ratio, with disposable personal income in turn depending on GDP, taxation, undistributed profits, etc. The personal saving ration is then found to fluctuate more or less inversely with the cycle, but not regularly, and this movement is explained largely with reference to the availability of consumer credit.

For the present purpose, it is useful to compare consumption not with disposable personal income but with the total of nonconsumption (GDP minus consumption), in order to avoid Friedmanite objection that explaining consumption in terms of national income or a variant of it means explaining it largely in terms of itself. Durables and nondurables will be discussed separately here, because of differences in their behavior. Chart 4–4 shows first differences in the relevant series.

Consumption of durables has fluctuated more than consumption of nondurables, absolutely and proportionately. It has a conspicuous tendency to lead other classes of expenditure, including consumption of nondurables, at turning points. It also leads disposable personal income. The important and still largely unresolved question is how far these fluctuations in purchases of durables have been due to government regulation of the availability of consumer credit and how far they have been due to an endogenous cycle of a stock-adjustment kind. It is common ground that they have also been influenced by income. Government action to restrict or ease hire-purchase conditions has been a regular

---

[31] Stocks of finished goods did continue to rise fairly fast in the trough years 1958 and 1962, but stocks of materials kept in line with output more closely than they did in the years of rapid expansion.

[32] W. C. Mitchell, *What Happens During Business Cycles,* New York, 1951, pp. 299–305.

[33] Stockbuilding has also been important in connection with imports and hence the balance of payments, discussed later.

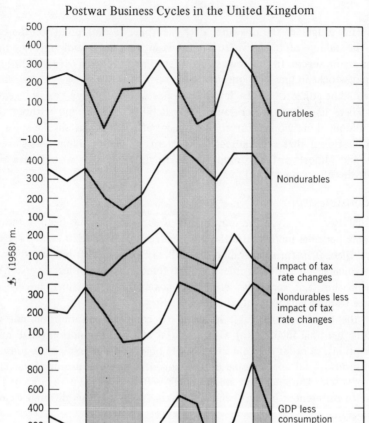

**Chart 4-4**  United Kingdom: consumption (first differences), 1953–1965.

feature of the cycle, and the timing of this action roughly but not exactly fits the observed fluctuations. However, not only is the timing imperfect; the relative magnitude of the changes in hire-purchase regulations does not correspond in a clear way to the observed change in expenditure on durables. The results of studies of the effects of hire-purchase control on expenditure on durables[34] are inconclusive, and they mostly do not take any account of the existing stock of durable goods, which would be a key variable in any stock-adjustment model[35].

Since hire-purchase conditions have not been satisfactorily integrated into a stock-adjustment model of the demand for consumer durables, probably the safest provisional hypothesis is that both elements have been present; hire-purchase regulations have played some part, and there has also been some endogenous tendency for sales to be low after a period when they have been very high, and vice versa. But there is much room for further research, and the issue is of some importance in assessing the effect of government action in bringing about turning points[36].

The movements in consumption of nondurables lend themselves more readily to straightforward Keynesian explanation (with allowance for the effects of fiscal policy), though there are still some loose ends.

The estimated direct effect on consumption of changes in tax, subsidy, and national insurance rates is shown in chart 4-4[37]. This measure of government policy has a clear-cut cyclical movement, leading the general cycle except in 1962; this means that changes in tax rates had a countercyclical influence in peak and trough years, but during parts of the upswing and downswing they

---

[34] Among them are L. Needleman, "The Demand for Domestic Appliances," *N.I.E.R.,* No. 12, November 1960; J. R. Cuthbertson, "Hire Purchase Controls and Fluctuations in the Car Market," *Economica* May 1961; L. R. Klein, R. J. Ball, A. D. Hazlewood, and P. Vandome, *An Econometric Model of the United Kingdom*, Oxford, 1961; F. R. Oliver, *The Control of Hire Purchase,* London, 1961; A. Silberston, "Hire Purchase Controls and the Demand for Cars," *Economic Journal,* March 1963; R. J. Ball and Pamela S. Drake, "The Impact of Credit Control on Consumer Durable Spending in the United Kingdom, 1957–1961," *Review of Economic Studies,* October 1963.

[35] An article by J. R. N. Stone and D. A. Rowe, "The Market Demand for Durable Goods," *Econometrica,* July 1957, presents a model of this type and fits—with some success—to interwar annual data and quarterly data for the years 1950–1955.

[36] In connection with the present paper, experiments were made with a number of econometric models of automobile demand in the United Kingdom, along the same general lines as those followed by Stone and Rowe. The coefficients of the hire-purchase variables in the regressions persistently turned out small and non-significant. However, this finding, though suggestive, is not conclusive, because none of the models provided a fully satisfactory explanation of fluctuations, and it is possible that some alternative specification would produce a different result.

[37] These estimates are based on the method used by Dow, *op. cit.,* pp. 196–204. (Dow gives his figures in chart form only, and they have therefore been reconstructed here on the basis of the procedure he describes, and also have been brought up to date.) It must be emphasized that they have a large margin of error, because rather arbitrary assumptions are made about the timing of the impact of the measures. Dow gives two alternative series, based on different assumptions about the length of lags, and the figures in Chart 4–4 are a simple average of the two. These estimates, moreover, relate to the estimated effects on total consumption, not merely on nondurables. (A more sophisticated procedure is suggested for forecasting purposes in W. A. B. Hopkin and W. A. H. Godley, "An Analysis of Tax Charges," *N.I.E.R.,* May 1965.

strengthened tendencies present elsewhere. If these estimated effects of tax changes are deducted from the total change in consumption of nondurables, a rough estimate is derived of changes that are not due directly to government action. The fluctuations in this residual are larger (until 1964–1965) than those in the effects of tax changes, and are mainly responsible for fluctuations in the total. In the last two cycles, as may be seen from Chart 4-4, they show a rough conformity with movements in nonconsumption, in the Keynesian manner. But the rise in consumption of nondurables was larger in the trough years 1958 and 1962, and smaller in the recovery years 1959 and 1963, than the Keynesian multiplier would have predicted: it appears that there is a resistance to cuts below a certain level in the rate of growth of consumer expenditure on nondurables[38]. The pattern before 1958 is more irregular, especially in the years 1955–1956. The chief explanation is probably that there was a sharp rise in 1955 and fall in 1956 in the ratio of personal income to GDP, because of the relative movements of wages and prices, which resulted in a more rapid growth of income from employment than in GDP in 1955, and the converse in 1956.

The tendency to lead the general cycle, exhibited by consumption of durables and by that part of consumption of nondurables attributable to tax changes, has given consumption a strategic role in the cycle even though its fluctuations have been smaller than those in nonconsumption. This point will be taken up again presently.

### IMPORTS

Imports have shown large fluctuations, larger proportionately than those of GDP. In particular, imports have risen very steeply in peak years. Their behavior has thus served, proximately, to mitigate the amplitude of fluctuations in the demand for domestically produced goods and services resulting from given fluctuations in total final expenditure. But it by no means follows that the behavior of imports has been a stabilizing factor in a more fundamental sense. For the rapid increase in imports in peak years made the balance of payments adverse, and so led to changes in government policy.

Three types of explanation of the cyclical behavior of imports have been offered:

1. In peak years, demand outstrips domestic productive potential and the excess demand "spills over" into imports. Imports are thus a nonlinear function of the *level* of aggregate demand.

2. The high *rate of increase* in demand in the upswing causes industry to have difficulty in meeting it, because, even if there is some surplus capacity overall,

[38] Since first differences are being considered here, the anomalously high level of nondurable consumption in 1958 and 1962 is sufficient to explain its anomalously low rate of growth in 1959 and 1963.

increases in production take time to organize. So again demand spills over into imports[39].

3. The observed fluctuations in imports are to a large extent fluctuations in stockbuilding rather than in final use. As just mentioned, stockbuilding has increased sharply in peak years. On the assumption that the import content of total stockbuilding is high, this could account for most of the fluctuations in the ratio of imports to GDP[40].

It has not yet been established where the truth lies between these hypotheses, which could have substantially different policy implications. The statistical evidence for the stockbuilding hypothesis is impressive (the close similarity between the movements of stockbuilding and of imports is apparent from Chart 4-1). But there is some difficulty in explaining why stockbuilding should have such high import content as the hypothesis requires. [41].

In the postwar period, the amplitude of fluctuations in imports relative to the amplitude of fluctuations in GDP has been much larger than formerly (compared with pre-1914, even the absolute amplitude has been greater). It is not clear whether this has been because stockbuilding has fluctuated more or because the economy has been operating closer to full employment, with a greater tendency toward excess demand at cyclical peaks. Whatever the reason, it has—through its effects on the balance of payments—introduced a new strategic element into the cycle[42].

---

[39] F. Brechling and J. N. Wolfe, "The End of Stop-Go," *Lloyds Bank Review,* January 1965. The evidence put forward by Brechling and Wolfe is criticized by P. M. Oppenheimer, "Is Britain's Worsening Trade Gap Due to Bad Management of the Business Cycle?", *Bulletin of the Oxford University Institute of Economics and Statistics,* August 1965.

[40] Insofar as the level and rate of increase of demand are among the factors influencing stockbuilding, this hypothesis is not unrelated to the other two.

[41] The Treasury's forecasting procedure uses the assumption that the import-content of stockbuilding is as high as one-half. ("Short-term Economic Forecasting in the United Kingdom," *Economic Trends,* No. 130, August 1964, p. 9.) This estimate is derived from the coefficient found by regressing imports on stockbuilding and other variables, not from direct evidence. The proportion of imports in total *stocks* is substantially lower than this; it is perhaps about one-third. There is nothing surprising in the marginal (stockbuilding) import-content being higher over a period of years than the average (stock) import-content, since imports have been rising faster than output of home-produced goods. It would be slightly more surprising, however, if this difference held consistently within the cycle. A difficulty with the stockbuilding view in regard to the peak years is that the rapid increase in imports at that stage of the cycle has largely taken the form of an increase in imports of finished manufactures, and stockbuilding might be expected to have less influence on these than on imports of materials.

### III

Before trying to weave together the various threads, brief reference may be made to two other elements that have contributed to the special character of postwar cycles: employment behavior and price behavior.

#### EMPLOYMENT AND UNEMPLOYMENT

The relationship between fluctuations in output and fluctuations in employment has been very different in postwar cycles from what it was earlier. First, the decline in the amplitude of employment fluctuations, compared with those prior to World War II, has been much greater than the decline in the amplitude of output fluctuations. Second, the cycle in employment since the war has persistently lagged in time behind that of output; this did not happen previously. Third, employment fluctuations have been due, to a greater extent than formerly, to fluctuations in participation rates rather than in unemployment[43].

Table 4-3 shows the average amplitude of fluctuations in employment, calculated in the same way as the amplitude measures given earlier, and of those in GDP[44]. Even after allowance for lags, proportional fluctuations in employment since the War have been not much more than one-third of those in GDP. In the interwar period employment fluctuated about as much as GDP, and in the pre-1913 period, if the figures are to be trusted, it actually fluctuated more. When the postwar period is compared with that prior to 1913, it appears that the decline in the amplitude of employment fluctuations owes much more

---

[42] Balance of payments difficulties caused by increases in imports at cyclical peaks were not a characteristic of the British cycle in the three-quarters of a century before 1939. The Bank of England did often have trouble from loss of gold reserves at the peak of the cycle, but for other reasons (before 1914, chiefly, internal drain of gold under the working of the Bank Charter Act of 1844). The postwar pattern is a throwback to a still earlier period: in the first half of the nineteenth century, cyclical peaks *were* often accompanied by an accelerated increase in imports, probably connected with stockbuilding, and these led to loss of reserves and restrictive action by the Bank of England. (A. D. Gayer, W. W. Rostow, and A. J. Schwartz, *The Growth and Fluctuations of the British Economy, 1790–1850,* Oxford, 1953, pp. 784–795, and R. C. O. Matthews, "The Trade Cycle in Britain, 1790–1850," *Oxford Economic Papers,* February 1954.

[43] This change has been less marked than the other two, but has made a contribution to the diminution of the size of fluctuations in unemployment. In the interwar period, 92 per cent of the difference between the average annual increase of employment in upswings and that in downswings was accounted for by changes in unemployment; in the postwar period, 60 per cent.

[44] Reference cycle measures understate the amplitude of employment fluctuations in postwar years, because of the lag of employment cycles. Two measures are therefore given. Before World War II, there was no occasion when the turning point in employment was clearly different from the reference cycle date.

to the reduction in the output-elasticity of employment than it does to the greater stability of output. This would not be true of a comparison with interwar years; but, even so, if the output-elasticity of employment had been as high as it was in the interwar period, unemployment in postwar cyclical recessions would have risen far above the level now regarded as politically acceptable.

TABLE 4–3   United Kingdom: Average Amplitude of Fluctuations in Unemployment and Gross Domestic Product (GDP)

|           | GDP | Employment |
|-----------|-----|------------|
| 1951–1964 | 1.8 | 0.3*       |
|           |     | 0.7†       |
| 1920–1937 | 5.8 | 5.1        |
| 1872–1913 | 2.5 | 3.2        |

* Reference cycles   † Employment cycles

Sources: GDP, as in Table 4–1. Employment, unpublished series prepared for forthcoming Social Science Research Council study of "Postwar Growth in the British Economy," by R. C. O. Matthews, C. H. Feinstein, and J. Odling-Smee.

The low postwar output-elasticity of employment has to be viewed in conjunction with the lag of employment after output. In aggregate annual data, this appears as a year at most postwar turning points. In quarterly data, the lag is less than this, but there are signs that it has been increasing.

The short-run relationship between employment, unemployment, and output in Britain has been much studied[45], as has the same phenomenon in the United States. The limited and lagged adjustment of employment can be analzyed as the consequence of a gradual adjustment of employment to a desired level in relation to output. A question then arises: How much of the observed results can be attributed to the lag in adjustment, on the one hand, or to a less than unit elasticity of desired employment to output, on the other? In reality, the distinction is not so clear-cut, because some of the same factors will tend to influence the length of the lag and this desired elasticity. It is likely, *a priori*, that the low *ex post* output-elasticity of employment is connected with the generally high pressure of demand for labor: other evidence besides the straightforward comparison of prewar and postwar experience can be cited in

---

[45] R. R. Neild, *Pricing and Employment in the Trade Cycle*, Cambridge, 1963, Chapter 3; W. A. H. Godley and J. R. Shepherd, "Long-term Growth and Short-term Policy," *N.I.E.R.*, August 1964; F. P. R. Brechling, "The Relationship Between Output and Employment in British Manufacturing Industries," *Review of Economic Studies*, July 1965; R. J. Ball and E. B. A. St. Cyr, "Short-Term Employment Functions in British Manufacturing Industry," *Ibid.*, July 1966.

support[46]. A general shortage of labor increases the effective costs of hiring and firing, and encourages firms to hold on to the temporarily redundant labor in recessions. In addition to this "labor hoarding," firms in certain sectors of the economy have been chronically short of labor; in boom periods the shortage has been particularly acute, but in recessions their labor force has still not been above the desired level, so they have had no inducement to cut it down and they have even increased it as demand for labor slackened elsewhere. The services have been cases in point.

The lag of employment and unemployment behind output has created certain problems for policy. Fluctuations in the demand for goods and service relative to productive potential are what the government wants ultimately to control. But there is no direct way of judging whether demand is growing faster than productive potential. Moreover, the most recent unemployment statistics available are less subject to revision and less erratic in their fluctuations than are the statistics of output. Hence, it is tempting to be guided by labor market indicators, even though they are recognized as subject to lags[47]. In any case, the state of the labor market rather than of the goods market is what is relevant to the rate of increase of wage rates, which is also a direct concern to the authorities. This creates a danger that the authorities may persist in deflationary or reflationary measures after the trend in the economy has already begun to turn.

PRICES

Most investigators of the United Kingdom data have found that the increase in wage rates can be expressed as a lagged function of the demand for labor and of price increases, and that the increase in prices can be expressed as a lagged function of the increase in input costs (*not* input costs per unit of output—that is, rises in average costs which are due to decreases in the degree of utilization of capital and labor in recessions are not passed on in prices)[48]. The *level* of the demand for labor has a clearer effect on wage increases than does the *increase* in the demand for labor, so the cycle in wages tends to lag behind that in employment. Moreover, employment itself tends to lag behind output; and prices lag behind costs. The cumulative effect of these lags is probably the main explanation for the curious fact, noted earlier, that prices have moved inversely with the cycle[49]. This inverse movement has in fact been quite regular (Table 4-4). It has been due only to a very small extent, to the behavior of indirect

---

[46] Thus Ball and St. Cyr, *ibid.*, pp. 192–193, found that the speed of adjustment was faster in industries with above average unemployment. It is also significant that in Northern Ireland, where unemployment has been persistently higher than in the rest of the United Kingdom, employment has fluctuated more.

[47] In the most recent downswing, the issue was further clouded by a substantial reduction in normal hours of work.

TABLE 4–4    United Kingdom: Percentage Increase from Year to Year in Gross Domestic Product Implicit Price Deflator

|  | Market Price | | Factor Cost | |
|---|---|---|---|---|
|  | Upswing years | Downswing years | Upswing years | Downswing years |
| 1952 | – | 8.7 | – | 9.1 |
| 1953 | 2.9 | – | 3.0 | – |
| 1954 | 1.7 | – | 2.0 | – |
| 1955 | 3.9 | – | 3.7 | – |
| 1956 | – | 6.4 | – | 6.2 |
| 1957 | – | 3.7 | – | 3.9 |
| 1958 | – | 4.0 | – | 4.6 |
| 1959 | 1.0 | – | 1.6 | – |
| 1960 | 1.1 | – | 1.6 | – |
| 1961 | – | 3.3 | – | 3.2 |
| 1962 | – | 3.9 | – | 3.4 |
| 1963 | 1.6 | – | 1.9 | – |
| 1964 | 2.2 | – | 1.7 | – |
| 1965 | – | 4.7 | – | 3.6 |
| Average | 2.1 | 5.0 | 2.2 | 4.9 |

taxes, since it has been almost equally pronounced whether prices have been measured at market price or at factor cost.

There has been a clear cyclical movement in the share of profits in national income, just as there was in earlier times. But from what has already been said about the behavior of employment and prices, it can be seen that the reasons for

[48] Among the leading contributions to the extensive literature on the United Kingdom are A. W, Phillips, "The Relation Between Unemployment and the Rate of Change of Money Wage Rates in the U.K., 1861–1957," *Economica*, November 1958; R. G. Lipsey, "The Relation Between Unemployment and the Rate of Change of Money Wage Rates in the U.K., 1862–1957: A Further Analysis," *Economica*, February 1960; L. A. Dicks-Mireaux, "The Inter-relationship Between Cost and Price Changes, 1946–1959: A Study of Inflation in Post-war Britain," October 1961; Neild, *Pricing and Employment, op. cit.*; Dow, *op. cit*; pp. 330–363; J. Johnston, D. D. Bugg, and P. J. Lund, "Some Econometrics of Inflation in the United Kingdom," and J. D. Sargan, "Wages and Prices in the United Kingdom: A Study in Econometric Methodology," in P. E. Hart, G. Mills, and J. K. Whitaker (eds.) *Econometric Analysis for National Economic Planning* London, 1964; W. A. H. Godley and D. A. Rowe, "Retail and Consumer Prices," *N.I.E.R.*, No. 30, November 1964; W. A. H. Godley and C. Gillion, "Pricing Behaviour in Manufacturing Industry," *N.I.E.R.*, August 1965.

the movement have changed. In interwar cycles, and still more so before 1914, prices were responsive to the pressure of demand, and this was probably the main reason why the share fluctuated over the cycle. In the postwar period, the price response has not been the same as it was previously. But in contrast to earlier times, employers have not been able or willing in recessions to reduce employment nearly in proportion to the reduction (relative to trend) in output; therefore, there has been a rise in labor costs per unit of output, with an adverse effect on profit margins[50].

IV

The three cycles under review have not been identical. The interconnections of the system are complicated. And, as has repeatedly been said, there is much that is not understood about the factors affecting the various components of demand. In the following oversimplified synthetic account of the course and causes of the cycle, these sundry cautions are to be taken as read. From the more detailed treatment in Section II, above, the reader will be able to see for himself the various necessary qualifications and the points on which a different view might be held.

RECOVERY PHASE

The rate of expansion was rapid in the opening years of each of the upswings (1953, 1959, 1963). This is the stage of the cycle with the largest changes of direction in the economy. On each occasion there were forces making for recovery, independent of government action: a recovery in exports, which must be treated as exogenous, and recoveries in stockbuilding and consumer durables, which were at least partly endogenous. These together would have outweighed the still continuing decline in manufacturing investment. Superimposed on them, however, came government stimulus, mainly to consumption, in the form of tax remissions and easing of credit. As the economy was patently working below capacity at the beginning of each upswing and as the balance of payments seemed satisfactory for the moment, the decision of the authorities to encourage expansion was generally applauded at the time.

REMAINDER OF THE UPSWING PHASE

Once the recovery had got undeway, further stimulus from government action did not play a major part (1964 is an exception)[51]. Private fixed capital

---

[50] It is easy to construct a theoretical model in which the lagged relationship of wages and prices amplifies fluctuations in demand or even produces a self-sustaining cycle through the effects of the distribution of income on consumption. But it is difficult to discern any systematic tendency of this sort in the data.

formation, on the other hand, became more important. With excess capacity diminished by the foregoing recovery, manufacturing investment resumed its rise. Consumer durables slackened toward the end of the upswing. But any deflationary effects from this side were outweighed by the very sharp increase in stockbuilding that took place at the end of each upswing, reflecting a delayed reaction by producers to the preceding rise in demand. Possibly because of this rise in stockbuilding, there was also an abnormal increase in imports. This was not fully foreseen, but on each occasion the view was widely expressed that the economy was in, or was approaching, an "overheated" condition. However, on two of the three occasions (1955 and 1964), electoral considerations were influential in causing the government to defer taking deflationary measures that might have been thought appropriate. On two occasions (1960 and 1964), an inflow of short-term capital temporarily distracted the authorities' attention from the adverse balance of payments on current account.

DOWNTURN PHASE

By the end of each of the peak years, 1955, 1960, and 1964, the government had begun restrictive action. But the slackening in the rate of growth in the early stages of the downturn was partly, and perhaps mainly, due to causes independent of government action. The main sources of the slackening were stockbuilding and consumer durables. The sharp reversal in stockbuilding from its previously abnormally high level would certainly have happened anyway. The magnitude of the endogenous element in the decline of consumer durables is more debatable and represents one of the most important unsettled questions about the cycle. Total private investment continued to rise at this stage, because of the effect of decisions already taken and partly also because the recession was not then pronounced enough to do much damage to confidence.

REMAINDER OF THE DOWNSWING

There have been two complete cycles since 1953, but the provisional data for 1966 suggest for the third cycle pattern similar to the other two. On each occasion, the main factor making for a further decline in activity was fixed capital formation. There was also some slackening in the rate of growth of exports, and stockbuilding continued to decline. A special feature of this phase was that the government felt impelled for balance of payments reasons to impose further restrictions on demand when it was generally recognized to be already

---

[51] Nineteenth century British cycles also often showed this pattern, in which a factor important in initiating the upswing ceases to be so important once the upswing is under way. Government action in postwar upswings has thus played the role that in late nineteenth century cycles in Britain was usually played by exports to the United States and by good harvests.

moving downward. The crises leading to these measures (1957, 1961, 1966) were not due to the state of the current balance of payments, which was improving; they were essentially crises of confidence in the pound. Special factors played some part (discussions of possible exchange-rate adjustments in 1957 and revaluation of the Deutsche Mark in 1961), but these had the effect because confidence had already been shaken by the underlying weakness in the balance of payments revealed in the preceding boom years. The effects of the measures were not savage (in 1966 they were more severe than in the other two years). But they had a direct effect on consumption and on private non-manufacturing investment, through their effects on demand generally and on confidence they no doubt contributed, though it is difficult to say how much, to the decline in manufacturing investment. On the most skeptical interpretation of their efficacy, they at least meant that the decline in manufacturing investment was not yet neutralized by expansion elsewhere.

In broadest outline, the profile of the British postwar cycle is therefore as follows:

Government action plays an important part in promoting the early stages of the upswing (though it is not the only factor). This recovery sets in train cumulative effects for which the government does not have the main responsibility. Fixed capital formation rises. Then there is a sharp increase in stockbuilding, a delayed result of the preceding rise in demand. This is in its nature a transitory phenomenon. Its reversal, probably combined with some endogenous tendency for sales of consumer durables to fall off after a period of rapid increase, creates a slackening of the boom; this is strengthened by government action to protect the balance of payments. If this were the end of the story, the cycle would be very mild. But it is not, for two reasons. First, after a significant delay, private fixed investment declines. Second, confidence-induced balance of payments crises cause the government to take further deflationary measures, especially in the monetary field. An important unsettled question is how far the second of these reasons is responsible for the first, and how far the decline in private fixed investment represents a delayed reaction from the preceding boom and would have happened anyway. But on any reckoning, the government's measures strengthen and prolong the downswing. The extent of the downswing creates a slack in the economy and increases the arrears of investment in producers' fixed capital, in stocks, and in consumer durables. It therefore prepares the way for the strong revival which ensues in the next phase.

The later stages of the downswing have features which resemble more than superficially those characteristics of earlier business cycles which Schumpeter embraced under the heading of "the secondary wave" [52]. A recurring theme in business cycle history is that crises created by illiquidity and damage to

[52] J. A. Schumpeter, *Business Cycles,* New York, 1939, pp. 145–161.

confidence are likely to occur after recession is already underway. The original boom and downturn create a vulnerable situation, but the liquidity-confidence crisis is not an inevitable consequence; if it does occur its severity depends on the strength of the financial system. The crisis, if it occurs, leads to a "secondary wave" (first down, then up) added to the downswing phase of the primary wave. It carries activity downward to a greater extent and for a longer time than would have resulted from the operations of the underlying real forces, and the kickback in the recovery is also correspondingly stronger. The postwar British case has not, of course, been identical with the Schumpeterian prototype. The illiquidity resulting from the boom has been illiquidity of the monetary authorities in terms of foreign exchange, brought about by the high imports of the boom, not illiquidity of private traders or banks; the underlying financial weakness has been the small reserves of the authorities, not private financial malpractice, and it is the authorities' solvency in terms of foreign exchange that has been the subject of loss of confidence. However, earlier crises often extended to include this sort of loss of confidence too. The common feature is the potential financial weakness created by the exchange of monetary assets for real assets at the peak of the boom[53].

The government's action in the secondary wave has been destabilizing, both in pushing activity down to a lower level and in creating the scope and need for a rapid expansion thereafter. Does it follow that, in its absence, the economy would have been subject only to very mild cycles, associated with exogenous fluctuations in exports and tendencies to overshooting in stockbuilding and consumer durables? The difficulty in answering this question concerns private fixed investment (especially in manufacturing) and whether it would have fallen off anyway after the boom. Given the circumstances of the time, it probably would have, at least to some extent. But the tendency of investment to rise to unmaintainable levels has itself been associated with the depth of the foregoing recession and the speed of the recovery from it; and this in turn goes back to government policy in the secondary wave. So the strength of endogenous cyclical tendencies in private investment remains very unclear.

The question of what the net effects of government policy have been is an extremely hypothetical one, since what is at issue is how the economy would have behaved if the government had acted differently, not merely at a single point of time but consistently over a longer period. It is arguable that a consistently neutral government policy would have resulted in a different kind of fluctuation rather than in no fluctuation at all. Government action may have increased the sharpness of year-to-year movements, but it has probably lessened

---

[53] This kind of government-induced secondary wave has been a point of difference between cycles in Britain and in other countries in the postwar period. Outside Britain, it has not been a characteristic feature of the cycle.

the overall duration of the cycle (thus helping to account for the diminution in duration of cycles, noted above in Section I). Admittedly, the downswing has for the time being been prolonged by restrictive measures; but once this has happened, government contribution to the reflation ensured that the downward movement did not go too far—and maybe it would have gone quite a long way even in the absence of the restrictive measures. The sharp pace of the expansion was partly government-induced, and its cumulative effects made a fairly early reversal inevitable; but a more prolonged private investment boom might have created a more complete temporary exhaustion of investment opportunities and a more prolonged setback.

Whether the overall effect of government policy has been stabilizing or destabilizing (a complicated question to define, let alone answer)[54], it cannot be denied that government policy did differ considerably from what it ought to have been if the objective had been to maintain activity at a stable and consistent level. It is difficult to believe that the reasons for this lay primarily in faulty forecasting of trends in demand, or of the effects of instruments chosen to affect it. Over the past fifteen years, techniques of forecasting and controlling demand have made great advances; the data available for the purpose have improved greatly; both civil servants and cabinet ministers have developed a better understanding of the principles involved. Yet fluctuations have, if anything, become more severe. There have been some wrong forecasts, and also some wrong judgments about the existing balance of demand and supply; but the main fault of policy has been infirmity of purpose about the level of demand to be aimed at. Lacking effective policy instruments to act directly on the balance of payments, the authorities have had to aim not at the level of activity ideally desirable, but at the best level compatible with avoiding a balance of payments deficit. Their judgments of what this level is have not been consistent. The "waves of optimism and pessimism" of old-fashioned business cycle theory have played a role in the postwar British cycle—not (or not only) in the attitudes of businessmen, but in the attitude of the authorities about what level of activity the balance of payments would stand. Had a consistent view been adopted about this, steps would have had to be taken to prevent either the upswings or the downswings or both from proceeding to the lengths they did. These inconsistencies of view were influenced, though not wholly determined, by the electoral timetable, and also, of course, by the state of the reserves[55]. They have tended to become progressively worse, because the underlying balance of payments problems have been getting more acute and at the same time the pressure of opinion in favor of a growth-oriented policy has been getting stronger. This is what has offset the potential good effects of the improvements in technical economic expertise.

What are the ways in which policy can be altered in order to produce a higher degree of stability in the future?[56] First and foremost, obviously, by the adoption of more consistent and realistic aims [57]. In addition to this, there undoubtedly exists room for improvements in forecasting, and in particular for a greater attention to the less immediate consequences of present actions. Numbers of areas where knowledge is imperfect have been pointed out. Knowledge about the forces operating on the supply side is still more imperfect. The rate of increase of productivity is inevitably very hard to predict, but there is also a wide area of ignorance about the seemingly more straightforward question of the labor supply. In the most recent past, particularly, this has made it difficult to judge what the balance of supply and demand in the labor market is or is likely to become.

How much have the cycles mattered? To answer this properly, it would be necessary to go into questions about the underlying forces affecting growth and balance of payments performance, which cannot be considered here. But my

---

[54] The conclusion that it was destabilizing was reached by Dow in the much-quoted passage referred to earlier. In reaching this conclusion, Dow was influenced by the frequent tendency for government action to push activity in the same direction as other forces were already pushing it. This criterion is not by itself a satisfactory one, however, because the objective of fiscal and monetary policy in principle is not just to keep activity stable but to keep it stable at the right level. By the beginning of 1953, 1959, and 1963, activity had fallen to a level that by common consent was too low. The fact that other forces may have been tending in the direction of raising it does not necessarily mean that the government was to be blamed for helping the process along. The same applies in reverse to peak years.

[55] This interpretation of government policy has much in common with the cycle model put forward by Professor Gelting in his contribution to this volume, in which government income-creation is a function of the level of foreign exchange reserves and the latter is a function of past income levels. In Britain, government income-creation should be regarded as a function of the current level of activity as well as of the state of the reserves: both have some influence. A cyclical result can easily be derived from this, as from Professor Gelting's model. But what has been involved in Britain has been rather more than a stock adjustment process: The state of the reserves has influenced government policy not only because of the need to adjust the reserves to a desired level, but also because changes in the climate of opinion brought about by movements in the reserves (and by other factors) appear to have caused changes in the actual beliefs of the authorities about what is feasible.

[56] In asking this question I do not mean to rule out the view that an improvement in this direction does not have a very high priority. It could be argued that it is best for the authorities to go on attempting to find out, by trial and error, what level of activity has been made consonant with balance of payments equilibrium as a result of their latest efforts (productivity drives, incomes policy, restrictions on capital export, etc.), even at the risk of recurring cycles.

[57] In the "wave of pessimism" prevailing at the time of writing, the view has gained ground that, given the obstacles to influencing the balance of payments by other means, the level of activity to be aimed at as a permanency is one not much above that of the trough years of the postwar cycles (the view that has been consistently advocated by Professor Paish and is associated with his name); but signs of a retreat from this view are already apparent.

tentative answer would be that they have not mattered much. Cycles have had a markedly disturbing influence on certain individual industries, such as the motor industry. For the rest, they have caused more concern to the authorities than to the public. The restrictions on spending that people have been conscious of have, to a large extent, been no more than a cyclical expression of a more general limit to what the economy is able to produce. It is often claimed that fluctuations have had a discouraging effect on investment; but the ratio of investment to income over the period has had a strong upward trend, so the damage cannot have been too bad. It is also sometimes argued that fluctuations have made the balance of payments worse than it would have been if the same average level of activity had been maintained consistently; this is possible, but the extent of the effect is debatable, and it is not plausible to maintain that it has been the main source of the country's balance of payments difficulties.

Are cycles likely to continue fairly mild in the United Kingdom in the future? Unless balance of payments difficulties enforce deflation of a far more serious order than anything so far, major depressions are not likely to occur. The possibility of a more serious and prolonged decline or stagnation in private investment than has hitherto occurred cannot be ruled out. The steady downward trend of the pretax profit rate has already been referred to, and it may not be possible indefinitely to offset the effects of this by tax concessions. But such an eventuality would not lead to a major general depression. The reason is not so much that the authorities are particularly skilled at stabilization, but that there is acknowledged to exist an enormous backlog of investment opportunities in the public sector, and these could and would be speeded forward if private investment should stagnate for any considerable length of time.

TABLE 4–5  GDP and Components 1950–1965 = £m. 1958

| | Total final expenditure | GDP | Consumers expenditure | Imports | Exports | GDFCF | PACE | Inventory investment |
|---|---|---|---|---|---|---|---|---|
| 1950 | 22484 | 18864 | 13098 | 3620 | 3947 | 2459 | 3255 | −275 |
| 1951 | 23412 | 19539 | 12919 | 3873 | 3907 | 2469 | 3502 | 615 |
| 1952 | 23081 | 19497 | 12855 | 3584 | 3825 | 2479 | 3857 | 65 |
| 1953 | 24263 | 20396 | 13433 | 3867 | 3985 | 2748 | 3962 | 135 |
| 1954 | 25172 | 21163 | 13979 | 4009 | 4210 | 2982 | 3947 | 54 |
| 1955 | 26308 | 21895 | 14543 | 4413 | 4470 | 3150 | 3832 | 313 |
| 1956 | 26683 | 22257 | 14672 | 4426 | 4665 | 3296 | 3806 | 244 |
| 1957 | 27229 | 22682 | 14978 | 4547 | 4785 | 3471 | 3751 | 244 |
| 1958 | 27339 | 22740 | 15365 | 4599 | 4711 | 3485 | 3673 | 105 |
| 1959 | 28606 | 23702 | 16075 | 4904 | 4838 | 3768 | 3744 | 181 |
| 1960 | 30384 | 24888 | 16724 | 5496 | 5108 | 4132 | 3824 | 596 |
| 1961 | 31186 | 25732 | 17113 | 5454 | 5259 | 4524 | 3964 | 326 |
| 1962 | 31474 | 25920 | 17463 | 5554 | 5344 | 4499 | 4091 | 77 |
| 1963 | 32802 | 27034 | 18282 | 5768 | 5576 | 4575 | 4153 | 216 |
| 1964 | 34890 | 28601 | 18970 | 6289 | 5783 | 5347 | 4228 | 562 |
| 1965 | 35585 | 29231 | 19284 | 6354 | 6049 | 5533 | 4373 | 346 |

TABLE 4-6    Private Fixed Capital Formation 1950-1965 £m. 1958

|      | Total private GDFCF | Manufacturing | Other | Dwellings |
|------|------|------|------|------|
| 1950 | 1324 | 624  | 628  | 72  |
| 1951 | 1187 | 656  | 459  | 72  |
| 1952 | 1110 | 619  | 379  | 112 |
| 1953 | 1218 | 605  | 421  | 192 |
| 1954 | 1467 | 641  | 568  | 258 |
| 1955 | 1685 | 754  | 645  | 286 |
| 1956 | 1848 | 896  | 647  | 305 |
| 1957 | 1963 | 965  | 694  | 304 |
| 1958 | 2008 | 913  | 773  | 322 |
| 1959 | 2171 | 860  | 911  | 400 |
| 1960 | 2493 | 970  | 1039 | 484 |
| 1961 | 2757 | 1122 | 1108 | 527 |
| 1962 | 2664 | 1061 | 1088 | 515 |
| 1963 | 2639 | 957  | 1170 | 512 |
| 1964 | 3068 | 1073 | 1370 | 625 |
| 1965 | 3142 | 1173 | 1353 | 616 |

TABLE 4-7    Public Sector Expenditure 1950-1965 £m. 1958

|      | Total | PACE | Public Sector G.D.F.C.F. excluding dwellings | Dwellings |
|------|------|------|------|------|
| 1950 | 4435 | 3255 | 800  | 380 |
| 1951 | 4776 | 3502 | 890  | 384 |
| 1952 | 5221 | 3857 | 930  | 434 |
| 1953 | 5486 | 3962 | 1005 | 519 |
| 1954 | 5462 | 3947 | 1037 | 478 |
| 1955 | 5297 | 3832 | 1062 | 403 |
| 1956 | 5254 | 3806 | 1102 | 346 |
| 1957 | 5259 | 3751 | 1190 | 318 |
| 1958 | 5150 | 3673 | 1212 | 265 |
| 1959 | 5341 | 3744 | 1323 | 274 |
| 1960 | 5463 | 3824 | 1365 | 274 |
| 1961 | 5731 | 3964 | 1481 | 286 |
| 1962 | 5926 | 4091 | 1510 | 325 |
| 1963 | 6089 | 4153 | 1590 | 346 |
| 1964 | 6507 | 4228 | 1815 | 464 |
| 1965 | 6761 | 4373 | 1886 | 502 |

TABLE 4–8  Consumption (First Differences): 1953–1965 £m. 1958

|      | Durables | Nondurables | Impact of tax rate changes | Nondurables less impact of tax rate changes | GDP less consumption |
|------|----------|-------------|----------------------------|---------------------------------------------|----------------------|
| 1953 | 227      | 351         | 135                        | 216                                         | 321                  |
| 1954 | 256      | 290         | 91                         | 199                                         | 221                  |
| 1955 | 209      | 355         | 20                         | 335                                         | 168                  |
| 1956 | −71      | 200         | −                          | 200                                         | 233                  |
| 1957 | 166      | 140         | 94                         | 46                                          | 119                  |
| 1958 | 173      | 214         | 156                        | 58                                          | −329                 |
| 1959 | 323      | 387         | 241                        | 146                                         | 252                  |
| 1960 | 174      | 475         | 118                        | 357                                         | 537                  |
| 1961 | −2       | 391         | 73                         | 318                                         | 455                  |
| 1962 | 60       | 290         | 30                         | 260                                         | −162                 |
| 1963 | 384      | 435         | 214                        | 221                                         | 295                  |
| 1964 | 254      | 434         | 75                         | 359                                         | 879                  |
| 1965 | 21       | 293         | 10                         | 283                                         | 316                  |

# COMMENTS

G. D. N. WORSWICK
National Institute of Economic and Social Research, London

Professor Guitton has introduced the felicitous expression a business cycle "of good family"—*de bonne famille*. How do we recognize a cycle of good family?

First, he must be seen to be well behaved. His manners must be such that, when he goes up or down stairs or leaves or enters the room, he is recognizably a gentleman.

Second, it is not enough that he should have the superficial characteristics of good behavior. *Why* he behaves well must be understood. A cycle of good family must be seen to be obeying certain rules which have been imparted by good parents or in the best schools.

From this point of view, the characteristic of a wellbred cycle is that, for the greater part, it is endogenous. A wellbred cycle may occasionally marry a foreigner, as the best English aristocratic families have occasionally refreshed themselves by marriages to American heiresses, but the family must not overdo it. Random shocks are permitted, but must not occur with such frequency as to obliterate the endogenous movement.

There is, of course, more than one good family. In the theoretical literature, there is the very finely bred cycle of Harrod and Samuelson, whose physiognomy is sharply recognizable. The family to which I was introduced when I was learning economics, and for which I have always had a special affection ever since, is the type formulated by Kalecki. The cycle is not so purebred, and it has a rather more dashing ancestry. The discerning observer can see a Marxian trace in the physiognomy, in addition to the more familiar Keynesian features. Again, there is a group of Schumpeterian theories, altogether a more boisterous family, whose behavior is more than a little suspect. The point I am trying to make is that *the* business cycle, the cycle that used to be discussed up to the 1930's, had these "good family" characteristics.

136

From this point of view, the parentage of the fluctuations of the British economy since 1950 is in some doubt. While in some respects—for example, in the movement of private investment in manufacturing—they show the outward signs of good behavior and good breeding, their credentials need close inspection. Whatever else may be said about the British economy in the past 15 years, it has been managed by the government or, if not managed, then mismanaged. In North America, much has been made of the distinction between automatic stabilizers of one kind and another and discretionary moves. In England, this distinction is less commonly made. One reason for the difference is that, in the U.S. case, discretionary moves, acts of government expressly designed to alter the course of the economy, cannot be made quickly (on the taxation side), are comparatively difficult to make, and have not occurred frequently. On the other hand, the British arrangements give to the authorities an exceptional degree of freedom to act quickly and on any scale they may choose in the fiscal and monetary fields, a freedom they have exercised. They may be constrained by political considerations, but certainly not by constitutional ones.

In the early postwar period, there was still a substantial lumping of discretionary moves in the regular April Budget; but since then, there has been an increasing tendency to spread discretionary moves, fiscal and monetary, throughout the year. This tendency has been criticized, but the informed consensus seems to be in favor of spreading rather than concentrating discretionary moves.

I think Professor Matthews is quite right when he brings out explicitly the basic problem of analyzing the fluctuations of the British economy in recent years, namely, the difficulty of separating movements which may be attributed to the endogenous behavior of the system from movements in response to deliberate changes made by the authorities.

It is even possible that academic economists have gone too far in explaining British fluctuations in terms of acts of government, to the comparative neglect of endogenous movements. Certainly in much writing about the movement of the contemporary British economy, the word "government" appears with great frequency. Thus I am glad that Mr. Dow, whose views on the movements of the economy are quoted by Matthews, is attending this conference. If I understand Dow's position correctly, it is that the cyclical character of the movements of the British economy is adequately accounted for by government policy. Matthews does not accept this interpretation, as can be seen from his concluding paragraphs. I find myself more on Matthews's side than Dow's side, but I hope they will come to grips on this point in the course of the discussion.

I should like to point up one or two of the very interesting features brought out by Matthews, and to mention, though not to solve, one or two outstanding queries.

1. I would draw attention to the very striking change that he observes in the phasing of price movements in relation to output movements, so that nowadays prices tend to move upward faster in the so-called downswing than in the upswing. My first thought was that perhaps the very striking inverse relationship between the rates of increase of output and of prices might have been accentuated by using the GDP implicit price deflators for the price index. On inspection, there appears to be a little justification, but only a little, for this thought. The accompanying table reproduces the GDP market price deflator, in the form which Matthews presents it, and also shows the year-to-year changes in the index of retail prices and in the wholesale price index for manufactured goods. The broad inverse relationship is unaffected, but there are sufficient differences of detail to suggest that this particular phenomenon deserves closer scrutiny than was necessary for Matthews' purposes.

TABLE 4–9   United Kingdom Percentage Increase over Previous Year in Various Price Indicators

|  | Upswing Years | | | Downswing Years | | |
|---|---|---|---|---|---|---|
|  | GDP* | Retail† | Wholesale‡ | GDP* | Retail† | Wholesale‡ |
| 1952 |  |  |  | 8.7 | 8.8 | (2.4) |
| 1953 | 2.9 | 3.1 | (−2.0) |  |  |  |
| 1954 | 1.7 | 1.8 | (0.2) |  |  |  |
| 1955 | 3.9 | 4.5 | 3.4 |  |  |  |
| 1956 |  |  |  | 6.4 | 4.9 | 3.2 |
| 1957 |  |  |  | 3.7 | 3.7 | 3.3 |
| 1958 |  |  |  | 4.0 | 3.0 | 0.7 |
| 1959 | 1.0 | 0.6 | 0.4 |  |  |  |
| 1960 | 1.1 | 1.0 | 1.5 |  |  |  |
| 1961 |  |  |  | 3.3 | 3.4 | 2.3 |
| 1962 |  |  |  | 3.9 | 4.2 | 2.0 |
| 1963 | 1.6 | 2.0 | 1.3 |  |  |  |
| 1964 | 2.2 | 3.3 | 3.1 |  |  |  |
| 1965 |  |  |  | 4.7 | 4.8 | 4.2 |
| Average | 2.1 | 2.3 | 1.9 | 5.0 | 4.7 | 2.6 |

* Gross Domestic Product. Market price implicit deflator.
† Retail price index.
‡ Wholesale price index of all manufactured goods. The figures for 1953 and 1954, in parentheses, are the index of wholesale prices, excluding food. The averages for wholesale prices exclude the years 1952–1954.

2. Matthews draws attention to the diminished role of export changes as prime movers of changes in the economy, as compared with the interwar years.

Meanwhile, a new aspect of the relationship between exports and domestic demand has come into the picture. In the past, a change in exports was considered to be a change in primary expenditure leading to corresponding changes in domestic demand. In recent years, attention has been given to the influence the other way round, on the grounds that, for example, a spontaneous fall in domestic demand may push out additional exports; a fair amount of work has been done on this hypothesis. Some traces of this influence can be found, though the work is not conclusive. I shall have another word to say about this later.

3. The greater variability of imports, and also its relation to stockbuilding, are noted by Matthews. One might have hoped to find that the pressure of demand in the domestic economy would give a fairly simple explanation for import behavior on the grounds that, by previous standards, the average pressure of demand has been rather high. Oddly enough, in the econometric analyses of this question, the "pressure of demand" variable does not get a significant coefficient.

4. I think the behavior of private manufacturing investment and other private investment in 1966, prior to the July measures, may prove a rewarding study. On general conjunctural grounds, a downturn analogous to previous downturns had been expected some time in 1965 and early 1966, but it failed to materialize. This raises the interesting question of whether, on that occasion, had it not been for the July 'stop', there might have been a curve of manufacturing investment with a point of inflexion rather than a maximum. Tax policy was undoubtedly aimed to protect and stimulate private investment, but the prevailing view is that such policy is ineffective in the absence of confident demand expectations. There is a hint in the experience of 1965–1966 that this view may be perhaps too pessimistic.

In general, I would like to say that more work needs to be developed on the supply side of an economy which has been run at a pretty high level of employment. There are some paradoxical phenomena. For example, in equations attempting to explain exports, those which include a price variable quite often get a significant coefficient, but with the wrong sign.

I should like to support Matthews in stressing the importance of separating the study of cyclical behavior from policy implications. I agree with him that stabilization as such, in the sense of merely removing fluctuations, may not have as high priority as other policy objectives. His manner of presentation is so modest that the fact that his analysis leads to two controversial conclusions might be overlooked. The first I have already mentioned, namely, the difference between his interpretations and that of Mr. Dow of the influence of government policy. The second is even more striking, namely, that in Matthews's view, whatever may have been the cause of the fluctuations, those fluctuations themselves (which some call 'stop-go') have not done much harm.

Chapter Five

# CYCLICAL DEVELOPMENTS IN FRANCE, GERMANY, AND ITALY SINCE THE EARLY 1950's

J. C. R. DOW

Department of Economics and Statistics, OECD

The accompanying material on cyclical developments in France, Germany, and Italy represents a report on work in progress. To a large extent the studies are no more than systematic presentations of the main relevant series. The general aim may be described most simply as that of assembling the ingredients required to construct an econometric, short-term forecasting model at a later stage. At the present stage of the work, it seems most convenient to present the data largely in graphical form. The work was undertaken to provide a stronger basis for a current routine of short-term economic forecasting. Since the forecasts deal with changes in activity over periods of one or two years, the analysis is primarily in terms of annual changes.

---

This chapter is included at the request of the editorial committee, and against the wishes of the principal author. Produced as a basis for discussion, it should ideally have been revised more substantially before publication. It was a report on work in progress; the lapse of time since its preparation makes it unrepresentative of current work at OECD. Three OECD studies, completed since the chapter was prepared, now supplement it substantially: Bent Hansen, *Fiscal Policy in Seven Countries, 1955–1965*; Michael K. Evans, *An Econometric Model of the French Economy*; F. G. Adams, H. Eguchi, and F. Meyer zu Schlochtern, *An Econometric Analysis of International Trade*.

The three studies included in this chapter were prepared by members of the National Accounts and Economic Forecasting Division, Department of Economics and Statistics, Organization for Economic Cooperation and Development (OECD). Those responsible for the individual studies were P. Gutmann (France), P. Schwanse (Germany), and Miss J. Sutherland (Italy).

In each of the three countries, output expanded fairly rapidly in the period studied (on average by more than 5 per cent a year) and also fairly continuously. There was no year in any of the countries in which national output fell from one calendar year to another. But there were distinct variations in the *rate* of expansion, and these variations are the subject of the studies.

It seems helpful to conceive of the "capacity" of the economy as growing at a fairly steady rate, and to compare the actual increase of output with this norm. When actual output grows more slowly than potential output, the degree of underutilization of capacity ("slack") will grow; when it grows more rapidly, slack will decrease (or overfull employment will increase). This concept underlies the dating of successive phases of quick or slow expansion. Thus a "downturn" (phase of slow growth) has been dated *from* the point at which slack appears to have started to increase *until* the point at which it appears to have stopped increasing; and vice versa for an "upturn" (phase of quick growth). In practice, this amounts to much the same thing as the removal of the trend from the time series of output. There is no reason, however, why economic capacity should grow at a perfectly steady rate, for the rate of growth of both the labor force and the stock of capital is liable to variations. Attempts, of varying crudeness, have therefore been made to construct estimates of the growth of capacity; these make use of available statistics of labor unemployment or underutilization of capacity, so as to correct the trend of actual output.

While the underlying principle has been to compare the level of output with the level of economic capacity, it is difficult to display changes in trend effectively if the data are shown graphically in index number form, since changes in rates of growth are relatively small. It is therefore frequently convenient to display them in the form of changes over successive 12-month (or shorter) periods. However, this method of presentation may give a misleading impression of turning points. If, for instance, the cycle should take a pure sinusoidal form, the rate of increase of output would start to decline a quarter-phase before output would start to grow less rapidly than capacity (Chart 5-1) [1].

---

[1] If the data are shown in the form of changes, then the turning points should be dated (on the principle set out earlier) close to the point where the curve of output crosses the line showing the average rate of change over the period. (In practice, this will, in most cases, be very close to the growth rate of capacity.)

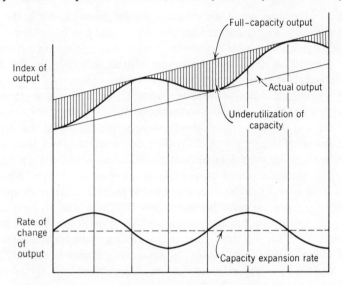

**Chart 5–1**    Actual output, "capacity" output, and rate of change of output: Hypothetical data.

As the chief interest in these studies was the behavior of aggregate output, cycles were defined in terms of output. Although the behavior of many other series is closely parallel to that of output, there often are significant differences in timing; therefore, in establishing turning points, other series were used where they helped to date changes in the trend of output.

Each of the three national studies has the same form, and consists of the following sections:

1. General description of cyclical developments in the economy studied; establishment of main turning points

2. First analysis in terms of final expenditure data to establish which main categories of expenditure accounted for the change in trend in output; notes on policy influences;

3. Detailed analysis of behavior of the following:
    (a)   Exports.
    (b)   Private fixed investment expenditure.
    (c)   Stocks of goods.
    (d)   Consumer expenditure
    (e)   Imports.

The statistical data varied considerably as between the three countries; for the present purpose they were most adequate for France, least adequate for

Italy, and in an intermediate position for Germany. These variations have affected the relative length and completeness of the studies.

A separate study of the economic impact of fiscal changes has been undertaken at OECD [2]. At the time of writing, however, estimates were available only for Germany; for the other two countries, less systematic methods have had to be used to allow for fiscal effects. The effects of monetary policy, though doubtless of considerable importance at times, have been assessed much more impressionistically.

The three countries which are the subject of the present study are the three major economies of continental western Europe; geographically, they are close neighbours. It is therefore to be expected that they will have been affected by common external influences, and that developments in one of them will have affected developments in the others. Clear evidence of this appears. Each country was affected by a fall in exports in 1958; this seems to have originated not in a falling off in demand within the countries but in a falling off in demand in the United States. More recently, however, the cycle has not been simultaneous. The major fluctuations have been due to successive phases in which demand has been allowed to grow too rapidly—or expansion has been caused by an overexpansionary policy of the authorities—and phases where a corrective policy has been applied. These phases have not coincided in the three countries, and the differing degrees of demand pressure existing at times between them have had marked effects on their mutual trade and, consequently, on demand pressures in the partner countries. Part of the inflationary or deflationary impulses originating in one country has, in effect, been exported to the others.

---

[2] A group of experts was appointed (first under the Chairmanship of Professor Zijlstra, then under that of Professor Walter Heller) to study the use made of fiscal policy; the hindrances, institutional and otherwise, to its use as an instrument of economic policy; and the ways of reducing such hindrances. The report of this group has been published as *Fiscal Policy in the Balanced Economy*, along with Professor Bent Hansen's background study of seven countries: Belgium, France, Italy, Germany, Sweden, the United Kingdom, and the United States.

## France

The annual increase of France's gross national product (GNP) at constant prices was 4.8 per cent during the period 1950–1965. In that period, there were cycles in the rate of growth of total output as measured by gross domestic produce (GDP) with major slowdowns in 1953, 1959, and 1965, and with high rates of expansion in 1951, 1957 and 1962 (Chart 5-2). Since adverse harvests in 1956, 1961, and 1963 disturbed the regularity of the cycles somewhat, the contraction and expansion periods are more clearly described by nonagricultural output and industrial output, which showed largely parallel movements. It is clear from Chart 5-2 that the cycles were not purely French but moved in sympathy with the European OECD cycles.

A relationship was established between the pressure of labor demand and the departure of output from its full employment or capacity rate of growth [1].

The derived index of capacity output utilization which was used to date turning points, is shown in Chart 5-3 along with other cyclical indicators [2]. The turning points selected, defined in terms of quarters, are shown in both Chart 5-3 and Table 5-1. Since national accounts data for calendar years have to be used later in describing many of the expenditure trends, annual approximations to the turning points are also tabulated; for three years (1949, 1951, and 1959), the annual data are rather poor approximations.

---

[1] The pressure of labor demand is measured as active civilian population, plus outstanding vacancies, *less* unemployment as a percentage of the active civilian population; and output is measured by the index of industrial production including construction. The full employment or capacity growth rate is measured by the growth of output between two years (1956 and 1964) when the pressure of labor demand was very high and about the same in each year. The ratio of output to full employment capacity is here called full employment– capacity output utilization (or more simply capacity output utilization)–the inverse of internal slack. The amplitude of capacity output utilization was about ten times the amplitude of the pressure of labor demand; variations in capacity output utilization were roughly estimated as equal to the pressure of labor demand after correcting unemployment (minus vacancies) multiplied by a factor of ten.

[2] From Chart 5–3 it appears that outstanding vacancies and unemployment moved closely in harmony, with the former a little ahead of the latter; and that a decrease in outstanding vacancies preceded by a period the rises in the increase of the number of hours worked and of the number of outstanding vacancies. These in turn took place before a new increase in employment.

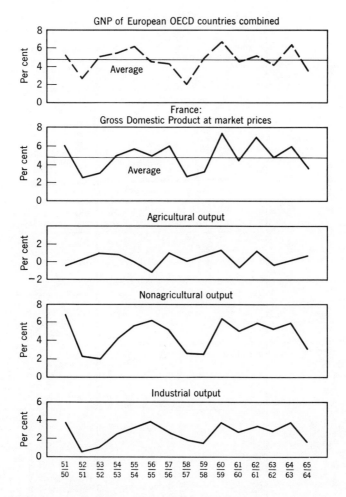

**Chart 5-2** France fluctuations in output, 1950–1965. (Percentage rates of change, annual basis.)

146

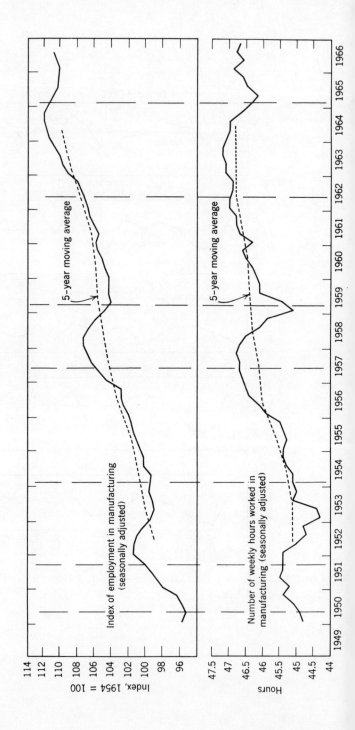

Index of employment in manufacturing (seasonally adjusted)

5-year moving average

Number of weekly hours worked in manufacturing (seasonally adjusted)

5-year moving average

Index, 1954 = 100

114
112
110
108
106
104
102
100
98
96

Hours

47.5
47
46.5
46
45.5
45
44.5
44

1949 1950 1951 1952 1953 1954 1955 1956 1957 1958 1959 1960 1961 1962 1963 1964 1965 1966

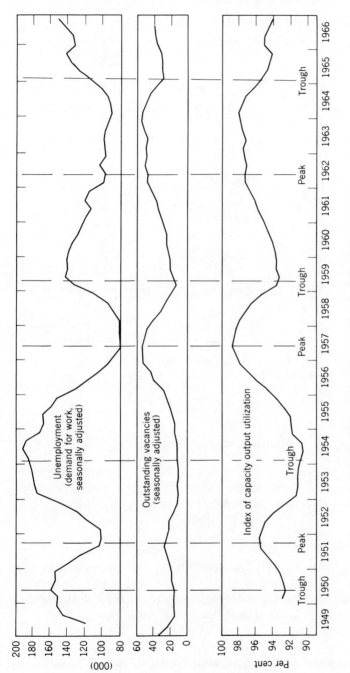

**Chart 5-3** France: selected cyclical series, 1949, 1950 . . . 1966.

147

TABLE 5-1    France: Dating of Cyclical Turning Points, 1949–65

| Dating by Quarters | | | Approximation in terms of calendar years | |
|---|---|---|---|---|
| Peak | Trough | | Peak | Trough |
| 1949.1 | | | 1949* | |
| | 1949.3 | 1st upturn | | 1950 |
| | 1950.2 | | | |
| 1951.3 | | 1st downturn | 1951* | |
| 1952.1 | | | | |
| | 1953.1 | 2nd upturn | | 1953 |
| | 1954.2 | | | |
| 1956.4 | | 2nd downturn | 1957 | |
| 1957.2 | | | | |
| | 1959.1 | 3rd upturn | | 1959* |
| 1962.1 | | | 1962 | |
| 1964.2 | | | 1964 | |
| | 1965.1 | 3rd downturn | | 1965 |

* As will be seen from Chart 5-3, the calendar years in these cases give a poor indication of the peak or trough.

## First Analysis of Final Expenditure Data

Changes in final expenditure at constant prices between the years selected as representing turning points over the six periods are given in Table 5.2; quarterly data for such expenditure series (or proxies) are shown in Chart 5-4.

### CHRONOLOGICAL ANALYSIS

FIRST UPTURN, 1950–1951. The Korean War led to a large rise in exports (reversed, however, in the course of 1951–Chart 5-4) and an increase in public consumpton (defense). The war atmosphere probably stimulated private consumption [3]; changes in stocks of goods were a dampening factor.

[3] There were significant fluctuations in savings ratios; see the later discussion of consumption in France.

TABLE 5-2    France: Annual Average Percentage Rates of Change in Final Expenditure and Its Main Components*

|  | 1950 to 1951 | 1951 to 1953 | 1953 to 1957 | 1957 to 1959 | 1959 to 1962 | 1964 to 1965 |
|---|---|---|---|---|---|---|
| Private consumption | 4.4 | 2.2 | 3.0 | 0.9 | 3.6 | 1.8 |
| Public consumption | 0.8 | 1.3 | 0.3 | 0.2 | 0.4 | 0.2 |
| Gross fixed capital formation | 0.9 | −0.2 | 1.6 | 0.6 | 1.5 | 1.0 |
| Of which: Government | - | 0.2 | 0.3 | 0.1 | 0.2 | 0.3 |
| Exports | 1.7 | −0.1 | 0.6 | 0.9 | 1.2 | 1.5 |
| Final sales | 7.7 | 3.1 | 5.3 | 2.6 | 6.4 | 4.5 |
| Changes in stocks of goods | −0.9 | −0.5 | 0.5 | −0.5 | 0.4 | −1.0 |
| Final expenditure | 6.9 | 2.7 | 5.7 | 2.1 | 6.8 | 3.5 |

*  Changes between years selected as representing turning points.

FIRST DOWNTURN, 1951–1953. The 1953 recession was due largely to the readjustments following the inflation resulting from the Korean War. Exports fell at first, then rose a little (Chart 5-4). Private consumption may have been affected by the reaction to developments in 1950–1951. Fixed investment declined, possibly because of credit measures.

SECOND UPTURN, 1953–1957. The expansion was led by an initial rapid rise in exports (Chart 5-4). Fixed investment demand was strong (Table 5-2).

SECOND DOWNTURN, 1957–1959. Exports at first rose very little (later they increased strongly in response to the devaluations of 1957 and 1958; see Chart 5-5). Fixed investment, buoyant at first, decelerated continuously.

THIRD UPTURN, 1959–1962. At the start, exports were among the main elements in the upswing. Fixed investment (especially machinery and equipment) increased rapidly in 1960, and continued to increase at a strong pace (about 8 per cent annual rate) during the remainder of the period. As the upturn developed, public consumption as well as private consumption was stimulated by the mass arrival of repatriates from Algeria.

THIRD DOWNTURN, 1964–1965. The 1963 Stabilization Plan was followed by a deceleration of public expenditure and of gross fixed capital formation; 1965 saw a fall in private productive investment. The accumulation of stocks was the lowest in 12 years. Exports, however, remained relatively strong.

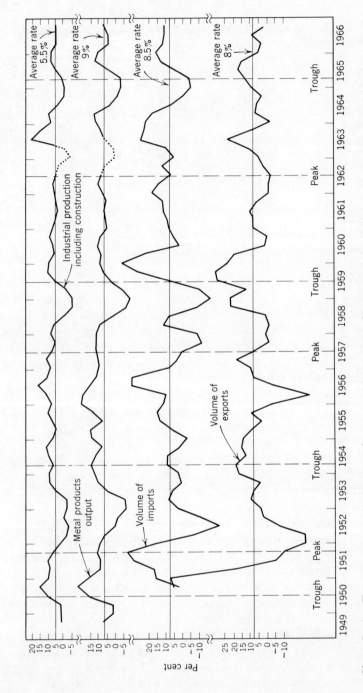

**Chart 5–4**   France: output, imports, and exports, 1949–1966. (Quarterly changes in seasonally adjusted data smoothed by three-quarter (1.2.1) weighted average.

150

## Analysis of Main Components of Demand

EXPORTS

Annual data are·shown in Chart 5-5 for changes in the volume of French exports
(excluding exports to French overseas territories), changes in France's share of
her export markets (derived from the total volume of imports of France's
principal clients), changes in the ratio of world to French prices [4] lagged three

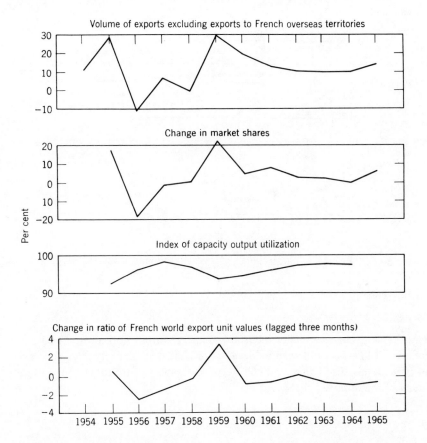

**Chart 5—5**   France: percentage changes in export shares, in the index of
capacity utilization and in the ratio of world to French export unit values,
annually 1954–1965.

[4] Ratio of world export unit value for manufactures to French export unit value for
manufactures.

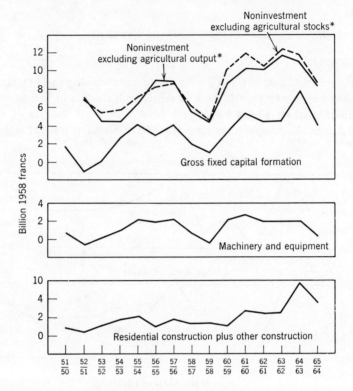

**Chart 5–6**   France: changes in fixed investment and noninvestment outlays, 1950–1965.

*Two-year moving average leading by one-half year.

months, and changes in the index of capacity output utilization. The pace of inflation in France, followed by devaluations, created relatively large differences in price levels. Both this, and the degree of capacity utilization, may explain much of the observed changes in market shares.

INVESTMENT

From Chart 5-6 it appears that fixed investment is related rather closely to noninvestment (excluding agricultural stocks or agricultural output). Both correlation coefficients give $R^2$ of approximately 0.6; the correlation between investment in machinery and equipment and noninvestment is less close. It appears that, with the main exceptions of 1956 and 1964, when residential

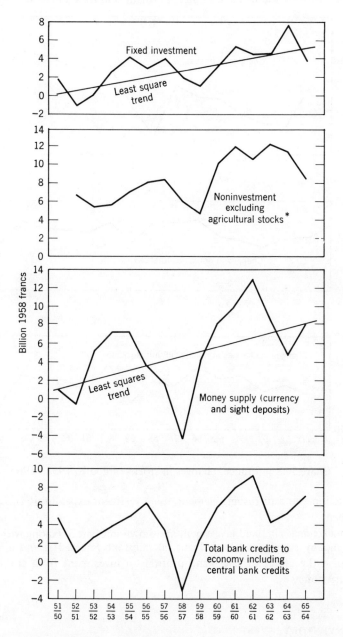

**Chart 5–7** France: changes in fixed investment, noninvestment, money supply, and bank credits, 1950–1965. (Annual percentage changes in deflated series.)

*Two-year moving average leading by one-half.

153

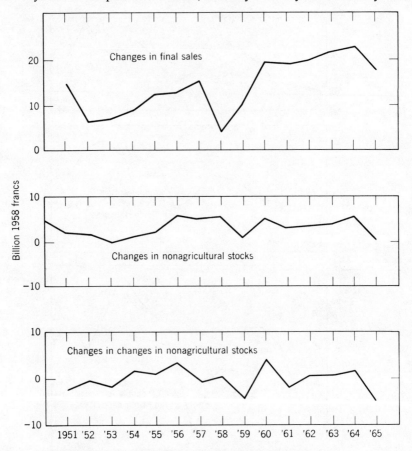

**Chart 5–8**   France: changes in stocks of goods, 1951–1965.

construction was a disturbing element, noninvestment expenditure was causal to investment.

Annual changes in fixed investment are shown in Chart 5-7 along with changes in the money supply and bank loans, at constant prices. It seems difficult to distinguish the effect of sales (and profits) on investment from any effect of monetary policy.


INVENTORY INVESTMENT

Changes in final sales, and changes (also changes in changes) in nonagricultural stocks are presented in Chart 5-8. On the whole, investment in stocks (excluding

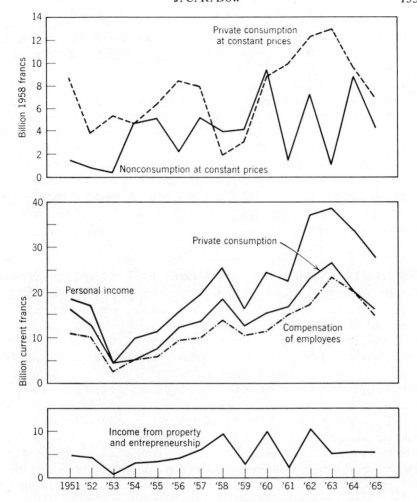

**Chart 5–9**    France: changes in private consumption, nonconsumption and personal income, 1951–1965.

agricultural stocks) moved more or less in sympathy with the trend in sales, turning points in the former sometimes tending to lag.

CONSUMPTION

From Chart 5-9 it is clear that there is little relationship between the change in private consumption and in nonconsumption expenditures (at constant prices). Much of the year-to-year fluctuation in the latter is associated with fluctuations in agricultural output and stocks. Though the corresponding changes in agricultural income are one element in personal income (income from enterprise), they do not dominate the picture. This must be due in part to the behavior of corporate profits. But it is also evident that fluctuations in the personal-saving ratio are correlated with year-to-year fluctuations in nonconsumption and personal income from enterprises (compare Charts 5-9 and 5-10), and this must inhibit multiplier effects from such short-period oscillations. It is also evident that short-period oscillations in the personal-saving ratio are inversely correlated with the personal-tax ratio (Chart 5-10) [5]. Therefore, it might be feasible to try to explain fluctuations in consumption spending in terms of those in nonconsumption spending by allowing for the behavior of corporate profits, personal enterprise saving, and changes in tax ratios. It would probably also be necessary to consider the capital formation of independent traders as an alternative call on disposable income [6].

IMPORTS

Imports of goods and services represent between 14 and 15 per cent of GNP. The long-run elasticity of the volume of merchandise imports with respect to GNP is about 2. This estimate appears to hold when the growth rate is some 5 per cent; when that rate falls to 2.5 per cent the import elasticity approaches zero.

Annual changes in (a) the volume of imports (b) the index of industrial production including construction, (c) final expenditure, less services, (d) capacity output utilization (as defined earlier), and (e) nonagricultural stocks as a percentage of final expenditure are shown in Chart 5-11. As expected, most of the variations in imports may be explained in terms of expenditure ($R^2 = 0.59$); capacity output utilization or stocks add little ($R^2 = 0.65$). An attempt was also made to explain changes in the volume of imports by changes in industrial production *less* construction, changes in the volume of consumer expenditure *less* services and changes in stocks of goods. The multiple correlation coefficient was higher ($R^2 = 0.88$). The simple correlation between the change in imports and the change in final sales was also relatively high ($R^2 = 0.78$) [7].

---

[5] The change in the average savings ratio is more closely correlated with the change in the marginal tax ratio than with that in the average-tax ratio. At first this is puzzling. But it may well be that the collection of taxes on personal income from enterprises is either ineffecient or delayed, and that fluctuations in such income cause fluctuations in both the savings ratio and the tax ratio.

[6] In the September 1966 issue of *Etudes et Conjontures,* a multiple correlation analysis based on annual data at 1959 prices was presented in an attempt to explain private consumption by disposable income (minus the financing of capital formation by independent traders and minus imputed food self-produced and consumed) *and* by the one-year lagged private consumption (past consumption habits). The multiple correlation coefficient of the absolute levels was 0.9995, and the multiple correlation coefficient of the first differences was 0.98.

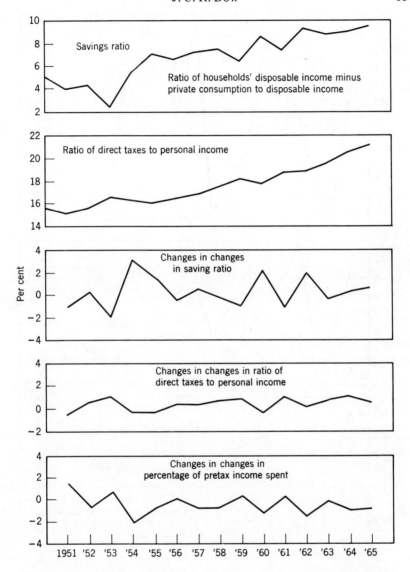

**Chart 5–10**    France: changes in savings and tax ratios, 1951–1965.

[7] Largely as a consequence of this relationship, faster than average increases in final expenditure are associated ($R^2$ = 0.6) with deterioration of the foreign balance (exports *less* imports of goods and services).

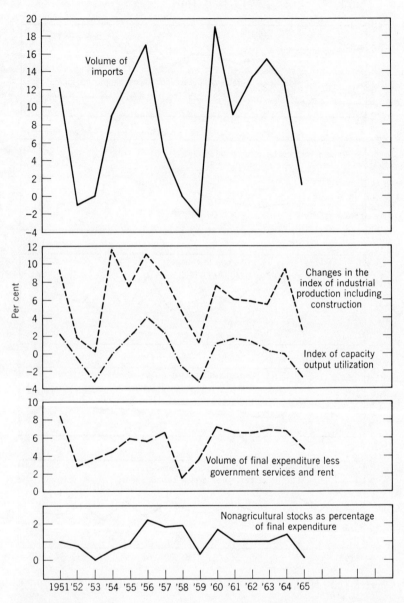

**Chart 5–11**  France: changes in imports and domestic activity, 1951–1965.

## Germany

Germany's GNP at constant prices increased on average by 6½ per cent a year over the period 1950–1966. At the beginning of the period, unemployed resources were substantial, permitting a particularly rapid rate of expansion; but as full employment was approached. the rate of expansion tended to slow down (Chart 5–12). Superimposed on this general trend were cycles in the rate of expansion (especially high rates in 1951, 1955, 1960, and 1964; especially low rates in 1954, 1958, and 1963). Up to 1958, these cycles tended to parallel those in the GNP of all OECD countries combined.

Only a small part of the fluctuation was due to harvest variations; nonagricultural output (in principle, the more relevant series for the present purpose) shows much the same pattern as total output (Chart 5-12). Of the fluctuations in nonagricultural output, the greater part was directly due to fluctuations in manufacturing output [1]. This is convenient for later analysis in that the series for industrial or manufacturing output, for which monthly and quarterly data are available, can be used as a proxy for total nonagricultural output.

In Chart 5-13, the trend of industrial output is shown, along with an estimate of the "full employment" or "capacity" level of output. To obtain the latter, actual output was adjusted by the use of labor market indicators. It was found that there was a fair correlation ($R^2 = 0.73$) between the yearly change in industrial output and the yearly change in the percentage of unfilled vacancies less the percentage of unemployed. Full employment, of capacity output, was arbitrarily defined as the level of output that would be expected with unemployment of 1 per cent. If actual output is adjusted to the full employment level in accordance with the above relationship, the result is the series of dots on curve A in Chart 5-13, approximated by the straight line. The resultant index is shown as curve B [2] .

---

[1] On Chart 5–12, the scale for nonagricultural and manufacturing output corresponds to the respective contributions to total GNP.

[2] This index may overestimate the degree of slack in the early years; labor was then in excess supply, but there may have been insufficient capital equipment to provide full employment. An independent estimate of the degree of capital utilization shows much the same cyclical movements, but a different trend. The latter estimate (by R. Krengel in *Vierteljahrsheft zu Wirtschaftsforschung*, 1964) is based on an estimate of the capital stock derived from a cumulation of industrial investment; the trend in output is compared with this estimate of capacity.

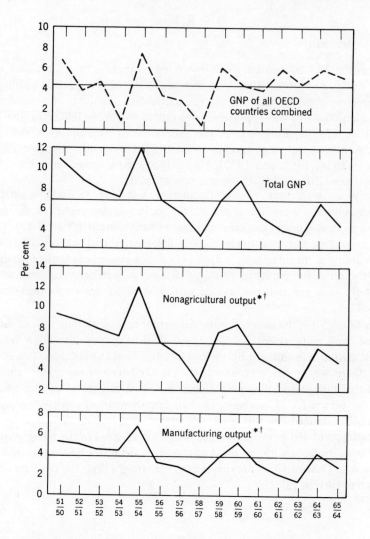

**Chart 5–12**    Germany: fluctuations in output, 1950–1965*.
(Percentage rates of change between calender years.)

*Expressed as contributions to percentage change in GNP.

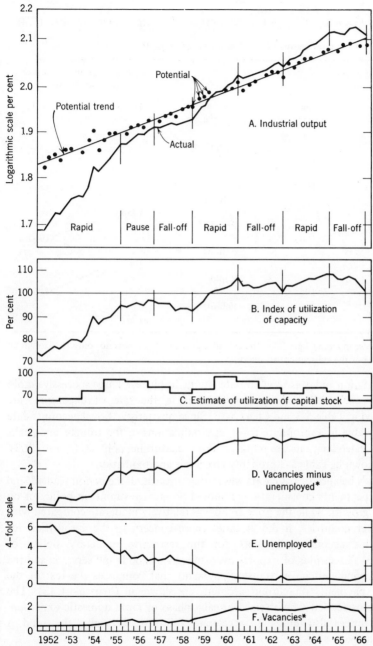

**Chart 5–13** Germany: actual output, potential output, and Underutilization of capacity, 1952–1966.

*As percentage of total labor force.

TABLE 5-3    Germany: Dating of Cyclical Turning Points, 1952–1967.

| Dating by Quarters | | | Approximation in terms of calendar years | |
|---|---|---|---|---|
| Trough | Peak | | Trough | Peak |
| 1952.1 | | Rapid | 1952 | |
| | 1955.4 | Passive | | 1956 |
| | 1957.2 | Fall-off | | 1957 |
| 1959.1 | | Rapid | 1958 | |
| | 1961.1 | Fall-off | | 1961 |
| 1963.1 | | Rapid | 1963* | |
| | 1965.2 | Fall-off | | 1965 |
| 1966.4 | | | 1967 | |

\* As will be seen from Chart 5-13, the calendar year 1963 contains not only the trough but the beginning of the subsequent recovery.

The utilization index is used to date the main phases. Three successive rapid expansions, each followed by a falling off in the rate of expansion, are distinguished in Table 5-3 and Chart 5-13. Since quarterly national accounts data are not available in appropriate form, approximations of the troughs and peaks in terms of calendar years are required. For most turning points (but not 1963), the years shown in Table 5-3 probably give a fair approximation.

Germany's balance of payments was strong throughout the period studied, and balance of payments considerations imposed no great restraint on policy or on the rate of growth. While the price trend was relatively moderate compared with that in other countries, it did at times cause concern to the authorities; for instance, this accounted in part for the restrictive monetary policy of 1965–1966. Ths surplus of exports over imports of goods and services, and the steadily growing deficit on transfer payments that comprises the rest of the balance of payments on current account, are shown in Chart 5-14 [3]. The export surplus tended to worsen after each phase of rapid domestic expanson. The rise in prices also tended to accelerate, following, typically, the trend of output with a year's lag.

[3] In most years total capital movements were also a positive item in the overall balance.

CHRONOLOGICAL ANALYSIS

Changes in final expenditure by main categories during each of the phases outlined earlier are given in Table 5-4. The changes shown are between selected calendar years, rates of change being expressed (since the periods differ in length) as annual rates. In Table 5-5 and Chart 5-15, the same data are displayed in another form, the change in each item being expressed as the contribution it made to the annual average percentage change in final expenditure over each period. This permits a first analysis of the causes of fluctuations.

*Rapid expansion, 1952–1956.* Over these years, the expansion was very rapid, GNP at constant prices growing by 8½ per cent a year. The main expansionary forces clearly were the rise in exports (19 per cent a year) and in investment expenditure (14½ per cent). As a result, there was a very substantial, sustained increase in consumer expenditure (8½ per cent a year), and a rise in imports that was even more rapid (though smaller in absolute magnitude) than the rise in exports.

*Moderate expansion, 1956–1957.* This phase is not perfectly represented by the annual national accounts figures (compare Charts 13 and 15). It is clear that the main reason for the moderate growth was the weaker trend in investment. This may have been connected with the tightening of monetary policy which took place from the middle of 1956 (see later section of this chapter subtitled Monetary Policy).

*Falling-off in expansion, 1957–1958.* The main factor in this period was the pause in the expansion of exports. Investment demand remained relatively weak, though there was the beginning of a revival in private investment. An inventory cycle, originating in the previous period, seems to have been a minor contributing factor.

*Renewed expansion, 1958–1961.* The 1952–1956 experience was repeated on a more moderate scale (an increase in GNP of 7 per cent a year). Both export demand and investment expenditure again rose substantially (10 and 11 per cent a year, respectively), bringing in their wake renewed expansions in consumer expenditure (6½ per cent) and imports (14½ per cent).

*Falling-off in expansion, 1961–1963.* The rate of increase in GNP was halved (3½ per cent a year). Exports slackened (7 per cent a year increase against 10 per cent in the previous period). But the main factor appears to have been another weakening of investment demand (which again may have been connected with the tighter monetary policy).

*Rapid expansion, 1963–1965.* Investment demand recovered (9½ per cent annual increase, against 4½ per cent in the preceding period), and exports rose

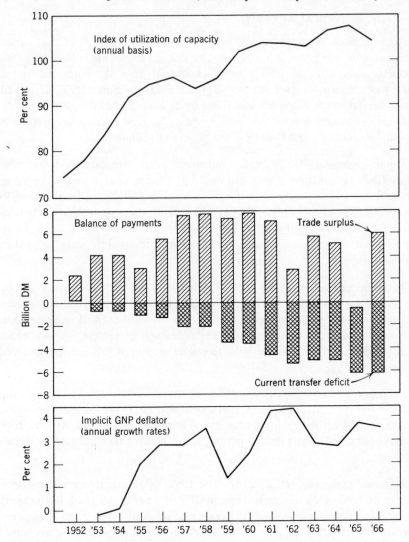

**Chart 5–14**   Germany: the balance of payments and the trend of prices, 1952–1966.

rather faster (9 per cent against 7 per cent). For the first time in a period of rapid expansion, consumer demand rose as rapidly as GNP [4].

[4] For further discussion, see the later section on consumer expenditure in Germany.

*Falling-off in expansion, 1965 onward.* At the time of writing it seemed likely that GNP over the years 1965–1967 would show an increase of less than 2 per cent a year–the greatest slowing down so far. Exports continued to rise rapidly. But investment demand started to decline in 1966; one major factor in these changes probably was monetary policy.

### EFFECTS OF FISCAL POLICY

Government expenditure on goods and services has been on a rising trend–most rapid in the years 1957–1963 and reduced to small proportions in 1966 (Table 5–4). Tax rates in most years were lowered, thus tending to offset the automatic effect of rising values of GNP on tax yields [5].

An estimate of the impact on the economy of changes in the government budget is shown in Chart 5–16 (for the period 1955–1965 only). It represents the increase each year in total government domestic spending *less* the estimated impact on personal spending of the increase in personal taxes, the net result being multiplied by the estimated value of the multiplier and expressed as a percentage of GNP [6].

Fiscal policy was hardly used as a way of influencing general demand, but in some years the fiscal impact was in fact anticyclical. In 1958, it was strongly so–partly as a result of the increase in defense spending and partly because of automatic effects. Without these influences, there might have been an actual fall in GNP in that year. Again if it had not been for the fiscal effects in 1961–1963 (a phase of falling-off in expansion) the rise in GNP might have been 2 per cent a year less than it was. In 1965, too, the effect was strongly expansionary [7].

### MONETARY POLICY

Chart 5-17 shows (along with the annual changes in private investment) the size of the money supply, the change in bank credit to the private sector, and the course of interest rates. Although these data are hardly adequate as quantitative indications of the impact of monetary policy, they may provide some indication of the direction of its effect. Changes in private investment are further analyzed below.

---

[5] The automatic effects were contractive even if the effect of rising prices on government expenditure is included as an automatic effect.

[6] These are crude estimates by Dr. Bent Hansen in connection with his OECD study of fiscal policy. The estimates shown do not allow for the effect of taxation on corporate income and corporate finance. In 1955 and 1956, tax changes reduced the sums available to companies by an amount equivalent to ½ per cent of GNP; and in 1958, 1962, and 1963, tax changes increased them by a like amount.

[7] This does not mean that the net effect was necessarily stabilizing. The pressure of demand was high, and measures to correct it were later deemed necessary.

TABLE 5-4  Germany: Annual Average Percentage Rates of Change in Final Expenditure and its Components, 1952 to 1966* (Based on data at constant 1954 prices)

| | 1952 to 1956 | 1956 to 1957 | 1957 to 1958 | 1958 to 1961 | 1961 to 1963 | 1963 to 1965 | 1965 to 1966 | 1952 to 1966 |
|---|---|---|---|---|---|---|---|---|
| Consumer expenditure | 8.7 | 6.2 | 4.8 | 6.4 | 4.5 | 5.8 | 3.2 | 6.9 |
| Government expenditure on goods and services | .1.8 | 4.3 | 8.3 | 8.3 | 10.2 | 2.7 | 0.3 | 5.5 |
| Gross fixed asset formation | 14.6 | 0.5 | 6.2 | 11.2 | 4.3 | 9.4 | 0.6 | 9.4 |
| Of which: Government construction | 20.9 | 3.5 | 12.3 | 9.8 | 16.6 | 8.5 | 4.0 | 13.4 |
| Residential construction | 10.8 | 1.2 | 3.0 | 7.8 | 0.8 | 5.8 | 3.9 | 6.6 |
| Other construction | 18.4 | 3.6 | 6.5 | 8.4 | 0.7 | 9.2 | 1.3 | 9.6 |
| Machinery and equipment | 14.2 | -1.2 | 6.3 | 13.7 | 4.3 | 10.8 | -1.2 | 9.7 |
| Change in stocks of goods (as a percentage of GNP) | (2.0) | (2.5) | (1.7) | (2.3) | (0.9) | (1.7) | (0.3) | (1.8) |
| Exports of goods and services | 19.1 | 16.2 | 3.6 | 10.1 | 6.9 | 8.7 | 10.4 | 11.1 |
| Of which: Goods | 18.0 | 15.0 | 2.2 | 11.2 | 7.7 | 9.3 | 11.4 | 11.0 |
| Total final expenditure | 10.1 | 7.2 | 4.4 | 8.4 | 4.9 | 7.2 | 2.6 | 7.6 |
| Imports of goods and services | 21.0 | 15.0 | 9.5 | 14.5 | 9.8 | 12.8 | 2.1 | 13.4 |
| Of which: Goods | 19.4 | 14.4 | 9.6 | 14.8 | 10.9 | 13.8 | 1.6 | 13.1 |
| Gross national product | 8.5 | 5.8 | 3.3 | 7.0 | 3.8 | 5.7 | 2.7 | 6.6 |

Sources: Based on data in *Wirtschaft und Statistik*, October 1963 and January 1967, and in W. Kirner, *Ermittlung von Investitionsgrössenordnungen für Wirtschaftsbereiche*, Berlin, 1965.
* Changes between years selected as representing turning points.

TABLE 5.5 Germany: Contribution of Components to Changes in Final Expenditure, 1952–1966 (Contribution to Annual Average Percentage Rates of Change; Based on Data at Constant 1954 Prices)

| | 1952 to 1956 | 1956 to 1957 | 1957 to 1958 | 1958 to 1961 | 1961 to 1963 | 1963 to 1965 | 1965 to 1966 | 1952 to 1966 |
|---|---|---|---|---|---|---|---|---|
| Consumer expenditure | 4.5 | 3.1 | 2.4 | 3.2 | 2.2 | 2.8 | 1.5 | 3.5 |
| Government expenditure on goods and services | 0.2 | 0.4 | 0.8 | 0.9 | 1.1 | 0.3 | 0.0 | 0.7 |
| Gross fixed asset formation | 2.5 | 0.1 | 1.1 | 2.1 | 0.8 | 1.9 | 0.1 | 1.7 |
| *Of which:* Government construction | 0.3 | 0.1 | 0.2 | 0.2 | 0.3 | 0.2 | 0.1 | 0.2 |
| Residential construction | 0.4 | 0.0 | 0.1 | 0.3 | 0.0 | 0.2 | 0.1 | 0.3 |
| Other construction | 0.5 | 0.1 | 0.2 | 0.3 | 0.0 | 0.3 | 0.0 | 0.2 |
| Machinery and equipment | 1.3 | -0.1 | 0.6 | 1.4 | 0.5 | 1.2 | -0.1 | 1.0 |
| Change in stocks of goods | -0.1 | 0.6 | -0.6 | 0.2 | -0.4 | 0.7 | -1.1 | -0.2 |
| Exports of goods and services | 3.1 | 3.2 | 0.7 | 2.0 | 1.3 | 1.7 | 2.1 | 1.9 |
| *Of which:* Goods | 2.6 | 2.4 | 0.4 | 1.8 | 1.2 | 1.5 | 2.0 | 1.7 |
| Total final expenditure | 10.1 | 7.2 | 4.4 | 8.4 | 4.9 | 7.2 | 2.6 | 7.6 |
| Imports of goods and services | 2.8 | 2.5 | 1.7 | 2.7 | 1.9 | 2.8 | 0.5 | 2.3 |
| *Of which:* Goods | 2.1 | 1.9 | 1.3 | 2.1 | 1.7 | 2.4 | 0.3 | 1.8 |
| Gross national product | 7.4 | 4.8 | 2.7 | 5.7 | 3.0 | 4.5 | 2.1 | 5.4 |

167

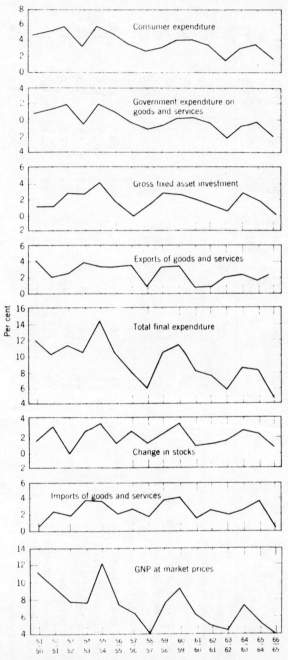

**Chart 5–15** Germany: contribution of components to changes in final expenditure, 1950–1966.

168

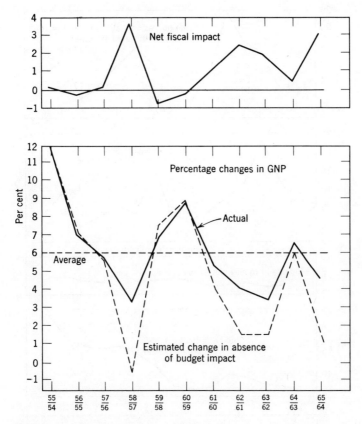

**Chart 5–16**    Germany: net impact on the economy of changes in the government budget, 1955–1965.
For description, see text.

## Analysis of Main Demand Components

### EXPORTS

Annual changes in the volume of exports are compared in Chart 5-18 with annual changes in the weighted average of the imports of Germany's trading partners (described on the chart as demand in export markets). Each falling-off in German exports was associated with a falling-off in demand abroad; the sharpest decrease was in 1958.

The correspondence, however, was far from exact. Until 1959, Germany increased her share of export markets fairly consistently, by 6–8 per cent a year (Chart 5-18, center). After 1959, when full employment had been attained,

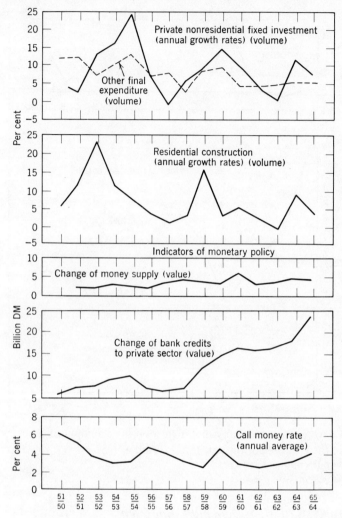

**Chart 5–17**  Germany: private investment and indicators of monetary policy, 1950–1965.

the increase ceased. Also, phases of particularly rapid domestic expansion (as in 1955 and 1964) were associated with a minor loss of export markets; and a falling-off in domestic expansion (as in 1958 and 1963) was associated with a minor gain. The loss in 1962 might be explained by the revaluation of the mark in 1961.

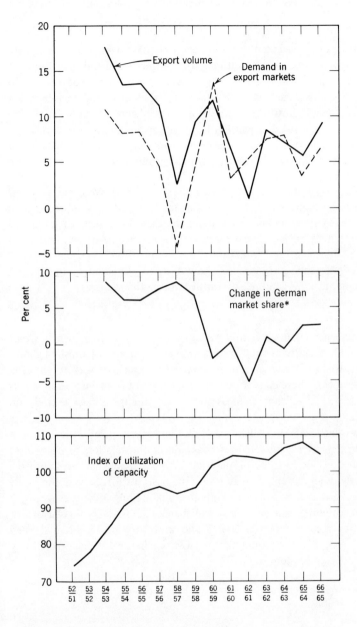

**Chart 5–18** Germany: changes in volume of exports and export markets, 1951–1965.

*Difference between actual change and change in markets.

INVESTMENT

Most of the phases of investment growth have extended over three years, both upward and downwards, whereas those of "other" demand have not. A comparison of Charts 5-17 and 5-18 suggests that the relation to the growth of exports was somewhat closer; however, the correspondence here was far from exact, and not all of the turning points could conceivably be explained in these terms. An export-led expansion is a fashionable hypothesis, though its logic is far from self-evident, particularly for Germany where the balance of payments did not, as in the United Kingdom, impose phases of "stop–go" on economic policy.

Other possible hypotheses seem to be either that there were more or less autonomous cycles in investment, possibly associated with the unprecedented rapid growth, particularly in the early years, or that the effects of monetary policy were extremely severe. Uncertainty on this score may be less important for forecasting, inasmuch as "intentions" data are utilized. The present data suggest that if indicators of intentions show a trend unrelated to the current trend of the economy, this is no reason for distrusting them.

INVENTORIES

Changes in final sales (that is, excluding stocks) of goods are shown in Chart 5-19 together with changes in total stocks, changes in stocks of finished goods, and changes in stocks of materials. An estimate of changes in stocks of *imported materials* suggests that these constitute only a small part of the changes in stocks of all materials [8], and that changes in stocks impinge almost entirely on domestic output.

The data in Chart 5-19 show little sign of an inventory cycle of the kind that would be expected, or of any obvious rationale in the relation of changes of stocks of finished goods to those in materials. Some available current indicators of the recent rate of stockbuilding may give some basis for forecasting. But while these data reveal a tendency for a year of high stockbuilding to be followed by a year of low stockbuilding, and *vice versa*, the changes are not very regular. If, for lack of a better assumption, the changes in inventory formation had been assumed to be zero, then this would have been wrong in most years, typically by the equivalent of ½–1 per cent of GNP.

---

[8] the ratio of imports of industrial materials to industrial output was calculated. An excess of the ratio over the three-year moving average was taken to reflect an increase in stocks of imported materials.

CONSUMER EXPENDITURE

Chart 5-20 shows that consumer expenditure grew at rates varying between 4 and 11 per cent a year. As a first hypothesis, it might be expected that these variations were related to the rate of increase of nonconsumption expenditure, but, in fact, thére was no obvious relation. There were some large swings in the rate of change of nonconsumption (for example, in 1958 and 1959) without any observable effect on the growth of consumption.

The explanation seems to lie in the rather curious behavior of savings. Chart 5-20 shows annual changes in real personal income before tax (a curve clearly reflecting, to some extent, the swings in nonconsumption expenditure); annual changes in the portion of personal income left after deduction of taxes (the changes have in fact been minor); and changes in real income after taxes. Over the long term, the ratio of saving to income after taxes appears relatively stable, so that personal savings can be explained fairly well in terms of disposable income [9]. But the year-to-year residuals in such a calculation are large, erratic, and frequently anticyclical. When the curves for changes in savings (as estimated from the behavior of disposable income), the actual changes in savings, and the unexplained residual are examined, it is apparent that the residual helps to account for the low consumption increase in 1954 and 1963 and the high one in 1959. (The curves are shown on an inverted scale for ease of comparison with the consumption series). The behavior of the residual therefore requires an explanation; in some other countries, the behavior of noncorporate investment has been an important factor.

IMPORTS

An attempt was made to explain changes in nonfood imports in terms of (a) expenditure changes (a weighted average of manufacturing output—75 per cent—and of final expenditure series—25 per cent—was used), (b) the pressure of demand, (the change in new orders less deliveries, expressed as a ratio to deliveries was used as a measure, lagged by three quarters; and (c) price changes (rate of change of the rate of domestic prices to import prices, lagged by three quarters). The equation was fitted to annual data for the years 1954–1964 ($R^2 = 0.910$): the results are shown in Chart 5-21.

---

[9] The estimating equation was:

$$\Delta S' = -1.22 + 0.38 \, \Delta \, Yd - 2.09 \, \Delta r \quad [R^2 = 0.696]$$
$$(1.27) \, (0.11) \qquad (0.35)$$

where $Yd$ equals total disposable personal income in constant prices and $r$ represents employee compensation as a percentage of total personal income.

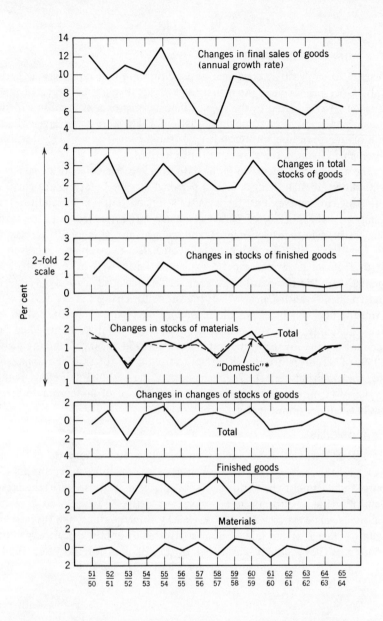

**Chart 5–19** Germany: changes in stocks of goods (volume), 1950–1965. (Expressed as annual percentage rate of GNP.)
*The differences between total and domestic changes are estimated changes in stocks of imported materials. See text.

174

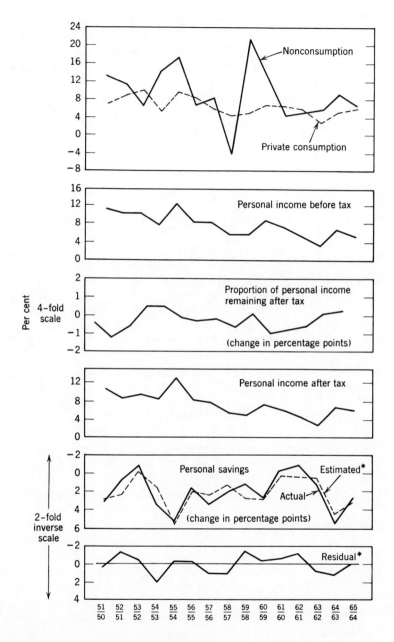

**Chart 5–20** Germany: annual rates of change in volume of consumers' expenditure, 1950–1965.

*For the method of estimation, see text.

175

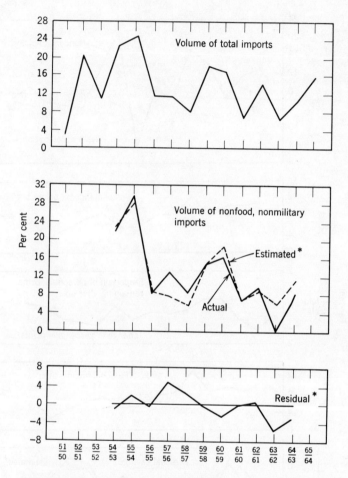

**Chart 5–21** Germany: annual rates of change in imports, 1950–1965.

*For the method of estimation, see text.

Expenditure changes lead to more than proportionate changes in imports (the parameter was estimated to be 1.22). While this might have been expected, the disproportionate effects should probably have been picked up by the pressure of the demand variable, for which the indicator used may not have been a satisfactory measure.

## Italy

In the period 1955 to 1965, Italy's GNP at constant prices grew at an annual average rate of 5.3 per cent. There was no year in which output failed to register an increase, but there were distinct variations in the rate of increase (Chart 5-22). In 1955 and again from 1959 to 1963, the rate of increase exceeded the average; in most other years (1956, 1958, and, especially 1964 and 1965), it was less than the average.

Part of the fluctuation was due to harvest factors; for present purposes these are neglected. As shown in Chart 5-22, the variations in the annual rates of growth of nonagricultural output resemble closely variations in industrial output. Since figures for industrial output are available quarterly (and seasonally adjusted), they are used to define turning points.

In many countries, changes in the percentage of unemployment provide a good indicator of cyclical fluctuations in the pressure of demand. For Italy, however, this did not seem to be true for the period studied [1], and Rey's index of capacity utilization in the "industrial-production-index industries" was used [2]. The potential of full capacity rate of growth of output is estimated as the rate of growth between successive peaks of output for each of the 22 series included in the production index. These estimated potential rates of growth, which vary between the component series and may also vary between periods, were aggregated to provide a potential rate for the total of industrial production.

---

[1] There appears to be little relation between the fluctuations on the rate of growth of output and changes in the percentage of unemployment (Chart 2–23). The reasons for this lack of relationship have not been fully explored, although inadequate and variable coverage of the statistical series, particularly for unemployment, may be one factor.

[2] Up to and including 1964, the index was taken from G. Rey, "Una misura della capacità produttiva utilizatta nel settore industriale," *L'Industria,* No. 3, 1965, where the method of calculation is fully described. For 1965 and 1966, the index was estimated by extrapolating the implied potential rate of growth and comparing it with actual changes in the industrial production index.

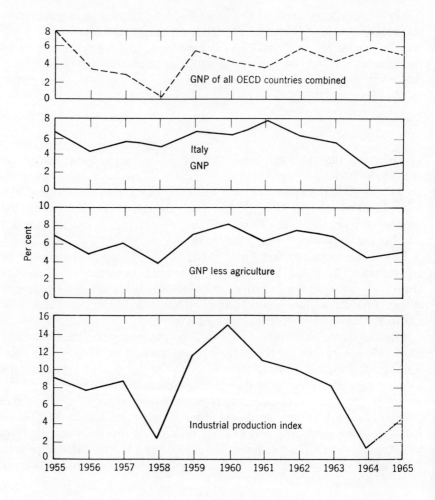

**Chart 5–22**    Italy: Fluctuations in output, 1955–1965.* (Percentage rates of change between calendar years.)

The percentage variation of actual output about this estimated potential rate thus provides an index of capacity utilization (Chart 5-23). This index was used to determine the turning points shown in Table 5-6.

TABLE 5-6    Italy: Dating of Cyclical Turning Points, 1955–1965

| Dating by Quarters | | | Approximation in terms of calendar years | |
|---|---|---|---|---|
| Trough | Peak | | Trough | Peak |
| | 1955.1 | Flat | | 1954 |
| | \| | | | \| |
| | 1957.2 | Downturn | | 1957 |
| 1958.2 or 3 | | Upturn | 1958* | |
| | 1960.3 | | | 1960 |
| | \| | Flat | | \| |
| | 1963.2 or 3 | Downturn | | 1963 |
| 1965.1 | | Upturn | 1965 | |

* Calendar year gives poor indication of peak or trough.

## Analysis of Aggregate Expenditures

In general, annual national expenditure data, at constant prices (Table 5-7) have been used to analyze the cyclical experience of the period 1955–1965. But annual data—the only data systematically available for most of the period—often cut across the different phases distinguished by the index of slack in Chart 5-23, particularly in the downturn from the second quarter of 1957 to the third quarter of 1958. Therefore, wherever possible, yearly figures have been supplemented by partial indicators available on a quarterly basis, as shown in Chart 5.24.

### CHRONOLOGICAL ANALYSIS

*First downturn: 1957 second quarter to mid-1958.* From 1954 to 1957, preceding the first downturn, GNP was increasing by 5.5 per cent a year (Table 5-7). The fastest rising component was exports of goods and services (average increase, 17 per cent a year). Gross fixed investment—notably dwellings—also rose fast, and consumer expenditure advanced steadily (4 per cent a year).

Between 1957 and 1958 the rate of increase of GDP slowed to 4.9 per cent; the main factors in the slowing down were investment and exports. Investment in dwellings rose by only 3 per cent (previously 15 per cent a year), and investment in machinery and equipment fell by 5½ per cent (previous rate of increase 8½ per cent). As shown in Table 5-8, these two factors alone contributed heavily to the change in pace of final expenditure—from an increase of 6.0 per cent in 1954–1957 to 4.8 per cent in 1957–1958.

TABLE 5–7 Italy: Annual Average Percentage Rates of Change in Final Expenditure and its Components, 1954 to 1965 (Based on Data in 1954 Prices)

| | 1954 to 1957 | 1957 to 1958 | 1958 to 1960 | 1960 to 1963 | 1963 to 1965 | 1954 to 1965 |
|---|---|---|---|---|---|---|
| Consumer expenditure | 4.2 | 4.0 | 5.3 | 7.4 | 2.2 | 4.9 |
| Of which: Food and rent | 3.5 | 5.4 | 4.9 | 5.1 | 2.3 | 4.2 |
| Other | 5.0 | 2.6 | 5.6 | 7.0 | 2.1 | 5.5 |
| Government expenditure on goods and services | 2.3 | 5.5 | 4.2 | 5.1 | 3.9 | 3.9 |
| Gross fixed asset formation | 9.3 | 2.8 | 10.6 | 9.8 | -7.4 | 5.9 |
| Of which: Public works | -0.1 | 19.7 | 10.9 | -0.5 | 5.0 | 4.3 |
| Residential construction | 14.7 | 3.2 | 4.2 | 12.2 | -0.2 | 8.2 |
| Other construction | 11.4 | 12.2 | 8.1 | 9.3 | -6.9 | 6.7 |
| Machinery and equipment | 7.6 | 5.5 | 16.8 | 11.6 | 15.7 | 4.3 |
| Change in stocks of goods* | (0.65) | (0.59) | (1.07) | (1.51) | (0.84) | (0.99) |
| Exports of goods and services† | 17.0 | 12.9 | 18.7 | 11.8 | 15.7 | 15.2 |
| Total final expenditure | 6.0 | 4.8 | 8.1 | 8.0 | 2.3 | 6.1 |
| Imports of goods and services† | 11.8 | 3.9 | 23.9 | 17.8 | -2.1 | 12.0 |
| Gross national product at market prices | 5.5 | 4.9 | 6.4 | 6.5 | 3.1 | 5.4 |

Based on data in OECD, *National Accounts Statistics*, 1956–1965, Paris 1967, and on national sources.

* As a percentage of GNP.
† Including factor income.

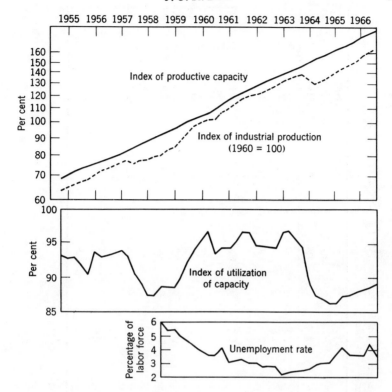

**Chart 5–23**    Italy: Productive capacity, and actual output, and the unemployment rate, 1955–1965.

A more precise dating of the downturn that occurred during 1957 and, in particular, any precise account of the sequence of any of the changes in demand is difficult. In an attempt to bring out the main features, quarterly data are shown in Chart 5-24 [3].

From Chart 5-24 it appears that the rate of growth of industrial output began to slow down about mid-1956 and continued to decline until the third quarter

[3] The chart shows quarterly percentage changes in the volume of industrial output, imports, and exports. Since these are rates of change, the timing of peaks and troughs for the series shown differ from that indicated in Chart 5–23, which is used to define the different phases of development during the period 1955–1965. For this reason, positions corresponding to turning points in output, imports, and exports are also shown on Chart 5–34. To determine these positions, the average of the quarterly rates of change for the whole period was calculated for each series; then the point between two successive quarters when the observed quarterly rate of change rose above this average rate, or vice versa, was identified. In the first case, the turning point was identified as a peak, and in the second as a trough.

TABLE 5-8  Italy: Contribution of Components to Changes in Final Expenditure, 1954 to 1965 (Contribution to Annual Average Percentage Rates of Change—Based on Data in 1954 Prices)

| | 1954 to 1957 | 1957 to 1958 | 1958 to 1960 | 1960 to 1963 | 1963 to 1965 | 1954 to 1965 |
|---|---|---|---|---|---|---|
| Consumer expenditure | 2.6 | 2.3 | 3.0 | 4.0 | 1.2 | 2.8 |
| Of which:  Food and rent | 1.1 | 1.6 | 1.4 | 1.4 | 0.6 | 1.2 |
| Other | 1.5 | 0.7 | 1.6 | 2.6 | 0.6 | 1.6 |
| Government expenditure on goods and services | 0.3 | 0.7 | 0.6 | 0.6 | 0.4 | 0.5 |
| Gross fixed asset formation | 1.6 | 0.6 | 2.0 | 1.9 | -1.4 | 1.0 |
| Of which: Public works | – | 0.4 | 0.3 | – | 0.1 | 0.1 |
| Residential construction | 0.7 | 0.2 | 0.3 | 0.7 | – | 0.4 |
| Other construction | 0.3 | 0.4 | 0.3 | 0.3 | -0.2 | 0.2 |
| Machinery and equipment | 0.6 | -0.4 | 1.2 | 1.0 | -1.3 | 0.3 |
| Change in stocks of goods | 0.2 | – | 0.6 | -0.1 | -0.1 | 0.1 |
| Exports of goods and services* | 1.3 | 1.2 | 2.0 | 1.5 | 2.2 | 1.7 |
| Total final expenditure | 6.0 | 4.8 | 8.1 | 8.0 | 2.3 | 6.1 |
| Imports of goods and services* | -1.0 | -0.4 | -2.4 | -2.3 | 0.3 | -1.3 |
| Gross national product at market prices | 5.0 | 4.5 | 5.8 | 5.7 | 2.6 | 4.6 |

Source:  See Table 5-7
*National Accounts Statistics.*
* Including factor income.

of 1957 [4], although there was never an absolute fall in output. The rate at which exports were rising also lessened over the same period; no leading or lagging of output can easily be discerned. The two indicators of investment demand, shown in Chart 5-24 are the indices of the output of investment goods and the volume of imports of investment goods. These two series slowed down a little later than total output and exports, and were falling throughout most of the period of downturn. It would seem then that the check to exports was the first element in this downturn, followed very shortly by falling rates of investment, which continued well into the period, even though the rise in exports had quickened in pace [5].

*First upturn: mid-1958 to third quarter of 1960.* After about mid-1958, output picked up rapidly (Chart 5-22); industrial production rose to the third quarter of 1960 at an annual rate of 13.7 per cent. The GNP rose at an annual rate of 6.4 per cent between the years 1958 and 1960 (Table 5-7). The main factors in the upturn were investment in machinery and equipment, exports, and stockbuildng. The rate of increase in consumer expenditure also rose quite sharply, suggesting a multiplier effect. The marked change in the rate of stockbuilding is difficult to interpret [6]. On a year-to-year basis, there was little change in the rate between 1957 and 1958 or between 1958 and 1959; it was only in 1960, the peak year of this upturn, that the rate changed sharply.

As shown in Chart 5-24, exports rose sharply in the early part of this period and, to judge from the output series for investment goods, investment demand began to contribute materially, two or three quarters later, to the recovery in total demand.

*Plateau: end 1960 to mid-1963.* The moderately high rate of increase of output—6½ per cent a year—achieved during the upturn was maintained for more than three years.

The composition of demand during these three years of sustained "boom" underwent a significant shift toward consumption; for the first time since 1954, consumer expenditure rose, on average, almost as fast as final expenditure (Table 5-7). An increasing share of resources was devoted to fixed investment, which expanded at an annual rate of some 10 per cent; a slower pace of exports and a

[4] Although the rate of growth of output was falling over this period, it was only during the downturn from the second quarter of 1957 to mid-1958 that it fell below the *capacity* rate of growth of output.

[5] A number of Italian observers have attributed the first downturn to the check in U. S. and European demand, hence in Italian exports. See, for example, F. Di Fenezio and G. Miconi, "Cycles brefs enregistrés en Italie pendant les vingt dernières années," *Revue Économique*, N. 3 May 1965. In that article, this first downturn period is referred to as the "European Cycle."

[6] The recorded figures of stockbuilding are probably the least reliable element in the Italian national accounts.

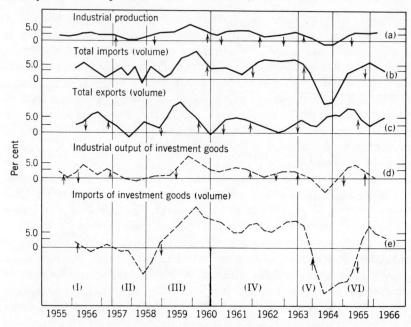

**Chart 5–24** Italy: Rates of growth of economic indicators, by quarters, 1955–1965. (Weighted moving averages).

Note: Arrow pointing up = peak; arrow pointing down = trough.

constant rate of stockbuilding were associated with this shift. Prices rose sharply between 1960 and 1963: the GNP deflator increased by as much as 5.9 per cent at an annual rate; that is, faster than in any earlier period since 1954.

*Second downturn: mid-1963 to first quarter of 1965.* The second downturn was the most severe check experienced by the Italian economy during the 10-year period. From mid-1963 to the first quarter of 1965, GNP rose at an annual rate of only 1.8 per cent and industrial production did not rise at all. The index of capacity utilization fell sharply, from 96½ to 85 (Chart 5-23).

On a year-to-year basis, the check to rising expenditure and output between 1963 and 1965 is striking, even though demand began to pick up in the course of 1965. The major factor associated with the downturn of the economy was investment in machinery and equipment, which fell at an annual rate of almost 16 per cent between 1963 and 1965.

The contributions of investments, exports, and imports to changes in GNP are illustrated by the curves in Chart 5-25 [7]. Investment in machinery and

[7] Quarterly estimates of the major components of GNP are available beginning with 1961.

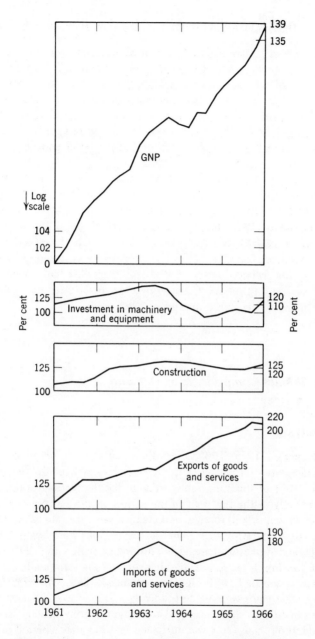

**Chart 5–25**  Italy: Indices of gross national product and components, quarterly, 1961–1965 (1960 = 100).

185

equipment, which had risen rapidly throughout 1961 and 1962, was checked suddenly in the first quarter of 1963 and remained virtually unchanged until the fourth quarter of the year, when it fell sharply. This fall is reflected also in the sharp decline in the imports of investment goods and of imports generally (Chart 5-24). By contrast, exports of goods and services rose strongly through this period, at an annual rate of 15½ per cent. However, this rise was insufficient to offset the impact of falling investment, and in the latter part of this period real GNP fell in absolute terms.

*Second upturn: first quarter of 1965.* At the time of the Conference, full national accounts data were not available for the year 1966, but Chart 5-25 gives some idea of the principal factors contributing to the expansion which began in the first quarter of 1965. In the main, exports of goods and services led and sustained the increased rate of expansion during much of this period. Although investment stopped falling in the first quarter of 1965, it did not begin to rise steadily until the second quarter of 1966, although GNP had already risen by as much as 6 per cent. In the third quarter of 1966, investment was still well below the peak attained in the fourth quarter of 1963.

## Analysis of Main Components of Demand

### EXPORTS

During the period 1955–1965, the volume of exports of goods grew at an annual average rate of 15.8 per cent, increases varying from 3.2 to 24.2 per cent (Table 5-9). Most of this variation was due to the fluctuations in Italian markets abroad, especially in the first half of the period. In all years but one (1963), the share of Italian exports in foreign markets increased, the rate of increase varying from year to year. Although there is no obvious correlation between the fluctuations and domestic demand conditions as represented by the index of capacity utilization, it seems possible that some of the variation in the growth of exports was associated with domestic demand. Thus, in 1959 and 1965, particularly large gains were made following a year of low capacity utilization; 1961 does not fit into this pattern. Conversely, relatively small gains were made in 1962 and 1964, and a loss was sustained in 1963 after a period of continued high capacity utilization.

Preliminary econometric results relating the growth of markets to actual export behavior tend also to suggest that, as domestic pressure rises, the rate of increase of exports tends to become less great. These results also indicate that relative export price performance may also be a factor accounting for changes in

TABLE  5–9   Italy:   Annual  Percentage  Increases  in  Exports  and  Related  Series,
1955–1965

|      | Growth of volume of exports* | Causes of growth | | Under-utilization of capacity‡ |
|------|------|------|------|------|
|      |      | Growth of market† | Increase in shares | |
| 1955 | 17.0 | 10.5 | 6.5  | −7.43 |
| 1956 | 18.3 | 10.8 | 7.5  | −7.46 |
| 1957 | 14.8 | 8.4  | 6.4  | −7.26 |
| 1958 | 6.2  | 0.5  | 5.7  | −11.95 |
| 1959 | 22.8 | 5.6  | 17.2 | −10.20 |
| 1960 | 20.7 | 12.0 | 7.3  | −5.21 |
| 1961 | 20.0 | 6.1  | 13.9 | −5.07 |
| 1962 | 12.2 | 8.0  | 4.2  | −5.01 |
| 1963 | 3.2  | 8.1  | −4.9 | −4.29 |
| 1964 | 15.0 | 11.4 | 3.6  | −11.20 |
| 1965 | 24.2 | 9.0  | 15.2 | −14.40 |

* Merchandise exports from *Monthly Economic Indicators*.
† Market growth is based on the growth of imports of France, of Germany, of other OECD members, and of countries that are not members of OECD–each group weighted by Italy's exports to these groups.
‡ For description, see text, pp. 176–177 above.

the share of markets abroad. There also seems to have been a sharp stimulus to exports between 1959 and 1961, provided by entry into the Common Market.

INVESTMENT

Investment seems more likely than other elements of demand to have been influenced by official policy. It is therefore appropriate to introduce at this point considerations of both monetary and public works policy. The development of public works has tended to be somewhat countercyclical (see Table 5-7). Thus, between 1954 and 1957–and also between 1960 and 1963–there was virtually no increase in public works when private investment was rising strongly. By contrast, public works rose sharply from 1957 to 1958 when total private investment was increasing only slowly; and between 1963 and 1965, some increase, albeit slight, in public works helped to mitigate the sharp fall in private investment.

For private investment, notably machinery and equipment, the rates of change have varied quite sharply (Chart 5-26). No simple relationship, however, appears between changes in private investment and in the other elements of expenditure taken together, perhaps because of changes in policy. Quarterly changes in the money supply and in credit to the private sector are compared in Chart 5-26 with changes in the value and volume of investment. The fairly close correlation of changes in money supply and in credit with investment does not necessarily give any indication of causality. The fact that the rate of change of

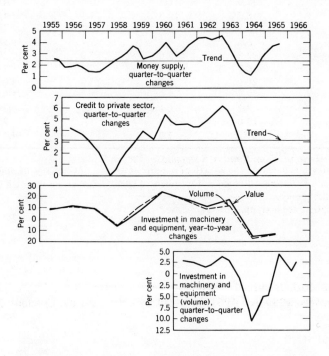

**Chart 5–26**    Italy: rates of change in money supply, credit, and investment, 1955–1965.

credit to the private sector fell and rose between 1956 and 1959 at the same time that the rate of change of investment fell and rose may well reflect a decrease in the demand for credit as the rate of investment was cut back, and *vice versa*. However, it does seem possible to attribute at least part of the variation in the rate of change of investment late in the period to the influence of monetary policy. Thus, although the rate of increase of investment and of credit began to slow down at the beginning of 1963, policy measures taken in the second half of that year to restrict credit must have reinforced the trend.

CONSUMER EXPENDITURES

Annual changes in the volume of consumer spending are compared in Chart 5-27 with changes in the volume of GNP excluding private consumption. The most striking feature is the lack of relationship between these two series. In the period 1955–1961, changes in consumption were remarkably regular notwithstanding the variation in the rates of change of the other components of GNP taken together. Only late in the period did the rate of change of consumption vary. It seems possible that some lagged relationship with GNP excluding consumption could be found; for example, the sharp fall in the rate of change of nonconsumption was followed a year later by a sharp reduction in the rate of growth of consumption.

Changes in consumption are more closely related to changes in the compensation of employees [8] (deflated by the consumer price index), also shown in Chart 5-27. This would suggest that the combined effect on consumer expenditures of changes in tax rates, in the household savings ratio, and in transfer payments was small, and that, in the main, fluctuations in consumer expenditure reflect changes in employment and hours worked [9]. Changes in the volume of consumer expenditure on goods, other than food and rent, are most closely related to changes in the compensation of employees (deflated by consumer price changes) [10].

Changes in stocks of goods and the relationship that these changes may have with such variables as imports and output, are particularly difficult to assess for Italy. Changes in agricultural stocks, associated with harvest fluctuations, are possibly an important component which might mask cyclical changes, but so far no satisfactory method has been found to eliminate changes in agricultural stocks from changes in total stocks. One attempt, which may be worth reconsideration, was made by calculating deviations about a three-year moving average of real agricultural output and imports taken together (Chart 5-28).

---

[8] No official series are available for total personal income or for total personal disposable income.

[9] Systematic data on employment and hours worked over a long period are difficult to obtain (or at best to interpret) for Italy.

[10] A simple relationship between percentage changes in consumption, excluding food and rent, ($C$) and percentage changes in the real compensation of employees ($W$) was obtained: $C = 0.85\ W - 0.66\ (R^2 = 0.95)$.

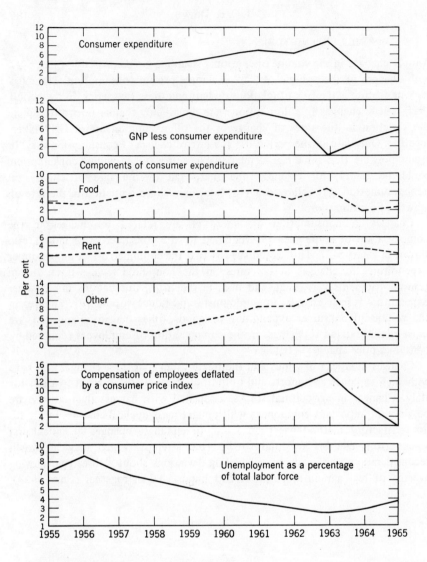

**Chart 5–27**  Italy: annual percentage changes in consumer expenditure and related series, and in unemployment rate.

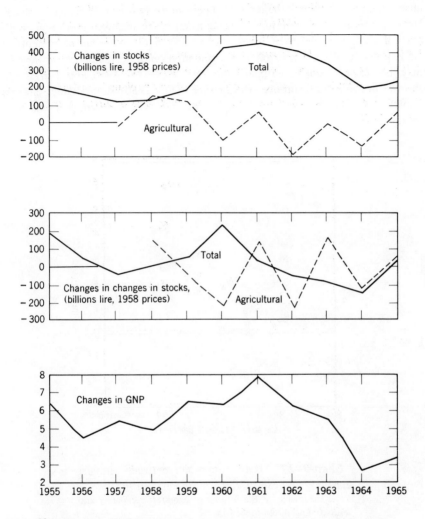

**Chart 5–28**    Italy: annual changes in stocks of goods, 1955–1965.

Chart 5-28 also shows (a) changes in total stocks and (b) changes in these changes, and it compares them with (c) percentage year-to-year changes in NGP. Notwithstanding the inclusion of agricultural stock changes, there is a rough cyclical pattern in the total series, loosely coincident with the movements of GNP, possibly because of involuntary accumulation or decumulation, as the case may be. (For example, compare the two series for 1960 and 1961.) For short-term forecasting purposes, the absence of any explanation of stock changes is particularly acute, given the large swings that have occurred, particularly in recent years.

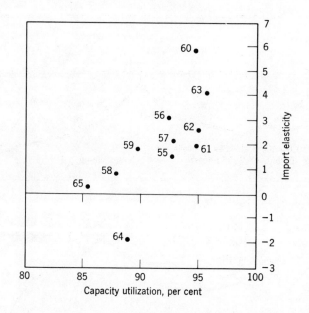

**Chart 5—29**    Italy: relation between import elasticity and capacity utilization, 155–1965.*
* As measured by the indices of productive capacity and industrial production; see Chart 2.

IMPORTS

Chart 5-29 shows the ratio of change in imports to change in GNP (import elasticity) for each year. Imports rise more than proportionately as the degree of capacity utilization becomes fuller.

Some attempts were made to explain annual changes in imports in terms of changes in expenditure, changes in stocks, changes in the pressure of demand, and changes in the relative movement of domestic and import prices. The expenditure component is, of course, the major determinant. It proved somewhat difficult, however, to distinguish the "change in stocks" effect on imports from "pressure of demand" effect.

APPENDIX TABLE A   Italy: Annual Percentage Rates of Change in Components of Final Expenditure, 1955–1965

| | 1955 | 1956 | 1957 | 1958 | 1959 | 1960 | 1961 | 1962 | 1963 | 1964 | 1965 |
|---|---|---|---|---|---|---|---|---|---|---|---|
| Consumer expenditure | 4.2 | 4.3 | 4.1 | 4.0 | 4.7 | 5.9 | 6.9 | 6.3 | 8.9 | 2.3 | 2.1 |
| Government current expenditure | 1.7 | 3.4 | 1.7 | 5.5 | 4.4 | 4.0 | 4.8 | 5.4 | 5.1 | 4.0 | 3.7 |
| Gross fixed asset formation | 12.3 | 6.9 | 8.7 | 2.8 | 8.8 | 12.5 | 11.4 | 10.2 | 8.5 | -6.5 | -8.2 |
| Of which: Residential Construction | 20.8 | 10.8 | 12.8 | 3.2 | 7.6 | 1.0 | 9.2 | 15.4 | 12.1 | 6.0 | -7.0 |
| Other Construction | 9.8 | -1.3 | 10.7 | 15.1 | 11.0 | 11.2 | 7.4 | 7.4 | 1.6 | -2.2 | -2.9 |
| Machinery and Equipment | 8.5 | 9.7 | 4.6 | -5.5 | 10.9 | 23.0 | 15.7 | 8.5 | 10.6 | -17.6 | -13.8 |
| Exports of goods and services | 11.7 | 16.2 | 21.3 | 12.7 | 17.6 | 19.8 | 16.0 | 11.4 | 6.5 | 11.9 | 19.9 |
| Final Sales | 5.7 | 5.5 | 6.0 | 4.8 | 6.6 | 8.3 | 8.6 | 7.6 | 8.1 | 1.9 | 3.0 |
| Final expenditure | 6.8 | 5.2 | 5.8 | 4.8 | 6.8 | 9.2 | 8.5 | 7.3 | 7.7 | 1.5 | 3.1 |
| Imports of goods and services | 9.7 | 13.8 | 11.1 | 3.5 | 11.5 | 37.7 | 14.4 | 15.8 | 22.5 | -5.3 | 0.9 |
| GDP at market prices | 6.5 | 4.5 | 5.3 | 4.9 | 6.4 | 6.4 | 7.8 | 6.2 | 5.5 | 2.7 | 3.3 |
| Index of industrial production | 9.2 | 7.7 | 8.6 | 2.6 | 11.5 | 14.9 | 11.0 | 9.9 | 8.2 | 1.5 | 4.5 |

Sources: Based on data in Organization for Economic Cooperation and Development, *National Accounts Statistics, 1956–1965*, Paris, 1967; *Monthly Economic Indicators*; and Historical Statistics, OECD.

**APPENDIX TABLE B**  Italy: Indicators of Quarterly National Accounts, 1961–1965 (Indices, 1960 = 100)

| Quarters | Gross National product | Imports of goods and services | Exports of goods and services | Investment in machinery and equipment | Investment in construction |
|---|---|---|---|---|---|
| 1961 | | | | | |
| I | 104.8 | 109.3 | 106.0 | 112.0 | 106.7 |
| II | 106.5 | 113.0 | 111.5 | 113.1 | 108.4 |
| III | 108.7 | 117.7 | 119.3 | 117.9 | 109.5 |
| IV | 111.3 | 118.6 | 128.2 | 120.0 | 108.5 |
| 1962 | | | | | |
| I | 112.7 | 126.5 | 128.6 | 122.8 | 112.2 |
| II | 113.6 | 128.9 | 128.0 | 124.0 | 119.0 |
| III | 115.4 | 134.2 | 132.0 | 125.7 | 124.6 |
| IV | 116.3 | 144.1 | 133.8 | 130.0 | 126.8 |
| 1963 | | | | | |
| I | 116.9 | 146.7 | 137.9 | 134.3 | 126.5 |
| II | 120.8 | 162.6 | 138.2 | 140.1 | 128.1 |
| III | 122.3 | 169.4 | 142.3 | 140.6 | 129.7 |
| IV | 123.2 | 174.5 | 140.1 | 140.6 | 132.1 |
| 1964 | | | | | |
| I | 124.6 | 168.5 | 146.1 | 134.6 | 132.8 |
| II | 123.6 | 157.4 | 156.0 | 115.1 | 132.5 |
| III | 123.1 | 149.7 | 157.5 | 105.5 | 131.6 |
| IV | 125.1 | 144.5 | 163.9 | 102.7 | 130.9 |
| 1965 | | | | | |
| I | 125.3 | 147.6 | 177.2 | 94.4 | 127.6 |
| II | 127.9 | 153.8 | 187.0 | 94.8 | 126.1 |
| III | 129.4 | 155.9 | 190.0 | 101.6 | 125.5 |
| IV | 130.9 | 168.5 | 193.2 | 103.8 | 124.2 |

**Source:** ISCO, *Relazione Generale, 1965*, pp. 100–102.

APPENDIX TABLE C   Italy: Index of Slack, 1955–1966*

| Quarters | 1955 | 1956 | 1957 | 1958 | 1959 | 1960 | 1961 | 1962 | 1963 | 1964 | 1965 | 1966 |
|---|---|---|---|---|---|---|---|---|---|---|---|---|
| I | 93.1 | 90.3 | 93.5 | 89.2 | 88.4 | 93.9 | 94.1 | 96.4 | 94.1 | 94.4 | (85.1) | (86.8) |
| II | 92.7 | 93.5 | 93.9 | 87.3 | 88.6 | 95.5 | 94.2 | 94.6 | 96.6 | 88.9 | (85.0) | (87.0) |
| III | 92.8 | 93.2 | 93.1 | 87.2 | 89.7 | 96.6 | 94.9 | 94.4 | 96.6 | 86.1 | (86.1) | (88.4) |
| IV | 91.7 | 93.2 | 90.4 | 88.4 | 92.6 | 93.2 | 96.5 | 94.5 | 95.5 | 85.9 | (86.2) | |

Source: 1955–1964 figures are based on data from *Industria*, No. 3, 1965; 1965–1966 figures are estimates calculated by the OECD Secretariat.

* For description, see text.

# COMMENTS

LUIGI SPAVENTA

University of Perugia

The three papers on France, Germany, and Italy are based on material collected for the purpose of short-term forecasting—the analysis of past cyclical behavior of the three economies being, to some extent, a byproduct. Thus problems which are important for an interpretation of the past, but less relevant for forecasting, were left aside. Moreover, as the task of forecasting appears to be conceived in a rather mechanistic fashion, there is no analysis of structural aspects and of long-term factors which have had, and will have, a quantitative and qualitative influence on short-term developments (for instance, the labor supply situation in Germany and in Italy, or the impact of the Common Market). This also applies to the quantitative relationships between the relevant variables discussed in the papers. Instead of determining structural relationships of the usual kind for consumption, investment, and imports, the attempt is made to establish a line between the rates of change of each of these variables and the rates of change of gross national product (GNP) *minus* the variable to be explained. The results are seldom satisfactory. This is not surprising and does not authorize the inference that useful relationships are actually lacking. As Professor Bert Hickman pointed out in discussion, the procedure followed amounts to working directly on the reduced form of a model, bypassing the analysis of the underlying relationships, and therefore is not always legitimate.

I shall now consider some details. The formal similarity of the three studies, both in the order of presentation and in the methods used, makes it easy to deal with the three of them together.

Cyclical phases for the three countries are determined on the basis of upturns and downturns in the degree of utilization of productive potential. The criterion being correct in principle, the results obtained will clearly be different, depending

197

on how productive potential is measured. The measures adopted are different for the three countries.

For Germany, the ceiling is taken to be *full-employment* output, defined as the level of output associated with unemployment of 1 per cent. Because a measure of full-employment output can be arrived at in different ways, it is a pity that neither the method followed nor the value of the elasticity of output with respect to employment is specified in the paper. For Italy, a *full-capacity* notion is used: the measure of capacity is the one obtained by Dr. Rey, who applied a slightly modified version of the Wharton School method [1]. The measure used for France seems to be a mixture of the measures used for the other two countries: full-capacity output is obtained from the trend between two years in which the pressure of demand for labor was high.

I feel that, at least for Italy, a measure in terms of full-employment output would not yield the same results as one in terms of full capacity. At any rate, it would be desirable to use the same criterion for all countries or, even better, to use each of the three "country-criteria" for all three countries and then compare the results.

In the dating of the cycles, there seems to be a discrepancy for Italy between the dating finally adopted and that resulting from the fluctuations in the index of utilization of capacity: two troughs, although not of great importance, are neglected (February 1956 and January 1961) and the 1963 peak is anticipated by one quarter. When the 1956 trough is included, there is a close enough correspondence between the fluctuations in the index of utilization, based on calendar years, and those of the annual growth rate. For France, this correspondence is closer than it is for Italy. For Germany, however, it is lacking; none of the peaks obtained from the index of slack occur in years with particularly high growth rates, and only two of the troughs correspond to years with particularly low growth rates. This may cast some doubts on the index of slack used in the study, especially when the relative behavior patterns of the different indices used for France and Italy, and the respective growth rates, are considered.

In assessing the contribution of the main components of national expenditure to the growth of GNP, it might have been useful to determine the value of an *ex post* or an *ex ante* multiplier and its fluctuations over the period, in order to show the final effects of public expenditure, exports, and investment. This was done only for public expenditure in Germany, although published estimates are available, at least for Italy [2].

[1] Guido M. Rey, "Una misura della capacità produttiva utilizzata nel settore industriale," *L'Industria* (1965, No. 3).
[2] G. Fuà "Influenza del bilancio pubblico sulla formazione della domanda in Italia, 1955–1963," *Moneta e Credito*, March 1965.

The behavior of *exports* of the three countries is explained with reference to the degree of capacity utilization or demand pressure within the countries and to the behavior of foreign markets. It might be interesting to supplement the analysis with a consideration of changes in relative competitiveness connected with changes in labor costs per unit of output.

As for *investment*, attention is devoted almost exclusively to the relative behavior of rates of change of investment and rates of change of other expenditure items. Some relationship is found only for France. For the other two countries, alternative explanatory hypotheses are mentioned without being tested: exports, autonomous cycles, and monetary policy for Germany; monetary policy for Italy. It seems to me that a qualitative analysis of possible explanatory variables, one by one, is bound to yield unsatisfactory results for investment; among other reasons the effects of any one variable taken individually (for example, monetary policy) may be asymmetrical. It is surprising not to find any mention of a capital–stock adjustment mechanism, the working of which might well be at the bottom of the "more or less autonomous investment cycles" in Germany.

For all three countries, a relationship was sought, but not found, between rates of change of *consumption* and rates of change of nonconsumption expenditure. As I said at the beginning, the procedure followed is open to doubt. It would be very surprising if no satisfactory generalization, even for purposes of short-term forecasting, could be reached for consumption behavior. Several functions that include income distribution as an explanatory variable have been tried with good results in Italy: it might be interesting to try them also for the other two countries and to compare the values of the relevant parameters.

In spite of the formal similarities of the studies, a comparative analysis of the economies of the three countries under review in the period considered can hardly be obtained from them. When the degree of interdependence and the structural differences and similarities of the three economies are taken into account, such analysis would be of great interest for an appraisal of future developments. From this point of view, consideration of some structural factors and identification of some major structural relationships could help greatly.

To conclude, I venture to put forward two points which seem to emerge from the information provided in the papers. First, the growth process appears to have been more stable in Italy than in the other two countries, at least in terms of fluctuations of the rates of change of GNP. It should be emphasized, however, that there is no assurance that this same feature is going to persist in future years. Second, a comparison of cyclical behavior in the three countries seems to lend support to a remark by Professor Rothschild: namely, that one of the reasons for the relative mildness of postwar fluctuations in Europe is that, with the exception of 1958, cycles in individual countries do not coincide, so that the mechanism of international transmission has worked in reverse.

Chapter Six

# DENMARK, NORWAY, AND SWEDEN

JØRGEN H. GELTING
University of Aarhus

INTRODUCTION

The Scandinavian countries, like other small, industrialized countries, are heavily dependent on foreign trade. Exports of goods and services equal, roughly, 1/4 of gross domestic product in Sweden, 1/3 in Denmark, and 2/5 in Norway. Probably the Danish economy fits the characterization of an export economy less well than that of Norway and Sweden, in the sense that changes in domestic demand have a relatively stronger impact on exports. The elasticity of commodity imports with respect to gross domestic product (at constant prices) is between 1½ and 2, and the marginal propensity to import (goods and services, at current prices) between 1/3 and 1/2)[1]. Further, the flows of receipts and expenditures through the public sector are relatively large. Economic activity in the private sector is, therefore, highly sensitive both to developments abroad and to government policies, whereas any spontaneous change in private-sector activity will soon lose its momentum if not supported by government policies or by parallel tendencies in the international economy. The Scandinavian countries are entirely too small for the boomerang effect to assume major importance[2].

   Thus the question of the cyclical experience of the Scandinavian countries

---

[1] The postwar development of imports has been influenced by the relaxation and removal of restrictions on imports and by changes in relative prices. The estimates mentioned in the text and based on postwar experience are somewhat suspect, the estimate of the elasticity probably being too high and that of the marginal propensity too low. Further, it should be remembered that year-to-year movements are strongly affected by inventory investment.
[2] Though not negligible, the repercussions of intra-Scandinavian activity will not be discussed here. In each of the three countries studied, exports to the two others amounted in 1965 to roughly 1/5 of commodity exports to all countries.

concerns primarily the ways in which their economies have received and reacted to changing economic conditions in the outside world. In most countries, it is mainly through the foreign balance – particularly by their exports – that economic changes are transmitted from abroad. The principal markets for the exports of the Scandinavian countries are in western Europe. For these reasons, western European intratrade is used here as an indicator of the changes in international economic activity relevant to developments in Scandinavia. Figures 6-1 to 6-3 show annual changes in intrawestern European imports, and in gross domestic product and national expenditure components for each of the three Scandinavian countries during the period under review, 1952–1965 inclusive.

### INTERCOUNTRY DIFFERENCES

It is immediately apparent that the growth of total output in Denmark deviated more from the growth pattern of western European trade than did the growth of output in Norway or Sweden, and that developments in Norway and Sweden were almost parallel.

In Norway and Sweden, the changes in international economic activity appear to have been transmitted to the domestic economies mainly through varying earnings from exports of goods and services. In both countries, annual changes in exports conformed fairly closely to the changes in intrawestern European trade. The fluctuations of Norwegian shipping earnings – partly following a separate pattern – seem to have been a more important influence than commodity exports.

Through the fluctuations in earnings from total exports, the Norwegian economy has been exposed to stronger destabilizing influences than either the Swedish or the Danish. The annual increase in Norwegian exports of goods and services has averaged 2.3 per cent of gross domestic product (at current prices), with a standard deviation of 3.2 per cent; for Sweden, the corresponding figures are 1.1 per cent and 1.7 per cent; and for Denmark, 2.2 per cent and 1.0 per cent. On the basis of these figures, fluctuations in economic activity in Norway would be expected to be larger, and in Denmark smaller, than in the other two countries. But such has not been the case.

During the period under review, the average annual rate of growth of gross domestic product (at constant prices) was close to 4 per cent in each of the three countries. As in other western European countries, economic growth was exceptionally stable, when compared with earlier experience. In no one of the three countries did a significant absolute decline in gross domestic product occur in any year. However, the rate of growth showed greater variations in Denmark than it did in Norway and, particularly, in Sweden. In all three countries, growth was more rapid in the second than in the first half of the period; the change was most marked in Denmark. In both Norway and Sweden, near full-employment levels were maintained throughout the period. In Denmark, however, unemployment averaged about 10 per cent of insured workers from 1952 to 1958 inclusive; but in subsequent years, a decline in unemployment combined with an increase in the number of persons actively seeking employment made possible a high rate of expansion. In addition, productivity increased at a higher rate during the 1960's than in the preceding years. However, the greater instability of the growth rate in Denmark was not due entirely to the shift from a low average rate of growth in the 1950's to a high rate in the 1960's.

Why was a high degree of domestic stability attained in Norway and Sweden despite strong disturbances from abroad? On the other hand, why did economic activity in Denmark show relatively strong fluctuations, in spite of the stable growth of exports? In particular, how were the changes in each country influenced by international developments? Some clue to the answers is provided by the behavior of the balance on goods and services.

In Norway and Sweden, there has been a close correspondence between the annual changes in exports and imports of goods and services. In each country, the coefficient of correlation between annual variations of exports and imports of goods and services (in per cent of gross domestic product at current prices) was above 0.85. And in Sweden, the changes in imports were generally of about the same magnitude as the changes in exports. Consequently, the Swedish balance of goods and services has varied relatively little; furthermore, it has shown little systematic connection with the course of domestic activity. In other words, the international reflection ratio of the Swedish economy has been close to unity. The remarkable thing is that at the same time changes in total output have been moderate − as though a short-circuiting mechanism had switched a large part of the foreign impact from exports directly to imports. One view of the postwar performance of the Swedish economy is that, although the major components of gross national expenditure have fluctuated considerably, these fluctuations have − by luck or design − been mutually neutralizing in large part. This account certainly applies to Sweden's international transactions, but it is only part of the story.

As in most countries, inventory investment fluctuated widely during the period under review. A large part of the recorded changes took place in export industries, and showed synchronization with changes in exports and imports. A number of reasons may be adduced for this: goods in process vary with the volume of production; parallel movements in prices and output induce investment in inventories when output rises; and the depreciation of larger inventories offsets higher taxable profits. And insofar as imported commodities are prominent in inventory changes, the close connection between movements in exports, imports, and inventory investment is accounted for.

If, then, it is assumed that inventory investment is governed mainly by the course of exports and international prices, and in turn has an important effect on imports, it may follow that the foreign balance plus inventory investment constitutes the primary external factor affecting domestic economic activity. It turns out that the annual changes of foreign balance plus inventory investment are closely correlated with the growth of gross domestic product; that the standard deviation amounts to twice that of the foreign balance and more than two-thirds that of gross domestic product. The annual change of foreign balance plus inventory investment fluctuated relatively more than in Denmark, but much less than in Norway.

Apart from the foreign balance and inventory investment, private fixed investment is the expenditure component which would be expected to show the greatest amount of instability and to play a major role in changes in economic activity. It turns out that in Sweden there has been only a weak positive association between the changes in the foreign balance plus inventory investment and in private fixed investment. In Norway, these two elements tended to move

Code for Figures 6-1 to 6-4. *ET*: annual change (parts per thousand) in intrawestern European import trade; $Y_{const}$ : annual changes (parts per thousand) in gross domestic product at constant prices; $Y$: annual changes (parts per thousand) of GDP at current prices; $X$: exports of goods and services; $X - M$: net exports of goods and services; $L$: inventory investment; $I_P$: private fixed gross investment; $I_G$: government fixed gross investment. $C_P$: private consumption. $C_G$: government consumption.

TABLE FOR ET IN FIGURES 6-1, 6-2,
6-3    Annual (per thousand) changes in
intrawestern European imports

| | |
|---|---|
| 1952 | 21 |
| 1953 | 31 |
| 1954 | 100 |
| 1955 | 142 |
| 1956 | 114 |
| 1957 | 76 |
| 1958 | −21 |
| 1959 | 111 |
| 1960 | 187 |
| 1961 | 119 |
| 1962 | 114 |
| 1963 | 128 |
| 1964 | 137 |
| 1965 | 101 |

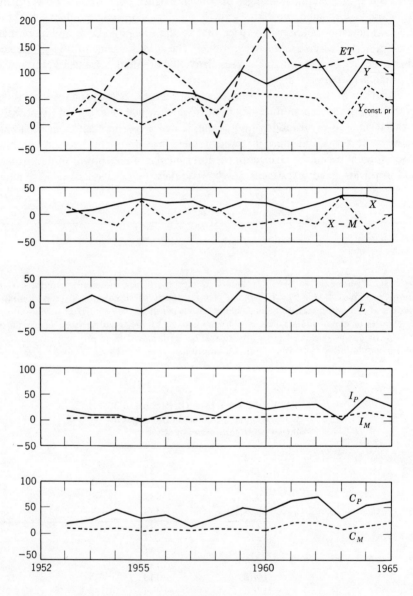

**Figure 6-1**

TABLE FOR FIGURE 6–1  Denmark

|  | $Y$ | $X$ | $X - M$ | $I_P$ | $I_G$ | $C_P$ | $C_G$ | $Y_{const,pr.}$ | $L$ |
|---|---|---|---|---|---|---|---|---|---|
| 1952 | 65 | 6 | 17 | 18 | 3 | 20 | 13 | 12 | −6 |
| 1953 | 70 | 9 | −2 | 10 | 5 | 28 | 10 | 59 | 18 |
| 1954 | 47 | 21 | −21 | 10 | 4 | 47 | 11 | 29 | −3 |
| 1955 | 46 | 32 | 24 | −2 | 2 | 30 | 6 | 3 | −13 |
| 1956 | 68 | 25 | −10 | 13 | 4 | 38 | 8 | 20 | 15 |
| 1957 | 64 | 28 | 12 | 18 | 3 | 16 | 7 | 51 | 8 |
| 1958 | 45 | 11 | 15 | 9 | 5 | 32 | 8 | 26 | −25 |
| 1959 | 106 | 27 | −20 | 34 | 4 | 51 | 10 | 64 | 27 |
| 1960 | 82 | 23 | −14 | 22 | 6 | 46 | 8 | 63 | 13 |
| 1961 | 111 | 9 | −6 | 31 | 11 | 68 | 24 | 59 | −16 |
| 1962 | 128 | 22 | −18 | 30 | 7 | 75 | 23 | 55 | 11 |
| 1963 | 63 | 36 | 33 | 1 | 5 | 34 | 11 | 5 | −22 |
| 1964 | 131 | 36 | −25 | 44 | 14 | 59 | 17 | 79 | 22 |
| 1965 | 120 | 28 | 2 | 27 | 7 | 63 | 24 | 44 | −3 |

# Denmark, Norway, and Sweden

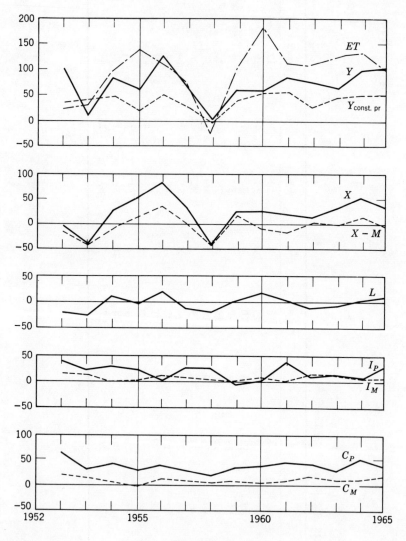

Figure 6-2

TABLE FOR FIGURE 6-2   Norway

| | $Y$ | $X$ | $X - M$ | $I_P$ | $I_G$ | $C_P$ | $C_G$ | $Y_{const.pr.}$ | $L$ |
|---|---|---|---|---|---|---|---|---|---|
| 1952 | 103 | -3 | -15 | 39 | 16 | 61 | 21 | 36 | -20 |
| 1953 | 14 | -37 | -41 | 24 | 14 | 30 | 14 | 40 | -27 |
| 1954 | 84 | 26 | -11 | 33 | 1 | 41 | 7 | 50 | 13 |
| 1955 | 63 | 52 | 15 | 25 | 1 | 28 | -1 | 23 | -4 |
| 1956 | 128 | 82 | 37 | 5 | 13 | 38 | 13 | 52 | 21 |
| 1957 | 68 | 33 | 2 | 28 | 8 | 30 | 10 | 31 | -11 |
| 1958 | 5 | -41 | -38 | 28 | 8 | 19 | 6 | -1 | -18 |
| 1959 | 64 | 26 | 18 | -3 | 2 | 34 | 10 | 43 | 2 |
| 1960 | 63 | 27 | -9 | 2 | 10 | 37 | 5 | 58 | 18 |
| 1961 | 87 | 20 | -14 | 39 | 2 | 46 | 10 | 61 | 4 |
| 1962 | 78 | 15 | 3 | 9 | 16 | 43 | 18 | 33 | -11 |
| 1963 | 67 | 33 | 1 | 16 | 16 | 29 | 12 | 48 | -7 |
| 1964 | 102 | 54 | 18 | 9 | 7 | 51 | 13 | 54 | 4 |
| 1965 | 105 | 35 | -1 | 34 | 8 | 39 | 18 | 54 | 10 |

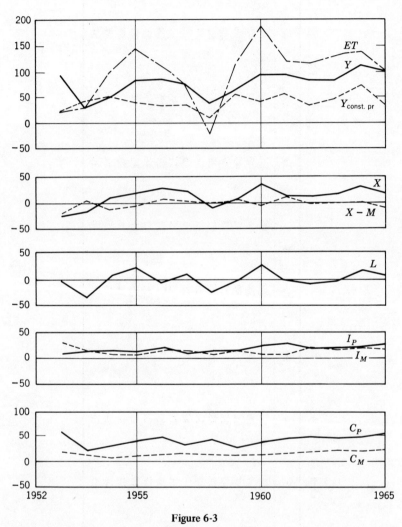

**Figure 6-3**

TABLE FOR FIGURE 6–3   Sweden

| | $Y$ | $X$ | $X - M$ | $I_P$ | $I_G$ | $C_P$ | $C_G$ | $Y_{const.pr.}$ | $L$ |
|---|---|---|---|---|---|---|---|---|---|
| 1952 | 94 | −26 | −20 | 7 | 31 | 58 | 20 | 22 | −2 |
| 1953 | 31 | −15 | 4 | 13 | 16 | 21 | 10 | 42 | −33 |
| 1954 | 51 | 12 | −12 | 13 | 5 | 31 | 5 | 51 | 9 |
| 1955 | 84 | 20 | −5 | 11 | 6 | 40 | 10 | 39 | 24 |
| 1956 | 85 | 28 | 6 | 18 | 12 | 44 | 11 | 34 | −6 |
| 1957 | 75 | 22 | 1 | 8 | 14 | 29 | 14 | 34 | 10 |
| 1958 | 39 | −9 | −3 | 11 | 6 | 40 | 9 | 9 | −24 |
| 1959 | 64 | 8 | 4 | 11 | 15 | 25 | 10 | 54 | −4 |
| 1960 | 92 | 35 | −6 | 23 | 5 | 35 | 9 | 40 | 26 |
| 1961 | 92 | 12 | 10 | 24 | 7 | 43 | 13 | 56 | −5 |
| 1962 | 83 | 11 | −3 | 14 | 18 | 45 | 17 | 35 | −9 |
| 1963 | 82 | 15 | −2 | 16 | 14 | 43 | 19 | 45 | −7 |
| 1964 | 108 | 28 | 1 | 16 | 18 | 45 | 16 | 72 | 14 |
| 1965 | 98 | 14 | −14 | 23 | 15 | 49 | 20 | 32 | 5 |

in opposition; this accounts in part for Norway's success in counteracting economic disturbances from abroad. In Denmark also, the growth in private fixed investment tended to vary opposite to the changes in foreign balance plus inventory investment — as a result of the sensitivity of imports to domestic economic activity. But the most striking thing is that the growth of private fixed investment was much more stable in Sweden than in the other two countries. It would appear then that a main factor in Swedish postwar stability has been the stabilization of private fixed investment. On the other hand, Swedish government investment (central plus local) has been rather less stable than private investment and has contributed only partly to stability. This lack of stability, however, has been due almost entirely to the behavior of local government investment.

The movements in imports in Norway, though equally closely related to those in exports, were of relatively smaller amplitude than those in Sweden. Thus changes in net exports of goods and services have been positively correlated with changes in gross domestic product. A sizable part of the fluctuations in exports of goods and services is accounted for by shipping, whose direct import content is fairly high. For obvious reasons, the marginal rate of spending out of domestic income from Norwegian shipping earnings is rather low, and the marginal propensity to save correspondingly high; a large part of the fluctuations in shipping receipts (net of changes in direct imports) is reflected in changes in the retained profits of Norwegian shipping companies. The timing of induced investment expenditures does not conform closely to the time pattern of shipping earnings, and here again the direct import content is high. Thus, the immediate impact of fluctuations in shipping receipts on the flow of incomes and demand in Norway is effectively cushioned. On the other hand, in Norway as in Sweden, a close correspondence as to both the direction and magnitude of changes is found between commodity exports and imports.

In Denmark, the picture was entirely different during the period reviewed. The growth of exports conformed largely to the pattern of European trade. But the fluctuations, as already mentioned, were quite moderate, and there was little correlation between the year-to-year movements of exports, on the one hand, and domestic output and imports, on the other. Only in small part can this be explained by the variations of the harvest, and thus of grain imports. The correlation between the annual changes in imports and in domestic product in Denmark was about as close as in the two other countries. Apparently then, in contrast to Norway — where the positive covariation of total output and the foreign balance reflected the effect of exports on domestic activity and on imports — the negative covariation of total output and the foreign balance in Denmark might indicate that changes in economic activity were mainly of domestic origin.

Another possible interpretation would be that the Danish postwar experience thus far has conformed to some extent to the cyclical pattern of the Danish economy before World War I. At that time, Denmark exported agricultural products almost exclusively; these enjoyed a relatively stable market in western Europe, and particularly in Britain. With exports generally insensitive to business conditions abroad, it was principally through changes in import prices that economic conditions in Denmark were affected by the international cycle. An international upswing led to a deterioration of the terms of trade without a compensating increase in the volume of exports. Both liquidity and income effects of the deterioration of the foreign balance tended to depress domestic economic activity; and the liquidity effect was strengthened by the tightening of capital markets abroad, on which Denmark regularly depended for large-scale borrowing. The only expansionary factor of major importance was the investment inducement from the expectation of rising prices. But as this investment largely took the form of increased inventories of imported goods, liquidity was further tightened. During an international downswing, and in particular during its early phase, Denmark benefited from an improvement of her terms of trade as a result of falling raw material prices, while export earnings were maintained relatively well. Typically, therefore, the Danish cycle tended to lag behind the international cycle. Indeed, with the gold standard in operation and interest-elastic international capital movements, the country hardly had an independent monetary system.

COMPARATIVE CYCLE HISTORY, 1952–1966

Within the period under review, the most striking deviation of developments in Denmark from those in the other two Scandinavian countries and in western Europe occurred in 1955. At a time when boom conditions prevailed in industrial Europe and North America, business was depressed in Denmark, and total output stagnated. This was, however, the result of deliberate policy measures begun in the summer of 1954 to cope with an increasing payments deficit.

In the preceding three years, developments in Denmark and Norway had been rather similar; indeed, in several respects they conformed to a widespread western European pattern. The Korean War had led to a deterioration in the terms of trade and a rise in imports, largely on inventory account. As the balance of payments deteriorated, contractionary fiscal and monetary policies were adopted; these policies, together with the subsequent fall in import prices, resulted in a recovery of the foreign exchange position and of domestic liquidity. From 1952 to 1954, residential and public construction in Denmark expanded and gradually induced an increase in private investment expenditures. Recovery of exports started in 1952, and from the spring of 1953 industrial exports rose rapidly. Relaxation of fiscal policies, as well as easier conditions in money and capital markets, supported the rise in total demand.

In Norway, gross receipts from shipping and commodity exports continued to decline until 1953, but in the following year they provided a stronger expansionary impetus than existed in Denmark. Residential and other construction rose strongly, as licensing was decentralized and relaxed. Also, as in Denmark, less stringent fiscal policies added to the growth of total demand.

Developments in Denmark and Norway were similar also in that, as expansion gathered momentum, balances of goods and services showed large deficits — in Norway in 1953 and in Denmark in 1954. The larger deficit was in Norway, where the shortfall on goods and services amounted to more than 4 per cent of gross domestic product, against 1½ per cent in Denmark. There were, however, two notable differences: first, in Norway exports appeared to accelerate more than imports, so that the foreign balance deteriorated less from 1953–1954 than from 1952–1953; in Denmark it was the other way round. Second — and of greater immediate importance to economic policies — in Norway there was both the ability and the willingness to finance the foreign deficit through borrowing abroad, but this was not true in Denmark. In fact, during the period 1952–1955 as a whole, Denmark's balance of goods and services was in surplus.

Both countries instituted restrictive economic policies in 1954 and 1955; however, their effects were much more drastic in Denmark than in Norway. In Denmark, total output hardly rose from 1954 to 1955, whereas in Norway there was a rise of close to 3 per cent, which was due in large part to continued export expansion. In 1956, domestic growth accelerated in Norway at the same time that the balance of payments position continued to improve. In Denmark, on the other hand, a moderate re-expansion in 1956 caused renewed deterioration of the balance of payments, to which, however, a number of special and abnormal circumstances also contributed.

Actually, then, 1952–1955 developments in Denmark constituted no repetition of the pattern prior to World War I. The terms of trade improved considerably after the war in Korea, and deteriorated only slightly from 1954 to 1955. The balance of payments deteriorated in 1954 not because of higher import prices but of domestic expansion, called forth in part by expansionary fiscal and credit policies. In turn, the adoption of these policies is explained sufficiently by the depressed state of the economy in 1952 (when 12.5 per cent of the insured workers were unemployed) and some recovery in the Danish foreign exchange position.

The decisive difference from conditions before World War I, however, was that free access to a smoothly functioning international capital market was lacking. In principle, the positive side of this change was that the Danish authorities were able to pursue independent monetary policies without regard to the state of capital markets abroad. In practice, the absence of capital imports acted to restrict the scope of domestic policies designed to attain high levels of economic activity and growth, since Danish foreign exchange reserves were extremely low (until 1958, gross reserves did not exceed $200 million), and since, at ruling levels of money wages and exchange rates, high employment proved irreconcilable with a favorable balance on goods and services account.

During the international recession of 1958, the performance of the Danish economy was more satisfactory, and the mechanism conformed fairly closely to the traditional pattern. While total output stagnated in Sweden and Norway, it continued to expand — though at a reduced rate — in Denmark. Despite the general decline in western European trade, Danish exports, particularly exports of industrial products, continued to advance; in fact, industrial exports rose more than they had in 1957, whereas both Norwegian and Swedish exports declined.

There is no obvious explanation for the favorable performance of Danish exports. It may have been that the relatively high level of unemployment in Denmark during the 1950's caused wages, and thus costs, to increase less than they did in competing countries, and that delivery periods were shorter. In the summer of 1956, various contractionary measures had been taken in order to improve the precarious foreign exchange position, and the year 1958 began with relatively low domestic activity. However, the high selectivity of the rise in exports from 1957 to 1958, both as to countries and commodities, may indicate that special factors were at work. At any rate, the continued rise in Danish exports, together with the fall in the value of imports as import prices were lower, produced an exceptionally large balance of payments surplus.

In both Norway and Sweden, imports at current prices declined, but in neither country was the decline sufficient to counterbalance the fall of exports. In Sweden, the terms of trade improved to about the same extent as in Denmark; but in Norway, where freight rates declined severely, the terms of trade (on goods and services) deteriorated from 1957 to 1958. In addition, the contractionary impact of the decline in exports was intensified by a restrictive fiscal policy (presumably unintended, in part), when income taxation was shifted to a pay-as-you-earn basis.

The setback of 1958 was rapidly overcome in both Norway and Sweden. In Norway, the growth of private fixed investment continued remarkably high in 1958. Credit conditions were eased in the second half of the year, and various other measures were adopted to stimulate total spending. More important, probably, was the fact that a large number of building licenses issued in 1957 affected construction in 1958. In all three countries, a state of excess demand has persisted in the postwar housing market, because of rent controls and other housing policies, so that the general problem has been to prevent excessive expansion of building activity rather than the opposite.

Initially, however, the dominant factor in the renewed upswing in Norway was the rise in exports that began in the second half of 1958. Later, in 1960–1961, the balance of the forces changed; private investment and consumer expenditures—the latter stimulated by a relaxation of fiscal policies in 1959—rose strongly, while export demand eased. Consequently, the balance on goods and services, which had improved greatly from 1958 to 1959, deteriorated in the next two years.

In Sweden, the fall in exports from 1957 to 1958 was much less severe than the decline in Norway. And private investment, stimulated by government policies, rose more in 1958 than it had in 1957. In the spring of 1957, it had been decided — presumably without any prevision of developments in 1958 — to abandon, in January 1958, the tax on fixed investment expenditures (excluding residential construction) which had been introduced in order to restrain the 1955–1957 investment boom. Later, in 1958, credit policies were eased, funds for investment expenditures were released from tax-exempt deposits, and the quantitative control of building activity was relaxed.

In Denmark, 1958 marked the beginning of a fundamental change in economic conditions. Unemployment was reduced from about 10 per cent of the insured workers in 1953–1958 to 4.3 per cent in 1960, and it remained low during the following years[3]. The dominant view was that this development was based mainly on the improvement of the terms of trade and the resumption of both public and private borrowing abroad. The terms of trade in 1958 improved impressively, when compared with 1957, but much less so when compared with earlier years. Actually, the main factor was the progressive removal of the structural weakness of the Danish economy: the commodity composition of exports. Whereas, after 1953, agricultural exports stagnated or rose only slowly, industrial exports expanded fairly steadily at a high rate. Consequently, at the end of the period under review, industrial exports amounted to just above 50 per cent of total commodity exports, against slightly less than 40 per cent in 1958, and 30 per cent in 1952.

The rise in the share of industrial exports in total exports presumably explains the change which can be observed (see Figure 6-4) in the relationship between domestic activity (represented by the level of unemployment) and the balance of goods and services (measured in percentages of gross domestic product). The major part of the movements in the balance of goods and services is readily accounted for by the level of employment and a trend factor, whereas changes in the terms of trade seem to have played only a minor role. Furthermore, some confirmation is provided for the presumption that the lower the level of unemployment, the more strongly the balance of goods and services reacts to a given change in the level of unemployment. Though the major part of this response of the foreign balance to domestic activity is accounted for by imports, the growth of industrial exports seems to have been slowed down in a

[3] Seasonal unemployment is relatively large in Denmark, particularly, of course, in construction, building, and agriculture. In manufacturing, unemployment averaged 2.0 per cent in the period 1960 to 1965, inclusive.

J⌀rgen H. Gelting

TABLE FOR FIGURE 6–4    Net exports
($X - M$) of goods and services in per cent of
GDP and unemployment ($U$), percentage of
insured workers unemployed, annual averages.
Denmark 1950–1965.

|  | $X - M$ | $U$ |
|---|---|---|
| 1950 | −3.21 | 8.7 |
| 1951 | −0.81 | 9.7 |
| 1952 | 0.84 | 12.5 |
| 1953 | 0.62 | 9.2 |
| 1954 | −1.45 | 8.0 |
| 1955 | 0.91 | 9.7 |
| 1956 | −0.09 | 11.1 |
| 1957 | 1.04 | 10.2 |
| 1958 | 2.49 | 9.6 |
| 1959 | 0.42 | 6.1 |
| 1960 | −0.91 | 4.3 |
| 1961 | −1.29 | 3.9 |
| 1962 | −2.76 | 3.3 |
| 1963 | 0.55 | 4.3 |
| 1964 | −1.71 | 2.8 |
| 1965 | −1.30 | 2.3 |

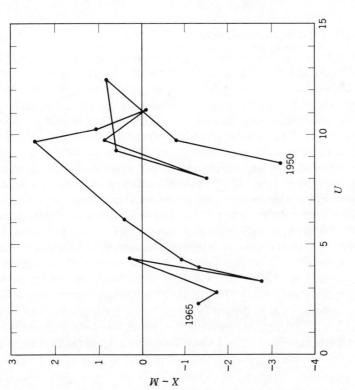

Figure 6-4

215

few years (particularly by 1961) of strong domestic demand pressure. In all three countries, the inflation of money wages accelerated from the 1950's to the 1960's, but to a greater extent in Denmark than in the other two countries. The extent to which this has so far affected relative export performance is quite uncertain. Developments in 1965 and 1966, however, point to an increased sensitivity of Danish industrial exports to fluctuations in international economic activity.

In view of the high rate of growth of Danish industrial exports after 1953, there can be little doubt that they were very profitable. Relatively high unemployment moderated the rise in wages and served to maintain, or even increase, the profitability of exports during the 1950's. It seems doubtful that the growth of exports could have been accelerated appreciably by further depreciation (beyond that undertaken in 1949) or by lower money wages. And the major part of imports − raw materials and controlled imports of manufactures − would be only slightly sensitive to relative prices. To the extent that depreciation was successful in providing a basis for an increase in domestic activity and more rapid industrial growth, wages would almost certainly have risen more.

### DANISH STOP-AND-GO EXPERIENCE

The remarkable improvement of the Danish foreign exchange position in 1958, together with the extended expansion of domestic activity relative to earlier experience, had strong secondary effects on both public and private investment expenditures. Expectations regarding the future level and growth of economic activity were revised drastically upward; this led to a strong investment boom, which was stimulated also by more liberal depreciation allowances after 1958. Furthermore, fiscal policies were relaxed considerably in 1961, and wages increased strongly in both the private and the public sector. A repetition, at a higher level, of the policies of 1954−1955 occurred in 1962−1963, after exchange reserves had been depleted by the domestic expansion and inflation in 1961. But after a brief but sharp contraction in 1963, which proved sufficient for the recovery of reserves, activity expanded again in 1964.

It will thus be seen that the course of economic activity in Denmark provides a fairly clear specimen of stop-go policies. A contraction or slowing down of expansion occurred in 1955, 1958, and 1963. Each time, the main cause was restrictive fiscal and monetary policies, although in the last two years the effects of domestic measures were reinforced by international developments. In contrast to the situation in Norway and Sweden, the Danish economy was exposed to only mild disturbances from abroad. Conditions were admittedly difficult in the 1950's, because of the commodity composition of exports and the narrow international margin. Little effort was made, however, to cope with these difficulties in a fundamental way, and the instability of the economy seems to have been due mainly to government policies, the shortcomings of which cannot be explained by lack of adequate policy instruments.

A simple model, which will reproduce some essential behavioral characteristics of the Danish economy, is the following:

Domestic product equals net income creation by the government plus private expenditure plus the foreign balance:

(1) $Y = G + D + F$

(2) $D = dY$ $\qquad d > 0$

(3) $F = A + fY$ $\qquad 0 < f < 1,$

where $A$ depends on international economic conditions.

Foreign exchange reserves at the end of the year equal reserves at the beginning of the year plus the foreign balance plus capital imports during the year:

(4) $R_t = R_{t-1} + F_t + K_t$.

Government net income creation is adjusted annually on the basis of the reserve position at the beginning of the year relative to some desired reserve position:

(5) $G_t = G_{t-1} + g(R_{t-1} - R^*)$. $\qquad g > 0$

Once this lagged model is off balance, it may generate cyclical fluctuations [4]. Evidently, this is a case of monetary schizophrenia: a Keynesian private sector and a quantity-theorist government.

As the balance of payments both directly (by income and liquidity effects) and indirectly (by motivating changes in public policy) exerts a strong influence on economic conditions in Denmark, and as changes in total bank deposits are related to changes in foreign exchange reserves, Danish monetary statistics seem to reflect a close dependence of total effective demand and economic activity on the quantity of money [5].

WICKSELLIAN PROCESSES AND INCOME REDISTRIBUTIONS

As mentioned previously, both the growth rate of real output and the rate of inflation in all three countries were higher in the 1960's than in the 1950's.

---

[4] Alternatively—and possibly more plausibly, equation (5) might be formulated as a step function.

[5] Annual changes in inventory investment—which are related to changes in both gross domestic product and the foreign balance—show a high correlation with changes in bank lending minus bank deposits. Changes in bank lending follow closely changes in deposits with a lag of one year.

Though inflation was international, domestic factors in general contributed relatively more to demand pressures. A disparity in price and wage trends emerged, with more rapidly rising incomes and prices in services, construction, and building and other sheltered industries than in export industries and industries exposed to foreign competition in the home market.

Partly as an effect of these developments, a trend has been observed — especially in Sweden and, to a lesser extent, in Denmark — toward a declining share of retained profits in the financing of private, particularly industrial, investment [6]. At the same time, savings by the central government (including social insurance funds) have increased considerably in relative importance; this has been true especially in Sweden. While year-to-year changes in the relative volume of debt financing of industrial investment depend mainly on the fluctuations of investment, the longer-term trend toward a decreasing share of retained profits as a source of finance seems, at least in Sweden, to be due largely to the rising share of wages in value added and the consequent downward pressure on profit margins.

It may appear paradoxical that under such conditions high levels of investment and economic activity can be maintained. But though interest rates have increased in all three countries during recent years, and are definitely higher than they were in the 1950's, real rates of interest have — in view of strengthened expectations of further inflation — probably increased little, if at all. Thus the Swedish and Danish booms of the 1960's may be said to provide examples of a Wicksellian inflationary process, simultaneously kept alive by a low real rate of interest and kept within bounds through contractionary fiscal policies. Evidently, this process carries with it considerable risk: if present trends continue, widening disparities between wage and profit levels in sheltered and in export industries may affect factor allocation so as to create serious balance of payments difficulties in the long run. If, on the other hand, the international inflationary boom should come to a sudden halt, leading to a wholesale downward revision of business expectations, the maintenance of domestic economic activity at a high level may prove to be most difficult.

However, in full-employment conditions (which are expected to continue), a certain switch from profits to wages and an increase in debt financing of private investment are to be expected. The last part of this statement is not merely a consequence of the first, but follows also from the decreasing riskiness of investment at high and presumably stable levels of activity. Compared with more unsettled conditions, firms may incur a larger debt relative to equity capital, without exposing themselves to additional risks.

---

[6] This was true in Norway also until 1962–1963; but in the following years, exports improved greatly and, at least for the time being, reversed the trend.

The shift from profits to wages in presumably due not merely to the squeeze between international prices and domestic wage increases called forth by domestic demand pressures. It is improbable that relative shares and real wages will, at a given level of employment (and a given complex of material resources, etc.), be the same irrespective of the available reserve of unemployed labor. In a tight labor market, each firm has a greater interest in retaining its work force because of the difficulties of finding replacements. Firms will, therefore, hesitate to release excess workers when demand weakens and production plans are cut back temporarily.

Further — quite apart from any such change in production schedules — firms will be increasingly concerned about reducing the labor turnover. From the point of view of the individual firm, the quit rate is a declining function, both of the wage rate paid by that firm and of the general level of unemployment. In addition, the risk of loss to the firm from a certain quit rate rises as the level of employment decreases. It follows that the optimal real wage rate varies inversely with the rate of unemployment. In other words, at full employment, wages rise relative to prices and profits because the marginal revenue product of labor increases.

Of interest in this connection is the change that has taken place in the cyclical behavior of the wage share in Swedish industry, which in the postwar period has not exhibited the pronounced countercyclical variation shown during the interwar period. The same is true of home market industries in Norway, whereas the traditional pattern is found in exports, largely because of developments in shipping where output prices have fluctuated widely [7].

RECAPITULATION

To recapitulate: economic activity in the Scandinavian countries in recent years has been much more stable than in earlier periods, and particularly the interwar period. Changes in international economic conditions have had a stronger effect on Norway's and Sweden's exports than on Denmark's; and fluctuations in economic activity in Norway and Sweden have been fairly closely synchronized with changes in international economic activity.

In Norway, the impact of export changes on domestic demand and activity has been cushioned in particular by the shipping industry's relatively low marginal propensity to spend in Norway and also by Norway's ability to borrow abroad, thus obviating the risk of having to reduce domestic activity undesirably in order to cope with balance of payments difficulties.

In Sweden, the cushioning mechanism appears to have been a relatively short

[7] In Denmark, the wage share in individual industries shows little systematic connection with activity. However, value-added figures are affected to an unknown extent by the inclusion of inventory changes in the statistics of output and input.

chain impact from exports to imports, resulting in a remarkably stable foreign balance. A change may, however, be in progress as a result of the altered commodity composition of Swedish commodity imports.

In the early part of the period, Denmark had serious balance of payments difficulties, and the policies adopted to cope with these difficulties were far from conducive to high and stable economic activity. With a rapid expansion of industrial exports and also improved terms of trade and capital imports, a much higher level of activity has been attained in the 1960's.

In all three countries, a wide spectrum of policy measures have been used. This is especially true of Norway, whose economy is subject to intensive government intervention.

In the early postwar years, the control of building through licensing was an important instrument of policy in Norway. The Norwegian system was, however, decentralized and relaxed at the beginning of the period under review, and completely abandoned for residential construction in 1960. In return, credit policies – implemented through a system of fairly detailed regulations – have assumed increasing importance.

The most striking aspect of policies in Sweden is the stabilization of private investment, which has been achieved partly through the temporary taxation of investment expenditures (through which the investment boom of the 1950's was suppressed) and partly through a system of tax-exempt and partially blocked investment funds, from which releases may be made at the discretion of the authorities for specified amounts, periods, and purposes. Experience so far indicates a strong and rapid response of investment to such releases.

In all three countries, fiscal policy has been important. In Denmark, the general view probably is that fiscal policy is the major instrument for controlling total demand and activity. An important practical consequence of this view has been the manifest instability of private consumption in Denmark, compared with the other two countries. In Denmark and Norway throughout the period, and in Sweden in the 1960's, public savings comprised a sizable part of total savings. At the same time, however, total government spending increased rapidly, and the net effect of fiscal policy may well have been expansionary.

During the last part of the period under review, economic activity was high and relatively stable in all three countries and economic growth – measured in the usual way – was rapid. But it may be said that – in the international economic climate – the relatively manageable problem of stability has drawn undue attention compared with that devoted to the rational allocation of resources.

# COMMENT

P. NØRREGAARD RASMUSSEN
University of Copenhagen

Despite similarities among the three Scandinavian countries, it is hard to treat those countries in one chapter. Their postwar histories differ significantly. It is clear that Professor Gelting has realized this difficulty; he has reacted by treating as a main point the question of foreign trade. One thing that the three countries have in common is the apparent lack of regular cycles; another is the importance of foreign trade. Thus, the focus of Gelting's paper is that there seem to have been differing economic fluctuations in the three countries in the sense that the rates of growth have varied. To what extent may the exogenous changes in the world market explain such swings over the past 15 years?

It appears that the fluctuations have been larger in Denmark than in Norway and Sweden. But according to the picture drawn by Gelting, this has not been due to more violent exogenous shocks to the Danish economy. In fact, the fluctuations of Danish exports seem to be smaller than those of Swedish and — in particular — Norwegian exports.

To start with the Norwegian case: Gelting tends to explain the lack of internal reactions to outside shocks by the predominant influence of shipping. This is a sector in which fluctuations in incomes are "effectively cushioned." The point apparently is that the propensities out of the gross income of that sector partly to import and partly to save are very high, while investments, on the other hand, are independent of current income. In consequence, outside shocks may not work their way through the Norwegian economy. Mr. Gelting's arguments are more refined, but I hope that my summary presents the heart of the matter.

There is an important point in this reasoning. But why then is the gross domestic product significantly better correlated with changes in total exports in Norway than in Sweden and, particularly, in Denmark? Mr. Gelting may be right, however, if fluctuations in Norwegian exports in general significantly exceed those of Swedish and Danish exports. In fact, this seems to be true.

221

For Sweden, Gelting's findings are particularly fascinating. According to him, total output has changed only moderately—"as if a short-circuiting mechanism switched a large part of the foreign impact from exports directly to imports." One fact behind this surprising mechanism is that changes in investment in inventories have moved in very much the same direction as changes in exports. The thesis, however, holds only if these inventories are carried by the export industries and consist of imported goods. The "short-circuiting mechanism" does not work if the pulp industries in an expanding market pile up pulp. The calculating machine factory must react toward an increase in sales by increasing its stock of imported components. An alternative mechanism, of course, would work if the import content of exports was very high. However, this does not seem to be the case.

Finally, in Denmark there have been greater fluctuations in gross domestic product despite a relatively stable growth of exports. Again simplifying, Gelting's judgment seems to be that a substantial part of these fluctuations has been a product of economic policy. Gelting may, however, be biased by being a Dane. I venture to guess that a non-Dane would have argued along the following lines: In Denmark, the situation toward the mid-1950's became particularly difficult because the European balance between demand and supply of agricultural commodities changed; scarcities disappeared. The heavy weight of agricultural exports had been a virtue but become a burden. The simultaneous shift toward exports of industrial goods gradually tended to make life easier. I think that Gelting is right in stressing this when explaining the recovery from 1958 onward. However, he tends to underrate the short-term effects of the improvement of the terms of trade in 1957–1958 and a number of other changes—including changes in policy—in explaining the very significant and fast shift between pre- and post-1958.

The gradual shift of Danish exports toward manufactured industrial goods has continued at a very steady rate over the last 15 years. Exports of manufactures have increased, year by year, by some 10 to 15 per cent. The remarkable thing is that this favorable development has continued even in years of an overall weakening of demand in European markets. For instance, in 1958 Danish exports of manufactured goods increased by close to 10 per cent, while exports from Western Europe as a whole stagnated. A detailed study[1] shows that this was due to the fact that Denmark at that time succeeded in exporting the right kinds of commodities, that is, commodities which, despite the slack in overall demand, were meeting the needs of an expanding market. An interesting comparison may be made with British exports, which seem to have tended

---

[1] *Statistiske Efterretninger*, 1959, Tillaeg nr. 8.

toward concentrating on the wrong kinds of commodities[2]. The Danish problems may be to continue the shift away from agricultural products, while the analogous British problem may be to change her mix of exported manufactured goods.

A further obvious reason for comparing Danish and British developments is that Denmark has been rather close to the "stop-a-go" policy associated with the United Kingdom. Gelting gives several hints in this respect.

During the upswings, an attempt has often been made to dampen the expansion by monetary measures. The result has been—although this is far from being the only cause—that the rate of interest on perfectly safe bonds today is close to 10 per cent. Even so, I think it can be maintained—as Gelting does—that the boom periods resemble a Wicksellian inflationary process. In particular, this may hold for the late 1950's. In order to explain this it may be necessary to take into account the high marginal rates of direct taxation. The combination of high marginal rates, beneficial rules of depreciation, and (very often exaggerated) price expectations is bound to lead to a very high propensity to invest.

To this might be added that, because of the structure of the capital market, the rate of return on bonds in Denmark tends to be higher than the rate in other countries. Time does not allow any discussion of details, but a general remark may be appropriate. On the basis of Gelting's paper—and several of the other papers as well—we may be able to reach some tentative, and admittedly vague, conclusions about the role of fiscal policy in the postwar cycles. However, on monetary policy it seems much more difficult to reach unanimous views. One reason for this is the well known and basic one: the investment function is much more difficult to estimate than the consumption function. Another, though not totally different, reason is that the institutional framework of the capital market varies greatly from country to country. Statistics on banking and on monetary flows in general are very hard to interpret for any country. And the difficulties become greater when comparisons of different countries are attempted. I want to stress this point because the papers before us show the immense benefit we have derived from the attempts to construct standardized National Accounts. I expect, however, that we shall meet greater difficulties in an attempt to construct standardized Flow-of-Funds Accounts, which could make international comparisons of money flows sensible and might improve our general understanding of the business cycle. Differences in the setting of the capital market will prove to be a major difficulty in international comparisons.

Time does not allow me to discuss all the points raised by Gelting. I do want, however, to draw attention to sections toward the end of his chapter where

---

[2] T. Barna, "What Is Wrong With Britain's Trading Position?", *The Times* (London), August 12, 1963.

some hints are given about a theory of changes in the distribution of income between profits and labor over the cycle. There are long-run theories about income distribution, although the two Cambridge centers disagree violently about it. But in the post-Keynesian generation, very few attempts have been made to explain changes over the cycle. Whether Gelting's proposal is fruitful or not is difficult to say—for one thing, because the empirical evidence is weak.

Gelting has a good final point: the problems of stability are relatively manageable but they have drawn "undue attention compared with that devoted to the rational allocation of resources." This, however, points to a deficiency in the present state of economics. We have very few possibilities for presenting a quantitative measure of the cost of a given misallocation. The real costs of a change in rent policy, a change in agricultural subsidies, a change in the degree of protection, and so on, can, on the basis of our present knowledge, be stated in qualitative terms. However, quantification is badly needed. Over the cycle, the loss in this respect may be due to "bad policy" or it may be due to a failure of the individual firm to optimize. But how can we divide the responsibility quantitatively? We know of the attempt to measure the gain from reallocation of manpower over the trend (the celebrated "Petty-effect"); and a few attempts have been made to measure the "cost of duties." Further, a Swedish economist, Mr. Werin[3], has attempted to measure the loss, in Sweden, as of 1957, through the misallocation of resources in general. From the point of view of methods, his study is extremely interesting, in spite of the fact that he obviously failed. His model proved that an optimal allocation in 1957 would have increased the gross domestic product of Sweden by less than half of one per cent! But generally, I know of only very few studies in this field.

This is naturally an immense problem. One virtue of it, however, is that we ought to be able to mobilize our Eastern colleagues in attempts to solve it. My impression is that they believe that the question of optimizing the allocation of resources has been the key problem in the socialized countries for a long time.

[3] Lars Werin, *A Study of Production, Trade and Allocation of Resources*, Stockholm, 1965.

Chapter Seven

# AUSTRIA AND SWITZERLAND

KURT W. ROTHSCHILD
School of Social and Economic Sciences, Linz

Two alternative approaches can be usefully chosen, to place historic events in perspective. On the one hand, similar objects may be studied, as for instance two highly industralized countries in the same region with comparable economic structures. Even slight deviations from a common course can then be taken as important indicators of some specific influences in the country studied. On the other hand, two contrasting objects — for example, developed and less-developed countries — may be observed, and significant clues may be drawn from the differences that are plainly visible.

When economic events in Austria and Switzerland are under consideration, both approaches may fortunately be used at the same time. In some respects, Austria and Switzerland are as alike as could be expected in nationally and historically divided Europe. Both countries are definitely small, with 7.2 million people in Austria and 5.9 million in Switzerland. Both are land-locked, mountainous, and poorly endowed with natural resources, apart from ample supplies of hydro-electric power[1]. Smallness and geographic and natural conditions have insured a dominant place for industry, foreign trade, and tourism in the two economies. These similarities between the two countries in the years following World War I have often been stressed[2].

In other respects, however, the gaps between Austrian and Swiss economic conditions are large. Switzerland is one of the wealthiest European countries, with a per capita income of $2,190. Austria is near the bottom of the

[1] In the past twenty years, Austria's oil discoveries have played an increasing role without, however, changing the economic picture fundamentally.
[2] As early examples, see, for example, the League of Nation's Report on Austria by W. T. Layton and C. Rist, *La Situation Economique de l'Autriche: Rapport Présenté au Conseil de la Société des Nations,* Geneva, 1925, and A. Basch and J. Dvoracek, *L'Autriche et son existence économique,* Prague, 1925.

225

industrialized world, with a per capita income of $1,180 (per capita gross
national product in 1964 at official exchange rates). Switzerland can look back
on undisturbed development for more than a century; Austria, in contrast, went
through two major wars, one occupation and three major breaks in its
constititional history in the past half-century. After 1945, the Austrian economy
had to recover from destruction and confusion, while the Swiss economy had
hardly been harmed by World War II. Switzerland's industrial structure is
characterized by a high share of modern industries (chemical products, precision
instruments and watches, machinery, etc.), while in Austria traditional industries
(basic metals, textiles, paper, food) have maintained a dominant position[3].
The similarities as well as the differences between the two countries should be
kept in mind when their growth and cyclical experience in recent years are
considered.


## Early Recovery and Return to Normality

The Conference of the International Economic Association held in 1952[4]
adopted the title, "The Business Cycle in the Post-War World." It took more or
less for granted the existence of the business cycle in some form. Today we ask
far more skeptically, "Is the Business Cycle Obsolete?" Looking back with all
the advantages of hindsight, we recognize how courageous it was in 1952 to
attack the question of the postwar cycle after only seven years of postwar
experience. Today, it is recognized that the immediate postwar period was
almost as irregular as the war years from which, after all, nobody tried to deduce
the probable development of cyclical behavior.

   The early postwar years in Europe were so dominated by the special forces of
pentup demand, the rebuilding of necessities, the reconstruction of external trade
links, etc., that cyclical influences had hardly any chance to appear[5]. Far more
important than any differences in the cyclical experience of single countries was

---

[3] These and some other divergences between the Austrian and Swiss situation are
discussed in Kurt W. Rothschild, *Österreich, Schweiz, Schweden: Ein Wirtschaftsvergleich*,
Austrian Institute for Economic Research, Vienna, 1964.

[4] For details, see E. Lundberg, (ed.), *The Business Cycle in the Post-War World*, London,
1955.

[5] This fact was clearly recognized by D. H. Robertson in his introduction to the country
papers presented at the Oxford conference. The extraordinary postwar influences "have
moulded," he wrote, "the actual course of events to a degree which makes it idle to suppose
that the economic record of the past seven years can be written in any direct and simple way
in terms of a theory of normal cyclical movement" (Lundberg, *op. cit.*, p. 3). Yet Robertson
hoped that the studies might reveal bits and pieces of the emerging postwar cycle.

.the sharp division between war-torn countries, on the one hand, and relatively undamaged countries, on the other. The remarkable feature of that period was the quick recovery of the war-torn countries. It was not dependent on any very specific policy: Germany, Italy, Austria, Eastern Europe, Japan, all presented a similar picture. The main reason for these various "economic miracles" was, no doubt, that very high growth rates can be achieved where reserves of skilled people and half usable capital equipment can be put to work. Of course, other events were necessary ingredients for this success story, as for instance a nonrestrictive monetary (or better, inflationary) policy, large-scale international aid, and above all the prevention of major depressions in the rest of the world[6]. But recessions in the less damaged part of the world were easily avoided precisely because of the expansive trend that emanated from the "miracle" countries.

I would suggest, therefore, that the search for clues about "normal" postwar cycles should start at a point of time which was outside the reach of the Oxford conference. Particularly with regard to Austria and Switzerland, the early postwar years are too clearly overshadowed by the special forces mentioned previously. These two countries stood more or less at opposite ends in the scale from complete disruption to "business as usual." Their growth experience was correspondingly different. Between 1948 and 1951, real per capita income grew by 43 per cent in Austria, but by only 5 per cent in Switzerland[7].

Little could be gained by including these abnormal years in considering present-day business cycles. I have chosen, therefore, to let the tale begin with 1953–1954. It is true that the special effects of the postwar situation had not completely vanished by that time; but conditions had definitely moved nearer to normality.

In Western Europe as a whole, industrial production, which had increased by more than 10 per cent a year in the period 1947–1951 ceased to grow by this amount in 1952 (Table 7-1). In Austria, prices and wages in 1951 had continued to rise by 30–40 per cent. But in 1952, an increase in bank rate from 3½ to 6 per cent, a rise in taxes coupled with decreases in government expenditures, restriction of credits, and related measures brought the inflation to a halt[8]. Production then stagnated, and unemployment increased to 249,000 in December 1952, against 152,000 a year earlier. However, this recession had nothing to do with "normal" cyclical swings. In 1952, the trade balance found its equilibrium, and the multiple exchange rates of the earlier postwar years were abolished.

---

[6] These factors had been absent in 1919–1921, when recovery was cut short in the war-torn countries of Europe.

[7] These figures, from the United Nations, *Statistical Yearbook, 1955,* p. 455, are rough estimates, but they reveal the wide gap in growth rates.

[8] F. Nemschak, *Zehn Jahre Österreichischer Wirtschaft 1945–1955,* Vienna, 1955, p. 10.

228                         Austria and Switzerland

TABLE 7-1    Industrial Production in Western Europe,
1947–1954*

| Year | (1953=100) | Annual percentage increase |
|---|---|---|
| 1947 | 59 | 15.7 |
| 1948 | 68 | 15.3 |
| 1949 | 76 | 11.8 |
| 1950 | 85 | 11.8 |
| 1951 | 94 | 10.6 |
| 1952 | 95 | 1.1 |
| 1953 | 100 | 5.3 |
| 1954 | 109 | 9.0 |

Source: United Nations, *Statistical Yearbook, 1955.*
* Index of mining and manufacturing production in
European countries, excluding Bulgaria, Czechoslo-
vakia, German Democratic Republic, Hungary, Poland,
Rumania, and the U.S.S.R.

Switzerland, of course, had returned to normality much earlier[9]. But the
world situation, as well as the dearth of Swiss statistics for earlier years, make it
advisable to limit our observation for Switzerland to the 1953–1966 period.

## The Question of Cyclical Developments

It is better not to put to authors of country studies the question, "Is the
Business Cycle Obsolete?" If they answered in the affirmative there would be
nothing to report about the cyclical experience of their countries.

If the cycle in its classical form—with ups and downs in major economic
aggregates (production, employment, foreign trade, prices)— is considered, then
it would be difficult indeed to detect one in the period under review[10]. In
Europe, it was only in 1958 that developments came near to anything that could
be called a slight recession in the postwar U.S. style. From the autumn of 1957
to the end of 1958, economic activity was more or less stagnant. But even in
1958, industrial production in most European countries (the main exceptions

[9] H. Böhi, in his short survey of Switzerland's cyclical history, puts the normalization of
the Swiss economy at 1948/9. See "Hauptzuge einer schweizerischen Konjunkturge-
schichte," *Schweizerische Zeitschrift für Volkswirtschaft and Statistik,* 1964, p.99.
[10] Austin Robinson's remark at the Oxford Conference still applies: "Would it be true to
say that the trade cycle has disappeared from the British economy since World War II? In
the sense in which we knew the cycle before the war it would undeniably be true to say that
it had." Lundberg, *op. cit.,* p. 37.

being Belgium-Luxemburg and Great Britain) was higher than in 1957. In the European countries that are members of the Organization for Economic Cooperation and Development (OECD), industrial output increased by 1.4 per cent, in contrast to a decline of 7 per cent in the United States during the same year.

Yet in spite of this absence of classical depressions, cyclical fluctuations continue to be a topical subject in capitalist countries. To keep swings in activity under control is the daily bread of economic policy. Under such circumstances, it remains meaningful to speak of cycles in a modified form. If a motor car moves along a certain road at rather uneven speeds, these irregularities may not worry us as long as the car moves in the right direction. But in all likelihood, the *causes* of the uneven progress would be of interest. Business cycle research in the present growth period (which may not last forever) is similar to this example. As long as economies continue to grow, we are free of the worst worries with which the classical cycle presented us. But if the growth process shows distinct phases of fast and of retarded growth, this cycle-like phenomenon deserves investigation [11].

There can be little doubt that such modified cycles do exist. A close examination of 90 statistical series of the Austrian economy (seasonally adjusted quarterly figures) reveals that only 26 of them show cyclically significant *absolute* fluctuations in the classical sense [12]. Most of them refer to economically less important entities. But as soon as the *changes* from quarter to quarter are compared, very clear swings in activity can be discovered in many of the series.

With this material, an attempt was made at "dating" the (cyclical) swings by adapting the method of the National Bureau of Economic Research (NBER) to the peculiarities of a growth period. While in the NBER cycle phases are marked by absolute turning points in economic time series, the divisions — in the Austrian case — were drawn with regard to trend lines. Whenever the growth rates lie above a (predetermined) trend value, they are described as periods of fast growth (corresponding to the expansions in the NBER cycles), while growth rates below the trend denote periods of damped growth (corresponding to the NBER contractions) [13]. When this method is applied to real gross national product (GNP) data and the trend values adopted are annual growth rates of 6 per cent for the period 1950–1956 and 4.5 per cent for later years, [14] a fairly well-behaved picture of three to four [15] "cycles" is obtained for the period since 1950 (Table 7-2).

The foregoing considerations were introduced in order to show ways of describing "cyclical" developments in postwar Europe. In the following sections dealing with the Austrian and Swiss economies, no detailed "phasing" of the above sort will be used. What is needed is a rough sketch of the fluctuating growth and the factors behind it. For this purpose, annual figures will be used.

TABLE 7-2    **Austria: Cyclical Phases, 1950–1966**

| Period (quarter and year) of | | Duration in quarters |
|---|---|---|
| Fast growth | Damped growth | |
| –III/1951 | | – |
| | III/1951–I/1953 | 6 |
| I/1953–IV/1955 | | 11 |
| | IV/1955–III/1956 | 3 |
| III/1956–III/1967 | | 4 |
| | III/1957–I/1959 | 6 |
| I/1959–I/1961 | | 8 |
| | I/1961–I/1963 | 8 |
| I/1963– | | |

**Source:** Unpublished investigations by Dr. H. Neiss, Austrian Institute of Economic Research

---

[11] Even if development is perfectly smooth, there remains the interesting question of what sort of cycle would have been experienced in the absence of policy measures. It would, however, be difficult to tackle such a question in a quantitative way when answers have to be based on only a few years of "normal" postwar behavior.

[12] These and the following remarks are based on unpublished investigations by Dr. Hubert Neiss of the Austrian Institute of Economic Research.

[13] In other words, the dividing line between periods of a good and a poor "Konjunktur" is, in the U. S. case, the line of zero growth, while in the foregoing example the line is drawn at some positive value of growth (the trend rate).

It can, of course, be objected that this method ensures that there will *necessarily* be "cyclical" swings in the economy. For, while the line of zero growth may never be crossed and the cycle could consequently disappear on the NBER pattern, there must always be values above and below the trend rate, if this presents some sort of long-run average (and not a *minimum* requirement for a growing economy).

But the swings would not be described as quasi-cyclical if (a) positive and negative deviations from the trend rate were erratic rather than continuous for some period, and/or if (b) the deviations were very small. In fact, neither (a) nor (b) applies to the Austrian data.

[14] The choice of the trend introduces, of course, an arbitrary element into the determination of the turning points. But slightly different values would not greatly affect the actual phases of the "cycle." Moreover, it should not be forgotten that the use of *absolute* turning points as sign posts is also an arbitrary choice.

[15] The "downturn" of 1955–1956 may be a statistical artifact or a random movement. Its inclusion in the "cyclical history" can be questioned.

## "Cyclical" Experience, 1953–1966

When annual data for real gross national product (GNP) and industrial production are used, the following picture of the overall development in Austria and Switzerland is obtained (Table 7-3). Both countries enjoyed rapid expansion from 1954 to 1957. In 1958, each suffered a definite setback. In Switzerland, the setback took the form of decline of 1.8 per cent in real GNP — the only decline in the postwar era. In Austria, it led to a drop in the growth rate of GNP from 5.9 per cent in 1957 to 4.1 per cent in 1958 and in industrial production from 5.7 per cent to 2.6 per cent. The slowing down in Switzerland began in 1957 but was completely overcome in 1959, while in Austria it came later and lasted well into 1959.

After 1959, expansion at high rates characterized both countries. In Switzerland, it lasted without interruption until about 1964; Austria experienced another sharp break in 1962, with growth rates of real GNP (2.4 per cent) and industrial production (2.2 per cent) even lower than in 1958–1959. In 1965 the two countries displayed slight, but noticeable, declines from the high activity of the previous years. Industrial production, which in all but the "recession" years had grown by more than 4 per cent, advanced only between 3 and 3.5 per cent. In the first half of 1966, the stage was set for a new recovery, but it was damped down in the later months through the recessionary trends in several European countries, particularly Western Germany. These dampening influences continued to affect Austria, and to a lesser extent Switzerland, in 1967 without, however, setting off cumulative processes in a downward direction. Before any special questions are considered, these ups and downs will be examined in more detail. In particular, developments in Austria, Switzerland, and OECD-Europe (henceforth called simply Europe) will be compared.

The only serious setback shared by both Austria and Switzerland — the 1958 "pause" — coincides with the only obvious all-European "recession" during the period observed. The Austrian and Swiss economies, which are highly dependent on foreign trade, were strongly affected[16]. With world imports falling by 4.9 per cent between 1957 and 1958 and Western European imports by 6.6 per cent[17], both countries had to accept reductions in their exports. In Austria, where industry had not yet fully recovered its competitive strength and where some basic export commodities (steel, timber, magnesite) are particularly sensitive to cyclical fluctuations, exports declined by 7.3 per cent. The more competitive and specialized export industries of Switzerland were better able to resist the storm; their sales abroad declined by only 1.5 per cent.

---

[16] In 1964, exports of commodities amounted to 17 per cent of GNP in Austria and to 21 per cent in Switzerland.
[17] From United Nations, *Yearbook of International Trade, 1964.*

TABLE 7-3    European Countries: Real Gross National Product and Industrial Production, 1953–1966

| | Real gross national product at market prices | | | Industrial production | | |
|---|---|---|---|---|---|---|
| | European OECD* | Austria | Switzerland | European OECD* | Austria | Switzerland |
| | | | Index numbers† | | | |
| 1953 | 81 | 72 | 84 | 65 | 56 | |
| 1954 | 85 | 78 | 89 | 70 | 64 | |
| 1955 | 90 | 86 | 93 | 77 | 75 | |
| 1956 | 94 | 91 | 99 | 81 | 79 | |
| 1957 | 98 | 96 | 102 | 85 | 83 | |
| 1958 | 100 | 100 | 100 | 86 | 85 | 84 |
| 1959 | 105 | 103 | 107 | 91 | 90 | 90 |
| 1960 | 112 | 111 | 113 | 100 | 100 | 100 |
| 1961 | 117 | 117 | 122 | 105 | 105 | 107 |
| 1962 | 123 | 119 | 128 | 110 | 107 | 113 |
| 1963 | 128 | 124 | 134 | 115 | 112 | 119 |
| 1964 | 136 | 132 | 141 | 124 | 120 | 124 |
| 1965 | 142 | 136 | 146 | 129 | 125 | 128 |
| 1966 | ... | 142 | ... | 134 | 129 | 132 |
| | | | Annual rates of growth in per cent | | | |
| 1953 | 6.6 | 3.9 | 4.5 | 8.7 | 2.0 | |
| 1954 | 4.9 | 8.6 | 5.6 | 7.7 | 14.3 | |
| 1955 | 5.9 | 11.1 | 5.3 | 10.0 | 17.2 | |
| 1956 | 4.4 | 5.1 | 6.0 | 5.1 | 4.9 | |
| 1957 | 4.3 | 5.9 | 2.9 | 4.4 | 5.7 | |
| 1958 | 2.0 | 4.1 | −1.8 | 1.4 | 2.6 | |
| 1959 | 5.0 | 2.8 | 7.2 | 5.9 | 5.6 | 7.1 |
| 1960 | 6.7 | 8.3 | 5.8 | 10.0 | 10.9 | 11.1 |
| 1961 | 4.5 | 4.7 | 7.3 | 5.1 | 4.7 | 7.0 |
| 1962 | 5.1 | 2.4 | 5.1 | 4.3 | 2.2 | 5.6 |
| 1963 | 4.1 | 3.9 | 4.7 | 5.0 | 4.2 | 5.3 |
| 1964 | 6.3 | 6.6 | 5.1 | 7.3 | 7.8 | 4.2 |
| 1965 | 4.4 | 3.0 | 4.2 | 4.1 | 3.5 | 3.2 |
| 1966 | ... | 4.3 | ... | 3.9 | 3.2 | 3.1 |

Sources: Organization for Economic Cooperation and Development (OECD), *Historical and Monthly Statistics; United Nations Yearbook of National Accounts; National Statistics.*
* European members of OECD.
† For gross national product, base period is 1958; for industrial production, it is 1960.

However, the greater resilience of exports did not prevent the economic setback in Switzerland from being greater than that in Austria. The reason is that domestic factors lessened the external blow in Austria, but intensified it in Switzerland.

To begin with, Austria had raced toward 1958 with more than average speed (for reasons still to be discussed). That momentum helped her to counterbalance the external shock. In addition, the introduction of tax relief in 1957 had given a fillip to investment which lasted well into 1958. Real gross investment in machinery and equipment, which had weakened in 1956 (a decrease of 5.7 per cent from 1955), rose by 11.9 per cent in 1957 and by another 8.8 per cent in 1958. The completion of important productive capacity in the iron and steel industry in 1956, a mild spring in 1957, and higher government expenditure fostered building activity, which had stimulating effects on many other branches of the economy.

By contrast, the Swiss situation of 1957 was characterized by deflationary elements. A strong boom in factory and residential construction—resulting from the influx of foreign workers, urbanization, and a growing foreign demand—had set off a quickened rise in prices and a sharp increase in imports. Adjusted for seasonal fluctuations, the import surplus rose from a monthly average of $27 million in 1956 to $41 million in the first quarter of 1957. This led to a reduction in the supply of central bank money and to a slight squeeze in credit markets. The situation was intensified when the discount rate was raised from 1½ to 2½ per cent in May 1957—the first change since 1936—in order to fight inflationary tendencies and the increase in the foreign trade deficit.

The tighter credit conditions did not take long to show their effects. Private building activity in 1957 was more than 8 per cent lower than the year before[18]. This, coming on top of the unexpected export stagnation, had an adverse effect on investment in machinery and equipment. Total fixed asset formation (construction and equipment) in real terms was almost 9 per cent lower than in 1957. The continued rise in consumption and government expenditure did not quite suffice to prevent a slight decline in total social product. In 1959, when a new export boom was on its way and the disinflationary policy was dropped (the discount rate was lowered to 2 per cent in February) the economy returned quickly to its upward course.

At this stage, a slight digression may be permitted. What will be said is rather banal, but perhaps I cannot do much better than draw some simple conjectures from our short postwar experience[19]. Probably all agree that in the postwar

---

[18] Calculated from value figures deflated by the Zurich index of building costs. See *Statistisches Jahrbuch der Schweiz* (1965), pp. 179 and 183.

[19] A period, which with its Korean, Cold, and Vietnam Wars, has so far been anything but a "normal" peacetime period.

years developed capitalism has shown a greater economic stability than before World War II. Many reasons have been adduced for this fact, such as faster technological progress, a greater pool of investment opportunities inherited from the depression and war, the greater role of the state, armament expenditures, the new political setting, the full employment obligation, and, of course, our improved knowledge of how to deal with economic fluctuations[20].

I do not want to go into the question of which of these different influences is the "real" cause of the increased stability and whether that stability is going to last. It suffices to note that a change *has* taken place. At the same time, fluctuations of a milder sort continue to appear in different countries and regions of the world. Here again it is not necessary to inquire into the reasons for these "autonomous" disturbances; we just register their existence.

It seems that some sort of see-saw mechanism has helped to keep postwar world production and trade on their upward courses. Autonomous disturbances[21] in one part of the world did not—as in prewar times—spread quickly and automatically to the rest of the world. The quick growth in individual areas which creates its own momentum; the existence of a singularly expansive phase in world trade and international payments (characterized by such institutional arrangements as the IBRD, IMF, OEEC, ECE, GATT, EUP, EEC, EFTA, UNCTAD, and a number of other capital-letter combinations): a redistribution of international liquidity which for the time being laid the ghost of the dollar shortage; and, last but not least, the ubiquity of full-employment policy—all helped to make undisturbed areas rather immune against infections from external sources. Instead of reflecting and intensifying external irritations—the classical prewar chain of events—these disturbances were more or less absorbed, and the continued growth and imports in "healthy" areas offered a support for the disturbed country whose recovery was correspondingly eased[22].

In the postwar era, the economic disturbances so far have not only been comparatively light but, on the whole, have occurred at different periods in different areas. This has helped each region to pull itself out of the threatening mess by the other regions' bootstraps [23].

---

[20] On all these matters, see the interesting discussions in S. Tsuru (ed.), *Has Capitalism Changed?* Tokyo, 1961.

[21] The word "autonomous" as used here is to be understood as "originating independently in one region."

[22] This postwar interregional resilience is ably described by A. Lamfalussy, "International Trade and Trade Cycles, 1950–1960," in Roy Harrod and Douglas Hague (eds.), *International Trade Theory in a Developing World*. London, 1963.

[23] This point was also stressed by Harrod in his contribution to the discussion on Lamfalussy's paper mentioned in the previous footnote. See Harrod and Hague, *op. cit.*, p. 502.

If a quick glance is taken at Western Europe and North America as a whole, it is not difficult to make out this nonsynchronized change of ups and downs. The U.S. recession of 1949 took place while Europe was moving on its steep recovery path. When Europe slowed down for the first time in 1952, the U.S. economy was still moving at full steam in the wake of the Korean War boom. The European economy had recovered when the United States entered its next recession in 1953–1954. Similarly, the European economy was in mid-boom in 1960, with industrial production expanding by 10 per cent, when there was a slackening in North America. And finally, the weakening in Europe's economic growth in 1965 took place while the longest U.S. postwar expansion and armaments boom was showing no signs of flagging [24].

The one exception to this see-saw development was the year 1958 [25]. This was the only year when a U.S. recession (which had started in the second half of 1957) and a "pause" in Europe coincided. This synchronization by itself is probably enough to explain the greater severity of the 1958 setback [26]. European GNP and industrial production, which in all other years after 1953 had grown by more than 4 per cent, registered increases of only 2 per cent and 1.4 per cent, respectively.

The cumulative effects were sufficiently strong to hit even those countries which had shown no signs of declining growth. Where the internal situation was one of "dis-expansion," events which otherwise would have resulted in reduced growth suddenly led to actual declines. This was true in Switzerland. Because of the "three-layered" recession (United States-Europe-Switzerland) a relatively mild anti-inflationary policy produced a fall of 2 per cent in real GNP. Most other European countries, suffering under the impact of only two layers (U.S. recession, general European "pause"), experienced merely some slowdown of their previous growth. This was true of Austria [27].

---

[24] A similar process of mutual aid through nonsynchronized swings also helps to explain the short life of more localized recessions. Thus the deep Italian recession of 1964 could hardly have been overcome so quickly if it had not taken place in an expanding environment. The same circumstances enabled Britain to operate stop-go policies without international repercussions.

[25] At this time (Spring, 1967), a repetition of the 1958 conditions seems possible. Much depends on the resilience of the U. S. economy and on the chances of a quick recovery in Germany and Britain.

[26] An explanation of the great depressions of 1873 and 1932 probably also requires a stress on the abnormal cumulation of adverse cyclical influences. Here, however, we are only concerned with *regional* synchronization of disturbances in an otherwise comparatively stable growth period.

[27] It may be asked what lessons—if any—can be learned from this development of the postwar international cycle. One obvious lesson would be that we should try to be lucky enough not to get any cumulation of disturbances. There may be some opportunities to give luck a chance. Individual countries should decide the major aspects of their economic policies in the light not only of their own inflationary situations or the world situation as a

After this digression, let me return to the discussion of Austria and Switzerland. With international trade returning to its expansionary path, 1959 and particularly 1960–1961 were years of strong revival for both countries. In 1962, the Austrian expansion slumped in the midst of a continuously growing world economy. Several factors contributed to this isolated development. Adverse weather conditions had badly affected real agricultural production, which fell 5½ per cent below the 1961 output. Because of the bad weather conditions, the building season had a late start, which retarded several branches of the economy. These "exogenous" events would, however, not have been so important if they had not been reinforced by stagnation of investment in machinery and equipment.

The 1962 standstill in investment in the face of strongly-rising consumption expenditures, a high foreign demand, and sufficient credit facilities is not easily explained. If anything, it proves that investment continues to be a rather volatile character, and that the search for a reliable investment function must reckon with considerable difficulties. Of course, some important "real" dampening factors can be enumerated. The weather led to some minor repercussions on investment projects. More important was the intensification of the steel recession which had begun in 1961. In 1962, European steel production was 3.2 per cent below the 1960 record figure, but Austrian output fell by 6.3 per cent. The reduced demand and prices forced the important Austrian steel sector to cut back its investment plans. Furthermore, some large investment projects—for instance, in the oil industry—happened to be completed in 1961 and were not immediately followed by similar large-scale investments.

But these special factors, important as they are, do not suffice to account fully for the 1962 standstill. Normally, in a fully employed economy, it would be expected that—apart from the balancing effects of large numbers—the freeing of investment capacity and finance in some fields would *induce* additional investment in other fields. If an explanation of why this did not happen in 1962 in Austria is desired, then it is necessary to retreat into the psychological sphere.

The difficulties in some branches which occurred after a glorious boom period, and a catching-up of wages and salaries with growing profits[28], had

---

whole, but also of cyclical stages in other regions. Past experience also suggests that it may not have been a bad thing that international policies for full employment were not too closely coordinated. This may have prevented dangerous synchronizations. The call for a coordinated "Konjunkturpolitik" in the Common Market certainly appeals to sentiments for order, but it should be realized that, in our basically unstable economic system given to contagious diseases, coordination may have to mean planning for an economic policy which is consciously kept *out of step,* even though internal conditions may demand parallel measures in all countries.

[28] Wage rates in 1960 and 1961 had increased between 6 and 7 per cent, compared with 1 per cent in 1958 and 5.4 per cent in 1959.

created an atmosphere of uneasiness which put a brake on investment plans. This atmosphere of indecision was further nourished by a rather unfortunate, largely politically motivated, campaign criticizing Austria's membership in the European Free Trade Association (EFTA) and demanding entry into the European Economic Community (EEC) as an absolute economic necessity. The noisy discussion created an uncertainty which certainly did not reduce the bewilderment in the decision-making process.

The stagnation in investment, on top of the setbacks in agriculture and building, could have produced a dangerous situation in Austria in 1962. Danger was avoided by the continued high propensity to consume, and by the uninterrupted expansion of external demand. Industrial production could bypass internal demand lacunae by moving abroad; the percentage of manufacturing output sold abroad rose from 33.8 in 1961 to 35.2 in 1962. With consumption and exports providing a continuous pull, investment could not remain stagnant for long. Slowly in 1963, and more quickly in 1964, it was again increasing, though the dampening effects of the integration controversy and of structural imbalance have not been completly overcome.

Finally, we come to the slight retardation in growth in both countries in 1965. Austria and Switzerland shared this cooling-off with most European countries, but displayed it in a more pronounced fashion. The causes were partly different. In Austria, retardation to a large extent just "happened." As in 1962, bad weather conditions afflicted agriculture and caused a decline of 9 per cent in real output. Similarly, building was held up in the beginning of the year and delayed the general upswing in the spring season.

The weather factor also retarded activities in other countries. In Austria, however, it was intensified by a growing diversion of demand to imported goods. This is one aspect of the structural imbalance mentioned earlier. Austria's industrial structure is dominated by basic and traditional industries. With rising incomes and more sophisticated consumption and investment requirements, demand turns increasingly to imported commodities. In years with sharply rising prices—1965, with a price increase of more than 5 per cent, was a case in point—structural and competitive elements combine to create a large import surplus. That surplus jumped from a record $417 million in 1964 to $501 million in 1965. The increase in imports (value) by 13 per cent, reductions in inventory purchases, and a cautious budget policy (as a weapon against price increases) lowered the growth rate of industrial production to 3.5 per cent, though consumption and exports expanded at a faster rate, and investment (increasing by 5 per cent) also fared much better in 1962. In 1966, a return to faster growth was cut short by export difficulties on the recessionary German market and increased import demand. The deterioration in the balance of payments reduced the liquidity position and put a brake on investment. In the spring of 1967, relaxations in credit restrictions were taken to counteract these developments.

In contrast to the Austrian retardation, which just "happened," the Swiss reduction in speed was consciously engineered. Switzerland, for long time a happy island of stable prices in the sea of inflationary Europe, caught the general disease at the beginning of the 1960's. Consumer prices, which until 1961 had never increased by as much as 2 per cent a year, suddenly rose by 4.3 per cent in 1962 and by more than 3 per cent in subsequent years. When, in addition, the strong domestic boom and price developments caused the import surplus to rise sharply (from $333 million in 1960 to $823 million in 1963 and $946 million in 1964), the time was considered ripe for stronger government action than Switzerland had been used to.

Instead of relying exclusively on the traditional fiscal and monetary instruments—the discount rate was raised from 2 to 2½ per cent in July, 1965, and to 3½ per cent in July 1966—resort was taken to more direct measures for curbing the growth in demand. Restrictions were put on the entry and investment of foreign capital and on bank lending; the control of new security issues was extended to domestic securities; an embargo was imposed in certain types of low priority building, and upper limits were fixed for all other building; Finally, the continuous intake of foreign workers was stopped and a slight reduction in their numbers initiated. The combined impact of these measures was unfavorable to production, which rose by only 3.2 per cent in 1965, but favorable to the trade balance, whose deficit was reduced to $711 million. The inflation in building costs slowed down, but consumer prices continued on their upward course.

I want to conclude this section by indicating in a simple way the sectors which took the lead in the various years of expansion and recession in Austria and Switzerland. For this purpose, only four large aggregates are chosen; gross domestic fixed asset formation, private consumption, government current expenditure, and exports[29]. The growth rates of these aggregates, measured at

[29] From the point of view of cyclical development, one might miss in this list inventories, the trade balance, and the goverment surplus or deficit. Inventories are excluded because data referring to inventory changes in the two countries belong to the less reliable quantities. Moreover, I believe that—at least in small countries intensively linked to the world economy—inventory changes will seldom be a major cause of cyclical fluctuations. They may be a proximate cause, but the real reason for the accumulation or decumulation of stocks will normally be changes in investment demand, exports, etc.

Trade *balances* and budget *balances* are important influences in economic activity. But increases in exports as such, even with imports rising at the same time, are likely to set off expansive impulses. (On this point, see K. W. Rothschild, "Export oder Exportüberschuss" *Konjunkturpolitik,* Vol. 7, 1961). The same applies to government expenditure as such. Since in the text I work with changes in *real* quantities, I prefer to restrict myself to exports and government expenditures. The estimation of balances in real terms is a tricky business. But it should be kept in mind that the other side of the balance sheet is not without influence. In particular, the continued weakness of Austria's performance in 1959 was due largely to a high import surplus.

TABLE 7-4   Austria and Switzerland: Leading Sectors on Expansion and Recession

| Austria: Rates of Change in | | | Switzerland: Rates of Change in | | |
|---|---|---|---|---|---|
| | Real GNP | Leading sectors† | | Real GNP | Leading sectors† |
| 1954 | 8.6 | I: 24.9 | | 5.6 | I:  10.4 |
| | | E: 22.0 | | | E:   5.0 |
| 1955 | 11.1 | I: 31.5 | | 5.3 | E:  10.5 |
| | | E: 11.8 | | | I:   9.7 |
| 1956 | 5.1 | E: 17.6 | | 6.0 | I:  12.6 |
| | | C:  6.0 | | | E:  10.3 |
| 1957 | 5.9 | E: 15.4 | | *2.9* | *C:   2.4* |
| | | I:  8.5 | | | *I:   5.3* |
| 1958 | *4.1* | *E: −4.4* | | *−1.8* | *I:  −8.7* |
| | | *G:   3.8* | | | *E:  −1.5* |
| 1959 | *2.8* | *G:   1.5* | | 7.2 | I:  16.2 |
| | | *C:   5.2* | | | E:  11.9 |
| 1960 | 8.3 | I: 13.8 | | 5.8 | I:  14.0 |
| | | E: 13.0 | | | E:   6.5 |
| 1961 | 4.7 | I:  8.5 | | 7.3 | I:  17.3 |
| | | E:  7.3 | | | G:  13.3 |
| 1962 | *2.4* | *I: −1.0* | | 5.1 | I:  10.7 |
| | | *G:   1.9* | | | G:   9.0 |
| 1963 | 3.9 | E:  6.6 | | 4.7 | G:   8.2 |
| | | G:  5.4 | | | E:   6.5 |
| 1964 | 6.6 | I:  9.0 | | 5.1 | I:   8.7 |
| | | E:  6.2 | | | E:   7.9 |
| 1965 | *3.0‡* | *G:   3.7* | | 4.2 | E:  11.4 |
| | | *C:   4.4* | | | C:   3.5 |

\* Years of recession are indicated by italics. In these years of slow growth, the two "leading" sectors are those with the lowest rates of increase. In the other years, those with the highest rates are considered "leaders".

† All are measured in real terms.

I = gross domestic fixed asset formation; C = private consumption; G = government current expenditure; and E = export volume.

‡ Gross national product (GNP) expanded more slowly than the slow-growing subsections, because a large part of additional consumption and investment was covered by imports at improved terms of trade and because of (nonrecorded) changes in stocks.

constant prices, are used in Table 7-4 to indicate which of them played a leading part in pushing the economy up in good years or holding it back in bad ones. The two most effective groups (fastest growing in good years, slowest growing in bad years) are set against the growth rate of real GNP.

As should be expected, investment and exports prove to be the most volatile influences. For Austria, investment appears in seven out of twelve years as one of the "prime movers," exports in nine. For Switzerland, the corresponding figures are ten and nine. The importance of the external trade link cannot be overlooked.

Consumption, quite naturally, provides the stable basis of growth in the moderately quiet period being reviewed. Only five times does it appear on the combined list of both countries. In 1956, it helped to maintain economic growth in Austria in the face of declining investment, while in 1959 and 1965 its expansion was too weak to counteract the insufficiency of government expenditure and the deflationary effect of high imports. In Switzerland, the anti-inflationary government policy reduced the pace of consumption in 1957 and thus prepared the way for the setback of 1958.

Government expenditure also was a secondary factor in influencing the course of events. It appears five times on the Austrian and three times on the Swiss list. But only three times is it in a leading position. In 1959 and 1965, an insufficient expansion of government expenditure prolonged the "recession" in Austria; while in Switzerland the government made the main contribution (in terms of growth rates, not in absolute quantities) to the maintenance of the boom in 1963.

This simple tableau shows clearly the difference in the course which the 1958 recession took in Austria and in Switzerland. In Switzerland, internal measures triggered a decline in expansion in 1957 (a slowdown of consumption and investment) which was intensified by external causes (decline in exports) in 1958. In Austria, the outside world was responsible for the pause in 1958, which dragged on into early 1959 because of an insufficient response in government expenditure.


### Growth and Labor Supply

The small economies of Austria and Switzerland, embedded as they are in the European and world economy, cannot normally be expected to display marked autonomous fluctuations. And in fact, if the *relative* performance of the two countries is measured—relative, that is, to the all-European development—the previously discussed cyclical patterns disappear (Table 7–5). What remain are the few individual deviations: the particular severity of the 1958 setback in Switzerland; continuation into 1959 of the 1958 setback in Austria; and the special Austrian setback in 1962.

But while the data on relative development iron out the short-term cycle, they disclose more clearly some tendencies pertaining to the period as a whole. For Austria, a strong above average growth is noticeable until 1958, and a

TABLE 7-5. European Countries: Relative Growth in Real Gross National Product, Total and Per Capita, 1954–1965*

| | Total GNP | | | Per Capita GNP | | |
|---|---|---|---|---|---|---|
| | Austria relative to Europe | Switzerland relative to Europe | Austria relative to Switzerland | Austria relative to Europe | Switzerland relative to Europe | Austria relative to Switzerland |
| 1954 | 92 | 105 | 88 | 90 | 108 | 83 |
| 1955 | 96 | 103 | 92 | 95 | 107 | 89 |
| 1956 | 97 | 105 | 92 | 95 | 106 | 89 |
| 1957 | 98 | 104 | 94 | 97 | 104 | 93 |
| 1958 | 100 | 100 | 100 | 100 | 100 | 100 |
| 1959 | 98 | 102 | 96 | 98 | 102 | 96 |
| 1960 | 99 | 101 | 98 | 102 | 101 | 101 |
| 1961 | 100 | 104 | 96 | 101 | 101 | 100 |
| 1962 | 97 | 104 | 93 | 98 | 99 | 99 |
| 1963 | 97 | 105 | 93 | 99 | 98 | 101 |
| 1964 | 97 | 104 | 94 | 100 | 98 | 102 |
| 1965 | 96 | 103 | 93 | 100 | 98 | 103 |

* These data were obtained by dividing the index (1958=100) of real gross national product (GNP) of one region by the GNP index of a second region. Rising index numbers indicate *relatively* faster growth in the first region and vice versa. Europe refers to OECD-Europe.

slightly poorer performance in later years; Switzerland entered a period of faster growth at the beginning of the 1960's. This divergence between growth rates leads to a sharp rise of the relative Austrian-Swiss index of real GNP from 88 in 1954 to 100 in 1958, and a consequent decline to 93 in 1962–1963.

The steeper rise in Austria in the mid-1950's is easily explained as the final stage of the recovery period in a war-torn and badly disorganized economy. Repairs and new investments were completed; foreign trade and economic policy began to function more smoothly. These improvements could be fully exploited, because the poststabilization "crisis" had increased unemployment to a rate of roughly 9 per cent in 1953. The subsequent boom could, therefore, draw on comparitively ample supplies of labor [30]. Total employment increased by 16.8 per cent from 1953 to 1959, compared with only 6.5 per cent in the 1959–1965 period. Although unemployment again rose slightly during the 1958 setback, it had disappeared by 1960–1961; only seasonal and frictional unemployment remained. With full employment reached for the first time in the postwar era, growth became more difficult, while inflationary stresses increased.

Switzerland presents a different picture. At the beginning of the period under discussion, the labor force was fully employed. Unemployment, already negligible in the 1950's, dwindled to microscopic proportions in the 1960's. But here, too, the above-average growth of GNP was heavily conditioned by labor supplies. Switzerland extended her employment of foreign labor on a unique scale. The number of foreign workers—which was 365,000 in 1959, an increase of about one half since 1954—was doubled in the five years 1960–1964. Foreigners represented 30 per cent of the total labor force in 1964. In 1965, the number was slightly reduced under the restrictionist program.

The pros and cons of such a massive import of foreign labor, which is a much discussed item in Switzerland, is not of concern in the present discussion [31]. What matters here is that the high relative growth of the Swiss economy after 1960 was due, to a large extent, to the availability of additional labor. This is clearly shown by the relative development of real *per capita* GNP (Table 7-5). Austria's faster growth in 1954–1958 is unaffected, because the additional labor came from within the country and permitted a better utilization of resources, with a consequent increase in output per inhabitant. In Switzerland, the faster growth was obtained through a parallel increase in the number of inhabitants. If this is taken into account, the disparity between Austrian and Swiss developments in the full employment period after 1959 disappears.

------------

[30] Previously untapped reserves of female labor also played an important role.

[31] See E. Tuchtfeldt, *Wachstumsprobleme der schweizerischen Volkswirtschaft*, Kiel, 1965, and literature quoted at p. 7f.

## Liquidity and Balance of Payments

The previous sections have been concerned mainly with real developments. Without going into details of credit and fiscal policy, we can say that at no time between 1953 and 1966 was economic development seriously hampered by monetary developments. Money supplies were forthcoming in sufficient quantities to permit real expansion, and to maintain that slight degree of inflation which both aided the expansionary process and was nourished by it.

Liquidity ratios (money supply divided by nominal GNP) were remarkably stable in both countries, fluctuating between 0.21 and 0.26 in Austria, and between 0.49 and 0.54 in Switzerland (Table 7-6). In both countries, some tightening of liquidity can be noticed in the years up to 1957, which probably aggravated the 1958 recession. The relaxation in the following years was more marked in Switzerland than in Austria, and provided a basis for the extensive boom in that country. With inflation becoming more pronounced, the Swiss National Bank introduced a number of restrictive measures, and the liquidity ratio declined from its high of 0.54 in 1962 to 0.49 in 1965.

This stable liquidity record was possible because, during the period under review, both countries were singularly free of balance of payments difficulties. From 1955 onward (in Switzerland also in earlier years), gold and foreign exchange reserves rose steeply. (A slight decline occurred in Austria after 1964, when the import surplus became more marked, and capital imports were discouraged for anti-inflationary reasons.) In 1966, official gold and foreign

TABLE 7-6    **Liquidity Ratios,\* 1954–1965**

|      | Austria | Switzerland |
|------|---------|-------------|
| 1954 | 0.26 | 0.52 |
| 1955 | 0.23 | 0.50 |
| 1956 | 0.22 | 0.50 |
| 1957 | 0.21 | 0.49 |
| 1958 | 0.22 | 0.53 |
| 1959 | 0.23 | 0.52 |
| 1960 | 0.22 | 0.52 |
| 1961 | 0.21 | 0.53 |
| 1962 | 0.22 | 0.54 |
| 1963 | 0.22 | 0.53 |
| 1964 | 0.22 | 0.51 |
| 1965 | 0.22 | 0.49 |

\* Ratio of money supply (currency and sight deposits) to nominal gross national product.

exchange reserves exceeded those in 1953 by 285 per cent in Austria and by 118 per cent in Switzerland. Their value amounted to 6.3 and 10.1 months of imports, respectively.

The favorable balance of payments position was maintained in spite of some inflationary spurts in Austria and the disturbance with which the division of Europe presented these two EEC-encircled EFTA members. Several reasons account for this positive development. Switzerland's position as an international financial center, and capital imports into Austria, have something to do with it. But one factor, in particular, should be mentioned: both countries—thanks to their natural beauty and a long tradition—benefited greatly from the rising tide of international tourism. Between 1953 and 1965, net income from tourism increased in the relation of 1:8 in Austria and 1:3.4 in Switzerland (from \$53 million to \$420 million and from \$107 million to \$367 million, respectively). This influx of foreign exchange stimulated and permitted a growing deficit in the balance of commodity trade.

Tourism is presented here as a typical example of the importance of structural factors in the postwar cycle. Where international growth industries take an important place in a country's export structure, the balance of payments will be, *ceteris paribus*, relatively undisturbed. The country will possess more elbow room in the choice and timing of its policy measures. There will be less need for such externally enforced stop-go policies as were found in the United Kingdom and Denmark.

Postwar Germany offers, of course, an outstanding example of the advantages of a favorable export structure. High world investment activity promoted continuous export surpluses because of the predominance of engineering and chemical products in Germany's export program. Swiss industry, too, is favored by the present trend toward precision instruments and chemical products. For her, tourism is a useful addition to an already favorable export structure. In Austria, where less-favored traditional branches like timber, steel, and textiles loom large in the export field, tourism belongs in the top group of trend-favored balance of payments items.

## Economic Policy

Little has been said about the instruments of economic policy in the two countries. While no detailed description will be attempted here[32] a few general remarks may be useful.

It goes without saying that the standard weapons of cycle policy can be found in both countries: discount rate and open market policy being applied by the central bank, fiscal measures by the government. In Austria there are also rules and gentlemen's agreements stipulating minimum reserve requirements for the commercial banks and influencing the volume of credit. (In Switzerland, similar measures are applied, in particular, to foreign deposits.)

But each of the two countries also has its own specialties. In Austria, there is a Paritätische Kommission für Preis-und-Lohnfragen, a commission consisting of top representatives from the government and from the workers', employers', and farmers' organizations (which possess some semi-official standing). It was constituted in 1957 (on the basis of some precedents in the immediate postwar era)[33], with the task of advising on wage negotiations and major price changes. Though without legal powers, it has at times been able to delay actions or to influence the extent of changes demanded. In a way, it could be called an institution of moral suasion. Whether or not it has been influential in reducing fluctuations is hardly possible to tell; we do not know what would have happened without it.

Ths Swiss specialty is the massive use of foreign labor with its cyclically important effects[34] on employment, wages, capital utilization, etc. To this, attention was drawn earlier in this discussion.

Let me conclude with two generalizations suggested by the comparison of Austrian and Swiss cyclical policy and experience: (1) The instruments of contemporary economic policy in developed capitalist countries are known sufficiently widely to make *basically* different policies unlikely. Special features in one country or the other may be due to special needs or to traditional causes; but they have rarely proved to be decisive. Under three circumstances, the differences in economic policy lie more in the timing of policy measures and in the extent to which they are applied, rather than in the measures themselves. In our complex world it is, however, very difficult to trace the effects of slight differences in timing and amount. Particularly where countries are so exposed to the outside world as Austria and Switzerland, cyclical policy can in times of general growth only have marginal effects[35]. With each country being in many

---

[32] A good comprehensive description for earlier years is given by H. Hahn (on Austria) and E. Dürr (on Switzerland) in *Die institutionelle Verankerung von Instrumenten der Konjunkturpolitik in neun europäischen Ländern und in den Vereingiten Staaten von Amerika,* 1958. Also F. A. Lutz, "Das konjunkturpolitische Instrumentarium der Schweiz," *Schweizerische Zeitschrift für Volkswirtschaft und Statistik*, Vol. 99. Nr.3, Sept. 1963. For single years, see the useful annual country pamphlets of the OECD and the Economic Surveys of the Economic Commission of Europe (ECE).

[33] For a full history of the "Paritätische Kommision," see the contribution to G. Neuhauser in T. Pütz, ed., *Verbände und Wirtschaftspolitik in Östereich,* Berlin, 1966.

[34] What these effects are has been disputed in Switzerland—whether they helped to dampen the boom or whether they heated it up. Much seems to depend on the stage of the cycle, the extent and the quality of immigration. See citations in note 31.

[35] This applies only to short-run cyclical policy which is carried out along reasonable lines. Long-term economic policy (for example, regional policy, investment planning, educational policy) may have considerable effects, though its results are not immediately visible. In these fields, there are also greater differences between the policies of various countries.

respects a "special" case, this makes it difficult to draw reliable quantitative conclusions from international comparisons about the effectiveness of cyclical policies (including full employment and anti-inflation policy). This is regrettable, for the future may well demand a greater capacity of providing the right kind of policy mix.

(2) The development of Austrian and Swiss policies displays, in a nutshell, a trend characteristic of the world as whole. The impact of modern industrialization and the quick spread of information and experience lead to a general convergence of policy methods. Differences with regard to political, social, and economic *targets* remain; but former dogmatic attitudes toward certain *instruments* [36] have begun to dwindle. This is true within the capitalist and socialist camp and even between them. Words like planning, markets, planification, and liberalization achieve a more technical meaning, and do not necessarily make anyone's blood boil.

This convergence of methods shows up nicely in recent cyclical measures in Austria and Switzerland. Austria, with a long tradition of protectionism, regulation of entry, etc., has used voluntary reductions in tariffs and other measures of liberalization as anti-inflationary weapons. In Switzerland, on the other hand, where economic liberalism is an article of faith (and of the constitution), direct controls over building and credit were introduced in 1964 on a scale which would meet with opposition even in more *dirigiste* countries [37].

This growing *Entideologisierung*, this more rational and pragmatic attitude vis-a-vis policy instruments—exemplified in recent Austrian and Swiss history but characteristic of the world as a whole—I regard as a hopeful development. We may be unable to foretell whether the cyclical propensities of present-day capitalism will continue to be mere changes between hot booms and cold "pauses," or whether we shall again be faced with recessions or even depressions. We may also find it difficult for some time to come to develop sufficient economic and socio-political knowledge for an exact timing and dosing of anti-cyclical policy. But the box of instruments at each country's disposal is growing, and there is more readiness for experimentation with various instruments. This should lead to a gradual improvement of our knowledge of the contemporary cycle mechanism and of our ability to cope with it. Neither politicians nor economists are likely to suffer from cyclical underemployment for some time to come.

---

[36] Not all such prejudices are necessarily irrational.

[37] Because of constitutional rules, these restrictions could only be prolonged beyond one year if approved by a people's referendum. This was the case in February 1965.

# COMMENT

JÜRG NIEHANS
Johns Hopkins University

There is nothing I can add to Professor Rothschild's excellent discussion of developments in Austria; I hope it does not violate the spirit of this chapter if I concentrate on Switzerland. This need not mean that I disagree with what Rothschild has to say about the Swiss case. Indeed, it will appear that I agree with most of his points. Certain minor differences can probably be explained by the fact that Rothschild had to rely largely on material reflecting the "official" point of view. I think, however, that the Swiss experience presents some interesting aspects that deserve a few supplementary remarks.

The main difficulty in studying economic developments in Switzerland is the paucity of statistical data and the absence of systematic macroeconomic analysis, not to speak of macroeconomic models. In interpreting developments, one is forced to rely on intuition to an even larger extent than in countries with a long tradition of macroeconomic research. Nevertheless, with respect to the main features the picture is reasonably clear.

Switzerland offers an example of business cycles in a highly industrialized economy without conscious and effective stabilization policies. In the field of monetary policy, the supply of money was dominated by the balance of payments. The influence of the central bank on the money supply, aside from seasonal fluctuations, was minimal. There was no active open market policy; the central bank had no authority over minimum reserves; and the volume of central bank credit is traditionally small. With certain exceptions, to be noted later, the central bank had to rely on moral suasion and various kinds of gentlemen's agreements. It was the guiding principle of monetary policy to deep interest rates moderate and reasonably stable — two terms which, however, were not always given the same interpretation. During the postwar period, there was also a growing realization that, in an open economy with free capital movements and stable exchange rates, the freedom to use monetary policy for domestic stabilization is narrowly limited.

Similar considerations apply to fiscal policies. There was at best a very tenuous relation between government expenditures and tax rates, on the one hand, and stabilization efforts on the other. According to the dominant doctrine, taxes — being too serious a matter to be used for stabilization purposes — should mainly reflect the long-term demand for public goods. However, there were some built-in stabilizers. Thanks to the progressive income tax, government revenues at constant tax rates were sensitive to business conditions. On the other hand, legislatures, while showing a high propensity for lowering tax rates in times of inflationary pressure, were usually slow in doing so. As a result, if one looks at the government sector in a statistical way, the record up the the end of the 1950's was actually quite good. The hidden hand, working through the tax structure and legislative inertia, made up for the lack of enlightened discretionary policies.

The remarkable fact is that in the absence of effective stabilization efforts, the Swiss economy developed in just about the same way as other economies in the postwar period, showing neither much more nor much less stability. Statistics show two "main" cycles reaching (from peak to peak) from 1948 to 1957, and from 1957 to 1964–1965, respectively. I am tempted to classify these as Juglar cycles. Their frequency seems to be of about the same order of magnitude as in earlier periods. These two cycles display in some respects a rather "classical" pattern. They are most clearly visible in investment and in private construction projects. There was a rather violent parallel movement of the import surplus and also a concurrent movement of interest rates (as measured by bond yields), reflecting consecutive periods of pronounced tightness and ease in the credit market. Stock prices led the investment cycle by one to two years, and a similar statement can be made about the incorporation of new firms. The volume of bankruptcies, on the other hand, moved inversely with a lag of one to two years. Both in 1949 and in 1958 there was a decline in output. All of these series show cycles not only in their rate of change or in their deviations from the trend but also in absolute terms.

At the same time, however, the Swiss cycles had some "unclassical" features. In particular, there was no significant unemployment. As a business indicator, unemployment was replaced by the varying number of foreign workers which, however, now reflects at least as much the social and political ability and willingness to absorb foreign labor as changes in the demand for labor as a whole. (The present ceilings on the employment of foreign workers have to be interpreted in the light of the fact that in the postwar period Switzerland was able to absorb foreign labor at a rate which has few, if any, precedents in the modern history of industrialized economies.) For the theorist, this seems to suggest the interesting possibility of a non-Keynesian (perhaps hyperclassical) cycle without excess capacity, without any difference between potential and actual output: each level of unemployment would represent "full employment" and, at each level of employment, labor would be combined with the existing capital stock in an optimal way.

The two basic cycles were modified by certain exogenous factors. As in the rest of the western world, the economic consequences of the outbreak of the Korean war helped to fill in the trough of 1950 and even created a secondary cycle of their own; this cycle was not reflected in stock prices, construction, new firms, or bankruptcies. A second factor was the restoration of convertibility. By increasing the mobility of capital, it changed the dynamic behavior of the Swiss economy. Before 1959, deficits in the current payments balance (created by cyclical upswings) contributed to an early tightening of the money supply with gradually increasing interest rates. This in turn acted as an automatic brake on investment, particularly construction. After 1959, however, the growing deficit of the current balance was largely neutralized by capital inflows. As a consequence, despite a growing trade deficit, there was no significant increase in interest rates until near the peak of the cycle. An important automatic stabilizer thus became inoperative.

The quantitative restrictions imposed in 1964 were a third exogenous factor. The government and the central bank regarded interest rates mainly as cost factors. To counteract inflationary price increases, they thought it necessary to restrain investment, but without increasing interest rates. As a consequence, they found themselves driven toward quantitative controls on construction and bank credit. Though these controls were discussed as matters of economic life and death, they were actually quite weak, and it is hard to identify their effect in economic time-series. While their imposition was indeed followed by a slowing down of the rate of expansion, the experience from earlier cycles seems to indicate that this slowing down was to be expected and that the restrictions were largely ineffective. A fourth factor, finally, was the rapid increase in government investment which began in the early 1960's. Combined with an ill-timed increase in social security benefits, it gave an added stimulus to the economy exactly at the time when the inflationary pressure otherwise showed signs of falling off. Without these exogenous factors, the postwar cycles in the Swiss economy would probably look even more "classical" than they do.

On the basis of these observations, I should like to express certain conjectures I have made about the cyclical mechanisms at work in the Swiss economy. The general problem appears to be the creation of endogenous cycles in a system of open, interdependent economies. I shall try to identify some elements of a solution of this problem which seem to be suggested by the Swiss case. First, certainly, are the fluctuations of total exports, which may be assumed to be caused by the occasional synchronization of fluctuations in the various export markets. Rothschild pointed out that such an upswing in exports contributed greatly to the expansion which began in 1958. However, cyclical fluctuations were not simply imposed from the outside; to a large extent, they were created by an endogenous response mechanism. An increase in exports would have multiplier effects on domestic demand and imports. In addition, there would be an accelerator effect on investment demand, the demand for inventories of imported raw materials, and the demand for consumer durable goods, particularly imported automobiles. In the early stages, expansion would be further stimulated by monetary ease created by the balance of payments surplus. However, in the course of the expansion, imports would soon overtake exports and there would be a growing current account deficit. (In this respect, the picture seems to be different from the one in the Scandinavian countries, suggesting a stronger contribution of endogenous mechanisms in Switzerland.) The import surplus would in turn tend to dampen the growth of the money supply and thus, combined with an increasing demand for credit, lead to a gradual increase in interest rates. Near the peak, there might develop an acute tightness in the credit market accompanied by liquidity problems in the banking system. With a lag of about one year, this would in turn lead to a rather strong falling off in private construction activity. At the same time, the accelerator mechanisms would have run their course, accentuating the fall in investment. After a short period of moderate slack, the economy would again become sensitive to developments in foreign markets. From a general point of view, one of the interesting aspects of these cycles seems to be the important role played by monetary factors.

Finally, I want to touch upon the question of whether the Swiss economy is more or less stable than it used to be. The answer largely depends on the meaning we give to the question. If by instability we mean the deviations from trend of certain series like output and employment, then the economy certainly was more stable in the postwar period than it was between the two world wars. If by instability we mean the fluctuations which would have occurred in the absence of conscious countercyclical policies, again, the economy was more stable in the postwar period, because there were hardly any symptoms of effective counter-cyclical efforts. However, if the question is whether stability has increased in the course of the two postwar decades, the answer is probably negative: most series have shown more variance in the 1960's than they showed in the 1950's. If, finally, the question is assumed to refer to future developments, recent experience seems to suggest an attitude of cautious skepticism. Indeed, if over the next decade the instability in the private sector increases at the same rate at which it increased from 1954 to 1964, the outlook for the 1970's would be clouded. Perhaps the time has passed when a country can afford to have no effective stabilization policies of its own. Of course, if the rest of the world follows good policies, Switzerland may still be able to enjoy a reasonable degree of stability even without more enlightened stabilization policies of her own.

# II  INTERNATIONAL TRANSMISSION OF ECONOMIC FLUCTUATIONS

Chapter Eight

# TRANSMISSION OF BUSINESS FLUCTUATIONS FROM DEVELOPED TO DEVELOPING COUNTRIES

RUDOLF R. RHOMBERG
International Monetary Fund, Washington*

The years since World War II have been an era of remarkable economic stability in comparison with earlier periods for which economic data are recorded. Declines in economic activity in industrial countries have been rare, and business cycle analysts have had to direct their attention to periodic advances and retardations of growth rates—or periods of expansion and of "pause"—rather than to actual booms and recessions of the old-fashioned kind. Cumulative processes of the type that led to severe and protracted depressions in the past have been prevented in the postwar period by appropriate economic policies, by a number of fortunate coincidences, or by an institutional environment more conducive to economic stability than was that of earlier periods[1].

The postwar stability of the world economy is particularly striking if attention is directed toward such broad international aggregates as world production or world trade. But the broad view hides many more or less isolated instances of insability, for example, individual countries, in individual commodities, or in particular sectors of one or more economies. These instances are, of course, of great importance to those affected directly; but as long as their

*Previously published in *IMF Staff Papers* (March, 1968). The author wishes to express his gratitude to his colleagues, Miss Lorette Boissonneault and Dr. Erich Spitäller, for assistance in the preparation of this chapter.
[1] See, for example, A. Lamfalussy, "International Trade and Trade Cycles, 1950–1960," in *International Trade Theory in a Developing World,* ed. by Roy Harrod and Douglas Hague (London, 1963), pp. 241–276.

incidence is random, and the response pattern of the world economy is not such as to transform these individual random shocks into cyclical swings, they do not constitute a threat to world economic stability. They may require action in the affected country, or policies influencing particular commodities or sectors, but they do not ordinarily require concerted efforts to sustain or to retard the rate of expansion of world demand as a whole.

The degree of over-all economic stability observed over the past 15 or 20 years should not, however, give rise to complacency. Fortuitous circumstances may not always favor the maintenance of a stable world economy. And while the institutional framework has certainly changed in such a way as to foster economic stability, there is not, as yet, sufficient evidence to indicate with certainty whether economic policy in the main industrial countries has reached a level of sophistication sufficient to ensure stability in all circumstances, or whether it merely has not yet been put to a test comparable to that which faced the policymakers in the 1930's.

The transmission of fluctuations of economic activity from developed countries[2] to developing countries—with which this paper is concerned—is a broad subject. The present study therefore has been limited in a number of ways, to confine itself to certain aspects of the topic.

First, an aggregative approach is chosen in which only two regions are distinguished, the developed countries as one group and the developing countries as another. While this approach is appropriate for assessing the magnitude of business fluctuations in developed countries, the transmission of these fluctuations to the developing countries, and the response of the latter, it does not show the effects which changes in economic activity in individual developed countries (or in subgroups of such countries) may have on the economies of individual developing countries (or subgroups of them). This is a severe limitation of the present discussion; it is intended to supplement, at a later stage, the findings reported here by studies of smaller groups of countries.

Second, the discussion deals only with short-term variations in economic activity and their international transmission. This excludes discussion of long-run variations in the production and prices of individual classes of commodities. Long-run fluctuations of this type may indeed have cyclical characteristics; however, they are usually not on world-wide scale but are specific to individual commodities or sectors. To whatever extent they are universal, moreover, they are more profitably studied in the context of economic growth rather than in that of short-term fluctuations.

Third, attention is directed to the transmissions of business fluctuations from developed to developing countries and not to transmission in the reverse

---

[2] In this study, the term "developed countries" will refer to member countries of the Organization for Economic Cooperation and Development (OECD) plus Australia, New Zealand, and South Africa.

direction. This is not to deny that individual developing countries may experience economic fluctuations with cyclical characteristics. But these countries, as a group, have not been subject to autonomous short-term fluctuations of sufficient magnitude to affect to a noticeable degree the economies of the developed countries as a group[3] .

Fourth, two limitations of a statistical character have had to be accepted: (a) The analysis is based on annual data. It would, of course be more satisfactory to use semiannual or quarterly values for an investigation of a cyclical process. Unfortunately, however, suitable data on regional trade flows and trade by commodities for time periods of less than one year are not available for a sufficiently long period. (b) The indicator of changes in economic activity in the developed countries chosen for this study is the combined (weighted) index of industrial production in these countries. For more detailed investigation of the topic of this chapter, it would be appropriate to base the analysis on a variety of cyclical indicators (such as changes in inventories, the rate of unemployment, and changes in orders) in different countries or regions, and to ascertain the influence which each of these may have on imports from, and capital exports to, the less developed countries. This study is, however, limited by the nature and quality of the annual data on trade and capital flows. For this reason, refinement of the data (indicating variations in economic activity in the developed countries) may not be warranted. The chapter confines itself, with two exceptions to be mentioned later, to an analysis of the apparent responsiveness of trade and capital flows between developed and developing countries to variations in economic activity, as indicated by the combined annual index of industrial production for the developed countries as a group. Its aim is to reach some broad generalizations regarding the dependence of developing countries on short-run variations in economic activity in developed countries.

After a brief discussion of the channels through which business fluctuations may be transmitted from developed to developing countries, and of the timimg and intensity of the fluctuations experienced in the postwar period, a statistical analysis of the influence of short-term fluctuations in aggregate economic activity in developed countries on their imports from developing countries is presented. Then the influence of changes in economic activity in developed countries on capital flows to developing countries is discussed. This is followed by consideration of the response mechanism of developing countries as a group to cyclical influences transmitted to them. The final sections of the chapter show why the effect of variations in economic activity in developed countries upon the economies of developing countries and their aggregate balance of

---

[3] See, for instance, A. Lamfalussy, *op. cit.,* and J. J. Polak and R. R. Rhomberg, "Economic Instability in an International Setting," *American Economic Review,* May 1962 (reprinted in *Readings in Business Cycles,* ed. by R. A. Gordon and L. R. Klein, Homewood, Illinois, 1965).

payments has been relatively slight and diffuse; it is argued that the response mechanism in developing countries has in fact contributed to the dampening of fluctuations in the world economy.

## Channels of Transmission

Trade in goods and services is the principal channel through which changes in economic activity in developed countries affect the economies of developing countries. Actual or anticipated changes in production in developed countries result in variations in demand for raw materials imported from developing countries. Since the supply of such materials is generally not very elastic, especially in the short run, variations in demand should be expected to cause changes in the same direction in the prices of these commodities. The more inelastic are supply and demand with respect to price, the larger will tend to be the induced variation in prices, and the smaller that in quantities, of exports of materials from developing countries. Demand for food, on the other hand, is less responsive to variations in economic activity, and cyclical changes in developed countries should not be expected to have a pronounced effect on exports of food products from developing countries. During the postwar period there has been a small, though rapidly growing, amount of exports of manufactured goods from developing to developed countries. The export volume of this class of products should be expected to show some cyclical responsiveness, although perhaps less than manufactured exports from developed to other developed countries, which consist to a large extent of investment goods.

Fluctuations in the exports of developing countries will tend to be mitigated by two factors which have the character of built-in stabilizers. One factor is the extent to which exportables are produced by foreign-owned companies. A change in such exports will be associated with a change in the same direction in repatriated earnings and will therefore reduce the variations in the current account balance resulting from fluctuations in exports. This influence is quite pronounced on some countries. From a sample of 29 countries, it has been estimated that it may amount, on average, to as much as 7 per cent of the value of exports; and in some oil-producing countries, it may range from small values to more than 40 per cent[4]. The second factor is the extent to which the production of exportables requires imports from the developed countries. The import content of exports of developing countries is difficult to assess, but it has been estimated at perhaps 5 per cent of the value of exports.

The transmission of business fluctuations through the current account of the balance of payments has been widely discussed in the literature. Less attention

---

[4] See Marcus Fleming, Rudolph Rhomberg, and Lorette Boissonneault, "Export Norms and Their Role in Compensatory Financing," *Staff Papers,* Vol. X (1963), p. 144, and Alasdair I. MacBean, *Export Instability and Economic Development* (Cambridge, Massachusetts, 1966), pp. 93–95.

has been devoted to the possible transmission of fluctuations through capital movements, especially in the context of relations between developed and developing economies. Since changes in economic activity in developed countries affect both the availability of capital and domestic investment opportunities, and since the transmission of these fluctuations to developing countries affects the business situation there, the possibility of a systematic variation of capital flows from developed to developing countries, in response to cyclical business fluctuations, cannot be excluded. If such an influence is found to exist, then developing countries may be harmed by the drying up of the private capital inflow from developed countries in addition to the reduction of export receipts which they experience as a result of a decline in economic activity in developed countries

Changes in public loans and grants from developed to developing countries would, in principle, affect the latter group of countries in the same way as variations in private capital flows. It is plausible to assume, however, that changes in public capital flows are not subject, to any great extent, to cyclical factors in the developed countries. It may be that decisions concerning the flow of public capital from individual developed countries are subject to considerations with regard to the balance of payments positions of these countries. However, longer-run viewpoints often prevail over these considerations, and public capital flows are not ordinarily altered abruptly in response to short-term changes in the budgetary or balance of payments situation. Moreover, it may be argued that cyclical influences will not greatly alter the overall balance of payments of the developed countries as a group. While some of these countries may experience balance of payments difficulties when there is a recession in economic activity in other countries of the group, the latter would tend to find their external payments position eased. The effect which such changes may have on the flow of public loans and grants to developing countries depends on the incidence of these balance of payments shifts among countries with different propensities to make such loans and grants.

A number of minor channels of transmission will be left out of account in this discussion, for example, profits made, or losses sustained, by nationals of developing countries as a result of investment in the stock markets of developed countries.

## Economic Fluctuations in Developed Countries

Fluctuations in economic activity in the main industrial countries during the postwar period were not only mild but also dissynchronous. In the years covered by the study, 1950–1965, the United States has had recessions in 1953–1954, 1958, and 1960–1961. Each of these downturns was short-lived, lasting about one year or less. Industrial production on an annual basis fell in 1954 and 1958, but not in 1960 or 1961. Recessions were even milder in industrial Western

Europe. Only two recessions, or pauses, in economic growth in that area can be clearly identified: one was in 1951–1952 when the annual index of industrial production failed to rise, and the other in 1958 when the index was only 2 per cent higher than in 1957 (Table 8–1). Western Europe did not share with North America that is, the United States and Canada) either the recession of 1953–1954 or that of 1960–1961; in fact, in 1953–1954 it experienced a vigorous recovery from the 1951–1952 recession. On the other hand, the European recession of 1951–1952 was not shared by the United States, where there was only a slight retardation in the growth of economic activity.

As a result of these divergent movements, the combined index of industrial production for the developed countries, which is taken in this study as an indicator of variation in economic activity in the entire group, showed two slight declines—one from 1953 to 1954 and one from 1957 to 1958. In addition, it showed particulary small increases from 1951 to 1952, from 1956 to 1957, and

**TABLE 8–1    North America, Western Europe, and All Developed Countries: Indices of Industrial Production**

|  | Index: 1958=100 | | | Changes in Index | | |
|---|---|---|---|---|---|---|
|  | North America[1] | Western Europe | Developed countries[2] | North America[1] | Western Europe | Developed countries[2] |
| 1950 | 80 | 62 | 65 | – | – | – |
| 1951 | 86 | 71 | 73 | 6 | 9 | 8 |
| 1952 | 89 | 71 | 75 | 3 | 0 | 2 |
| 1953 | 97 | 75 | 88 | 8 | 4 | 13 |
| 1954 | 92 | 82 | 87 | −5 | 7 | −1 |
| 1955 | 103 | 89 | 97 | 11 | 7 | 10 |
| 1956 | 107 | 94 | 101 | 4 | 5 | 4 |
| 1957 | 107 | 98 | 103 | 0 | 4 | 2 |
| 1958 | 100 | 100 | 100 | −7 | 2 | −3 |
| 1959 | 113 | 106 | 110 | 13 | 6 | 10 |
| 1960 | 116 | 117 | 118 | 3 | 11 | 8 |
| 1961 | 117 | 123 | 121 | 1 | 6 | 3 |
| 1962 | 126 | 129 | 130 | 9 | 6 | 9 |
| 1963 | 133 | 135 | 136 | 7 | 6 | 6 |
| 1964 | 142 | 145 | 147 | 9 | 10 | 11 |
| 1965 | 154 | 152 | 156 | 12 | 7 | 9 |

**Source:** United Nations, *Monthly Bulletin of Statistics.*
[1] United States and Canada.
[2] OECD, Australia, New Zealand, and South Africa.

from 1960 to 1961. This indicator does therefore reflect, even on the annual basis, all the recessions or pauses experienced by either North America or Western Europe.

## Transmission Through Foreign Trade

A number of recent studies deal with the dependence of exports of developing countries upon economic activity in developed countries during the postwar period. For instance, the world trade model of the International Monetary Fund (IMF)[5] contains equations for imports by the United States and Western Europe from one another and from the rest of the world[6]. The relevant income and price elasticities, evaluated at the means of the variables, are shown in Table 8–2. It appears that the U.S. demand for imports from the rest of the world is somewhat more elastic with respect to gross national product (GNP) than is that of Western Europe. The weighted GNP elasticity of imports by these two industrial regions combined from the rest of the world is slightly higher than unity. Estimated price effects on the volume of exports of the rest of the world are, in this model, low or nil.

TABLE 8–2    Incomes and Price Elasticities as Derived from IMF World Trade Model [1]

| | Imports from | | |
|---|---|---|---|
| Importing Region | United States | Western Europe | Rest of the world |
| United States | | | |
| Income elasticity[2] | – | 1.6 | 1.4 |
| Price elasticity[3] | – | –2.1 | –0.2 |
| Western Europe | | | |
| Income elasticity[2] | 0.8 | – | 0.9 |
| Price elasticity[3] | –2.2 | – | ... |

[1] The original model is described in Rudolf R. Rhomberg and Lorette Boissonneault, "Effects of Income and Price Changes on the U.S Balance of Payments," *Staff Papers,* (1964), pp. 59–124. The elasticities given here resulted from a re-estimate of the model, based on data for 1953–1965.
[2] Elasticity with respect to gross national product (GNP).
[3] Elasticity with respect to the ratio of import prices to the domestic GNP price deflator.

[5] A general description of this model is given in Polak and Rhomberg, *op. cit.,* and a more detailed account is found in Rudolf R. Rhomberg and Lorette Boissonneault,"Effects of Income and Price Changes on the U. S. Balance of Payments," *Staff Papers,* (1964), pp. 59–124. See also Grant B. Taplin, "Models of World Trade," *Staff Papers,* (1967), pp. 433–455.
[6] This residual region includes not only developing countries but also Australia, Canada, Japan, New Zealand, South Africa, the Soviet countries, and Mainland China.

TEST OF LAG PATTERN

The question arises whether the use of annual data obscures any lag in the response of imports to changes in economic activity. In work with quarterly import functions, it had been found that there is either no lag or a very short lag between changes in economic activity and the changes in imports induced by them[7]. The lag pattern was tested once more by the present author; he computed equations with (seasonally unadjusted) quarterly data from the first quarter of 1948 to the first quarter of 1966 for imports of merchandise and of total goods and services into the United States from developing areas. Industrial production (seasonally adjusted) was used as the independent variable. It was again found that the best results are achieved if imports are unlagged, or follow with a lag of one quarter behind the variable expressing changes in ecomomic activity. Lags of two or more quarters give distinctly worse results, and are in fact unacceptable when computations are carried out in first differences of logarithms. (These tests are shown in Appendix I.) It may be concluded that in the United States imports lag behind industrial production with an average lag of one to three months, and that the corresponding relation in terms of annual data should be unlagged.


CYCLICAL   DEPENDENCE   OF   EXPORTS   TO   DEVELOPED
COUNTRIES


In order to assess the dependence of export receipts of developing countries on year-to-year changes on economic activity in developed countries, annual changes in the logarithms of export values, export volumes, and export prices were regressed on annual changes in the logarithms of the index of industrial production in developed countries[8]. Equations of this form relate proportionate changes in the dependent variable to those in the independent variable; the

---

[7] R. R. Rhomberg and Lorette Boissonneault, "The Foreign Sector," in *The Brooking Quarterly Econometric Model of the United States*, ed. by J. S. Duesenberry and others (Chicago and Amsterdam, 1965); R. J. Ball and K. Marwah, "The U.S. Demand for Imports, 1948–1958," *Review of Economics and Statistics*, November 1962, pp. 395–401.

[8] These equations are of the following form:

$$\Delta \log X_t = a + b \Delta \log A_t,$$

Where $X_t$ refers, alternatively, to the value of exports, the volume of exports, or an index of export unit values, and $A_t$ stands for the index of industrial production in developed countries. In addition, similar equations in terms of logarithms and included a linear trend term were computed. These are of the following form:

$$\log X_t = a' + b' \log A_t + ct,$$

where $t( = 1, 2, 3, \ldots)$ is a trend variable. The two sets of computations are compared in Appendix II.

regression coefficients therefore indicate apparent elasticities of response of the former to changes on the latter. The estimated relationships are independent of the common upward trends observed in all the variables in question, since they are based on year-to-year changes.

Our present aim is not to derive the best possible explanatory equations for imports of developed from developing countries. If that were the objective, a number of other explanatory variables, such as relative prices, changes in inventories, and indicators of changes in demand by economic sector, would be introduced. Our aim is merely to establish the degree of dependence of exports to developed countries on our selected indicator of variations in economic activity in those countries.

Particular interest attaches to the question of the separate effects of changes in economic activity in the developed countries on the quantities and prices of their imports from developing countries, and to a comparison of these results with the corresponding responsiveness from other developed countries. This response pattern was tested for total merchandise trade as well as for four commodity categories, namely, food and beverages, raw materials, fuels, and manufactures. Annual data for the period 1953–1965 were used; the results are shown in Table 8–3, and further details are given in Appendix II.

TABLE 8–3   Elasticity Coefficients of Value Quantum, and Unit Value of Exports to Developed Countries from Developing Countries and Developed Countries with Respect to Industrial Production in Developed Countries[1]

| Exports from | Exports from developing countries | | | Exports from developed countries | | |
|---|---|---|---|---|---|---|
| | Value | Quantum | Unit value | Value | Quantum | Unit value |
| Total merchandise exports | 0.48 | 0.37* | 0.08 | 1.06* | 0.90* | 0.11 |
| Food and beverages (SITC 0–1) | −0.41 | 0.39 | −0.79 | 0.46 | 0.22 | 0.23 |
| Raw materials excluding fuels (SITC 2, 4) | 1.56* | 0.59* | 1.05* | 1.43 | 1.13* | 0.33 |
| Fuels (SITC 3) | −0.27 | 0.06 | −0.31 | 1.18 | 1.06 | 0.14 |
| Manufactures (SITC 5–8) | 2.03* | 0.35 | 1.66* | 1.02* | 0.92* | 0.12 |

[1] The elasticities were determined from regressions of first differences of the logarithms of value, quantum, or unit value on first differences of the logarithms of the index of industrial production of the developed countries. Elasticity coefficients with an asterisk (*) are significant at the 5 per cent level; others are not. Annual data for 1953–1965 were used. The commodity groupings are the United Nations Standard Industrial Trade Classifications (SITC). For details, see Appendix II.

According to traditional views, the export earnings of primary producing countries are more unstable than those of industrial countries. In the short run, the supplies of the commodities exported by primary producers are inelastic, and so is the demand for these products. Shifts in demand tend, therefore, to induce some variation in the volume of exports but larger variation in export prices. Supply shifts will produce offsetting changes in volume and price, but they usually lead to changes in value in a direction opposite to those of the underlying shifts in supply. By contrast, shifts in demand for exports of industrial countries are expected to induce larger variations in volume than in price, and shifts in supply of these exports are not very pronounced.

The findings presented here are not intended to support or contradict these views. In fact, they are not directly comparable with the findings of studies on the instability of prices and volumes in international trade. In the first place, the present study is not concerned with the overall instability of export proceeds, but merely with the effect of changes in economic activity in the (developed) importing countries on export proceeds of developing and developed countries. In other words, short-term changes in demand for reasons other than variations in economic activity, and short-term changes in supply in the exporting countries, are left out of account. Second, the distinction made is not between industrial and primary exporting countries, but rather between developed and developing countries. Among the former are some, like the United States, whose exports consist to a considerable extent of primary products. At the same time, exports of manufactured goods from developing countries, though initially small, have been rapidly expanded.

The extent to which exports of developing and developed countries have responded to variations in economic activity in the developed countries is shown in Table 8–3 for all commodities and for certain subgroups. The figures for total merchandise exports support the view that the volume of exports from developed countries is much more responsive than the volume of exports from developing countries. The estimated elasticities of the volume of exports with respect to industrial production in developed countries are, respectively, 0.37 for developing countries and 0.90 for developed countries (first line of Table 8–3). The expected difference in price responsiveness is, however, not found. Table 8–3 shows that the unit values of both groups of countries are only weakly responsive to changes in economic activity in the developed countries, and that there is no significant difference in the two estimated coefficients. As a result, changes in total export proceeds of developed countries are much more responsive to changes in industrial production in their own area (with an elasticity of 1.06) than are the export proceeds of developing countries (with an elasticity coefficient of 0.48). From this, it may be concluded that a change of 1 per cent in industrial production in developed countries would tend to change export proceeds of that group in the same direction by about 1 per cent, but those of developing countries by only about ½ of 1 per cent.

For the four commodity groups listed in Table 8—3, there is a clear indication that developing countries' export proceeds from raw materials are strongly responsive to variations in economic activity in developed countries, and that this responsiveness is to a great extent one of prices rather than one of quantities. Interestingly, there is a similar indication for manufactured products. Their price responsiveness is particulary high, whereas the elasticity coefficient for the volume of exports is small and statistically uncertain. For these two groups taken together—which account for not quite one half of the developing countries' exports to developed countries—export proceeds would tend to change by about 1¾ per cent in response to a change of 1 percentage point in the industrial production index of developed countries. Most of this change would be accounted for by price variations. For the other two commodity groups, food and fuels, quantities exported from developing countries to developed countries are found to be only weakly responsive to economic activity in the recipient area, and prices appear to be inversely affected. But as these elasticity coefficients are statistically not significant, not much weight should be given to this finding. If the true elasticity of export proceeds from these two commodity groups were to be set equal to their apparent quantum elasticities, the elasticity of developing countries' total export proceeds with respect to economic activity in developed countries would be close to unity. Even in that case, however, it would not exceed the responsiveness of total export proceeds of developed countries from other developed countries.

For the developed countries, the expected responsiveness of export volumes are found for all commodity groups, with the elasticity of food being very low and that for each of the three other commodity groups being about unity. Price responses are found to be small and statistically uncertain.

The equations for total merchandise exports could be computed on the basis of a somewhat longer time period, namely, 1950—1965. In this instance, the apparent elasticity of the volume of developing countries' exports to developed countries is almost the same as that found for the period 1953—1965, but the price responsiveness is somewhat higher. As a result, the elasticity of total export proceeds of developing countries from developed countries, computed for the longer period, is 0.71 [9]. The corresponding elasticity of export proceeds of

---

[9] The equation, cast in first differences of logarithms, is as follows:

$$\Delta\log V^{ld}{}_t = 0.0016 + 0.707 \; \Delta\log A_t$$
$$(2.0)$$
$$\bar{R}^2 = 0.17 \qquad d = 2.18$$

where $V^{ld}$ is the value of exports from developing to developed countries, and $A$ is the index of industrial production of developed countries. $\bar{R}^2$ is the coefficient of determination adjusted for degrees of freedom; $d$ is the Durbin-Watson statistic for serial correlation; and the number in parentheses below the regression coefficient is the $t$ ratio.

developed countries is somewhat lower than that computed for the shorter period, namely, 0.87.

Athough more intensive study would be necessary to reach firm views on this matter, it must be taken as doubtful that export proceeds of developing countries—as a group—to developed countries are more strongly affected by short-term changes in economic activity in developed markets than are the export proceeds of the developed countries themselves. If anything, the indication is the reverse[10]. As stated earlier, these conclusions are drawn for the aggregate of developing countries. Export proceeds of individual members of this groups may be very severely affected by declines in economic activity in their main export markets, or in the group of developed countries as a whole Moreover, the conclusion refers only to short-term changes; although the fluctuations in economic activity in North America and Europe did not occur at the same time and were rather quickly reversed, it can nevertheless be argued that export proceeds of developing countries would have shown not only greater stability but also a higher rate if even these minor setbacks to economic grwth in the developed countries could have been avoided.

## Transmission Through Private Capital Flows

Some general considerations that would lead to expectations that capital flows from developed to developing countries may respond to changes in economic activity have been advanced above. There is of course, the question of whether these influences are strong enough to be detected in the available data. This question is particulary acute, since the response of capital flows to changes in economic activity is unlikely to be a simple and simultaneous one.

Capital movements may be expected to respond to factors affecting the supply of funds—as reflected in past retained earnings of corporations and the general ease or tightness of the capital market—and to considerations of alternative investment opportunities at home and abroad. When retained earnings are high relative to investment at home, the incentive to invest abroad should be relatively strong, and vice versa. At the start of a recession, domestic investment opportunities, in relation to given investment opportunities abroad, tend to appear less promising than earlier; but earnings accumulated over the recent past are still high[11]. Investment abroad should therefore remain high,

---

[10] To repeat, this does not contradict the view that developing countries' export proceeds may be more unstable than those of developed countries, particularly since the former may be affected to a greater extent than the latter by instability resulting from supply shifts, or from demand shifts unrelated to changes in aggregate economic activity.

[11] If current profits are synchronous with the cycle in economic activity, then the peaks and troughs of accumulated retained earnings, that is, the funds available for investment at home or abroad, will tend to lag behind the peaks and troughs of the cycle.

or even rise, for some time after a recession has started. After the recession has continued for a while, retained earnings will decline and thus lower the supply of funds available for foreign investment. At the same time, the incentive to invest in foreign export industries, whose profits may be affected by the domestic recession in economic activity, may be impaired. Nevertheless, if the recession is still in progress, the continued reduction in domestic investment opportunities may offset these adverse affects on foreign investment. Shortly after the beginning of a recovery, past accumulated earnings are presumably at their lowest point, and domestic investment opportunities improve. As a result of both of these factors, investment abroad should continue to decline. Only after the recovery has gone on for some time will earnings improve and begin to counteract the negative effect of better domestic investment opportunities on foreign investment. Still later, earnings will have fully recovered, and domestic investment opportunities will tend to level off. At that point, foreign investment will again rise, and the cycle will have been completed. This hypothesis leads to the expectation that changes in foreign investment will follow changes in domestic economic activity with a substantial lag.

To test the actual lag pattern, it was again necessary to use quarterly data. Data for the United States were employed. Quarterly U.S. direct investment in developing countries, and alternatively the total net flow of private U.S. capital to these countries on a quarterly basis, were related to the quarterly index of industrial production, with various discrete lags. On the basis of this test it was concluded that a lag of capital flows behind economic activity of approximately 1 year was appropriate[12].

Unfortunately, continuous time series on the flow of capital from all developed to developing countries are not available for a very long period. Data beginning with 1956, published by the Organization for Economic Cooperation

---

[12] The best results were obtained with capital movements (five-quarter moving averages) lagged four and five quarters behind industrial production (seasonally adjusted). For instance, the equations for U.S. direct investment in less developed countries ($D$) are as follows (third quarter 1948 to third quarter 1965):

$$D_t = -330 + 6.5 A_{t-4} - 4.7t, \quad \bar{R}^2 = 0.235$$
$$\qquad\qquad (3.81) \quad\ (2.95)$$

$$D_t = -339 + 6.7 A_{t-5} - 4.8t, \quad \bar{R}^2 = 0.237$$
$$\qquad\qquad (3.85) \quad\ (2.98)$$

(Residuals are serially correlated in both equations.) The $t$ ratios (in parentheses below the coefficients) and $\bar{R}^2$ are highest for the equation with a five-quarter lag. Inferior results were obtained with shorter and longer lags (tested up to seven quarters). The implied elasticity (at the means of the variables) of U.S. direct investment in less developed countries with respect to U.S. industrial production of the preceding year is approximately + 5.

and Development (OECD), show that the flow of total private long-term net capital from industrial OECD countries to developing areas in 1958 was less than in 1957, and that the decline continued in 1959. After some recovery in 1960 and 1961, the capital flow declined again in 1962 and further in 1963[13].

In attempting to relate the hypothesis just outlined to annual data (the only data available for all countries), the trade data of developing countries were combined with changes in international reserves to compute a residual series which represents net capital flows to developing countries plus net credit balance on service account minus net deficit with the Soviet countries and mainland China on trade account. The data are shown in Table 8–4. Although the resulting series does not represent capital movements exclusively, its short-term variations can be considered representative of the changes in net capital flows[14]. The changes in the series shown in column 4 of Table 8–4 indicate reductions in the net flow of foreign exchange on service and capital account to developing countries in 1953 and in 1954, again in 1958 and 1959, and once more in 1961 and 1962; in addition, there was a decline in the rate of net inflow in 1964. Here again, the evidence is not clear as to the lag by which capital flows to developing countries follow economic activity in the industrial countries. The data may be consistent with a lag of anywhere from 6 to 18 months. But there is some indication, even in these impure data, that a relation of the type postulated exists.

When this series $(C^{dl})$ is related to the index of industrial production in developed countries lagged one year, the following results, in terms of first differences, are obtained:

$$\Delta C^{dl}_t = -0.23 + 0.06 \, \Delta A_{t-1}$$

(1)                                      (1.3)

$$\bar{R}^2 = 0.05 \qquad d = 2.16$$

The coefficient of $\Delta A_{t-1}$ is not significant at the 5 per cent level, but the magnitude of the effect, a change of $60 million in the annual capital flow for a change of 1 percentage point in industrial production, is not inconsistent with the value found for the response of U.S. capital alone ($6 million quarterly, that

---

[13] OECD, *The Flow of Financial Resources to Less-Developed Countries, 1956–1963,* Paris, 1964. The data (in billions of U.S. dollars) for the years 1956–1963, respectively, are as follows: 2.58, 3.23, 2.72, 2.44, 2.58, 2.59, 1.99, 1.87. These figures might be consistent with a distributed lag response, in which part of the reduction in capital flows to the developing countries occurs in the year of the recession and part in the year following the recession.

[14] It was possible to determine from data for part of the period that the trade deficit of developing countries with the Soviet countries and mainland China was not subject to cyclical variations, although it appears to show an upward trend.

TABLE 8–4    Developing Countries: Trade Balance with Developed Countries, Reserve Changes, and Residual Balance of Payments Items, 1950–1965

*(In billions of U.S. dollars)*

| | Net merchandise exports to developed countries[1] | Change in reserves (increases +)[2] | Net capital imports and other residual items[3] | Change in net capital imports, etc.[4] |
|---|---|---|---|---|
| | (1) | (2) | (3) | (4) |
| 1950 | 2.67 | 1.44 | −1.23 | – |
| 1951 | 1.40 | 0.48 | −0.92 | 0.31 |
| 1952 | −0.56 | −0.28 | 0.28 | 1.20 |
| 1953 | 1.10 | 0.48 | −0.62 | −0.90 |
| 1954 | 1.03 | 0.06 | −0.97 | −0.35 |
| 1955 | 1.05 | 0.41 | −0.64 | 0.33 |
| 1956 | 0.14 | 0.26 | 0.12 | 0.76 |
| 1957 | −2.58 | −0.86 | 1.72 | 1.60 |
| 1958 | −1.76 | −0.89 | 0.87 | −0.85 |
| 1959 | −0.51 | 0.11 | 0.62 | −0.25 |
| 1960 | −1.44 | – | 1.44 | 0.82 |
| 1961 | −1.89 | −0.73 | 1.16 | −0.28 |
| 1962 | −0.54 | −0.26 | 0.28 | −0.88 |
| 1963 | 0.39 | 0.99 | 0.60 | 0.32 |
| 1964 | 0.27 | 0.16 | −0.11 | −0.71 |
| 1965 | −0.39 | 1.30 | 0.91 | 1.02 |

[1] Merchandise exports of developing to developed countries less merchandise exports of developed to developing countries. Source: United Nations, *Monthly Bulletin of Statistics*.
[2] Change in reserves of the group described in the source as Less Developed Areas. Source: International Monetary Fund, *International Financial Statistics*.
[3] Column (2) minus column (1). This residual represents (a) the net flow of capital and aid into developing countries from all other countries plus (b) the net receipts on service account by developing countries, minus (c) the merchandise trade deficit of developing countries with the Soviet countries and Mainland China, plus (d) a statistical discrepancy reflecting the difference between developing countries' imports from developed countries and the exports to them reported by developed countries.
[4] Change from preceding year; based on data in column (3).

is, $24 million annually, for a change of 1 percentage point in U.S. industrial production).

It may be tentatively concluded that, in addition to the trade effect of fluctuations in economic activity in developed countries on the economies of developing countries, there may be an influence through systematic variations in capital flows, but that this influence is exercised with a lag which may be as long as one year.

## Response Mechanism of Developing Countries

The two preceding sections have indicated the intensity and time pattern of the transmission, through the balance of payments, of variations in economic activity in developed countries to the economies of developing countries. The purpose of this section is to consider the response pattern in the developing countries. Here again, considerable differences among members of the group of developing countries would be expected, and these differences and their explanation merit further study; but this paper concerns itself only with the global response pattern of the countries taken as a group.

The main features of the response pattern have been discussed extensively in the literature. Changes in export receipts, whether they occur through variations in the volume of exports or price changes, result in income changes in the export sector of the affected economies. These changes tend to lead directly to changes in the same direction in imports, as well as to a multiplier effect on the domestic economy which will result in further changes in the demand for imports. In addition, there may be a more direct connection between the demand for imports and changes in export receipts. Since foreign exchange reserves in most of these countries are not ample, and do not admit of large downward variations, the authorities may be compelled to tighten import restrictions fairly promptly after a decline in export receipts, unless this decline is offset by an inflow of capital or foreign aid. When export receipts increase, import restrictions may be, and often are, relaxed as soon as some increase in foreign exchange reserves has occurred.

The response to changes in the net capital inflow is similar, in more than one way, to the response to changes in export receipts. In the first place, an increase in receipts on capital account may lead to a relaxation of restrictions; and a reduction in the inflow, to a tightening of restrictions. Moreover, an increased capital inflow is often accompanied by, or is the financial equivalent of, increased investment expenditure, and has a multiplier effect similar to that of a change in exports.

As a result, it is not inappropriate to lump together export receipts and net capital inflows into a total of "gross foreign exchange receipts," and to expect changes in import expenditures to be related partly to the change in this total in the current year and partly to the change in the preceding year[15].

---

[15] In the monetary model of imports and income designed by J. J. Polak chiefly for application to developing countries, income and imports are related to current and past values of export receipts plus capital inflows plus the change in domestic credit creation. Application of this model has shown that the influence of lagged values of this causative variable diminishes rapidly as longer lags (beyond 1 or 2 years) are considered, and that a large part of the influence is accounted for by the current value and that of the preceding year. See J. J. Polak and Lorette Boissonneault, "Monetary Analysis of Income and Imports and Its Statistical Application," *Staff Papers,* (1960), particularly pp. 358–359

The reaction of imports to present and recent past foreign exchange receipts from exports and capital inflows may not exhaust the response mechanism. The private responses may be such that, with a given set of foreign exchange restrictions and financial policies of the countries concerned, import demand tends to remain behind, or to run ahead of, gross foreign exchange earnings. In addition, the authorities may find that, in adjusting their financial policies and foreign exchange measures to achieve balance of payments equilibrium, they either have insufficiently compensated or have overcompensated for the changes in gross foreign exchange receipts which have occurred. In such instances, foreign exchange reserves tend to change by amounts different from those anticipated, and the authorities may take additional corrective action. It is reasonable, therefore, to test the hypothesis whether in addition to current and lagged gross foreign exchange receipts, the past change in foreign exchange reserves (that is, the change in the preceding year) helps to explain current import expenditures.

Since the levels of import expenditures and gross foreign exchange receipts from exports and capital inflows are obviously related over time, the response mechanism is appropriately tested not in terms of the levels of these variables but in terms of annual changes. As a result, the variable for the change in foreign exchange reserves of the preceding year is expressed in first differences; that is, it is the change in the change in foreign exchange reserves which enters the equation. The result is as follows (data period 1952–1965):

$$\Delta V^{dl}{}_t = -0.173 + 0.795 \ \Delta G_t + 0.410 \ \Delta G_{t-1} + 0.407 \Delta \Delta R^l_{t-1}$$

(2)
$$(6.3) \qquad\qquad (4.4) \qquad\qquad (2.1)$$

$$\bar{R}^2 = 0.87 \qquad\qquad\qquad d = 1.95$$

In this equation, $V^{dl}$ represents the value of exports of developed to developing countries (that is the imports of developing from developed countries); $G$ equals $V^{ld} + C^{dl}$, which is the value of gross foreign exchange earnings of developing countries, (that is, the value of their exports plus the net capital inflow from developed countries, including developing countries' net balance on service account and their net trade balance with the Soviet countries and mainland China); and $R^l$ is the developing countries' international reserves (gold, foreign exchange, and reserve positions in the IMF). The coefficients of $\Delta G_t$ and $\Delta G_{t-1}$ are significant at the 1 per cent level, while the coefficient of $\Delta\Delta R^l_{t-1}$ barely misses significance at the 5 per cent level. This equation has a standard error of $450 million, or less than 2 per cent of the recent value of developing countries' imports from developed countries.

The addition of an indicator of the change in economic activity in developing countries, namely, the index of industrial production in these countries, did not add to the explanatory power of the equation; neither was that indicator by itself significantly related as an explanatory variable to changes in developing countries' imports from developed countries. This finding does not contradict the existence of a multiplier process or of a tendency of imports to respond to changes in economic activity in developing countries. It merely means that, in view of the generally low international reserves of these countries, the process of balance of payments adjustments—brought about through market forces, through financial policies, or through variations in import restrictions—is necessarily very rapid. As a result, changes in foreign exchange receipts are a better predictor of changes in imports than are changes in economic activity.

The interpretation of the response mechanism of developing countries to variations in their gross foreign exchange receipts from developed countries, as it emerges from this equation, is as follows. A change in gross foreign exchange receipts tends to result in a concurrent change in import expenditures of about four fifths of the change in receipts. One year after the change in foreign exchange receipts has occurred, there is a further induced change in the same direction in import expenditures by about two fifths of the change in receipts. If the rate of reserve accumulation in the preceding year is higher, or lower, than the rate was 2 years earlier, two fifths of this difference will tend to be added to, or subtracted from, import expenditures of developing countries. In every year, import expenditures tend to increase less or decrease more—by about $170 million—than they would have done on the basis of the influences expressed in the three variables just discussed.

The nature of the adjustment mechanism may be appraised by adding to equation (2) an identity for the current change in international reserves, which is defined as the value of gross foreign exchange receipts (exports plus net capital inflows) minus the value of imports:

$$\Delta R^l{}_t = V^{ld}{}_t + C^{dl}{}_t - V^{dl}{}_t.$$

Thus, the change in the change in international reserves is

(3) $\qquad \Delta\Delta R^l{}_t = \Delta V^{ld}{}_t + \Delta C^{dl}{}_t - \Delta V^{dl}{}_t = \Delta G_t - \Delta V^{dl}{}_t.$

By substituting (3) in (2), the following expression is obtained for the change in developing countries' imports from developed countries:

(4) $\qquad \Delta V^{ld}{}_t = -0.173 + 0.795 \ \Delta G_t + 0.817 \ \Delta G_{t-1} - 0.407 \ \Delta V^{dl}{}_{t-1}.$

The change depends about equally on changes in gross foreign exchange receipts in the current year and the preceding year, and is negatively affected by its own value in the preceding year and by a constant trend decline.

Table 8–5 shows the response of imports, the foreign balance, and international reserves in three cases. In Example A, gross foreign exchange receipts increase, after a period of constancy, by $ billion in year 1 and remain at that new level without further change; in Example B, they increase by $1 billion in every year; and in Example C, they fluctuate.

Table ⟨…⟩

Adjustment ⟨…⟩ of Developing Country Imports and Reserve Receipts to Changes in Their Receipts from Exports and Capital Inflows[1]

*(In billions of U.S. dollars)*

Effects on $\Delta V^{dl}_t$

| Year | $(V^{td}+C^{dl})_t$ (1) | $-0.173$ (2) | $0.795(V^{td}+C^{dl})_t$ (3) | $0.410(V^{td}+C^{dl})_{t-1}$ (4) | $0.407\Delta\Delta R^l_{t-1}$ (5) | Total effect $[(2)+(3)+(4)+(5)]$ (6) | $\Delta\Delta R^l$ (1)−(6) (7) | $\Delta R^l_t$ (8) |
|---|---|---|---|---|---|---|---|---|
| | | | | | Example A | | | |
| 1 | 1.0 | −0.173 | 0.795 | — | — | 0.622 | 0.378 | 0.378 |
| 2 | — | −0.173 | — | 0.410 | 0.154 | 0.391 | −0.391 | −0.013 |
| 3 | — | −0.173 | — | — | −0.159 | −0.332 | 0.332 | 0.319 |
| 4 | — | −0.173 | — | — | 0.135 | −0.038 | 0.038 | 0.357 |
| 5 | — | −0.173 | — | — | 0.015 | −0.158 | −0.158 | 0.515 |
| 6 | — | −0.173 | — | — | 0.064 | −0.109 | 0.109 | 0.624 |
| 7 | — | −0.173 | — | — | 0.044 | −0.129 | 0.129 | 0.753 |
| 8 | — | −0.173 | — | — | 0.052 | −0.121 | 0.121 | 0.874 |
| 9 | — | −0.173 | — | — | 0.049 | −0.124 | 0.124 | 0.998 |
| 10 | — | −0.173 | — | — | 0.050 | −0.123 | 0.123 | 1.121 |
| | | | | | Example B | | | |
| 1 | 1.0 | −0.173 | 0.795 | — | — | 0.622 | 0.378 | 0.378 |
| 2 | 1.0 | −0.173 | 0.795 | 0.410 | 0.154 | 1.186 | −0.186 | 0.192 |
| 3 | 1.0 | −0.173 | 0.795 | 0.410 | −0.076 | 0.956 | 0.044 | 0.236 |
| 4 | 1.0 | −0.173 | 0.795 | 0.410 | 0.018 | 1.050 | −0.050 | 0.186 |
| 5 | 1.0 | −0.173 | 0.795 | 0.410 | −0.020 | 1.012 | −0.012 | 0.174 |
| 6 | 1.0 | −0.173 | 0.795 | 0.410 | −0.005 | 1.027 | −0.027 | 0.147 |
| 7 | 1.0 | −0.173 | 0.795 | 0.410 | −0.010 | 1.022 | −0.022 | 0.125 |
| 8 | 1.0 | −0.173 | 0.795 | 0.410 | −0.009 | 1.023 | −0.023 | 0.102 |
| 9 | 1.0 | −0.173 | 0.795 | 0.410 | −0.009 | 1.023 | −0.023 | 0.079 |
| 10 | 1.0 | −0.173 | 0.795 | 0.410 | −0.009 | 1.023 | −0.023 | 0.056 |
| | | | | | Example C | | | |
| 1 | 1.0 | −0.173 | 0.795 | — | — | 0.622 | 0.376 | 0.378 |
| 2 | 1.0 | −0.173 | 0.795 | 0.410 | 0.154 | 1.186 | −0.186 | 0.192 |
| 3 | −1.0 | −0.173 | −0.795 | 0.410 | −0.076 | −0.634 | −0.366 | −0.174 |
| 4 | 1.0 | −0.173 | 0.795 | −0.410 | −0.149 | 0.063 | 0.937 | 0.763 |
| 5 | 2.0 | −0.173 | 1.590 | 0.410 | 0.381 | 2.208 | −0.208 | 0.555 |
| 6 | — | −0.173 | — | 0.820 | −0.085 | 0.562 | −0.562 | −0.007 |
| 7 | −1.0 | −0.173 | −0.795 | — | −0.229 | −1.197 | 0.197 | 0.190 |
| 8 | 1.0 | −0.173 | 0.795 | −0.410 | 0.080 | 0.292 | 0.708 | 0.898 |
| 9 | 2.0 | −0.173 | 1.590 | 0.410 | 0.288 | 2.115 | −0.115 | 0.783 |
| 10 | 1.0 | −0.173 | 0.795 | 0.820 | −0.047 | 1.395 | −0.395 | 0.388 |

[1] Computed from equations (2) and (3). Changes in the year preceding year 1 are assumed to be zero.

These examples illustrate the tendency, inherent in equation (4), of imports to overadjust to changes in gross foreign exchange receipts. Balance is restored through the effect of reserve developments on imports[16]. Column 8 of Table 8–5 shows the effects of the assumed changes in gross foreign exchange receipts on the over-all balance of payments. Example C illustrates the rapid balance of payments adjustment and the correspondingly weak effect of fluctuations in gross receipts on reserves. This may help to explain the small variation in reserves of developing countries, which remained virtually unchanged from 1953 to 1965 and varied within this period in a relatively narrow range, that is, between $8.4 billion (1962) and $10.7 billion (1956).

## Dampening the Effect of Business Fluctuations

The findings of this chapter cover (a) the effect of fluctuations in economic activity in developed countries on export proceeds of developing economies, through their effect on both quantities and prices; (b) the effect of these changes in economic activity on the flow of capital from developed to developing countries; and (c) the response mechanism of the developing countries as a group to these impulses. It is possible to gather these findings into a small model with the following five equations (with the variables as previously defined):

(5) [7]    $\Delta V^{ld}{}_t = 0.13 \Delta A_t$

(6)    $\Delta C^{dl}{}_t = 0.06 \Delta A_{t-1}$

(7)    $\Delta V^{dl}{}_t = -0.17 + 0.80 \Delta G_t + 0.41 \Delta G_{t-1} + 0.41 \Delta \Delta R^l_{t-1}$

(8)    $\Delta G_t = \Delta V^{ld}{}_t + \Delta C^{dl}{}_t$

(9)    $\Delta \Delta R^l_t = \Delta G_t - \Delta V^{dl}{}_t.$

The solutions for changes in the developing countries' imports, trade balance (B), and overall balance of payments (which equals the change in their reserves) are as follows:

---

[16] As a result of the constant term, exact balance is not restored in Examples A and B. In Example A, the foreign balance ($\Delta R^l$, which is the cumulation from year 1 to the year in question of $\Delta \Delta R^l$) would continuously improve as long as gross foreign exchange receipts remained constant, whereas in Example B it would steadily worsen as long as gross receipts continued to grow by a constant absolute amount.

[17] This linear equation is substituted for the logarithmic one shown in footnote 9. The equation is estimated over the period 1951–1965; the implied elasticity of the value of developing countries' exports with respect to industrial production in developed countries at the means of the variables is 0.7.

$$(10) \quad \Delta V^{dl}{}_t = -0.41\Delta V^{dl}{}_{t-1} +0.10\Delta A_t +0.16\Delta A_{t-1}+0.05\Delta A_{t-2}-0.17$$

$$(11) \quad \Delta B_t = 0.41\Delta V^{dl}{}_{t-1} +0.03\Delta A_t -0.16\Delta A_{t-1}- 0.05\Delta A_{t-2}+0.17$$

$$(12) \quad \Delta\Delta R^l{}_t = 0.41\Delta V^{dl}{}_{t-1}+0.03\Delta A_t -0.10\,\Delta A_{t-1}-0.05\Delta A_{t-2}+0.17.$$

Each of these magnitudes depends on economic activity in the developed countries in the current period and the two preceding periods, as well as on the change in imports in the preceding period. As long as changes in economic activity in the developed countries reverse themselves frequently, with each phase being of short duration, the influence of these fluctuations on the economies of the less developed countries, taken as a group, will be spread out over time and weakened through mutual offsetting. The developing countries will experience the effect of previous prosperous years during a year of recession in the developed countries. At a time when they are responding to a past recession, they will already be under the influence of the subsequent recovery in the industrial countries.

The trade and overall balances are affected chiefly by lagged variables, and only to a small extent by current industrial production. This suggests the possibility of forecasting the magnitudes of the cyclical components of these dependent variables—though not the variables themselves, which may be affected by factors left out of account in this study—for the year following the latest 12-month period for which the requisite data are available.

As a result of the response mechanism discussed in the preceding section and of the brevity of recessions in the developed countries, the developing countries have, as a group, exerted a stabilizing influence on the world economy. Declines in their exports have not been fully reflected in concurrent declines in imports, and part of the adjustment of imports has tended to occur after the recessions have ended. While it is true that developing countries have returned impulses emanating from the capital account, changes in developed countries' imports from developing countries and in their capital exports to these countries have not been synchronous. Consequently, the effect on developed countries' exports of the response by developing countries to these impulses has been, at least to some extent, offsetting rather than reinforcing.

The model also shows, however, that the pattern would have been different, had there been a protracted decline in economic activity in developed countries. In this case, the effects of declines in their imports from developing countries in successive years would begin to reinforce one another, and the effect of reductions in capital exports to developing countries would, some time after the beginning of a prolonged decrease in economic activity, start to reinforce the trade effects. As far as the economic relations of developed and developing countries are concerned, there would be a cumulative process in which developing countries would, after some time, return the full impact of a business decline in developed countries.

## Repercussions on Developed Countries' Exports

In order to determine the extent to which, over the period 1953–1965, fluctuations in exports from developed to developing countries were the apparent echo effect of variations in economic activity in the developed countries themselves, the model can be solved, taking as given changes in industrial production in the developed area and also the initial change in these exports for 1952–1953. The computed (simulated) changes are then compared with those actually observed (Table 8–6). The discrepancies can be interpreted as having arisen from causes other than short-term variations in economic activity in the developed countries. They may be the result of other factors operating in the developed economies, such as (a) autonomous changes in private and public capital flows to developing countries, that is, changes that are unrelated to changes in economic activity as measured in this study, or (b) changes in developed countries' imports independent of variations in economic activity. To some extent, however, they may be due also to factors operating within the developing region.

During the 1953–1954 recession, the difference between actual and computed exports of developed to developing countries was not large. In the 1958

TABLE 8–6   Exports of Developed to Developing Countries: Actual and Computed Changes, 1952–1965

*(In billions of U.S. dollars)*

|            | Actual | Computed[1] | Residual[2] |
|------------|--------|-------------|-------------|
| 1952–1953  | −1.02  | 1.91        | −2.93       |
| 1953–1954  | 0.87   | 1.08        | −0.21       |
| 1954–1955  | 0.96   | 0.92        | 0.04        |
| 1955–1956  | 2.10   | 1.38        | 0.72        |
| 1956–1957  | 2.66   | 0.61        | 2.05        |
| 1957–1958  | −1.13  | −0.22       | −0.91       |
| 1958–1959  | −0.40  | 0.58        | −0.98       |
| 1959–1960  | 1.96   | 1.82        | 0.14        |
| 1960–1961  | 0.42   | 1.16        | −0.74       |
| 1961–1962  | −0.35  | 1.17        | −1.52       |
| 1962–1963  | 1.15   | 1.53        | −0.38       |
| 1963–1964  | 2.20   | 1.74        | 0.46        |
| 1964–1965  | 1.88   | 2.08        | −0.20       |

[1] Computed from equation (10); computed values of exports in year $t$ were used to calculate exports in year $t + 1$.
[2] Actual minus computed values.

TABLE 8–7 Quarterly U.S. Imports from Developing Countries and U.S. Industrial Production Unlagged and Lagged One and Two Quarters[1]

| | ΔlogA | Quarterly Dummy Variables | | | Constant term | R̄² | D-W test[2] |
| | | 1 | 2 | 3 | | | |
|---|---|---|---|---|---|---|---|
| **Import of goods and services** | | | | | | | |
| ΔlogA: unlagged | 0.86 (3.2) | -0.029 (3.1) | -0.028 (2.9) | -0.015 (1.6) | 0.018 | 0.19 | 2.46* |
| one quarter lag | 0.94 (3.6) | -0.029 (3.1) | -0.031 (3.3) | -0.020 (2.1) | 0.020 | 0.22 | 2.47* |
| two quarters lag | 0.21 (0.7) | -0.026 (2.6) | -0.027 (2.6) | -0.018 (1.7) | 0.021 | 0.08 | 2.22 |
| **Merchandise imports** | | | | | | | |
| ΔlogA: unlagged | 0.94 (3.1) | -0.038 (3.5) | -0.043 (4.0) | -0.014 (1.2) | 0.022 | 0.26 | 2.47* |
| one quarter lag | 1.04 (3.5) | -0.037 (3.5) | -0.048 (4.4) | -0.018 (1.7) | 0.024 | 0.28 | 2.45* |
| two quarters lag | 0.15 (0.5) | -0.035 (3.0) | -0.043 (3.7) | -0.016 (1.4) | 0.026 | 0.15 | 2.21 |

[1] Regressions of the change in the logarithm of the value of imports on the change in the logarithm of industrial production (ΔlogA) with indicated lags. Quarterly data from first quarter 1948 to first quarter 1966 (73 observations) are used. Figures in parentheses below the regression coefficients are their t ratios.

[2] Durbin-Watson test statistic for serial correlation of residuals. The values indicated by an asterisk (*) fall in the indeterminate range on the test.

275

TABLE 8-8    Elasticity Coefficients of Value, Quantum, and Unit Value of Exports of Developing and Developed Countries to Developed Countries with Respect to Industrial Production in Developed Countries

| | First differences of logarithms | | | | |
| | Elasticity | | | | |
| | Value | t ratio[2] | Constant term | $\bar{R}^2$[3] | d[4] |
|---|---|---|---|---|---|
| *Value of Exports* | | | | | |
| Developing to developed countries | | | | | |
| 1. Total | 0.48 | 2.2 | 0.01 | 0.26 | 1.66 |
| 2. Food, etc. (SITC 0–1) | −0.41 | 1.0 | 0.02 | −[5] | 1.78 |
| 3. Raw materials (SITC 2, 4)[6] | 1.56 | 6.0* | −0.03 | 0.76 | 2.44 |
| 4. Fuels, etc (SITC 3) | −0.27 | 0.8 | 0.05 | −[5] | 1.12 |
| 5. Manufactures (SITC 5–8) | 2.03 | 4.8* | −0.01 | 0.66 | 1.78 |
| Developed to developing Countries | | | | | |
| 6. Total | 1.06 | 4.1* | 0.02 | 0.59 | 2.10 |
| 7. Food, etc. (SITC 0–1) | 0.46 | 2.1 | 0.02 | 0.23 | 1.97 |
| 8. Raw materials (SITC 2, 4)[6] | 1.43 | 2.1 | −0.01 | 0.24 | 2.37 |
| 9. Fuels, etc. (SITC 3) | 1.18 | 1.3 | −[7] | 0.06 | 1.47 |
| 10. Manufactures (SITC 5–8) | 1.02 | 5.0* | 0.02 | 0.68 | 1.83 |
| *Quantum of Exports* | | | | | |
| Developing to developed countries | | | | | |
| 11. Total | 0.37 | 2.7* | 0.01 | 0.36 | 2.79 |
| 12. Food, etc. (SITC 0–1) | 0.39 | 1.2 | −[7] | 0.04 | 2.88 |
| 13. Raw materials (SITC 2, 4)[6] | 0.59 | 2.7* | −[7] | 0.36 | 2.90 |
| 14. Fuels, etc. (SITC 3) | 0.06 | 0.3 | 0.04 | −[5] | 1.68 |
| 15. Manufactures (SITC 5–8) | 0.35 | 0.9 | 0.03 | −[5] | 2.08 |
| Developed to developed countries | | | | | |
| 16. Total | 0.90 | 5.0* | 0.02 | 0.69 | 1.88 |
| 17. Food, etc. (SITC 0–1) | 0.22 | 1.0 | 0.02 | −[5] | 2.59 |
| 18. Raw materials (SITC 2, 4)[6] | 1.13 | 2.3* | −[7] | 0.29 | 2.05 |
| 19. Fuels, etc. (SITC 3) | 1.06 | 1.6 | −[7] | 0.13 | 1.91 |
| 20. Manufactures (SITC 5–8) | 0.92 | 4.9* | 0.02 | 0.68 | 1.53 |
| *Unit Value of Exports* | | | | | |
| Developing to developed countries | | | | | |
| 21. Total | 0.08 | 0.4 | −[7] | −[5] | 1.52 |
| 22. Food, etc. (SITC 0–1) | −0.79 | 1.8 | 0.01 | 0.16 | 1.58 |
| 23. Raw materials (SITC 2, 4)[6] | 1.05 | 4.5* | −0.02 | 0.63 | 2.43 |
| 24. Fuels, etc. (SITC 3) | −0.31 | 1.6 | −[7] | 0.13 | 0.74 |
| 25. Manufactures (SITC 5–8) | 1.66 | 4.5* | −0.03 | 0.64 | 2.63 |
| Developed to developed countries | | | | | |
| 26. Total | 0.11 | 1.0 | −[7] | −[5] | 1.74 |
| 27. Food, etc. (SITC 0–1) | 0.23 | 1.4 | −[7] | 0.08 | 0.74 |
| 28. Raw materials (SITC 2, 4)[6] | 0.33 | 1.4 | −0.01 | 0.07 | 2.20 |
| 29. Fuels, etc. (SITC 3) | 0.14 | 0.4 | −[7] | −[5] | 1.32 |
| 30. Manufactures (SITC 5–8) | 0.12 | 1.0 | −[7] | −[5] | 1.55 |

[1] Annual data, 1953–1965. The equations are of the form $\Delta \log X_t = a + b \Delta \log A_t + u_t$ and $\log X_t = a + b \log A_t + ct + v_t$, where $X_t$ stands, respectively, for value, quantum, or unit value of exports, $A_t$ for the index of industrial production of developed countries, $t$ for a linear trend, and $u_t$ and $v_t$ for the residuals of the two equations.

[2] Ratio of coefficient to its standard error. Asterisk (*) indicates that the coefficient is significant at the 5 per cent level.

276

| Logarithms and trend term | | | | | | | |
|---|---|---|---|---|---|---|---|
| Elasticity | | Trend | | | | | |
| Value | t ratio[2] | Value | t ratio [2] | Constant term | $\bar{R}^2$ [3] | d[4] | |
| 0.91 | 3.4* | −0.002 | 0.3* | −0.57 | 0.96 | 1.33 | 1. |
| 0.51 | 1.0 | −0.006 | 0.5 | −0.21 | 0.32 | 1.30 | 2. |
| 1.34 | 5.0* | −0.021 | 3.8* | −1.87 | 0.84 | 1.45 | 3. |
| -0.26 | 0.5 | 0.044 | 4.4* | 0.91 | 0.98 | 0.67 | 4. |
| 2.53 | 6.7* | −0.020 | 2.5* | −4.7 | 0.98 | 2.09 | 5. |
| 1.20 | 4.6* | 0.011 | 1.9 | −0.84 | 0.99 | 1.45 | 6. |
| 0.98 | 3.7* | 0.006 | 1.1 | −1.11 | 0.98 | 1.55 | 7. |
| 1.19 | 2.0 | −0.005 | 0.4 | 1.46 | 0.87 | 1.86 | 8. |
| 1.06 | 1.0 | −0.004 | 0.2 | −1.70 | 0.60 | 0.97 | 9. |
| 1.09 | 5.0* | 0.025 | 4.7* | −0.86 | 0.99 | 1.31 | 10. |
| 0.58 | 5.0* | 0.009 | 3.8* | 0.76 | 0.99 | 2.44 | 11. |
| 0.25 | 1.1 | 0.006 | 1.3 | 1.46 | 0.94 | 2.66 | 12. |
| 0.66 | 3.9* | −0.005 | 1.4 | 0.72 | 0.95 | 2.46 | 13. |
| 0.41 | 1.8 | 0.034 | 7.0* | 0.96 | 0.99 | 1.48 | 14. |
| 0.40 | 1.3 | 0.025 | 3.9* | 1.07 | 0.99 | 2.22 | 15. |
| 1.01 | 5.7* | 0.013 | 3.5* | −0.13 | 0.99 | 1.56 | 16. |
| 0.22 | 1.3 | 0.022 | 6.1* | 1.43 | 0.99 | 2.31 | 17. |
| 0.48 | 0.9 | 0.015 | 1.3 | 0.99 | 0.93 | 1.47 | 18. |
| 1.24 | 1.8 | −0.004 | 0.3 | −0.46 | 0.86 | 1.26 | 19. |
| 1.11 | 6.1* | 0.017 | 4.5* | −0.86 | 0.99 | 1.70 | 20. |
| 0.34 | 1.5 | −0.011 | 2.3* | 1.41 | 0.66 | 1.17 | 21. |
| 0.26 | 0.4 | −0.012 | 0.9 | 1.52 | 0.35 | 1.29 | 22. |
| 0.75 | 3.0* | −0.018 | 3.4* | 0.62 | 0.53 | 1.51 | 23. |
| 0.62 | 1.9 | 0.009 | 1.3 | 3.18 | 0.49 | 0.61 | 24. |
| 2.11 | 6.8* | −0.045 | 7.0* | −1.96 | 0.80 | 2.32 | 25. |
| 0.16 | 1.4 | −0.002 | 0.6 | 1.69 | 0.56 | 1.41 | 26. |
| 0.76 | 2.8* | −0.016 | 2.7* | 0.56 | 0.32 | 1.04 | 27. |
| 0.73 | 3.0* | −0.020 | 3.9* | 0.65 | 0.74 | 1.83 | 28. |
| 0.17 | 0.3 | − | − | 2.32 | 0.17 | 0.94 | 29. |
| 0.01 | 0.1 | 0.003 | 1.3 | 1.95 | 0.84 | 1.49 | 30. |

$\bar{R}^2$ is the coefficient of determination corrected for degrees of freedom.
Durbin-Watson statistic for serial correlation test.
As a result of the correlation for the number of degrees of freedom, $\bar{R}^2$ equals zero.
Excluding fuels.
Smaller than 0.005.

recession (1957–1958), actual exports declined much more than computed exports, and exceeded, therefore, the decline that could be accounted for by the echo effect. The same is true of the 1960–1961 recession, when actual exports rose very much less than computed exports.

The marked declines, or reductions in the rate of growth, of exports of developed to developing countries in 1952–1953, 1957–1959, and 1960–1962 cannot be explained entirely as a reflection of declining business activity in the developed countries. They seem also to be related to substantial reductions in the rate of net capital flow from developed to developing countries, which exceeded by far the reductions that we have been able to ascribe to cyclical causes. Similarly, the large rise in exports from 1956 to 1957 seems to have been associated with a large incease ($1.6 billion) in the net capital flow to developing countries.

It is generally agreed that developing countries do not contribute to cyclical instability of economic activity in developed ones. It is possible however, to go further, and argue that they have contributed to stability of aggregate demand in developed countries. Indeed, this proposition is supported by inspection of the timing of changes in the international reserves of developing countries (see Table 8–4). Reductions occurred in 1952, 1957, 1958, 1961, and 1962. To the extent of these reductions, developing countries helped to support aggregate demand in the developed countries during these recessive periods.

## Appendices

### I.   TEST OF LAG OF IMPORTS BEHIND INDUSTRIAL PRODUCTION

Equations with lags of varying length were computed for (undeflated) quarterly U.S. imports of goods and services and merchandise imports. The independent variable is the seasonally adjusted index of U.S. industrial production. Since imports are seasonally unadjusted, quarterly dummy variables are included in these equations. The data cover 73 observations from the first quarter of 1948 to the first quarter of 1966. The equations without lag and with lags of one and two quarters, computed with first differences of logarithms, are shown in Table 8–7.

For imports of goods and services, and also for merchandise imports alone, the equation with a lag of one quarter is slightly superior to that without lag. But with a lag of two quarters the correlation is significantly reduced; and with longer lags, the results become progressively worse.

### II   REGRESSION EQUATIONS

Table 8–8 presents the detailed regression results discussed in connection with Table 8–3, as well as the alternative regression equations referred to in footnote 8.

# COMMENT

F. J. M. MEYER ZU SCHLOCHTERN
Organization for Economic Cooperation and Development, Paris

The vastness of his subject has obliged Dr. Rhomberg to impose limitations on his analysis. He has restricted himself to flows between two, albeit heterogeneous, groups of countries alone—the developing and the economically advanced countries. He has used only industrial production as an indicator of economic activity, and he has limited his study to the period since World War II. Such restrictions conceal part of the underlying structural relationships [1]. But even with this global approach, his interesting analysis arrives at some illuminating findings. These comments will analyze the results further, while remaining largely within the boundaries established by the study. The following points will be treated: (a) imports of advanced countries from developing countries; (b) net capital imports and residual items; (c) exports of advanced countries to developing countries; and (4) conclusions.

## Imports of Advanced Countries from Developing Countries $(V^{ud})$

### THE ELASTICITIES

The elasticity of import unit values with respect to industrial production depends largely on the period chosen. The elasticity based on the period 1950–1965 (Table 8-9) seems more acceptable in view of the elasticities by commodity group in Table 8-3 of the Rhomberg study. The elasticities for the

---

[1] A more disaggregative study has been completed by Kanta Marwah: "Towards an Econometric Model of World Import–Export Flows," presented at the Economic Commission for Europe *ad hoc* group of experts on import–export projections, May 29–June 2, 1967.

279

TABLE 8-9    Elasticities of Value, Volume, and Unit
Value of Imports of Advanced Countries from
Developing Countries with Respect to Industrial Pro-
duction of Advanced Countries

|  | 1953–1965 | 1950–1965 |
|---|---|---|
| Value | 0.48 | 0.71 |
| Volume | 0.37 | 0.40* |
| Unit Value | 0.08 | 0.30 |

* Estimated at 0.40 in view of Rhomberg's statement
(p.263): In 1950–1965 the "elasticity of the volume
of developing countries' exports to developed countries is almost the same as that found for the period
1953–1965."

unit values of Food, etc., and Fuels, etc., are not significantly different from
zero. The negative values are hardly acceptable, theoretically. The elasticities for
Raw Materials, Excluding Fuels and Manufactures—1.05 and 1.66, respectively—
are significantly positive; these two groups constitute 40 per cent of the exports
of developing countries to advanced countries. When the elasticities for Food,
etc., and Fuels, etc., are put at zero, the weighted elasticity is close to ½. The
elasticity for total exports in the period 1950–1965 is closer to this value than
the elasticity for the total in the shorter period, 1953–1965, covered by the
Rhomberg study.

It is important to note that the short-run elasticity for the volume of trade is
quite different from the long-run elasticity. Since the elasticities used in the
study are based on annual percentage changes, short-run effects will dominate.
Table 8-3 gives 0.4 as the elasticity for the volume of trade. Longer time
intervals—for instance two years—will bring the elasticity close to the long-run
elasticity, which is near unity.

COMPETITION FROM OTHER AREAS

It can be argued that some products produced by developing countries will
compete with products produced by other areas. The elasticity calculated
between industrial production and realized imports of the advanced countries
from the developing countries may therefore differ from the elasticity between
industrial production and overall demand for their products [2]. On the
European market, suppliers other than developing countries have increased their
market share for primary products (Table 8-10).

---

[2] The influence of other suppliers is particularly important for raw materials. The Marwah
study shows high price-substitution elasticities between regions exporting primary products.

TABLE 8-10  OECD Europe's Share of Exports of Primary Products* from North America and Eastern Europe (In per cent)

| Exporting Area | 1953–1954 | 1964–1965 |
|---|---|---|
| North America | 17.5 | 20.0 |
| Eastern Europe | 3.8 | 7.5 |
|  | 21.3 | 27.5 |

Source: Organization for Economic Cooperation and Development (OECD), Foreign Trade Statistics.
* SITC groups 1, 2, 3, and 4; for commodities included in these groups, see Rhomberg's Table 8-3.

STOCKBUILDING

Products of developing countries that are brought by advanced countries can be exported immediately to the latter, but they also can first enter into stocks held in the country of production [3], and be exported later. This means that the speculative movements of stocks will be reflected partly in exports of the same period and partly in capital movements; therefore, the coefficient of industrial production has a downward bias [4].

CONCLUSION

The above arguments imply that the elasticities shown will be minimum values. In a more elaborate approach, the elasticities would probably be higher. An elasticity of 1.00 instead of 0.71 seems not unreasonable, Rhomberg's equation (5) becoming $\Delta V_t^{ud} = 0.18\Delta A_t$ instead of $\Delta V_t^{ud} = 0.13\Delta A_t$.

NET CAPITAL IMPORTS AND RESIDUAL ITEMS ($C^{du}$)

The trade balance is on an f.o.b. basis; that is, it excludes transportation costs. A large part of these costs will have to be paid by the developing countries to insurance and shipping companies in the advanced countries. This can be taken roughly into account by assuming that these costs are 10 per cent of the imports of the developing countries. Then, a new definition of net capital imports can be given as

$$\Delta C_t^{du\prime} = \Delta C_t^{du} - 0.10\,\Delta V_t^{du}.$$

[3] See J. F. W. Rowe, *Primary Commodities in International Trade,* Cambridge, England, 1965, pp. 41–42.
[4] In the Rhomberg study, the coefficients are reduced-form coefficients, with industrial production taking the place of other variables, like stock movements.

In explaining the net capital flow, Rhomberg has assumed that at the start of a recession domestic investment opportunities seem less promising than formerly, but that earnings accumulated over the recent past are still high. On the other hand, recessions are often brought about by tight money and lack of funds for investment anywhere. Another explanation can be given, however. Exports of developing countries will affect profits. A sharp rise in exports will increase profits of the exporting industries. This rise in profits will make it attractive to invest in exporting countries, and these investments will have an influence on exports of advanced countries, since developing countries most import of their investment goods, and most investment goods imported by developing countries come from advanced countries [5]. The correlation of $C^{dw'}$ with past imports $V_{t-1}^{ud}$ gives the following results:

$$\Delta C_t^{dw'} = 0.27\, \Delta V_t^{ud}$$
$$R^2 = 0.37.$$

## Exports of Advanced Countries to Developing Countries

In the equation $\Delta V_t^{du} = f(\Delta G_t, \Delta G_{t-1}, \Delta\Delta R_{t-1}^{u})$, the variable $\Delta\Delta R_{t-1}^{u}$ poses some problems. It can be assumed that the policies of authorities in developing countries depend on the *level* of their reserves rather than their change. Their policies will be attuned to a desired level of reserves $(R^u)$; thus,

$$V_t^{ud} = f(R_{t-1}^{u} - R^{u}).$$

$R^u$ can be assumed to be constant in the short period:

$$\Delta V_t^{ud} = f(\Delta R_{t-1}^{u}).$$

Replacing $\Delta\Delta R_{t-1}^{u}$ by $\Delta R_{t-1}^{u}$ will affect the time lag and the coefficient. Unfortunately, $\Delta R_{t-1}^{u}$ cannot be expressed easily among the exogenous variables of the model. This problem may be solved as follows:

$$R_t^{u} = R_{t-1}^{u} + \Delta R_t^{u}$$

and
$$\Delta R_t^{u} = \Delta R_{t-1}^{u} + \Delta\Delta R_t^{u},$$

of which
$$\Delta R_{t-1}^{u} = \Delta R_{t-2}^{u} + \Delta\Delta R_{t-1}, \ldots.$$

With assumed initial conditions of $\Delta R^u$, this dynamic system can be solved through time.

Another explanation for the significant parameter for reserves is that their reserves are positively correlated with the export prices obtained by the developing countries. These prices will often influence the investment climate in

---

[5] Such an influence has been found by R. E. Krainer, "Resource Endowment and the Structure of Foreign Investment," *Journal of Finance*, March 1967.

these countries, and will therefore be correlated positively with exports of advanced countries, which consist in large part of investment goods.

## Conclusions

In a more elaborate equation than the one presented by Rhomberg, the elasticity of imports of advanced countries from developing countries ($V^{ud}$) with respect to industrial production will be close to unity:

$$\Delta V_t^{ud} = 0.18\Delta A_t.$$

The net capital flow will also include transport payments by developing countries to advanced countries. This can be roughly estimated at 10 per cent of exports of the advanced countries to the developing countries, as has been said. The remaining part will show a correlation with past export performance. The resulting equation becomes

$$\Delta C_t^{du} = 0.10\ \Delta V_t^{du} + 0.27\Delta V_{t-1}^{ud}.$$

In the export function of advanced countries, the variable expressing the change in the growth of reserves ($\Delta\Delta R_{t-1}^{u}$) poses some problems. There are reasons to put $\Delta R_{t-1}^{u}$ in the equation instead of $\Delta\Delta R_{t-1}^{u}$. Without further analysis, it is difficult to see whether the significance of the variable is caused by government policy either to attain a certain level of reserves, or to avoid changes in the reserves, or by the parallelism mentioned above between reserves and export prices.

The first two changes can be incorporated in Rhomberg's model. The reduced form of his export equation would then be:

$$\Delta V_t^{du} = -0.36\,\Delta V_{t-1}^{du} + 0.15\,\Delta A_t + 0.22\,\Delta A_{t-1} + 0.05\,\Delta A_{t-2}$$

instead of his (10):

$$\Delta V_t^{du} = -0.41\Delta V_{t-1}^{du} + 0.10\Delta A_t + 0.16\Delta A_{t-1} + 0.05\,\Delta A_{t-2}.$$

# III ECONOMIC FLUCTUATIONS UNDER SOCIALISM

Chapter Nine

# CYCLICAL FLUCTUATIONS UNDER SOCIALISM

ALEC NOVE
University of Glasgow

Many of the contributors to this book will have read Josef Goldmann's very interesting views on this subject, published in Scandinavia [1] and elsewhere. Some may know of an earlier contribution to the discussion, by the Argentine economist Juan Olivera [2], which has certain points in common with Goldmann's argument. Both emphasize a kind of political ("subjective") imperative, to go ahead as fast as possible, and so to overinvest. As soon as the crisis which compelled cuts in investment is overcome, the same tendency reasserts itself. Goldmann would attribute the cuts to the exhaustion of raw material supplies and foreign exchange reserves, while Olivera gave greater emphasis to exhaustion of the people's patience with low living standards; but no doubt each would agree that the factors named by the other did play a significant role in the "crises" which beset a number of East European countries.

My own task is not to question either the analysis or the statistics of fluctuations in such countries, but to concentrate on the Soviet Union. Does the history of the USSR provide evidence of the presence or absence of cyclical fluctuations, of some kind of trade cycle? It so, of what kind? If the evidence for the Soviet Union refused to fit into a pattern applicable to, say, Czechoslovakia, Hungary, and Poland, this in no way disproves the validity of generalizations derived from the experience of those three countries, but one might be entitled to dissent from conclusions purporting to apply to "collectivist countries" in general.

---

[1] *Economics of Planning,* Oslo, Vol. 4, No. 2, 1964.
[2] "Cyclical Economic Growth under Collectivism," *Kyklos,* Vol. 13, 1960, pp. 229–252, and my comment, *ibid,* p. 256.

What is meant here by fluctuations? Any considerable variation in growth rates and/or the rate of increase in investments will be examined to see whether it would "fit" into a pattern which could be called cyclical. Obviously, the mere fact of variation is not of itself evidence of "crises" in the sense discussed in the present paper. For example, there could be:

(a) Substantial year-by-year variation in the harvest, owing to weather conditions (Table 9-1) therefore contains a column for crops, as well as for total agricultural production). (b) A drastic once-and-for-all shift in government policy, occasioned (for instance) by the removal or death of the leader. (However, if, as in Mexico, the succession of a president *always* leads to economic fluctuations every six years, because the outgoing president spends all available funds to the greater glory of himself, leaving the incoming president with an empty treasury, then that would be a species of "trade cycle".) (c) A change in the international situation that could lead to a major shift of resources into armaments. And (d) a discernible secular trend toward lower rates of growth.

None of the foregoing are strictly part of the conception of *cyclical* trends, and so care must be taken to note the effects of such factors and to discount them where necessary.

A more difficult question is raised by the Russian word *shturmovshchina*, "storming," uneven production related to plan timetables. Anxiety to fulfill a plan tends to cause a rush to increase output towards the end of any plan period (month, quarter, year), with a consequent exhaustion of resources and personnel and a sharp fall in output at the beginning of the next period. The effects of such practices spread widely, since there is a tendency for deliveries of materials and components to be made toward the end of the plan period, compelling plants which would otherwise prefer an even tempo to pile up work for the last weeks or days. That this is a major problem in the traditional Soviet planning system is not to be doubted. It does constitute a species of fluctuation, but so does the Christmas shopping rush in London. Without denying its importance (or asserting any equivalence between the significance of the annual plan and that of December 25), *this* kind of fluctuation will be ignored here, as too short-term and too regular in character. (Even in the West, business practices are affected by the date at which annual accounts are made up.) However, it is another matter with five-year plans, since these cover a longer time-span. If evidence were to show a tendency to invest heavily in the last year of the plan period, with a slack year at the beginning, then this might be treated as analogous to a trade cycle.

The statistical series shown in Table 9-1, being aggregated, inevitably conceal considerable fluctuations, or changes in policies, affecting particular industries. For example, investments in coal were drastically cut in the middle 1950's in favor of oil, electricity, and gas. However, this made no perceptible difference in growth rates; it simply led to a switch of resources within the fuel sector. Of

TABLE 9-1. Soviet Union: Indicators of Economic Fluctuations, 1928–1966 (Percentage increase over previous year)

| | National income | Gross ind. prod. | Gross agric. prod. | Crops | Investment* |
|------|------|------|------|------|------|
| 1928 | 8.7 | 19.4 | 2.4 | 3.5 | |
| 1929 | 15.6 | 20.0 | −2.4 | −0.9 | |
| 1930 | 21.1 | 21.7 | −3.5 | 8.6 | 71.2 |
| 1931 | 16.9 | 20.5 | −2.6 | 0 | 39.4 |
| 1932 | 11.2 | 14.8 | −6.1 | −0.8 | 16.8 |
| 1933 | 6.6 | 5.4 | −5.6 | −3.2 | −14.3 |
| 1934 | 15.1 | 19.2 | 5.0 | 3.3 | 30.9 |
| 1935 | 19.2 | 22.3 | 12.3 | 10.4 | 18.0 |
| 1936 | 29.3 | 28.5 | −8.4 | −14.5 | 36.9 |
| 1937 | 12.0 | 11.2 | 22.9 | 27.1 | −9.7 |
| 1938 | 9.0 | 11.7 | −10.4 | −20.0 | 3.8 |
| 1939 | (11)‡ | 16.1 | 0.8 | 4.2 | 14.1 |
| 1940 | (11)‡§ | 11.8§ | 16.7§ | 24.0§ | 7.0§ |
| | | | | | |
| 1946 | −6.0 | −16.3 | 13.3 | 14.0 | 20.3 |
| 1947 | 19.1 | 20.8 | 27.9 | 40.0 | 9.9 |
| 1948 | 24.1 | 26.9 | 11.5 | 12.1 | 20.3 |
| 1949 | 18.0 | 19.5 | 2.1 | −1.0 | 18.9 |
| 1950 | 20.1 | 22.7 | 0 | −4.0 | 20.3 |
| 1951 | 12.7 | 16.8 | −6.1 | −11.3 | 13.2 |
| 1952 | 10.8 | 11.4 | 8.6 | 11.6 | 11.8 |
| 1953 | 9.3 | 12.0 | 3.0 | 0 | 5.2 |
| 1954 | 12.3 | 13.1 | 4.8 | 3.1 | 18.1 |
| 1955 | 11.9 | 12.3 | 11.0 | 14.1 | 13.3 |
| 1956 | 11.2 | 10.6 | 13.2 | 15.0 | 16.1 |
| 1957 | 6.9 | 10.2 | 2.9 | −1.5 | 12.9 |
| 1958 | 12.4 | 10.3 | 10.6 | 14.8 | 16.2 |
| 1959 | 7.5 | 11.4 | 0.6 | −4.8 | 13.3 |
| 1960 | 7.6 | 9.9 | 1.9 | 5.0 | 7.8 |
| 1961 | 6.9 | 9.0 | 3.1 | 1.4 | 4.5 |
| 1962 | 5.7 | 9.8 | 1.2 | 0 | 4.8 |
| 1963 | 3.9 | 8.2 | −7.2 | −8.7 | 5.1 |
| 1964 | 9.4¶ | 7.0 | 14.2 | 28.7 | 9.0 |
| 1965 | 7.0 | 8.6 | 0.6 | −9.7 | 9.0 |
| 1966 | 7.5 | 8.6 | 10.0 | ? | 6.0 |

Sources: *National income*: 1928–1938: *Sotsialisticheskoe stroitel'stvo*, 1934, pp. 20–21, 1926, p. xxxii, 1933–1938, p. 18. 1946–1964: *Narodnoe khozyaistvo SSSR* (hereinafter *N. Kh.*), 1965, p. 589. 1966: *Pravda*, January 29, 1967.

*Industrial production*. 1928–1940: *Promyshlennost, SSSR,* 1964, p. 34 1946–1965: *N. Kh.,* 1965, p. 122.

*Agricultural production and crops:* 1928–1940: *Selskoe khozyaistvo SSSR* 1960, p. 79; *N. Kh.,* 1965, p. 259.

*Investment:* 1928–1956: *N. Kh.,* 1956, pp. 172, 173; 1957–1965: *N. Kh.,* 1965, p. 528.

* Investments are given gross of *part* of the depreciation fund (not of that part deemed to be devoted to "capital repairs"). Figures include collective farm investments. Omission of vast disinvestment in private and collective agriculture in 1930–1934 causes considerable overstatement for those years. Private investment in housing is included only for the years 1957 and after. The index is derived from a value series "in constant prices."

† Some sources give 30.3.

‡ Average of the two years, 1939 and 1940.

§ Figures significantly affected by annexation of new territory.

¶ Figures amended upward four times. All 1964 data may have been affected by the fall of Khrushchev.

289

led to some dislocation, as does any sharp change in an existing pattern. This happens in all economies. It could legitimately be argued that the decision-making process in the USSR is such as to make such policy shifts drastic and disorganizing, because a change in existing patterns requires central decision-making at a high political level, and decisions are often delayed until the case for action is so overwhelming that a drastic campaign must be mounted, with correspondingly severe pains of adjustment. This is so, but the tendency will not be held to constitute a "cyclical fluctuation," *unless* the adjustment is so great as to affect overall growth rates. (Even so, it is doubtful if it can be called cyclical.)

A statistical warning must be given. The figures presented are Soviet official indices of growth. For reasons which cannot be gone into here, they tend to inflate growth rates (and probably also investment volume). The period before 1950 is more liable to such "inflation" than more recent years. The point, however, has little bearing on *this* study. If growth rates claimed are +20 per cent, +3 per cent, and +10 per cent, this is a fluctuation, and its extent remains little affected by the possibility that the "real" figures were respectively +13 per cent, −2 per cent, and +7 per cent. Admittedly, a recomputation with different weights, or a different methodology, would yield different results. But the procedure chosen here seems to be the least unsatisfactory of any.

There are various other statistical inadequacies in the table. Thus the national income series for the 1930's is taken from past data which appear not to have been corrected downward to take account of a downward amendment of harvest figures, athough this is reflected in the agricultural production index. This may help to explain some rather odd relationships between the figures for national income and those for industry and agriculture. The coverage of investment statistics is also inconsistent, as is noted in the footnote to the table. In all years, the indices given have some peculiarities of definition. Thus national income excludes "unproductive" services; gross industrial production is calculated by adding together the output of every Soviet enterprise (gross of the value of goods and services purchased from other enterprises); and gross agricultural production is the sum of the volume of all crops and livestock products, without correction for consumption within agriculture. However, for the purpose of the present discussion, corrective coefficients and precise adjustments are not needed, since the shape of the curves and their various zigzags are little affected.

## An Early Soviet Crisis

The years 1922–1923 constitute a most interesting example of an economic crisis. This crises followed the beginning of NEP (New Economic Policy), that is, from a highly centralized economy ("war communism") to one in which (a) peasants were free to sell farm surpluses, subject to a tax in kind; (b) state trusts and enterprises were ordered to operate "commercially" by reference to market criteria, instead of being dependent on state orders and state financing; and (c) a legal private sector operated not only in agriculture, where it was dominant, but in small-scale industry and (especially) trade.

In 1922, industrial output was a small fraction of prewar output, and agriculture was still suffering from the after-effects of the disastrous 1921 harvest. The terms of trade favored the peasants, but the food shortage was so acute in farming areas that peasants had little opportunity to take advantage of favorable trade terms. State trusts, left to their own devices and starved of credit (as part of the effort to contain the inflation), began to sell fixed assets and stocks of materials in desperate efforts to raise money. Then, in 1923, a better harvest led to a drastic change in the terms of trade between village and town. Food production recovered rapidly, while manufacturing industry was still disrupted and extremely inefficient. The result was the emergence of the famous "price scissors." If the 1913 ratio between industrial and agricultural prices is taken as 100/100, this relationship became 180/60 in the autumn of 1923, when the peasants threw the proceeds of a fairly good harvest into the market. Despite the shortage of manufactures, the state trusts which ran large-scale industry found it exceedingly difficult to sell their output. The peasants, faced with relatively high prices of goods they wished to buy, threatened to reduce output as a protest against the unfavorable terms of trade.

During 1924, a sharp rise in industrial production and measures to reduce costs in state industry "closed" the blades of the scissors. This particular crisis was over. It was not repeated in that form, and so must be seen as a crisis of adjustment to a new system in the aftermath of the cataclysm and breakdown of 1917–1921. It is true that the terms of trade again moved sharply against the village a few years later. However, this was part of the state's deliberate policy, to finance its vast investment program.

## The "Great Leap Forward" Crisis, 1929–1933

More relevant to this discussion is a study of the period of the first five-year plan. This, as shall be shown, fits into the pattern discussed by Goldmann. The plan was an extremely ambitious one, whose "optimal variant" called for: national income to increase by 110 per cent over that of 1927–1928 (the economic year ended on September 30 at that time); fixed investment to increase more than threefold, agricultural production by 55 per cent, and industrial production by more than 125 per cent; labor productivity in large-scale industry to double; per capita personal income to increase rapidly, with real wages up by 77 per cent; and costs and prices to fall substantially. This was a fantasy plan. It is remarkable that even in the last edition of his book, Dobb [3], holds that it could be taken seriously, and that its disproportions arose out of subsequent amendments to heavy-industry targets (allegedly owing to war danger), plus peasant troubles and worsening terms of trade. Of course it was taken seriously at the time, but in retrospect it *was* a fantasy, and some of its authors must have thought so. Be that as it may, many of the overoptimistic industrial target figures were actually increased in 1929–1931, requiring its planners to aim not for the impossible but for the miraculous. A full account of the repeated upward amendments of targets would fill a book. There was the slogan "fulfill the five-year plan in four years." Plan goals for key industrial commodities were set higher and higher. The pages of *Planovoe khozyaistvo* and *Problemy ekonomiki* of those years abound in evidence of this. Kuibyshev, the head of Gosplan, was particularly guilty. The figures in Table 9-2 are examples of upward amendments.

Jasny has pointed out [4], and rightly, that there exists a peculiarly unbalanced document, adopted by the 17th party conference, held in February 1932, as the directive for the drafting of the second five-year plan. To give one example only: the coal output target for 1937 was provisionally fixed at 250 million tons (1932 figure: 64.3 million). Luckily the final version of the second plan was much more realistic, and the figure was reduced to 152 million (actual 1937 figure: 128 million).

What happens if, under strong political pressure, the planning technicians accept an impossible plan? (If any objections were to lead to instant imprisonment on a charge of being a right-wing deviationist, few would take the risk of warning against unrealism.)

By "impossible" is meant a plan that calls for buildings to be completed at a pace that cannot be maintained, requires materials that cannot be made or transported in time, and/or provides inputs insufficient to produce the planned outputs. In the Soviet case, there was an impossible strain on material inputs and also on labor, which was untrained and ruined valuable machines in consequence. Nevertheless, forward momentum was maintained at top pressure. The results were as follows:

(a) There was a *de facto* downward amendment of plans for nonpriority sectors. (b) A system of rationing and administrative allocation was introduced. This became a necessity when (planned) demand exceeded supply, in order to enforce the politically determined priorities. The so-called command economy of centralized resource allocation, devised at this period, was created in response to this situation. It was not thought out *ex ante* as a "model" [5]. (c) Despite this,

[3] Maurice Dobb, *Soviet Economic Development Since 1917*, London, 1966.
[4] *Soviet Industrialization, 1928–1952*, Chicago, 1961.
[5] This point is made by Cz. Bobrowski, in *Formation du systeme sovietique de planification* Paris, 1956.

TABLE 9-2    Soviet Union: Goals for Key Commodities Under First Five Year Plan*

| Commodity | 1927–1928 Actual | 1932–1933 "Optimal" plan | 1932–1933 Amended plan† | 1932 Actual |
|---|---|---|---|---|
| Grain (mill. tons) | 74 | 105–108 | 115 | (72)‡ |
| Coal (mill. tons) | 35 | 75 | 95–105 | 64.3 |
| Oil (mill. tons) | 11.7 | 21.7 | 40–55 | 21.4 |
| Iron ore (mill. tons) | 6.7 | 20.2 | 24–32 | 12.1 |
| Pig iron (mill. tons) | 3.2 | 10 | 15–15§ | 6.2 |
| Sawmill products (index) | 100 | 340 | 600 | 187 |

Source: S. Bessonov, *Problemy ekonomiki*, No. 10–11, 1929, p. 27 and *Promyshlennost'
SSSR*, 1957.
* The economic year until 1933 was October 1–September 30. The five-year plan was to be
"fulfilled in four years;" 1932–1933 targets were "brought forward" to December 1932.
† On December 29, 1929.
‡ The exact figure for the grain harvest of 1932 is not available.
§ On January 30, 1930, amended again to 17–18 million tons.

in the hectic atmosphere of declamatory overoptimism, too much was constantly being attempted. Supplies ran out, delays occurred, transport was overloaded, and there were fuel crises. Owing to peasant resistance to collectivization, and also to inefficiency and inexperience, there was a decline in farm output and, in particular, a catastrophic fall in numbers of livestock, which adversely affected living standards and also deliveries of agricultural raw materials to industry. (d) The first five-year plan coincided with the great depression, and the Russians suffered with other raw material exporters from a worsening in the terms of trade. This led to increased exports and contributed to domestic shortages of food, amounting in some areas to an appalling famine.

All these factors culminated in a critical situation in 1932–1933. Growth rates, even those of industrial output, were sharply checked. Agricultural production fell. Desperate shortages, bottlenecks of all kinds, impeded production. The population suffered great hardships, and millions were on the move in search of bearable living, creating havoc with labor-turnover statistics. In 1933, investment was severely cut back, even though the plan called for a further increase.

Some of the participants in the present Conference had attended a Warsaw conference in 1966, and read A. Vainshtein's (still unpublished) conference paper. Vainshtein had been among those who had earlier sought to warn against wildly overoptimistic planning, and had spent 20 years behind bars for his heresy. In his 1966 paper, Vainshtein returned to this theme: the rate of increase in investment was grossly excessive; it would not be absorbed; the resultant overstrain wasted resources. Table 9-1 shows an increase of 70 per cent for the single year 1930 [6]. This, as Vainshtein pointed out, was plain absurdity.

It proved necessary to call a halt. It is true that 1932 saw the end of the first five-year plan, and so the slowdown in 1933 could be treated as an example of "five-year *shturmovshchina*." In this instance, the evidence is strong that the exhaustion of resources and of people in the period, which Jasny has called "hurrah-planning," [7], compelled a halt in any case. It is interesting to compare the 1932–1933 crisis in the United States and in the Soviet Union, for it is as well to remember that the West was in no position at that time to lecture Stalin on economically rational utilization of resources. (This, however, is beyond the subject matter of this chapter.)

## The Late 1930's

The next period that requires examination is 1936–1940. These years call for special comment in several respects:

(a) The substantial rise in output claimed for 1936 is peculiarly suspect, statistically. This is so not only because the national income total seems incredibly high for a year of bad harvest, but also because it was a year in which wholesale prices were sharply raised, and most specialists would agree that this affected the so-called "unchanged 1926–1927 prices," at which national income and its various elements were computed, thus adding abnormal quantities of "water" to the figures [8]. This is not to deny that 1936 (and 1935) were very good years for Soviet industry. Only, they were not that good.

(b) The year 1937 was the last one of the second five-year plan. It was also the best harvest year of the interwar period. Given the pressure to fulfill targets (that is five-year *shturmovshchina*), an unusually high rate of growth might have been expected. Yet industrial output grew only slowly, and investment actually fell. Was this due to exhaustion of resources in the preceding three years? If so, then it would be another example of a fluctuation brought on by trying to run too fast. But was this in fact the case? Other factors obscure the answer to the question, as shall be shown in this paper.

(c) The year 1937 was also one in which Soviet expenditure on arms made an upward climb, as the Nazi menace loomed. The resultant redeployment of resources was bound to affect the investment program to some extent. From 1936 to 1940, arms expenditure in the budget rose almost fourfold.

(d) Last, but far from least, 1937 and 1938 were the years in which the Great

---

[6] Less, if disinvestment in the private sector is taken into account.

[7] *Op. cit.,* which contains a vivid picture of the period.

[8] Even the late Professor Baykov, who accepted most Soviet indices, took exception to the 1936 figures for this reason.

Purge reached its climax. Thousands of planners, managers, technicians, and experts of all kinds and all levels were arrested. Other thousands trembled in fear of arrest and avoided responsibility. This must have had adverse effects on the economy. This factor is now mentioned in Soviet histories of the period as one of the major causes of the marked slowdown in industrial growth in those years.

It has been pointed out (for instance by Jasny) that war preparations can hardly account for the pattern of development of those years, since weapons needed metal, and the metallurgical industry failed to grow after 1937. Thus, steel output was 17.7 million tons in 1937 and only 18.3 million in 1940, an insignificant rise, far below plan. This certainly strengthens the belief that the purge had a good deal to do with the slowdown. But it is also true that metal would have been diverted into arms production and the re-equipping of arms factories (including the conversion of tractor works to tank production), and the resultant shortages could have led to a disruption of all other investment programs, exacerbated by the disorganizing effects of the terror. There is also, undeniably, the possibility of shortages arising from too rapid a growth in output and investment in the three years 1934–1936, which in turn was made possible by the completion of many projects begun but not finished during the first five-year plan period. Evidence on the importance of this factor is lacking; it is not enough to find quotations to show that supply shortages occurred, since these shortages occur somewhere in the USSR in any and every year, as the inevitable consequence of attempting full utilization of resources (or what some analysts call "taut planning"). In any case, the consequences of the great purge and of the arms program loom rather larger, and make it virtually impossible to identify the operation of other factors.

Statistical recomputations made by various western scholars (for instance, Nutter) indicate a poor performance by Soviet industry in 1938–1940, and this is certainly true for civilian industry. However, this does not necessarily mean that output failed to rise. Thus, to take one example, tractor production fell from 112,900 in 1936 to 51,000 in 1937 and to 31,600 in 1940, no doubt because of a switch to tanks. Since military output was secret, its contribution to the output index cannot be measured by the authors of western recomputations. It is, naturally included in the Soviet official index. The "gross output of the arms industry" in 1938 was 36.4 per cent greater than in 1937, and investment works in defense rose by 70 per cent [9].

When the entire period 1928–1940 is reviewed, the extreme ups and downs on investment (last column in Table 9-1) stand out sharply. The idea that a planned economy ensures a steady and constant level of investment expenditure (unlike the situation in the West, which relies on unplannable private and corporation savings) can hardly survive an examination of the record. However,

---

[9] *Finansy SSSR za 30 let*, p. 181.

those were extraordinary years. The period of the "Soviet great leap forward" (1929–1932) was described by Stalin himself as a "revolution from above." It was a period of dominance of political arbitrariness over calculation, of the struggle over economic rationality. The slogans of the time–"there is no fortress the Bolsheviks cannot take," etc., etc.,–predisposed officialdom to excesses, while arguments about balance and caution came to be associated with Bukharin and the right-wing enemies of the "general line." This, plus the collectivization disaster, led to an overcommitment of resources, an overextension of effort, and the "about face" of 1933. But the next downswing seems to have been of a different kind, or to have been overlaid by other considerations, such as the direct damage done by political terror, or the switch of capital goods industries into weaponry.

## The Postwar Years

Since World War II, the pattern seems to have been quite different. The "minus" in 1946 was evidently due to the strains of reconversion of war industry. The very large increases in the next years appear equally to have been due to postwar reconstruction and recovery. (The recovery of agriculture was sharply checked in 1949, partly because of weather, but even more owing to Stalin's price policies and his heavy taxes on peasants.) A downward trend in industrial growth tempos became apparent as the reconstruction period came to an end, considerably before Stalin's death. This was inevitable, and could hardly be fitted into a trade-cycle pattern. Obviously, when new factories need to be built, rather than old ones reactivated, the capital-output ratio tends to rise. In addition, 1951 saw a large increase in expenditure for arms; this was the time of the Korean War and Russia's rapid development of nuclear weapons, accompanied by a bigger call-up of troops. This, too, must have caused some decline in economic growth and investment. The year 1953 was abnormal in one important respect: Stalin died. Malenkov adopted a policy of pleasing the consumer: there was a big rise in the planned output of consumer goods; there were lower taxes on peasants; there was a marked reduction in forced savings (mass bond sales); and there were wage increases. Efforts were made to halt the arms race. Investment increased little and its structure began to change, with more attention to agriculture and the needs of the citizen. However, Malenkov was ousted in February 1955, in the name of a policy which reasserted the priority of heavy industry. There followed the period of Khrushchev's dominance, in which investment policy fluctuated, with agriculture's share in total investment first rising and then falling, while expenditure on housing increased spectacularly, only to fall both relatively and absolutely after 1960. (In 1958, housing absorbed 25.4 per cent of total investment, as against 18.4 per cent in 1950. By 1960, the percentage had fallen to 16.3.) There was the episode of the adoption of the sixth five-year plan (1956–1960), followed by its abandonment because—it was alleged—it was out of balance in the sense of requiring investment on an unfeasibly large scale. This would suggest that the planners (or some of them) were conscious of the need to avoid overstrain and overcommitment of resources, that is, that they were trying to avoid the kind of fluctuations to which overinvestment would have led (one Soviet economist, however, assured me that this was not so, that the plan was opposed by Khrushchev on political and personal grounds). Khrushchev pressed strongly for greater attention to his own "favorites": nonsolid fuels, chemicals, maize, and so on. However, all these things, while they show that many drastic changes occurred, do not add up to evidence of fluctuations in the sense discussed in this Chapter. National income rose by percentages which varied with the harvest, with a general trend toward deceleration.

The last years (1960–1964) of Khrushchev's tenure of office witnessed a sharp decline in the rate of increase in investment, accompanied by a *relative* fall in output of consumer goods, compared with producer goods, as well as very modest results in agriculture (except in 1964). No doubt the slowdown in investment was due in some part to the sharp rise in military expenditure decreed in 1961. Another factor was the marked slowdown in the intake of new labor during the years 1957–1963, owing to the dramatic decline in the birth and survival rates during and just after the war. This may be illustrated by the following figures of the numbers (in millions) attending primary schools, that is, children in the age group 7–11:

| 1950–1951 | 1952–1953 | 1954–1955 | 1955–1956 | 1958–1959 | 1964–1965 |
|-----------|-----------|-----------|-----------|-----------|-----------|
| 20.1      | 13.4      | 12.9      | 13.8      | 17.7      | 20.0      |

The "1954–1955" children had been born in 1942–1947, and joined the labor force during 1957–1962. This is a "fluctuation" indeed, but hardly of the "cyclical" variety.

The sheer administrative muddle which characterized Khrushchev's last years in power probably also contributed to fluctuations. He is known to have caused difficulties by excessive emphasis on the chemical industry and by too drastic cuts in investments in coal, metallurgy, and bricks. His successors have corrected these disproportions, which were causing unnecessary strains and shortages. As an example of such correction, which at the same time provides statistical evidence of the kind of fluctuations which do occur—and must be unconducive to good order and rational resource utilization—investment figures for the chemical industry may be examined [10]:

---

[10] Data, except those for "1965, plan," are from *Narodnoe khozyaistvo,* 1965, p. 534. The "1965 plan" figure is from A. Zverev, *Voprosy ekonomiki,* 6, 1964, p. 46. (The plan was drawn up before 1964 figures became available.)

|                                       | 1958 | 1960 | 1964 | 1965 plan | 1965 |
|---------------------------------------|------|------|------|-----------|------|
| Total (million rubles)                | 455  | 890  | 1948 | 2757      | 1924 |
| Per cent of total industrial investment | 4.5  | 7.0  | 11.7 | –         | 10.7 |

Sources: See footnote 10.

These figures demonstrate both the violence of the upswing in investment in this relatively neglected sector of Soviet industry, and the drastic nature of the downward amendment made by Kosygin after Khrushchev's fall.

But this, however painful, is evidence of sectoral policy zigzags and campaigns. It does not add up to a picture of "macroeconomic" fluctuations. A similar series of changes in agricultural policy—for instance, in the cropping pattern—can be used as evidence of the undesirability of centrally organized campaigns to grow more maize, or less grass, or more livestock, but here again the matter is not really relevant in the present context, save insofar as the performance of agriculture affects the growth of the economy as a whole.

The tendency to overinvest must be seen as a constant feature of Soviet planning. Its very constancy has led, in postwar years especially, to a continuing strain which seems not to vary significantly in intensity. There is an annual appeal by the minister of finance for an end to what he calls *raspylenie sredstv*—or the scattering of resources among too many projects, few of which can be completed in time and some of which are "frozen" for years on end. The causes of this phenomenon are: (a) The fact that investment resources are free to the recipient, which leads to too many applications from below for slices of the cake; (b) the more projects are started, the greater is the hope of local officials and managers that further allocations will be made to enable the work to be completed; (c) the general "mystique" of maximizing growth, which causes the center to approve "taut" plans; (d) the absence of any financial penalty for prolonging the period of construction, or for possessing uncompleted buildings and uninstalled machinery; (e) the measurement of profits as a percentage of costs, without considering the value of the capital employed; and (f) a delibrate underestimation of cost, in order to persuade the top planners to approve a given project.

Recent measures are designed to correct these tendencies: capital charges, interest-bearing and returnable credits, charges on unused equipment and hoarded stocks (and greater freedom to dispose of both), the computation of profits as a percentage of capital—all are designed to check or penalize excessive investment demand. It remains to be seen whether pressure for maximizing growth will so diminish as to provide the "slack" necessary to avoid continuous strain in the investment goods sector. It may be, of course, that the spread of "market" relations into Soviet type planning will lead to fluctuations of another kind—more familiar to the West—that are due to overproduction and the resultant difficulties in selling. The very success of an expansion of output has brought this day nearer. In years in which almost everything was in short supply, such problems did not arise. Three Soviet examples can be cited:

|  | Output (thousands) | |
|---|---|---|
|  | 1960 | 1965 |
| Sewing machines | 3096 | 800 |
| Cameras | 1794 | 1052 |
| Clocks and watches | 16302 | 14813 |

In all these instances, demand has been insufficient to sustain production at planned levels. This is also true of certain "unpopular" types of textiles and clothing.

As more decisions come to be taken at enterprise and trust levels, and with reference to sales expectations, the chances of trade cycles developing must increase, especially in the early stages of the conversion of the system, since—

(a) The "Stalin" model provided for the assessment of requirements (of enterprises and consumers) by the planning organs, which collected evidence in the form of applications (*zayavki*). In the imperfect conditions of a Soviet "market", and with prices still subject to administrative control, microplans may go adrift.

(b) The center is unaccustomed to the operation of fiscal and other indirect forms of control.

(c) There is not, and cannot be, any capital market, so structural changes will still require central ("political") decision.

However, further consideration of these issues is far afield from the subject matter of this paper.

It would seem possible, very tentatively, to conclude that the type of fluctuations observed by Goldmann cannot be identified within the USSR since the war, and perhaps not since 1934. The very large zigzags in growth and investment which have indeed occurred are due to other causes, or do not constitute fluctuations in the meaning which Goldmann gives to the word, or are not large or broad enough to "qualify." This is a proposition but forward for argument's sake, rather than with any great confidence, and leads to the following question: If there is indeed a difference in this respect between Russian experience on the one hand and Czech, Polish, or Hungarian experience on the other, what is the cause, or are the causes, of this difference?

The following points are put forward for discussion:

1. The East European experience has in fact reflected political decisions,

under somewhat odd circumstances which may not in fact be repeated, certainly not in the extreme form of, say, 1952 or 1955.

2. These circumstances included a tendency to copy Russia, and in doing so to go further than the Russians went, owing to the habit (at the period) of slavish imitation. The best example is that of Hungary. Rakosi forced the adoption in 1950–1952 of ambitious investment targets, whose pattern was derived not from Hungarian but from Soviet experience despite the vast differences in size and resource endowment of the two countries. In 1953, Nagy succeeded Rakosi, and policy changed. Investment in heavy industry was cut, and more consumer goods were put into the plan. This happened not for Hungarian reasons but because Malenkov had come to power in Russia and was pursuing a pro-consumer policy. In 1955 Malenkov fell, for good Russian reasons. This led in Hungary to the return of Rakosi and the readoption of a very ambitious and "hard" investment program. The policy zigzag in Hungary seems to have been greater than in Russia, though the chapter on Hungary in this book shows that the actual growth rates in 1955–1956 were not decisively affected. (No doubt political events disrupted the process.) The tail wagged harder than the dog to which it was attached, *pour ainsi dire*. In other words, in Hungary (and perhaps in Czechoslovakia and Poland, too), *so long as they had subordinate status*, the cycles identified by Goldmann must be seen as having part of their origin and pecularities in this status. (It matters not whether the policies were adopted by orders from Moscow, or whether the local leadership copied Moscow of its own violation.) To put the point in another way: Even under Stalin, Soviet plans were a response, however distorted, to Soviet conditions, and the lessons of the wild "hurrah-planning" period may not have been lost on Stalin. Before 1956, however, the policies of both communist-ruled countries were greatly influenced by Soviet policies or their leaders' conception of such policies, rather than by the realities of their situation.

3. The process of planning involves the identification by planning technicians of the feasible, and a reconciliation of the feasible with the demands of the political leadership. Lack of experience or inadequate information can lead the planning technicians into error, and the political atmosphere (as in the period 1929–1932 in the USSR) could make it impossible for them to communicate to the leadership, views as to what is in fact feasible, so that impracticable plans are adopted. These plans must, by definition, give rise to the exhaustion of resources and irregular progress from bottleneck to bottleneck. It would seem that communications between planners and politicians have greatly improved, especially since Stalin's death. Of course, disagreements are possible. There is ample evidence of a clash between Khrushchev and the planning experts in 1963–1964 over the chemical investment program. (It may not be irrelevant to note that it was Khrushchev who lost out in the struggle.)

4. The Olivera article cited at the beginning of this Chapter referred to a

growing conflict between the time-preferences of the citizens and of the authorities, and also of the growing disparity between the growth of labor productivity and that of consumption, as characteristic of "collectivism." In his view, these things give rise to a cyclical tendency with repeated upsurges of discontent among the citizenry. However, the citizens may not be interested in time-preference and labor productivity or investment statistics. They are interested in their own living standards, and will accept any rate of investment provided these standards rise. If living standards do not rise, and/or if expectations are severely disappointed, then social-political pressures do indeed develop. But the leaders of the various countries are now well aware of this. It has become a political imperative to satisfy this demand, so as to avoid political embarrassment and dangers. Needless to say, this is not always done, and, as in Hungary in 1966, there can be public expressions of strong dissatisfaction. But the essential point is that "collectivist" governments in recent years have tried consciously to avoid adopting investment programs of a type and scale which cut basic living standards, and have tried genuinely to provide for a steady rise in real incomes.

5. Finally, it must be noted that the excesses in Hungary, Poland, and Czechoslovakia were contemporaneous with a social revolution, as were those in Russia in 1929–1933. Social revolutions have a logic of their own, one that is not conducive to moderation.

If the foregoing analysis is anywhere near the truth, it would seem to follow that the kind of ups and downs analyzed by Goldmann and (in a different way) by Olivera will be smoothed out in the future, and may be replaced by fluctuations of a type more familiar in western countries. Of course, it is possible to envisage an eastern country (say Hungary) exhausting its foreign exchange reserves and taking deflationary measures, including the reduction of its investment program. But one need look no further than London for a western example of the same thing. The Hungarian proposals for reform provide for a significant increase in freedom for management in industry, including (in some limited respects) freedom as purchasers of imports; there are also to be more investments outside the direct control of the central planners. (Overstrain can be the result of decentralized planning too, as the experience of Yugoslavia has amply demonstrated.)

However, to pursue these thoughts and speculations would require another paper. The USSR is not so dependent on foreign trade, and its reforms are (so far) more cautious and limited than those of most of its allies. Of course, its investment programs must be expected to give rise to some strains and shortages. In most years, they would cancel each other out, to some extent (for example, not enough steel this year, sulphuric acid next year, cement the year following, but never all at once). But on occasion there might be a more general shortage, for instance of fuel, or of a wide range of materials, especially building materials, which would result in some form of modified "stop-go," perhaps accentuated in due course by problems of demand saturation for some items in the internal market.

In balance, and in concluson, the recent economic history of the USSR does not fit any pattern of *cyclical fluctuations*.

# COMMENTS

HERBERT S. LEVINE
University of Pennsylvania

The credentials I bring to this discussion are those of one who has worked on Soviet economic planning, not those of a specialist in business cycles. Indeed, until now, a "leading indicator" has always meant to me a high priority target in a Soviet plan. It is from this Soviet planning approach, therefore, that I come to (or at) Alec Nove's paper.

Professor Nove has taken us on a brief but highly informative trip through Soviet economic history. He has sketched in several major quantitative movements and has offered explanations enriched by the insights of a man who has spent many years studying Soviet economic developments. He refers to some theories of the causes of cycles in planned economies, which have to do primarily with the attempt "to run too fast." And he reaches the conclusion that, in the Soviet experience with central planning (from 1928 on), such cycles can be observed rather clearly in the early 1930's but not so clearly in the middle and late 1930's, and that in the postwar period, though investment fluctuates widely, there is little evidence of an economic cycle. His paper ends with the speculation that, if the economic reforms now being introduced in the Soviet Union bring with them a significant increase in decentralized decision-making, economic fluctuations similar to those that occur in the West may begin to appear.

It is clear that we have come a long way from the Universities-National Bureau Conference of 20 years ago where, in a session on cycles in planned economies, the speaker chose not to talk about the Soviet Union at all [1]. But perhaps we could have come a little further. Though Nove does mention some

---

[1] See Gottfried Haberler, "Business Cycles in a Planned Economy," in Universities-National Bureau Committee, *Conference on Business Cycles*, New York, 1951.

theories of the cycle in planned economies, what is needed now is more investigation, theoretical and empirical, of the mechanisms in centrally planned economies that might lead to economic fluctuations. Great difficulties beset such research but, if we are to further our understanding of economic fluctuations under socialism, it needs to be done. In my comments, therefore, I would like to explore, in a very preliminary fashion, some theoretical aspects of possible cyclical behavior under Soviet-type planning. But before doing that, I must first quibble a bit with Professor Nove over some matters of statistical data [2].

1. The statistical series that Nove presents is based on official Soviet data. He calls the reader's attention to this, alludes to the inflationary bias and other inadequacies of the data, but adds: "The point, however, has little bearing on *this* study. If growth rates claimed are +20 per cent, +3 per cent, and +10 per cent, this is a fluctuation, and its extent remains little affected by the possibility the 'real' figures were respectively +13 per cent, −2 per cent, and +7 per cent" (p.290). This is an overjustification of his position. Although what he could have done in the way of improving upon official data for the purposes of uncovering year-to-year fluctuations in the Soviet economy is not immediately clear, he is certainly wrong in his assertion that the use of official data can have little effect on his study. Since a major distortive element in Soviet aggregate data is the weighting systems used, a reweighting of basic physical series, or a different deflation of current value aggregates, might not merely change all annual growth data in the same direction (downward), but might have differential effects in different years, depending upon the composition of the aggregates. Thus the turning points in the series of annual growth rates might be affected, and this, of course, could seriously affect our picture of cyclical movements. In a survey of some recent, thorough Western recalculations of Soviet economic performance covering the period 1928 to the early 1960's (excluding the war years), it was discovered that for the gross national product (GNP) series there were seven occasions on which year-to-year growth rates moved in the direction opposite to that shown by the official series presented by Nove, four occasions for the investment series, and six occasions for the industrial output (including military) series [3].

---

[2] Some points which were not raised at the Conference are included in these comments.
[3] GNP (1928–1961) from R. Moorsteen and R. Powell, *The Soviet Capital Stock, 1928–1962*, Homewood, Illinois, 1966, p. 361; investment (1928–1961) *ibid.*, p. 360; industry (1928–1940), R. Powell in A. Bergson and S. Kuznets (eds), *Economic Trends in the Soviet Union*, Cambridge, Massachusetts, 1963, pp. 178–179; industry (1951–1965), J. Noren in *New Directions in the Soviet Economy*, Joint Economic Committee, 89th Congress, Washington, D.C., 1966, p. 280. The work of Moorsteen and Powell is part of the project on the measurement of Soviet economic growth organized by Abram Bergson. Their results, therefore, are closely related to the results published earlier by Bergson (*The Real National Income of Soviet Russia Since 1928,* Cambridge, Massachusetts, 1961).

This does not necessarily mean that Nove should have used these Western recomputations rather than the official Soviet data. For as the authors of the Western studies warn, the year-to-year variations in their data are not so reliable as the longer period growth trends [4]. The issue becomes one of judgment, and I am not sure that Nove used poor judgment in deciding to use the official series. What I am arguing is that he overstated the case for their use. It is clearly possible that official Soviet data, with the type of distortions they contain, could give on occasion a wrong picture of the movement of annual growth rates and could displace turning points in such a series. It is one thing to say that this is the best that can be done with the available data (Soviet and non-Soviet). It is quite another to say that the results would be unaffected if better data were available.

The investment series that Nove presents is investment in fixed capital. If investment in inventories had been included, the annual rates of growth would have fluctuated even more widely [5]. Inventory investment has been a growing part of total investment in recent years. According to official data, it comprised about 40 per cent of total net investment in 1965 [6]. This may have an effect on the stability of the economy in the near future [7].

It is to be regretted that Nove looked only at aggregated series. Analysis of some disaggregated data, say within the industrial sector, might have provided interesting information about leads and lags which might have added to our understanding of the prewar fluctuations that were observed and also of the postwar experience in which fluctuations in industrial growth were not observed. The French economist Eugène Zaleski has studied disaggregated series for industry and agriculture in the early 1930's. He finds that there was great variation in the behavior of the different series and that, generally, producer goods suffered less in the downturn than consumer goods. But he concludes: "The rule which makes consumption in general and agriculture in particular play the role of shock absorbers worked only partially. In effect, once a perturbation reached a producer goods sector, it apparently became very hard to contain, at least immediately. In essence, what we have is a movement which is *generalized but whose effects vary with the nature of the activity,* and of course with the priority that the government wished or was able to accord to the activity [8]."

---

[4] see for example, the comments of Powell in Bergson and Kuznets, *Economic Trends*, p. 159.

[5] Moorsteen and Powell, p. 360.

[6] *Narodnoe khoziaistvo SSSR v 1965 godu* (hereinafter referred to as *N. Kh. v 1965*), p. 592.

[7] It is not clear whether the effect will be destabilizing or stabilizing. Under Soviet conditions, if the inventories are primarily inputs rather than finished goods outputs, the effect may be stabilizing. More on this later.

[8] Translation of passage in E. Zaleski, *Planification de la Croissance et Fluctuations Economiques en U.R.S.S.*, Tome 1, Paris, 1962, p. 278.

There are problems raised by the relative absence of data for periods of less than one year. Again, it is not clear that Professor Nove could have done much about this, but the absence of quarterly (and monthly) data does leave the possibility that mild cycles of short duration may exist but be unreflected, or not clearly reflected, in the annual data [9]. Against this it might be argued that, since the key planning document is the annual plan, quarterly data are not too important. However, plans and commands are changed many times during the operation of an annual plan; therefore, quarterly data would provide useful information about how Soviet planners respond to errors and shocks in the system.

Finally, it is possible that economic fluctuations are partially obscured by the uneven falsification of data from below. The overreporting (and at times, underreporting) of data from below is a serious problem in the Soviet Union, since those reporting the data have a stake in the data they report, for their rewards depend upon them. It may be that there is more overreporting in those years when actual growth was not high, which would tend to smooth out the reported growth series.

2. In contemporary theories of the business cycle in Western market economies, the focus is on aggregate demand and its fluctuations. Key roles are played by expenditure decisions of consumers, profit expectations of business-men, and the complex communication network of buying and selling. Impulses are propogated through the system in cumulative, self-reinforcing movements which in both the upswing and the downswing cause the system to overrespond; thus counterpressures and resistances are built up, leading to a reversal of direction and to cumulative movements in the opposite direction.

In thinking about the possibility of business cycles in centrally planned systems, economists have sought similar propogation mechanisms. But the differences between the two systems make a direct transference impossible. The primary difference is the way in which effective demand is manifested. In a centrally planned economy of the Soviet type, demand is communicated to business firms in quantitative plans, not through the actions of other firms or consumers [10]. And aggregate demand has always been kept at a high–often excessively high–level. It was assumed by many Western economists that, under such conditions, economic fluctuations would not exist. But the fact that a propagation mechanism similar to that in Western economies does not exist should not be taken as proof that no propagation mechanism can exist. With a

---

[9] A simple case would be an eight-quarter cycle, containing the following sequence of quarterly growth rates, in per cent: 1, 2, 3, 4, 4, 3, 2, 1. In a table of annual data, these would, of course, be shown as two annual growth rates of 10.4 per cent each.

[10] To some extent this has been affected by the recent experiments in certain consumer goods industries.

high-level floor maintained on the demand side, it might be well to look for sources of economic fluctuations on the supply side.

A major barrier to the development of a well articulated theory of economic fluctuations, or to an explanation of the short-period-to-short-period flow of economic activity in the Soviet economy, is out limited knowledge of the behavioral characteristics of economic decision-makers in the Soviet Union: political leaders, planners, firm managers, and households. In the West, behavioral functions of consumers and businessmen occupy a crucial position in cycle theory.

Work on the Soviet economy, however, has produced some insights into the behavior of Soviet economic decision-makers which can, perhaps, serve as primitive building blocks for a propagation mechanism. For example, in order to attain economic objectives, Soviet planners tend to launch broad campaigns rather than to employ particularized, fine-tuning methods. This is an element in the Soviet system which could lead toward overdoing things which might necessitate reversal, and thus lead in the direction of economic fluctuations. On the other hand, the Soviet firm, which has more decision-making opportunities than is generally realized (even before the current reforms), appears to have behavioral characteristics that would dampen economic fluctuations. Western studies portray the Soviet firm as a self-protecting, conservative element that would lead in the direction of economic stability and routinized, not excessive, noninnovative growth [11].

In Western theory, the actions of government (excluding actions related to "built-in stabilizers") are usually treated as part of the impulse system rather than the propagation system. But it should come as no surprise that the few cycle theories on the Soviet economy which we do have depend heavily on observed or hypothesized behavioral characteristics of political leaders.

Among the first of such theories is the one suggested by Alexander Gerschenkron [12]. This is a long-swing theory, in which the swings do not recur regularly but appear on a number of occasions in Russian history back to the time of the removal of Mongol domination. Gerschenkron argues that in certain periods, when Russia came in conflict with more advanced Western nations, the Russian state would apply pressure to the internal economy, to force it to develop rapidly and thus help Russia to achieve military parity with her adversaries. These periods of rapid growth were frequently followed by long periods of relatively little growth (this did not happen, however, after the rapid growth period, 1890–1900). The plan era, beginning in 1928, fits into this

---

[11] See, for example, J. Berliner, *Factory and Manager in the USSR,* Cambridge, Massachusetts, 1957.

[12] See his *Economic Backwardness in Historical Perspective,* Cambridge, Massachusetts, 1962, pp. 17–18.

Gerschenkron pattern. The upswing lasted from 1928 to the late 1950's. And the Soviet Union may now be in the downswing of this long cycle.

The shorter-cycle theory of Josef Goldmann, discussed in Nove's paper, also depends upon an assumed behavioral characteristic of political leaders [13]. Goldmann argues that political leaders, under certain circumstances, have a subjective tendency to maximize the rate of growth. Plans are constructed in an overly tight way: insufficient inputs to produce the planned outputs. This leads to overstrain in the economy, shortages, bottlenecks, and production crises [14].

This proclivity on the part of political leaders to "run too fast" could theoretically also give rise to an inventory cycle of the following sort [15].

*Upswing:* Political leaders, through planners, put pressure on producers for increased output. Flow of output grows faster than stocks of inputs. Thus, in upswing, the ratio of input inventory to output flow tends to decline. There may even be inventory disinvestment.

*Upper Turning Point:* The inventory-output ratio reaches a critically low point where random delivery failures, temporary bottlenecks, begin to propagate through the system (insufficient buffer stocks of inputs to absorb these shocks). The rate of growth of output begins to turn down.

*Downswing:* Planners, alarmed by inventory tightness, reduce pressure by reducing output targets (slightly) and allowing increased inventory accumulation. Thus, in downswing, inventory-output ratio increases.

*Lower Turning Point:* When the inventory-output ratio reaches a more "comfortable" level, the planners begin to call for higher rates of growth of output.

A program of high output targets is usually accompanied by, or induces, a program of high investment which may add an overinvestment cycle to the excessive output target cycle. In practice the two may always go together, but theoretically they are separable. Moreover, the central planning overinvestment cycle should be distinguished from overinvestment in the Western business cycle.

---

[13] J. Goldmann, "Short- and Long-term Variations in the Growth Rate and the Model of Functioning of a Socialist Economy," *Czechoslovak Economic Papers*, 5, Prague, 1965, pp. 35–46. For a theory of an econometric cycle in China, see A. Eckstein, "Trends and Cycles in Communist China's Economic Development and Foreign Trade," Paper presented at the University of Chicago, Center for Policy Study, Conference on China, the United States, and Asia, February 5–9, 1967.

[14] See J. Hicks, "The Empty Economy," *Lloyds Bank Review,* July 1947, pp. 1–13, and H. Levine, "Pressure and Planning in the Soviet Economy," in H. Rosovsky (ed.), *Industrialization in Two Systems: Essays in Honor of Alexander Gerschenkron* New York, 1966.

[15] This inventory model is purely a theoretical construct on my part. I have not examined the evidence on whether it is, or ever was, operative in the Soviet economy.

In the latter, more investment goods than are needed are produced. In the former, overinvestment refers both to a commitment of resources beyond the producer goods sector's capacity to produce (and thus to a waste of resources) and to an overcommitment of resources in the construction sector. In construction, if construction time is at first given, the greater the investment, the greater the number of projects undertaken. This increases the pressure on the control bureaucracy and on the supply system for construction materials, which in turn leads to the further lengthening of construction periods on existing projects. This causes supply tightness and failures in the rest of the economy, since the output expected from new factories (now behind construction schedules) was included in the input plans of other firms in the economy. Both tend to lead to a cyclical downturn in the rate of growth of investment.

As Professor Nove indicates in his discussion, it can be argued that there were two cycles of this excessive growth pressure type in the Soviet Union during the period 1928–1940. But in the postwar period, the growth of national income and industrial output are rather stable, though the rate of growth or investment does vary widely. Why are there cycles observable in the prewar period, but not in the postwar period?

First, during the 1930's, the Soviet leaders were pressing for massive structural changes; and thus, the pressure they applied to the economy was widespread. There is much less structural change in the postwar period, special pressure being applied to individual sectors (for example, the chemical program mentioned by Nove) but not spread throughout the economy. Second, there may have been a learning process at work which has led to a conscious lessening of the strain put on the economy [16]. Third, in regard to the Gerschenkron long swing, pressure from the center, at least since the mid-1950's, has been reduced. Fourth, the Soviet firm, over time, may have increased ita ability to protect itself from overstrain by hoarding buffer stocks, and by other means.

The absence of fluctuations in the postwar period should not, however, be overstated. As said earlier, there are some statistical problems. The absence of quarterly data limits our ability to observe short fluctuations. And the possible uneven overreporting of data from below may tend to smooth our fluctuations in growth data.

Also, our inability to perceive a strong, cumulative propagation mechanism at work in the postwar period should not be taken as proof that there have been no fluctuations in Soviet economic activity. Many Western economists, including Bert Hickman in his paper in this volume, argue that Western propagation

[16] Khrushchev, in his speech on the Seven-Year Plan at the Twenty-First Party Congress, stated that "the Seven-Year Plan is being drawn up in such a way that it can be carried out without overstrain," and he then went on to describe some of the negative consequences of overly tight plans; see 7 *Year Plan Target Figures*, Soviet Booklet #47, London, 1957, p. 33.

mechanisms are damped (this is especially so now, with government automatic stabilizers) and that what gives rise to recurrent cycles are the random impulses or shocks striking the system from within and without [17]. That such random shocks exist in regard to the Soviet economy is clear from Nove's discussion. Furthermore, a study by George Staller of fluctuations in planned and market economies show that while the growth of Soviet national income fluctuated very little there was even less fluctuation in a number of Western countries; however, Soviet industry fluctuated less than industry in any of the other countries sampled [18].

Why is it that with the growth of investment fluctuating as widely as it did in the Soviet Union in the postwar period the growth of output did not fluctuate more widely? Again the question is perplexing because we think in terms of demand phenomena. When we think in terms of supply phenomena and the effects or growth, it is the rate of growth of the capital stock (with changes in the capital-output ratio ignored) rather than the rate of change of investment which is of prime importance. Because of the magnitudes involved, the annual rates of growth of the "productive" (basically, nonresidential) capital stock in the period 1950–1965 vary within the narrow range of 9 to 12.2 per cent [19], while the rates of growth of fixed investment vary between 4.5 and 20.3 per cent. Furthermore, the decrease in the rate of growth of investment, evident since 1960, has been related in part to the attempt, discussed earlier and by Nove, to reduce the overhand of uncompleted construction. To the extent that this was successful, it would work in the direction of increasing the rate of growth of the capital stock.

One final comment: As Nove indicates, the rate of growth of industrial output was very stable from 1952 to 1959. Then it shifted to a lower, again rather stable, level. It just may be possible that in the period 1960–1966, Soviet industry found itself in the down phase of a longish cycle in which transitions to new technologies in some important industries were being undertaken (chemicals, oil and gas, complex machinery). Such a transition period involves dislocations, but when (if?) the transition is completed, the new technologies mastered, new technicians trained, and new plants completed and in operation,

---

[17] See Ragnar Frisch, "Propagation Problems and Impulse Problems in Dynamic Economics," *Essays in Honor of Gustav Cassel,* London, 1933, and Irma Adelman and Frank L. Adelman, 'The Dynamic Properties of the Klein-Goldberger Model," *Econometrica,* 1959 (both reprinted in R. A. Gordon and L. R. Klein, eds., *Readings in Business Cycles,* Homewood, Illinois, 1965, pp. 155–185, 278–306).

[18] "Fluctuations in Economic Activity: Planned and Free-Market Economies, 1950–1960," *American Economic Review,* June 1964, pp. 385–395.

[19] Soviet official data, *N. Kh. 1965,* p. 59. Moorsteen and Powell, pp. 332, 361–362, for the period 1950–1961, show a range of 9.3 to 10.8 per cent for the annual rates of growth of nonresidential fixed capital, and a range of 5.7 to 19.9 per cent for fixed investment.

rates of industrial growth may move up again. Much will depend, however, on other developments in the economy, including, to be sure, the course of the economic reform.

Chapter Ten

# THE RATE OF ECONOMIC
# GROWTH IN HUNGARY, 1924-1965

ANDREW BRÓDY
Institute of Economics, Budapest

I shall present in this chapter several long-run series, prepared in a simple and crude way, which are neither exact nor reliable. They are useful, however, in showing the fundamental interconnections and orders of magnitude. I would like to use these figures to prove two fundamental points: first, that the compilation of these time series is possible, as the appropriate basic statistics are available; second, that their compilation is necessary, as they can substantially modify views of the past and therefore affect decisions concerning the immediate future as well as those bearing on long-term plans. The analysis is not complete; indeed, it is quite fragmentary. Many of the time series necessary for a really comprehensive picture are lacking (suffice it here to point to the gaps in the series for net industrial product, investment, size and distribution of the labor force, and living standards). Nevertheless, the few series that have been reconstructed permit certain conclusions.

The data used in this study are presented in the Appendix. I think the margins of error involved in the data remain for the most part within the margins of error inherent in the diagrammatic representation, and the tendencies shown visually by the diagrams give a roughly correct picture.

* The original Hungarian version of this discussion was published in *Közgazdásagi Szemle,* which has consented to the publication of this English edition.

312

## Growth of National Income

### DATA AND SOURCES

The postwar data used here are from the Statistical Yearbooks of the relevant years. The prewar data are based on the national income calculations of K. Matolcsy and I. Varga, which the Economic Research Institute continued for a few years after the war. A good summary of the prewar data and of the Judik-Notel study relating to investment is in a paper by A. Eckstein[1]. Several supplementary figures are taken from the book by S. Ausch[2].

An attempt has been made in each case to prepare indices at constant prices. This may not have been entirely successful for the postwar investment series, for it was impossible to eliminate small price changes (for example, the abolition of the turnover tax on certain investment goods in 1950). Still more uncertain are the import series which, for the prewar era, have been (for lack of anything better) deflated by the price index implicit in the current and constant price data for national income, and for the postwar era calculated from the data in foreign exchange forints. This means that the data (and the diagram) probably show a growth in imports which overstates the real growth prior to 1952 and understates it thereafter. (Up to the "Korean boom" of 1952 the prices of Hungary's imports were rising, and since then they have shown a gradual decline.)

Figure 10-1 shows the chief time series drawn to logarithmic scale. The year 1949 is the base year (=100), not because it is a particularly reliable or average year, but merely to conform to postwar statistics which use the same time base. The analysis is in any case concerned with relative tendencies only.

### THE THREE CHIEF PERIODS OF GROWTH

On the basis of the rate of growth of national income, the period may be divided into three radically different subperiods. In the first subperiod, the Horthy era, the overall rate of growth was about 2 per cent per annum in spite of the great depression. Particularly striking is the pronouncedly cyclical character of investment, which falls to a dangerously low point in the crisis and recovers only as the war approaches. The series for imports follows this pattern rather closely, but begins to lag behind national income after 1938 because of the war and foreign exchange restrictions and Hungary's enlarged geographical area, which reduced the need for import expansion.

[1] International Association for Research on Income and Wealth, *Income and Wealth*, V, London, 1955, pp. 152–223.

[2] *Az 1945–1946. evi inflacio es stabilizáció (The Inflation of 1945–1946 and the Stabilization)*, Budapest, 1958.

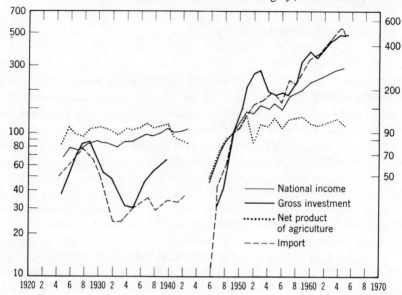

**Fig. 10-1.**    Long periods.

In the second subperiod, the era of postwar reconstruction, the rate of growth was exceptionally fast — about 25 per cent per annum. This period clearly did not end in 1949, but lasted well into 1951. It is a widespread but incorrect practice to equate its close with the end of the Three-Year Plan (1949). It is true that at that time the economy had approximately regained the level of the "last year of peace," that is, 1938. But seen in perspective, this "last year of peace" was not the high point of Hungarian prewar development; indeed, it started out as a year of depression, and only the announcement of the Daranyi Program, together with large government and defense investments, brought recovery in its later stages. The national income grew by at least 13 per cent in the following two years, accompanied by a 22 per cent growth in investment, thus reaching a peak which was only regained in the course of 1950. But 1950 cannot be regarded as the end of the period either.

The unparalleled rate of growth of national income, resulting in the main from the even faster reconstruction of industry, came to an end only when industry had absorbed the large industrial labor force which was available. The simultaneous growth in productivity boosted output greatly beyond the 1950 level. After this, however, the very fast influx of new untrained workers reduced the growth rate, and even caused a fall in industrial productivity for a short time.

The exceptionally fast growth of national income during the reconstruction period was accompanied by an even faster, though rather uneven and jerky, growth of investment. In these 4½ years, the annual volume of investment rose more than sevenfold (again carrying with it the corresponding growth of imports), which implies an annual growth rate of about 55 per cent. Thus the growth of investment was not in step with the general development of the economy; this proved to be harmful for several reasons. First, it slowed down the growth rates of consumption. (It is known that real wages fell after 1950; certain calculations led to the conclusion that this process had begun immediately after 1948, with stagnation of real wages and actual reduction in certain areas.) Second, it resulted in the development of an investment cycle. Third, it could not but cause disorganization and confusion in investment activity. I shall return later to the last two reasons.

In the third subperiod, lasting from 1952 until the present, the average rate of growth of national income was about 5.5 per cent. During the first half of the period, it was subject to fluctuations, while in the second half of the period the growth path was more even and growth was somewhat faster (5.3 per cent per annum in 1952–1956, 5.7 per cent per annum in 1957–1965). In both halves of the period, however, the development of investment still continued to show strong cyclical tendencies, characterized by peaks in 1953, 1960, and 1964, and troughs in 1957, 1961, and 1965. The fall between 1953 and 1957 was about 34 per cent. Even compared with the drop during the Great Depression (about 70 per cent between 1929 and 1935), this is still a large decline. Nor can the declines in investment of more than 10 per cent in 1961 and about 10 per cent in 1965 be regarded as healthy phenomena, despite that moderation of the cycle which has taken place. Thus the investment cycle has not stopped; although it has become less pronounced, there are still fluctuations.

In this period, however, the overall rate of growth of investment was not so clearly divorced from the development of national income. But this statement is true of only the *average* rate of growth: in several years, and even over longer periods, the growth rate of investment was more than double the rate of national income's growth; only the repeated declines, which necessarily followed, tended to restore equilibrium. It is characteristic of the new cycle, however, that the growth of investment in general proceeded without any decline and even with some increase in real wages. But for precisely this reason the tensions in the foreign trade balance were accentuated, and this necessarily led in turn to a slowing down of the growth of real wages and thus of the standard of living.

This preliminary, crude analysis from approximate data permits two conclusions which might somewhat modify the accepted picture of Hungary's economic development.

First, if the subperiods within the era under consideration have been correctly demarcated, then the notion of a "necessary decline during the period of building socialism" becomes highly debatable (at least as far as Hungary is concerned, but probably for other socialist countries also, and for similar reasons). In fact, what happened was that with the completion of reconstruction the necessarily faster growth rate of the reconstruction period was replaced by a normal rate of economic development. Under socialism, this development was substantially faster than could be achieved by capitalism. Thus the "falling rate" concept can appear only if the examination of developments is confined to the period after 1949 or 1950, divorced from the earlier time series. When this is done, *of course* the growth rate of 1949–1956 (a period that contains two postwar reconstruction years of fast growth) is higher than that for 1957–1965, although – as shown earlier – the post-1956 growth has in fact been somewhat faster, and certainly much steadier[3].

Second, however, although any general law of the "falling rate" can be disregarded, the problem of substantial investment cycles becomes correspondingly more acute. Although the text that follows examines the question more closely, this study can deal with only surface phenomena, and not with their causes, let alone their cure. The preceding analysis, however, shows that theoretical research on socialist growth cycles is both justified and necessary.

## *Growth of Agriculture and the Distortions of Accounting*

Although the periods described above are discernible in the data of agricultural output, there was no significant difference between the rates of growth of the Horthy era and the postreconstruction period. It is hardly possible to speak of growth, as the picture given by the series is rather one of stagnation. For the period as a whole, there is a growth rate of, almost, 0.8–0.9 per cent, with disruptions and occasional declines of varying magnitude.

If changes in agriculture are studied more deeply, however, some difference between the two contrasting periods can be discerned. It is known that between the wars agricultural employment grew in absolute terms, although its share of the total declined. After the reconstruction period, however, the numbers employed in agriculture decreased rapidly, and the area of cultivated land diminished. The same rate of growth was therefore achieved by means of a significant rise in labor productivity and a noticeable increase in the value added per unit of land.

It is clear that the fluctuations in national income are decisively influenced by agricultural production. In bad years, the sudden decline in net agricultural output depresses the whole of the national income. This phenomenon was absent only in a few war years, and possibly also in recent years, but it is

---

[3] This does not mean that in the future any decline in the growth rate is improbable. After the complete redeployment of the country's labor force, a new period will probably start. (see the writer's article in *Közgazdasági Szemle*, November 1965.)

understandable in view of that fact that throughout the period under consideration agriculture accounted for a significant part of the national income. In the 1920's, this share was almost 50 per cent, and even at the outbreak of war, it equaled the contribution of industry. Only after the war did it start to decline rapidly.

Recent research has shown that the peculiarities of the price system played a major role in the decline of agricultural share. If the shares of the major economic sectors were calculated on the basis of some consistent price system instead of the one currently in use (for example value type, production cost, two channel, or world market prices), the share of agriculture would become significantly larger. It can therefore be said that, if a more balanced price system were used for the calculation, the share of agriculture in the national income would not be much smaller than that of industry, even in recent years.

But if this is so — and the results of several inquiries prove it unequivocally — then it follows that the use of a different price system would alter quite significantly the time path of national income and its components. Unfortunately, the tools needed to carry out such a recalculation with any precision are lacking; full-scale input-output tables would be required, at least for the 1930's and the immediate postwar period. This is why it is not possible to assess exactly how the recalculation would affect the individual indices. However, some conclusions regarding the direction of these effects can be drawn from what has been discussed so far.

With relatively higher agricultural prices and lower industrial prices, the growth rate of net agricultural output would certainly be higher; for since the liberation, agriculture has been using increasing quantities of capital goods of industrial origin in order to compensate for diminishing resources of land and labor. For the same reason, the growth rate of net industrial production would be somewhat lower. This would probably be accompanied by some decrease in the growth rate of total national income because of the increased weight given to agriculture.

There is no need to propose that a "continuously equilibrating" price system be substituted in the future for present accounting methods. It would not be possible to do this until the price system currently in use had been improved; for it would be very difficult to operate a system of accounting which was divorced from planning methodology and the price system actually in use. However, parallel calculations of time series which use this approach should be made, and historical data should be reconstructed as much as possible on the same basis. This is all the more necessary because the impending price revision within the framework of the new system of management will have the effect of slowing down the growth figures for national income because of the elimination of certain disproportionate elements. This retardation, however, will only be apparent, and will be due entirely to the new and "better" price system. Care must be taken, therefore, not to lay the blame for this apparent decline at the door of the initial difficulties which the new management system will bring in its wake. However "backward" the present price system would seem to be within two or three years, it would still have to be used for parallel calculations for clear indications of the changes that have occurred.


## Investment and National Income

### FLUCTUATION IN INVESTMENT

Perhaps the most surprising feature emerging from comparison of postwar and interwar data is the extent to which the investment ratio and the growth rates of investment and national income have fluctuated. Since in both periods investment has been very cyclical and uneven, it has been difficult to find a more exact basis of comparison. If 1938 is regarded as an average year (neither particularly good nor particularly bad) it is apparent that the almost eightfold rise in investment since then has failed to multiply national income or its growth rate even by the factor 3[4].

The incremental level or growth rate of national income arising from extra investment is not, of course, a proper measure of the effectiveness of that investment. Nevertheless, it is an important tool of analysis and reveals that the increased investment effort did not attain its desired and expected results.

In seeking the reason for this disappointment, it should not be forgotten that a considerable portion of the investment effort proved to be "organizing cost" for the socialist economy. In fact, a portion of Hungarian investment did nothing to increase the national wealth or productive potential simply because it could not have done so. What kind of investment was this? In the first investment period, starting from 1948, small-scale industry was virtually eliminated within a few years. During that period, one part of industrial investment merely replaced small-scale production by larger-scale, though not always more modern, techniques. Before the war, half the labor force worked in small-scale enterprises; now part of large-scale industry has to be devoted to providing employment for these people. Since less than the whole of small-scale industry became unusable, it was possible to create a portion of the necessary work places by increasing the number of shifts; nevertheless, the "reorganizing

---

[4] The data on accumulation are not cited here, as they yield rather imprecise data series because of the uncertainty attaching to the calculation of depreciation. It has, however, become clear that accumulation fluctuates even more, and becomes divorced from the growth of national income. Investment had multiplied eightfold; net capital accumulation increased nine- to fifteenfold.

investment" can hardly be regarded as negligible, despite the fact that it cannot be measured exactly.

In the second investment period after 1958 (and to some extent at the beginning of the collectivization movement in the early 1950's), part of the agricultural investment served — as it still does — to replace rural capital goods which could not be utilized on collective farms. The part replaced do far is estimated at 10 billion forints, but I think this is a very conservative estimate. (It will be shown later in this chapter that even this lower estimate represents several years of agricultural investment.) It takes no account of an item characteristic of Hungary's agriculture, a leakage which cannot be identified with either diminution or depreciation of national wealth, but constitutes a simple conversion of fixed capital to other uses. As cooperative farming developed, a stock of rural buildings which had served as stores, barns, stables, etc., under conditions of small-scale peasant production (valued at 100 billion forints), was converted to human habitation. Even if it had been necessary to replace only 30-40 billion forints' worth of these structures (by new buildings for stables, stores, workshops, etc.), this was still a huge burden which did nothing to increase productive potential (unless it was accompanied by technical progress of some sort).

All these cost items should therefore be left out of account when assessing the effectiveness of investment. Naturally, the effectiveness of such replacements could in itself by quite large, but this does not change the fact that they were replacements of already operating assets. A further cause of diminishing effectiveness might be the cyclical character of investment. It is difficult — probably impossible — to carry out long-term planned investments under conditions of constant fluctuation and uncertainty concerning the total volume of investment. In such conditions, it is impossible to maintain permanent cadres and an organizational framework to carry out investment at the necessary level of competence and expertise. Imagine, for instance, the problems of staffing at all levels of skill under conditions where the labor force in State construction grew from some 60,000 in 1949 to almost 200,000 three years later, only to fall back to 114,000 in the following three years, while the regional and central distribution of construction activity was subject to constant change. As can be seen from the statistics (though this is more difficult to prove), the same phenomenon affects other activities involved in investment: investment planning, the importation of equipment, engineering production, assembly and installation of plant and equipment, and related activities. It is known that the "spread effect" of investment on other sectors, for example, metallurgy, building materials, and other supplying branches, is very significant: owing to the "accelerator," a fluctuation in investment entails a fluctuation that is two to three times larger in the supplying industries, which ultimately causes fluctuations throughout the economy.

But not only does the total of investment fluctuate; violent fluctuations also occur in various sectors.

Figure 10-2 shows that the sectors fluctuated at least as much (perhaps rather more) in the period after 1958 as they had done in depression and in conversion to a war economy. Whereas conversion to a war economy was accompanied by certain well defined tendencies (growth of industrial, mining, and transport investment at the expense of agricultural and communal investment), such trends can hardly be discerned after the war. To the extent that they do appear, they last for a mere two or three years, giving place to entirely opposite trends, again lasting two or three years, only to change yet again. This is demonstrated by the behavior of investment in heavy industry. (The appropriate time series are available only from 1949 onward.)

Figure 10-3 illustrates the absence of long-term investment policies during the period of economic planning. Ideas about the distribution of investment were likely to change every two or three years, and often were completely reversed thereafter. In this respect, the post-1957 period shows greater stability, which probably played a part in the achievement of a faster growth-rate in this period.

These fluctuations in the distribution of investment aggregate the mistakes by concentrating and amplifying the harmful effects of the investment cycles in certain key fields of production. Thus for example, industry's share of total investment rises at the peak of the cycle and falls at the bottom. In other words, within the general cycle, industrial investment displays even greater cyclical variations. Within industry itself, investment in metallurgy plays a similar role, as indicated by the shift from 1,890 million forints in 1953 to 289 million in 1957 and then to 1,916 million in 1963.

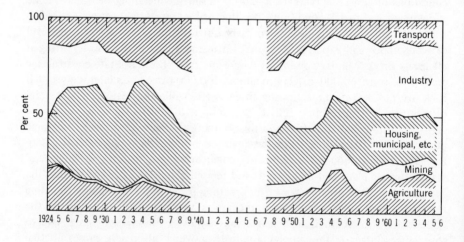

**Fig. 10-2.**     Sectoral distribution of investment

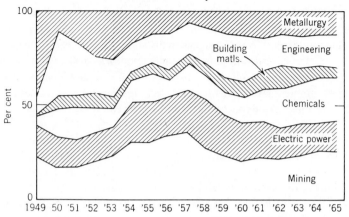

**Fig. 10-3.**   Shares of investment in heavy industry.

It is obvious that engineers, architects, skilled laborers, etc., who gain experience in connection with investment in metallurgy can hardly use their experience when they transfer to the chemical or transport investment fields. The planning and realization of investment in metallurgy is just as much an independent field of production activity, requiring the same degree of specialist expertise, as designing and manufacturing TV sets. There would be hesitation about imposing production plans on the latter industry, as this would necessarily lead to disorganization in the factory and production. Yet this is done every day in those fields of investment where planning and execution are divorced from each other and not integrated in geographically defined factories.

Metallurgy is an example of this. Exceptionally violent cycles have also occurred in the engineering and construction industries. This, of course, is quite natural, as there cannot be periodicity in one field without having it cause periodicity in others. The expansion of one sector at the cost of others will later on entail the expansion of the neglected sectors at the cost of the first. In this way, activity becomes cyclic in fields which have hitherto been exempt from this characteristic.

These fluctuations, and the consequent investment cycles, are certainly harmful, and express measures should be taken against them. But it is easier to say this than to carry it into practice. In a small country, the cost of modernizing productive capacity is very high in relation to total sectoral investment in any sector. Such "large chunks" would probably always swell the investment share of a particular sector. This tendency could be offset in two ways: by possibly embarking on smaller constructional tasks (many past projects were characterized by unjustified "gigantomania") and by avoiding the frittering of resources.

If investment cycles are to be damped in the future (the prerequisite of more effective, better organized, and steadier economic growth, and of an increasing national income), it will not be sufficient to adopt a more cautious and careful approach to the allocation, planning, and handling of the total volume of investment. It will also be necessary to refrain from sudden changes in times of peaceful economic development. For this reason, an investment pattern acceptable for long periods ahead needs to be evolved.

### DISTRIBUTION OF INVESTMENT

In order to evolve a pattern which is "satisfactory on the average," it is not enough to analyze the data relating merely to the last 15 years. Nevertheless, it is worth looking at the pattern which has emerged so far.

If, on the basis of Figures 10-1 to 10-3 and the tables in the Appendix, the postwar sectoral investment shares are averaged, then the following pattern is obtained:

|  | Per cent |
|---|---|
| Agriculture and forestry | 18 |
| Mining | 8 |
| Industry and construction | 36 |
| Transport (roads, bridges, communications) | 13 |
| Communal (housing fund, public service, and utility installations) | 25 |
| Total | 100 |

What sort of development could follow from this pattern for the individual sectors? Some idea (on the assumption that capital requirements are constant) may be formed if the value of fixed assets in each sector is related to the net investment figures of the corresponding year. (This is useful for a first rough analysis only.) In 1960, the estimated total net value of fixed assets was 400 billion forints, distributed as follows:

|  | Billion forints |
|---|---|
| Agriculture, forestry | 50 |
| Mining | 10 |
| Industry and construction | 80 |
| Transport (roads, bridges, communications) | 90 |
| Communal (housing fund, public service, and utility installation) | 170 |
| Total | 400 |

Total investment in 1960 was 37 billion forints. After 13 billion forints are deducted for depreciation and replacement, the net investment of 24 billion forints implies an annual growth of about 6 per cent in fixed assets. This corresponds to the rate of growth characterizing the period. How would this increase be distributed among the sectors? The answer is given in Table 10-1.

TABLE 10-1. **Hungary: Estimated Postwar Growth of Investment and Fixed Assets (Billion Forints)**

| | Fixed assets | Investment (av. pattern) | Capital consumption | Net fixed capital formation | |
| --- | --- | --- | --- | --- | --- |
| | | | | Absolute | Per cent |
| Agriculture | 50 | 6.7 | 1.7 | 5.0 | 10.0 |
| Mining | 10 | 3.0 | 0.3 | 2.7 | 27.0 |
| Industry, and construction | 80 | 13.3 | 5.9 | 7.4 | 9.2 |
| Transport | 90 | 4.8 | 1.1 | 3.7 | 4.1 |
| Communal | 170 | 9.2 | 4.0 | 5.2 | 3.0 |
| Total | 400 | 37.0 | 13.0 | 24.0 | 6.0 |

The figures show, to a first approximation, the expected fixed capital formation and by implication the approximate net increase in the output of each sector. Since these figures differ from the actual growth rates, some explanation is called for.

In the first place, probably not all investment in mining represents true investment — the industry does not grow at anything like this rate — and a significant part is a State subsidy in the guise of investment funds.

The growth of net industrial production is also smaller (by one to two per cent) than average fixed capital formation, though theoretically it ought to be greater as, one supposes, the machinery requirements of industrial production ought to diminish under the circumstances assumed here. The shortfall of two to three points (actual rate, 7–8 per cent per annum, theoretically attainable rate 9–10 per cent) could probably be made good by raising the effectiveness of investment through damping down the fluctuations, and by rationalizing economic management, as may be expected under the new system of management.

The share of transport and communications appears too low. The lower rate of growth of these branches will sooner or later become an impediment to industrial and agricultural growth, and it is of great importance for the remaining economic sectors that the rate should be increased.

Agriculture demands even more explanation. It contributes approximately 30 billion forints to the national income. (This is in terms of the existing pricing system; in real terms, it would come to almost 40 billion forints.) Because of its huge capital requirements, net assets of about 150–200 billion forints are needed. Only part of this is reflected in the statistics. The statistical practice treats part of the livestock (valued approximately 20–30 billion forints) as working capital (it should rather be treated as fixed capital) and ignores altogether the value of land, which would come to 100–150 billion forints even on a conservative reckoning. If, therefore, the 5 billion forints of net investment (which should be reduced still further because of amortizations on the new additions) is compared with the total fixed asset requirements, it is clear that it supports a growth rate of only 2–3 per cent per annum. If, in addition, account is taken of the "reorganizing cost" already mentioned (that is, the replacement of entirely useless implements – houses, stables, etc.), it should not come as a surprise that the growth rate of net agricultural production hardly reaches 1 per cent.

It must also be remembered that, at the outbreak of World War II, Hungary's agriculture was still burdened with feudal institutions and was about a decade behind the times. Its main and perennial problems were a tragic lack of capital investment and an utter inability to increase intensive modes of production. It is well known that modern agriculture is much more capital-intensive than was the feudal system. Also, it is known that the greatest damage caused by the war was to agriculture and transport.

As Figure 10–2 shows, the restoration of transport was more or less completed during the period 1947–1950. This was not so in agriculture.

All the foregoing would have justified increased agricultural investment and great patience in awaiting its results. For the reasons outlined, investment will appear to be "ineffective" for some time to come.

These ideas are far from being proposals for a future investment policy, although the basic approach is correct. More detailed inquiries and calculations would be needed in order to obtain the correct investment ratios and the permissible limits of their fluctuations.

This chapter has tried to show, however, that this kind of analysis cannot rely solely on postwar data. It will be possible to solve, or even to identify, the problems only if sufficiently long time-series are available. Nor can any sectoral problems be identified, let alone solved, without regard to historical development.

I had to indicate the fields in which the reconstruction, supplementation, and exploration of long time-series (other than those of national income, production, and expenditure) in the greatest possible detail could signally contribute to economic planning and decision-making, I would call attention to the need for a series reflecting the movement of national income components, and also for a series showing the mutual relationships of individual sectors. It would also be very helpful (as indicated earlier) to have the pattern of sectoral relationships reconstructed for a two- or three-year period. These tasks could be solved, provided the necessary resources were made available.

## Appendix

TABLE 10-2.    Hungary: Main Time-Series (Indices, 1949 = 100)

| Year | National income | Gross investment | Net production of agriculture | Imports |
|------|-----------------|------------------|-------------------------------|---------|
| 1924–1925 | 65  | 37  | 82  | 49  |
| 1925–1926 | 78  | 50  | 106 | 54  |
| 1926–1927 | 75  | 67  | 97  | 61  |
| 1927–1928 | 78  | 84  | 94  | 75  |
| 1928–1929 | 85  | 88  | 105 | 76  |
| 1929–1930 | 88  | 66  | 107 | 66  |
| 1930–1931 | 86  | 52  | 106 | 52  |
| 1931–1932 | 82  | 48  | 103 | 36  |
| 1932–1933 | 79  | 38  | 96  | 24  |
| 1933–1934 | 87  | 31  | 106 | 24  |
| 1934–1935 | 87  | 30  | 104 | 27  |
| 1935–1936 | 92  | 36  | 107 | 31  |
| 1936–1937 | 98  | 47  | 116 | 33  |
| 1937–1938 | 96  | 53  | 109 | 35  |
| 1938–1939 | 100 | 59  | 111 | 29  |
| 1939–1940 | 108 | 65  | 115 | 33  |
| 1940–1941 | 100 | .   | 93  | 34  |
| 1941–1942 | 101 | .   | 89  | 33  |
| 1942–1943 | 109 | .   | 85  | 36  |
| 1945–1946 | 45  | .   | 48  | 11  |
| 1946–1947 | 61  | 30  | 65  | 43  |
| 1947–1948 | 80  | 41  | 83  | 58  |
| 1949 | 100 | 100 | 100 | 100 |
| 1950 | 121 | 159 | 112 | 110 |
| 1951 | 141 | 215 | 133 | 137 |
| 1952 | 139 | 262 | 83  | 159 |
| 1953 | 157 | 276 | 115 | 169 |
| 1954 | 150 | 194 | 110 | 184 |
| 1955 | 164 | 184 | 127 | 192 |
| 1956 | 146 | 190 | 106 | 167 |
| 1957 | 180 | 182 | 124 | 237 |
| 1958 | 191 | 225 | 128 | 219 |
| 1959 | 204 | 317 | 133 | 275 |
| 1960 | 225 | 372 | 119 | 339 |
| 1961 | 239 | 342 | 114 | 355 |
| 1962 | 250 | 394 | 116 | 399 |
| 1963 | 264 | 454 | 122 | 453 |
| 1964 | 277 | 476 | 126 | 510 |
| 1965 | 282 | 478 | 113 | 515 |

TABLE 10-3    **Hungary: Investment Shares (Per cent at current prices)**

| Year | Agriculture | Mining | Industrial and Construction | Transport, etc. | Housing and municipal communal |
|------|-------------|--------|-----------------------------|-----------------|--------------------------------|
| 1924–1925 | 22.2 | 0.5 | 37.6 | 12.8 | 26.9 |
| 1925–1926 | 23.6 | 0.3 | 24.3 | 13.8 | 38.0 |
| 1926–1927 | 21.2 | 0.5 | 21.8 | 14.1 | 42.4 |
| 1927–1928 | 16.4 | 0.1 | 18.9 | 16.2 | 48.4 |
| 1928–1929 | 15.2 | 1.0 | 24.3 | 10.7 | 48.8 |
| 1929–1930 | 15.7 | 0.9 | 23.1 | 11.0 | 49.3 |
| 1930–1931 | 12.3 | 1.5 | 25.7 | 16.8 | 43.7 |
| 1931–1932 | 11.4 | 1.7 | 26.0 | 16.9 | 44.0 |
| 1932–1933 | 12.1 | 0.9 | 20.8 | 22.0 | 44.2 |
| 1933–1934 | 14.2 | 0.5 | 12.3 | 21.5 | 51.5 |
| 1934–1935 | 16.5 | 2.0 | 7.8 | 23.6 | 50.1 |
| 1935–1936 | 14.8 | 1.8 | 15.8 | 20.7 | 46.9 |
| 1936–1937 | 11.8 | 2.9 | 28.0 | 15.4 | 41.9 |
| 1937–1938 | 10.8 | 2.8 | 27.9 | 20.5 | 38.0 |
| 1938–1939 | 9.3 | 3.2 | 30.0 | 25.5 | 32.0 |
| 1939–1940 | 8.9 | 4.5 | 31.4 | 27.0 | 28.2 |
| 1947–1948 | 8.1 | 6.9 | 31.5 | 25.7 | 27.8 |
| 1948 | 8.3 | 7.3 | 32.5 | 25.5 | 26.4 |
| 1949 | 8.8 | 6.8 | 34.1 | 16.9 | 33.4 |
| 1950 | 9.8 | 5.9 | 36.1 | 19.3 | 28.9 |
| 1951 | 10.6 | 7.0 | 41.8 | 13.6 | 27.0 |
| 1952 | 12.8 | 8.6 | 39.5 | 14.7 | 24.4 |
| 1953 | 13.2 | 10.0 | 39.5 | 10.5 | 26.8 |
| 1954 | 22.7 | 10.9 | 32.1 | 6.8 | 27.5 |
| 1955 | 23.8 | 10.4 | 32.3 | 8.5 | 25.0 |
| 1956 | 15.5 | 13.7 | 34.6 | 8.7 | 27.5 |
| 1957 | 11.3 | 12.8 | 31.5 | 7.9 | 36.5 |
| 1958 | 12.6 | 10.0 | 34.3 | 10.6 | 32.5 |
| 1959 | 18.1 | 8.5 | 35.4 | 12.3 | 25.7 |
| 1960 | 20.8 | 6.9 | 35.5 | 12.0 | 24.8 |
| 1961 | 17.5 | 8.9 | 38.5 | 9.4 | 25.9 |
| 1962 | 18.6 | 8.0 | 37.4 | 11.0 | 25.0 |
| 1963 | 20.3 | 7.7 | 34.8 | 12.4 | 24.8 |
| 1964 | 21.0 | 8.2 | 34.5 | 11.8 | 24.5 |
| 1965 | 17.5 | 8.4 | 40.0 | 12.1 | 22.0 |

Andrew Bródy                                   327

TABLE 10-4    Hungary: Investment Shares Within Heavy Industry (Per Cent)

| Year | Mining | Metallurgy | Electric power | Engineering | Chemicals | Building materials |
|------|--------|-----------|---------------|-------------|-----------|-------------------|
| 1949 | 22 | 43 | 17 | 11 | 4 | 3 |
| 1950 | 17 | 11 | 16 | 35 | 14 | 7 |
| 1951 | 17 | 17 | 14 | 28 | 17 | 7 |
| 1952 | 20 | 24 | 15 | 20 | 13 | 8 |
| 1953 | 23 | 26 | 14 | 20 | 10 | 7 |
| 1954 | 30 | 17 | 21 | 15 | 12 | 5 |
| 1955 | 30 | 13 | 21 | 15 | 16 | 5 |
| 1956 | 34 | 13 | 20 | 19 | 9 | 5 |
| 1957 | 36 | 7 | 22 | 16 | 14 | 5 |
| 1958 | 28 | 9 | 25 | 19 | 13 | 6 |
| 1959 | 24 | 12 | 21 | 24 | 12 | 7 |
| 1960 | 21 | 13 | 19 | 25 | 14 | 8 |
| 1961 | 23 | 14 | 19 | 18 | 17 | 9 |
| 1962 | 22 | 12 | 16 | 17 | 21 | 12 |
| 1963 | 24 | 13 | 18 | 17 | 20 | 8 |
| 1964 | 26 | 12 | 16 | 17 | 23 | 6 |
| 1965 | 26 | 12 | 17 | 18 | 22 | 5 |

# COMMENT

RICHARD D. PORTES
Oxford University

The end of 1949 was the end of the Three-Year Plan in Hungary. The first year of the First-Five Year Plan was 1950. This was also the time at which output (net material product) attained its 1938 level. Thus the Hungarian literature has tended to take 1949 as the end of the reconstruction period and the base year for all postwar series. In his discussion Dr. Bródy argues that the reconstruction period lasted until 1952, when employment reached its previous (wartime) peak. If this argument is accepted, says Bródy, then it must be concluded that, at least in the Hungarian case, there has been no tendency for the growth rate to decline in the postwar (that is, postreconstruction) period. Bródy's argument also implies that the slowing of growth in 1952 no longer appears to be exclusively the result of the admittedly poor policies followed by the government in 1951 and 1952, but primarily a consequence of the ending of the reconstruction period.

Bródy briefly discusses the reliability of the data he cites, especially in regard to the distortions introduced by a price system which undervalues agricultural and overvalues industrial output. This distortion of course affects measured growth rates, since Hungarian agriculture has grown much more slowly than industry. For present purposes, however, in dealing with cyclical fluctuations, there is no doubt that his data correctly show the turning points, peaks, and troughs: declines in national income in 1952, 1954, and 1956; declines in total gross fixed investment in 1954, 1955, 1957, and 1961. It should be stressed that total investment, including inventories, did *not* fall in 1957 or 1961: there was a large increase in inventories in 1957 to restore stocks depleted during the last months of 1956, when production virtually ceased; in 1961, there was a large increase in uncompleted investment projects. On the other hand, total investment *did* fall in 1952, when stocks of agricultural goods were reduced

328

because of the disastrous harvest; in 1956, because of the already mentioned reduction in stocks of consumer goods; in 1958, when stockbuilding fell to a more normal level after the great increase in 1957; and in 1965, when stockbuilding again fell significantly, in part because of a conscious attempt to reduce extremely high inventories. It is clear from this brief summary that the forces affecting stockbuilding are often totally unrelated to changes in fixed investment, and these two components of total investment frequently move in opposite directions.

Bródy then turns to a discussion of fluctuations in investment, which he calls investment "cycles". His main point is that these fluctuations have generated tensions and distortions which have depressed the actual long-term growth rate of output below what would have been attainable along a more even growth path. This is because of the disruption and disorganization in planning and execution of investment projects caused by the sudden shifts in the volume and distribution of investment. The harmful effects of fluctuations in the total of investment or in its rate of growth are exaggerated by fluctuations in the sectoral distribution within the total. In the investment booms, the share of industry rises; that of heavy industry rises within total industrial investment; and that of metallurgy rises within the total going to heavy industry. The increases in the shares of investment going to certain sectors during the boom also result in lagged fluctuations in other sectors, because the uneven expansion of capacity generates bottlenecks which must be eliminated before growth can proceed further. Although it is implicit in his analysis, Bródy does *not* explicitly make the point which Goldmann has made, namely, that excessive investment in the boom leads to such disruption and tensions that investment must *necessarily* be cut and the growth rate of output reduced, in order to allow some time to reorganize and regroup.

The major question arising out of Bródy's paper is whether the fluctuations in investment, which appear clearly in both absolute magnitudes and rates of growth, can properly be called "cyclical". There are several criteria which have frequently been used in the literature, and during this Conference, to characterize cyclical behavior. First, it might be asked whether the fluctuations in investment are *cumulative*. Is there a process of multiplier-accelerator interaction which makes any swing in investment generate a further movement in the same direction? It seems clear that this is not the case. The Hungarian data confirm the intuitive belief that if central planning means anything, it is that the planners can avoid this particular sort of cumulative process by "shortcircuiting" the multiplier-accelerator process.

A second criterion, whether fluctuations in investment are ultimately self-reversing, raises the whole set of questions associated with Goldmann's work. Without entering into a general discussion of these questions, it should be noted that the Hungarian investment booms of 1951–1952 and 1959–1960 did generate bottlenecks of the type Goldmann describes, necessitating subsequent downturns in investment and the rate of growth. I would therefore disagree with Professor Nove, who seemed in his discussion to attribute at least the earlier downturn primarily to pressure from Moscow. There certainly was such pressure, but it was not a necessary condition for the switch toward consumption. The economic causes would have been quite sufficient, even without political ones.

The question also arises whether the fluctuations in investment are accompanied by associated fluctuations of other important macrovariables. In Hungary, this has by and large *not* been the case. Output shows some association with investment for certain years, but there are several years in which the two seem to vary quite independently. Employment seems almost totally impervious; with all the unsteadiness of postwar growth in Hungary, industrial employment has increased each year, and the annual growth rates show remarkably little variation. The price level has been strictly controlled, since almost all nonagricultural prices are set centrally; certainly since 1956 this control has been quite effective. The balance of trade *has* shown some relationship to the level and rate of growth of investment; this aspect is discussed later.

The picture that emerges from all this is apparently not one of investment *cycles*. Fluctuations, yes; cycles, no. But some generalizations about the paths of investment and output in the postwar period are nevertheless valid for the socialist countries as a group.

First, the fluctuations in investment have shown some synchronization between countries in Eastern Europe. There are several obvious reasons for this parallel development. There have been similar, in some cases identical, influences on policy. The plans themselves have been coordinated to some extent. The general development strategies of the various Eastern European countries have been broadly similar. Finally, the economies have increasingly been closely connected through foreign trade. It is interesting to note that the intercountry relation between changes in investment is considerably closer than that between changes in income.

Second, the degree of instability of Eastern European countries seems to vary inversely with the range and depth of their natural resource endowments, and directly with their dependence on foreign trade and the share of agriculture in total output. In descending order of stability from the USSR are, first, East Germany, which has been very closely connected with the Soviet economy through foreign trade, while also having (over most of the postwar period) a substantial reserve of unused plant capacity which has been gradually drawn into production, thereby eliminating bottlenecks; then comes Poland, with large reserves of labor and rich natural resources; then Czechoslovakia and Hungary, which are rather less stable, being small, poorly endowed, and highly trade dependent; then Rumania, with ample natural resources but a high proportion of agricultural output and severely fluctuating harvests; and finally Bulgaria, without Rumania's natural resources but with a similarly important and unstable agricultural sector.

An interesting question for Hungary has been raised in Professor Matthews's Conference paper on Great Britain. Are imports stabilizing, *qua* leakages from the expenditure stream, or destabilizing, in that the balance of payments constraint may force the planners to adopt destabilizing policies? It appears that in the Hungarian investment boom of 1959–1960, imports were stabilizing; the balance of payments deficit which did develop was covered by loans, mainly from the USSR; and, in fact, much of the investment was imported machines financed by these loans. On the other hand, imports seem to have been destabilizing in the following few years, when investment was lowered; this allowed a faster expansion of consumption, which required substantial imports of consumer goods, external finance for which was understandably not forthcoming. The resulting balance of payments problems forced a further slowdown in investment in 1965.

It is often thought that money is merely a passive tool of accounting and control within the producing sectors in Soviet-type economies. This is a rather oversimplified view. In particular, there were monetary aspects of the recent investment booms in both Hungary (1959–1960) and Czechoslovakia (1959–1961). In both countries, the planners decided to allow a certain degree of decentralization by increasing the amounts retained by the enterprises out of their current profits. Enterprises could use this extra liquidity to make small, decentralized investments on their own initiative. This monetary ease led to chaos: the expansion of decentralized investment coincided with the planned expansion of large-scale centrally planned and financed projects, and the enterprises were bidding against the planners for investment goods. The situation became so intolerable in Hungary that at the end of 1960 the greater proportion of these funds was simply taken away from the enterprises by blocking the bank accounts in which they had accumulated. This is indeed selective monetary restriction.

Central allocation can never be fully effective and all-embracing. To the extent that decentralized decisions, operating through market processes, are allowed to affect resource allocation, monetary variables will be important. In the case just described, they influenced both the locus of investment decisions and the level of investment, and in a manner similar to their effects in Western economies. The study of fluctuations in Eastern Europe cannot be confined to the role of real variables alone.

Chapter Eleven

# FLUCTUATIONS IN THE GROWTH RATE IN A SOCIALIST ECONOMY AND THE INVENTORY CYCLE

JOSEF GOLDMANN

Czechoslovak Academy of Sciences, Prague

This chapter is concerned with the mechanism of fluctuations in the rate of growth in Czechoslovakia, given in "Hospodářský rust v ČSSR" (*Economic Growth in Czechoslovakia*, Prague, 1966), as well as in my previous papers[1]. Disequilibrium in the economy, caused (or intensified) by the selection of too high rates of growth, and revealed particularly in the operation (or intensification) of the raw material and foreign trade barriers, was analyzed in my earlier publications in connection with the well known consequences of overinvestment, linked to the planned rate of economic growth. The special role of fixed capital investment was found to be that the investment cycle, originally started at the beginning of the 1950's, gives the operation of the raw material and foreign trade barriers its specific, oscillating character.

In the present analysis, the exposition of the mechanism of fluctuations in the growth rate is extended somewhat; the impact of oscillation in inventories (and not only the echo-effect of changes in the rate of fixed capital formation) is examined in detail[2].

---

[1] *Economics of Planning,* Vol. 4, No. 2, 1964, and Vol. 6, No. 2, 1966; *Eastern European Economics*, Vol. IV, No. 1, 1965.

[2] See *Hospodářský rust v ČSSR*, p.102, where the central problem of this paper is discussed.

## Summary of Previous Analysis

The exposition of the mechanism of quasi-cyclical fluctuations in the growth rate, given in several of my earlier publications, may be summarized as follows:

> In a relatively small, industrially developed socialist country, there is a tendency for the raw-material base to lag behind the growth of manufacturing industries whenever the rate of growth exceeds certain optimum level[3]. This is due to tendencies toward underfulfillment of production (and investment) plans in the extractive and raw-material industries and toward overfulfillment of such plans in the higher-stage manufacturing industries, resulting in the formation of what has come to be known as the raw-material barrier.
>
> This in turn will bring about additional imbalances in foreign trade. That barrier, likewise, is bound to slow down economic growth, particularly in a small country with a limited raw-material endowment.
>
> In the given context, agriculture is playing a similar role, in view of the economic and institutional factors making for slow agricultural growth. This relatively slow development will cause additional strain whenever the over-all growth rate exceeds the rate of balanced growth.
>
> The results of economic disequilibrium, ensuing from a growth rate in excess of the rate of balanced growth, will be intensified by the well known effect of overinvestment, induced or necessitated by the planned rate of growth. Overinvestment, consequently, is not an independent cause of the subsequent decline in the rate of growth, but one of the factors accompanying excessive growth.

## Joint Impact of Synchronized Investment and Inventory Cycles

In this chapter, an attempt is made to examine how far the echo-effect of fluctuations in fixed-capital investment (resulting in oscillation in the flow of completed new capacity) is synchronized with, and accentuated by, an inventory cycle. Such a cycle may be due to "speculative" hoarding of raw materials and goods in process in periods of rapid growth, and to subsequent dishoarding in periods of slow growth, when maturing investment projects in the basic industries, jointly with relatively declining demand resulting from a low growth rate, cause an easing of the supply position.

The result of long-term trends and fluctuations in inventory accumulation and in capital goods under construction (described in more detail in previous

---

[3] See M. Kalečki, "Nástin metody aestavováni perspektivniho plánu" (Outline of a Method of Constructing a Long-Term Plan), in *Náčrt teorie růstu socialistické ekonomiky* (Outline of the Theory of Growth of a Socialist Economy), Prague, 1965, p. 137.

studies [4] is that a considerable part of accumulation, reaching about 1/3 on the average, for the years under investigation, is tied up in the rise of stocks and of capital goods under construction. Therefore, the total volume of inventories and uncompleted construction corresponds to more than 2/3 of the national income.

> This supplies an answer to the question, how is it possible that the high share of accumulation in national income and the considerable lead of the rate of growth of the output of means of production over the production of consumer goods, which prevailed practically throughout the whole period, did not have the expected effect, that is, a sustained rate of rapid economic growth? It is now known that fixed-capital (and inventory) formation need not always induce such growth. Far from resulting in acceleration – or at least stabilization – of the rate of growth, a high rate of capital formation did not even prevent a notable deceleration. Statistical data give an interesting, though necessarily approximate, picture of two of the main escape channels through which parts of the national income are "falling out" of the reproduction process[5].
>
> In the context of this chapter, however, I am not concerned much with the (long-term) declining trend in the growth rate – which is due, *inter alia*, to excessive accumulation of inventories and, to a lesser extent, of capital goods under construction – but with the quasi-cyclical effect of oscillation in the rate of such accumulation.

A somewhat deeper insight into the decelerating effect of excessive accumulation of inventories and capital under construction—and the accelerating effect of disaccumulation—is made possible by a more complex, incremental analysis, using year-to-year changes in the accumulation data, instead of the accumulation figures themselves. In 1961, for instance, of the increment in national income (of about 15 billion crowns), approximately 2/3 was used to increase accumulation and about 1/3 to increase consumption. The expansion of inventories and of capital under construction was, however, larger than the rise in consumption or in fixed capital accumulation, net of capital under construction[6].

In this respect, there is an important analogy between economic developments in 1966 and in 1961. In 1966, as in 1961, the expansion of inventories and of capital under construction was larger than the increase in consumption or the increase in fixed capital formation, net of capital under construction.

But in 1964, developments contrasted sharply with those in 1961 or in 1966. In 1964, the increase in national income was far smaller than – but the increase in consumption was as large as – the corresponding figure in 1966. This was due

---

[4] *Czechoslovak Economic Papers* Vol. 5, 1965, p. 43.

[5] See *Economics of Planning* Vol. 4, No. 2, 1965, pp. 96–97.

[6] That is, the increment in the flow of new fixed assets going into operation.

to the fact that in 1964 there was a large decrease in inventories and in capital under construction. In 1964, the combination of a fairly high rate of increase in consumption with a relatively low rate of growth of national income was not achieved — as many economists believed — at the cost of accumulation of fixed capital, net of capital under construction. On the contrary, fixed capital brought into operation rose by more than 5 billion crowns. Such a development, which at first sight seems somewhat inconsistent, was made possible by a disaccumulation of excessively high inventories and capital under construction. As a result "disposable" national income (that is, national income reduced by a rise in the volume of inventories and capital under construction, or increased for a decline) was considerably higher than national income, according to the current definition. On the other hand, in 1961 and 1966, disposable national income was considerably lower than national income, as currently defined, for the reason that the rate of increase of inventories and capital under construction was high. (See Figures 11-1 and 11-2.)

If the process of reproduction is compared with a pipeline, into which the factors of production enter and from which flow final products, either for consumption or for raising the volume of productive and "nonproductive" capacity in operation, then it may be said that in 1966 (as in 1961) there was a large increase — relative to factor input — in the volume of the factors of production inside the pipeline. For this reason, the output of final products for consumption or fixed capital formation was relatively low as compared with the input of factors of production.

On the other hand, in 1964 an opposite process was taking place. Inventories and capital under construction declined. Therefore, the output of final products was considerably larger than might have been expected from the input of factors of production.

Thus, the accumulation of inventories and of capital under construction represents one of the main factors which make for alternating intensification and alleviation of economic tension, for intensification or alleviation of economic imbalance, and for the resultant fluctuations in the rate of economic growth.

## Diagrammatic Presentation

Graphically, the relationship between "statistical" and "disposable" national income may be presented as in Figure 11-1, borrowing the usual balance sheet technique from the National Accounts System:

> The balance between the increment in national income produced (increment of resources) and the increment in national income allocated (increment of allocations) will be represented by two columns for each year. In the most straightforward case, the left-hand column will stand for the national income increment, while the

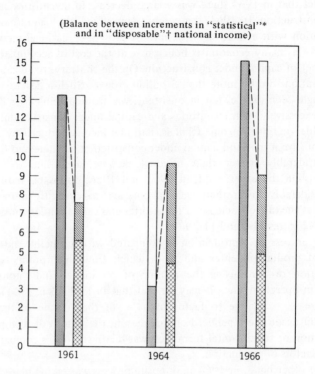

(Balance between increments in "statistical"*
and in "disposable"† national income)

**Fig. 11-1.** Czechoslovakia: relationship between "statistical" and "disposable" national income. From *Economic Growth in Czechoslovakia*, Prague, 1966, p. 68.

*Increments in:*

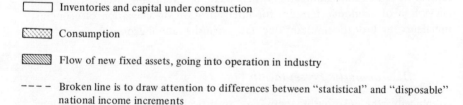

"Statistical" national income

Inventories and capital under construction

Consumption

Flow of new fixed assets, going into operation in industry

– – – – Broken line is to draw attention to differences between "statistical" and "disposable" national income increments

\* Statistical national income: national income as currently defined in Czechoslovakia.
† Disposable national income: national income reduced for the increase (or increased for the decline) in volume of inventories and capital under construction.

right-hand column, of the same height, will be built up from the following components, reading from the base line: consumption increment, increment in the flow of new fixed assets going into operation, and increment in inventories and capital under construction.

Decrements in any of these values will be shown below the base line, except for inventories and capital under construction. Here, the procedure is somewhat more complicated. If there is an increment of this component, then it will appear in the right-hand column as an increase in allocations. If, however, there is a decrement in this component, then it will be shown as a part of the left-hand column, since such a decline in inventories and capital under construction increases the volume of additional resources available for raising consumption and/or the flow of new fixed assets.

In other words, the changing position (on the diagram) of inventories and capital under construction reflects the pipeline effect. Increment of this component reduces the national income increment available for raising consumption or increasing the flow of new fixed assets. On the other hand, a decrement of this component (that is, inventories and capital under construction) raises the national income increment available for these purposes. On the diagram, the dotted lines draw attention to the resultant differences between "statistical" and "disposable" national income.

As mentioned earlier, decrements in national income, consumption, or the flow of new fixed assets are shown below the base line. In the more complex case, where a statistical national income decrement is combined with a decline in inventories and capital under construction, the latter will have to be subtracted from the statistical national income decrement to obtain the disposable national income decrement, to which must correspond a decline in consumption and/or the flow of new fixed assets. If the decline in national income is arithmetically smaller than the decline in inventories and capital under construction, then consumption and/or the flow of new fixed assets will actually rise in spite of the fall in "statistical" national income.

These relationships are shown in Figure 11-1 for selected, typical years of quasi-cyclical fluctuations: 1961, a year of imminent deceleration; 1964, a year of early acceleration; and 1966, in some respects similar to 1961.

When the same technique is applied to the entire period 1950–1966, the relationship between statistical and disposable national income is seen to change significantly within the quasi-cycle (Figure 11-2). Thus, it is clear that the three years selected were not chosen arbitrarily but represent extreme cases of the pipeline effect on economic equilibrium and on the rate of growth of changes in inventories and in capital under construction.

A practical conclusion may be drawn from this analysis. It is true that at present the disequilibrating effect of excessive accumulation of inventories and of capital under construction is recognized in Czechoslovakia. However, countermeasures taken so far relate only to the credit and financial spheres. But it is necessary to pay attention to the fact that changes in inventories and in capital under construction appear to be closely connected with the quasi-cycle. Thus, it seems that a more comprehensive program mix will have to be applied.

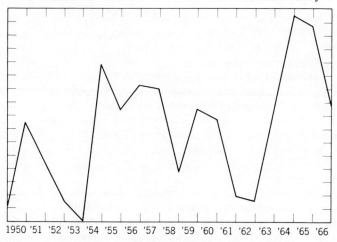

**Fig. 11-2.** Czechoslovakia: quasi-cyclical changes in relationship between "statistical" and "disposable" national income: the pipe-line effect. Upward movement indicates that "disposable" national income is overtaking "statistical" national income (and *vice versa* for downward movement). In other words, upward movement indicates release from – and downward movement damming-up – in the pipeline. *Note*: Interval on vertical scale represents 1 billion crowns.

Economic instruments in the field of credit and finance will have to be complemented by the use of economic instruments that would result in some moderation of the rate of growth. This would go to the roots of excessive inventory accumulation, especially if applied in combination with the measures already taken.

It may be surprising to economists outside Czechoslovakia that in this analysis all increases in inventories and capital under construction have been taken as reducing the disposable national income. It might be argued that, with an increase in national income, some increase in inventories and capital under construction is unavoidable. It can be shown, however, that at their present excessive levels no further increase would be necessary, at least for some years to come, even with a high growth rate of national income.

*Mechanism of Quasi-Cyclical Fluctuations
and the New Economic System*

The great – and, so far, little-appreciated – extent to which changes in the rate of formation of inventories and of capital under construction are bound to generate oscillation is brought out clearly by the following comparison. In 1964,

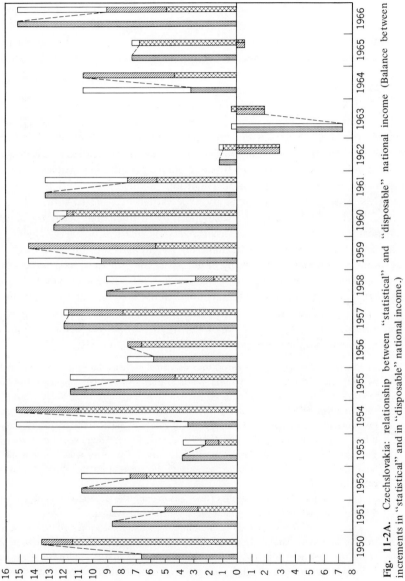

**Fig. 11-2A.** Czechoslovakia: relationship between "statistical" and "disposable" national income (Balance between increments in "statistical" and in "disposable" national income.)

"disposable" national income was 6.5 billion crowns higher than national income, as currently defined. On the other hand, the opposite was true in 1966; that is, disposable national income was about 6 billion crowns lower than national income, according to the current definition. It is obvious that a negative change in the relation between "statistical" and "disposable" national income in the range of more than 12 billion crowns—roughly 7 per cent of national income—must have had a decisive effect on economic equilibrium, bringing about increased tension in the economy and rendering quite probable another period of deceleration in the rate of growth.

Against such an eventuality there is the fact that, at present, apart from rolling stock and building materials, the raw materials barrier does not seem operative to any greater extent. In this connection, however, another factor must be taken into consideration. The behavior of enterprises − particularly under conditions of the new system of economic planning and management − is influenced not so much by given conditions in the sphere of supply of raw materials and goods in process as by expectations relating to future developments. Uncertainty in this sphere is, possibly, a more significant signal than statistical data, which, in any case, are relatively few and not very reliable. An enterprise that expects a worsening of its supply position will obviously "economize" supplies, and possibly even restrict the growth of its production. It will do so in order to safeguard a smooth flow of its own output for future months[7] . For this reason, increasing uncertainty as to further developments in the supply position may in itself bring about unfavorable developments. Expectations, being subjective factors, may in themselves become objective factors determining the development of real economic processes.

> However, the behavior of enterprises described earlier (and sometimes referred to as a kind of "socialist speculation") is not as irrational as might appear at first sight from the macroeconomic point of view.
>
> Under capitalism, the inventory-turnover ratio forms one of the major problems of production management. An enterprise will carefully balance the costs and risks of minimizing inventories against the expenses incurred by holding excessive inventories. The smoother the supply (and transport) situation, the lower will it be possible to hold the inventory-turnover ratio, optimizing this relation on the basis of economic calculations.
>
> This principle, however, applies (or ought to apply) to production management in Socialism as well, particularly under the new economic system.
>
> Therefore, excessive inventory accumulation, sometimes referred to as speculation, is, as a rule, dictated by the given—or rather the expected—supply situation, and is in line with the principle of economic calculation at the enterprise level. Such rational behavior of production managers relating to inventory accumulation, even if

---

[7] As to the impact of the simultaneous "hoarding" of materials and goods in process, see the foregoing discussion.

rather dangerous from the macroeconomic view as a cycle-generating factor, should be taken as a significant indicator of changes in economic equilibrium and of imminent alterations in the rate of growth that are bound to result from these changes.

For these reasons, it may well be that the mechanism of fluctuations in the growth rate still continues to operate, especially in the present situation. Autonomous factors inside the economy, which in the past made for quasi-cyclical changes in the rate of growth, may continue to operate, particularly—but not only—because of the restricted extent, so far, of the operation of the new system of economic planning and control.

The traditional system of planning and management was rightly criticized as lacking any economic mechanism which would call for rapid reaction to economic tensions at a time when they are only *in statu nascendi,* below the surface of current economic life. When the new economic system is fully implemented and the market mechanism becomes sufficiently objective, signals from the market and other information will more rapidly indicate turning points in the rate of growth. Thus, following comprehensive analysis, such signals will give rise to adequate countermeasures, which will make it possible to reduce the amplitude of fluctuations and to shorten their duration. As a result, far-reaching economic losses, due to underexploitation of productive resources in the trough phase of the quasi-cycle, may be lessened to a considerable extent.

## Interrelation of Objective and Subjective Factors

The complex interaction of objective and subjective factors — at both central and enterprise levels — in the process of growth-rate variations appears more clearly in historical perspective.

The success of economic planning in the period of postwar reconstruction and the gradual release of large output and labor-productivity reserves in those years, in conjunction with the deterioration of the international situation, resulted in 1950–1951 in the revision of current plans (or plan projects) with a view to a considerable rise in the rate of economic growth far beyond the optimum level. The economic difficulties and disproportions that followed could not be overcome except by a remarkable cut during 1953–1954 in the rate of growth and in the volume of investment. The radical economic measures of that period were not due so much to political changes; they were, in fact, the unavoidable outcome of preceding economic developments. Making possible the solution of the disproportions inherited from the preceding period, they simultaneously set up the indispensible preconditions for the implementation of the *Neue Kurs* after Stalin's death.

After a gradual recovery beginning in 1954, a new period of very rapid development started about 1958. At that time many investment projects initiated in the early 1950's, particularly in the basic industries, were completed and put into full operation; this played a decisive part in overcoming, or substantially alleviating, the economic disproportions that had brought about the fall in the rate of growth in 1953 and 1954. All available data show that 1958, like 1950–1951, was one of the most successful years in the history of economic planning in Czechoslovakia – but not only in that country.

However, these objective conditions, in conjunction with certain subjective tendencies which have a particularly wide radius of action in the traditional model of economic planning and management, gave rise to a new wave of industrialization and a new investment drive, culminating in 1959–1960. For reasons mentioned earlier, these developments necessarily caused–or aggravated–disproportions, such as had appeared in 1953–1954, and induced a similar, though far steeper, decline in the rate of growth of industrial production in the period 1961–1963. While in Czechoslovakia there was even a fall in output in 1963, some consolidation took place in 1964–1966, and there was a new upturn in the rate of growth.

As to the interrelation between objective and subjective factors in the genesis of quasi-cyclical movement in the growth rate, the following conclusion may be drawn from this analysis. The phase of deceleration is objectively unavoidable. Once strain and economic tensions have been allowed to develop rather far in a planning system, reacting only indirectly and with some time lag to market signals (if any), the only immediate solution can be to reduce the rate of growth.

Things are more complicated as far as acceleration is concerned. Certain subjective tendencies toward maximizing the rate of growth assert themselves continuously. However, it is only under conditions such as those prevailing about 1950 or 1959 that voluntarism in planning has an exceptionally wide field of action under conditions of general optimism, owing to high rates of growth and a relatively satisfactory supply position. Conditions like those in the 1958–1960 period, when the 1950–1952 investment wave gradually matured, may recur cyclically, as happened in 1966. The process of acceleration, though resulting from subjective decision-making, nevertheless has its specific, objective foundation.

## Convergence?

Fluctuations in the growth rate may be observed in some socialist, as well as in capitalist, countries. However, the wave-like movement in the rate of growth, analyzed earlier, obviously differs in principle from cyclical development under capitalism. While a fall in output is quite exceptional under socialism, quarterly, if not annual, data show that a decline occurs more or less regularly in developed capitalist countries, particularly in the United States, Canada, Scandinavia, etc.

In the postwar period, capitalist countries succeeded in alleviating the amplitude of cyclical fluctuations carrying out an active and complex economic policy, which is based upon what has become to be known as the new economics[8]. It is true, of course, that local wars, and particularly war preparations, were important factors in raising effective demand—directly in home countries and indirectly, via foreign trade, in others. Thus, a relatively stable rate of growth could be achieved over a fairly long period. Nevertheless, few economists in the West hold that under capitalism the trade cycle is already obsolete. One need not be a dogmatist to maintain that the economic cycle follows necessarily from the very essence of the capitalist system and can only be mitigated by state intervention. On the other hand, fluctuations in the rate of growth are not inherent to the socialist order, but ensue from insufficient knowledge of the economic laws of socialism and from shortcomings in their application.

Selection of optimum rates of growth, coupled with a thorough overhaul of the system of economic planning and management and elimination of a relapse into overinvestment, would contribute to the prevention of economic overstrain and disproportions that otherwise might arise again in the future. Thus, it might be possible to secure more regular and, in the long run, more rapid economic growth.

The basic causes of both deceleration and acceleration are linked to the development of the relation between supply and effective demand, under capitalism as well as under socialism. While, however, in a capitalist economy deceleration is due to deficiency of effective demand, the opposite applies to a socialist economy. There, deceleration is due to economic strain and tension which ensue from the lagging of supply under the intensified operation of the raw-material, foreign-trade, and production-capacity barriers.

It is for this reason that the way out of the trough in the growth rate (that is, the transition into acceleration) differs in capitalism and socialism. In the classical model of Marx, acceleration will start when the moral and physical *Verschleise* of fixed productive capital gradually balances the relation between supply and demand; under modern conditions, acceleration will be brought about by coordinated application of the new instruments of economic policy, including local wars and more intensive war preparations. Under socialism, the transition into acceleration is rendered possible, first of all, by maturing production capacities, the construction of which was started in the period centering about the peak of the preceding investment cycle. Thus, supply is increased while simultaneously the fairly low rate of growth (and low investment activity) reduces the demand relative to supply, particularly in the basic branches of industry.

An analogous argument applies to the transition into deceleration. Under capitalism, maturing investment projects accentuate the excess of supply relative to effective demand, thus strengthening the basic contradiction of capitalism.

---

[8] Paul A Samuelson, *Economics*, New York, 1962. 6th ed., pp. 150, 264f., 337f., 786f..

Under socialism, the excess of effective demand is accentuated at the peak of the quasi-cycle by maximal investment activity, connected with an increase in the volume of capital under construction. Thus, in both social systems there are analogous processes, proceeding, however, in opposite directions.

The inventory cycle, analyzed above, apparently increases the amplitude of fluctuations in both social systems. In this field, too, cyclical development again operates in opposite directions. Under capitalism, inventories are reduced in the initial phase of a decline (or deceleration) in output, further increasing supply, compared with current output[9]. In a socialist economy, inventories rise steeply at this phase, as a result of the speculative tendencies mentioned above, which accentuate the excess of effective demand.

It is especially in this context that the role and importance of complex *Konjunkturforschung* show up must clearly. As has been fittingly noted by a Yugoslav economist, the virtual ignoring of quasi-cyclical fluctuations in a number of socialist countries on the basis of a fictitious "law of steady economic growth in Socialism," has necessarily led to the further fiction that there is no room for *Konjunkturforschung* in a socialist economy. The costs to the economy of such dogmatic fiction are, however, being increasingly realized.

## Summary and Discussion

As a result of the analysis in this chapter, the presentation of the mechanism of wave-like movements in the growth rate (Figure 11-3) may be summarized as follows:

The top section of the diagram presents data on year-to-year changes in investment activity, covering two full cycles. In the second section, the echo-effect of these fluctuations is shown in two significant peaks in the increments of the flow of new investment in industrial capacity. With a time lag of about eight or nine years, corresponding to the length of the construction and gestation period under given conditions, the two peaks in investment activity at about 1951–1952 and 1959–1960 are reflected in similar peaks in the increments of the flow of new fixed assets coming into operation in industry in the 1959–1960 and 1964–1966 periods.

The third section in the diagram indicates a fairly satisfactory synchronization of this wave-like movement both in investment activity and in the flow of new fixed capital with the rate of growth of the output of producer goods industries.

Finally, the last section presents a further echo-effect of the investment cycle, appearing in significant inventory changes that are due to expectations relating

---

[9] Samuelson, *op cit.*, p. 257.

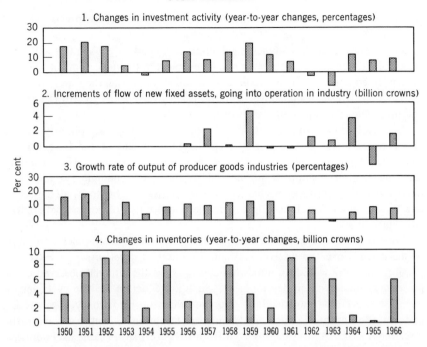

**Fig. 11-3.** Czechoslovakia: mechanism of wave-like movements in growth rate. (The echo-effect of investment waves in new-output-capacities flow, in growth rate of producer goods industries, and in inventory formation.) Fluctuations in investment activity (top section) give rise to an echo-effect in two significant peaks in the increments of the flow of new industrial capacity, with a time lag of about eight or nine years (second section). There is fairly satisfactory synchronization of the above wave-like movements with the rate of growth of the output of producer goods industries (third section). A further echo-effect of the investment cycle shows in significant changes in inventory formation (fourth section). From *Economic Growth in Czechoslovakia*, Prague, 1966, pp. 36, 37, 44, 68.

to further developments in the supply position. In those years when the increase in the flow of investment in new industrial capacity is at a maximum, the supply position is improving. Enterprises will adjust themselves to such a change by lowering their inventory – turnover ratios, thus alleviating further the supply position in the economy as a whole. As a result, there will arise a strong tendency toward reduction of inventories. The successive improvements in the supply position are thus characterized by a positive feedback effect, and the process of relative or absolute disaccumulation of stocks will gain momentum.

When, however, under conditions of relative economic equilibrium, the rate of growth of industrial output expands again, new tension and strain develop with a resultant deterioration in the supply position. Enterprises adjust to such changes by raising their inventory – turnover ratios, thus worsening still more the supply position in the economy as a whole. As a result, the growth rate will decline.

Such unfavorable developments will come to an end only when the combined effect of the falling rate of growth and a new peak in the increments of the flow of new fixed capital again alleviate tension and strain, easing the supply position so that objective—and subjective—conditions are given for the growth rate to rise and for a new investment and inventory cycle to start.

A process, similar to that described in the next to last paragraph, may well be in its initial phase at the present stage of development of the Czechoslovak economy, as jointly with the effects of more or less unavoidable frictions resulting from transition from the old to the new economic system. Final judgment and quantitative evaluation of the relative weight, to be attributed to one or the other factor making for deceleration, must, of course, be left to a later stage of analysis.

Some objections against our interpretation of present developments will now be discussed. First, the interval between the onset of deceleration in 1961 and, possibly, in 1967 would be somewhat shorter than the intervals observed in the preceding quasi-cyclical development. Such a reduction in the cycle length might, however, be explained by the fact that, of the two cycle-generating factors, the inventory cycle is gaining in importance, compared with the investment cycle. As can be observed from data for mature capitalist countries, inventory cycles have a strong tendency to reduce the wave-lengths of economic fluctuations.

Another objection might relate to the fact that the flow of investment in new industrial capacity, compared with the stock of existing capacity, is too small to induce fluctuations in the growth rate. However, the interpretation of the complex interrelation in the dynamics of supply and demand factors must be based on incremental analysis. Increments in supply, absolutely small in size, may have a fairly large effect on relative changes in the supply-demand ratio. Such changes in their turn will bring about cumulative reactions in enterprise behavior (relating to inventory formation) which was described earlier.

A third objection is possible on the following grounds: The interpretation in this chapter of the mechanism making for fluctuations in the growth rate assumed a causal nexus which operates in a definite one-way direction: (a) The beginning of an investment wave, for example, in the 1950—1952 period—as shown in the top section of Figure 8-3—brings about a lagged maximum in the flow of investment in new industrial capacity, that is, in the 1957—1959 period in this example (second section in Figure 11-3). (b) This leads to a peak in the rate of growth of output of the producer goods industries (third section), synchronized with an increase in the flow of new fixed assets. (c) Finally, the cycle-generating echo-effect of investment waves is accentuated by the inventory cycle, as described earlier (fourth section). The slight, but significant, time-lag of the inventory-investment series behind the industrial growth-rate series will be discussed later.

Such an interpretation of the causal nexus between investment waves and fluctuations in the growth rate is in sharp contrast with another explanation. Some economists hold that the causal nexus operates the other way round. According to them, it is precisely the peak in investment activity which makes for a high rate of growth, particularly in producer goods industries.

This theory is, in fact, based on the Keynesian trade cycle under capitalism. There, it is quite clear that, under conditions of underemployment of the factors of production, a rise in investment activity beings about an increase in demand and, therefore, in industrial output. In an economy like that of Czechoslovakia, conditions of relatively full employment of the factors of production prevail—at least under the previous planning and control system, and excluding the trough phase in the growth rate of output. There is no need, therefore, for additional investment to raise the degree of utilization of output capacity and manpower. On the contrary, it is exactly the peak in the investment drive which intensifies economic strain and tensions, induces inventory hoarding, and thus sets up conditions for a decline—not for a rise—in the rate of growth of output in the phase immediately following.

This is only another instance that shows the importance of carefully differentiating between a demand-oriented capitalist economy and a supply-oriented economy of the Czechoslovak type. In the latter, acceleration is due not to additional investment (that is, to additional demand) but to the coming into operation of additional capacity (that is, it is due to additional supply).

Finally, there is an interesting time-lag problem. A careful examination of Figure 11-3 shows that inventory investment reaches a maximum at a point when the growth rate of output has passed its peak. This fact, however, seems to be in agreement with the thesis that it is inventory investment which, with a kind of multiplier effect, reinforces the deceleration in the growth of output which would follow from the fading of the echo-effect (of changes in investment activity) in the flow of new fixed assets in industry.

Another interpretation is also possible. It may be held here, too, that the causal nexus operates in the opposite direction. It may well be that it is the deceleration in the rate of growth that makes for higher inventory investment, as a result of a temporary decline in demand. A definite answer to such an objection will be possible only when more data relating to the structure of inventory investment are available and analyzed. There is the question of whether the changes in inventory formation relate primarily to stocks of raw materials and goods in process or to stocks of finished products ready for shipment. It may well be that there is a two-way interaction, with a significant feedback effect[10].

The time-lag of inventory investment behind the industrial growth rate is not only apparent in the phase of deceleration of industrial growth; though lagged correlation is not so close in this case, the lag appears in the phase of accelerated industrial growth as well. Industrial growth is already accelerating when inventory formation is near a minimum. This fact seems to be in line with the earlier interpretation that the causal nexus works primarily from inventory investment toward the rate of output growth, and not the other way round.

In conclusion, another remark may be permitted. Reference has been made above to the problem of the interaction of subjective and objective factors in bringing about a quasi-cyclical movement in the growth rate. In this connection, another "political" interpretation must be taken into consideration. As mentioned already, some economists, particularly in the West, hold that deceleration was due to the political changes after Stalin's death in 1953, and to similar political changes in the early 1960's. Thus in his paper, "Cyclical Fluctuations under Socialism"[11], Professor Alec Nove writes as follows, referring to both Professor Olivera's and my explanation of the quasi-cycle: "Both emphasize a kind of political ("subjective") imperative, to go ahead as fast as possible, and so to overinvest. As soon as the crisis, which compelled cuts in investment, has been overcome, the same tendency reasserts itself. Goldmann would attribute the cuts to the exhaustion of raw material supplies and foreign exchange reserves, whole Olivera gave a greater emphasis to exhaustion of the people's patience with low living standards; but, no doubt, each would agree that the factors named by the other did play a significant role in the "crises" that beset a number of East European countries"[12].

First of all, pressure toward excessive growth and overinvestment there certainly is, though not only—not even predominantly—political pressure; and, certainly, growthmanship is not a specific characteristic of planning under socialism[13].

It is true that certain subjective tendencies toward maximizing the rate of growth make themselves felt continuously. However, as mentioned earlier, it is only under conditions such as those that prevailed about 1950, or 1959, or 1966, that voluntary planning has a wide field of action. The process of excessive acceleration, with resultant overinvestment, though ensuing from

---

[10] Postponement or abandonment of some investment projects will result in the cancellation of orders placed with the engineering industries, although work on these orders may already have begun. Thus inventories will be increased still further because of the rise in "work in progress" which is not likely to be completed.
[11] Chapter 9, above.
[12] The "political" aspect was stressed even more in another paper by Professor Nove in *Economic Journal*, June 1966, p. 276.
[13] See *Everyman's Dictionary of Economics*, p. 199: " . . . emphasis on economic growth to the exclusion or at the expense of other economic objectives and to the concentration on investment as the only dominant source of economic growth . . ."

subjective decision-making, nevertheless has its specific objective foundation. Political or professional pressure might, potentially, operate continuously. However, it could hardly be implemented in such periods as 1954 or 1962, since the objective preconditions for a new upturn in the rate of growth of new investment were not given then.

Now to the quantitative aspects of Professor Olivera's arguments: More detailed examination of statistical data (which hardly were at Olivera's disposal) shows that not purely political considerations—relating to the desirability of securing a pronounced rise in the standard of living—but extreme economic tension and overstrain within the sphere of production were the factors that made deceleration unavoidable.

Thus, from a table given in *Economic Growth in Czechoslovakia* (p.36), it can be seen that between 1952 and 1953 the rate of growth of producer goods industries was reduced by approximately ½, while that of consumer goods industries was reduced by nearly 2/3. Such a development does not seem to be in line with the view that deceleration in 1953 was brought about by the desire to raise consumption rapidly.

In the 1960–1963 period, there was, at least, no significant difference in the decline in the rates of growth of producer and consumer goods industries, respectively, but another fact may be even more relevant. In that period, the structure of investment was changed in an interesting way, but not in favor of the consumer. While investment for "productive" purposes was reduced only hesitatingly, the burden of the cut in investment activity was borne predominantly by the "nonproductive" sphere.

In addition, in the years 1963–1964, for instance, the planned rate of growth for producer goods industries was several times higher than that for the consumer goods sector. These facts hardly corroborate the "political" interpretation of quasi-cyclical fluctuations, which might be opposed with the more detailed statistical information given earlier.

# COMMENT

FRANCIS SETON,
Oxford University

A great deal has been said in this discussion about "well behaved" trade cycles—cycles conforming to a respectable theory that could claim to be *"de bonne famille."* No one, however, would expect a good Socialist to pride himself on his ancestry, and if a socialist trade cycle can be found at all, he certainly will play down all family connections and firmly identify himself with the disinherited class. His manners will come straight from the heart, and not from any book of etiquette. How, then, can he be recognized? The obvious thing about the heart, I suppose, is that it *pulsates*—even if it does not go up and down—and that is the residue of common humanity which the socialist cycle must be expected to share with his capitalist namesake. But is there anything else? Two further characteristics have emerged from the overall discussion of the business cycle contained in this book.

First, there is the notion that the cyclical pulse must be *all-pervasive*; it must communicate itself to the total aggregates of economic activity — national income, domestic product, or what have you. Second, there must be a quality of progressive or cumulative reinforcement about the beats; each upswing (or acceleration), and possibly also each downswing (or deceleration), must grow on what it feeds." To this I would like to add a third characteristic which has not, perhaps, been stated quite so explicitly: each phase must in some sense depend on the occurrence and opposite direction of its predecessor; it must not be wholly initiated by unrelated causes disturbing the normal course of events; if it were, there would be exogenous shocks or "irregular" fluctuations rather than cyclical movements as we have learned to distinguish them. As Professor Menshikov has put it: the downward movement is in a sense the "corrective" (some would say the deserved penalty) for the debauchery which has gone before.

350

Now it is easy enough to find aggregates in socialist economies that perform the required "pulsation." In all these economies, even in the Soviet Union, the growth in investment activity quickens and slackens in turn; and in the larger Peoples' Democracies (with the apparent exception of Poland), it even dips below zero at certain intervals. Dr. Goldmann has called attention to these movements in Czechoslovakia, Poland, and the German Democratic Republic, and Dr. Bródy's discussion deplores their nefarious influence on the Hungarian economy. The question that must be asked, however, is whether they share the three characteristics I have mentioned as the badges of full-cycle status: pervasiveness, self-propulsion, and a modicum of self-reversion.

As for pervasiveness, the picture differs sharply as between the Soviet Union and the Peoples' Democracies. Professor George Staller, in the *American Economic Review* of June 1964, published two variants of an "index of total output fluctuations" to measure the behavior of 8 socialist and 18 nonsocialist economies during the 1950's. The index is based on the departure of annual growth ratios from their least-square trend values, and Staller comes up with a figure for the socialist group as a whole which is twice that for the capitalist sample — with Yugoslavia leading in the former and Turkey in the latter. *Within* the socialist group, however, the Soviet Union appears as a model of steadfastness, with a total fluctuation index (a la Staller) below that of any other country, though not very far below those of France and the Scandinavian countries! I am aware, of course, that much uncertainty attaches to the appropriateness of the Staller indices as comparative measures of cyclical variability, or even of "unsteadiness" in general. More particularly — as Mr. Portes has pointed out to me — the failure to express the annual deviations of growth ratios as percentages of the trend values from which they deviate must overstate the variability of high-growth time paths compared with those of lower growth; intuition prompts that an expansion showing annual growth rates between 9 and 11 per cent should be considered less "variable" than one which oscillates between 2 and 4 per cent. Staller's index, however, would give a verdict of equality between them, so long as their absolute amplitudes remain the same. If this criticism is justified, the faster-growing socialist countries would compare much less unfavorably with the nonsocialist economies than Staller's indices imply, and the position of the Soviet Union in the general league table would be even further improved. While it remains true that Staller did not extend his observations to the 1960's, when the Soviet Union was entering slightly choppier seas, the crude calculations for 1960–1965, which I was able to carry out at short notice (on the basis of Professor Nove's and Dr. Bródy's papers), have convinced me that this would not make very much difference — at least as far as the relative positions of Britain, the Soviet Union, and Hungary are concerned. We may take it, then, that there were strong *pervasive* fluctuations in the growth rates of the Peoples' Democracies, but very little pervasiveness of such movements in the Soviet Union.

352          Comment

Leaving pervasiveness aside, can we discover any process of self-propulsion at work in those important series which nonetheless pulsate or fluctuate? As Dr. Bródy tells us, these series for Hungary are fixed investment and agricultural output. In Czechoslovakia, as we know from Dr. Goldmann's work, fixed investment and also stock building fluctuate the most. In the Soviet Union also, the most volatile major series — though, as I have indicated before, it is far less volatile there than it is anywhere else — is, once more, fixed investment. Unfortunately, neither Bródy nor Goldmann offers guidance regarding the self-propelling character (or otherwise) of investment swings, though Goldmann — if I understand him correctly — seems to hint that unequal degrees of plan fulfillment in extractive and manufacturing industries may lead to supplementary "catching-up" investment whenever the economy is overheated. Bródy refers to the violent changes in the direction of investment in Czechoslovakia. If we may surmise that it is always easier to obtain investment funds to stop bottlenecks than to effect equivalent cuts in investment in other sectors where projects are already under way, we can easily imagine a ratchet effect of investment-aggrandizement, whereby increased investment leads to bottlenecks, and bottlenecks lead to increased investment. In Nove's discussion, some prominence is given to the tendency to "fritter away" investment resources on a multiplicity of projects. This may be the effect of lower echelons of economic administration (whether regions or ministries) consistently claiming more than they can chew — as insurance in case some of their claims are disallowed — and inveigling the central authorities into long-term commitments from which they cannot easily extricate themselves, once the projects are under way. As the frittering process leads to an alarming lengthening of gestation periods and large backlogs of unfinished construction, the central authorities may be led to allocate additional investment funds to projects near the stage of completion. These are institutional factors peculiar to fully planned economies (though doubtless not unknown in market ones), and their strength may well increase with the degree to which investment decisions are decentralized. In the Soviet Union, such decentralization was relatively extensive shortly after the regionalization measures of 1957; it was subsequently decreased, but may well be on the point of rising again, though under the new reforms fixed capital will no longer be virtually costless to the lower echelons of economic administration. In most Peoples' Democracies, the decentralization of investment has in recent years been greater than in the Soviet Union — with probably inadequate provision for financial responsibility for investment choice at the periphery.

Apart from these empirically documented factors, however, it should be quite easy to construct self-propelling models of investment growth in centrally planned economies, corresponding quite closely to the early Hicksian or Kaldorian models of cumulative income expansion[1]. All that needs to be done

[1] J. R. Hicks, *Contribution to the Theory of the Trade Cycle,* Oxford, 1949; Nicholas Kaldor, "A Model of the Trade Cycle," *Economic Journal* 50, March, 1940.

is to cast investment in the role of income, dividing it into "pipeline investment" and "completions," somewhat as income is divided into investment and consumption. It might then be quite plausible to argue that completions were a function of total investment in some previous period (involving perhaps a "marginal propensity to complete"), and that pipeline investment was some function of the *growth* in total investment (involving perhaps some sort of "gestation accelerator"). The interaction of these two principles could produce cumulative movements in investment in either direction; any nonlinearities dependent on the planners' views on the tolerable ceilings or floors to the ratio of uncompleted to operating capital stock could then produce the familiar reversals at high and low points. The planners would then have to live with this cycle until they became conscious of the "spontaneous forces" which their own idiosyncratic behavior had unleashed, and had learned to vary their actions accordingly. (I am plagiarizing a somewhat specialized terminology.)

Let us now consider the third characteristic of trade cycles – the element of self-reversion. Here the literature of socialist countries is a little more explicit: Kalĕcki, as quoted by Goldmann, speaks of a "raw material" and a "foreign trade" barrier which come into operation in relatively small, industrially developed countries whenever their rates of growth exceed certain "optimum" levels. Goldmann himself speaks more generally of "disproportions" (an overworked term in the literature) forcing a reduction in growth rates at the downturn, while the upturn is occasioned by the maturing of long-gestating investment projects, particularly in extractive industries. To his mind, the excessive growth rates of 1950–1951 in Czechoslovakia necessarily entailed the investment cuts of 1953–1954, while a new period of rapid expansion started in 1958 when many basic investment projects inherited from the early 1950's could be put into operation. But this in turn unleashed "subjective tendencies" which led to new excesses in investment whith their inevitable aftermath of disproportions and the subsequent decline of the early 1960's.

In the Soviet Union, a high ratio of uncompleted works to total investment has repeatedly led to blanket moratoria on new starts in construction – a crude and violent measure which can greatly reduce the growth and efficiency of investment activity as workers and resources are suddenly switched to a smaller range of projects. On the whole, as Nove reminds us, the practice of taking macroeconomic barometer readings intermittently, and only acting when these have reached putative danger levels, opens the way to sudden *volte-faces* in policy and to the kind of "overshooting" which is an ingredient of many trade-cycle situations. We need not, I imagine, go into the semantic issue of whether such policy decisions ought to be classed as exogenous variables, or whether they are sufficiently conditioned by the timing and context in whch they occur to put them in the endogenous class.

If the notion is accepted that Peoples' Democracies show movements with all the characteristics of trade cycles (pervasiveness, self-propulsion, and self-reversion) and that the last two of these are present also in the investment cycle of the Soviet Union, then we are led to ask immediately what it is in the Soviet economy that prevents the investment tail from wagging the national income dog, as it apparently succeeds in doing in the Peoples' Democracies. It seems rather difficult to answer this question. No doubt, there is a good deal in Nove's suggestion that there was an overenthusiastic adoption of Soviet-type investment policies at very inappropriate times and places, and that the reaction to their unfavorable effects was correspondingly sharper. But this applies to the Peoples' Democracies only in the early 1950's. There was sufficient independence later on for it to be overcome. More should perhaps be made of the fact that these countries suffer from a much higher dependence on foreign trade (if "suffer" is the right word), and some of them also on agriculture, whose fluctuations have often been phased in such a way as to reinforce the fluctuations in general investment activity. The foreign trade and raw material barriers from which the Soviet Union is more or less immune must obviously be powerful destabilizers.

In contrast to market economies, however, it seems clear that the socialist countries should be enabled to keep their fluctuations in bounds, owing to the absence of the signals and "carriers" which are apt to propagate them from one sector to another. Employment is kept stable whatever happens to output, and prices are unresponsive to variations in activity. Clearly, however, some of this must be achieved at considerable hidden cost in overall efficiency. The price of stable employment may be excessive fluidity of labor between occupations, with its corollary of lowered levels of skill and competence in any one of them. Labor productivity must also vary considerably when employment keeps steady in the face of fluctuations in output, though this is no doubt masked by aggregative figures. Lastly, the continuing production of output which a "pulsating" investment program cannot always fully utilize must exert variable pressure on the proportion of truly *useful* or *demanded* products in the total volume of output. If this were reflected in prices, as it would be in a market economy, it would certainly aggravate the cyclical effects throughout the economy. In fact, what market economies attempt to achieve through demand management, with less interference with economic criteria and signalling devices, socialist countries may achieve by allowing efficiency and rationality to vary unobtrusively, as the slack in the economy requires.

It is not yet clear how the economic reforms now under way in socialist countries will alter this situation. On the one hand, the introduction of capital costs and interest charges may remove certain institutional causes of the investment cycle. On the other hand, such changes as the shift from output targets to sales targets and the establishment of direct-order systems between customers and suppliers may strengthen the forces promoting efficiency at the expense of those making for stability. The same is clearly true of the increased powers of hiring and firing — and the added incentives to do the latter — which will accrue to individual factory managers in the future. It is difficult to assess how far the ostensible decentralization of pricing decisions in selected fields will open the way to a genuine responsiveness of prices to changes in demand; the powers so delegated in some Peoples' Democracies are still too narrowly circumscribed, and may be eroded by inflation. The Soviet Union is, in any case, far less adventurous than other socialist countries in this respect.

What does seem clear is that, at least in the Soviet Union, there are two secular trends which may increase the danger of fluctuations in the future. In the first place, a revolution of rising expectations is evident in the field of agricultural living standards. Although farm incentives have greatly increased in the last few years, they are still insufficient to stem the tide of internal emigration (especially of young and skilled males) from the countryside to the towns. The government, it seems, does not expect to be able to narrow (or reverse) the incentive gap sufficiently to cause much difference in this trend in the near future. Urban inflows will therefore continue at a time when stronger postwar age cohorts are entering the labor market and when the most productive technological changes in the Soviet Union are likely to be in the labor-saving direction. All this must clearly generate a new tendency for employment problems to arise. It is dangerous to suggest that the Soviet system is ill-equipped to deal with these; on the contrary, it should be dealt with more easily there than in many other systems. But the new situation must impose some changes in economic structure — perhaps a greater concern for the creation of employment opportunities in certain geographic areas, and a greater emphasis on selected labor-intensive branches, such as trade and services, in which there is also a greater leeway to be made up. To the extent that these branches are less amenable to central control than the traditionally favored steel mills, power stations, and the like, and to the extent that they are more consumer-oriented, the chance of fluctuations in the restructured economy seems to be definitely increased.

At the same time — and this is the second trend — the rising living standards of the Soviet population in general are bound to make consumers more selective in their purchases. More and more of them can afford to hold off the market for a time, if they do not like what is being offered. T'.c chance for sales problems to arise in these circumstances is obviously increased. There is no reason, of course, why the Soviet system should not develop responses to prevent such problems from escalating into general demand deficiencies. But new tricks will have to be learned, and some degree of demand management may eventually become necessary. The need for this will be even greater if investment demand is to be more decentralized, if consumer durables take on greater importance in family budgets, and if small-scale or shorter-lived modernization schemes come to make up a larger share of total investment activity as technology becomes cheaper and more flexible.

# IV ECONOMETRIC STUDIES

Chapter Twelve

# EXPERIENCE WITH ECONOMETRIC ANALYSIS OF THE U.S. "KONJUNKTUR" POSITION

MICHAEL K. EVANS
and LAWRENCE R. KLEIN
University of Pennsylvania

Economists in public agencies, private business, and academic life have displayed professional expertise since World War II in appraising the macroeconomy and in making policy recommendations regarding the main aggregative magnitudes— employment, gross national product (GNP), prices, investment, interest rates, etc. On the whole, professional opinion has been in agreement and correct, when compared with similar thought of an earlier era. There have, however, been disagreements and surprises. Unexpected deficits, inflationary pressures, or increases in unemployment have been experienced.

We do not mean to paint too rosy or harmonious a picture of professional life, but we do mean to point out that the trained economist has been able to go far in the application of general tools, especially those contained in the received body of doctrine known as macroeconomics. We should like to push this point a bit further now, and argue that, as well as general macroeconomics has done, it is capable of being pushed to a higher degree of refinement by the methods of econometrics; also that technical, quantitative methods can be applied to macroeconomic problems. We feel that econometric methods are now capable of making a further contribution, over and above the fine work already

The authors wish to express their gratitude to Nancy Blossom, Edward Green, Michael Hartley, Morris Norman, K. Sarma, and George Schink for invaluable and dedicated research assistance.

359

accomplished in general macroeconomics, to the economic stabilization and eventual obsolescence of the business cycle.

For the past four years, we have been regularly engaged in econometric analysis of the U.S. *konjunktur* position; we now would like to report on the promise held out by the experience. From the summer of 1963, we have been meeting quarterly with economists of a group of major U.S. corporations to assess the near-term outlook through the eyes of an econometric model. All of our industrial colleagues are attached to large firms dealing with national and world markets. (We could equally well have met with government economists.) Preliminary forecasts of economic activity are prepared before each quarterly meeting, and assumptions about exogenous variables are discussed at each meeting, together with specific information on strikes, bargaining progress, new models, effects of government regulations, market performance, etc. After each meeting, forecasts are recomputed on the basis of consensus about exogenous variables and special factors.

At the end of the first month of a quarter, we have a nearly complete set of preliminary data estimates for the preceding quarter. We estimate this preceding quarter with the model and adjust parameters where needed in order to make the model nearly duplicate the quarter just completed. This can usually be done by adjusting the constant terms of equations. (We do not add the previous period's residual to every equation, but adjust constants where equations are substantially off the mark and show some persistent bias over the past six quarters.) We also make use of information on economic disturbances, such as strikes. (The closing of the Suez Canal is another example of a piece of information that could not be ignored in model analysis of the current situation as of 1957.)

Once we have "zeroed in" on the preceding quarter, we solve the model for eight quarters—the one just beginning and the next seven. Not much can be said about individual quarterly values beyond that range; in fact, the second half of our extrapolation period is considerably more hazy than the first. Beyond two years, we can make only general trend extrapolations without pinpointing particular quarterly values.

The same model is used repeatedly in these forecast calculations, but every year or two parameters are re-estimated and the model is re-specified. The lagged inputs and exogenous variables are changed every quarter as data are revised and new information becomes available. Between quarterly forecast periods, there may be interim revisions of forecasts when new policy decisions are announced, or when major revisions in data are made.

We have emphasized *forecasting* in these remarks, but the pure attempt to foretell the pattern of future events is not the only use of econometric models in analyzing the current economic situation. It is our conviction that the intelligent implementation of economic policy, either public or private, demands a high accuracy in forecasts. The public official must know with some degree of precision what his actions are trying to avoid or bring about. Similarly, the private executive must know what to expect for his national operation, including economic outcome of actions by public officials.

To be of use in establishing economic stabilization policies, econometric models should be applied in a more general way than pure forecasting. It is equally important to say what economic activity might be if a variety of possible actions were undertaken. Hypothetical projections are as useful as pure forecasts. Moreover, there is considerable uncertainty surrounding the values placed on many exogenous variables. (As an example, it was practically impossible to say in late 1965 what U.S. defense expenditures would be in 1966.) A single forecast is therefore not recommended. A range of forecasts covering all the uncertain values of exogenous variables is the most revealing and fruitful. For public officials, this range is required to show what would be the effect of various alternative actions open to them.

Other important applications beyond pure forecasting are *simulation* and *multiplier* analyses. By simulation, we mean starting the model from given (initial) conditions and letting it develop its own subsequent lag inputs, given a specified time path of exogenous variables. For the system

$$f_i(Y_{1t}, \ldots, Y_{nt}, Y_1, {}_{t-1}, \ldots, Y_{n,t-p}, X_{1t}, \ldots, X_{mt}) = 0 \qquad i=1,2,\ldots,n,$$

we fix lags of endogenous variables

$$Y_{i,t_0-1}, \ldots, Y_{i,t_0-p},$$

and values of exogenous variables over the simulation period $(t_0,t_1,t_2,\ldots,t_q)$

$$X_{jt_0}, \ldots, X_{jt_q},$$

and solve for

$$Y_{it_0}, \ldots, Y_{it_q}.$$

For a particular $X_{jt_0}, \ldots, X_{jt_q}$, we have a simulation. Our best estimates in forecast situations make up a "control" simulation. Plausible alternatives may involve tax cuts or tax increases, war escalations or peace settlements, high or low bargains, easy or tight money. These are quantitatively simulated in terms of exogenous input or parametric changes. Other, or *ex post*, forecasts involve solving the model over historical periods, for which computed values of $Y_{it}$ can be compared with observed ones. Past economic events, such as the Revenue Act of 1964, can be simulated against a hypothetical solution with taxes left unchanged, in order to see how much economic growth can be attributed to the tax cut and how much would have come about without the cut. Such judgment is important in considering future tax policy.

In modern econometric analysis, the multiplier concept has been extended to encompass the effects of change in any exogenous variable, parameter, or combination of the two. For a simple change in any exogenous variable we compute

$$\frac{Y_{it}^d - Y_{it}^c}{X_{jt}^d - X_{jt}^c}$$

as the multiplier expression that shows the change in $Y_{it}$ ($Y_{it}^d$ = "disturbed" value; $Y_{it}^c$ = "control" value) by a change in $X_{jt}(X_{jt}^d$ = "disturbed" value; $X_{jt}^c$ = 'control" value). These multipliers can be evaluated at *impact* (first time period), *dynamically* (at points along the simulation path), or in equilibrium (after the simulation has come to long-run equilibrium). In later sections, we shall discuss simulations of the model and its major multiplier values, and also analyze forecast performance.

The original forecasts made in 1963, 1964, and part of 1965 were from the Wharton and the Evans models [1]. These two models were then merged into a single, larger system, using features of both. This is known as the Wharton-Econometric Forecasting Unit Model (Wharton-EFU) [2].

## Forecasting Properties of the Model

A first order of business in examining an econometric model is to establish its ability to predict. Modern computer technology has made it easier for the research economist to search his data thoroughly for high correlation coefficients and good *ex post* forecasts. Such methods tend to reduce the usefulness of standard statistical tests for determining the reliability of the estimated equations; the verification of the accuracy of the parameter estimates and the usefulness of the model tend more and more to depend on the record of *ex ante* forecasts. Even if the model is used primarily for policy simulations, the fact that it describes the real world accurately should be shown.

Unfortunately, the true *ex ante* forecasting record presently available for the Wharton–EFU model (and its predecessors) is not long; it covers only four years, 1963–1966. This was a period of uninterrupted expansion, so there has been no chance to test the predictive ability of the model at turning points of the entire economy. However, expenditures on consumer durables, inventory investment,

[1] L. R. Klein, "A Postwar Quarterly Model: Description and Applications," *Models of Income Determination*, Vol. 28 of *Studies in Income and Wealth*, Princeton, New Jersey, 1964; M. K. Evans, "Multiplier Analysis of a Postwar Quarterly U.S. Model and a Comparison with Several Other Models," *Review of Economic Studies*, October 1966.
[2] M. K. Evans and L. R. Klein, *The Wharton-Econometric Forecasting Model*, Philadelphia, 1967. A list of equations used in the model and of definitions of the variables is obtainable in this publication.

housing, imports, and exports all fluctuated during the period, so turning points are not entirely absent. (A survey of more than 50 forecasts since 1959 shows that years of recession have been predicted more accurately than years of continued expansion.)[3]. We would have preferred a longer and more varied period on which to base our predictive record, but the available period seems adequate for present purposes.

As explained in the first section of this chapter, forecasts are generated each quarter up to eight quarters ahead. (Forecasts of more than a year ahead, however, are often fuzzy because of lack of knowledge about exogenous variables. Consequently, these outlying quarters are omitted in the examination that follows.)

The comparison of predicted and actual values is complicated by a massive revision of data in mid-1965 and continuing changes since then. One way to assess the overall forecasting efficacy of the Wharton-EFU model, while sidestepping this problem, is to compare its predictions with certain other forecasts publicly released at the same time. Since these forecasts were all based on the same data and the same information about exogenous variables, they give a realistic picture of the overall predictive performance of the various models. The comparison of several annual predictions and the actual data are given in Table 12-1.

The slight downward error in the predictions of all models in 1965 and 1966 is due to the unforeseen rise in defense expenditures. The predictive accuracy of the Wharton-EFU model appears to be superior on the basis of then current information; and the record seems accurate enough to warrant an investigation of the detailed forecasts of that model.

It is not possible to compare quarterly and sectoral forecasts of the Wharton-EFU and other models, since, in general, these are not available for the latter. Instead, the predictive record will be based exclusively on comparison with actual values. To minimize complications arising from data revisions, we compare predicted with actual changes, defined as follows:

Predicted Changes: the predicted values at time $t + j$, minus the latest actual value available *at the time of prediction.*
Actual Changes: values taken from the July 1965 *Survey of Current Business;* these are 1963.II–1965.II pre-revised data.
Actual Changes: values taken from the January 1967 *Survey of Current Business.* 1965.III–1966.IV

(In a few instances, predictions three and four quarters ahead, originally based on the old data, were compared with extrapolations of those data instead of new data. This was done because the revisions in certain components of GNP

[3] M. K. Evans, *Macroeconomics, An Econometric Approach,* New York, 1969.

TABLE 12-1    Predictions of U.S. Gross National Product (GNP), Annually 1963–1966
(In billions of current dollars)

| Year | Wharton-EFU [a] | CEA [b] | Michigan model [c] | Avg of 50 [d] | Actual GNP old data [e] | Actual GNP new data [f] |
|------|------|------|------|------|------|------|
| 1963 | 585 [g] | 578 | 578 | 573 | 584 | 591 |
| 1964 | 625 | 623 | 619 | 616 | 623 | 632 |
| 1965 | 662 | 660 | 652 | 656 | 666 | 684 |
| 1966 h) | 728 | 722 | 725 | 725 | 732 | 743 |
| Av. abs. error | 2.7 | 5.5 | 7.7 | 8.7 | | |

[a]  Forecasts made in November or December of previous year (except 1966; see note g).

[b]  Forecasts of Council of Economic Advisors, taken from the *Economic Report of the President* available in mid-January.

[c]  Forecasts released in early November (except 1966). Details available from Professor Daniel B. Suits, Department of Economics, University of Michigan, Ann Arbor, Michigan.

[d]  Average of approximately 50 forecasts publicly released in the fourth quarter, compiled by the Federal Reserve Bank of Philadelphia.

[e]  Values of GNP based on most recent figures available at time of prediction.

[f]  Values of GNP available from most recent national income accounts at time of writing (February 1967).

[g]  Forecast actually made in early 1963.

[h]  In late 1965 and early 1966, a substantial escalation of the Vietnam conflict led to widespread escalation of GNP forecasts. A special additional release was tabulated by the Federal Reserve Board, based on new forecasts made during January. Our predictions were made with the Wharton-EFU model at the end of January. A revised prediction from the Michigan model was not available, so we increased the November forecast by $12 billion, the average difference between the fourth quarter and January tabulations of the FRB.

(consumer durables, fixed business investment, and inventory investment) differed from the old data by steadily increasing amounts [4].

As suggested in the previous section, we usually make several alternative forecasts each quarter in order to assess the effects of different monetary and fiscal policies. For purposes of the predictive record, however, we have used the "control solution," which incorporates our own best estimates of exogenous variables, as a basis for comparison in all cases.

---

[4]  The adjustments, in billions of dollars, used were $0.5, $1.0, and $0.5 a quarter, respectively. Except for these adjustments, the quarter-to-quarter changes in the revised data were used for extrapolation.

The first forecasts were made in early 1963 for eight quarters ahead. This pattern has been continued, except for a break following the massive data revision in mid-1965. The complete model was then re-estimated, because the nature and definition of many of the series had changed. The re-estimate was not completed until the end of the year, so that two quarters of predictions are missing [5].

With these modifications, detailed comparisons of predicted and actual changes are presented in Tables 12-2 to 12-5 for all major components of GNP one and two quarters ahead, for GNP up to four quarters ahead, and for the annual end-of-the-year forecasts. (The latter are actually five-quarter forecasts, made before the fourth-quarter results are known.) These forecasts are possibly more important than the others because of the preponderance of calender-year planning by both business and government. They are usually more accurate than forecasts made at other times of the year, because more is generally known at the end of the year than in mid-year about monetary and fiscal policies for the next four quarters (although this was not true of defense expenditures in late 1965).

Many of the results follow familiar patterns. The average absolute error of prediction for GNP one and two quarters ahead is much smaller than the absolute value of the sum of these errors for the individual components. The error of prediction of GNP for a four-quarter average is much less than the average of the errors from predictions one, two, three, and four quarters ahead. This occurs because many erratic quarter-to-quarter fluctuations cancel out. Such a result suggests that there is little evidence that errors accumulate; instead, the predictions tend to regress to the actual values. For the four-quarter average forecasts, the error ($3.6 billion) is smaller than the forecast error for only two quarters ahead ($4.3 billion).

It is hard to choose a completely objective measure for assessing the relative performance of each of the sector predictions. As mentioned previously, these cannot be compared with other models because comparable detail is not available. If the average absolute error is compared with the average absolute actual change, it appears that steadily increasing series, such as consumption of nondurables and services, are predicted much better than fluctuating series, such as inventory investment. This may in fact be the case, but such a test would suggest it even if it were not true. Similar comments can be applied to various naive models and other mechanistic tests.

In general, we think that the predictions of consumption of nondurables and services and fixed business investment were the best. For the first, the predicted values tracked the actual values closely in almost all quarters, including the

_____

[5] Some interim forecasts based on a hastily adjusted version of the old model proved unreliable and are not included here.

TABLE 12-2  Predictive Record of the Wharton-EFU Model One Quarter Ahead *(In billions of current dollars)*

| Variable | 1963-II A† | P‡ | Eφ | 1963-III A† | P‡ | Eφ | 1963-IV A† | P‡ | Eφ | 1964-I A† | P‡ | Eφ | 1964-II A† | P‡ | Eφ |
|---|---|---|---|---|---|---|---|---|---|---|---|---|---|---|---|
| $C_{ns}$ | 2.4 | 3.7 | 1.3 | 4.7 | 2.8 | −1.9 | 2.5 | 3.0 | 0.5 | 6.3 | 3.9 | −2.4 | 5.1 | 2.9 | −2.2 |
| $C_d$ | 0.4 | 0.3 | −0.1 | 0.7 | −2.4 | −3.1 | 1.4 | −1.9 | −3.3 | 2.3 | 0.7 | −1.6 | 1.1 | 0.1 | −1.0 |
| $I_p$ | 1.5 | 3.9 | 2.4 | 1.8 | 2.2 | 0.4 | 1.2 | 2.2 | 1.0 | 2.0 | 2.3 | 0.3 | 0.8 | 2.3 | 1.5 |
| $I_h$ | 0.8 | −0.8 | −1.6 | 0.3 | −0.2 | −0.5 | 0.8 | 0.2 | −0.6 | 0.7 | −0.3 | −1.0 | −0.7 | −1.0 | −0.3 |
| $\Delta I_i$ | 0.0 | 3.8 | 3.8 | 0.6 | 2.6 | 2.0 | 2.2 | 1.6 | −0.6 | −3.9 | −0.3 | 3.6 | 1.2 | 4.6 | 3.4 |
| $F$ | 0.9 | −0.1 | −1.0 | −0.1 | −0.9 | −0.8 | 1.6 | 0.4 | −1.2 | 1.9 | −1.1 | −3.0 | −2.0 | −3.0 | −1.0 |
| $G$ | −0.5 | 0.8 | 1.3 | 1.9 | 5.1 | 3.2 | 2.0 | 5.2 | 3.2 | 0.4 | 5.2 | 4.8 | 4.4 | 5.8 | 1.4 |
| GNP | 5.6 | 11.6 | 6.0 | 9.8 | 9.2 | −0.6 | 11.8 | 10.8 | −1.0 | 9.8 | 10.4 | 0.6 | 9.8 | 11.6 | 1.8 |

| Variable | 1964-III A† | P‡ | Eφ | 1964-IV A† | P‡ | Eφ | 1965-I A† | P‡ | Eφ | 1965-II A† | P‡ | Eφ | 1966-I A† | P‡ | Eφ |
|---|---|---|---|---|---|---|---|---|---|---|---|---|---|---|---|
| $C_{ns}$ | 6.8 | 5.6 | −1.2 | 4.4 | 4.8 | 0.4 | 5.7 | 5.3 | −0.4 | 6.4 | 4.8 | −1.6 | 7.5 | 5.6 | −1.9 |
| $C_d$ | 1.7 | 1.5 | −0.2 | −2.4 | −2.1 | 0.3 | 5.7 | 4.0 | −1.7 | −1.4 | −0.4 | 1.0 | 3.0 | −0.3 | −3.3 |
| $I_p$ | 1.5 | 2.8 | 1.3 | 0.8 | 2.3 | 1.5 | 2.0 | 1.6 | −0.4 | 0.7 | 3.0 | 2.3 | 2.6 | 1.6 | −1.0 |
| $I_h$ | −0.5 | −0.4 | 0.1 | −0.6 | 0.2 | 0.8 | 1.1 | 1.5 | 0.4 | 0.1 | −1.1 | −1.2 | 0.3 | −0.6 | −0.9 |
| $\Delta I_i$ | −0.9 | 1.5 | 2.4 | 2.9 | 1.7 | −1.2 | 1.1 | 0.9 | −0.2 | −1.1 | 1.4 | 2.5 | 0.0 | 2.2 | 2.2 |
| $F$ | 1.3 | −0.2 | −1.5 | 0.7 | −0.3 | −1.0 | −2.7 | −1.3 | 1.4 | 2.1 | 2.0 | −0.1 | 0.0 | 1.5 | 1.5 |
| $G$ | −0.1 | 1.8 | 1.9 | 0.5 | 1.6 | 1.1 | 1.0 | 2.0 | 1.0 | 2.6 | 2.8 | 0.2 | 4.2 | 3.5 | −0.7 |
| GNP | 9.8 | 12.6 | 2.8 | 6.2 | 8.2 | 2.0 | 14.0 | 14.1 | 0.1 | 9.4 | 12.4 | 3.0 | 17.6 | 13.5 | −4.1 |

| V* | 1966-II A† | P‡ | Eφ | 1966-III A† | P‡ | Eφ | 1966-IV A† | P‡ | φ | All quarters Average absolute change | Average absolute error |
|---|---|---|---|---|---|---|---|---|---|---|---|
| $C_{ns}$ | 6.7 | 7.7 | 1.0 | 5.9 | 9.3 | 3.4 | 3.9 | 6.6 | 2.7 | 5.3 | 1.6 |
| $C_d$ | −3.4 | −1.1 | 2.3 | 2.7 | 2.6 | −0.1 | −0.3 | −1.2 | −0.9 | 2.0 | 1.5 |
| $I_p$ | 0.4 | 1.7 | 1.3 | 2.5 | 2.3 | −0.2 | 1.6 | 2.3 | 0.7 | 1.5 | 1.1 |
| $I_h$ | −1.2 | −0.7 | 0.5 | −1.9 | 0.1 | 2.0 | −2.8 | 0.9 | 3.7 | 0.9 | 1.0 |
| $\Delta I_i$ | 4.1 | 2.1 | −2.0 | −2.6 | −2.9 | −0.3 | 7.1 | −0.5 | −7.6 | 2.1 | 2.4 |
| $F$ | −0.7 | 0.4 | 1.1 | −0.8 | 0.4 | 1.2 | −0.3 | −0.9 | −0.6 | 1.2 | 1.2 |
| $G$ | 4.7 | 3.4 | −1.3 | 6.5 | 4.9 | −1.6 | 4.0 | 5.6 | 1.6 | 2.5 | 1.8 |
| GNP | 10.6 | 13.4 | 2.8 | 12.3 | 16.7 | 4.4 | 13.2 | 12.8 | −0.4 | 10.8 | 2.3 |

Symbols are defined as follows:

$C_{ns}$ = consumption of nondurables and services  
$C_d$ = consumption of durables  
$I_p$ = investment in fixed plant and equipment  

$\Delta I_i$ = inventory investment  
$F$ = net foreign balance  
$G$ = government purchases of goods and services  

P† = predicted change  
Eφ = absolute error

366

TABLE 12–3  Predictive Record of the Wharton-EFU Model Two Quarters Ahead (*In billions of current dollars*)

| Variable | 1963-III A† | P‡ | E$ | 1963-IV A† | P‡ | E$ | 1964-I A† | P‡ | E$ | 1964-II A† | P‡ | E$ | 1964-III A† | P‡ | E$ |
|---|---|---|---|---|---|---|---|---|---|---|---|---|---|---|---|
| $C_{ms}$ | 7.1 | 7.8 | 0.7 | 7.2 | 5.1 | -2.1 | 8.8 | 8.6 | -0.2 | 11.4 | 11.9 | 0.5 | 11.9 | 9.4 | -2.5 |
| $C_d$ | 1.1 | 0.7 | -0.4 | 2.1 | -2.9 | -5.0 | 3.7 | -1.6 | -5.3 | 3.4 | 2.2 | -1.2 | 2.8 | 2.7 | -0.1 |
| $I_p$ | 3.2 | 4.9 | 1.7 | 3.0 | 2.7 | -0.3 | 3.2 | 4.0 | 0.8 | 2.8 | 3.8 | 1.0 | 2.3 | 3.6 | 1.3 |
| $I_h$ | 1.1 | -1.0 | -2.1 | 1.1 | -0.6 | -1.7 | 1.5 | -1.1 | -2.6 | 0.0 | -0.2 | -0.2 | -1.2 | -1.0 | 0.2 |
| $\Delta I_i$ | 0.6 | 2.8 | 2.2 | 2.8 | 0.5 | -2.3 | -1.7 | 0.9 | 2.6 | -2.7 | 0.2 | 2.9 | 0.3 | 5.1 | 4.8 |
| $F$ | 0.8 | -0.1 | -0.9 | 1.5 | -1.1 | -2.6 | 3.5 | 0.1 | -3.4 | -0.1 | -1.1 | -1.0 | -0.7 | -3.0 | -2.3 |
| $G$ | 1.4 | 2.8 | 1.4 | 3.9 | 7.1 | 3.2 | 2.4 | 7.2 | 4.8 | 4.8 | 7.2 | 2.4 | 4.3 | 6.8 | 2.5 |
| GNP | 15.4 | 17.9 | 2.5 | 21.6 | 10.8 | -10.8 | 21.6 | 18.2 | -3.4 | 19.6 | 24.0 | 4.4 | 19.6 | 23.5 | 3.9 |

| Variable | 1964-IV A† | P‡ | E$ | 1965-I A† | P‡ | E$ | 1965-II A† | P‡ | E$ | 1965-III A† | P‡ | E$ | 1966-II A† | P‡ | E$ |
|---|---|---|---|---|---|---|---|---|---|---|---|---|---|---|---|
| $C_{ms}$ | 11.2 | 11.0 | -0.2 | 10.1 | 11.0 | 0.9 | 12.1 | 11.0 | -1.1 | 12.3 | 10.7 | -1.6 | 14.2 | 12.4 | -1.8 |
| $C_d$ | -0.7 | 2.2 | 2.9 | 3.3 | 1.0 | -2.3 | 4.3 | 5.8 | 1.5 | 0.9 | -0.3 | -1.2 | -0.4 | 0.7 | 1.1 |
| $I_p$ | 2.3 | 4.2 | 1.9 | 2.8 | 1.8 | -1.0 | 2.7 | 5.1 | 2.4 | 2.9 | 4.0 | 1.1 | 3.0 | 5.0 | 2.0 |
| $I_h$ | -1.1 | -0.1 | 1.0 | 0.5 | 0.8 | 0.3 | 1.2 | 1.5 | 0.3 | -0.1 | -0.9 | -0.8 | -0.9 | -1.0 | -0.1 |
| $\Delta I_i$ | 2.0 | 0.6 | -1.4 | 4.0 | 3.9 | -0.1 | 0.0 | 3.2 | 3.2 | 0.0 | -2.0 | -2.0 | 4.1 | 1.4 | -2.7 |
| $F$ | 2.0 | -0.2 | -2.2 | -2.0 | -0.6 | 1.4 | -0.6 | -0.7 | -0.1 | 1.0 | 1.5 | 0.5 | -0.7 | 1.4 | 2.1 |
| $G$ | 0.4 | 3.6 | 3.2 | 1.5 | 3.0 | 1.5 | 3.6 | 3.8 | 0.2 | 6.0 | 4.3 | -1.7 | 8.9 | 7.0 | -1.9 |
| GNP | 16.0 | 21.3 | 5.3 | 20.2 | 20.9 | 0.7 | 23.4 | 29.8 | 6.4 | 23.0 | 17.3 | -5.7 | 28.2 | 26.8 | -1.4 |

| Variable | 1966-III A† | P‡ | E$ | 1966-IV A† | P‡ | E$ | All quarters V* Average absolute change | Average absolute error |
|---|---|---|---|---|---|---|---|---|
| $C_{ms}$ | 12.6 | 14.8 | 2.2 | 9.8 | 15.9 | 6.1 | 10.7 | 1.6 |
| $C_d$ | -0.7 | 0.1 | 0.8 | 2.4 | 3.1 | 0.7 | 2.3 | 1.9 |
| $I_p$ | 2.9 | 3.8 | 0.9 | 4.1 | 5.6 | 1.5 | 2.9 | 1.3 |
| $I_h$ | -3.1 | 0.4 | 3.5 | -4.7 | -0.1 | 4.6 | 1.3 | 1.4 |
| $\Delta I_i$ | 1.5 | 0.3 | -1.2 | 4.5 | -3.2 | -7.7 | 2.1 | 3.0 |
| $F$ | -1.5 | 0.0 | 1.5 | -1.1 | 0.2 | 1.3 | 1.3 | 1.6 |
| $G$ | 11.2 | 6.9 | -4.3 | 10.5 | 8.7 | -1.8 | 4.9 | 2.4 |
| GNP | 22.9 | 25.5 | 2.6 | 25.5 | 30.2 | 4.7 | 21.4 | 4.3 |

For footnotes, see Table 12–2.

TABLE 12-4  Predictive Record of the Wharton-EFU Model: Total GNP 1, 2, 3, and 4 Quarters Ahead *(In billions of current dollars)*

| | One quarter ahead | | | Two quarters ahead | | | Three quarters ahead | | | Four quarters ahead | | | Four-quarter average ending in given quarter | | |
|---|---|---|---|---|---|---|---|---|---|---|---|---|---|---|---|
| | Actual change | Predicted change | Error | Actual change | Predicted change | Error | Actual change | Predicted change | Error | Actual change | Predicted change | Error | Actual change | Predicted change | Error |
| 1963-II | 5.6 | 11.6 | 6.0 | 15.4 | 17.9 | 2.5 | | | | | | | | | |
| 1963-III | 9.8 | 9.2 | -0.6 | 21.6 | 10.8 | -10.8 | 27.2 | 21.8 | -5.4 | | | | | | |
| 1963-IV | 11.8 | 10.8 | -1.0 | | | | | | | | | | | | |
| 1964-I | 9.8 | 10.4 | 0.6 | 21.6 | 18.2 | -3.4 | 31.4 | 16.5 | -14.9 | | | | | | |
| 1964-II | 9.8 | 11.6 | 1.8 | 19.6 | 24.0 | 4.4 | 31.4 | 33.5 | 2.1 | 41.2 | 22.9 | -18.3 | 26.0 | 14.9 | -11.1 |
| 1964-III | 9.8 | 12.6 | 2.8 | 19.6 | 23.5 | 3.9 | 29.4 | 37.5 | 8.1 | 41.2 | 46.0 | 4.8 | 26.5 | 27.1 | 0.6 |
| 1964-IV | 6.2 | 8.2 | 2.0 | 16.0 | 21.3 | 5.3 | 25.8 | 32.9 | 7.1 | 35.6 | 48.9 | 13.3 | 23.6 | 30.2 | 6.6 |
| 1965-I | 14.0 | 14.1 | 0.1 | 20.2 | 20.9 | 0.7 | 30.0 | 26.0 | -4.0 | 39.8 | 42.7 | 2.9 | 23.8 | 27.7 | 3.9 |
| 1965-II | 9.4 | 12.4 | 3.0 | 23.4 | 29.8 | 6.4 | 29.6 | 31.5 | 1.9 | 39.4 | 35.9 | -3.5 | 23.9 | 24.0 | 0.1 |
| 1965-III | 14.6 | n.p. | ... | 23.0 | 17.3 | -5.7 | 34.9* | 29.0 | -5.6 | 41.3* | 36.2 | -5.1 | 24.3* | 24.0 | -0.3 |
| 1965-IV | 18.4 | n.p. | ... | 33.0 | n.p. | ... | 36.9* | 27.6 | -9.3 | 50.9* | 35.5 | -15.4 | 30.3* | 27.1 | -3.2 |
| 1966-I | 17.6 | 13.5 | -4.1 | 36.0 | n.p. | ... | 50.6 | n.p. | ... | 51.6* | 34.6 | -17.0 | 29.1* | 23.0 | -6.1 |
| 1966-II | 10.6 | 13.4 | 2.8 | 28.2 | 26.8 | -1.4 | 46.6 | n.p. | ... | 61.2 | n.p. | ... | 38.8 | n.p. | ... |
| 1966-III | 12.3 | 16.7 | 4.4 | 22.9 | 25.5 | 2.6 | 40.5 | 40.5 | 0.0 | 58.9 | n.p. | ... | 39.2 | n.p. | ... |
| 1966-IV | 13.2 | 12.8 | -0.4 | 25.5 | 30.1 | 4.6 | 36.1 | 39.5 | -3.4 | 53.7 | 53.1 | -0.6 | 33.5 | 33.4 | -0.1 |
| Average Absolute Error | | | 2.3 | | | 4.3 | | | 5.6 | | | 9.0 | | | 3.6 |

n.p. = no prediction made.
All actual changes through 1965-II are based on the old data: 1965-III and later are based on the new data except where * indicates an extrapolation of the old data has been used.

TABLE 12-5    Predictive Record of the Wharton-EFU Model Annual Forecasts made during the 4th Quarter of the Previous Year *(In billions of current dollars)*

| Variable | 1963[a] | | | 1964 | | |
| --- | --- | --- | --- | --- | --- | --- |
| | Actual change | Predicted change | Error | Actual change | Predicted change | Error |
| $C_{ns}$ | 13.6 | 14.1 | 0.5 | 19.6 | 19.2 | −0.4 |
| $C_d$ | 4.6 | 2.6 | −2.0 | 4.9 | 0.9 | −4.0 |
| $I_p$ | 3.2 | 4.9 | 1.7 | 5.6 | 7.7 | 2.1 |
| $I_h$ | 1.0 | −0.8 | −1.8 | 0.8 | 0.3 | −0.5 |
| $\Delta I_i$ | 1.2 | 1.9 | 0.7 | −0.7 | 2.9 | 3.6 |
| $F$ | 0.0 | −1.1 | −1.1 | 2.6 | −0.5 | −3.1 |
| $G$ | 6.4 | 9.4 | 3.0 | 5.9 | 10.4 | 4.5 |
| GNP | 30.0 | 31.0 | 1.0 | 38.7 | 40.9 | 2.2 |

| Variable | 1965 | | | 1966[c] | | |
| --- | --- | --- | --- | --- | --- | --- |
| | Actual[b] change | Predicted change | Error | Actual change | Predicted change | Error |
| $C_{ns}$ | 23.7 | 22.9 | −0.8 | 28.5 | 26.7 | −1.8 |
| $C_d$ | 5.1 | 3.9 | −1.2 | 4.3 | 2.6 | −1.7 |
| $I_p$ | 5.4 | 5.9 | 0.5 | 9.1 | 10.6 | 1.5 |
| $I_h$ | 0.1 | 0.7 | 0.6 | −2.6 | −1.2 | 1.4 |
| $\Delta I_i$ | 2.9 | 0.0 | −2.9 | 4.0 | −1.8 | −2.2 |
| $F$ | −1.3 | −0.2 | 1.1 | −1.9 | 1.1 | 3.0 |
| $G$ | 7.0 | 5.8 | −1.2 | 17.9 | 13.8 | −4.1 |
| GNP | 42.9 | 39.0 | −3.9 | 59.3 | 55.4 | −3.9 |

[a]  Forecast actually made in 1963, as model was not available before then.
[b]  Actual data based on extrapolation of old data.
[c]  Forecast made at the end of January 1966. For additional footnotes, see Table 12-2.

period of the large personal income tax cut. In all except the 1966.I forecasts, large errors of prediction in this sector can be traced to errors in predicting personal disposable income elsewhere in the model. In 1966.I, almost the entire error was due to a sudden and sharp rise in farm prices; while our constant dollar figures were reliable, the current dollar estimates were considerably underestimated. Investment in plant and equipment rose rapidly throughout the entire 1963–1966 period at an average annual rate of more than 13 per cent a year. The model predicted this increase very well at a time when most opinion, including the McGraw-Hill investment anticipations, suggested a lower rate of growth.

The most poorly performing sector was inventory investment, although the average error of prediction two quarters ahead is no larger than the error for one quarter ahead. Part of the error was caused by erratic fluctuations that were due to stockpiling for expected steel strikes and then decreasing stocks when strikes did not occur. Our adjustments for this movement were not successful.

The forecasts for consumer durables and housing present a mixed record. Early forecasts of consumer durable purchases were very poor and were responsible for a poor 1963.IV forecast (two quarters ahead). Since that time, the equations have been re-formulated and have yielded considerably better predictions. The predictions from the residential construction equation were moderately good until the most recent forecasts, when an almost unprecedented tightening of credit led to near collapse of the new housing market. While our housing equation contains a term representing tightness of credit, it is only a proxy variable, unable to handle situations of this severity. Further work is necessary for this equation.

Predictions of net foreign balance and government purchases of goods and services are largely exogenous. Although endogenous equations for imports and exports are used in the model, they depend largely on exogenous estimates of world trade and prices. Furthermore, no endogenous export equation was actually used for prediction during much of the period.

We have not discussed the predictive accuracy of the equations explaining wages, prices, interest rates, unemployment, income distribution, and other supply phenomena. Early versions of the Wharton-EFU model and its predecessors were skimpy in these areas. While substantial expansion of the model has been made recently, a complete set of forecasts for these variables is not yet available.

We believe that the forecasting record of the Wharton-EFU model is a contribution to the needs of business and government. It should dispel any lingering views that an econometric model cannot be used for effective short-term forecasting. Naturally, further improvements are intended. We are aware of the weak spots of the forecasts, and work is proceeding in those areas. In particular, attempts are being made to enlarge the supply side and to introduce more monetary variables into the system.

### Multiplier Analysis

Multiplier analysis is another very important use of econometric models. It does little good to predict future patterns of behavior without suggesting the amount of policy action, if any, that is necessary. Both blades of the scissors—accurate forecasting and methods of control—are needed to make econometric analysis a useful policy tool.

In this section, we discuss the results of several simulations calculated for the 40 quarter (hypothetical) period 1966–1975 by use of the Wharton-EFU model. The method of calculation is as follows. First, for these 40 quarters a "control solution" was calculated in which values of government expenditures and other exogenous variables were chosen to keep the unemployment rate at approximately 4 per cent. Since the model is nonlinear, the multipliers will vary depending on the level of unemployment (and capacity utilization) that is chosen. An unemployment rate of 4 per cent seemed to be a useful, although perhaps slightly optimistic, level to choose. This resulted in annual increases of 4 per cent in constant-dollar GNP and of 2 per cent in the GNP deflator. Both of these seem reasonable in light of previous experience. Several "disturbed" solutions were then calculated, in which the following exogenous variables were changed by the indicated amounts (changes for variables 1–6 are all in constant dollars):

1. A $1 billion increase in government defense expenditures ($G$ in Table 12-2)
2. A $1 billion increase in government nondefense expenditures ($G_d$)
3. A $1 billion increase in exports (for example, through an increase in the index of world trade) ($F_e$)
4. A decrease in personal income tax rates equal to a $1 billion decrease in taxes for 1965.IV levels of personal income ($T_p$)
5. A decrease in corporate income tax rates equal to a $1 billion decrease in taxes for 1965.IV levels of pretax corporate profits ($T_c$)
6. A decrease in excise tax rates equal to a $1 billion decrease in taxes for 1965.IV levels of national income ($T_b$)
7. A 5 per cent increase in the ratio of free reserves to required reserves, which corresponds to a $1 billion increase in the amount of money that banks have to lend ($FR$). (Other monetary policies are not considered because they act on the interest rate, and thus influence the economy, in the same manner.)

For each of these cases the dynamic path of the differences between the disturbed and control solutions of several key variables is presented in Tables 12-6 to 12-10.

The changes in GNP and other variables that are due to a change in government expenditures represent no problem of interpretation and can be considered as straightforward multipliers. However, this is not true of the other simulations. This is the reason why the generalized multiplier expression was defined in the first section of this paper as

$$\frac{Y_{it}^d - Y_{it}^c}{X_{jt}^d - X_{jt}^c}$$

When the change in tax rates is considered, the fact that $X_{jt}^d - X_{jt}^c$ represents the change in tax revenues at current incomes, not at original incomes, should be stressed. In other words, we are normalizing the changes in the endogenous variables by a quantity which increases over time. In this way, the change in the $Y$'s resulting from a change in government spending and a change in tax rates can be compared directly, even though the change in tax revenues is increasing over time [6]. Similar comments apply to changes in other exogenous variables.

[6] Strictly speaking, this is not an accurate procedure since $Y_{it}^d - Y_{it}^c$ depends on all the previous changes in the $X_i$ as well as the present change. But since the multiplier values change very little from one period to the next, this error is small.

TABLE 12-6 Changes in Constant-Dollar Gross National Product (GNP) Per $1 Billion Change in Selected Variables* *(In billions of 1958 dollars)*

| Quarter | $G$ | $G_d$ | $F_e$ | $T_p$ | $T_b$ | $T_c$ | FR |
|---------|------|------|------|------|------|------|------|
| 1 | 1.98 | 2.19 | 1.75 | 1.13 | 1.80 | 0.11 | 0.00 |
| 2 | 2.35 | 2.96 | 2.15 | 1.50 | 1.99 | 0.15 | 0.00 |
| 3 | 2.13 | 2.21 | 2.05 | 1.26 | 1.45 | 0.18 | 0.16 |
| 4 | 2.03 | 2.10 | 1.99 | 1.25 | 1.54 | 0.22 | 1.50 |
| 5 | 1.94 | 1.71 | 1.95 | 1.22 | 1.68 | 0.27 | 1.96 |
| 6 | 1.91 | 1.69 | 1.95 | 1.19 | 1.47 | 0.30 | 2.09 |
| 7 | 1.95 | 1.78 | 1.98 | 1.26 | 1.45 | 0.34 | 2.15 |
| 8 | 2.03 | 1.88 | 2.02 | 1.32 | 1.54 | 0.38 | 2.10 |
| 9 | 2.06 | 1.90 | 2.05 | 1.37 | 1.68 | 0.38 | 2.03 |
| 10 | 2.06 | 1.89 | 2.06 | 1.39 | 1.44 | 0.39 | 1.95 |
| 11 | 2.07 | 1.90 | 2.08 | 1.38 | 1.41 | 0.40 | 1.83 |
| 12 | 2.07 | 1.91 | 2.08 | 1.42 | 1.46 | 0.41 | 1.73 |
| 20 | 2.13 | 2.05 | 2.14 | 1.55 | 1.57 | 0.50 | 1.46 |
| 40 | 1.93 | 2.02 | 2.13 | 1.62 | 1.54 | 0.60 | 1.92 |

*For definitions of variables, see text.

TABLE 12-7 Changes in Unemployment Rate, Per $1 Billion Change in Selected Variables* *(In per cent)*

| Quarter | $G$ | $G_d$ | $F_e$ | $T_p$ | $T_b$ | $T_c$ | FR |
|---------|------|------|------|------|------|------|------|
| 1 | 0.25 | 0.23 | 0.20 | 0.06 | 0.10 | 0.01 | 0.00 |
| 2 | 0.29 | 0.31 | 0.23 | 0.10 | 0.14 | 0.01 | 0.00 |
| 3 | 0.25 | 0.23 | 0.22 | 0.08 | 0.08 | 0.01 | 0.01 |
| 4 | 0.23 | 0.20 | 0.20 | 0.07 | 0.09 | 0.02 | 0.15 |
| 5 | 0.21 | 0.16 | 0.19 | 0.06 | 0.10 | 0.02 | 0.17 |
| 6 | 0.21 | 0.16 | 0.19 | 0.06 | 0.08 | 0.02 | 0.16 |
| 7 | 0.22 | 0.16 | 0.19 | 0.06 | 0.06 | 0.02 | 0.15 |
| 8 | 0.22 | 0.17 | 0.19 | 0.07 | 0.07 | 0.02 | 0.12 |
| 9 | 0.22 | 0.17 | 0.19 | 0.07 | 0.07 | 0.02 | 0.10 |
| 10 | 0.22 | 0.17 | 0.18 | 0.07 | 0.06 | 0.02 | 0.08 |
| 11 | 0.21 | 0.17 | 0.18 | 0.07 | 0.05 | 0.02 | 0.05 |
| 12 | 0.21 | 0.16 | 0.17 | 0.07 | 0.04 | 0.02 | 0.03 |
| 20 | 0.20 | 0.15 | 0.16 | 0.06 | 0.05 | 0.02 | −0.05 |
| 40 | 0.15 | 0.12 | 0.12 | 0.04 | 0.03 | 0.02 | −0.07 |

*For definitions of variables, see text. A negative figure represents a *rise* in unemployment.

TABLE 12-8 Changes in the Implicit Gross National Product (GNP) Deflator, per $1 Billion Change in Selected Variables* (1958 = 100)

| Quarter | $G$ | $G_d$ | $F_e$ | $T_p$ | $T_b$ | $T_c$ | FR |
|---------|-----|-------|-------|-------|-------|-------|-----|
| 1 | 0.07 | 0.02 | 0.00 | 0.00 | −0.13 | 0.00 | 0.00 |
| 2 | 0.03 | 0.05 | 0.00 | 0.02 | −0.11 | 0.00 | 0.00 |
| 3 | 0.04 | 0.06 | 0.00 | 0.02 | −0.10 | 0.00 | 0.00 |
| 4 | 0.05 | 0.07 | 0.00 | 0.03 | −0.10 | 0.01 | 0.01 |
| 5 | 0.05 | 0.07 | 0.00 | 0.04 | −0.10 | 0.01 | 0.03 |
| 6 | 0.05 | 0.08 | 0.01 | 0.04 | −0.09 | 0.01 | 0.05 |
| 7 | 0.05 | 0.08 | 0.01 | 0.04 | −0.08 | 0.01 | 0.06 |
| 8 | 0.05 | 0.08 | 0.01 | 0.04 | −0.07 | 0.01 | 0.08 |
| 9 | 0.05 | 0.08 | 0.01 | 0.04 | −0.07 | 0.01 | 0.09 |
| 10 | 0.06 | 0.08 | 0.01 | 0.04 | −0.06 | 0.01 | 0.10 |
| 11 | 0.06 | 0.08 | 0.01 | 0.04 | −0.07 | 0.01 | 0.11 |
| 12 | 0.06 | 0.08 | 0.01 | 0.04 | −0.08 | 0.01 | 0.12 |
| 20 | 0.09 | 0.09 | 0.02 | 0.05 | −0.08 | 0.01 | 0.14 |
| 40 | 0.13 | 0.13 | 0.03 | 0.06 | −0.04 | 0.01 | 0.20 |

*For definitions of variables, see text.

TABLE 12-9 Changes in Fixed Business Investment, Per $1 Billion Change in Selected Variables* *(In billions of 1958 dollars)*

| Quarter | $G$ | $G_d$ | $F_e$ | $T_p$ | $T_b$ | $T_c$ | FR |
|---------|-----|-------|-------|-------|-------|-------|-----|
| 1 | 0.00 | 0.00 | 0.00 | 0.00 | 0.00 | 0.00 | 0.00 |
| 2 | 0.21 | 0.28 | 0.16 | 0.24 | 0.39 | 0.02 | 0.00 |
| 3 | 0.25 | 0.36 | 0.20 | 0.28 | 0.38 | 0.04 | 0.08 |
| 4 | 0.24 | 0.30 | 0.20 | 0.27 | 0.34 | 0.06 | 0.25 |
| 5 | 0.25 | 0.33 | 0.21 | 0.30 | 0.38 | 0.08 | 0.56 |
| 6 | 0.27 | 0.31 | 0.24 | 0.32 | 0.47 | 0.11 | 0.81 |
| 7 | 0.28 | 0.35 | 0.26 | 0.34 | 0.46 | 0.12 | 1.02 |
| 8 | 0.31 | 0.38 | 0.29 | 0.33 | 0.48 | 0.15 | 1.20 |
| 9 | 0.33 | 0.39 | 0.31 | 0.37 | 0.49 | 0.16 | 1.31 |
| 10 | 0.33 | 0.39 | 0.33 | 0.39 | 0.51 | 0.17 | 0.37 |
| 11 | 0.32 | 0.37 | 0.34 | 0.38 | 0.45 | 0.17 | 1.38 |
| 12 | 0.32 | 0.36 | 0.34 | 0.39 | 0.45 | 0.17 | 1.38 |
| 20 | 0.29 | 0.33 | 0.24 | 0.36 | 0.39 | 0.17 | 1.20 |
| 40 | 0.21 | 0.27 | 0.28 | 0.32 | 0.34 | 0.16 | 1.21 |

*For definitions of variables, see text.

TABLE 12-10  Changes in Personal Disposable Income (DI) and Corporate Profits (π) Per $1 Billion Change in Selected Variables*, *(In billions of current dollars)*

| Quarter | G DI | G π | $G_a$ DI | $G_a$ π | $F_e$ DI | $F_e$ π | $T_p$ DI | $T_p$ π | $T_b$ DI | $T_b$ π | $T_c$ DI | $T_c$ π | FR DI | FR π |
|---|---|---|---|---|---|---|---|---|---|---|---|---|---|---|
| 1  | 1.14 | 0.50 | 1.29 | 0.63 | 0.87 | 0.47 | 1.61 | 0.47 | 0.91 | 1.01 | 0.16 | 0.05 | 0.00 | 0.00 |
| 2  | 1.35 | 0.71 | 1.70 | 1.02 | 1.09 | 0.66 | 1.80 | 0.70 | 0.74 | 1.56 | 0.21 | 0.08 | 0.00 | 0.00 |
| 3  | 1.29 | 0.67 | 1.36 | 0.85 | 1.07 | 0.64 | 1.68 | 0.65 | 0.50 | 1.37 | 0.23 | 0.09 | 0.09 | 0.06 |
| 4  | 1.27 | 0.67 | 1.35 | 0.83 | 1.07 | 0.64 | 1.71 | 0.68 | 0.56 | 1.43 | 0.27 | 0.11 | 0.77 | 0.58 |
| 5  | 1.21 | 0.70 | 1.12 | 0.79 | 1.05 | 0.65 | 1.70 | 0.72 | 0.87 | 1.28 | 0.31 | 0.14 | 1.01 | 0.87 |
| 6  | 1.16 | 0.73 | 1.07 | 0.85 | 1.04 | 0.68 | 1.65 | 0.76 | 0.57 | 1.49 | 0.33 | 0.16 | 1.09 | 1.04 |
| 7  | 1.20 | 0.75 | 1.11 | 0.89 | 1.06 | 0.69 | 1.70 | 0.79 | 0.60 | 1.43 | 0.35 | 0.19 | 1.12 | 1.18 |
| 8  | 1.25 | 0.79 | 1.17 | 0.93 | 1.09 | 0.71 | 1.72 | 0.83 | 0.64 | 1.49 | 0.38 | 0.21 | 1.08 | 1.31 |
| 9  | 1.28 | 0.81 | 1.18 | 0.96 | 1.11 | 0.72 | 1.75 | 0.88 | 0.83 | 1.43 | 0.38 | 0.22 | 1.00 | 1.44 |
| 10 | 1.29 | 0.81 | 1.18 | 0.98 | 1.11 | 0.73 | 1.77 | 0.91 | 0.50 | 1.63 | 0.39 | 0.24 | 0.92 | 1.55 |
| 11 | 1.32 | 0.81 | 1.21 | 0.98 | 1.15 | 0.73 | 1.75 | 0.90 | 0.53 | 1.51 | 0.40 | 0.24 | 0.83 | 1.61 |
| 12 | 1.32 | 0.82 | 1.24 | 0.98 | 1.16 | 0.74 | 1.80 | 0.92 | 0.54 | 1.56 | 0.41 | 0.24 | 0.75 | 1.62 |
| 20 | 1.54 | 0.88 | 1.38 | 1.11 | 1.27 | 0.75 | 1.89 | 1.02 | 0.59 | 1.64 | 0.45 | 0.28 | 0.34 | 2.10 |
| 40 | 1.67 | 1.13 | 1.57 | 1.56 | 1.43 | 0.81 | 2.02 | 1.19 | 0.66 | 1.91 | 0.52 | 0.34 | 0.29 | 3.50 |

*For definitions of variables, see text

The tables show the effects of these various policies on several alternative economic goals: full employment, price stability, and maximum growth. Balance of payments equilibrium is not represented explicitly, because it depends both on the reaction of world trade and prices to a change in GNP in the United States and on the direction of capital movements, particularly when monetary policy is changed. However, the balance of payments situation will deteriorate the more, the faster prices rise, because the sum of the short-run price elasticities of imports and exports (in the model) is more than two. Since equity considerations may also be a factor in alternative monetary and fiscal policies, we have included the effects on income distribution. The variables whose paths are traced out here are thus constant-dollar GNP, the unemployment rate, the implicit GNP deflator, fixed business investment (representing growth), and personal disposable income and corporate profits. In all the calculations, the differences between the disturbed and control solutions have been normalized so that all changes are relative to a $1 billion change in the exogenous variables.

A few salient features of these generalized multiplier values are worth noting:

1. The long-run effects on GNP of each of these policy changes are quite similar when normalized by the amount of the change, except for shifts in the corporate income tax rate, which have a much smaller effect per dollar. While the various short-run multipliers are quite different, it is certainly not unreasonable to suppose that any $1 billion original injection of spendable funds into the economy will in the long run produce approximately the same effect on GNP. The corporate income tax multiplier is much lower because of the small marginal propensity to spend out of retained earnings. In the long run, approximately ¾ of the after-tax profits accrue to dividends, which are presumed to be spent in the same ways as other personal disposable income. However, there is little relationship between changes in retained earnings and changes in fixed business investment, over any time period.

2. In the short run, changes in government spending have a substantially greater effect on GNP than do any of the changes in the tax rates. This is a familiar result, and occurs because the short-run marginal propensity to consume (mpc) is much less than unity. Defense spending has a greater initial impact than does nondefense spending; this occurs primarily through the effect of the former on orders, and thus on inventory investment. It is not surprising that this difference becomes negligible in the long run, since inventory investment adjusts with short lags and changes little thereafter.

Among the tax rate changes, the corporate income tax has almost no initial effect, since the change in after-tax profits is distributed to dividends quite slowly, and corporate saving does not affect fixed business investment except with a substantial lag. The short-run effects of the excise tax changes are greater than those of the personal income tax change in the example given, but this is not always the result. The excise tax cut considered here for the simulation was similar to the 1965 excise tax cut, which centered on highly price-elastic consumer durables. If a further change in excise taxes were to be applied to some product with a very inelastic demand, such as tobacco or gasoline, its effect would be smaller than that of the personal income tax.

The change in monetary policy has a much longer lag than that for any of the other policies examined, because it acts through fixed investment with lags from two up to ten quarters. However, it is fully as effective as the other policies in the second and succeeding years.

3. The short-run and long-run government expenditure multipliers are quite similar. In other models, including the present version of the Brookings model, government expenditure and other multipliers increase steadily [7]. The cause of the trendless behavior of our government multipliers seems to be an approximate counterbalancing of two forces: the gradual increase in mpc for consumer nondurables and services, and the stock-adjustment forces affecting consumer durables, fixed business investment, and inventory investment. Since the true values of the multipliers in the real world are not known, no compelling case can be made for stating that the impact multiplier should be approximately the same as, smaller than, or larger than the long-run multiplier. A strong case can be made, however, for introducing stock-adjustment functions in every component of aggregate demand for which the equilibrium stock of durable goods depends on past, as well as present, income or output.

4. The trade-off between price stability and full employment is somewhat blurred, since the price increases are substantially different for the various policies examined. Since the supply curve for fixed business investment is less elastic than for the overall economy, a policy change which primarily affects investment will cause a greater change in the overall price level than will be caused by alternative policies. Since exports have a relatively elastic supply curve, price changes will be minimized for an exogenous shift in exports. Because of differing supply elasticities in various sectors, a change in government expenditures will affect prices somewhat more than equal changes in tax rates.

5. The trade-off between high growth rates and full employment, at least in the long run, appears to be more serious than is sometimes assumed. Since labor and capital are substitute factor inputs in the long run, a policy that increases capacity the most may have a small positive or even a negative effect on employment. This would suggest that policies cannot be directed only toward rapid growth, but rather towards a policy of full employment as well.

---

[7] For a comparison of several of these models, see M. K. Evans, "Multiplier Analysis of a Postwar Quarterly U.S. Model," *op. cit.* See also J. S. Duesenberry, G. Fromm, L. R. Klein, and E. Kuh, (eds.) *The Brookings Quarterly Econometric Model of the United States,* Chicago and Amsterdam, 1965; G. Fromm and P. Taubman, *Policy Simulations with an Econometric Model,* Washington, 1966.

In summary, these simulations suggest that a change in government spending is the most effective policy move in the short run because it has the most rapid effects. However, in the long run the choice is much less clear clear-cut. All the policy alternatives examined here, except the change in corporate tax rates, result in approximately the same change in GNP; thus the choice of which policy action to use must be made on other grounds. An increase in exports, if achieved through market forces (not the simple expedient of granting subsidies) would be preferable, for it clearly increases the net foreign balance and leads to very little change in prices; while the changes in the unemployment rate and fixed business investment are similar to those for the government expenditure multipliers. Among the alternative fiscal policies, a decrease in excise taxes lowers the price level, a decrease in personal income taxes raises it slightly, while an increase in government spending has a somewhat greater effect on prices. Both tax changes have a larger effect than spending changes on investment but a smaller effect on unemployment; again the trade-off between these two variables is noted. It would seem that a change in government spending would be more beneficial for ending a recession or inflation, while either tax change would be preferable for keeping the economy growing near full employment. Conversely, a tax increase would have little effect on lowering the price level, but would reduce investment and capacity more than a cutback of equal magnitude in government expenditures.

## Historical Simulations [9]

Simulations of a model can be made forward in time over periods not yet reached, or over purely hypothetical and unrealistic phases. Alternatively, models can be solved for historical periods, either to try to duplicate history or possibly to indicate what might have happened if exogenous circumstances had been different. In this section, we shall consider some historical simulations to see what the model would have done had it been used for prediction in the past, to see how closely it moves with the actual time path of economic variables, and to see what its internal dynamics are. (We are here treating only nonstochastic simulations. Stochastic simulations have not yet been made for this particular model.)

---

[8] This statement should not be misconstrued. A larger increase in GNP will, *ceteris paribus*, lead to higher employment. But a policy which leads to a greater total capacity at the same level of aggregate demand will result in lower employment.

[9] Research on simulations of the model has been carried out by Professor George Treyz of Haverford College on a Research Participation Grant from the National Science Foundation to the University of Pennsylvania. He has kindly made some of his simulations available to us.

TABLE 12-11   Short-Run Forecast Errors, Wharton-EFU Model, 1952.III–1962.II

| Length of prediction | Mean absolute error | Standard deviation as per cent of mean actual | Mean absolute error | Standard deviation as per cent of mean actual |
|---|---|---|---|---|
| | GNP (*bill. curr.$*) | | GNP (*bill. 1958 $*) | |
| 1Q | $ 5.81 | 1.7% | $ 5.71 | 1.6% |
| 2Q | 6.79 | 1.9 | 5.90 | 1.8 |
| 3Q | 6.35 | 1.8 | 6.25 | 1.8 |
| 4Q | 6.52 | 1.9 | 7.32 | 2.0 |
| 5Q | 7.42 | 2.0 | 8.82 | 2.2 |
| 6Q | 8.54 | 2.2 | 10.33 | 2.5 |
| 7Q | 8.79 | 2.2 | 10.60 | 2.7 |
| 8Q | 8.99 | 2.2 | 10.89 | 2.8 |
| | Consumption (*bill. curr. $*) | | Nonresidential fixed investment (*bill. curr. $*) | |
| 1Q | $ 3.28 | 1.5% | $ 0.74 | 2.2% |
| 2Q | 3.45 | 1.6 | 1.54 | 4.3 |
| 3Q | 3.27 | 1.5 | 1.53 | 4.5 |
| 4Q | 3.14 | 1.5 | 1.40 | 4.5 |
| 5Q | 3.18 | 1.4 | 1.66 | 5.2 |
| 6Q | 3.69 | 1.5 | 2.04 | 5.7 |
| 7Q | 3.95 | 1.5 | 2.32 | 6.4 |
| 8Q | 4.50 | 1.5 | 2.52 | 6.9 |
| | Residential investment (*bill. curr.$*) | | Exports (*bill. curr. $*) | |
| 1Q | $ 0.84 | 4.8% | $ 0.64 | 3.7% |
| 2Q | 0.88 | 4.8 | 0.71 | 3.9 |
| 3Q | 0.91 | 4.8 | 0.76 | 4.1 |
| 4Q | 0.98 | 5.5 | 0.82 | 4.5 |
| 5Q | 1.08 | 6.2 | 0.89 | 4.8 |
| 6Q | .19 | 6.8 | 0.98 | 5.0 |
| 7Q | 1.29 | 7.2 | 1.08 | 5.3 |
| 8Q | 1.39 | 7.4 | 1.15 | 5.6 |
| | Imports (*bill. curr.*) | | Disposable income (*bill curr. $*) | |
| 1Q | $ 0.62 | 3.9% | $ 2.79 | 1.1% |
| 2Q | 0.59 | 4.0 | 2.71 | 1.2 |
| 3Q | 0.62 | 4.0 | 2.67 | 1.0 |
| 4Q | 0.65 | 4.1 | 2.81 | 1.0 |
| 5Q | 0.73 | 4.4 | 3.29 | 1.0 |
| 6Q | 0.76 | 4.3 | 3.62 | 1.1 |
| 7Q | 0.75 | 4.2 | 3.81 | 1.1 |
| 8Q | 0.76 | 4.0 | 4.14 | 1.1 |

TABLE 12-11    (Continued)

| Length of prediction | Mean absolute error | Standard deviation as per cent of mean actual | Mean absolute error | Standard deviation as per cent of mean actual |
|---|---|---|---|---|
| | GNP deflator (*1958:100*) | | | |
| 1Q | 0.22 | 0.3% | | |
| 2Q | 0.47 | 0.6 | | |
| 3Q | 0.56 | 0.7 | | |
| 4Q | 0.61 | 0.7 | | |
| 5Q | 0.64 | 0.8 | | |
| 6Q | 0.66 | 0.8 | | |
| 7Q | 0.66 | 0.9 | | |
| 8Q | 0.64 | 0.8 | | |
| | Manufacturing wage bill (*bill. curr. $*) | | Manufacturing employment (*mill. pers.*) | |
| 1Q | $2.89 | 4.1% | 0.39 | 2.8% |
| 2Q | 2.96 | 4.2 | 0.45 | 3.3 |
| 3Q | 2.70 | 3.9 | 0.41 | 3.0 |
| 4Q | 2.75 | 4.0 | 0.43 | 3.2 |
| 5Q | 3.06 | 3.7 | 0.47 | 3.2 |
| 6Q | 3.58 | 4.0 | 0.52 | 3.3 |
| 7Q | 3.90 | 4.1 | 0.54 | 3.4 |
| 8Q | 4.27 | 4.3 | 0.55 | 3.6 |
| | Nonmanufacturing wage bill, private nonfarm (*bill. curr. $*) | | Nonmanufacturing employment private nonfarm (*mill. pers.*) | |
| 1Q | $2.56 | 2.4% | 0.53 | 2.0% |
| 2Q | 2.65 | 2.5 | 0.56 | 2.2 |
| 3Q | 2.58 | 2.4 | 0.55 | 2.1 |
| 4Q | 2.59 | 2.3 | 0.62 | 2.2 |
| 5Q | 2.80 | 2.4 | 0.68 | 2.4 |
| 6Q | 2.98 | 2.5 | 0.74 | 2.6 |
| 7Q | 3.03 | 2.5 | 0.78 | 2.8 |
| 8Q | 3.04 | 2.6 | 0.81 | 3.0 |

SHORT-RUN PROJECTIONS

In analogy to actual forecasting situations, we have extrapolated the model ahead every quarter from 1952.III–1962.II for the next eight quarters. This is precisely the pattern we follow in actual forecasting practice; we start with new initial conditions each quarter, and project ahead for eight quarters. The projections discussed in this section are *ex post* forecasts. The only difference between our usual practice and the procedure used in these simulations is that in practice we adjust the constants so that we start an eight-quarter solution that is nearly correct in the preceding quarter. This makes a difference in our practical results, but this practice was not followed in the simulation calculations. Also, tax and transfer functions changed parametrically over the simulation period to reflect the changing laws that parameterize these functions.

All 76 endogenous variables included in the Wharton-EFU model have been extrapolated, and we have condensed the presentation here by reporting on a few leading variables: GNP (current and constant prices), consumption, investment, exports, imports, disposable income, price level, employment, and wage bill. Results in the form of mean absolute error (level terms) and ratio of standard deviation of error to mean actual values (percentage terms) are given in Table 12-11.

The error in GNP forecasting, either in current or in 1958 dollars, is just under $6 billion for a one-quarter projection and rises relatively little over eight quarters to a figure as large as $9–11 billion. The percentage errors look small, but they are calculated on a large base that moves in limited jumps from quarter to quarter. About ½ of the error is in consumption expenditures. The private nonresidential fixed investment error ranges between $0.75 billion and $2.5 billion, while the residential investment error is about $1.0 billion. Disposable income is projected with a smaller error, but this series is stabilized by taxes and transfers so that it has less dynamic movement than GNP. Wage payments (manufacturing or nonmanufacturing) are less closely estimated than is aggregate disposable income. The estimate of the overall price index seems to be fairly close. In eight-quarter projections, its average error is much less than a full index point. The standard deviations of error, expressed as a percentage of the mean observed values, are mostly under 5 per cent for the main components of national income and product, but the more volatile investment components have coefficients of variation as high as 7.5 per cent in eight quarters. These would be expected to be less reliably forecast than the smoother, more dependable components.

The discrepancies observed over this 10-year period are not unusual, either for models of this type of for other methods of analysis. For a standard of comparison, however, Table 12-8 presents our errors along with those reported for the model of the Office of Business Economics (OBE) of the U.S. Department of Commerce [10].

The error analysis of OBE refers to forecasts from one to four quarters ahead, made in the fourth quarter of each year 1952–1964. The model makes use of certain key variables on anticipations, which are available only at the end of each year, for succeeding four quarters. The simulations are helped considerably by starting after adjustments of constant terms in selected equations, so as to give

---

[10] M. Liebenberg, A. Hirsch, and J. Popkin, "A Quarterly Econometric Model of the United States: A Progress Report," *Survey of Current Business,* May 1966, pp. 13–39.

nearly correct results in the fourth quarter from which the projections are made. Our simulations have no adjustments. The comparisons in Table 12-12 are for only those major variables that have been presented in this form of analysis in the basic paper on the OBE model. The Wharton-EFU errors in the table are based on projections from the fourth quarter of each year, 1952–1961.

The OBE results are generally superior, and show the advantages to be gained by adjusting for initial errors and taking account of persistence or serial correlation of error in complete system solution. Some of the equations of the model have serially correlated errors. Even if individual errors are random in time, the process of generating complete system solutions of dynamic systems with lags induces serial correlation of errors in the simulation path; therefore, error correction can be extremely important. Whether or not the OBE *ex post* forecasts are helped in a relative sense by the use of anticipatory variables remains to be seen. Eventually, corresponding simulations of the Wharton-EFU model, obtained by using such variables, will be available.

While the OBE results are closer, *ex post*, for most variables in Table 12-12, this finding is not uniform. The EFU projections of price level and disposable income (after the first quarter) are superior. Consumption and residential investment projections are very nearly as good in the OBE model.

The OBE forecast errors *ex post*, are close to the *ex ante* values found in the

TABLE 12-12 Comparison of Short-run Forecast Errors, Wharton-EFU Model and OBE Model

|  | EFU | OBE | EFU | OBE | EFU | OBE |
|---|---|---|---|---|---|---|
|  | GNP | | GNP | | Consumption | |
|  | (bill. curr. $) | | (bill. 1958 $) | | (bill. curr. $) | |
| 1Q | 3.5 | 2.5 | 3.7 | 2.9 | 2.1 | 1.9 |
| 2Q | 6.2 | 2.6 | 5.7 | 2.6 | 2.4 | 2.0 |
| 3Q | 6.9 | 4.1 | 7.7 | 3.7 | 3.7 | 3.0 |
| 4Q | 6.5 | 3.7 | 7.3 | 3.4 | 3.5 | 3.6 |
|  | Nonresidential fixed investment | | Residential investment | | GNP deflator (1958:100) | |
|  | (bill. curr. $) | | (bill. curr. $) | |  | |
| 1Q | 0.7 | 0.6 | 0.9 | 0.7 | 0.2 | 0.3 |
| 2Q | 1.2 | 0.6 | 1.1 | 0.6 | 0.4 | 0.3 |
| 3Q | 1.4 | 0.7 | 1.0 | 0.8 | 0.5 | 0.5 |
| 4Q | 1.4 | 0.8 | 0.9 | 0.8 | 0.6 | 0.7 |
|  | Disposable income (bill. curr. $) | |  | |  | |
| 1Q | 2.1 | 1.4 |  | |  | |
| 2Q | 1.5 | 1.5 |  | |  | |
| 3Q | 2.6 | 3.0 |  | |  | |
| 4Q | 3.1 | 3.3 |  | |  | |

previous section for the Wharton-EFU model. Adjustments prior to forecasting were made in the genuine situation, *ex ante.*

### LONG-RUN PROJECTIONS

Another way of simulating the model historically is to fix exogenous variables over many periods—enough to cover several cyclical movements—and to solve forward from the starting point of fixed initial conditions. We have done this by simulating over a long stretch of the sample period, when exogenous variables can be fixed at their observed historical values. The objective here is to see whether the generated endogenous series have the trend and cycle dynamics of the corresponding observed data. We are not enquiring whether 1962 can be forecast accurately from the vantage point of 1952, or whether any intermediate point after 1954 can be so forecast, but whether we can generate some reasonable growth rates and business-cycle characteristics in a period of 12 years.

Again, we have simulations of all 76 variables, and this time we cover 48 quarters. Selected simulation paths are available in tables and graphs. That for GNP is presented as Chart 12-1. GNP projections in current and 1958 dollars follow the trends of the economy for 12 years, in a sense that actual and projected values are close at the beginning and the end of the period. The first business-cycle turning point (1953–1954 recession and recovery) is near the initial conditions and well picked out by the solutions. The 1957–1958 recession-recovery is not discerned at 1952.III even with correct exogenous variables, but some of the 1960–1961 business-cycle movement is depicted Very large residuals that appear between observations 10–21 (1954.IV–1957.III) would be considerably reduced, to the order of magnitude of $5.0 billion and smaller, if short extrapolations of a year or less were made in this period with new initial conditions.

For disposable income, price level, and consumption expenditures, the simulations remain close for almost three years, and then drift low. There would be a drastic reduction in error over the period of large discrepancy beginning 1955.I if the solution were started again with new lag values as initial conditions. Investment simulations are different in that they end on the track for the last three years, after having left the track at the end of the first three years. Again, the intermediate period of 1955–1958 would have been predicted much more closely from the end of 1954, using new initial conditions. There are definite business-cycle movements in the investment series, although some are missed, and the long-run trend is correct. For economic policy and decision-making, the best use of econometric models would seem to be in the short-run prediction and simulation. Over longer periods, the most that can be expected is correct trend generation.

Long-period simulations from other models are not readily found. However, these results may be compared with those obtained from the Brookings model over a similar period. The Brookings model has been simulated over 38 sample quarters, 1953.III–1962.IV [11]. The Wharton-EFU model is basically expressed in 1958 prices, while the Brookings model is basically expressed in 1954 prices; therefore to obtain comparable summary statistics of simulation accuracy, we tabulate

$$\frac{1}{T}\sum_{t=1}^{T}\left\{\frac{|X_t^{\text{actual}}-X_t^{\text{pred}}|}{X_t^{\text{actual}}}\right\}100 = \text{mean absolute percentage error.}$$

These are comparable as between the two models.

For main variables, such as GNP and investment, the EFU simulations are close at the beginning and the end of the period of calculation. The Brookings simulations are less close at the end of the run, but it should be stressed that the sample period of fit for many of the Brookings equations ended with 1960. The Brookings model simulations, like the EFU simulations, pick out the business– cycle turns quite well in 1953–1954, having been started from initial conditions near those cyclical quarters. Both models are poor in picking out later cyclical turns. Both have later turns but not at the precise points where the economy turned in 1957–1958 or 1960–1961. If the models are started again at the beginning of 1957–1958, they do better in displaying their relevant cyclical phases. The Brookings model does not show the 1960–1961 cycle as well as the EFU model does, but in long-run cyclical performance the two are roughly similar. This fact can be seen by comparing their mean absolute errors in simulation (Table 12-13). For aggregate GNP, the two systems are very close, with a slight edge in performance for the Brookings model; however, the results vary by components.

## Some Future Possibilities in Macroeconometric Research

In 1952, at a similar conderence, discussing "The Business Cycle in the Postwar World", each econometric model applicable to the types of problems considered was of obvious relevance. Now that we have had a poliferation of models throughout the world, we must justify our concentration in this paper on yet another model of the United States.

The Wharton-EFU model is probably the largest and most detailed that has been repeatedly applied to the study of actual economic problems when those probems were first discussed [12]. The applications have been both in the field

[11] These simulations are reported in the paper by A. L. Nagar, "Stochastic Simulation of the Brookings Econometric Model," delivered before the meetings of the Econometric Society, San Francisco, December 1966.
[12] The OBE model and some private corporation models of comparable size have, in fact, been repeatedly applied for internal use.

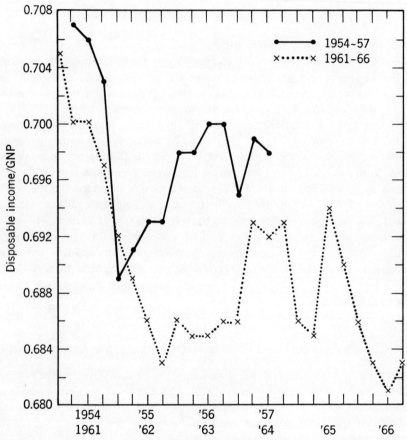

**Chart 12–1** Actual and predicted U.S. Gross National Product, annual rates by quarters, 1952.III 1964.II. (In billions of current dolar.[4])

TABLE 12-13    Mean Absolute Percentage Errors, Wharton-EFU Model
and Brookings Model (*In per cent*)

|                                          | EFU  | Brookings |
|------------------------------------------|------|-----------|
| GNP (*constant dollars*)                 | 2.32 | 2.03      |
| GNP (*current dollars*)                  | 2.79 | 2.70      |
| GNP deflator                             | 1.56 | 1.46      |
| Aggregate business investment*           | 6.28 | 8.49      |
| Aggregate consumption*                   | 3.19 | 1.55      |
| Disposable income (*current dollars*)    | 2.90 | 1.75      |

* EFU model data in current prices; Brookings model data in constant
prices.

of alternative policy formation and in forecasting. The Brookings model (of the
United States) and the Osaka model (of Japan) are larger than the EFU model,
but they have not been continuously updated and extrapolated within months
of the actual occurence of economic events.

The experience gained with the EFU model suggests that through the use of
models the economy can be tracked well enough to use models for public and
private business policy. For the near term, the EFU model is being, and will
continue to be, used with minor alterations in its present form for work in
applied economics. There is always, however, a new model on the drawing board
to supercede, eventually, those currently being used.

The work with the Brookings and Osaka models indicates that much larger
and more detailed systems are capable of providing solutions in the neighborhood of actual economic performance. It is certain that future work in improving
the EFU model will be in the direction of introducing more sectors (especially
supply and monetary sectors) and more markets to make it closer in size to these
larger systems. We have already found that useful industry projections can be
superimposed on EFU model solutions by using input-output and final demand
equations, like those in the Brookings model. The larger monetary sector of the
Brookings model can serve as a framework from which to build more detail on
cash holding and interest rates into the Wharton-EFU model.

Apart from integrating sector detail into a large macro model by using
input-output methods, we can also graft detailed models of individual industries
or sectors to a general master model. This approach, too, is being followed, with
improvements, in the present Wharton-EFU model.

In a paper presented at the 1952 conference, it was hinted that it would be
possible to combine ordinary economic time-series data in relationships with
data on expectations. This promise has been fulfilled in the EFU model [13].

---

[13] The original Wharton Model and the OBE model also make use of anticipatory data in
essential ways.

Our two-track model can use purely objective data in either short- or long-run projections (simulations). Certain equations (consumer durables, car expenditures, business investment, and housing) can be suppressed and replaced by alternative equations that are based on the use of anticipatory or contractual variables, such as buying plans, consumer attitudes, investment intentions, and housing starts. These forms of the system can be extrapolated ahead only as far as anticipatory data are given forward in time; although this limits the applicability of this kind of analysis, it is useful and interesting to carry out the analysis. As we have just begun this second of the two-track operations of the EFU model, its performance cannot yet be judged. We do know, however, that it was misleading in the old Wharton model in mid-1963. In subsequent periods, the Wharton model performed reasonably well. We expect to make fuller tests of simulation solutions of the EFU model, using the anticipatory data. Of course, the scope of these data can be extended to inventory, price, employment, and other forms of expectation.

The future EFU model will thus be large, eventually including 500-1,000 simultaneous nonlinear equations, and it may use more anticipatory data. It will incorporate new research on estimation of parameters, realistic assessments of standard errors, and better lag distributions. While we have made the transition from annual to quarterly models in the last ten years, so that almost all cycle-oriented econometric research is with quarterly series, we have not yet used monthly data. That, however, is one of the next items on the agenda of research in model building. We shall have even a finer tracking of the dynamic economy. We have often considered, and used in an experimental way, cross-section sample data for econometric model building. In a rough way, we have used anticipatory data from sample surveys, but we have not yet tried to generate a closed system of macroeconomic data from microeconomic observation. That remains as a possible avenue of research, but it is not clear that it will be as fruitful as the other lines of approach suggested here.

Michael K. Evans and Lawrence R. Klein

TABLE 12-14 **Actual and Predicted U.S. Gross National Product,**
**Annual Rates by Quarters, 1952.III–1964.II** *(In billions of current dollars)*

| Quarter | Actual | Predicted | Error Actual | Error Percentage |
|---|---|---|---|---|
| 1952-III | 345.377 | 352.866 | −7.489 | −2.168 |
| -IV | 357.855 | 358.754 | −0.899 | −0.251 |
| 1953-I | 356.383 | 365.497 | −0.114 | −0.031 |
| -II | 367.679 | 361.621 | 6.058 | 1.648 |
| -III | 365.928 | 358.972 | 6.956 | 1.901 |
| -IV | 361.160 | 355.501 | 5.658 | 1.567 |
| 1954-I | 360.531 | 354.495 | 6.036 | 1.674 |
| II | 359.828 | 353.173 | 6.655 | 1.850 |
| -III | 364.835 | 358.801 | 6.034 | 1.654 |
| -IV | 372.912 | 360.573 | 12.340 | 3.309 |
| 1955-I | 388.179 | 372.320 | 15.859 | 4.085 |
| -II | 392.658 | 377.552 | 15.106 | 3.847 |
| -III | 402.404 | 383.458 | 18.947 | 4.708 |
| -IV | 409.996 | 386.628 | 23.369 | 5.700 |
| 1956-I | 410.657 | 384.811 | 25.846 | 6.294 |
| -II | 416.692 | 392.861 | 23.832 | 5.719 |
| -III | 420.632 | 398.412 | 22.219 | 5.282 |
| -IV | 429.875 | 406.207 | 23.668 | 5.506 |
| 1957-I | 436.910 | 416.450 | 20.460 | 4.683 |
| -II | 439.890 | 421.841 | 18.049 | 4.103 |
| -III | 446.277 | 427.736 | 18.541 | 4.155 |
| -IV | 441.139 | 431.558 | 9.581 | 2.172 |
| 1958-I | 434.507 | 437.603 | −3.096 | −0.713 |
| -II | 438.431 | 443.943 | −5.512 | −1.257 |
| -III | 450.534 | 456.219 | −5.685 | −1.262 |
| -IV | 464.840 | 468.290 | −3.449 | −0.742 |
| 1959-I | 473.763 | 467.739 | 6.024 | 1.272 |
| -II | 486.852 | 470.643 | 16.209 | 3.329 |
| -III | 484.027 | 460.665 | 23.362 | 4.827 |
| -IV | 488.111 | 470.638 | 17.472 | 3.580 |
| 1960-I | 502.984 | 475.527 | 27.457 | 5.459 |
| -II | 504.318 | 473.589 | 30.729 | 6.093 |
| -III | 504.189 | 479.588 | 24.601 | 4.879 |
| -IV | 502.816 | 487.963 | 14.853 | 2.954 |
| 1961-I | 503.541 | 497.021 | 6.520 | 1.295 |
| -II | 515.231 | 508.064 | 7.166 | 1.391 |
| -III | 524.342 | 518.406 | 5.935 | 1.132 |
| -IV | 537.931 | 529.138 | 8.794 | 1.635 |
| 1962-I | 547.284 | 538.103 | 9.181 | 1.678 |
| -II | 557.182 | 549.187 | 7.995 | 1.435 |
| -III | 564.424 | 556.214 | 8.211 | 1.455 |
| -IV | 571.985 | 563.180 | 8.805 | 1.539 |
| 1963-I | 576.969 | 566.742 | 10.288 | 1.773 |
| -II | 583.170 | 569.756 | 13.414 | 2.300 |
| -III | 592.951 | 578.405 | 14.546 | 2.453 |
| -IV | 603.569 | 589.323 | 14.246 | 2.360 |
| 1964-I | 613.734 | 597.332 | 16.402 | 2.673 |
| -II | 624.509 | 611.408 | 13.101 | 2.098 |

387

TABLE 12-15  Quarterly Dynamic Multipliers of Government Expenditure on Gross National Product [a]

| Country | Model | Quarter | | | | | | | | | |
|---|---|---|---|---|---|---|---|---|---|---|---|
| | | I | II | III | IV | V | VI | VII | VIII | IX | X |
| Canada | (Rhomberg) | | | | | | | | | | |
| | (I) Flexible exchange rate | 1.5 | 2.4 | 2.8 | 3.3 | 3.6 | 3.6 | 3.5 | 3.2 | 2.9 | 2.4 |
| | (II) Fixed exchange rate | 1.8 | 3.1 | 3.7 | 4.5 | 5.0 | 5.2 | 5.2 | 5.0 | 4.6 | 4.1 |
| | (III) Fixed exchange rate | 1.8 | 3.1 | 3.7 | 4.7 | 5.4 | 5.8 | 6.0 | 6.1 | 6.0 | 5.8 |
| Japan | (Osaka) | 1.3 | 1.7 | 2.2 | 2.4 | 2.2 | 2.3 | 2.2 | 2.2 | | |
| U.S. | (Brookings) | 1.6 | 2.0 | 2.4 | 2.1 | 2.2 | 2.1 | 2.7 | 2.8 | 2.8 | 2.7 |
| | (Wharton-EFU) | 2.0 | 2.4 | 2.1 | 2.0 | 1.9 | 1.9 | 2.0 | 2.0 | 2.1 | 2.1 |

Sources: Rudolf R. Rhomberg, "A Model of the Canadian Economy Under Fixed and Fluctuating Exchange Rates," *Journal of Political Economy*, February 1964, pp. 1–31.

Shinichi Ichimura, "Dynamic Properties of the Osaka Econometric Model of the Postwar Japanese Economy, 1952–1961" mimeographed, no date.

M. K. Evans and L. R. Klein, "Experience with Econometric Analysis of the American 'Konjunktur' Position," Chapter 12.

Gary Fromm and Paul Taubman, "Policy Simulations with an Econometric Model," Brookings Institution, Washington, September 1966, Table 12-5.

[a] Multipliers for Canada and the United States are in constant dollars and those for Japan are in current dollars.

# COMMENT

PIETER DE WOLFF

University of Amsterdam

### STRUCTURE OF THE MODEL

This model is not as complex as some of the other models for the U.S., for example, the Brookings model. Nevertheless, it contains six producing sectors, namely, manufacturing, services, housing, agriculture, government, and foreign. (Government and agriculture are largely autonomous.) Consumption, investment, and imports are separated into various categories. In addition, the model contains two production functions.

The whole model is strongly dynamic. Most of the equations contain lags (up to 40 and 60 quarters in the capital stock equations). Quasi-accelerators appear in a few equations. For example, PB (nonfarm unincorporated business income) depends on the increase of the real national product (with different lags). The system, however, is too complicated to derive its dynamic behavior from these properties; therefore, the simulation experiments are particularly important.

Nonlinearities arise in the model from the identities stating that value equals volume times price, and also from the Cobb-Douglas production functions.

It is not surprising that the Wharton School indicator of capacity utilization, $C_p$, has been used in the model. This indicator is mainly based on the comparison, industry by industry, of actual and potential production. The latter is derived from trends adapted to peak values of actual production. Curiously, however, from equations (14) and (15) it follows that

$$C_p = \left( \frac{N_m h_m}{N_m^c} \right)^{4/3}.$$

Hence, potential production depends essentially on only the degree of employment of the civilian labor force in manufacturing. This is in line with Dutch models, which use a similar method because capital stock data are lacking. The

389

question arises: Why have Evans and Klein not used separate capacity indicators, one for capital and one for labor?

It is surprising to note that $p_m$, the deflator for gross output, is linearly dependent on $C_p$. Here, a curvilinear relation would have been expected.

Two measures of unemployment are used: $U$ for males of age 25–34 and $U_n$ for total unemployment. A complicated relation between the two is assumed; its static version expresses a hyperbolic relation, with a minimum for $U_n$ being 2½ per cent. The distinction is made because the wage rate, $wr_m$, depends on accumulated difference of the two during four consecutive quarters. The static relationship might lead to a perverse effect if total unemployment ever fell below 2½ per cent. More explanation would be welcome.

Professor Klein's preference for "real" models is well known, but the monetary content of the present model is larger than it is in his earlier models. The relations between $i_L$ and $i_S$ are practically the same as in the earlier versions, but the effect of monetary policy (through the influence of $FR$ and $i_d$ on $i_S$ and $i_L$) is now much more important, as interest rates are present in many behavior equations, especially in those explaining investment ($I_{pm}$, $I_{pr}$, $I_{pe}$, and $I_h$). In many cases, the effects of these variables are strongly lagged (at least two or three quarters), leading to a delay in the effect of monetary policy measures, which seems to be quite reasonable.

The model contains a large number of exogenous variables, dummies, forward indicators, demographic variables, variables related to the autonomous farm and foreign sectors, instruments (government and monetary variables), and a few others. These give rise to several questions:

Is is logically justifiable to use indicators and other explanatory variables in the same equation?

The indicators used to explain consumption ($C_{na}$ and $C_a$) do not seem to improve the result at all, but probably only increase the degree of multicollinearity. (The investment indicators seem to do better in this respect.) But, when forward indicators are used to improve forecasts, how are they treated in the discussion of alternative forecasts arising from different assumptions about the economic policy to be pursued?

Wages are treated as endogenous variables in the Dutch model, in spite of the existing wages policy. They are explained by productivity, cost of living, and unemployment. This last variable enters in a clearly curvilinear way (this part of the relation represents the so-called Phillips curve), and I am astonished that in Evans's and Klein's similar equation such effects are missing.

In small countries, the assumption is often—and correctly—made that the foreign sector is independent of internal developments. The same assumption has been made by Evans and Klein, but it is of doubtful accuracy for a large country like the United States.

It would also be very interesting to know what methods have been used to forecast the government and monetary variables.

FORECASTING PROBLEMS

Forecasts based on a model are subject to two different kinds of errors, namely, those caused by erroneous estimates of the exogenous variables (which again may be subdivided between controlled and uncontrolled variables) and those which are due to incorrect specifications. Evans and Klein report three series of experiments.

1. *Actual forecasts for 1963.II–1964.IV, one and two quarters ahead.* In this case, the two types of errors are obviously combined. The record is good, but changes in gross national product (GNP) are generally overestimated slightly, in contrast to normal experience with this type of forecasting. The results for the other variables (components of GNP, etc.) are usually less good, as could be expected. Still, the results are remarkable. The one-quarter error is, on the average, roughly twice as large as the two-quarter one. The correlation between $GNP_{act.}$ and $GNP_{pred.}$ is not very high in either case. The slopes of the regression lines differ considerably from unity, and again there is a clear difference between the one- and the two-quarter estimates. In the one-quarter estimates, below-average changes are usually overestimated, and above-average ones tend to be underestimated. For the two-quarter estimates, it is the other way round.

2. *Eight-quarter forecasts on a historical basis (ex post).* This experiment is interesting, as errors are now due only to the model. In this case too, the results are satisfactory. Errors tend to increase with the length of the forecasting period but at a decreasing rate. It would, however, have been easier to compare the performances for different variables if the errors had been expressed as percentages of the standard errors of the variables to be forecast.

3. *Long-term forecasts on the same basis as (2) for 48 quarters.* In this case the results are not particularly encouraging. The trend is fairly well represented, as are certain minor fluctuations, but the important cyclical movements around 1956–1960 have been missed almost entirely. These results are difficult to explain. Under the given circumstances, a model may do better in explaining fluctuations caused by exogenous forces rather than those which result from erratic disturbances. In short-term forecasting, the latter type is picked up to the extent that it occurs, whereas in long-term forecasting it is neglected. It is difficult, however, to consider that the cycle mentioned is mainly of erratic origin. It is also possible that the trend solution(s) of the system is (are) more correct than those explaining the cyclical fluctuations.

In this connection, it is interesting to consider the policy experiments carried out by Evans and Klein. I agree completely as to the value of such experiments.

The value of the model is greatly increased when it can be used for a discussion of policy problems in addition to its role in forecasting. Moreover, the long-term effects of the various policy simulations seem to be quite reasonable. But, when the time-shapes of the policy-impacts on various variables are studied, it is evident that the model tends to generate very short and heavily damped cycles (their length is of the order of six to eight quarters). This again raises some doubt with respect to the possibilities of the model explaining correctly the actual short-term fluctuations. However, too hasty conclusions should not be drawn. In some cases, much longer cycles are produced, for example, by changes in FR. Obviously, more has to be known about the dynamic properties of the system before definite conclusions can be reached.

### FURTHER OUTLOOK

I agree with Evans and Klein that it will be useful to develop larger models, preferably with sectoral disaggregation either in the model itself of through connected separate systems. Better statistical information will also be of paramount importance. And it may be very fruitful to try to derive a consistent set of macro data from micro information.

I should also like to add that it is very important that knowledge of the properties of the model should be increased, and that the effects of errors of measurement should be studied. In this connection, the experience of the Dutch Central Planning Bureau indicates that, even where considerable progress has been made in improving the models in use, the record of the forecasts of exogenous variables is not yet satisfactory.

[*Editorial Note*: Certain of Professor de Wolff's comments pertain to the equations and symbols of a preliminary version of the Evans-Klein paper. This preliminary version was available at the Conference, but was considered too long for publication here. We believe that Professor de Wolff's context makes his remarks understandable, despite condensation of the main Evans-Klein paper.]

Chapter Thirteen

# DYNAMIC PROPERTIES OF MACROECONOMETRIC MODELS: AN INTERNATIONAL COMPARISON

BERT G. HICKMAN
Stanford University

Economic theorists have been analyzing the dynamic properties of simplified difference-equation models of the business cycle for many years. As Samuelson showed in his famous 1939 article[1], the interaction between the multiplier and accelerator is capable of producing a variety of time paths of national income — damped or explosive, cyclical or noncyclical — according to the values of the underlying structural parameters: in the sequel, this basic lesson has been modified and amplified in numerous models by the addition of such factors as autonomous trends, ceilings and floors, and ratchet effects. On a more pedestrian, but nonetheless useful, level, numerical examples of the time paths associated with particular values of, say, the marginal propensity to consume and the acceleration coefficient are frequently given in elementary textbooks.

It is not yet so widely appreciated that analogous investigations of the dynamic properties of macroeconometric models are not only a natural extension of these analytical techniques but are potentially more revealing than the original applications. Because the econometric models are often much larger systems, there may be fewer qualms about their realism. Because they are fitted

I am indebted to Jay Siegel for his able computational assistance and to Robert Coen for his constructive comments on the text. I regret that circumstances prevented C. J. OHerlihy from preparing his formal discussion (at the conference) in time for inclusion here.

[1] Paul A. Samuelson, "Interactions Between the Multiplier Analysis and the Principle of Acceleration," *Review of Economic Statistics,* May 1939, pp. 75–78.

to actual data, their relevance to the real world economies which they purport to represent may be accepted with more confidence. Because their parameters are numerically specified, it is no longer necessary to speculate about the entire range of possible behavior. One may simply ask: What time path is generated by the single estimated structure?[2]. These advantages remain even after allowance is made for the imperfections of macroeconometric models in their present state of development.

This chapter compares a selection of 16 macroeconometric models for 10 countries[3]: Australia, Canada, the Federal Republic of Germany, Greece, Holland, India, Italy, Japan, the United Kingdom, and the United States of America. They could be examined from several points of view; for example, the specification of the model and the method of statistical estimation, or the forecasting record, or the information that the model conveys about the structural characteristics of a given economy. For the purposes of this chapter, I have concentrated on the stability implications of the models, with particular reference to the impact and dynamic multipliers they generate. However, this discussion also contains a substantial amount of information on the general structure of the models and on key parameters of the principal demand functions[4].

No exhaustive survey of existing models has been attempted, but there is no reason to believe that the models selected for comparison represent a biased sample as regards their cyclical properties. Some models have been excluded because dynamic multiplier estimates were not available, or could not be computed without undue effort[5]. The selection has also been influenced by the desire to achieve breadth and comparability of international coverage. Thus more space is devoted to annual than to quarterly models because the latter are unavailable for most countries. Greater comparability has also been sought by excluding several pioneering models that were fitted only to prewar data[6], and a few long-run growth models which appear less interesting from the cyclical viewpoint[7].

## Impact and Dynamic Multipliers

Forming multiplier estimates from linear macroeconometric models is a straightforward generalization of the familiar Keynesian concept. Just as in the

[2] The sensitivity of the solution to changes in the values of the parameters within, say, a given range of sampling error may also be studied.

[3] Twelve annual models and four quarterly models; see Tables 13–1 and 13–2.

[4] See Marc Nerlove, "A Tabular Survey of Macro-Econometric Models," *International Economic Review*, May 1966, pp. 127–175, for a qualitative comparison of the basic structural features of 25 models.

simplest Keynesian system, the estimates are derived from the reduced-form solution of the original structural equations. In the reduced form, each current endogenous variable is expressed as a function only of predetermined (exogenous or lagged-endogenous) variables[8]. The coefficient of each predetermined variable in a given reduced-form equation is the multiplier of that variable on the endogenous variable explained by the equation. The reduced-form multiplier coefficients are functions of the parameters of the structural equations, so that it is always possible in principle – though difficult in practice for large models – to relate the multiplier estimates explicitly to the structural parameters.

Since a structural analysis of the multiplier determinants can be most revealing, the foregoing remarks may be clarified by a simple hypothetical example, which illustrates the major features of the subsequent analysis. Assume the following structural system:

(1)   $C = c(Y - T)$

(2)   $I = a(Y - Y_{-1})$

---

[5] Excluded for this reason were (a) L. R. Klein, R. J. Ball, A. Hazlewood, and P. Vandome, *An Econometric Model of the United Kingdom,* Oxford, 1961; (b) G. Fromm, "Inventories, Business Cycles, and Economic Stabilization," in *Inventory Fluctuations and Economic Stabilization,* Part IV, Joint Economic Committee, U.S. Congress, 87th Session, Washington, 1962; (c) T. C. Liu, "An Exploratory Quarterly Model of Effective Demand in the Postwar U.S. Economy," *Econometrica,* July 1963, pp. 301–338; (d) T. M. Brown, "A Forecast Determination of National Product, Employment, and Price Level in Canada from an Econometric Model," in *Models of Income Determination,* Studies in Income and Wealth, Princeton, New Jersey, 1964; (e) L. R. Klein and Y. Shinkai, "An Econometric Model of Japan, 1930–1959," *International Economic Review,* January 1963, pp. 1–28; (f) H. Ueno, "A Long-Term Model of the Japanese Economy, 1920-1958," *International Economic Review,* May 1963, pp. 171–193; (g) N. V. A. Narashimham, *A Short-Term Planning Model for India,* Amsterdam, 1956; (h) D. B. Suits, *An Econometric Model of the Greek Economy,* Athens, 1964. In addition to the unavailability of dynamic multiplier estimates, models (a) and (f) lack comparability with the models surveyed herein because they employ a production index rather than gross national product as the basic activity variable; also model (h) lacks adequate endogenous investment coverage for dynamic extrapolation. The model of J. S. Duesenberry, O. Eckstein, and G. Fromm, "A Simulation of the U.S. Economy in Recession," *Econometrica,* October 1960, pp. 749–809, is omitted because it deals only with recession behavior.

[6] J. Tinbergen, *Business Cycles in the United States of America, 1919–1932,* Part II of *Statistical Testing of Business Cycle Theories,* Geneva, 1939, and *Business Cycles in the United Kingdom,* 1870–1914, Amsterdam, 1951; L. R. Klein, *Economic Fluctuations in the United States,* 1921–1941, New York, 1950.

[7] S. Valavanis, "An Econometric Model of Growth: U.S.A., 1869–1953," *American Economic Review,* May 1955, pp. 208–221; R. E. Caves and R. H. Holton, *The Canadian Economy: Prospect and Retrospect,* Cambridge, Massachusetts, 1959, pp. 129–140.

[8] In a linear model, let $y$ and $x$ be vectors of endogenous and predetermined variables and let $A$ and $B$ be coefficient matrices. Then the structural model is $Ay + Bx = 0$, and the reduced form is $y = Cx$, where $C = -A^{-1} B$ is the matrix of reduced form coefficients.

(3)   $M = mY$

(4)   $T = tY$

(5)   $Y = C + I + G + E - M.$

In this simple model, national income $(Y)$ is defined as the sum of consumer expenditure $(C)$, net investment $(I)$, government expenditure $(G)$, and exports $(E)$ minus imports $(M)$. Consumption is assumed to depend on disposable income $(Y - T)$, whereas taxes net of transfers $(T)$, and imports $(M)$ are functions of $Y$. Investment is related to the one-year change in national income by a simple acceleration coefficient. All variables are measured in constant dollars. All relationships are linear, and the constant terms are omitted for convenience. On the assumption that government spending and exports are determined exogenously, there are five equations in the five endogenous variables, $C, I, M, T,$ and $Y$. Their reduced-form solutions are:

(6)   $C = \dfrac{c(1-t)}{1-k}$   $(G+E) - \dfrac{ac(1-t)}{1-k}$   $(Y_{-1})$

(7)   $I = \dfrac{a}{1-k}$   $(G+E) - \dfrac{a(1-k+a)}{1-k}$   $(Y_{-1})$

(8)   $M = \dfrac{m}{1-k}$   $(G+E) - \dfrac{am}{1-k}$   $(Y_{-1})$

(9)   $T = \dfrac{t}{1-k}$   $(G+E) - \dfrac{at}{1-k}$   $(Y_{-1})$

(10)  $Y = \dfrac{1}{1-k}$   $(G+E) - \dfrac{a}{1-k}$   $(Y_{-1}),$

where  $k = c(1-t) + a - m.$

Equation (10) expresses $Y$ as a function of the two exogenous variables $G$ and $E$ and of the lagged endogenous variable $Y_{-1}$. Thus the time path of $Y$ will be determined partly by the time paths of $G$ and $E$ and partly by the system of induced responses summarized in the reduced-form coefficients. The simplest way of studying the dynamic properties of the model itself — that is to say, its response system — is to assume a permanent increase of one dollar in exogenous expenditure and then to trace the resultant behavior of $Y$ over time: through repeated use of equation (10)[9]. The initial effect of $G$ on $Y$, for instance, is measured by the "impact multiplier," or the coefficient of $G$ in this

---

[9] In small systems it is also comparatively simple to obtain a complete dynamic solution by an analysis of the characteristic roots of the "final" equation for, say, national product, but this is computationally difficult for larger ones.

reduced-form equation. In the present example, if $G$ should rise by one dollar, $Y$ would increase by $1/(1 - k)$ dollars in the same year. The response for the second year, however, would be modified by the lagged term for $Y$ — the multiplier would be equal to $1/(1 - k) [1 - (a/1 - k)]$ — and similarly for subsequent years. It is to take account of such variations over time that dynamic multipliers are calculated by successive iteration.

In the present illustration, the value of the impact multiplier, $1/(1 - k) = 1/[1 - c(1 - t) - a + m]$, is determined by the parameters of the consumption, investment, import, and tax functions. In general, the multiplier will be larger, the greater the scope for induced expenditure on domestically produced goods and services. Similarly, the multiplier will be affected by the scope of endogenous leakages — including business saving, taxes, and imports — from the income stream. Thus, the demand equations and saving and tax functions of the models discussed in this paper will be of particular interest when their multiplier properties are analyzed.

The multiplier values of a model will also be strongly influenced by whatever lags are involved in the structural equations. Suppose, for instance, that in the illustrative model the equation for investment were changed from $I = a(Y - Y_{-1})$ to $I = a(Y_{-1} - Y_{-2})$. This would change the reduced-form equation from

$$(10) \quad Y = \frac{1}{1 - k} \quad (G + E) \quad - \frac{a}{1 - k} \quad (Y_{-1}), \quad \text{to}$$

$$(11) \quad Y = \frac{1}{1 - (k - a)} \quad (G + E) + \frac{a}{1 - (k - a)} (Y_{-1}) - \frac{a}{1 - (k - a)} (Y_{-2})$$

where $(k - a) = c(1 - t) - m$. The value of the impact multiplier would be reduced, because no induced investment would occur in the first year of an exogenous expenditure change. This is true of several of the models to be examined later. Similarly, some of the models include both current and lagged endogenous determinants in the equations for consumption or investment demand; this has the effect of reducing the impact multipliers by decreasing the immediate or short-run marginal propensities to consume or invest.

The dynamic multipliers will also be sensitive to the lags in the system. If there are no lags at all, the model is static; all adjustments occur in the same year as the exogenous disturbance, and there is no distinction between impact and long-term multipliers. Once lags are introduced, however, the impact and long-run multipliers may differ from one another, the system may or may not tend to long-term equilibrium, and the time path may or may not evidence oscillations. Therefore, close attention should be paid to lags in the structural equations and to the behavior of the dynamic multipliers of the group of models.

The foregoing refers to linear models. Complications are introduced into multiplier analysis whenever nonlinearities appear in the structural equations. If a general reduced-form solution is still desired, it is necessary first to linearize the structural equations of the model[10]. In place of a general solution through linearization, however, impact and intermediate-run multipliers may be calculated by nonlinear methods for particular initial conditions and particular values of the exogenous variables. This procedure has the advantage of greater exactness than can be attained from a linear approximation to the original structure and is increasingly being used in simulation studies of large models.

### An Overview of the Models

A quick overview of the structural features of the main group of models to be compared is given in Table 13-1. All the models are of Keynesian persuasion, although they differ considerably in size and complexity. Among the components of aggregate demand, consumption expenditure and at least some components of investment are explained endogenously in all cases. Export demand is usually exogenous. Government spending is completely exogenous in all the models except that for India, in which public consumption is exogenous but public investment is aggregated with private investment in the investment function.

With regard to leakages from the income stream, imports are endogenous in 10 of the models and tax receipts in nine. Depreciation is endogenous in four of the models and four contain explicit equations for corporate saving. Personal saving is implicit in the consumption functions of all the models, of course, but the income concept used in several of these functions embraces corporate saving as well. Finally, in the two Australian models, a linear relationship between disposable personal income and GNP takes the place of explicit functions for taxes, depreciation, and corporate saving.

Apart from the common use of an income-expenditure framework for the determination of real GNP, there is considerable diversity among the models. This is due in part to the fact that the demand functions are specified in different ways, as will soon be shown. It also results, however, from the differing coverage afforded to variables other than real GNP and its expenditure components. Seven models explain employment, eight explain prices, but only five include both variables endogenously. Moreover, only three models contain endogenous monetary variables. All but three, however, provide some information on the functional distribution of income, usually in the form of a separation of labor from property income.

---

[10] For an excellent description and application of the linearization procedure, see A. S. Goldberger, *Impact Multipliers and Dynamic Properties of the Klein-Goldberger Model*, Amsterdam, 1959.

Another type of diversity concerns the size of the models. Thus one model for the United Kingdom contains only six endogenous variables or structural equations, whereas the Canadian model has 69. The number of endogenous variables is heavily dependent on the extent to which definitional equations and other nonstochastic relationships are proliferated, however, so that a better standard of comparison is provided by a count of stochastic equations[11]. On this basis, the range is from 4 to 31 equations.

All the models contain lagged endogenous variables; hence all are dynamic and may be solved for intermediate-run multipliers. Four of the models are completely linear, implying invariant multiplier sequences irrespective of the level of the economy. In two others − those for Italy and Germany − the nonlinearities appear in equations which break off from the rest of the system, leaving a complete linear model in the remaining endogenous variables including GNP. In the other nonlinear models, however, multipliers must be obtained either by linearization methods or by particular solutions.

Most of the models are fitted only to postwar data, but the parameters of three reflect prewar experience as well. Most of the models were estimated by consistent statistical methods, although three were fitted by ordinary least squares.

## Consumption Functions

The many changes rung on the concept of the consumption function by the model-builders in the group is readily apparent from Table 13-2. Eight of the models provide explanations only of aggregate expenditure on consumer goods and services whereas the others distinguish among several components. An important theoretical reason for disaggregating consumption expenditure is treatment of the acquisition of a durable good as a household investment decision rather than as a consumption decision, and thus to regard the latter as applying to the use of the services of the durable good rather than to its original purchase. This is the rationale for the disaggregation of durables in the Suits model of the U.S. economy, since Suits' equations for automobiles and other durables include the relevant stocks among the explanatory variables. None of the other models in which consumer expenditure is disaggregated, however, contains an "investment formulation" of the durable goods equation. Rather, the disaggregation is performed to take account of specialized exogenous determinants of certain consumption components, or to employ different lag schemes for different components.

---

[11] For instance, the Canadian model was designed for fiscal analysis and therefore contains large blocks of *a priori* tax and transfer functions grafted to a rather small aggregative behavioral model.

TABLE 13-1. Principal Structural Features of Annual Econometric Models for Ten Countries[a]

| Country | Model | Number of | | | Model contains functions explaining | | | | | | | | |
|---|---|---|---|---|---|---|---|---|---|---|---|---|---|
| | | Endogenous variables | Exogenous variables | Stochastic equations | Consumption | Investment | Exports | Imports | Tax yields | Depreciation | Corporate saving | Employment | Prices |
| Australia | (Kmenta) | 18 | 12 | 15 | yes | yes | no | yes | no | no | no | yes | yes |
| | (Nevile) | 9 | 5 | 7 | yes | yes | no | no | no | no | no | no | no |
| Canada | (May) | 69 | 131 | 11 | yes | yes | no | yes | yes | no | yes | yes | yes |
| Germany | (K-T) | 20[b] | 19 | 15 | yes | yes | yes | yes | yes | yes | no | no | yes |
| Greece | (Pavlopoulos) | 18[c] | 25 | 12 | yes | yes | no | yes | yes | no | no | no | yes |
| Holland | (CPB) | 38 | 21 | 13 | yes | yes | yes | yes | yes | no | no | yes | yes |
| India | (Marwah) | 9[d] | 5 | 7 | yes | yes | no | yes | yes | no[e] | no | no | yes |
| Italy | (Ackley) | 34 | 10 | 28 | yes | yes | no | no | yes | no | no | yes | no |
| Japan | (EPA) | 59 | 27 | 31 | yes | yes | yes | yes | yes | yes | yes | yes | yes |
| U.K. | (Ball) | 6 | 3 | 4 | yes | yes | no | yes | no | no | no | no | no |
| U.S.A. | (K-G) | 25[b] | 17 | 15 | yes | yes | no | yes | yes | no | yes | yes | yes |
| | (Suits) | 32 | 21 | 16 | yes | yes | no | yes | yes | yes | yes | yes | no |

TABLE 13-1. *(continued)*

| Model Includes | | | | Period of fit | Method of fit[g] |
|---|---|---|---|---|---|
| Monetary Variables | Income distribution | Lagged endogenous variables | Nonlinear variables | | |
| no | yes | yes | yes | 1946–1961 | LS, TSLS |
| no | yes | yes | no | 1949–1960 | LS |
| no | yes | yes | yes | 1927–1941<br>1946–1961 | LS, TSLS |
| no | yes | yes | yes | 1950–1960 | TSLS |
| no | yes | yes | no | 1949–1959 | TSLS |
| yes | yes | yes | yes | 1923–1938<br>1949–1960 | LI, TSLS |
| yes | no | yes | yes | 1939–1960 | TSLS |
| no | no | yes | yes | 1951–1960 | LS |
| no | yes | yes | yes | 1954–1965 | LI, TSLS, LS |
| no | yes | yes | no | Unstated | TSLS |
| yes | yes | yes | yes | 1929–1941<br>1946–1952 | LI |
| no | yes | yes | no | 1947–1960 | LS |

**Sources:** See references at end of paper.

[a] Models for Germany and Japan are semiannual.

[b] Augmented model including tax functions.

[c] Augmented model with disposable national income endogenous.

[d] Augmented model (variant 3) including tax and import functions.

[e] Model excludes depreciation, since basic activity variable is net national product (NNP).

[g] LS = Least Squares

TSLS = Two-stage least squares

LI = Limited-information maximum likelihood

TABLE 13-2    Basic Characteristics of Consumption Functions

| Country | Model | Consumption variable | Explanatory variables | | |
|---------|-------|----------------------|------------------------|---|---|
| | | | Current endogenous | Lagged endogenous | Exogenous |
| Australia | (Kmenta or Nevile) | Motor vehicles | Disposable nonfarm personal income | None | Tax rate on motor cars |
| | | Other cons. | Disposable nonfarm personal income | None | None |
| Canada | (May) | Durables | Disposable nonfarm wage income | None | Residential construction<br>Common stock price<br>Credit restriction (dummy) |
| | | Nondurables | wage income | Nondurable cons. | Household debt<br>Household liquid assets<br>Time trend |
| | | Services | wage income | Service cons. | Time trend |
| Germany | (K-T) | Total cons. | Wage component of national income<br>Nonwage component of national income | Total cons. | None |
| Greece | (Pavlopoulos) | Total cons. | Disposable national income | Total cons. | None |
| Holland | (CPB) | Total cons. | Disposable labor income[a] | Disposable nonlabor income [b] | None |
| | | | Consumer prices | Total cons.<br>Bank deposits | |

402

| | | Total cons. | National income | Liquid assets | Population |
|---|---|---|---|---|---|
| India | (Marwah) | Total cons. | | | |
| Italy | (Ackley) | Total cons. | Disposable national income | Disposable national income | Population |
| Japan | (EPA) | Total cons. | Disposable personal income | Total cons. | None |
| U.K. | (Ball) | Total cons. | Gross domestic product | Total cons. | None |
| U.S.A. | (K-G) | Total cons. | Disposable personal income | Total cons. | Population |
| | | | Disposable personal farm income | Personal liquid assets | |
| | | | Disposable personal nonwage, nonfarm income | | |
| | (Suits) | Auto and parts | Disposable personal income net of transfers | Stock of cars | Household liquid assets |
| | | Other durables | Disposable personal income | Stock of other durables | .. |
| | | Nondurables | ,, | Nondurable cons. | .. |
| | | Services | ,, | Services cons. | .. |

[a] Disposable labor income is actually lagged 1/4 of a year.
[b] Disposable nonlabor income is actually lagged 3/4 of a year.

TABLE 13-3. Estimates of Short-Run and Long-Run Marginal Propensities to Consume (MPC)

| Country | Model | Consumption concept | Income concept | Short-run MPC[a] by income type | | | | Long-run MPC by income type | | | |
|---|---|---|---|---|---|---|---|---|---|---|---|
| | | | | Total | Wage | Farm | Other | Total | Wage | Farm | Other |
| Australia | (Kmenta) | Auto | Disposable non-farm personal | 0.123 | | | | 0.123 | | | |
| | | Other | | 0.911 | | | | 0.911 | | | |
| | | Total | | 1.034 | | | | 1.034 | | | |
| | (Nevile) | Auto | ” | 0.130 | | | | 0.130 | | | |
| | | Other | | 0.978 | | | | 0.978 | | | |
| | | Total | | 1.108 | | | | 1.108 | | | |
| Canada | (May) | Durable | Disposable nonfarm wage | 0.091 | | | | 0.091 | | | |
| | | Nondurable | | 0.343 | | | | 0.519 | | | |
| | | Services | | 0.225 | | | | 0.506 | | | |
| | | Total | | 0.659 | | | | 1.116 | | | |
| Germany | (K-T) | Total | National | 0.666 | 0.708 | | 0.602 | 0.822 | 0.874 | | |
| Greece | (Pavlo-poulos) | Total | Disposable national | 0.609 | | | | 0.820 | | | 0.743 |

| | | | | | | | | | | | |
|---|---|---|---|---|---|---|---|---|---|---|---|
| Holland | (CPB) | Total | Disposable personal | 0.69 | 0.86 | | 0.41 | 0.69 | 0.86 | | 0.41 |
| India | (Marwah) | Total | National | 0.836 | | | | 0.836 | | | |
| Italy | (Ackley) | Total | Disposable national | 0.183 | | | | 0.835 | | | |
| Japan | (EPA) | Total | Disposable personal | 0.447 | | | | 0.833 | | | |
| U.K. | (Ball) | Total | Gross domestic product | 0.251 | | | | 0.677 | | | |
| U.S.A. | (K-G) | Total | Disposable personal | 0.50 | 0.55 | 0.34 | 0.41 | 0.66 | 0.74 | 0.46 | 0.55 |
| | (Suits) | Auto | Disposable personal | 0.177 | | | | ? | | | |
| | | Other durable | | 0.176 | | | | ? | | | |
| | | Nondurable | | 0.224 | | | | 0.282 | | | |
| | | Services | | 0.091 | | | | 0.194 | | | |
| | | Total | | 0.668 | | | | ? | | | |

[a] First half-year in German and Japanese models and first year in other models.

Income is the principal explanatory variable in all the consumption functions. In conformity with the usual theoretical specification of a Keynesian model, some variant of disposable personal income is the concept most commonly used in these equations, although some use national income instead. Three of the models also distinguish between labor and property income, in order to allow for differing consumption propensities as between these income types.

Many of the equations contain lagged values of consumption or income, implying different marginal propensities to consume in the short and long run. Other dynamic influences on consumption are present in the lagged terms for liquid assets in two of the models and for stocks of durable goods in the Suits model of the United States.

Estimates of the marginal propensities to consume implied by the various consumption functions are shown in Table 13-3. The most interesting comparisons concern the aggregative propensities, but a few preliminary words are in order about the methods by which the aggregative estimates were derived in those models which contain more than one consumption equation.

In the three models featuring separations between wage and nonwage income, the respective income shares were used as weights in averaging the separate marginal propensities. The weights for the German model are based on 1961 income data, those for Holland on 1957 data, and those for the Klein-Goldberger model of the United States on averages for 1928–1952. Most variables in the Dutch model are measured as percentage rates of change; hence their coefficients represent elasticities. Estimates of marginal propensities by income type must be inferred from the corresponding elasticities and for particular levels of income and consumption. Those shown in Table 13-3 are based on 1957 levels.

Four of the models provide separate estimates of the marginal propensities for different categories of goods and services. Since the same income variable enters linearly in all the equations of a given model, the aggregate marginal propensity is simply the sum of the marginal propensities for the several consumption components.

As already mentioned, several of the models distinguish between short- and long-term propensities by including lagged income or consumption in the equations. For those equations containing a lagged consumption term (Table 13-2), long-term marginal propensities shown in Table 13-3 are calculated in the usual way [12]. Where lagged income is involved, the coefficients of the current and lagged income variables are summed to give the long-run propensity. It is impossible to infer long-run propensities from the durable goods equations in Suits' model, however, since no distinction is made between net investment and

---

[12] Let $C = a + bY + cC_{-1}$. Then the short-run marginal propensity is equal to $b$, and the long-run one $= b/(1 - c)$, since $C$ is stationary in long-run equilibrium.

replacement demand in the specification of the equations. (Net investment in consumer durable goods would be zero in long-term equilibrium, and replacement demand is a function of neither income nor the stock of durables in his formulation.) Finally, for those models employing static consumption functions, the short- and long-term marginal propensities are equal by specification.

When estimated marginal propensities for the various countries are compared, it is important to remember that different income concepts are used in the consumption functions. The marginal propensities for Holland, Japan, and the United States are directly comparable in this respect, since all of them refer to disposable personal income. The short-term values range from 0.447 for Japan to 0.69 for Holland, implying substantial amounts of personal saving from income increments occurring in the same year.

The marginal propensities for Germany and India relate to national income, thereby allowing implicitly for leakages in the form of direct taxes, and of corporate as well as for personal saving. The relatively high values of the short-term propensities for these countries − 0.666[13] and 0.836, respectively − therefore imply even higher ones relative to personal income, and, hence, correspondingly low marginal rates of personal saving.

The British model goes even further in the aggregation of income leakages, since consumption is regressed directly on gross domestic product. Hence the low marginal propensity is not surprising, although − as shown later − it is in the lower range of the group when the other models are put on a comparable income basis.

The Italian and Greek models employ a concept of disposable national income in the consumption function, lumping together personal and corporate saving. The short-run marginal propensity for Italy is remarkably low, implying a substantial adjustment lag, but the long-run value of 0.835 is of the same order as the roughly comparable estimates for Germany and India. Both the short-run and long-run propensities for Greece are similar to those for Germany.

Finally, the Australian and Canadian models relate consumption to disposable nonfarm personal income and disposable nonfarm wage income, respectively. Since consumption expenditure by all income earners is related to only the nonfarm wage component of income received, it is not especially surprising that the short-run marginal propensity for Australia and the long-run one for Canada exceed unity. These values do not imply instability, since other leakages serve to reduce the marginal propensities with respect to GNP below unity, as shall be shown presently.

---

[13] The time unit in the German model is a half-year; the marginal propensity for a full year is even higher (0.775). The Japanese model is also semiannual, but the distributed lag in the consumption function does not operate until a full year has passed.

## Investment Equations

The investment equations in the collection are, if anything, more varied (Table 13-4). With regard to coverage, they range from a single explanation of aggregate private and public net capital formation in the Indian model to separate equations for five categories of private investment in the Italian one. Inventory investment is explained independently in most of the models, although it is aggregated with fixed investment in the Indian model and the Klein-Goldberger model for the United States, and is treated exogenously in the German model.

In Nevile's Australian model, and in the models for Canada, Germany, Holland, Japan, and the United States, some form of profit income is the main explanatory variable in the business fixed investment (plant and equipment) function. This formulation may be justified theoretically either by the argument that realized profit on existing capital determines expected profit on new capital, or by the argument that self-financing of investment expenditure is preferred by business either because of a lower opportunity cost for internal funds or because of lack of access to capital markets. The remaining models — those for Australia (Kmenta), Greece, India, Italy and the United Kingdom — use some measure of real output as the basic variable to determine business fixed investment[14]. The fixed-investment equations for the Italian model are accelerator or stock adjustment formulations, but the equations for Australia, India, and the United Kingdom contain no terms in capital stock or lagged income. Incidentally, although neither feature is essential in a profits formulation of the investment function, the fixed-investment equations of the two U.S. models and the Greek model include capital stock, and that of the Dutch model includes a capacity-utilization index.

In marked contrast to fixed investment, inventory change is determined by an accelerator or stock-adjustment equation in all models in which it is explained separately, except the one for Greece.

Four models feature separate treatment of residential construction. The most elaborate of these is Suits's formulation for the United States, which involves a stock-adjustment model (with desired stock a function of the spread between the ceiling rate on insured mortgages and the private bond rate) and which also allows for the influence of construction costs on the real value of residential construction expenditure. Kmenta's equation for Australia includes disposable income and the excess of households over dwelling units as explanatory variables; housing investment in the German model depends on national income and the interest rate, and in the Greek model it is made a function of disposable national income and the number of marriages.

---

[14] Pavlopoulos relied on a profits formulation in his theoretical specification of the fixed investment function, but was forced to use real national income as a proxy for profits, owing to the unavailability of profits data in the Greek national accounts.

TABLE 13-4.  Basic Characteristics of Investment Functions

| Country | Model | Investment variable explained | Explanatory variables | | |
|---|---|---|---|---|---|
| | | | Current endogenous | Lagged endogenous | Exogenous |
| Australia | (Kmenta) | Residential construction | None | Disposable nonfarm personal income; Excess of households over dwelling units | None |
| | | Business fixed investment | None | GNP | Net immigration |
| | | Change in nonfarm inventories | None | Ratio of nonfarm inventories to GNP | None |
| | | Expenditure of financial enterprises | None | GNP excluding farm income | None |
| | (Neville) | Gross private fixed investment | Corporate income | Corporate income | None |
| | | Change in nonfarm inventories | None | Change in GNP | None |
| | | Expenditure of financial enterprises | None | GNP excluding farm income | None |
| Canada | (May) | Business fixed investment | None | Business fixed investment; Gross disposable nonfarm income | Common stock prices; Unfilled orders for nonresidential construction; Time trend |
| | | Change in nonfarm inventories | Change in nonfarm production | Ratio of inventories to sales; Change in consumer durable purchases | |
| Germany | (K-T) | Business fixed investment | None | National nonwage income | Unemployment; Interest rate |
| | | Privately financed residential construction | None | National income | Interest rate |

(Table continued on following pages)

TABLE 13-4 *(continued)*

| Country | Model | Investment variable explained | Explanatory variables | | |
|---|---|---|---|---|---|
| | | | Current endogenous | Lagged endogenous | Exogenous |
| Greece | (Pavlopoulos) | Business fixed investment | None | Gross national income<br>Stock of plant and equipment | Govt. gross fixed investment |
| | | Residential construction | None | Disposable national income | Number of marriages |
| | | Change in agricultural inventories | Gross agricultural production | None | Agricultural exports |
| | | | Demand for agricultural products | | |
| Holland | (CBP) | Business fixed investment | Capacity utilization index<br>Prices of investment goods | Disposable non-labor income<br>Bank deposits | None |
| | | Change in inventories | Total output excluding inventories and invisibles<br>Profits per unit of output | Ratio of change in inventories to sales | Import prices |
| India | (Marwah) | Aggregate public and private net capital formation | National income | Aggregate public and private net capital | None |

| Country | Model | | | | |
|---|---|---|---|---|---|
| Italy | (Ackley) | Business fixed investment: | | | |
| | | (a) Mining, manufacturing, and construction | Value added in sector | Value added in sector | None |
| | | (b) Electric, gas and water | ,, | Investment in sector | Time trend |
| | | (c) Transportation and communication | ,, | Value added in sector | ,, |
| | | (d) Financial services, trade | ,, | ,, | ,, |
| | | Change in inventories | Gross domestic product | Inventories | None |
| Japan | (EPA) | Business fixed investment | None | Disposable corporate profits | Interest rate on bank loans |
| | | Change in inventories | GNP | Inventories | Interest rate on bank loans |
| U.K. | (Ball) | Gross private fixed investment | Gross domestic product | Gross private fixed investment | None |
| | | Change in inventories | Gross domestic product | Inventories | None |
| U.S.A. | (K-G) | Gross private domestic investment | None | Gross disposable nonwage income<br>Stock of private capital<br>Business liquid assets | None |
| | (Suits) | Business fixed investment | None | Disposable corporate profits<br>Stock of plant and equipment | None |
| | | Residential construction | Housing starts | Housing starts | Construction costs |
| | | Housing starts | None | Housing stock | Spread between FHA and VA ceiling interest rates and bond yields<br>Military purchases |
| | | Change in durable goods inventories | Sales of consumer durables | Durable goods inventories | None |
| | | Change in nondurable goods inventories | Sales of consumer durables | Nondurable goods inventories | None |

Only a small role for monetary factors is evident in this large group of investment functions. Neither interest rates nor liquidity variables appear in the Australian, Canadian, Greek, Indian, or Italian models. Interest rates affect business fixed investment in the German and Japanese models, inventory investment in the Japanese model, residential construction in both the German model and the Suits model for the United States. Liquidity variables are present in the aggregate investment function for the United States (Klein-Goldberger) and the business fixed investment function for Holland.

Estimates of the short- and long-run marginal propensities to invest implied by the investment equations are shown in Table 13-5. For the functions emphasizing a profits formulation, the concept of marginal propensity to invest is directly analogous to that of marginal propensity to consume. In the accelerator or capital-stock adjustment models, however, the marginal propensity to invest refers essentially to output produced rather than to income received; it is thus related to the capital coefficient. The specific income (or output) concept for each equation is repeated in Table 13–5 as a reminder tht marginal investment propensities are not always comparable between countries.

The first thing to notice about these investment propensities is that part or all of investment demand is lagged a full year behind its income determinant in most of the models (a half-year for Germany and Japan). This means that an impact multiplier is a seriously inadequate device to summarize the response mechanism, and that dynamic multipliers must be inspected as well.

Another point brought out by Table 13-5 is that many of the investment functions have peculiar dynamic properties. The response of net investment expenditure to a once-and-for-all change of output must be zero in the long run, since net investment will continue only until capital stock has fully adjusted to the higher level of output. Quite properly, all the inventory investment functions do imply zero net investment in long-run equilibrium[15]. With the fixed investment equations, however, various difficulties appear.

First, aggregate net capital formation is the dependent variable in the investment function for India, which is of the form $I_t = a + bY_t + cI_{t-1}$, with $0 < c < 1$. This function implies that a permanent increase in the level of national income would induce a permanent increase in the level of net investment expenditure, or, in other words, that a perpetually rising capital stock is consistent with a constant national income. This is clearly an improper equation for dynamic analysis.

---

[15] No "equivalent marginal propensity" calculation has been attempted from the elasticities of the Dutch inventory investment function. Its "quasi-accelerator" form implies a larger response in the short run than in the long run, but the function apparently also implies a non-zero long-term response. It may therefore be an exception to the statement in the text.

Second, the fixed investment equations of the Italian model imply zero investment in the long run, despite the fact that the dependent variable is gross investment. As Ackley remarked in his exposition of the model, "Strictly speaking, this is correct only if capital lasts forever – that is, if depreciation is zero"[16]. This unrealistic assumption limits the value of the model for long-period dynamic analysis.

Third, the models for Australia (Kmenta), Germany, and Holland imply the same marginal response of gross investment to profits or output irrespective of the time allowed for adjustment. There is no logical contradiction in assuming a permanent increase of replacement investment in the long run, but rather special and unlikely conditions would be required for the rise of replacement demand exactly to offset the fall of net investment as capital stock approaches equilibrium, as is implied by the equations in question. The nature of the required conditions can be explored with the aid of the following simple model:

(12) $\quad \Delta K_t = b(K^*_t - K_{t-1})\qquad (0 < b \leq 1)$

(13) $\quad K^*_t = aY_t$

(14) $\quad D_t = dK_{t-1}$

(15) $\quad I_t = \Delta K_t + D_t.$

In this formulation, net investment ($\Delta K$) is assumed to be a constant fraction ($b$) of the gap between desired stock ($K^*$) and actual stock ($K$). Desired stock and depreciation ($D$) are related respectively to output ($Y$) and actual stock. Finally, gross investment ($I$) is the sum of net investment and depreciation. Substitution of (12-14) into (15) yields the following expression for gross investment:

(16) $\quad I_t = abY_t - (b-d)K_{t-1}.$

Assume a once-and-for-all increase of $Y$ from an initial equilibrium position. In the first year of adjustment, only the income term will contribute to the increase of investment expenditure, which will amount to $ab\Delta Y$. The lagged term for capital stock will also make a contribution in subsequent years, however, provided that $b \neq d$. Thus, only if the speed of adjustment of desired to actual stock were equal to the depreciation rate on capital stock would a once-and-for-all increase of output induce a permanent and constant stream of gross investment. It is much more likely, however, that the speed of adjustment is greater than the rate of depreciation on fixed capital, implying a diminishing stream of gross investment over time rather than a constant one.

---

[16] Gardner Ackley, *Un Modello Econometrico dello Sviluppo Italiano nel Dopoguerra*, Rome, 1963, p. 24.

TABLE 13-5   Estimates of Short-Run and Long-Run Marginal Propensities to Invest (MPI)

| Country | Model | Investment variable explained | Income concept | MPI with relation to income in | | |
|---|---|---|---|---|---|---|
| | | | | Same year[a] | Preceding year[b] | Long run |
| Australia | (Kmenta) | Residential construction | Disposable non-farm personal income | 0 | 0.113 | 0.113 |
| | | Business fixed investment | GNP | 0 | 0.140 | 0.140 |
| | | Expenditure of financial enterprises | GNP excluding farm income | 0 | 0.012 | 0.012 |
| | (Nevile) | Gross private fixed investment | Corporate income | 0.705 | 0 | 1.448 |
| | | Change in nonfarm inventories | GNP | 0 | 0.310 | 0 |
| | | Expenditure of financial enterprises | ,, | 0 | 0.013 | 0.013 |
| Canada | (May) | Business fixed investment | Gross private nonwage income | 0 | 0.484 | 0.557 |
| | | Change in nonfarm business inventories | Nonfarm output | 0.129 | 0 | 0 |
| Germany | (K-T) | Business fixed investment | National non wage income | 0 | 0.231 | 0.231 |
| | | Residential construction | National income | 0 | 0.053 | 0.053 |
| Greece | (Pavlopoulos) | Business fixed investment | Gross national income | 0 | 0.165 | ? |
| | | Residential construction | Disposable national income | 0 | 0.025 | 0.051 |
| Holland | (CPB) | Business fixed investment | Disposable non labor income | 0 | 0.36 | 0.36 |
| India | (Marwah) | Aggregate public and private net capital formation | National income | 0.089 | 0 | 0.340 |

| Country | Model | Investment | Explanatory variable | | | |
|---|---|---|---|---|---|---|
| Italy | (Ackley) | Business fixed investment | | | | |
| | | (a) Mining, manufacturing, and construction | Value added in sector | 0.158 | 0 | 0 |
| | | (b) Electricity, gas, water | " | 1.823 | 0 | 0 |
| | | (c) Transportation, commerce | " | 0.840 | 0 | 0 |
| | | (d) Finance, service, trade | " | 0.481 | 0 | 0 |
| | | Change in inventories | Gross Domestic product | 0.162 | 0 | 0 |
| Japan | (EPA) | Business fixed investment | Disposable corporate profit | 0 | 1.47 | 2.56 |
| | | Change in inventories | GNP | 0 | 0 | 0.277 |
| U.K. | (Ball) | Gross private fixed investment | Gross domestic product | 0.080 | 0 | 0 |
| | | Change in inventories | Gross domestic product | 0.283 | 0 | 0 |
| U.S.A. | (K-G) | Gross private domestic investment | Gross disposable nonwage income | 0 | 0.78 | ? |
| | (Suits) | Business fixed investment | Disposable corporate profits | 0 | 0.60 | ? |
| | | Change in durable goods inventories | Sales of consumer durables | 0.291 | 0 | 0 |
| | | | Sales of producer durables | 0.591 | 0 | 0 |
| | | Change in nondurable goods inventories | Sales of consumer nondurables | 0.427 | 0 | 0 |

[a] The time unit is a half-year for the German and Japanese models.
[b] These MPI's refer only to functions with no current income term. No "second year response" is calculated for distributed lag or stock adjustment functions, although the cumulated long-run response is given whenever it is defined by such functions.

**TABLE 13-6. Basic Characteristics of Import Functions**

| Country | Model | Import variable explained | Explanatory variables | | |
|---|---|---|---|---|---|
| | | | Current endogenous | Lagged endogenous | Exogenous |
| Australia | (Kmenta) | Imports of goods and services | | Change in GNP | Lagged exports<br>Net immigration |
| Canada | (May) | Merchandise imports | Consumer durable purchases<br>Consumer nondurable purchases<br>Change in nonfarm business inventories<br>Private investment in machinery and equipment<br>Ratio of import price index to NNP price index | None | Time trend |
| Germany | (K-T) | Imports of goods and services | GNP | None | Import price index<br>Tariff rate |
| Greece | (Pavlopoulos) | Imports of goods and services | Gross national income | None | Export earnings |

| | | | | |
|---|---|---|---|---|
| Holland | (CPB) | Imports of commodities | Total output less inventory change and net invisibles<br>Change in inventories<br>Price of total output<br>Margin between prices of imports and total output<br>Cap. util. index [a] | Cap. util. index[a] | None current |
| India | (Marwah) | Imports of goods and services | National income | None | None |
| Japan | (EPA) | Imports of raw materials and fuel<br>Other imports | Index of industrial production<br>Change in inventories<br>Business fixed investment<br>GNP less business fixed investment | None | None<br>Customs rate |
| U.K. | (Ball) | Imports of goods and services | Gross domestic product | Inventories | None |
| U.S.A. | (K-G) | Imports of goods and services | Disposable national income<br>Ratio of import and GNP prices | Imports of goods and services | None |
| | (Suits) | Imports of goods and services | Private GNP | None | None |

[a] Capacity utilization index enters with a lag of one-half year.

TABLE 13-7.  Estimates of Short Run and Long Run Marginal Propensities to Import

| Country | Model | Import variable explained | Income concept | Marginal propensity to import with relation to income in | |
|---|---|---|---|---|---|
| | | | | Short run | Long run |
| Australia | (Kmenta) | Imports of goods and services | GNP | 0.34[a] | 0 |
| Canada | (May) | Merchandise imports | Consumer durable purchases | 0.641 | 0.641 |
| | | | Consumer nondurable purchases | 0.283 | 0.283 |
| | | | Change in nonfarm inventories | 0.353 | 0.353 |
| | | | Investment in machinery and equipment | 0.797 | 0.797 |
| Germany | (K-T) | Imports of goods and services | GNP | 0.424 | 0.424 |
| Greece | (Pavlopoulos) | Imports of goods and services | Gross national income | 0.066 | 0.066 |
| India | (Marwah) | Imports of goods and services | National income | 0.088 | 0.088 |
| U.K. | (Ball) | Imports of goods and services | Gross domestic product | 0.392 | 0.360 |
| U.S.A. | (K-G) | Imports of goods and services | Disposable national income | 0.006 | 0.032 |
| | (Suits) | Imports of goods and services | Private GNP | 0.06 | 0.06 |

[a] The short-run response is lagged one year behind the change in GNP in this equation

Fourth, the Australian (Nevile), Canadian, Japanese, and U.K. models imply an even higher marginal propensity for gross investment in long-run equilibrium than in the first year of adjustment. The distributed lag of gross investment in the Canadian model, however, follows a rising and falling pattern rather than the geometric lag of my example; it is conceivable under these circumstances that the long-run marginal propensity for (replacement) investment could exceed the short-run one for (net) investment even if the depreciation rate were smaller than the speed of adjustment. As for the Japanese equation, it implies a constant perpetual gross investment stream after the first year of adjustment to a once-and-for-all increase of profit income. Since a capital-stock term is omitted from the investment function, it is implicitly assumed that the speed of adjustment is equal to the depreciation rate, which is estimated elsewhere in the model to be about 0.08. This rate of adjustment is much too slow to appear realistic. Since Ball's and Nevile's models lack depreciation functions, it is impossible to make a similar estimate of the implicit speed of adjustment [17].

Finally, capital stock enters the gross investment equations of the Greek model and both U.S. models with a negative coefficient. This means that a diminishing stream of induced gross investment would accompany a sustained increase of national income or profits, as indeed appears realistic *a priori*. In order to estimate the long-term MPI's, however, it would be necessary to infer the equations for net investment demand and depreciation which underlie the gross investment functions. This task has not been attempted, since inventory investment is aggregated with fixed investment in the Klein-Goldberger equation, and depreciation is either unexplained (Pavlopoulos) or is not a function of capital stock (Suits) in the other models.

## International Trade

At least one model for each country, with the exception of Italy, includes an import function (Table 13-6). As in the investment and consumption functions cases, the variety of specifications mitigates against across-the-board analysis of the marginal propensities, although direct comparisons are possible among countries with similar explanatory variables (Table 13-7). No transformation of import elasticities into import propensities has been made for the Dutch model; nor are any propensities given for Japan where imports depend on the composition as well as the magnitude of GNP. It is clear from the multipliers presented later, however, that the import leakage for both countries is substantial.

---

[17] For a variety of reasons, the other models with constant long-run marginal gross investment propensities—those for Australia (Kmenta), Germany, and Holland—also lack sufficient information to estimate the implicit speed of adjustment.

TABLE 13-8. Basic Characteristics of Export Functions

| Country | Model | Export variable Explained | Explanatory variables | | |
|---|---|---|---|---|---|
| | | | Current endogenous | Lagged endogenous | Exogenous |
| Germany | (K-T) | Exports to (a) Europe | None | None | European industrial production<br>Time trend |
| | | (b) North America | German export prices | None | U.S. industrial production<br>U.S. wholesale prices weighted by German exports |
| | | (c) Latin America | German export prices | None | L.A. industrial production<br>Export prices of U.S., U.K. and Japan weighted by shares of these countries in L.A. exports |
| Holland | (CPB) | Commodity exports | Dutch export prices | Dutch export prices | Exports of closely competing countries |
| | | | Cap. util. index[a]<br>Price of total output | Cap. util. index[a] | Prices of competing exports |
| Japan | (EPA) | Commodity exports | None | Japanese export price index | Exports from noncommunist countries to total world<br>Export price index of 11 industrial countries |

[a] Capacity utilization index enters with a lag of 5/12 of a year.

In most models, the import functions are linear relationships implying equal short-term and long-term responses. The Kmenta equation for Australia, however, employs a simple accelerator relation lagged one year, so that the response is purely transitory. The Klein-Goldberger formulation for the United States, by contrast, involves a geometric buildup to the equilibrium propensity, whereas the Dutch and U.K. models feature an initial burst of imports followed by a decline to the ultimate equilibrium.

The marginal import propensity estimated by Pavlopoulos for the Greek economy appears to be too low, in view of the fact that imports averaged 1/5 of GNP during the 1950's. According to Suits' model for Greece, the marginal propensity to import with respect to disposable income is 0.227[18].

Exports are endogenous in only three of the models (Table 13-8). In the German model, moreover, export *prices* (and hence exports) are only nominally endogenous. They are completely determined by exogenous variables, and may be eliminated from the system without affecting the solution for the mutually interacting endogenous variables.

### The Impact Multipliers

The first-year multipliers for an exogenous increase of real government expenditure on real GNP are presented in Table 13-9. These are one-period impact multipliers for the annual models. The German and Japanese models are semiannual, however, and the one-year multipliers shown in the table were obtained by letting the models run for two periods.

The table also shows the marginal relationships between the major expenditure categories and GNP. In general, the GNP multiplier is equal to $1/1 - (MPC + MPI + MPE - MPM)$, where the marginal propensities to consume, invest, export, and import are all measured relative to GNP and may differ for different exogenous impulses. These marginal propensities can be read from the original demand functions, however, only for a model in which all demands are assumed to depend directly on GNP. As indicated earlier, this is true only of the British model in this survey. Yet, unless the various spending propensities are related to GNP, it is difficult to be precise about the major structural features accounting for the magnitude of the multiplier in a given model, let alone to make comparisons among models. Fortunately, it was possible to derive such GNP propensities for all but one model in the group. The exception is the Dutch model, which is discussed separately later.

[18] *Op. cit.,* p. 53.

TABLE 13-9. Short-Run "Marginal Propensities" with Respect to Real Gross National Product (GNP), and One-Year Multipliers of Real Government Expenditure on Real GNP[a]

| Country | Model | Marginal propensity to | | | | | | Spend[b] | One-year Multiplier |
| | | Consume | Invest | | | Export | Import | | |
| | | | Total | Fixed | Inventory | | | | |
|---|---|---|---|---|---|---|---|---|---|
| Australia | (Kmenta) | 0.596[c] | 0 | 0 | 0 | 0 | 0 | 0.596 | 2.48 |
| | (Nevile) | 0.596[c] | 0.098 | 0.098 | 0 | 0 | 0 | 0.694 | 3.28[d] |
| Canada[e] | (May) | 0.186 | 0.129 | 0 | 0.129 | 0 | 0.090 | 0.225 | 1.29 |
| Germany[f] | (K-T) | 0.601 | 0.066 | 0.066 | 0 | 0 | 0.424 | 0.243 | 1.32 |
| Greece | (Pavlopoulos) | 0.484 | -0.116 | 0 | -0.116 | 0 | 0.061 | 0.307 | 1.44 |
| Holland | (CPB) | n.a. | n.a. | n.a. | n.a. | n.a. | n.a. | n.a. | 0.48[g] |
| India[h] | (Marwah) | 0.730 | 0.077 | n.a. | n.a. | 0 | 0.077 | 0.730 | 3.70 |
| Italy | (Ackley) | 0.137 | 0.375 | 0.234 | 0.141 | 0 | 0 | 0.512 | 2.05 |
| Japan | (EPA) | 0.316 | 0.326 | 0.069 | 0.257 | 0.001 | 0.128 | 0.515 | 2.06 |
| U.K. | (Ball) | 0.251 | 0.363 | 0.283 | 0.080 | 0 | 0.392 | 0.222 | 1.29 |
| U.S.A. | (K-G)[f] | 0.194 | 0 | n.a. | n.a. | 0 | 0.007 | 0.187 | 1.23 |
| | (Suits) [i] | 0.226 | 0.067 | 0 | 0.067 | 0 | 0.060 | 0.233 | 1.30 |

[a] See footnotes [e], [h], [i] for modifications of income concept. Estimates for Germany and Japan are averages of semiannual values.

[b] Marginal propensity to spend is sum of consumption, investment, and export propensities, less import propensity.

[c] Includes automobile demand represented in model by separate equation.

[d] Calculated by Nevile from coefficients correct to five decimal places. The rounded marginal propensities shown above imply a multiplier of 3.27.

[e] Refers to nonfarm gross domestic product.

[f] Endogenous tax yield case.

[g] Assumes 15 per cent underutilization of capacity (severe unemployment).

[h] Refers to net national product (NNP) instead of GNP, and to simplified model with price level suppressed.

[i] Refers to private GNP (GNP less output of government services).

n.a. = not available.

TABLE 13-10. Impact Multipliers for Selected Endogenous Variables in the Dutch Model[a]

| Variable | Initial level of unemployment | | |
| --- | --- | --- | --- |
| | 1% | 2% | 15% |
| Gross national product | 0.15 | 0.26 | 0.48 |
| Consumption | −0.03 | −0.02 | 0.01 |
| Business fixed investment | 0.10 | 0.05 | −0.06 |
| Exports | −0.34 | −0.25 | −0.03 |
| Imports | 0.74 | 0.73 | 0.72 |

[a] Based on an exogenous increase of government expenditure. The multipliers for all variables except exports and imports are in constant dollars.

Two methods were used to derive the GNP propensities. In some of the simpler models a relationship between, say, consumption and GNP was obtained by substituting in the consumption function the relevant relationship(s) between the original explanatory variable(s) and GNP. In the more complex models — those for Canada, Greece, Japan, and the United States — the values were inferred from complete reduced-form solutions presented by the original model-builders. The marginal propensity to consume GNP, for example, was obtained as $\partial C/\partial Y = (\partial C/\partial G)/(\partial Y/\partial G)$. The inferred spending propensities relate specifically to an initiating change in government expenditure; they may change for other exogenous variables in the same model. The reader should recall also that values of the multipliers and spending propensities even for a given exogenous impulse are not constant in nonlinear models.

The multipliers range from 0.48 for Holland to 3.70 for India, with those for Canada, Germany, Greece, the United Kingdom, and the United States in the neighborhood of unity and those for Italy and Japan about two in value. What factors account for the similarities and differences among these estimates? A complete answer must be sought in detailed study of Tables 13-1 to 13-9, but some summary remarks will convey the gist of the story.

Among the multipliers clustered in the region of unity, no single factor accounts for their low values. The multipliers for Canada, Greece, and the United States are small primarily because of small consumption and investment propensities, whereas that for Germany is pulled down primarily by a high import leakage[19]. The Italian and Japanese multipliers are virtually equal, but for quite different reasons. Since different combinations of structural features

[19] As mentioned earlier, the marginal import propensity is probably underestimated in Pavlopoulos' model, biasing the multiplier upward. Suits obtained an impact multiplier of 0.98 with his model, in which the corresponding reduced-form marginal propensities were respectively 0.356, 0.052, and 0.429 for consumption, inventory investment, and imports.

can and do yield similar multipliers, no simple generalization can account for the range of multiplier values. It is more informative, therefore, to compare the factors affecting the several spending propensities than to compare the multipliers themselves.

First, the scope of endogenous demand functions within a model bear importantly on the value of the multiplier. Consumption and fixed investment are endogenous in all models. Only the German model treats inventory investment as exogenous, although it is aggregated with fixed investment in two other models. Exports are endogenous in the Dutch and Japanese models, but only in the former are they of any consequence in the short-run response mechanism (compare Tables 13-9 and 13-10). Import functions are lacking in one Australian model (Nevile) and in the Italian model. The impact and dynamic multiplier values for these two models would probably be much lower if allowance were made for induced import leakages.

Second, the values of the impact multipliers are strongly affected by lags in the demand functions. Thus part or all of induced investment demand is lagged a full year in the models for Australia, Canada, Greece, Holland, and the United States, and a half year in those for Germany and Japan, thereby diminishing the impact multipliers compared with a static system. The distributed lags in the consumption functions for Canada, Germany, Greece, Italy, Japan, the United Kingdom, and the United States (Klein-Goldberger) have a similar effect even though some consumption response occurs in the first period. Kmenta's import function for Australia is lagged a full year and the Klein-Goldberger import function includes a distributed lag — each lag tending to increase the computed impact multiplier.

Third, the multipliers depend on the marginal spending propensities with respect to GNP, whereas the structural demand equations often relate expenditures to other variables, such as personal income or profits. Thus, the multiplier relationships are affected by the degree to which induced changes in such items as tax receipts, transfer payments, business saving, and depreciation are incorporated in the models. An individual quantification of these income leakages was not attempted because of the complicated nature of the relevant structural relationships. Their combined impact may be judged from a comparison of the marginal propensities for the structural functions given in Tables 13-3, 13-5, and 13-7 with the reduced-form propensities in Table 13-9 [20].

The Dutch model requires special consideration. It includes a curvilinear indicator of capacity utilization in several of the structural equations, with the result that the multiplier effects of an exogenous expenditure change depend on the initial slack in the economy. The estimates presented in Table 13-10 show the impact multipliers for three different levels of unemployment. It is apparent from the table that the low multipliers for the model are primarily a reflection of the openness of Holland's economy and its heavy dependence on foreign trade. Import leakages are large, and an increase of domestic activity diverts substantial resources from production for exports unless unemployment is high. Since the structural relationships of the Dutch model are nearly linear at the 15 per cent unemployment rate, the corresponding GNP multiplier of 0.48 is the one most comparable to the estimates for other countries.

For most of the models included in this survey, the impact multipliers are lower than the values often implied in public discussions and textbook examples. For the most part, this is due to the fact that simple econometric models often omit important leakages and reaction lags included in the larger ones. It is also of considerable importance, however, that consistent estimating methods were used in most of the models, since it is known that ordinary least-squares estimates of spending propensities and multipliers for simultaneous equation systems are subject to upward bias.

With regard to reaction lags, the impact multipliers for some of these models are biased downward by the assumption that investment demand lags a full year behind income change (Australia, Canada, Greece, Holland, and the United States), since part of the adjustment doubtless takes less time. Similarly, models with geometric lags in the consumption equations) Canada, Germany, Greece, Holland, Japan, the United Kingdom and the United States) or the investment functions (Canada, India, Italy, and the United Kingdom) may underestimate the speed of adjustment and hence the impact multipliers, if there is serial correlation in the residuals. The importance of both types of bias is reduced, however, when attention is turned to dynamic multipliers with their longer adjustment periods.

## The Dynamic Multipliers

The dynamic multiplier estimates presented in Table 13-11 are interesting from several points of view. Because they allow for reaction lags, they are more informative than impact multipliers about the ultimate income response to an

---

[20] Precise estimates of the multiplier effects of incorporating endogenous tax functions are available for three of the models. The impact multiplier of the Klein–Goldberger model of the United States was reduced from 1.39 to 1.23 when allowance was made for induced changes in tax receipts and transfer payments (Goldberger, *op. cit.*, Tables 3.2 and 3.3). A similar reduction from 1.28 to 1.14 occurred when indirect taxes were made endogenous in the German model. (Heinz König and Vincenz Timmerman, "Ein Ökonometrisches Model für die Bundesrepublik Deutschland," 1950–1960, *Zeitschrift für die Gesamte Staatswissenschaft* October 1962, Tables 1 and 3). Finally, allowance for the built-in stability provided by induced changes in revenues from direct taxes diminished the impact multiplier for Greece from 1.60 to 1.44 (P. Pavlopoulos, *A Statistical Model for the Greek Economy, 1949–1959*, Amsterdam, 1966, Tables 7.6 and 7.7).

TABLE 13-11.  Dynamic Multipliers of Real Government Expenditure on Real Gross National Product

| Country | Model | YEAR | | | | | | | | | |
|---|---|---|---|---|---|---|---|---|---|---|---|
| | | 1 | 2 | 3 | 4 | 5 | 6 | 7 | 8 | 9 | 10 |
| Australia | (Kmenta) | 2.48 | 3.30 | 4.19 | 4.47 | 4.64 | 4.62 | 4.56 | 4.46 | 4.36 | 4.27 |
| | (Nevile) | 3.28 | 7.87 | 10.95 | 10.58 | 6.94 | 2.21 | -6.93 | -8.67 | -1.79 | 9.60 |
| Canada | (May)[a] | 1.29 | 1.63 | 1.79 | 1.91 | 2.00 | | | | | |
| Germany | (K-T)[b] | 1.32 | 1.63 | 1.67 | 1.68 | 1.67 | | | | | |
| Greece | (Pavlopoulos) | 1.44 | 2.08 | 2.47 | 2.72 | 2.89 | 2.98 | 3.04 | 3.07 | | |
| Holland | (CPB)[c] | | | | | | | | | | |
| | (1%) | 0.15 | -0.39 | -0.75 | -0.92 | -0.81 | -0.63 | -0.56 | -0.56 | -0.58 | -0.59 |
| | (2%) | 0.26 | -0.06 | -0.23 | -0.38 | -0.39 | -0.36 | -0.35 | -0.35 | -0.36 | -0.36 |
| | (15%) | 0.51 | 0.68 | 0.92 | 0.98 | 1.02 | 1.06 | 1.08 | 1.11 | 1.11 | 1.11 |
| India | (Marwah)[d] | 3.70 | 4.48 | 5.23 | 5.93 | 6.61 | | | | | |
| Italy | (Ackley) | 2.05 | 4.77 | 6.94 | 7.79 | 7.11 | 5.24 | 2.85 | 0.75 | -0.46 | -0.53 |
| Japan | (EPA)[b] | 2.06 | 3.54 | 4.71 | 5.56 | 6.14 | 6.48 | | | | |
| U.K. | (Ball) | 1.29 | 1.39 | 1.53 | 1.66 | 1.78 | 1.38 | 1.97 | 2.04 | 2.10 | 2.16 |
| U.S.A. | (K-G) | 1.23 | 1.95 | 2.21 | 2.26 | 2.26 | 2.23 | 2.19 | 2.15 | 2.12 | 2.09 |
| | (Suits)[e] | 1.30 | 1.62 | 1.58 | 1.54 | 1.34 | | | | | |

[a] Refers to nonfarm gross domestic product.
[b] Annual averages of semiannual values.
[c] Multipliers are given for initial unemployment rates of one, two and 15 per cent.
[d] Refers to net national product.
[e] Refers to private GNP (GNP less output of government services).

exogenous expenditure increase. In addition, they convey a considerable amount of information about the time path and inherent stability of a model's response mechanism.

The multiplier estimates for Australia (Kmenta), Canada, Greece, Holland, Japan, and the United States were published by the original model builders, those for Australia (Nevile), Germany, India, Italy and the United Kingdom from the models themselves have been computed for this report by the writer. The multipliers for Holland and Japan are nonlinear solutions, and those for Australia (Kmenta), Canada, and the United States (Klein-Goldberger) are from linearized models. The remaining models are either entirely linear or have a self-contained linear subsystem for real income[21].

It is possible to make an across-the-board comparison of five-year multipliers. Notice that with few exceptions the fifth-year values are substantially larger than the impact multipliers. Even after allowance for a five-year buildup, however, the multipliers for Canada, Germany, Holland, the United Kingdom, and the United States range no higher than two in value. Considerably larger responses are characteristic of the remaining models.

It appears from these multiplier results that the great majority of the models are dynamically stable. The only sequences which definitely suggest a powerful endogenous cycle mechanism are those for Australia and Italy. Moreover, extrapolation of the Italian results up to 17 years gave evidence of damped cycles, as did Kmenta's general dynamic analysis of his Australian model[22]. A characteristic equation analysis of the Klein-Goldberger model for the United States uncovered a damped oscillatory component with a period of seven years[23]; but as Table 13-11 shows, the endogenous fluctuation is very mild, and would be easily dominated by changes in external conditions. Suits's model of the United States also appears heavily damped, and its author asserts that the system can be treated as in equilibrium after five years.

The remaining models suggest a monotonic approach to equilibrium, although several of the sequences are too short to establish that overshooting will not occur eventually. However, May states that the Canadian responses are highly damped, and quotes a 22-year multiplier of 2.3 which is not far above the five-year value of 2.0[24]. The only doubtful case is the Japanese sequence

[21] This is not strictly true of the Indian model, which is nonlinear in prices. The multipliers in Table 13-11 were estimated from a submodel, which is linear in real variables on the assumption of constant prices. This is the same submodel for which Miss Marwah quoted an impact multiplier for real income–that is, one in which the endogenous price formation and liquidity preference functions are suppressed and the import and tax functions are interpreted in real terms.

[22] Jan Kmenta, "Australian Postwar Immigration: An Econometric Study," unpublished Ph. D, dissertation, Stanford University, June 1964, pp. 234–235.

[23] Goldberger, *op. cit.,* p. 127.

[24] Sidney May, "Dynamic Multipliers and Their Use for Fiscal Decision-Making," *Conference on Stabilization Policies*, Economic Council of Canada, Ottawa, 1966, p. 175.

which is still rising strongly after five or six years of expansion, although at a steadily diminishing rate, and which conceivably could oscillate if extrapolated for a longer period.

If these multiplier results are accepted at face value, they imply that business cycles are not inherent in the response mechanisms of most of the countries surveyed. When it comes to evaluating this important implication, most of the internal evidence is on the side of the stabler models.

Thus most of the models with large or cyclical multipliers are the pioneering attempts of single researchers working with systems which may inadequately represent the economic structure of the country concerned. For example, the Italian model has no import function to moderate the response mechanism. Moreover, the number of observations available to fit the model was so limited that arbitrary restrictions were involved in choosing among various specifications of the investment and consumption functions. The fixed investment equations finally selected gave stabler results than those obtained from some plausible alternatives; indeed, they were chosen for this reason, but they nonetheless introduced an arbitrary second-order lag which is the principal "cycle-maker" in the model. (These equations also make no allowance for replacement demand, implicitly assuming that capital lasts forever.)

As for the Indian model, it was observed earlier that its investment function provides an inadequate foundation for dynamic analysis, since it places no ceiling on the growth of capital stock, relative to income. Moreover, there appears to be little justification for treating public investment as endogenous, given the large scope of economic planning in India.

Nevile's model for Australia is cyclically explosive. However, it too is overly simplified, and Kmenta's modifications converted it to a stable system with heavily damped cycles, as may be seen by comparing the multiplier sequences in Table 13-11. This result was brought about chiefly by Kmenta's incorporation of an import function, although he also modified the fixed investment equations. Thus among the models with large or cyclical multipliers, only the one for Japan is sufficiently polished and detailed to inspire much confidence in its dynamic implications on the part of an outside observer. But even this model yields multipliers that appear suspiciously high, despite the high growth rate of the Japanese economy. Multipliers derived from the quarterly Osaka model for Japan are considerably smaller than those for the model of the Economic Planning Agency.

All this is not to say that the dynamic implications of the stabler models should be accepted without reservation. The Greek and British simulations, in particular, may be of questionable validity because of the inadequate samples underlying the models. It is safe to conclude from the earlier analysis, moreover, that the investment functions of all the models are in need of improvement. It is perilous to ignore stock-adjustment processes in dynamic extrapolations, and the investment functions should certainly be consistent with long-term equilibrium between stocks and flows.

In fact, it is doubtful that multiplier sequences should be extrapolated for more than two or three years in this group of models[25]. Many of the models were designed primarily for short-term forecasting rather than for dynamic analysis of the economic system. Apart from inadequate treatment of stock-flow relations, they are demand-dominated models which give little or no attention to supply factors or to limitations of resources. Most of the models omit all reference to monetary variables, and only three include endogenous monetary variables in the structural equations. Indeed, it is only for the Dutch model that monetary variables are endogenous in the multiplier simulations of Table 13-11[26].

For all these reasons, there remains enough uncertainty about the adequacy and realism of the models to justify a skeptical attitude toward their implications. Nonetheless, the weight of their evidence suggests strongly that modern mixed enterprise systems are characterized by stable response mechanisms and small dynamic multipliers.

If that be so, then the cycles of experience must be kept alive by exogenous stimuli. These stimuli need not themselves follow a cyclical pattern, of course, since regular fluctuations may be produced by erratic shocks acting on a damped dynamic response mechanism[27]. It may be objected that models incorporating nonlinear output buffers would be more realistic and would be capable

---

[25] The authors of the Australian (Nevile), German, Italian, and British models did not themselves perform such extrapolations, although Nevile made a formal dynamic analysis of his model.

[26] As mentioned in footnote [21], the real income multipliers for India are based on a linear submodel which ignores interactions with price and liquidity variables. For purposes of comparison, I have calculated the following five-year multiplier sequence from the complete nonlinear model, using as a reference base the solution given by K. Marwah ("An Econometric Model of Price Behavior in India," unpublished Ph. D. dissertation, University of Pennsylvania, 1963, Table 6.4): 1.60, 3.48, 5.39, 6.06, 6.15. Because the new multipliers allow for induced price increases, they are smaller at first than those for the truncated model. After the second year, however, the balance is redressed by the influence of a lagged endogenous liquidity in the consumption function, and the new multipliers approximate the original ones.

[27] Cf. Ragnar Frisch, "Propagation Problems and Impulse Problems in Dynamic Economics," *Economic Essays in Honor of Gustav Cassel*, London, 1933, Frisch credits Knut Wicksell with the basic idea, quoting Wicksell's 1907 analogy that "If you hit a wooden rocking-horse with a club, the movement of the horse will be very different to that of the club." As Irma and Frank Adelman showed in a stimulating study, the dynamically-stable Klein-Goldberger model generates cyclical fluctuations with aggregative properties similar to those actually observed in the U.S. economy, when subjected to continuous random shocks. ("The Dynamic Properties of the Klein-Goldberg Model", *Econometrica*, October 1959, pp. 596–625.)

of generating endogenous cycles[28]. Given the large leakages and damped responses implied by the present models, however, it is unnecessary to introduce ceilings and floors in order to limit the movements of national income, so that the burden of proof is on those who believe that the cumulative process is inherently explosive unless constrained.

## Supplementary Note:
## Dynamic Multipliers for Quarterly Models

This note is planned to supplement the previous results on annual models for Canada, Japan, and the United States by reference to multipliers computed from recently developed quarterly models.

The Canadian model was constructed by Rudolf Rhomberg from data for 1952-I to 1959-IV. The parameters were estimated by the method of limited-information maximum likelihood. The model consists of 19 structural relationships, including 17 behavioal equations and two identities. The principal feature of the model is the endogenous determination of the Canadian balance of payments (including capital flows) under alternative regimes of fixed and fluctuating exchange rates. Real GNP is determined along Keynesian lines, and prices and interest rates are endogenous. Neither employment nor income distribution is explained in the model, and a linear relationship between disposable personal income and GNP takes the place of explicit functions for tax revenues, corporate saving, and depreciation.

Several dynamic multipliers computed from Rhomberg's model are shown in Table 13-12 for a period of 10 quarters. Each of the three sequences refers to the response of real GNP to a sustained unit increase of real government expenditure, but the responses differ substantially according to the assumption made about the exchange mechanism. The government expenditure multiplier is smallest under a flexible exchange rate system (I), intermediate under a fixed exchange regime with exogenous money supply (II), and largest when the money supply is assumed to respond endogenously to changes in foreign reserves under a fixed exchange rate system (III). Rhomberg states that all three systems show strongly damped cycles with a period of about 6.5 years. Equilibrium is approached closely within 60 to 80 quarters.

If the quarterly estimates are averaged, the flexible exchange model yields the following annual multipliers for the first two years: 2.5, 3.7. The corresponding averages for the two fixed exchange models are 3.3, 5.1 (II), and 3.3, 5.8 (III). All these multipliers are substantially higher than those for May's Canadian model examined earlier: 1.3, 1.6. The principal explanation for this difference

---

[28] The Dutch model does include a capacity ceiling, but it is nevertheless stable and nonoscillatory.

TABLE 13-12 Quarterly Dynamic Multipliers of Government Expentidure on Gross National Product

| Country | Model | I | II | III | IV | V | VI | VII | VIII | IX | X |
|---|---|---|---|---|---|---|---|---|---|---|---|
| | | | | | | Quarter | | | | | |
| Canada | (Rhomberg) | | | | | | | | | | |
| | (I) Flexible exchange rate | 1.5 | 2.4 | 2.8 | 3.3 | 3.6 | 3.6 | 3.5 | 3.2 | 2.9 | 2.4 |
| | (II) Fixed exchange rate[a] | 1.8 | 3.1 | 3.7 | 4.5 | 5.0 | 5.2 | 5.2 | 5.0 | 4.6 | 4.1 |
| | (III) Fixed exchange rate[b] | 1.8 | 3.1 | 3.7 | 4.7 | 5.4 | 5.8 | 6.0 | 6.1 | 6.0 | 5.8 |
| Japan | (Osaka) | 1.3 | 1.7 | 2.2 | 2.4 | 2.2 | 2.3 | 2.2 | 2.2 | | |
| U.S. | (Brookings) | 1.6 | 2.0 | 2.4 | 2.1 | 2.2 | 2.1 | 2.7 | 2.8 | 2.8 | 2.7 |
| | (Wharton-EFU) | 2.0 | 2.4 | 2.1 | 2.0 | 1.9 | 1.9 | 2.0 | 2.0 | 2.1 | 2.1 |

Sources: Rudolf R. Rhomberg, "A Model of the Canadian Economy Under Fixed and Fluctuating Exchange Rates", *Journal of Political Economy*, February 1964, pp.1–31.
Shinichi Ichimura, "Dynamic Properties of the Osaka Econometric Model of the Postwar Japanese Economy, 1952–61" (mimeographed, no date).
M. K. Evans and L. R. Klein, "Experience with Econometric Analysis of the American 'Konjunktur' Position", Chapter 12.
Gary Fromm and Paul Taubman, *Policy Simulations with an Econometric Model*, Washington, 1966, Table 5.
Note: Multipliers for Canada and the United States are in constant dollars; those for Japan are in current dollars. For distinction between (a) and (b) estimates see Rhomberg paper cited above.

appears to lie in the high value of the marginal propensity to consume in Rhomberg's model. With respect to GNP, this propensity is 0.837 in his model, compared with a first-year value of 0.186 in May's model. The lags in May's consumption and labor income functions operate to raise the long-run marginal propensity to a value of 0.41 (by the 22nd year), but this is still below Rhomberg's estimate, which applies to both the short run and long run, owing to the absence of lags in either the function which relates consumption to disposable income or that which relates disposable income to GNP. Rhomberg's estimated marginal propensity is clearly high in relation not only to May's estimate for Canada but to the other models discussed in this paper, and Rhomberg himself has reduced its value from 0.837 to 0.58 in a subsequent annual prototype model[29]. The impact multiplier for the latter model is 1.5, a value which is much closer to May's estimate of 1.3 than the estimates of Rhomberg's quarterly models.

Another important difference between Rhomberg's quarterly model and May's model is in the formulation of the investment equations. An increase of

[29] Rudolf R. Rhomberg, "Effects of Exchange Depreciation in Canada, 1960–1964", *Conference on Stabilization Policies*, Economic Council of Canada, Ottawa, 1966, pp. 99–125.

income in Rhomberg's model has only transitory effects on fixed investment, whereas an increase in the interest rate is assumed permanently to reduce the level of investment. As a result of this formulation, investment is reduced in the long run by an exogenous increase of government expenditure. This largely explains the low level of Rhomberg's equilibrium multipliers — respectively 0.73, 1.0, and 2.0 under the alternative foreign exchange regimes — compared with May's long-run multiplier of 2.3. Apart from the foregoing peculiarity, Rhomberg's investment functions take no account of the effects of capital accumulation on investment demand in the longer run — a deficiency shared by May's model and most others in this survey.

Despite the foregoing qualifications on Rhomberg's multiplier results, his model serves as a healthy reminder that monetary feedbacks may strongly affect the dynamic response of real income to exogenous stimuli.

The Osaka econometric model of Japan consists of 215 equations, of which 108 are stochastic relationships. The model was estimated by two-stage least squares from quarterly observations for the period 1952—1959. The model features a separation of heavy industry, textiles, other manufacturing, agriculture, and tertiary industry, and distinguishes further between small- and large-scale enterprises in the manufacturing sectors. The monetary and international sectors are also highly developed. Investment functions are included for eight categories of private fixed investment and six categories of inventory investment. Consumption is disaggregated into three categories, and imports into four. Exports are also endogenous in the model, although they are treated as exogenous in the present multiplier simulations.

The dynamic multipliers of government investment expenditure on GNP in money terms are shown for eight quarters in Table 13-12. The annual averages for the first two years are respectively 1.9 and 2.2, or considerably lower than the values of 2.1 and 3.5 cited earlier for the Economic Planning Agency (EPA) model of Japan. As noted earlier also, the multiplier sequence of the EPA model continues to rise at least through the sixth year, and reaches a value of 6.5 at that time, whereas equilibrium is apparently reached at a lower level during the second year of operation of the Osaka model. To judge from the published information in English, the discrepancy between these estimates is not traceable to differences in the consumption propensities, but to the investment or import functions. The discrepancies cannot be analyzed here, however, owing to the complicated structure of the Osaka model and the lack of published information on the reduced-form expressions for investment and imports. It is to be hoped that the modelbuilders themselves will be able to isolate the structural features responsible for these discrepancies and to eliminate them by further testing to uncover the "true" structure.

For the U.S. economy, the full-blown Brookings model embraces more than 300 relationships; however, the multipliers shown in Table 13-12 were computed from a smaller version of 177 equations. The model was estimated by least squares for the period 1948–1960. Among the distinctive features of the model is a considerable disaggregation of both final demand (six categories of consumption, four of inventory investment, and five of fixed investment) and industrial activity (eight producing sectors). Employment, tax revenues, income distribution, prices and wage rates are also explained in considerable detail, and the model has a well developed financial sector. The Wharton model is smaller than the Brookings model − 76 equations compared with 177 − but it is large enough to accommodate considerable disaggregation of final demand and industrial production and to provide for the endogenous explanation of wages, prices, employment, interest rates, tax revenues, and income distribution. The stochastic equations were estimated by the method of two stage least squares and for the sample period 1948–1964 [30].

The 10-period multipliers for both U.S. models are reproduced in Table 13-12. The multiplier sequence of the Brookings model gradually approaches an apparent equilibrium value of 2.7 or 2.8, which is reached in the seventh quarter and sustained thereafter. In contrast, the Wharton model implies a virtually stable equilibrium value of 2.0 or 2.1 from the very beginning. As Evans and Klein remark, "The cause of the trendless behavior of our government multipliers is not a lack of dynamic structure but an approximate counter-balancing of two forces: the gradual increase in marginal propensity to consume for consumer nondurables and services, and the stock-adjustment forces affecting consumer durables, fixed business investment, and inventory investment" [31]. These same opposing forces are represented in the Brookings model, but without the neat offsetting over time that happens to occur in the Wharton model.

The two-year multipliers for the four models of the U.S. economy examined in this paper are as follows:

| Year | K-G | Suits | Brookings | Wharton |
|------|-----|-------|-----------|---------|
| 1    | 1.2 | 1.3   | 2.0       | 2.1     |
| 2    | 2.0 | 1.6   | 2.4       | 2.0     |

The quarterly models imply second-year multipliers similar to those of the annual models, but the build-up is more rapid during the first year of operation of the quarterly models. As mentioned earlier, the impact multipliers of the Klein-Goldberger and Suits models are biased downward by the assumption that all (Klein-Goldberger) or part (Suits) of the investment response lags a full year behind the exogenous disturbance. The quarterly structure of the newer models overcomes this deficiency and is probably the main factor responsible for the larger value of their first-year multipliers.

[30] For details, see M. K. Evans and L. R. Klein, *Supra* pp. 359-370.
[31] *Ibid.*, p. 376.

434    Dynamic Properties Macroeconometric Models: International Comparison

In conclusion, this examination of quarterly models for three countries confirms the general conclusions reached from the survey of annual ones. The quarterly models are also dynamically stable. The Canadian model implies endogenous cycles, but they are heavily damped. Moreover, the intermediate-run multiplier responses of this model are biased upward by an overestimate of the marginal propensity to consume. The Osaka quarterly model of the Japanese economy is much stabler than the semiannual model of the Economic Planning Agency. Finally, the two quarterly models of the U.S. economy are not only stable, but also yield equilibrium multipliers of the same order of magnitude as the Klein-Goldberger model. Disaggregation of demand and elaboration of the lag structure and financial sector have affected the stability implications drawn from the Klein-Goldberger model only marginally, if at all.

## References for Annual Models

Australia
  1. Kmenta, Jan, "Australian Postwar Immigration: An Econometric Study," unpublished Ph.D. dissertation, Stanford University, June 1964.
  2. Nevile, J.W., "A Simple Econometric Model of the Australian Economy," *Australian Economic Papers,* September 1962, pp. 79–94.
Canada
  3. May, Sidney, "Dynamic Multipliers and Their Use for Fiscal Decision-Making," *Conference on Stabilization Policies,* Economic Council of Canada, Ottawa, 1966, pp. 155-187.
Germany, Federal Republic of
  4. König, Heinz, and Vincenz Timmerman, "Ein Ökonometrisches Model fur die Bundesrepublik Deutschland, 1950–1960", *Zeitschrift für die Gesamte Staatswissenschaft,* October 1962, pp. 598–612. (Referred to as K-T.)
Greece
  5. Pavlopoulos, P., *A Statistical Model for the Greek Economy, 1949–1959,* Amsterdam, 1966.
Holland
  6. Verdoorn, P.J., and J.J. Post, "Short-and Long-Term Extrapolations with the Dutch Forecasting Model 63-D," in *Model Building,* Entretiens de Monaco en Sciences Humaines, Centre International d'Etude des Problemes Humains, 1964.
India
  7. Marwah, Kanta, "An Econometric Model of Price Behavior in India," unpublished Ph.D. dissertation, University of Pennsylvania, 1963.
Italy
  8. Ackley, Gardner, *Un Modello Econometrico dello Sviluppo Italiano nel Dopoguerra,* Rome, 1963.
Japan
  9. Economic Planning Agency, "New Medium-Term Macro-Model," Tokyo, January 14, 1967 (mimeographed, in Japanese). (Referred to as EPA.)

*United Kingdom*
  10. Ball, R.J., "The Significance of Simultaneous Methods of Parameter Estimation in Econometric Models," *Applied Statistics*, March 1963, pp. 14-25.

*United States*
  11. Goldberger, Arthur S., *Impact Multipliers and Dynamic Properties of the Klein-Goldberger Model*, Amsterdam, 1959.
  12. Klein, Lawrence R., and Arthur S. Goldberger, *An Econometric Model of the United States, 1929–1952*, Amsterdam, 1964. (Referred to as K-G).
  13. Suits, Daniel B., "Forecasting and Analysis with an Econometric Model," *American Economic Review*, March 1962, pp. 104-132. (Reprinted in R.A. Gordon and L.R. Klein (ed.), *Readings in Business Cycles*, Homewood, Illinois, 1965.)

Chapter Fourteen

# COMPARISON OF THE PREWAR AND POSTWAR BUSINESS CYCLES IN THE NETHERLANDS: AN EXPERIMENT IN ECONOMETRICS

P. J. VERDOORN AND J. J. POST
Central Planning Bureau, The Hague

A comparison of the postwar years with the interwar period shows that cyclical fluctuations in the Netherlands have been greatly reduced. There can be little doubt about this, or about the fact that the reduction holds for both the amplitude and the period of the average cycle.

### DIFFERENCES IN CYCLICAL IMPACT

Real gross national product (GNP) and employment may be taken as yardsticks. As shown by the following tabulation, both the fluctuations of GNP—measured as percentage deviations of the exponential trends for each of the time intervals considered—and the length of the average period have decreased by some 40 or 50 per cent. For employment, in fact, the standard deviation has been reduced by 70 per cent, and the average period by half of that amount.

|  | Standard Deviation (per cent of trend) | | |
|---|---|---|---|
|  | 1923–1938 | 1949–1964 | Percentage change |
| GNP of enterprises | 5.20 | 2.98 | −42 |
| Wage earners employed | 5.10 | 1.52 | −70 |
|  | Average Period (years) | | |
| GNP of enterprises | 9.3 | 5.3 | −43 |
| Wage earners employed | 9.2 | 5.9 | −36 |

436

As is clear from Figure 14-1, simultaneous reduction of the amplitude and period of the fluctuations does not point to the vanishing of systematic movements of a cyclical nature. It is only the reduced intensity of the phenomenon that creates this impression. This illusion is reinforced by a generally declining trend during the 1923–1938 period that aggravated the cycle, whereas the period after World War II has been characterized by a spectacular upward trend. It is by virtue of the latter trend that the cyclical troughs of the last two decades create the impression of short periods of zero growth rather than of cyclical depressions. The best witness for the persistence of the cycle, therefore, is a variable such as unemployment. At the same time, unemployment (as a percentage of the working population) shows the largest

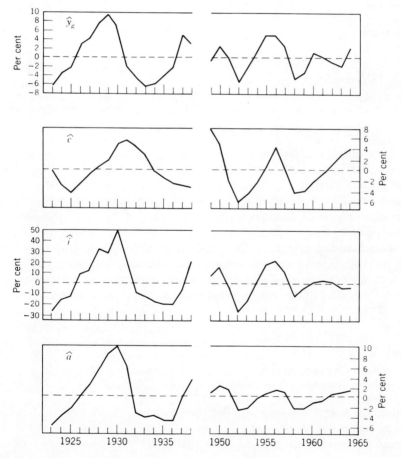

**Fig. 14-1.** Main endogenous variables (percentage deviations from trend). (For list of symbols, see Appendix A.)

difference between the two periods. These differences are even more pronounced if comparison is limited to employment in manufacturing and construction (see the tabulation that follows). Structural factors, however, tend to make the *level* of unemployment unreliable as an overall yardstick of the cyclical component of economic conditions.

| | Percentage of Working Population Unemployed | |
| --- | --- | --- |
| | 1923–1938 | 1949–1964 |
| *Unemployment Total* | | |
| Lowest value | 3.7 | 0.8 |
| Average | 9.4 | 2.1 |
| Highest value | 17.5 | 4.7 |
| *Unemployment in Manufacturing (including construction)* | | |
| Lowest value | 5.6 | 0.3 |
| Average | 18.1 | 1.4 |
| Highest value | 35.2 | 4.2 |

### DIFFERENCES IN MAIN IMPULSES

From the economist's point of view, a major question is whether or not the differences in the behavior of GNP and employment coincide with that of the main impulse variables. It appears that the reduction by 46 per cent of the average period of world demand (represented by competing exports in Table 14-1 and in Figure 14-2) corresponds closely with the 43 per cent GNP decrease of that period.

As might have been expected, the amplitude reduction of the latter is smaller than that of competing exports, namely, 42 per cent against 63 per cent. Typical for such an open country as the Netherlands is the striking correspondence between the values of the average period found for these two variables:

| | Average Period (years) | |
| --- | --- | --- |
| | 1923–1948 | 1949–1964 |
| GNP of enterprises | 9.3 | 5.3 |
| Competing exports (volume) | 9.6 | 5.2 |

Although international prices follow the reduction of the volume of trade, their average period shows only a slight reduction. In this respect, the pattern of international impulses has changed either incidentally or systematically.

If we consider private investments and wages as endogenous, then the main internal impulse is *autonomous expenditure*, defined as total government

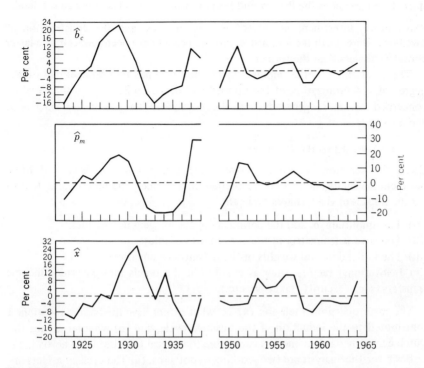

**Fig. 14-2.** Main impulse variables (percentage deviations from trend). (For list of symbols, see Appendix A.)

TABLE 14-1.  **Main Impulse Variables**

|  | Standard Deviation (per cent of trend) | | |
|---|---|---|---|
|  | 1923–1938 | 1949–1964 | Percentage change |
| Competing exports (volume) | 12.4 | 4.6 | −63 |
| Competing exports (prices) | 14.8 | 5.5 | −63 |
| Import prices | 16.2 | 7.4 | −55 |
| Autonomous expenditure | 11.8 | 6.2 | −39 |
|  | Average Period (years) | | |
| Competing exports (volume) | 9.6 | 5.2 | −46 |
| Competing exports (prices) | 8.8 | 7.7 | −12½ |
| Import prices | 8.1 | 6.7 | −17 |
| Autonomous expenditure | 7.1 | 5.5 | −22½ |

439

expenditure, investment by government enterprises, and the construction of dwellings. Here, both the amplitude and the period have been reduced, the latter considerably less than the former.

The total effect of the impulses mentioned depends to a large extent on the degree of synchronization of the upward and downward swings of the variables concerned or, more generally, on the covariance matrix of the exogenous variables.

### TWO WORKING HYPOTHESES

Given the reaction equations between the endogenous variables, and those between the endogenous and the predetermined ones, the determining factors for the impact of the business cycle are:

(i) The amplitude, $\sigma$, and the period, $T$, of the exogenous variables.
(ii) The covariance matrix of the exogenous variables.
(iii) The initial data and weights of the definitional equations.
(iv) Institutional factors, such as changes in the regulations governing income transfers (social security, taxation, etc.).

The main questions then are: (a) To what extent have the factors mentioned contributed to the reduction of the business cycle, and (b) whether or not the Dutch economy has become less vulnerable to cyclical impulses from abroad.

Basic for the analysis are two working hypotheses: (a) The cyclical effects are investigated with the Model 63-D as currently used for the Central Economic Plan. The equations are shown in *Appendix A*. Since the sampling period used for estimating the coefficients of the reaction equations covered the period 1923–1938 as well as the years 1949–1960, and the residuals for the two periods can be considered as about equally satisfactory, the conclusion seems justified that *a single set of reaction equations describes the basic reaction pattern of the Dutch economy during both periods*. This, as a matter of fact, does not hold for the definition equations, where fairly important shifts occur in the relative importance of, for example, the different categories of expenditures. (b) For the present purpose it is useful to work on the hypothesis that the average time-shape and period of the relevant impulse variables can be approximated and measured by curves.

In the case of short-time series, this method provides a simple and objective estimate of the period T of the cycles studied:

(1)
$$\cos \frac{2\pi}{T} = \rho$$

---

[1] R. Ferber and P. J. Verdoorn, *Research Methods in Economics and Business*, New York, 1962, Sec. 7.6.1.

where $2\pi = 360°$ and $\rho$ is the coefficient of serial correlation between the variables studied[1]. $T$, as estimated from (1), usually corresponds closely with the estimate obtained by averaging three alternative measures, namely, (i) the peak-to-peak average, (ii) the trough-to-trough average and (iii) twice the average number of time units intervening between two successive intersections with the trend.

This estimate of $T$, combined with the empirical value of $\sigma$, made it possible to represent the *average* cyclical behavior of an impulse variable for each of the two periods by a sinusoid[2] and to simulate its average effect with the help of Model 63-D.

### DIFFERENCES IN FIRST-YEAR EFFECTS

The first-year effect of a simple decrease by 10% of the more important exogenous variables produces considerable differences. The effect of a fall in world demand on GNP and profits amounted to 16 and 17%; the effect on private investment was 50%.

One interesting point with regard to the effect of changes in world demand on Dutch exports is the fact that the sizable partial elasticity of 1.32 in (4) of Appendix B:

$$b = 1.32b_c + \ldots + 4.63\Delta\tilde{w}_{1\ -5/12} + \ldots,$$

is reduced to 1.193 in period I and to about unity in period II, thus resulting for all practical purposes in proportionality with world demand. When evaluating the plausibility of the elasticity of 1.32, one is apt to overlook its character as a partial elasticity, and the fact that an increase of exports tends to diminish surplus capacity, $\tilde{w}$, and hence to effectuate a downward shift of the export-supply curve.

With regard to international prices, it should be noted that both the standard deviation and the average period for the prices of imports and competing exports tend to be the same, and that the correlation betwen their first differences is as high as 0.930 and 0.919, respectively. An approximate picture of the average effect of international price movements is, therefore, obtained by adding the corresponding columns for $p_m$ and $p_b$ [3]. The combined effects in the second period are, as a rule, somewhat larger than in the first. In both periods, a fall in the international price level tends to reduce employment while strengthening the balance of payments position by fostering exports.

---

[2] Some justification for representing the cyclical part of the development of national aggregates by a simple sinusoid is provided, for example, by C. E. Armstrong, "The Short-term Business Cycle," *Rev. Ec. Stat.*, May, 1936, pp. 62–66.

[3] The relation with the volume of world demand is much less close (Table 14-1).

442   Comparison of the Prewar and Postwar Business Cycles in the Netherlands

Interesting are the changes of sign for autonomous expenditure. Since the reaction equations (1) − (13) of Model 63-D have been equally applied to both periods, the cause of these changes (like the causes of the effects of the variables just discussed) is the combined result of two factors:

(a) Five of the 13 reaction equations (those for $I$, $b$, $m$, $a$, $l$ and $p_b$) are rather strongly curvilinear in the rate of unemployment, $\tilde{w}$; the more that the still available manpower and, hence, the surplus capacity, becomes exhausted, the larger will be the impact of a given change of $\Delta\tilde{w}$ on the variables concerned. This curvilinearity is introduced by a semilogarithmic transformation. Thus, for exports:

$$b = \ldots + \zeta\Delta\tilde{w}_1 = \ldots \zeta \ \ 4.34\Delta ln(\tilde{w} + 2) - 0.20\Delta\tilde{w} \ .$$

The sharply rising effect of a change of $\tilde{w}$ for lower initial values is illustrated by Figure 14-3[4]. Since the boom year of 1929 has been chosen as representative for period I and 1957 for period II, the initial values of $\tilde{w}$ are quite different, namely, 4.26 per cent and 1.61 per cent, respectively. Consequently, the reactions on an induced change of unemployment are much stronger in period II than in period I.

(b) With regard to the weights of the definition equations, it should be noted that the share of autonomous expenditure in total expenditure in period I was only half of that of period II (Table 14-2).

TABLE 14-2.   Percentage Composition of Total Expenditure[a]

| Variables | 1929 | 1957 | 1964 |
|---|---|---|---|
| Consumption | 54.5 | 44.4 | 45.1 |
| Private investment | 7.1 | 9.8 | 9.6 |
| Autonomous expenditure | 6.2 | 13.9 | 13.3 |
| Exports: commodities | 23.0 | 25.6 | 27.6 |
| Services[b] | 9.2 | 6.3 | 4.4 |
|  | 100.0 | 100.0 | 100.0 |
| (Imports) | (31.2) | (33.2) | (32.9) |

[a] Excluding inventory formation.
[b] Net balance.

Also the distribution of income underwent some change, owing to the increased share of wages and indirect taxation (Table 14-3).

[4] For general comments on the equations and the forecasting results with 63-D, see United Nations, *Construction and Practical Application of Macro-Economic Models for Purposes of Economic Planning (Programming) and Policy Making.* New York, 1968, The role of the capacity-impact curve is more fully discussed in P. J. Verdoorn and J. J. Post, "Capacity and Short-Term Multipliers," *Econometric Analysis for National Economic Planning,* Colston Papers, No. 16, London, 1964, pp. 179–198.

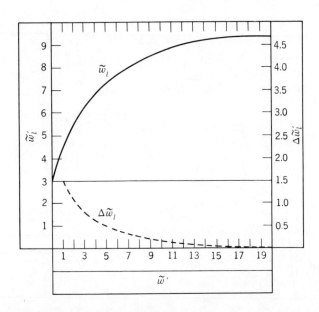

**Fig. 14-3.** The capacity-impact-curve.*

* The effect of an increase of 1 per cent in unemployment as a function of the initial level of unemployment

| Initial value of $w$ (in pct) | Value of $\Delta w$ coefficient | | | |
|---|---|---|---|---|
| | 2 | 4 | 8 | 16 |
| 0.5 | 2.52 | 5.05 | 10.09 | 20.18 |
| 1.0 | 2.10 | 4.20 | 8.40 | 16.79 |
| 2.0 | 1.54 | 3.08 | 6.15 | 12.31 |
| 4.0 | 0.94 | 1.88 | 3.76 | 7.51 |
| 8.0 | 0.43 | 0.86 | 1.71 | 3.42 |
| 16.0 | 0.07 | 0.14 | 0.28 | 0.56 |

TABLE 14-3. **Percentage Composition of Gross National Product at Market Prices**

| Variables | 1929 | 1957 | 1964 |
|---|---|---|---|
| Wages | 36.3 | 41.8 | 47.5 |
| Nonwage incomes | 46.9 | 39.1 | 32.6 |
| Depreciation | 11.2 | 9.7 | 9.5 |
| Indirect taxes | 5.6 | 9.4 | 10.4 |
| | 100.0 | 100.0 | 100.0 |

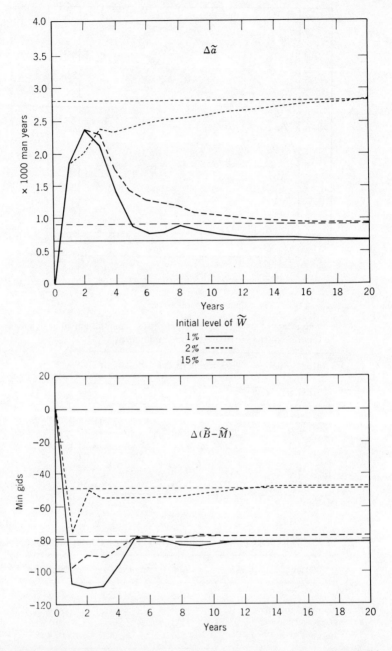

**Fig. 14-4.** Cumulated effects of a sustained increase (by 100 million guilders) of autonomous expenditure.

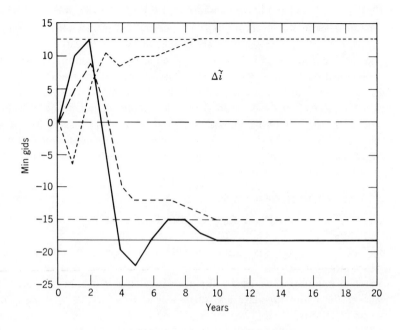

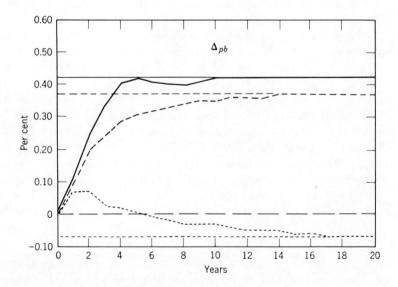

**Fig. 14-4.** (Continued from previous page)

445

The changes in the structure of the economy just mentioned may oppose or reinforce each other. For example, the change of sign for investment is explained by the fact that in period I the effect of a reduction of autonomous expenditure is determined by the favorable effect on the balance of payments, which raises the amount of available liquidities and stimulates investment (see Eq. 13). In period II, however, the even more favorable effect on the balance of payments (Table 14-1, the last two columns, last line) is overcompensated by the much higher negative effect of the accompanying increase of unemployment. True, the increase itself is the same as in period I, but given the much lower initial level of $\tilde{w}$, its effect has become twice as large.

### THE MAXIMUM-IMPACT APPROACH

Table 14-1 presents only the first-year effects of an arbitrarily chosen decrease of variables by 10 per cent. The problem of evaluating the effect of a given "mix" of cyclical impulses during a number of consecutive years is complicated by three circumstances:

(a) The impulses given at $t = 0$ are propagated in $t = 1$, $t = 2$, ..., etc., by means of the many time-lags and quasi-accelerators ($\Delta x_t = x_t - x_{t-1}$) of the reaction equations;

(b) The "impulse mix" is composed of the changes of variables that differ as to period and phase;

(c) Model 63-D represents the reactions of the economic system in terms of relative first differences, and not in terms of trend deviations.

The first difficulty can be easily dealt with for a nonrecurrent impulse or a sustained change of the exogenous variables. A method for estimating the effect of the latter has been presented by the authors in an earlier paper[5]; and examples, based on Model 63-D, of the time-path to be expected under conditions of sustained change are given in Figure 14-4. The effects of random deviations superimposed on a system of linear trends that represent the jointly exogenous variables has been studied by Irma Adelman and Frank L. Adelman with the Klein-Goldberger model[6]. In their approach, the systematic fluctuations of the exogenous variables have been replaced by random oscillations, thereby avoiding the second difficulty cited earlier.

To bring out as fully as possible the cyclical component of the impulses, another approach has been followed, namely, to estimate the maximum impact

---

[5] P. J. Verdoorn and J. J. Post, "Short and Long Term Extrapolations with the Dutch Forecasting Model 63-D," *Model Building*, Entretiens de Monaco en Sciences Humaines, Centre International d'Etude des Problèmes Humains, 1964, pp. 89–123. Also, see some further comments in the U. N. publication cited in footnote 4.

[6] "The Dynamic Properties of the Klein-Goldberger Model," *Econometrica*, October 1959, pp. 596–625.

of the average cyclical movement of the main exogenous variables. For this purpose, sinusoids have been used to approximate the average time-shape of the exogenous variables, the amplitude and period for each variable corresponding with averages found for the series concerned in period I and period II, respectively.

Evidently this maximum impact is reached when, starting from a situation of equilibrium of the endogenous variables, $y(t = 0) = y(t = -1) = y(t = -2) \ldots, = 0$, the exogenous variables begin to affect the system, with their different amplitudes and periods, but with the same phase, that is, with peak values at $t = 0$. This is no doubt a strong assumption. Differences in phase are often considerable. Many of the rather low values found in the covariance-matrix (Appendix C) hint in this direction. The very weak relationship between world demand $(b_c)$ and autonomous expenditure $(x)$, with roughly corresponding average periods, may well serve as a relevant example. Differences in phase tend to dampen the impact of the business cycle and, more important still, the economy does not begin its downswing from a period of equilibrium.

Actually, the lagged values of the predetermined variables tend to mitigate the beginning of the recession, and thus may dampen the amplitude of the cyclical movements of the system. The maximum impact found in this way, therefore, is of a theoretical rather than a practical nature. Nevertheless, it allows some inferences to be drawn about the differences between the prewar and the postwar business cycles.

## RELATIONSHIPS BETWEEN FIRST DIFFERENCES AND TREND DEVIATIONS

The next point presents less fundamental difficulties. If the sinusoid assumption is accepted, the relation between the relative first differences and the trend deviations is clear. Writing

$\tilde{y}_t$ for the absolute values,

$y_t$ for the percentage differences: $y_t = 100 \, \Delta \, \tilde{y}_t / \tilde{y}_{t-1}$,

$\bar{y}_t$ for the exponential trend of $y_t$ : $\bar{y}_t = e^{\alpha + \beta t}$, and

$\hat{y}_t$ for the percentage deviations from this trend : $\hat{y}_t = 100 \, (\tilde{y}_t / \bar{y}_{t-1})$,

the problem of the relationship between $y_t$ and $\hat{y}_t$ arises, since Model 63-D yields its results in terms of the former, whereas the study of cyclical impact demands conclusions in terms of the latter.

First, it is easy to see that $y$ can be regarded as the first difference of $\hat{y}$:

$$\frac{d\hat{y}}{dt} = 100 \, \frac{d\tilde{y}/\bar{y}}{dt} = 100 \, \frac{\bar{y} \, d\tilde{y}/dt - \tilde{y} \, d\bar{y}/dt}{\bar{y}^2},$$

$$= 100 \, \frac{e^{\alpha + \beta t} \, d\tilde{y}/dt - \beta \tilde{y} e^{\alpha + \beta t}}{\bar{y} e^{\alpha + \beta t}},$$

$$= 100 \frac{(d\tilde{y}/dt - \tilde{y}\beta)}{\bar{y}},$$

(1)
$$= 100 \frac{[\Delta\tilde{y}/\tilde{y} - \beta]}{(\bar{y}/\tilde{y})}$$

If $\bar{y} \cong \tilde{y}$ is assumed, then this takes the following form:

(2)
$$\boxed{\frac{d\hat{y}}{dt} = y - 100\,\beta}$$

that is, the trend deviations $\bar{y}$ correspond roughly to the integral of the differences between $y$ and the exponential trend-value of the original series $\tilde{y}$.

If the period of observations $(t = 1, \ldots, n)$ is not too short, the approximation

(3)
$$\frac{1}{n} \sum_{t=1}^{n} y_t \cong \beta$$

may be expected to be generally valid. *The values of y, therefore, correspond by and large with the deviations of y from their mean.*

Second, representing $y$ by a sinusoid of the general form

(4)    $$y = A \cos\,(2\pi t/T + \varepsilon) = A \cos\,(\omega t + \varepsilon),$$

where the angle $2\pi(= 360°)$ is expressed in radians, the periodicity is expressed in radians per time-unit: $\omega = 2\pi/T$. When annual data are used, the period itself is $T = 2\pi/\omega$ years.

The integral of the last expression is

(5)    $$\int y\,dt = \frac{1}{\omega} A \sin\,(\omega t + \varepsilon) = \frac{1}{\omega} A \cos\left(\omega t + \varepsilon - \frac{\pi}{2}\right).$$

It follows that the period of the integral of $y$ is the same as that of $y$ itself, but that the amplitude will be different for $\omega \neq 1$. Since $T = 6.3$ for $\omega = 1$, and remembering equation (2), we find that, theoretically,

$$\sigma_{\hat{y}} > \sigma_y \quad \text{if } T > 6.3 \text{ years,}$$

$$\sigma_{\hat{y}} = \sigma_y \quad \text{if } T = 6.3 \text{ years,}$$

$$\sigma_{\hat{y}} < \sigma_y \quad \text{if } T < 6.3 \text{ years.}$$

TABLE 14.4. Some Values of the Average Period and the Actual and Estimated Standard Deviation[a]
(I = 1923–1938; II = 1949–1964)

| | Variable | Average period (in years) | | | | Standard deviation (in per cent) | | | | | |
| | | I | | II | | I | | | II | | |
| | | $T_y$ | $T_{\hat{y}}$ | $T_y$ | $T_{\hat{y}}$ | $\sigma_y$ | $\sigma_{\hat{y}}$ | $\sigma_{\hat{y}}^*$ | $\sigma_y$ | $\sigma_{\hat{y}}$ | $\sigma_{\hat{y}}^*$ |
|---|---|---|---|---|---|---|---|---|---|---|---|
| $l$ | Wage rate | 7.2 | 10.1 | 4.4 | 4.9 | 2.5 | 4.3 | 4.1 | 3.1 | 2.6 | 2.4 |
| $b$ | Exports | 5.7 | 10.0 | 10.6 | 9.9 | 10.0 | 14.2 | 15.8 | 10.7 | 6.8 | 16.7 |
| $m$ | Imports | 4.3 | 9.7 | 3.9 | 4.5 | 7.0 | 10.1 | 10.8 | 10.9 | 7.7 | 7.8 |
| $b_c$ | World demand | 5.2 | 9.6 | 4.4 | 5.2 | 8.5 | 12.4 | 13.0 | 6.2 | 4.6 | 5.1 |
| $z$ | Profits | 6.3 | 9.5 | 5.5 | 8.7 | 8.4 | 13.6 | 12.7 | 6.0 | 6.4 | 8.3 |
| $c$ | Consumption | 4.5 | 9.5 | 5.9 | 8.1 | 2.0 | 3.0 | 3.0 | 3.2 | 3.9 | 4.2 |
| $y_g$ | GNP | 5.3 | 9.3 | 5.0 | 5.3 | 3.5 | 5.2 | 5.2 | 3.6 | 3.0 | 3.0 |
| $a$ | Employment | 5.8 | 9.2 | 4.6 | 5.9 | 3.3 | 5.1 | 4.9 | 1.5 | 1.5 | 1.5 |
| $p_c$ | Consumption prices | 5.8 | 9.0 | 4.9 | 6.8 | 3.2 | 4.7 | 4.5 | 3.2 | 2.9 | 3.5 |
| $p_b$ | Competing export prices | 6.1 | 8.8 | 4.9 | 7.7 | 9.6 | 14.8 | 13.4 | 5.2 | 5.5 | 6.4 |
| $p_m$ | Import prices | 4.8 | 8.1 | 4.8 | 6.7 | 12.0 | 16.2 | 15.6 | 7.4 | 7.4 | 8.0 |
| $i$ | Gross investments | 4.6 | 7.8 | 4.6 | 5.9 | 15.9 | 22.0 | 19.7 | 13.4 | 12.1 | 12.6 |
| $x$ | Autonomous expenditure | 3.8 | 7.1 | 4.0 | 5.5 | 10.5 | 11.8 | 11.8 | 6.7 | 6.2 | 6.0 |
| $K$ | Profits per unit | 4.4 | 6.9 | 4.7 | 8.1 | 2.0 | 2.2 | 2.2 | 1.2 | 1.4 | 1.6 |

[a] Lower case symbols refer to volume or prices; capitals to variables valued at current prices. For a full description of variables, see Appendix A. The ranking of variables is according to $T_{\hat{y}}$ in period I.

According to (5) it should be possible to approximate the standard deviation, $\sigma_{\hat{y}}$, of $\hat{y}$ as:

$$\sigma_{\hat{y}}^* = \frac{1}{\omega}\,\sigma_y = \frac{T}{2\pi}\,\sigma_y \; .$$

In order to test this hypothesis, $\sigma_{\hat{y}}^*$ has been calculated and tabulated in Table 14-4 for the main endogenous and exogenous variables. Usually, the estimate for the average period based on $y$ (i.e., $T_y$) is smaller than the one based on $\hat{y}$ (i.e., $T_{\hat{y}}$) as a consequence of the larger impact of random disturbances on the relative first differences. As the object of simulation is $\hat{y}$, the series of the latter has been used for estimating $T$. According to Table 14-4, the correspondence between $\sigma_{\hat{y}}^*$ and $\sigma_{\hat{y}}$ is satisfactory for the two periods. This correspondence justifies indirectly the use of a sinusoid to represent the average cyclical impulses during a given period.

TABLE 14-5.   **The Maximal Impulse Mix in Percentage Rates of Change**

| | Period I (1923–1938) | | | | |
|---|---|---|---|---|---|
| | 1 | 2 | 3 | 4 | 5 |
| $b_e$ | −0.73 | −11.28 | −11.28 | −7.03 | − |
| $D$ | $D$ 14.94 | −24.18 | −24.18 | −14.94 | − |
| $p_m$ | −12.92 | −18.28 | −12.92 | − | 12.92 |
| $p_b$ | −11.53 | −14.76 | −11.53 | − | 11.53 |
| $x$ | −9.80 | −13.86 | −9.80 | − | 9.80 |

| | Period II (1949–1964) | | | | |
|---|---|---|---|---|---|
| | 1 | 2 | 3 | 4 | 5 |
| | −7.75 | −7.75 | − | 7.75 | 7.75 |
| | −17.80 | −25.18 | −17.80 | − | 17.80 |
| | −11.24 | −11.24 | − | 11.24 | 11.24 |
| | −5.27 | −7.44 | −5.27 | − | 5.27 |
| | −8.41 | −8.41 | − | 8.41 | 8.41 |

THE INPUT OF SINUSOIDAL IMPULSES

The impulse mix, as derived from the sinusoids representing the time-shapes of the average cyclical fluctuations of the exogenous variables, is shown in Table 14-5, where $b_c$ equals world demand (volume of competing exports), $D$ equals net invisibles on current account, $p_m$ equals import prices, $p_b'$ equals competing export prices, and $x$ equals autonomous expenditure (volume).

A few comments are in order:

(a) The empirical periods of the impulse variables for periods I and II are rounded off to whole years.

(b) Although actually endogenous, $D$, because of its erratic character, is considered as exogenous as in Model 63-D.

With regard to the propagation of the effect of the impulse mix, it is important to note that a vital combination of factors has been neglected, namely:

(i) The lagged values of the endogenous and exogenous variables at the top of the boom. Also, no allowance is made for the existence of a surplus or deficit in the balance of trade at $t = 0$. Technically, therefore, the exercise is to be considered a problem of variation.

(ii) Such institutional variables as the average tax rates ($T_s''$ and $T_k'$), as well as the other terms of income transfers included in $O_L'$ and $O_s'$ (see equations (35-36) in Appendix B), are treated as constants. This procedure reinforces the theoretical character of the simulation. But the continuous changing of the tax schedules and social security measures makes it practically impossible to construct an average equation that can be taken as representative for so long a period as 1923–1938 or 1949–1964. In reverse, the procedure followed has the advantage of allowing some inferences as to the different effects of these institutional factors on the cyclical behavior of the economy in periods I and II.

THE THEORETICAL MAXIMUM IMPACT

With the international peak years 1929 and 1957 (unemployment rates, $\tilde{w}$, in the Netherlands of 4.3 and 1.6, respectively) selected as starting points ($t = 0$), the results obtained for the first five years of the theoretical cycle are given in Appendices D1 and D2. As mentioned earlier, these results are the outcome of a problem of variation. Therefore, in the cumulated theoretical impact, they should be superimposed on the current trend values ($\bar{y}_1, \bar{y}_2, \ldots, \bar{y}_5$) and the lagged reactions that are due to the upswing in the prepeak period.

In order to facilitate the comparison with the actual impact of the business cycle, the maximum theoretical impact is compared in Table 14-6 with the largest downward range of the deviations actually observed in the relevant intervals of periods I, and II. In the table, one correction is made so as to lessen the academic character of the comparison: in period I, the variables $c$, $y_g$, and $Z$ are roughly corrected for income transfers to wage earners. ($O_L'$ in 63-D is

TABLE 14-6. Theoretical Maximum of the Cumulated Cyclical Impact and Observed Maximal Range

| Variable[a] | | I (1923–1938: $w_0 = 4.3$) | | | II (1949–1964; $\tilde{w}_0 = 1,6$) | | |
|---|---|---|---|---|---|---|---|
| | | Observed maximal range (deviation from trend) | | Theoretical Maximum Impact (per cent) | Observed maximal range (deviation from trend) | | Theoretical Maximum Impact (per cent) |
| | | Years | Per cent | | Years | Per cent | |
| $c$ | Consumption | 1931–1938 | – 9.0 | –11.0[b] –19.1[c] | 1956–1958 | – 8.8 | – 12.2 |
| $b$ | Exports | 1928–1933 | –39.1 | –38.1 | 1955–1957 | –10.1[d] | 0 |
| $i$ | Investment | 1930–1936 | –69.5 | –52.5 | 1956–1958 | –33.9 | –33.3 |
| $m$ | Imports | 1929–1935 | –29.9 | –23.0 | 1956–1958 | –20.2 | –11.5 |
| $y_g$ | GNP | 1929–1933 | –15.8 | –20.5[b] –26.6[c] | 1956–1958 | – 9.7 | – 7.2 |
| $a$ | Employment | 1930–1933 | –14.5 | –12.1 | 1956–1958 | – 3.7 | – 6.0 |
| $\tilde{w}$ | Unemployment (pct.) | 1930–1933 | + 9.1 | + 6.3 | 1956–1958 | + 1.9 | + 3.1 |
| $l$ | Wage rate | 1930–1936 | –14.0 | –25.2 | 1957–1962 | – 8.6 | –18.6 |
| $p_c$ | Consumption prices | 1929–1933 | –12.9 | –19.4 | 1957–1962 | – 3.6 | –13.2 |
| $Z$ | Profits | 1929–1933 | –40.5 | –38.4[b] –51.3[c] | 1955–1958 | –12.5 | –24.2[e] –31.0[c] |

[a] Lower-case symbols refer to volumes or prices. For a full description of variables, see Appendix A.
[b] Corrected for effect of income transfers to wage income and government wages.
[c] Uncorrected.
[d] In this case the maximal range in the negative direction accompanied the top of the boom (1955–1957) rather than the recession.
[e] Corrected for net invisibles on current account.

predetermined and does not automatically take into account unemployment benefits, etc.)[7]. A second adjustment is made in period II, so as to correct profits for the unusual development of net invisibles on current account during the years 1955–1962.

Table 14-6 and its underlying tables in the appendices D1 and D2 lead to some important conclusions; certain of them are illustrated in Figure 14-5.

Most spectacular, undoubtedly, is the absence of any impact on exports. The starting point on the very steep interval of the capacity impact curve and the larger percentage reduction of autonomous expenditure compared with that of world demand, together with the heavily increased weight of the former in the impulse mix, explain this anomaly.

TABLE 14-7.   **Change of Cumulated Theoretical Impact**
(Actual "impulse mix" for periods I and II)

| Variable[a] | Per cent[b] | Variable[a] | Per cent[b] |
|:---:|:---:|:---:|:---:|
| $l$ | −26 | $a$ | −50 |
| $p_c$ | −32 | $\tilde{w}$ | −51 |
| $i$ | −35 | $Z$ | −52 |
| $c$ | −36 | $y_g$ | −69 |

[a] See Appendix A.
[b] In per cent of prewar impact.

This is not to say that the economy has become less vulnerable to cyclical impulses. Appendices D1 and D2, row II.1, show the—hypothetical—ravages if the impulse mix of the first period is applied to the second. The intensification of the cumulated effect is shown in Table 14-8. The conclusion is that the sensitivity of the economy as a consequence of the steeper interval of $\tilde{w}_1$ and the increased share of $\tilde{i}$ and $\tilde{x}$ in total output has grown instead of diminished.

TABLE 14-8.   **Change of Cumulated Theoretical Impact**
(Prewar impulse-mix; actual weights)

| Variable[a] | Per cent[b] | Variable[a] | Per cent[b] |
|:---:|:---:|:---:|:---:|
| $y_g$ | −19 | $Z$ | +17 |
| $i$ | +2 | $c$ | +12 |
| $w$ | +6 | $1$ | +31 |
| $a$ | +8 | $p_c$ | +31 |

[a] See Appendix A.
[b] Per cent of prewar impact.

---

[7] Government wages have likewise been corrected so as to take into account their approximate effect on the variables mentioned.

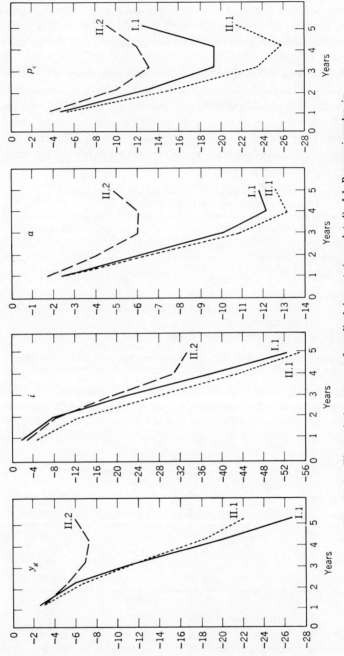

**Fig. 14-5.** Theoretical pattern of cyclical impact (cumulated). I.1 Prewar impulse in prewar period I.2 Prewar impulse in postwar period II.1 Prewar impulse in postwar period II.2 Postwar impulse in postwar period.

454

The stronger deflationary tendency in period I, if a decline of world demand and autonomous expenditure are synchronized, is reflected by the decrease of the impact on GNP, although there is an increase of consumption and investment. The relative improvement of GNP is caused by a more favorable current account of the balance of payments.

There are, however, compensating forces. One is the higher built-in stability of the system that is not reflected in Model 63-D, where the average tax rates and other income transfers are predetermined variables. Relevant are the higher level and greater progression of direct taxes, compared with period I. Unemployment insurance and benefits are likewise cases in point. Changes in taxation being rather manifold in period II, the time series available do not allow a quantification of this particular aspect.

Nevertheless, it seems beyond doubt that this factor explains, in part, why the discrepancies between the theoretical impact and the actually observed maximal range are larger in period II than in period I.

Other reasons are the general reduction of the income tax in 1955 and the institution of old-age pensions in 1957. Together with other factors, these measures tended to weaken the recession and prevented unemployment from rising to its theoretically expected level. This again kept the decline of the wage rate (from its trend) within reasonable limits.

In a later stage, government policy was aimed at stimulating the revival. Although the measures were perhaps timed too late, they certainly prevented a lingering of unemployment at a high level and thus stimulated the upswing of wages.

Table 14-6 leads to two further conclusions of a more general nature.

(a) As might have been expected, the theoretical maximum impact does not always correspond closely with the maximum for the observed range of the trend deviations. On the whole, however, there is a satisfactory correlation between the two sets of values. It holds for period I as well as for period II. This can be taken as proof that the cyclical movements of the endogenous variables of the Dutch economy since World War II are not the result of a pure random endogenous process, but are the same systematic response to cyclical impulses of exogenous variables as were given in the 1930's. True, the depressions of 1952 and 1957 can be considered as partly government induced in order to relieve inflationary tension. In this way, government policy hastened the beginning of each crisis. But the cyclical impulses were there, and the pattern of their impact on the economy likewise was largely according to the rules of the game as set by Model 63-D.

(b) Relevant for the present purpose is the fact emerging from Appendices D1 and D2 that the theoretical period, $T_{\hat{y}}$, is generally longer than the time indicated by twice the maximum range. This seems to suggest that the built-in stability mentioned earlier, and also the changed attitude of the government since the 1930's have actually helped to shorten the depression that itself was, at least partly, government induced.

Finally, it should be remembered, that the foregoing reasoning is entirely from the economist's point of view. The formal statistical proof that the fluctuations of the trend deviations during period II cannot be considered as random would have required an altogether different study from the one described in this paper.

## Summary

1. When the years 1949–1964 (period II) are compared with 1923–1938 (period I), the *endogenous variables* show both a considerably smaller amplitude and a much shorter period.

2. The same holds for such main *exogenous variables* as world import demand, international prices, and autonomous expenditures.

3. In order to verify whether or not the reduction of the amplitude and average period of the endogenous variables can be considered as the consequence of the reduced amplitude and period of the impulse variables, the *theoretical maximum impact* of the average cyclical morement of the exogenous variables on the endogenous variables has been estimated for period I and period II.

For this purpose, the time-shape of the average cycle in period I and of that in period II have been approximated by sinusoids for the five main exogenous variables. The maximal "impulse mix" is obtained by letting these sinusoids affect the economy by simultaneously sloping downward from their peak values at $t = 0$, that is, by starting with the same phase (Table 14-5). These impulses are then fed into the short-term business-cycle Model 63-D. The theoretical impact for any year ($t = 1, \ldots, 5$) is then obtained as the sum of the effects of the impulses received in that year and the propagation of the impulses of preceding years, and the maximum impact is easily found (Appendices D-1 and D-2)

4. The theoretical maximum impact thus estimated for the different endogenous variables appears to agree satisfactorily in period I as well as in period II with the *observed maximum range* for the series concerned (Table 14-6).

5. This can be considered as an indication that the *reduction of the cyclical movements of the endogenous variables is systematically related to that of the impulse variables*. Also, the averages for the amplitudes and periods of the endogenous variables appear to be the result of the normal responses of the Dutch economy, as represented by Model 63-D, to changes in the exogenous variables.

Therefore, insofar as the fluctuations of the exogenous variables and, more specifically, those of the international variables are conditioned by "the business cycle," the cyclical behavior of the endogenous variables is likewise to be attributed to the business cycle. Thus, the present material does not suggest that in the Netherlands the business cycle − at least the "imported cycle" − is obsolete. So far, only its amplitude and period have been reduced.

6. Further experiments have shown that although the fluctuations have become less the sensitivity of the Dutch economy for a given cyclical impulse has become greater (Table 14-8). The first-year effects, previously examined, have already pointed to this conclusion.

7. The main reasons are: (a) the prevalence of nearly full and overfull employment in period II, and (b) the larger share of commodity exports and autonomous expenditure in total expenditures.

8. Although this is not brought out by the Model as such, the increased sensitivity is probably offset by a higher *built-in stability*, which is due to such factors as the greater progressivity of direct taxes, increased unemployment benefits, etc.

## *Appendix A    List of Symbols*

Symbols without special indication refer to relative changes. Absolute quantities are indicated by $\sim$. Capital symbols refer to values, lower-case symbols to volumes or prices.

|  |  |  |
|---|---|---|
|  | $a$ | Number of persons employed in enterprises (man years). |
|  | $a_0$ | Number of persons employed in the government sector (man years). |
| $B$ | $b$ | Export commodities. |
|  | $b_c$ | Competing exports. |
| $C$ | $c$ | Total private consumption. |
|  | $c^r$ | Deposits at end of year. |
| $D$ |  | Net invisibles. |
| $\tilde{E}$ |  | Balance of payments (percentage of total output less inventory changes and net invisibles). |
| $F$ |  | Depreciation. |
| $H$ |  | Excess increase of wage costs over labor productivity (equation 27). |
| $I$ | $i$ | Gross investment of enterprises (excluding government enterprises and construction of dwellings). |
|  | $k$ | Quantitative import restrictions (1932–1937). |

| | | |
|---|---|---|
| | $k'$ | Rate of liberalization (1949–1955). |
| $K$ | | Gross profits per unit of output (equation 29). |
| | $l$ | Average gross wages per standard year of 300 days. |
| $L$ | | Wage bill of enterprises. |
| $L^B$ | | Disposable labor income. |
| $M$ | $m$ | Imports of commodities. |
| $N$ | | Inventory changes (percentage of total output less inventory changes and net invisibles). |
| $O'_L$ | | Income transfers to labor income, including government wages and direct taxes on cash receipts. |
| $O'_*$ | | Income transfers to nonlabor income, including direct taxes on cash receipts. |
| $P$ | | Population of working ages (14-65 years). |
| $P_B$ | | Total labor force (wage-earners plus registered unemployed). |
| | $p_{b_l}$ | Export prices. |
| | $p_b$ | Prices of competing exports. |
| | $p_c$ | Prices of consumption goods. |
| | $p_i$ | Prices of investment goods. |
| | $p_m$ | Import prices. |
| | $p_{m-v'}$ | Margin between import price adjusted for the incidence of indirect taxes and the price of total output (less inventory changes and net invisibles (equation 28)). |
| | $p_{v''}$ | Price of total output (less inventory changes and net invisibles). |
| | $p_x$ | Prices of autonomous expenditure. |
| $\pi w$ | | Equation 32. |
| | $r_e$ | Exchange rate. |
| | $r_k$ | Short-term rate of interest. |
| $\tilde{T}_c$ | | Minimum temperature $0°$ centigrade (sum of monthly averages). |
| $T_k$ | | Indirect taxes minus subsidies (amount). |
| $\tilde{T}'_k$ | | Incidence of indirect taxes minus subsidies ($\tilde{T}_{k'} = T_k / V'$). |
| | $t^*$ | Prewar decreasing trend (1923 = 15; 1938 = 0). |
| $T_z$ | | Direct taxes paid by nonwage earners cash receipts. |
| $T''_a$ | | Variation in the incidence of direct taxes on nonlabor income (equation 39). |
| $V$ | $v$ | Total output. |
| $V'$ | $v'$ | Total output less inventory changes and net invisibles. |
| | $v_a$ | Total output less inventory changes and net invisibles (components reweighted by intensities of labor demand, (equation 22)). |
| | $v_m$ | Total output less inventory changes and net invisibles (components reweighted by import requirements, (equation 23)). |
| $\tilde{W}$ | $\tilde{w}$ | Registered unemployment as percentage of employed and unemployed wage earners. |

$\tilde{w}_1$   Curvilinear indicator of use of capacity (equation 31).

$X$   $x$   Autonomous expenditure (government expenditure, investment of government enterprises and construction of dwellings).

$Y_g$   $y_g$   Gross national product at market prices.

$Z$   $z$   Nonlabor income.

$Z^B$      Disposable nonlabor income.

## *(Appendix B    Model 63D[1])*

*I.   Reaction equations*

  (i) *Expenditure categories*

(1*)  $C = 0.68\,L^B_{-1/4} + 0.15\,Z^B_{-3/4} + 0.43\,\Delta p_c + 0.08\,c^r - 0.19\,\Delta C_{-1} - 0.76$ .

(2)   $I = 0.71(Z_{-1} - T''_z) + 0.68\,c^r + 0.63\,p_i - 9.05\,\Delta\tilde{w}_1 + 0.88$ .

(3)   $N = 0.30\,v' - 1.17\,\tilde{N}_{-1}/\tilde{V}'_1 + 0.17\,p_m + 35K + 0.32\,t^* - 0.04$ .

(4)   $b = 1.32\,b_c - 1.78(p_b - p'_b) - 0.82\left(\underset{b}{p} - \underset{b}{p'}\right)_{-1} + 4.63\,\Delta\tilde{w}_{1\,-\frac{5}{12}} - 0.47\,\Delta p'_v$
$\qquad\qquad\qquad\qquad\qquad\qquad\qquad\qquad\qquad\qquad\qquad + 0.22$ .

  (ii) *Factors of production and capacity*

(5*)  $m = 0.99\,v_m + 0.28\,\Delta v_m + 2.10\,N - 0.37\,p_{m-v'} + 0.44\,\Delta p'_v -$
$\qquad\qquad\qquad\qquad -2.53\,\Delta\tilde{w}_{1\,-\frac{1}{12}} - 0.31k + 0.23k' + 0.64$ .

(6)   $a = 0.25\,v_a + 0.28K + 0.05\,c^r + 0.11\,p_{m-v'} - 1.05\,\Delta\tilde{w}_{1-1} + 0.50$ .

(7*)  $\Delta\tilde{w} = -0.52\,a + 0.34\,\dfrac{\Delta\tilde{P} - \Delta\tilde{a}_0}{\tilde{P}_{B_{-1}}} - 0.03\,\Delta\tilde{T}_c + \Pi_w - 9.68$ .

  (iii) *Wages and prices*

(8)  $l = 0.43\,p_c + 0.33\{(v' - a)_{-1} - 0.68(v' - a)_{-2}\} - 0.93(\Delta\tilde{w}_1 - 0.68\,\Delta w_{1_{-1}}) -$
$\qquad\qquad - 2.14(\Delta\tilde{w}_{1_1} - 0.68\,\Delta\tilde{w}_{2_2}) + 0.68\,l_{-1} + 0.52$ .

(9) $p_c = 0.38\,H_{-1/2} + 0.26\,p_{m-4/10} + 0.55(m-v)_{-4/10} + 0.19\,T'_{K-1/3} - 0.11\,c^r + 0.24$ .

(10*)  $p_i = 0.23H + 0.43\,p_m + 0.39\,p_{i_{-1}} + 0.90$ .

(11)   $p_b = 0.20H + 0.38\,p_m + 0.48\,p'_b - 1.43(\Delta\tilde{w}_1 - 0.48\,\Delta\tilde{w}_{1_{-1}}) - 0.80$ .

(12*)  $p_x = 0.47H + 0.46\,\Delta H + 0.25\,p_m + 0.40\,p_{x_{-1}} + 0.60$ .

---

[1] The estimates of the parameters are limited-information-maximum-likelihood estimates, except for the equations with an asterisk, where two-stage least squares have been applied.

(iv)  *Liquidities*

(13)  $c^r = 1.97\widetilde{E} + 1.12\widetilde{E}_{-1} + 0.47\,V' - 8.84\,r_{k-1} + 1.67\,N_{-2} + 0.38\,r_e -$
$$- 1.00\,p_{v'_{-1}} - 2.46.$$

## II.  *Definition equations[2]*
### (i)  *Relations between value and volume variables*

(14)   $C = c + p_c$

(15)   $X = x + p_x$

(16)   $I = i + p_i$

(17)   $B = b + p_b$

(18)   $M = m + p_m$

(19)   $V' = v' + p_{v'}$

(20)   $V = v + p_{v'}$

### (ii)  *Expenditure totals*

(21)    $v' = 0.48c + 0.15x + 0.10i + 0.27b$

(21a)   $v' = 0.60c + 0.07x + 0.08i + 0.25b$

(22)    $v_a = 0.46c + 0.20x + 0.16i + 0.18b$

(23)    $v_m = 0.45c + 0.15x + 0.11i + 0.29b$

(24)    $p_{v'} = 0.48p_c + 0.15p_x + 0.10p_i + 0.27p_b$

(24a)   $p_{v'} = 0.60p_c + 0.07p_x + 0.08p_i + 0.25p_b$

(25)    $V = 0.44C + 0.14X + 0.10I + 0.25B + 0.92N + 0.06D$

(25a)   $V = 0.52C + 0.06X + 0.07I + 0.22B + 0.87N + 0.09D$

### (iii)  *Balance of payments*

(26)    $\widetilde{E} = 0.27B - 0.35M + 0.01\,D + 0.93\widetilde{E}_0$

(26a)   $\widetilde{E} = 0.25B - 0.34\,M + 0.10D + 0.98\widetilde{E}_0$

### (iv)  *Costs and margins*

(27)     $H = l - (v' - a)_{-1/2}$

(28)    $p_{m-v} = p_m - p_{v'_{-1/2}} + 0.06\,T'_{K-1/3}$

(29)     $K = p'_v - 0.27\,l - 0.30p_m - 0.06\,T'_{K-1/3}$

### (v)  *Unemployment*

(30)     $\widetilde{w} = \Delta\widetilde{w} + \widetilde{w}_0$

(31)    $\Delta\widetilde{w}_1 = 4.34\Delta l\,n(\widetilde{w} + 2) - 0.20\Delta\widetilde{w}$

(32)    $\Pi_w = \Pi\{\widetilde{P}_{-1}/\widetilde{P}_{B-1}\}$   $\Pi = 3.94$ for the period 1923–38
$$= 4.55 \text{ ,, \quad ,, \quad ,, } \quad 1949\text{–}60\text{ff}$$

(vi) *Incomes*

(33)    $L = a + l$

(34)    $Z = 3.79V - 1.07L - 0.24T_K - 1.23M - 0.25F$

(34a)   $Z = 3.04V - 0.77L - 0.12T_K - 0.91M - 0.24F$

(35)    $L^B = 0.88L + 0.88O'_L + 0.21l$

(35a)   $L^B = 0.88L + 0.88O'_L + 0.14$

(36)    $Z^B = 1.49Z + 1.49O'_Z$

(36a)   $Z^B = 1.34Z + 1.34O'_Z$

(37)    $y_g = 1.48v - 0.48m$

(37a)   $y_g = 1.43v - 0.43m$


(vii) *Taxes*

(38)    $T_K = V' + T_{K'}$

(39)    $T_z'' = \Delta(\widetilde{T}_z / \widetilde{Z}_{-1})$


The complete model consists of 39 equations and also has 39 endogenous variables. The endogenous variables of the system fall into six groups:

Resources                          $a, l, L, Z, T_k, y_g, m, M$
Monetary variables                 $c^r, \widetilde{E}$
Expenditures                       $c, p_c, C, p_x, X, i, p_i, I, N, b, p_b, B, v,$
                                   $p_c, V, v, V$
Unemployment                       $\Delta\widetilde{w}, \widetilde{w}$
Secondary incomes and taxes        $L^b, Z^b, T''_\bullet$
Composite variables                $v_a, v_m, H, p_{m-v}, K, \Delta w_1, \Pi_w$

---

[2] In the definitional equations, the 1957 weights are inserted; equations with 1929 weights are characterized by the addition of an "a" to their numbers.

*APPENDIX C  Covariance Matrix of the Exogenous Variables*

| | | $b_c$ | $T_z''$ | $O_i$ | $r_k$ | $T_k'$ | $p_m$ | $p_b'$ | $s_a$ | $l$ |
|---|---|---|---|---|---|---|---|---|---|---|
| $x$ | I | -0.036 | -0.293 | -0.424 | -0.221 | -0.546 | -0.119 | -0.095 | -0.093 | 0.574 |
| | II | 0.200 | 0.210 | -0.451 | 0.222 | 0.091 | -0.042 | -0.038 | -0.247 | 0.287 |
| $b_c$ | I | | -0.196 | -0.694 | 0.051 | -0.508 | 0.851 | 0.793 | 0.137 | 0.386 |
| | II | | -0.250 | -0.071 | 0.417 | 0.324 | 0.546 | 0.439 | 0.443 | 0.302 |
| $T_z''$ | I | | | 0.053 | -0.077 | 0.621 | -0.044 | -0.222 | 0.080 | -0.200 |
| | II | | | -0.058 | 0.369 | -0.028 | 0.290 | 0.337 | -0.061 | 0.289 |
| $O_L'$ | I | | | | 0.124 | 0.561 | -0.574 | -0.523 | -0.007 | -0.541 |
| | II | | | | -0.028 | -0.112 | 0.106 | 0.189 | -0.062 | 0.082 |
| $r_k$ | I | | | | | 0.070 | -0.084 | 0.034 | 0.169 | -0.257 |
| | II | | | | | -0.194 | 0.669 | 0.563 | 0.274 | 0.721 |
| $T_k'$ | I | | | | | | -0.473 | -0.586 | 0.409 | -0.718 |
| | II | | | | | | -0.015 | 0.112 | 0.315 | -0.317 |
| $p_m$ | I | | | | | | | 0.930 | -0.260 | 0.429 |
| | II | | | | | | | 0.919 | 0.340 | 0.512 |
| $p_b'$ | I | | | | | | | | -0.401 | 0.409 |
| | II | | | | | | | | 0.182 | 0.328 |
| $s_a$ | I | | | | | | | | | -0.493 |
| | II | | | | | | | | | 0.131 |

Note: I = 1923–1938

II = 1949–1964

462

## APPENDIX D1  Theoretical Cyclical Changes Per Annum (percentages)[a]

| | | 1 | 2 | 3 | 4 | 5 | Σ |
|---|---|---|---|---|---|---|---|
| $c$ | I.1 | − 0.07 | + 0.01 | − 2.94 | − 7.01 | − 9.12 | −19.13 |
| | II.1 | − 0.24 | − 1.02 | − 3.86 | − 7.71 | −8.56 | −21.39 |
| | II.2 | − 0.11 | − 0.77 | − 2.98 | − 4.94 | − 3.41 | −12.21 |
| $i$ | I.1 | − 1.71 | − 5.42 | −13.90 | −16.68 | −14.75 | −52.46 |
| | II.1 | − 4.45 | − 7.82 | −14.20 | −16.03 | −12.34 | −54.84 |
| | II.2 | − 2.70 | − 5.75 | −11.65 | −10.59 | − 2.57 | −33.26 |
| $b$ | I.1 | − 4.32 | − 7.71 | −11.85 | −10.64 | − 3.56 | −38.08 |
| | II.1 | − 1.29 | − 2.67 | − 7.83 | − 8.25 | − 1.86 | −21.90 |
| | II.2 | − 0.09 | + 1.62 | + 0.29 | − 0.36 | + 0.79 | + 2.25 |
| $m$ | I.1 | −10.94 | − 7.29 | − 4.60 | − 0.15 | + 2.82 | −20.16 |
| | II.1 | −12.00 | − 9.02 | − 5.39 | + 0.02 | + 4.27 | −22.22 |
| | II.2 | − 8.12 | − 3.19 | − 0.16 | + 0.43 | + 0.69 | −10.35 |
| $y_g$ | I.1 | − 2.67 | − 3.21 | − 5.96 | − 7.76 | − 6.95 | −26.55 |
| | II.1 | − 3.04 | − 3.41 | − 5.54 | − 6.14 | − 3.43 | −21.56 |
| | II.2 | − 3.10 | − 2.14 | − 1.57 | − 0.36 | + 1.32 | − 5.85 |
| $\Delta\tilde{w}$ | I.1 | + 1.21 | + 1.93 | + 2.03 | + 1.09 | − 0.20 | + 6.06 |
| | II.1 | + 1.21 | + 2.12 | + 2.23 | + 1.18 | − 0.27 | + 6.47 |
| | II.2 | + 0.88 | + 1.28 | + 0.93 | + 0.03 | − 0.62 | + 2.50 |
| $a$ | I.1 | − 2.35 | − 3.74 | − 3.94 | − 2.11 | + 0.39 | −11.75 |
| | II.1 | − 2.35 | − 4.11 | − 4.33 | − 2.29 | + 0.53 | −12.55 |
| | II.2 | − 1.71 | − 2.48 | − 1.80 | − 0.05 | + 1.20 | − 4.84 |
| $l$ | I.1 | − 2.46 | − 6.63 | − 7.68 | − 6.14 | − 2.27 | −25.18 |
| | II.1 | − 3.10 | − 9.11 | −10.73 | − 8.89 | − 4.61 | −36.44 |
| | II.2 | − 2.31 | − 6.22 | − 5.93 | − 3.44 | − 0.72 | −18.62 |
| $p_c$ | I.1 | − 4.56 | − 8.66 | − 6.14 | − 0.03 | + 6.84 | −12.55 |
| | II.1 | − 5.01 | −10.18 | − 8.25 | − 2.27 | + 4.35 | −21.36 |
| | II.2 | − 3.70 | − 6.40 | − 3.11 | + 1.17 | + 2.94 | − 9.10 |
| $Z$ | I.1 | − 9.20 | −13.99 | −15.68 | −11.16 | − 1.31 | −51.34 |
| | II.1 | −11.59 | −16.56 | −18.37 | −11.80 | + 1.79 | −56.53 |
| | II.2 | − 8.37 | −10.54 | − 9.18 | − 2.94 | + 6.35 | −24.68 |

[a] I.1  Theoretical effect of prewar impulse in the prewar period.
 II.1  Theoretical effect of prewar impulse in the postwar period.
 II.2  Theoretical effect of postwar impulse in the postwar period.

## APPENDIX D2  Cumulated Theoretical Cyclical Impacts
## (cyclical minima are italicized)[a]

|              |       | 1        | +2       | +3      | +4      | +5      |
|--------------|-------|----------|----------|---------|---------|---------|
| $c$          | I.1   | − 0.07   | − 0.06   | − 3.00  | −10.01  | *−19.13* |
|              | II.1  | − 0.24   | − 1.26   | − 5.12  | −12.83  | *−21.39* |
|              | II.2  | − 0.11   | − 0.88   | − 3.86  | − 8.80  | *−12.21* |
| $i$          | I.1   | − 1.71   | − 7.13   | −21.03  | −37.71  | *−52.46* |
|              | II.1  | − 4.45   | −12.27   | −26.47  | −42.50  | *−54.84* |
|              | II.2  | − 2.70   | − 8.45   | −20.10  | −30.69  | *−33.26* |
| $b$          | I.1   | − 4.32   | −12.03   | −23.88  | −34.52  | *−38.08* |
|              | II.1  | − 1.29   | − 3.96   | −11.79  | −20.04  | *−21.90* |
|              | II.2  | − 0.09   | + 1.53   | + 1.82  | + 1.46  | + 2.25  |
| $m$          | I.1   | −10.94   | −18.23   | −22.83  | *−22.98* | −20.16  |
|              | II.1  | −12.10   | −21.12   | *−26.51* | −26.49  | −22.22  |
|              | II.2  | − 8.12   | −11.31   | *−11.47* | −11.04  | −10.35  |
| $y_g$        | I.1   | − 2.67   | − 5.88   | −11.84  | −19.60  | *−26.55* |
|              | II.1  | − 3.04   | − 6.45   | −11.99  | −18.13  | *−21.56* |
|              | II.2  | − 3.10   | − 5.24   | − 6.81  | *− 7.17* | − 5.85  |
| $\Delta\tilde{w}$ | I.1   | + 1.21   | + 3.14   | + 5.17  | *+ 6.26* | + 6.06  |
|              | II.1  | + 1.21   | + 3.33   | + 5.56  | *+ 6.74* | + 6.47  |
|              | II.2  | + 0.88   | + 2.26   | + 3.09  | *+ 3.12* | + 2.50  |
| $a$          | I.1   | − 2.35   | − 6.09   | −10.03  | *−12.14* | −11.75  |
|              | II.1  | − 2.35   | − 6.46   | −10.79  | *−13.08* | −12.55  |
|              | II.2  | − 1.71   | − 4.19   | − 5.99  | *− 6.04* | − 4.84  |
| $l$          | I.1   | − 2.46   | − 9.09   | −16.77  | −22.91  | *−25.18* |
|              | II.1  | − 3.10   | −12.21   | −22.94  | −31.83  | *−36.44* |
|              | II.2  | − 2.31   | − 8.53   | −14.46  | −17.90  | *−18.62* |
| $p_c$        | I.1   | − 4.56   | −13.22   | −19.36  | *−19.39* | −12.55  |
|              | II.1  | − 5.01   | −15.19   | −23.44  | *−25.71* | −21.36  |
|              | II.2  | − 3.70   | −10.10   | *−13.21* | −12.04  | − 9.10  |
| $Z$          | I.1   | − 9.20   | −23.19   | −38.87  | *−50.03* | −51.34  |
|              | II.1  | −11.59   | −28.15   | −46.52  | *−58.32* | −56.53  |
|              | II.2  | − 8.37   | −18.91   | −28.09  | *−31.03* | −24.68  |

[a] I.1 Theoretical effect of prewar impulse in the prewar period.
   II.1 Theoretical effect of prewar impulse in the postwar period.
   II.2 Theoretical effect of postwar impulse in the postwar period.

## APPENDIX E1:   *Trend Deviations of Main Impulses*
(Percentages of trend values)

|  | $b$ | $D$ | $p_m$ | $p_b'$ | $x$ |
|---|---|---|---|---|---|
| Trend coefficient, 1923–1938 | − 0.97 | − 5.34 | − 5.80 | − 6.41 | − 2.00 |
| 1923 | −16.8 | −21.6 | −11.8 | −11.5 | − 9.0 |
| 1924 | − 8.5 | −12.7 | − 2.0 | 0.1 | −11.3 |
| 1925 | − 2.0 | 0.1 | 4.5 | 5.0 | − 4.0 |
| 1926 | 1.8 | 17.0 | 3.0 | 2.7 | − 5.2 |
| 1927 | 15.3 | 24.2 | 8.5 | 4.5 | 0.5 |
| 1928 | 19.3 | 41.1 | 15.7 | 12.7 | − 1.7 |
| 1929 | 22.4 | 33.6 | 18.8 | 20.2 | 11.8 |
| 1930 | 13.7 | 36.2 | 14.6 | 15.4 | 21.0 |
| 1931 | 3.8 | − 2.9 | − 0.8 | − 1.1 | 25.8 |
| 1932 | −11.3 | −26.7 | −15.7 | −16.9 | 9.2 |
| 1933 | −15.5 | −35.8 | −20.3 | −18.7 | − 2.3 |
| 1934 | −11.6 | −42.0 | −20.6 | −21.1 | 10.9 |
| 1935 | − 8.7 | −29.4 | −19.1 | −16.9 | − 3.8 |
| 1936 | − 7.8 | − 3.4 | −10.8 | − 4.7 | −12.6 |
| 1937 | 11.1 | 39.1 | 28.4 | 21.7 | −18.8 |
| 1938 | 6.8 | 55.8 | 28.4 | 26.0 | 0.1 |
| Trend coefficient, 1949–1964 | 6.52 | 5.77 | 0.21 | 0.95 | 4.91 |
| 1949 | − 8.0 | −21.8 | −17.3 | −12.6 | − 2.4 |
| 1950 | 3.1 | −20.3 | − 8.0 | − 8.2 | − 5.1 |
| 1951 | 11.8 | 7.3 | 14.2 | 8.1 | − 4.7 |
| 1952 | − 1.4 | 16.5 | 13.2 | 10.0 | − 3.4 |
| 1953 | − 3.8 | 9.5 | 1.7 | 3.9 | 9.7 |
| 1954 | − 1.6 | − 1.0 | − 1.1 | − 0.0 | 4.0 |
| 1955 | 2.8 | 16.9 | 0.3 | 0.2 | 4.6 |
| 1956 | 3.6 | 11.6 | 3.5 | 2.6 | 10.2 |
| 1957 | 3.4 | 17.9 | 8.5 | 4.0 | 10.1 |
| 1958 | − 5.9 | 1.7 | 2.3 | 2.5 | − 6.3 |
| 1959 | − 5.4 | 1.3 | − 0.7 | 2.0 | − 8.1 |
| 1960 | 0.7 | − 1.0 | − 0.9 | 2.9 | − 2.9 |
| 1961 | − 0.0 | 0.1 | − 3.2 | − 3.3 | − 2.4 |
| 1962 | − 1.8 | −14.5 | − 4.0 | − 3.5 | − 4.1 |
| 1963 | 0.6 | − 4.3 | − 3.4 | − 3.5 | − 4.1 |
| 1964 | 3.5 | − 8.0 | − 0.8 | − 2.5 | 8.0 |

## APPENDIX E2  Trend Deviations of Some Endogenous Variables

(Percentages of trend values)

| | c | b | i | m | $y_g$ | a | w | l | $p_c$ | Z |
|---|---|---|---|---|---|---|---|---|---|---|
| **Trend coefficient 1923–1938** | 1.76 | −0.94 | 0.08 | −0.83 | 1.17 | 0.38 | 0.49 | −1.25 | −2.64 | −2.24 |
| 1923 | 0.1 | −24.6 | −26.0 | −18.1 | −6.5 | −6.1 | | −3.1 | −6.9 | −15.2 |
| 1924 | −2.7 | −7.4 | −16.1 | 7.9 | −3.4 | −4.3 | −1.7 | −4.4 | −2.3 | −4.9 |
| 1925 | −4.1 | 0.4 | −12.8 | 3.5 | −2.2 | −2.5 | −2.6 | −3.2 | 1.1 | −2.0 |
| 1926 | −2.3 | 6.2 | 9.4 | 3.6 | 2.8 | 0.1 | −3.7 | −2.0 | −0.0 | 5.7 |
| 1927 | −0.8 | 16.6 | 11.7 | 8.2 | 4.3 | 2.3 | −4.1 | −0.7 | 1.9 | 9.6 |
| 1928 | 0.6 | 22.7 | 31.5 | 13.9 | 7.8 | 5.7 | −5.6 | 2.3 | 6.2 | 21.2 |
| 1929 | 1.9 | 22.7 | 27.5 | 17.1 | 9.6 | 8.5 | −5.6 | 6.3 | 8.2 | 23.5 |
| 1930 | 5.0 | 14.8 | 50.3 | 15.4 | 6.6 | 10.2 | −6.7 | 8.5 | 6.8 | 12.8 |
| 1931 | 5.7 | 7.3 | 21.8 | 10.3 | −1.9 | 6.1 | −3.8 | 8.0 | 1.8 | −8.9 |
| 1932 | 4.6 | −11.9 | 8.0 | 5.2 | −4.7 | 3.4 | 0.9 | 2.9 | −4.5 | −15.9 |
| 1933 | 2.8 | −16.3 | −13.0 | 0.6 | −6.1 | −4.3 | 2.4 | 0.4 | −4.7 | −17.0 |
| 1934 | −0.3 | −14.5 | −18.1 | 8.6 | −5.9 | 3.6 | 2.2 | −1.1 | −4.0 | −14.3 |
| 1935 | −1.4 | −11.6 | −19.2 | −12.8 | −4.1 | 5.0 | 3.8 | −4.7 | −5.4 | −11.5 |
| 1936 | −2.3 | −6.2 | −19.2 | 7.4 | −2.0 | 4.8 | 4.2 | −5.5 | −3.8 | −2.8 |
| 1937 | −2.8 | 12.9 | −4.8 | 3.3 | 4.9 | 0.1 | 1.4 | −2.3 | 1.8 | 13.9 |
| 1938 | −3.2 | 5.1 | 20.8 | 0.4 | 3.0 | 3.3 | | −0.1 | 5.6 | 16.4 |
| **Trend Coefficient 1949–1964** | 4.33 | 9.41 | 7.36 | 8.30 | 5.28 | 1.97 | −0.09 | 7.14 | 2.61 | 6.75 |
| 1949 | 8.0 | −20.4 | 7.0 | −6.0 | −0.8 | 0.7 | | −0.8 | −7.4 | −10.0 |
| 1950 | 5.0 | 0.7 | 15.1 | 15.2 | 2.6 | 2.1 | 0.7 | −1.0 | −1.9 | 6.4 |
| 1951 | −2.1 | 4.1 | −3.1 | 3.3 | −0.3 | 1.4 | 1.2 | 2.1 | 6.5 | 0.8 |
| 1952 | −5.9 | 3.3 | −27.0 | −15.7 | −5.4 | −2.5 | 2.8 | 0.8 | 3.8 | 2.1 |
| 1953 | −4.7 | 5.5 | −15.2 | −7.4 | −2.3 | −2.1 | 1.6 | −2.3 | 0.4 | 0.1 |
| 1954 | −2.3 | 8.7 | 1.2 | 6.5 | 1.3 | −0.4 | 0.7 | −0.8 | 1.5 | 4.5 |
| 1955 | 0.5 | 9.1 | 17.4 | 5.8 | 5.0 | 0.8 | 0.0 | 0.6 | | 12.5 |
| 1956 | 4.7 | 2.7 | 21.8 | 10.6 | 5.2 | 1.6 | −0.3 | 1.5 | −1.2 | 8.6 |
| 1957 | 0.3 | −1.0 | 10.6 | 4.6 | 2.5 | 1.0 | 0.1 | 4.8 | 1.8 | 7.7 |
| 1958 | −4.1 | −0.5 | −12.1 | −9.6 | −4.4 | −2.2 | 1.6 | 2.1 | 1.2 | |
| 1959 | −3.9 | 1.7 | 4.3 | −5.7 | −3.3 | −2.1 | 1.0 | −2.8 | −0.4 | 2.1 |
| 1960 | −2.1 | 5.2 | 1.6 | 1.6 | 1.2 | −1.0 | 0.2 | −2.0 | −0.7 | 7.3 |
| 1961 | −0.8 | −1.1 | 3.2 | 0.4 | 0.2 | −0.6 | −0.1 | −2.2 | −1.7 | 0.3 |
| 1962 | 1.1 | −3.6 | 2.5 | −2.8 | −1.0 | 0.7 | −0.1 | −3.8 | −1.8 | 4.8 |
| 1963 | 3.2 | −6.6 | 3.7 | −1.1 | −1.7 | 1.1 | 0.0 | −1.3 | −1.7 | 9.7 |
| 1964 | 4.3 | −3.6 | −2.8 | 4.6 | 1.9 | 1.7 | | 5.7 | 2.1 | 5.4 |

# COMMENT

KARL A. FOX
Iowa State University, Ames

The discussion by Verdoorn and Post makes use of a relatively well known model of the Dutch economy, the CPB Model 63-D. This model reflects the work of a number of excellent and practical econometricians, beginning with Professor Jan Tinbergen and including Verdoorn and Post themselves.

I shall briefly recapitulate the logical structure of the Verdoorn-Post discussion and then proceed to a critique and reformulation of their handling of the exogenous variables in arriving at their "maximal impulse mix."

## LOGICAL STRUCTURE OF THE PAPER

The authors seek to explain why postwar cycles in the Netherlands have been less severe than prewar cycles, and to determine whether the Dutch economy has become inherently more vulnerable or less vulnerable to cyclical impulses from abroad.

In answering these questions, they use annual time-series of 59 variables for 1923–1938 and 1949–1964, organized into an econometric model of the Dutch economy (CPB Model 63-D). The variables are classified into exogenous and endogenous categories from the standpoint of a Dutch economic policymaker. A theoretical *cycle impulse mix* is determined for each of the periods 1923–1938 and 1949–1964 in a reproducible way, using the standard deviations and serial correlation coefficients of selected exogenous variables as bases for determining the amplitudes and periods of sinusoid cycles for these variables[1]. A *maximal cycle impulse* mix is obtained by assuming that all five of the most important exogenous variables turn down simultaneously.

---

[1] The intercorrelation matrix of the major exogenous variables is displayed but apparently not used. The sinusoid for each variable is based strictly on the standard deviation and serial correlation coefficient of that variable.

The *maximal impulse mix* is propagated through the CPB model, and the resulting cycles in selected endogenous variables are calculated. These are compared (a) by using the 1923–1938 impulse mix in both periods, starting at the 1929 and 1957 cycle peaks, respectively, and (b) by using the 1949–1964 impulse mix in 1949–1964, starting at the 1957 cycle peak.

The results obtained are summarized in several tables and charts. It appears that the responses of gross national product, investment, and employment to a given impact did not change greatly between 1923–1938 and 1949–1964. However, the maximal impulse mix was less violent in 1949–1964, as the standard deviations of the exogenous variables were much smaller than in 1923–1938.

The 13 reaction equations were the same in both periods; so also were the definition equations; likewise, equations (22-23), (38-39), and (27-33). The chief differences between the two periods are in the weights applied in forming certain expenditure totals and in certain equations involving incomes and average tax rates. *A priori*, I would not expect these changes to make much difference in the sensitivity of the Dutch economy to exogenous impulses.

### CRITIQUE, REFORMULATION AND EXTENSION: THE NATURE OF "EXOGENOUS" THREATS TO DOMESTIC ECONOMIC STABILITY

The Verdoorn-Post method assumes that business cycles are *not* obsolete, and it goes so far as to assume that the exogenous variables follow sinusoid patterns. I believe this is done primarily to achieve a reproducible rationale for the magnitude and time-shape of the maximal impulse mixes. Also, it seems plausible that *cycles* of several years duration in the chief exogenous variables would pose a greater threat to the Dutch economy than would random time paths for these same variables.

I propose first to reformulate the Verdoorn-Post experiment, assuming that the business cycle is indeed obsolete. Then, I shall briefly consider the mechanism which generates the variables Verdoorn and Post define as exogenous in this experiment.

Professor Kuhn has remarked that "what a man sees depends both upon what he looks at and also upon what his previous visual-conceptual experience has taught him to see."[2]

Most of us taking part in the discussion of business cycles have been taught to see cycles rather than random time series. But suppose we start on the assumption that *cycles are obsolete.* All we have for the Netherlands, then, is an econometric model expressing endogenous variables ($y$) as a function of exogenous "data" variables ($z$) and "instrument" variables ($x$).

[2] Thomas S. Kuhn, *The Structure of Scientific Revolutions*, Chicago, 1962, p. 112.

Then, for each of two time periods, 1923–1938 and 1949–1964, we have time-series observations for all variables. We wish (a) to compare fluctuations in the $y$'s in the two periods and (b) to explain differences in their fluctuations as between the two periods.

Assume that we have a single $y$, a single $x$, and a single $z$:

$$t = 1923, \ldots, 1938$$

(1)　$y(t) = bx(t) + cz(t) + u(t)$

$$\text{or } t = 1949, \ldots, 1964,$$

where all variables are deviations about their means for a given period. If the instrument $x$ had not been used but had been held constant throughout the period, then $x(t)$ would have been zero, and equation (1) could be rewritten as

(2)　$y(t) = cz(t) + u(t),$

where $u(t)$ is assumed to be a random disturbance not serially correlated and not correlated with $z(t)$.

For simplicity of notation, drop $(t)$. Then,

(2')　$y = cz + u,$

and the variance of $y$ can be expressed as

(3)　$s_y^2 = c^2 s_z^2 + s_u^2 .$

Now, suppose $s_y^2 (\text{II}) < s_y^2(\text{I})$, where (II) denotes 1949–1964 and (I) denotes 1923–1938. One or more of the following inequalities must account for the difference:

$$s_{u(\text{II})}^2 < s_{u(\text{I})}^2; \text{ and/or } s_{z(\text{II})}^2 < s_{z(\text{I})}^2; \text{ and/or } c_{(\text{II})}^2 < c_{(\text{I})}^2.$$

Note that　$\dfrac{\partial s_y^2}{\partial s_z^2} = c^2; \quad \dfrac{\partial s_y^2}{\partial c} = 2c s_z^2 .$

Suppose now that two exogenous variables (rather than only one) affect the endogenous variable $y$. Then equation (2') becomes

(4)　$y = c_1 z_1 + c_2 z_2 + u.$

The variance of $y$ during a time period of $n$ years is

(5)　$\dfrac{1}{n-1} \Sigma y^2 = \dfrac{1}{n-1} [\Sigma(c_1 z_1 + c_2 z_2)^2 + \Sigma u^2 + 2\Sigma(c_1 z_1 u + c_2 z_2 u)].$

Assume that $u$ is uncorrelated with $z_1$ and $z_2$, so $\Sigma z_1 u = 0$, $\Sigma z_2 u = 0$, and (5) leads to

(6)　$s_y^2 = c_1^2 s_{z_1}^2 + c_2^2 s_{z_2}^2 + 2c_1 c_2 r_{12} s_{z_1} s_{z_2} + s_u^2 ,$

where $r_{12}$ is the correlation coefficient between $z_1$ and $z_2$ during the $n$-year period.

The direct effects, $c_1^2 s_{z_1}^2$ and $c_2^2 s_{z_2}^2$, are additive and positive; the sign of the joint effect depends on the signs of $c_1$, $c_2$, and $r_{12}$.

If the $s_y^2$ in periods I and II are compared, the sources of possible difference include $s_u^2$, $c_1^2$, $c_2^2$, $s_{z_1}^2$, $s_{z_2}^2$, and $r_{12}$. If the coefficients $c_1$ and $c_2$ are the same in both periods, the remaining sources of difference are $s_{z_1}^2$, $s_{z_2}^2$ and $r_{12}$.

The effects of changing $c_1$ and $c_2$ are

$$(7.1) \qquad \frac{\partial s_y^2}{\partial c_1} = 2c_1 s_{z_1}^2 + 2c_1 r_{12} s_{z_1} s_{z_2} \quad \text{and}$$

$$(7.2) \qquad \frac{\partial s_y^2}{\partial c_2} = 2c_2 s_{z_2}^2 + 2c_1 r_{12} s_{z_1} s_{z_2}.$$

The point of equations (7.1) and (7.2) is that the total effect on the variance of the endogenous variable ($y$) resulting from a change in one structural coefficient (say, $c_1$) is a function not only of the variance of the corresponding exogenous variable ($z_1$) but also of the coefficient ($c_2$) of the other exogenous variable ($z_2$) and the covariance ($r_{12} s_{z_1} s_{z_2}$) of the two exogenous variables. The effects of a change in one coefficient cannot be safely be judged on an intuitive basis; explicit account must be taken of the complete structure of the economic model, and of the joint time-shape of all the exogenous variables.

If there is only one endogenous "target" variable, $y$, then only one instrument variable, $x$, is needed (in principle) to compensate for the effects of the exogenous variables and to attain a desired value of $y$. Structurally,

$$(8) \qquad y(t) = bx(t) + [c_1 z_1(t) + c_2 z_2(t)] + u(t)$$

The attempt may be made to forecast $z_1(t)$ as $\hat{z}_1(t)$ and $z_2(t)$ as $\hat{z}_2(t)$ and to apply a stabilization rule $x(t) = \alpha[c_1 \hat{z}_1(t) + c_2 \hat{z}_2(t)]$.

If so, write

$$(9) \qquad [y(t) - b\alpha[c_1 \hat{z}_1(t) + c_2 \hat{z}_2(t)]] = [c_1 z_1(t) + c_2 z_2(t)] + u(t),$$

restoring to the left hand side the effects of the stabilization instrument $x$ used according to the rule indicated [3].

Professor Verdoorn has the equivalents of the $b$, $c_1$, and $c_2$ coefficients in his

[3] One of the most important exogenous variables in the Verdoorn-Post experiment is the policy instrument $x$, autonomous expenditure. Presumably the planned use of this variable helped to reduce fluctuations in endogenous variables during 1949–1964. If records of forecast values of $z_1$ and $z_2$ and planned changes in $x$ had been kept, it would be possible through equation (9) to reconstruct the time path that $y$ would have followed if $x$ had been held constant.

basic model (Appendix B). He displays the equivalents of $r_{12}$ in Appendix C and $s_{z_1}$ and $s_{z_2}$ on page 439 and in table 14-4.

However, he calculates all variables $y$, $z_1$, $z_2$, $x$ as deviations from their respective trends. Then, he imposes the assumption that *there is a cycle* in each exogenous variable and approximates it with a sinusoid wave. He arrives at reproducible results, but perhaps in a cumbersome way.

A simpler alternative would have been to run the 1923–1938 time-series on exogenous variables through the 1949–1964 model. The effects of the change in *each* equation from 1923–1938 to 1949–1964 could have been displayed separately. The joint effects of *all* changes in the equations could then have been shown.

Conversely, the 1949–1964 time-series on exogenous variables could have been run through the 1923–1938 model.

These two demonstrations might have shown that changes in the coefficients of the CPB Model 63-D had not much effect on the sensitivity of the economy to specified fluctuations in the exogenous variables[4].

The chief exogenous variables mentioned in the Verdoorn-Post discussion are world demand for competing exports ($b_c$), prices of competing exports ($p_b$), and prices of imports. Prices of exports and imports were highly correlated during 1949–1964; neither of these price series was very highly correlated with $b_c$ during that period.

Professor Verdoorn's exogenous variable $x$ (autonomous expenditure) can in principle be used as the chief instrument of stabilization (and growth) policy.

Let me write a model of a two-country closed system, based on Professor Hickman's model but omitting $T$ and $Y_{-1}$:

*Country 1:*

(10.1)  $Y_1 = C_1 + I_1 + G_1 + E_1 - M_1$    (10.3)  $I_1 = i_1 Y_1$

(10.2)  $C_1 = c_1 Y_1$    (10.4)  $M_1 = m_1 Y_1$

---

[4] The effects of applying the same exogenous impulse at different initial levels of unemployment in 1929 and in 1957 do not depend on changes in the *structure* of the model.

The emphasis in equations (3), (6), (7.1) and (7.2) on explaining the *variance* of the endogenous variable, $s_y^2$, may be questioned, as the severity of economic fluctuations is usually measured in terms of the variable itself. But if the standard deviation $s_y$, is used to summarize the magnitude of these fluctuations in a given period, $s_y^2$ as an intermediate step, as in all variants of least squares approaches must be calculated. Also, $s_y^2$ might be considered as a quadratic performance measure or welfare measure, in which a deviation of 2 per cent from a desired value of $y$ is regarded as four times as bad as a deviation of 1 per cent. If so, the attempt would be made to steer the economy in such a way as to minimize the sum of squared deviations rather than the sum of absolute deviations.

*Country 2:*

$$(10.5) \quad Y_2 = C_2 + I_2 + G_2 + E_2 - M_2 \qquad\qquad (10.7) \quad I_2 = i_2 Y_2$$

$$(10.6) \quad C_2 = c_2 Y_2 \qquad\qquad\qquad\qquad\qquad (10.8) \quad M_2 = m_2 Y_2$$

In Country 1, it may (initially and naively) be assumed that $E_1$ (exports) is exogenous and that $G_1$ (government expenditure) is the main policy instrument. Four variables, $Y_1$, $C_1$, $I_1$, and $M_1$, are regarded as endogenous.

In the two-country model, of course, $E_1 = M_2$ and $E_2 = M_1$, so that the export variables become *endogenous* to the closed system, which may be displayed as follows:

| "Leading" Endogenous Variable | $Y_1$ | $C_1$ | $I_1$ | $Y_2$ | $C_2$ | $I_2$ | $M_1$ | $M_2$ | $E_1$ | $E_2$ | $G_1$ | $G_2$ | | |
|---|---|---|---|---|---|---|---|---|---|---|---|---|---|---|
| $Y_1$ | 1 | -1 | -1 | | | | 1 | | -1 | | -1 | | | 0 |
| $C_1$ | $-c_1$ | 1 | 0 | | 0 | | | | | | | | | 0 |
| $I_1$ | $-i_1$ | 0 | 1 | | | | | | | | | | | 0 |
| $Y_2$ | | | | 1 | -1 | -1 | | 1 | | -1 | | -1 | | 0 |
| $C_2$ | | 0 | | $-c_2$ | 1 | 0 | | | | | | | = | 0 |
| $I_2$ | | | | $-i_2$ | 0 | 1 | | | | | | | | 0 |
| $M_1$ | $-m_1$ | | | | | | 1 | | | | | | | 0 |
| $M_2$ | | | | $-m_2$ | | | | 1 | | | | | | 0 |
| $E_1$ | | | | | | | | -1 | 1 | | 0 | | | 0 |
| $E_2$ | | | | | | | -1 | | | 1 | | | | 0 |

This display is not in conventional matrix form. The vector to the extreme left is simply a list to help the reader identify rows of the coefficient matrix with equations in the models for Country 1 and Country 2. The vector of 10 endogenous and two exogenous variables, normally written as a column vector to the right of the coefficient matrix, is displayed as a set of 12 "column headings," each of which is to be multiplied by the coefficients in its column. Thus, the first row becomes

$$Y_1 - C_1 - I_1 + M_1 - E_1 - G_1 = 0 \ ,$$

or, rearranging terms,

$$Y_1 = C_1 + I_1 + G_1 + E_1 - M_1 \ ,$$

the first equation in the model for Country 1.

In this system there are now 10 endogenous variables and only two exogenous or autonomous ones, $G_1$ and $G_2$. Because of feedbacks through Country 2, the multiplier effect upon $Y_1$ of an increase in $G_1$ is larger than if imports $(M_1)$ were a genuine and complete leakage from the economy of Country 1. For example, let $c_1 = c_2 = 0.5$, $i_1 = i_2 = 0.2$, and $m_1 = m_2 = 0.3$.

If $M_1$ were simply a leakage, the multiplier in Country 1 would be

$$\frac{\partial Y_1}{\partial G_1} = \frac{1}{1-0.5-0.2+0.3} = \frac{1}{1-0.4} = \frac{1}{0.6} = 1.67 \, .$$

However, in the two-country system the corresponding multiplier becomes

$$\frac{\partial Y_1}{\partial G_1} = \frac{(1-0.5-0.2+0.3)}{(1-0.5-0.2+0.3)^2 - (0.3)^2} = \frac{0.6}{0.36-0.09} = 2.22 \, .$$

If the policymaker in each country understands the structure of the complete system, he will presumably take account of the fact that his multiplier is 2.22 rather than 1.67 in deciding by how much government expenditures should be modified[5].

[5] If $M_1$ is regarded as a leakage and $E_1$ as exogenous, then the multiplier for Country 1 can be derived by substituting equations (10.2), (10.3), (10.4) in (10.1):

$$Y_1 = c_1 Y_1 + i_1 Y_1 - m_1 Y_1 + G_1 + E_1; \quad \text{whence} \tag{11.1}$$

$$Y_1(1 - c_1 - i_1 + m_1) = G_1 + E_1, \quad \text{and} \tag{11.2}$$

$$Y_1 = \frac{G_1}{(1 - c_1 - i_1 + m_1)} + \frac{E_1}{(1 - c_1 - i_1 + m_1)}; \quad \text{so} \tag{11.3}$$

$$\frac{\partial Y_1}{\partial G_1} = \frac{1}{(1 - c_1 - i_1 + m_1)} = \frac{1}{k_1} \, . \tag{11.4}$$

The corresponding multiplier for Country 2, regarded as an open economy, would be

$$\frac{\partial Y_2}{\partial G_2} = \frac{1}{(1 - c_2 - i_2 + m_2)} = \frac{1}{k_2} \, . \tag{11.5}$$

In the two-country closed system, however, $E_1 = m_2 Y_2$, $E_2 = m_1 Y_1$, and $G_2$ is exogenous. So

$$Y_1 = \frac{1}{k_1}(G_1 + m_2 Y_2), \quad \text{and} \tag{11.6}$$

$$Y_2 = \frac{1}{k_2}(G_2 + m_1 Y_1) \, . \tag{11.7}$$

Substituting equation (11.7) in (11.6), we obtain

$$Y_1 = \frac{1}{k_1}\left[ G_1 + \left( \frac{m_2 G_2 + m_2 j m_1 Y_1}{k_2} \right) \right] \, . \quad \text{Then} \tag{11.8}$$

$$Y_1[k_1 k_2 - m_2 m_1] = k_2 G_1 + m_2 G_2, \quad \text{or} \tag{11.9}$$

$$Y_1 = \left( \frac{k_2}{k_1 k_2 - m_2 m_1} \right) G_1 + \left( \frac{m_2}{k_1 k_2 - m_2 m_1} \right) G_2, \quad \text{and} \tag{11.10}$$

$$\frac{\partial Y_1}{d G_1} = \frac{k_2}{k_1 k_2 - m_2 m_1} = \frac{(1 - c_2 - i_2 + m_2)}{(1 - c_1 - i_1 + m_1)(1 - c_2 - i_2 + m_2) - m_2 m_1} \, . \tag{11.11}$$

I am indebted to B. C. Sanyal, post-doctoral research associate at Iowa State University, for catching an error in my earlier calculation of the closed-system multiplier.

Conceptually, the basic structure of the two-country matrix could be elaborated into a world system, using as much detail as Professor Klein proposes for his Wharton School model. With more than two countries, the constraints relating total exports to total imports permit multilateral trade. Price-dependent demand and supply functions (where realistic) can be admitted for certain commodities in each of the trading countries or regions, so that the representation of international trade becomes a spatial equilibrium model for such commodities.

If the world model is partitioned into $k$ countries, then a "policymaker" in each country uses the instruments available to him to pursue his domestic objectives of growth and stabilization with greater or less awareness (1) of the properties of the coefficient matrix connecting the endogenous variables in the world economy and (2) of the intentions and expertise of each of the other policymakers.

Will such a world system produce *cycles* in the demand for exports, prices of exports, and prices of imports as these impinge upon the economies of individual countries? Or will it produce more or less random fluctuations in such variables? Will the system leads its $k$ policymakers either by an invisible hand (or by a visible econometric model) to a general good that was no part of their individual intentions? Are elderly politicians in all countries "waiting for Godot" – the cycle that never comes?

The countries and groups of countries discussed at this Conference accounted (as of 1965) for 75 to 80 per cent of world GNP. The business cycle seems to be completely surrounded, intellectually at least. And the "autonomous" cause of the business cycle (if there is to be one) must evidently be the impercipience of the policymakers who are supposed to avert it – or the impercipience of their economic advisers.

To frame the problem in this fashion puts "exogenous" threats to domestic economic stability in a less intractable light. I believe it was Christopher Morley who recorded an analogous insight:

> In a public house off Fleet Street (twas called the Red Lion),
> The Old Mandarin raised his glass to his friend, saying
> "I suddenly realize that you and I
> Are the men my father warned me against!"

Let us cultivate our model.

# V  BUSINESS CYCLE POLICIES

Chapter Fifteen

# POSTWAR STABILIZATION POLICIES

ERIK LUNDBERG
Stockholm School of Economics

This chapter, with its broad title, is intended to give a general survey of problems relevant to stabilization policies. It will attempt to try to concentrate on a number of issues to which more than the customary amount of attention should be given.

Stabilization policy should be defined with reference to a concept of actual or potential instability in economic development, relative to some accepted targets of stability. Therefore, some possible concepts of instability will first be considered, followed by an attempt to decide which measures within the sphere of government economic policy should be defined as stabilization policies.

## What Is Instability?

Economic change, implying some kind of instability, occurs continuously. New decisions concerning production, prices, sales, investment, consumption, savings, and government economic policy are being made more or less constantly by consumers, firms, organizations, government agencies, etc. These decisions successively create new situations for any number of economic units, disturb their position or development, and cause reactions throughout the economic system.

Economists have a propensity to consider change phenomena as important and interesting only if they fall into certain recognizable patterns. For example, changes may be classified by seasonal, cyclical, or trend patterns; all other changes are then considered irregular, nonclassified, or uninteresting. In this chapter, attention is concentrated on change phenomena that are called cyclical or conjunctural, which implies a kind of instability having certain properties that are difficult to define clearly, but are rather easily recognized. The desire is to find a kind of systematic economic instability that affects large sectors of the economy — sectors so large, in fact, that the entire economy is affected, as evidenced by variations in gross national product (GNP).

The distinction between cyclical or conjunctural instability and other economic changes may not be sufficiently clear, if economic change in the past is considered from only an empirical point of view. History never repeats itself exactly. For instance, the catastrophic U.S. depression of 1929–1933 and the very mild recessions of 1954 and 1960–1961 were so different that they can very well be classified in different categories. But if the assumption is made that the empirical evidence is sufficient to classify in one category the U.S. over the entire period 1919–1964, a question arises: How should, for instance, the British, Dutch, French, Japanese, or Swedish economic developments after World War II (hereafter called the postwar period) be classified? Is there empirical evidence that permits placing the experiences of these countries in the same category? It seems plausible to consider the Swedish and Swiss postwar instability experiences as rather different from the repeated balance of payments disturbances of such countries as the United Kingdom, Denmark, or Finland, or from corresponding balance of payments crises in a number of countries that export raw materials. During the interwar as well as the postwar period, several countries had spells of relative economic stagnation manifested by slow growth, or none at all. This was true, for example, of the United Kingdom during the 1920's and again in 1955–1959 and in 1964–1967; the United States during the 1930's and from 1953 to the beginning of the 1960's; France during nearly the whole interwar period; and Denmark during 1953–1957. Such periods of relative stagnation may be regarded as instability in the rate of economic growth, but they may not fit so well into the usual conception of business cycles. The repeated bursts of strong inflation during the postwar period — with excess demand conditions on the labor markets and above-trend increases in wages and prices — may be considered as a special kind of cyclical instability.

The various types of economic instability exemplified in the foregoing discussion might be described as short term and as important to the whole of the economy in question. "Important" is to be interpreted in light of the usual policy aims during the postwar period. However, it is not enough to refer only to empirical observations of instability; notions of potential instability must also be kept in mind in order to bring out essential characteristics of conjunctural behavior in various countries. It may be that the relatively even growth rate in the United Kingdom and the rather steady state of full employment in such countries as Norway and Sweden during the postwar period result, to a large extent, from government stabilization policies. Potentially, production and employment in these countries may have tended to fluctuate (as they did in the

United States and Canada), but government policy measures may have neutralized this tendency. This hypothetical statement implies that empirical evidence of some measured degree of instability is not a sufficient criterion for classifying instability phenomena. A characterization of the reaction pattern or mechanism of the economic system that is being observed should also be included. Thus, it may be possible to find a greater number of common features in the instability patters of economic development in the Western economies than are indicated by direct statistical observations.

PRINCIPAL CRITERIA

A certain degree of vagueness in the definition and demarcation of instability phenomena is unavoidable. It is better to keep such vagueness in mind, and to accept it as a realistic expression of the nature of the problems, rather than to put the problems into a straitjacket of false precision. One definition is spelled out in the actual choice of issues. But, of course, some very general criteria can determine the selection of problems. There are in fact three main criteria: the problems should refer in some ways to short-term deviations from balanced growth; they should be important; and they should be interesting from the point of view of stabilization policy.

Instability in the growth process has taken a variety of forms. The most simple one is the irregularity of the yearly rate of growth of real GNP. Variations of the annual growth rate between, for example, zero and 8 per cent are *prima facie* evidence of economic instability. This instability also implies corresponding variations in the rates of employment and unemployment. This kind of instability can easily be given a cyclical connotation. Even if growth has been proceeding without absolute setbacks, variations in the annual rates of growth (in real terms) usually convey the impression of cyclical swings.

There is a special form of instability in the behavior of GNP that is of considerable interest: in periods of relative stagnation, gaps may appear between actual and potential production as determined by full or normal use of labor and capital resources. Such "deflationary gaps" may, of course, be merely the result of recurring short-term retardations of actual growth (below capacity growth) and, thus, a consequence of the fluctuating growth rates. But production gaps lasting over a period of several years can be taken as a special form of instability.

Also of importance is the development of total demand, which cannot be adequately pictured as the rate of growth of production. Inflationary (as well as deflationary) developments should be regarded as deviations from balanced growth. In all countries during the postwar period, there has been a persistent long-term trend of rising prices, representing deviations from the price stability targets of economic policy.

## Comparisons of Cyclical Instability.

### VARIATIONS IN GROWTH RATES

The yearly and quarterly variations in production – as well as the variations in unemployment rates – in western countries during the postwar period seem rather insignificant when considered against the background of the interwar experiences. The postwar variations have been mostly retardations and accelerations of the growth rates; only in relatively few instances have there been absolute declines. However, instability experiences must be related to the new high ambitions with regard to the targets of rapid and stable growth, which have been accepted more or less explicitly by all countries in the years since the war. From this point of view, a retardation from 4 per cent to 1 per cent in the normal rate of growth is regarded as quite serious; it may imply a doubling of the unemployment rate (say, from 2 to 4 per cent) and cause trouble for the most exposed branches of activity, often rather highly dependent on export trade. Excessive price and wage movements, as well as balance of payments troubles, also are regarded as serious problems.

There is a limited degree of synchronization among countries in the variations in the general growth rate. The recession of 1957–1958 shows the greatest amount of synchronization: in all the countries studied there was a decline in the rate of growth of GNP, and in some (the United States, Canada, Belgium, Switzerland) there was even an obsolete decline. A tendency toward synchronization is evident also in the period following the Korean War boom, but the covariation is less marked than in 1957–1958 because of the deviant patterns for the United States and Canada, where recessions occurred in 1954. There is still less synchronization in 1960–1963 although a number of countries experienced some retardation of growth in those years. Generally, there is less synchronization in years of the most rapid growth. However, a rather general tendency toward relatively high growth rates is apparent for 1950, 1955, 1959–1960, and 1963–1964; but these years were not always the years when the top of the boom was reached.

When international comparisons of cyclical instability are attempted, difficulties arise in finding criteria for meaningful comparisons. In the postwar period, the various countries have presumably been exposed to shocks and disturbances of quite different kinds and in varying degrees. Would it not be helpful to compare sensitivities of the economies with regard to shocks of the same kind and relative order? Also, there is a rather vague and arbitrary line of division between what may be called external disturbances, on the one hand, and the reaction patterns of the economies, on the other. For instance, have the United Kingdom and Denmark been affected more frequently and deeply than

Sweden, Germany, and Switzerland by balance of payments disturbances? Or are the balance of payments disturbances related to the behavior patterns characteristic of the economies in question? These kinds of problems are, of course, especially pertinent with regard to the reaction of government policy. The actual postwar instability patterns in the various countries have been heavily influenced by policy changes—taken as exogenous factors or regarded as responses to actual or expected deviations from certain targets or norms.

EXPENDITURE COMPONENTS OF GNP

A small step in the direction of relevant comparisons may be taken by studying how the instability of the growth of GNP has been "determined" by variations in the expenditure components. When these components are examined, some interesting problems arise. Even apart from questions of functional relationships, it is not easy to obtain a clear picture of how the observed instability of output—the variation of the GNP growth rate—and the corresponding instability of the expenditure components are related, since variations in the growth of the components offset or reinforce each other to a varying extent. The arithmetical relationship between the instability of GNP and its components can be said to depend upon how much the growth of the components fluctuates, how much the growth of the components on the average contributes to the growth of GNP, and finally, the degree to which the weighted fluctuations of the components are synchronized with one another.

Gross and net instability coefficients of GNP growth (in real terms) are compared in Table 15-1. The gross instability coefficient of each country (1950–1964) is equal to the sum of the annual average variations of the growth of six GNP components (private consumption, fixed investment, inventory investment, government demand for goods and services, exports, and imports). The net instability coefficient is simply the average variation of the growth of total GNP. Obviously, the gross instability coefficient tends to be large for the small countries in the group, but the variations in the growth of the components tend to offset each other to a great extent. For example, contrast the size of the ratio of the gross to the net coefficient for Sweden and that for the United States: Should this difference be interpreted to mean that there are more stabilizing forces in the Swedish than in the U.S. economy? Or is the contrast mainly a result of differing stabilization policies? Actually, part of the much larger degree of offsetting among the growth variations of the components in the Swedish economy is due to the operation of an economy much closer to potential output and the ceiling of total supply. Another part is due to the difference in the importance of foreign trade, as variations in the growth of exports and imports tend to be mutually offsetting rather than additive. For Western Europe as a whole, the gross instability coefficient is lower than the corresponding figure for any of the individual countries; and the net instability coefficient is equal to the lowest corresponding figure for any of the individual countries. How much of the lower instability in Western Europe as a whole, compared with the United States, is due to a low degree of synchronization between the national economies, and to what extent is it due to a high degree of policy independence of the individual countries?

TABLE 15-1. **Gross and Net Instability Coefficients for Selected Countries***

|  | Gross coefficient | Net coefficient | Ratio of gross to net coefficient |
|---|---|---|---|
| Austria | 8.3 | 2.4 | 3.4 |
| Denmark | 8.8 | 2.5 | 3.5 |
| France | 4.5 | 1.4 | 3.3 |
| Germany | 5.0 | 1.9 | 2.7 |
| Italy | 4.8 | 1.4 | 2.4 |
| Netherlands | 10.9 | 2.3 | 4.7 |
| Norway | 6.3 | 1.4 | 4.5 |
| Sweden | 6.0 | 1.5 | 4.0 |
| Switzerland | 6.9 | 1.8 | 3.8 |
| United Kingdom | 4.6 | 1.4 | 3.2 |
| Canada | 6.8 | 2.7 | 2.6 |
| United States | 5.0 | 2.6 | 1.9 |
| Japan | 10.6 | 4.5 | 2.4 |

* For a description of the coefficients, see text.

INDUSTRIAL SECTORS

Comparisons of instability experiences may also be made by studying the cyclical movements within industrial sectors. A characteristic of the postwar period seems to be that the conjunctural movements have been concentrated in a rather limited number of branches of industry. There have been quite impressive variations in production, orders, prices, and sales (especially for exports and imports), as well as in investment in fixed capital and inventory, within such branches as iron and steel, iron ore, pulp and paper, textiles, shipbuilding, and certain subbranches of machinery production. These branches usually show much more international synchronization of cyclical development than is shown by GNP growth. In these branches of industry, international trade plays a strategic role in most countries; therefore, there is, an international price system having a common impact on profits, production, trade, and investment. Even if these branches have heavy weights in total industrial production, their relative importance in GNP is limited.

When the growth and instability in the postwar period of Western European countries and Japan are compared with the growth and instability in the United States and Canada, it is important to remember the very great differences in their conditions immediately after the war. In the United States, total output in 1948 exceeded by about 2/3 the prewar peak attained in 1937. In Western Europe, GNP at constant prices had only just regained its prewar peak, while the population was 8 per cent larger than before the war. Not until 1955 did Western Europe reach the same total and per capita production, in relation to the prewar peaks, that the United States had reached in 1948. But there were also great differences among the European countries. Such observations on postwar activity, relative to prewar peaks, may give some very rough indication of short-term growth possibilities as conceived from the supply side.

Within the limits of potential growth, the actual development of output during the postwar period was determined by factors of demand. In spite of its being somewhat vague with respect to actual measurement, the concept of demand pressure as it has appeared in the postwar debate may serve as a useful expression, if not a tool of analysis. The existence of strong and persistent general demand pressure may be considered a partial explanation for the absence of significant setbacks in most Western European countries. Elastic supply conditions—which imply a rapid response of total production to a real increase of demand—did not necessarily contribute to a quick reduction of the demand pressure, since additional income created by the rise in production and prices added new fuel to the inflationary fire. In Western Europe, the tendency toward continued generally strong demand pressure was due to a number of factors, among which the following should be given special attention: (a) a high and usually rising share of government in total expenditure; (b) a high and often rising investment ratio; (c) a shift in the foreign balance from a large current account deficit during the first Marshall Plan years to a balanced or even a surplus position in the early 1960's.

The conjunctural sensitivity of an economy cannot be understood, of course, only from the point of view of demand-supply relations of the type discussed. There are interrelations over time, manifested in accumulated experiences. In this respect it might be suggested that in the European countries which during the first part of the postwar period had realized rapid and continued growth there has occurred a build-up of strong expectations of continued substantial and essentially uninterrupted growth of markets and incomes. Such confidence in the future implies relatively strong overall resistance of fixed business and consumer investment expenditures in the face of short-run downward disturbances in some part of total demand (for instance in exports). Thus, downward disturbances in some part of the economy will be dampened, not only by the automatic stabilizers built into the fiscal system (plus stabilizing discretionary policy measures) but also by the acquired "growth habit" of the private sector of the economy. This kind of stability in growth expectations within the private sector is intermixed with anticipations of continued inflation. Generally prevailing expectations of a long-run steady rise of unit-wage costs and prices are intermingled in an unaccountable manner with anticipations of expanding markets. Under the conditions that have prevailed in most European countries during most of the time, a setback in some sector of final demand, including inventory investment, is in the short run prevented from spreading to other parts of the economy, so that total demand tends to continue rising. The setback is therefore reflected in a slowing-down of the rate of growth of real GNP rather than in a truly recessionary interruption of growth. In a "high pressure" economy, certain parts of private investment expenditures may even be automatically accelerated during periods of slack, as a result of quicker deliveries and a more elastic labor supply; investment costs may seem lower than during a past boom — and still more so when compared with conditions during an expected new boom. Such stabilizing business behavior may be expected among progressive corporations with reliable growth prospects. But since total investment in plant and equipment at constant prices usually has shown some decline during periods of slack, it appears that any such automatic stabilizing effects have not been sufficient to compensate fully for the instability tendencies arising from difficulties of financing investments in periods when profit margins are squeezed, markets are relatively dull, and inventories considerably above the desired range.

It was suggested earlier that a strong growth trend accompanied by excess demand pressure will, for several reasons, imply resistance against recessionary impulses originating from external shocks and minor setbacks in individual activities. Such a statement does not seem very clarifying or challenging, as it is close to circular reasoning when put so generally. There is no reason to believe that the rate of growth, but no other features of a trend, will be systematically related to cyclical instability. Only to the extent that the rate of growth and demand pressure are related can some conclusions be drawn. This may be done by comparing North American and some Western European experiences, especially during the 1950's. However, when such a comparison is made, it is important to remember that instability of the excess demand type, with tendencies toward wage inflation, was eventually combined with the threat of foreign exchange difficulties.

### Policy Factors

How do policy issues enter into this picture of instability? They cannot generally be isolated from events in the rest of the economy. In order to understand both short-term and long-term developments, an attempt should be made not only to assess the effects of policies which were actually carried out but also to understand why and how the measures came about. In some countries, policy changes can be explained to a large extent by referring to varying exchange situations. The basic possibilities for fast and stable growth have often been limited by balance of payments restrictions. This has been true particularly in the United Kingdom, but also at some times in the Netherlands, Denmark, Italy and Japan. In the United Kingdom, foreign exchange crises, or the serious threat of such crises, were the basis of restrictive policy measures in 1947, 1949, 1951, 1955, 1957, 1960–1961, and 1964–1965.

In his study of the postwar business cycle in Western Europe, Maddison concluded that the European economy no longer operates as it did in prewar years[1]. He related the essential difference not to a greater inherent stability of the private forces but to government intervention which succeeded both in limiting the range of fluctuations and in insuring that they take place at higher levels of output and employment. But he also concluded that the fluctuations in output and employment which did occur within a limited range were largely induced by specific government policy measures. Whereas the first part of this statement (referring to government's stabilizing influence in general) is the more important, the second part (relating actual instability to particular government intervention) is the more challenging. Milton Gilbert[2] also took the view that in most Western European countries growth should, or at least could, have proceeded without the slight recessions of 1951–1952 and 1957–1958 if no significant impediments from the policy side had been introduced. In the majority of countries, the prevailing trends of demand factors were strong—in some countries, so strong as to cause a more or less permanent tendency toward demand inflation. Therefore, the assertion goes, the setbacks that actually occurred were due mainly to restrictive government measures. Changes in economic policy were induced not only by the necessity of meeting actual or apprehended foreign exchange difficulties, but also by serious concern about inflationary developments.

There are some thorny problems in the way of regarding policy changes as causal factors in the cyclical development of an economic system. How to understand the word "cause" may be unclear, and how to interpret the concept of changes in policy is not self-evident. It is, of course, possible to imagine a stabilization policy so effective that no fluctuations in total activity would occur. The 1951–1952, 1957–1958, and 1961–1962 recessions could have been prevented by sufficiently inflationary policies before and during 1952, 1958, and 1961, respectively; or policies that included taxes and subsidies, licenses, and directives covering those branches where activity was considered too high or too low might have been introduced. Since such "effective" policy

[1] Angus Maddison, "The Postwar Business Cycle in Western Europe," *Banca Nazionale del Lavoro Quarterly Review,* June 1960.
[2] Milton Gilbert, "The Postwar Business Cycle in Western Europe," *American Economic Review,* May 1962.

measures were not carried out, economic policy might be blamed for the recessions. But it may be said that the experiences with the recessionary tendencies in Europe during 1961–1962 in some cases came rather close to this policy perfection. Is this relevant or not?

Other questions might be asked. If in the United Kingdom during 1951–1952, 1955–1956, and 1965–1966, no (or few) restraining policy measures had been introduced, would the country have experienced a longer expansion period and a shorter recession, or even no recessionary setbacks at all? To what extent would such a course of events have implied larger imports to the United Kingdom and thus prevented the recessionary impact on other countries' exports to the United Kingdom? Would a stronger and longer-lasting inflationary boom accompanying an easier policy have been followed by an earlier, or by a later and more severe, exchange crisis for the pound compared with the actual crises? Conclusions depend upon how the problem is put; it could be maintained that the cause of instability was not government policy but built-in weaknesses in the balance of payments; or that the actual recessions were a consequence of faulty and internationally uncoordinated economic policy measures. Similarly, questions might be asked about the possible effects of introducing, during the recession, policy changes that were less directly stimulating: Would the setback then have been deeper and more prolonged, or would the following period of expansion have developed along a lower path and in a less inflationary manner, with less risk to the country's foreign exchange position?

There is no clear line of demarcation between active policy changes and more or less automatic responses of certain policy measures. A change in tax schedules, for example, can clearly be regarded as a causal factor. On the other hand, a change in tax revenue or in the balance of the government budget has to be considered as a response of the economic system to the extent that there has been no change in either discretionary expenditures or in the schedule of rates of taxation and unemployment compensation. A rise in government investment expenditures may be the consequence of active policy efforts; it may be a rather passive response to changes in the availability of labor and materials when business conditions change. The same kind of considerations apply to changes in monetary policy. To what extent should the stringency of the money market following a balance of payments deficit be viewed as an automatic response of the central bank's selling of foreign exchange? To what extent is a change in, say, long-term interest rates due to a deliberate change in monetary policy, and to what extent is it due to changes in market conditions? In all such cases, it is necessary to distinguish between more or less automatic responses to changes in the economic system and deliberate policy actions. An active policy measure will certainly always contain an element of automatic response to economic changes.

All this means that a tabulation of government policy measures must be regarded critically. For example, careful analysis of circumstances is needed when a comparison is made of the "activeness" of stabilization policies in different countries. Differences in "policy needs" that are due to disturbances and the reaction sensitivity of the economy must be studied, and at distinction between active policy changes and passive responses must be made.

### Policy Effects

This section will give some examples taken from policy experiences in selected countries. The intention is not to present features characteristic of stabilization policy issues in these countries. The main purpose is to choose some cases of stabilization issues that have been prominent during the postwar period.

In order to bring some order into a discussion of possible policy effects on economic development during a period, the following points must be taken into account:

1. Some notions must be acquired about the strategic features of the economy that is being studied. At least some pieces of a model are necessary for this purpose. For example, to what extent do multiplier and acceleration effects seem to be stable and effective? How do changes in exports appear to be influenced by developments within the economy, and how do they affect the economy? Are price and wage movements spiral mechanisms?

2. What kind of external disturbances (which can be considered independent of policy changes) have affected the economy? Of course, the definition of external or exogenous factors depends on the choice of model; if there is no accepted model with which to work, there are no clear demarcations. However, it seems defensible to regard large parts of the export variations, changes in terms of trade, and variations in the capital account as external disturbances; therefore, it may seem reasonable in most cases to regard many of the changes in the balance of payments position as random factors disturbing the economy.

3. In order to judge the possible effects of government policy on actual economic development as described by current statistics, the first essential step is to ascertain the primary or direct impact of the various measures on demand. The second step should be to analyze the indirect effects, with account taken of the reaction system of the economy.

This way of dividing the problem does not provide an excuse for neglecting the close interrelation between the various steps. The effects on the economy of external disturbances cannot be studied in isolation; if they are sufficiently important, they are followed by policy reactions. But these reactions are also responses to the working of the economy, implying for instance a wage-price spiral. These interconnections mean that policy measures must be considered in part as reactions to earlier policies that may have had undesired and belated indirect effects; "overshooting" belongs to this category.

TIMING

In a study of the primary impact of policy measures, timing is an essential element. There is, and must be, much uncertainty about the various lags involved. Government authorities seem, as a rule, to have been late in observing that demand was expanding too rapidly and that a boom was coming. In a number of cases, the authorities have underestimated the current and prospective rate of demand expansion; expansive policies have been continued too long. Thus, a kind of overestimation of the economy has occurred, to be followed by restrictive policies that, from this point of view, have come too late. Restrictive policies during booms may have been mainly oriented toward impending balance of payments strains, observed at a late stage and likely to be underestimated. One reason (common to the countries studied) for underestimating the strength of the rise of demand during a revival may be the inventory disinvestment that regularly has occurred during such a period, and has had a dampening effect on production and imports. There has also been a lag – although usually not pronounced – in observing the approach of a recession, and a lag in introducing expansive measures.

The difficulties related to the observation lag have been aggravated by lags in the effect of policy measures on an economy with quickly changing "conjuncture moods." The periods of recession have usually been rather short, and therefore a large part of the stimulation effects may have had their main impact during the later revival. This may have been true especially of fiscal and credit policies affecting fixed investments, as there seems to have been a relatively slow investment reaction to expansive policies during recession.

The timing of policy effects cannot be ascertained without some notion of the relative size of the direct impact during the relative time periods. For the U.K. postwar cycles (up to 1960), Dow has made a pioneering effort in this direction [3]. His results, although rough and based on a number of explicit assumptions, give some conception of the order of size, as well as of the timing, of the direct effects of such measures as changes in tax rates, subsidies, grants and contributions, and hire purchase controls that have influenced disposable income and purchasing power of consumers: he also studied, very hypothetically, the impact of fiscal policy on investment.

FISCAL POLICY

Measures of the direct effects of fiscal policy, along such lines as Dow has tried, have been made in most countries. They are useful as a first approximation, in order to judge the relative size and timing of an expected direct impact. The Dutch, especially, have pioneered in estimating the total impact over a period of

---

[3] J. C. R. Dow, *The Management of the British Economy, 1945–1960,* Cambridge, England, 1960.

time; for this work, the econometric model developed by the Central Planning Bureau (CPB) has been used. A few words should be said about the high ambition implied in such a method of judging the effects of policy.

Without doubt the CPB model has been of great pedagogic value, partly because of the quantitative plausibility of its estimates of the direct and indirect effects of changes in policy parameters. In order to carry out an efficient stabilization policy, it often is not enough to know in what direction fiscal and monetary parameters should be changed, although this is certainly a primary condition for successful policy. The government authorities should also have some quantitative knowledge about both the projected size of the potential disequilibrium and the total expected effect of the policy changes considered. However, the problem is not just the simple one of putting alternative values of the parameters into the model (for example, government expenditures, tax rates, exchange rates); reading off the results after one and two years and in this way obtaining the differences (in GNP, export and import volume, prices, etc.) between the situations at the alternative parameter values. The model cannot be used as a mechanical device, but must be operated with skill as to choice of datum changes and to plausible assumptions of government and central bank reactions.

In a way, the CPB model can be applied as a systematic theory of policy. It is used for inferring short-term repercussions over the entire economic system. The research work done by the CPB and presented in a series of projections of the short-term trends of the economy has been an important basis for the good policy atmosphere in the Netherlands. The econometric models of the economy that have been presented and continuously revised seem to have created a common understanding of the way in which the Dutch economy works. But at the same time, there have been risks of mistakes; these risks might have been even greater if the analysis had been less precise and more modest, and if the conclusions had been presented in more qualitative and vague terms. In fact, with regard to forecasting future tensions in the economy as a basis for policy decisions, it sees that the Dutch technique of analysis was not efficient enough in the 1950's when it really mattered (for example, 1950–1951 and 1954–1956). Apparently the tendencies towards serious tensions were first discovered when there were clear indications of disequilibrium; the pertinent policy decisions were therefore made at too late a stage. Sophistication in the use of advanced econometric methods as such does not seem to help very much in situations of this sort. Perhaps the refined technique may even tend to create a kind of blindness with regard to simpler observations. There has, however, been a learning process going on, embodied in the coefficients of successive versions and also implying corrections of the results of the econometric analysis.

The CPB model has offered policy authorities the possibility of carrying out simulation exercises in the analysis of multiplier effects—on the entire

economy—of expenditure changes. This raises a question about the stability of
the coefficients, both during the various phases of a cycle and over longer
periods of time. The interesting problem, from a stabilization point of view,
concerns the possibilities of short-term variability of the coefficients over the
different phases of the cycle. The multiplier effects are derived mainly from the
demand side. However, there must be interrelations between demand and supply
during the greater part of expansion periods but, predominantly, only a
demand-governed development during contractions. It is unlikely that there is
much stable reversibility in some of the relations: for instance, the entrepre-
neurial reactions to increases of demand and liquidity during an expansion phase
must be expected to be quite different from reactions to a decline during a
contraction period. Variability in time lags may also be a serious complication
not usually considered in an econometric system. This possibility may be of
strategic importance in any discussion of the effects of policy changes.

When the attempt is made to isolate policy effects within the actual flow of
events during the cycle, certain pertinent problems arise that should be brought
out explicitly. In the description of a cyclical mechanism in the very simplest
terms, presented in order to demonstrate the strategic equilibrating and disequilibrating forces at work, there are always hidden presumptions of "given"
policy parameters. A sort of neutrality of government policy is presumed that,
however, is very difficult to define exactly. Are constant rates of interest or
constant rates of increase in the volume of money the relevant assumptions of
neutrality, or should it be assumed that some flexible adjustments of interest
rates and money supply are included in the automatic reactions of credit
markets during expansions and contractions? The same type of question arises
when a definition of neutral fiscal policy is attempted. It is easy to assume
constant tax rates as given parameters — and also to imagine some kind of
cyclical conformity of prices of government services.

The difficulties are greater on the expenditure side. It is reasonable to assume
automatic responses in payments of unemployment compensation (at given rates
and policy standards). But should an easing of government loan policies for
housebuilding be assumed following an "automatic" slack in general demand for
credit? Should it be taken as axiomatic that because of backlogs government
expenditures will be retarded during a boom and that, correspondingly, they will
be accelerated when resources become more easily available after the upper
turning point? The answers should be affirmative, but the actual measurement of
the relative importance of such automatic responses must be arbitrary within
wide limits. It can then be argued that a certain trend movement of government
expenditures (rather than constant expenditures) should be assumed as given,
when the actual instability of the economic system is discussed. The instability
problem should be analyzed from the point of view of a growing economy, and
this implies a rather strong trend in government demand for goods and services.

Parts of the deviations from some arbitrary trend should then be regarded as discretionary policy actions or disturbances.

MONETARY POLICY

As an illustration of the difficulty of isolating the relevant changes, consider the problem of the effects of monetary policy. It is customary to take the U.S. experience in the period 1946–1951 as an example of passive monetary policy. As the surplus liquidity inherited from the war years was combined with a policy aimed at interest rate stability, the business-cycle mechanism could operate without being disturbed by active changes in policy. But also, the inherited surplus liquidity could be regarded as a policy of very active ease that was more or less preserved in these years. During the period of inflation caused by the Korean war, measures had to be taken to preserve the high liquidity position and to prevent interest rates from rising.

In this connection, it is relevant to call attention to the incompetence of economists to point out clearly the general effects of monetary policy and to present specific evidence of such effects, with the exception of those on residential construction, installment buying, or international capital movements. For instance, the negative evidence of the findings in the Radcliffe Report or those given by Dow[4] can be matched by the positive conclusions of other authors. Modigliani, in an interesting study, reached the conclusion that monetary policy during the period 1947–1962 was relatively successful from the point of view of stabilization[5]. He measured the degree of success by the changes in money supply in relation to changes in nominal GNP, and was able to demonstrate that American monetary policy was quite well timed during this period. But he provides no information about the strength of the eventual effects and the length of time before they became operative. The results are quite inconclusive, also, since changes in money supply are unreliable indicators of changes in active policy as a whole.

Several attempts have been made to measure the lag distribution of the effects of monetary policy changes. The results must be considered rather inconclusive, however. If the results reached by Kareken and Solow[6] are assumed to give the correct order of size of the impact in the U.S., then an increase of 1 per cent in interest rates (as an indicator of credit restrictions) should result within a year's time in a substantially lower level of inventory

---

[4] J. C. R. Dow, *op. cit.*
[5] Franco Modigliani, "Some Empirical Tests of Monetary Management and the Rules Versus Discretion," *Journal of Political Economy,* June 1964.
[6] John Kareken and Robert M. Solow, "Lags in Monetary Policy," Part I of "Lags in Fiscal and Monetary Policy," in Commission on Money and Credit, *Stabilization Policies,* New York, 1963.

investment than otherwise would have been the case; the effects on fixed business investment, via changes in new orders, should be much slower (the maximum effect being reached after 2–3 years) but considerable[6]. The disturbing situation is that econometric analysis of this type—using time-series data and distributed lag techniques— give uncertain results within wide limits. The specifications of the models may vary widely without reducing significantly the high correlation coefficients usually reached. A number of highly regarded econometricians (like Tinbergen and Eisner) have attained good explanations of short-run investment variations without paying attention to interest rates and other monetary variables. One of the main difficulties in the interpretation of econometric research results, and therefore in choosing among alternative model structures, arises from the high degree of collinearity among the variables given by the time series.

It is reasonable to emphasize the sensitivity to, and therefore the potential effects of, restrictive monetary policy in specific business cycle situations— especially in periods around the upper turning points, when a rising share of firms and sectors of industry become dependent on outside finance. Increased interest rates, which may act as proxy variables for credit availability, may during such periods have a considerable, if lagged, impact on investment demand. Little or no influence may be apparent during the rest of the cycle; the inefficiency of monetary policy during contractions and depressions is a well preserved and probably realistic Keynesian doctrine dating from the 1930's. There may be a certain amount of nonlinearity in the relations: small increases in interest rates may have insignificant effects, while larger ones (surpassing certain threshold values) may be quite effective (too effective, in vulnerable situations). There are limited possibilities for taking care of such discontinuities by breaking up time-series and differentiating between the phases of the cycles. Meyer and Glauber have done this to a certain extent by applying "downswing and upswing models" to periods selected according to certain criteria[7]. In this way, and by looking closely into the behavior of the series in various quarterly periods, it was possible for them to ascertain that the interest rate variable was primarily effective in such years as 1953 and 1957–1958, when the rates were relatively high and the cyclical positions were sensitive to monetary policy.

It should be emphasized that effects of monetary and fiscal policies should not be judged in isolation. There often are package deals, where the intention is to have the various measures support each other. The effectiveness of restrictive monetary policy in a boom will then depend on how fiscal policy is carried out. In several countries, the potential efficiency of monetary policy has tended to

---

[7] John Meyer and Robert Glauber, *Investment Decisions, Economic Forecasting, and Public Policy*, Boston, 1964.

increase during the 1960's when compared with the 1950's, because of a higher frequency of budget surpluses. To mention one example: in Sweden during the 1960's a combination of rising wage costs, increased turnover taxes, and rising pension fees (paid by the entrepreneurs, mainly into a rapidly increasing government fund) has contributed to a squeeze on profit margins. The result has been that the business sector has depended to a substantially greater degree than during earlier booms on outside credit funds to finance a high level of investment. The dependence on bank credit and bond issues, especially by rapidly expanding corporations, has made the credit controls of the central bank a much stronger weapon than earlier. However, it has at the same time meant a high degree of disorganization of the credit and capital markets, with much rationing being based on grounds that have questionable effects on the allocation of the savings supply.

## Investment Policy

The potentialities of an efficient investment policy can perhaps be judged from a special Swedish experience. An investment tax was applied during several periods of inflation. The tax base was the actual investment expenditure for machinery and construction (excluding dwellings) incurred during the year and the rate was about 12 per cent. This was certainly a high extra investment cost. How high it was considered to be, and what effects it would have, depended very much on the anticipation of how long the tax would last. It is clear that if the tax when introduced was expected to continue for a long period or to be permanent, then it would tend to act as a cost-push factor and would be incorporated in the price system. The inflationary conditions ruling when the tax was introduced would have implied favorable conditions for transmitting the higher cost to the prices of finished goods. But if it was generally anticipated that the extra charge on investment would last for only one or two years, then the tax would have tended to have a strong postponement effect. To the entrepreneurs, the tax would mean an additional capital or interest cost of 12 per cent (although deductible like interest payments for taxation purposes). In a way, this is an example of the application of a type of flexible relation between short- and long-term interest charges that is needed for effective management of anticipations. In most countries, short - and long-term rates of interest have moved over the conjuncture in rather parallel fashion: for various reasons, the short-term rates have not been allowed to move high enough in relation to long-term rates during boom times in order to demonstrate the short perspective of the rate changes and thereby induce a postponement effect on investment.

A striking result of stabilization policy in Sweden during 1955–1959 was that industrial investment expenditures (calculated in real terms) on machines and buildings, which had remained fairly constant during the boom (they did not, in fact, expand noticeably above the peak reached in 1951) increased very substantially during the recession years 1958 and 1959. It could thus be maintained that the stabilization policy over the full course of the business cycle had been so successful in this sector that the increase in investment expenditures was shifted from the upward to the downward phase of the cycle. Investment surveys (a dangerous alternative to econometric analysis) carried out among a representative number of industrial enterprises confirmed the hypothesis that the combination of the investment tax and credit restrictions caused quite heavy reductions and postponements of investments. When the investment tax was abolished and credit policy was relaxed at the beginning of 1958, the natural consequence was that accumulated investment plans, which had been postponed on account of financing difficulties or excessive costs, were quickly realized during that year and also in 1959.

One weakness of monetary and fiscal policy, namely, to imply a "time-shape" of effects on investments that cannot be foreseen, is avoided to a considerable degree, in the Swedish investment fund technique. In this respect, the Swedish technique is superior to the usual forms of investment allowance measures. In principle, the investment fund system works in a symmetric way over the cycle; the system automatically combines ways of stimulating private investment during a recession with ways of damping investment during a boom. The fact that it is possible for a company to set aside funds for writing down the value of future investments means that there should be less incentive to invest in fixed capital during a boom just in order to create future write-offs. The way in which the investment fund technique presents numerous possibilities for controlling the time-shape of the use of funds released for financing investments is illustrated by a model referring to the year 1962. The investment surveys made during the fall of 1961 and the spring of 1962 had revealed a clear tendency toward a decline in industrial investment. A limited recession in construction activity and machinery production was expected to be concentrated in the winter of 1962–1963. As early as May 1962, the Labor Market Board announced the right of industrial companies to release investment funds for construction between July, 1962, and the end of April, 1963. Construction had to be started before the first of November, and funds were generally not available after April 1963. The release of funds for investment in machinery was also controlled as to timing by specifying that orders had to be given during the period November 1962–April 1963, and that investment funds would be released only on the condition that delivery was completed before the end of the year. Studies of the net effect on industrial investment arising from the release of funds give convincing evidence that the timing of the stimulus was also quite successful.

## *"Policy Cycles" and Full Employment*

In the discussions of the influence of policy on development, the term "policy cycle" has been used, especially with regard to the British experience. A generalized picture of the policy cycle in the United Kingdom would be very much the same as that in several other countries. Starting with a relatively successful anti-recession policy at the end of a period of slow growth and dampened activity, favorable conditions for rapid expansion have been created. Expansive fiscal and monetary policies have resulted in a substantial amount of surplus liquidity. Large budget deficits have created high liquidity reserves in the banking system at the same time that private business has been well supplied with cash. During recessions, decisions have to be made to expand public investment of various kinds and to increase housebuilding. Decisions on such expansive measures have necessarily been made with a certain time lag. Because the period of recessionary tendencies is short (say, one year), the maximum rates of public and housing investment may easily coincide with an acceleration of exports and of private investment which occurs with a new expansion phase of the cycle. (This apparently occurred in the United Kingdom, Sweden, and a number of other countries in 1953–1954, 1958–1959, and to some extent in 1962–1963.) As even at the bottom of these recessions the economy is close to the ceilings of full employment and full use of productive capacity, there will not be enough time to reverse the expansionary policy before inflationary tendencies appear.

The interrelations among the variations in demand pressure, productivity development, and the rates of wage and price increase are of central importance to the working of the economic system during revival and boom. In a loose way, the economic mechanism seems to function along the following lines, with the United Kingdom taken as a model[8]. Rapid expansion of demand (after 1952, 1958, and 1962) is accompanied by relatively large increases in labor productivity that neutralize a part of the current rise in wages and earnings of each employed person. There seems to be some time lag in the increase of prices, so that real incomes will rise more rapidly during the early part of the expansion than later, when wage costs advance more quickly because of a slower rise in productivity and exercise lag effects on prices. The rapid increases in real wages and employment are part of the explanation of the high rate of increase of consumption demand during the revival. From the point of view of stabilization policy, one strategic relation is the way in which change in the pressure of demand affects productivity. The short-term connection that seems to exist

---

[8] Dow, *op. cit.*, especially Chapter XVI.

places great difficulty in the way of controlling inflation. According to this hypothesis, the transition from high to low pressure as a result of a "successful" restrictive policy will be followed in the short run by a dampening of the growth of productivity and a corresponding rise in costs per unit of output, without having a restraining effect on the rise of wages—before the recession. The statistics of price, productivity, and wage developments during boom periods seem to be in accord with this pattern. However, there is no assurance that this tells more than a part of the story. The retardation in various sectors of the economy may have been determined partly by ceilings of capacity; to this extent, the slowing down of production and of the growth of productivity during the last year or two of the boom would not have been determined only by the dampening of demand as a result of policy restrictions. There are, apparently, no automatic equilibrating tendencies arising out of spiralling wages, prices, and nominal demand, except via balance of payments restrictions. Rising imports and declining exports will result in balance of payments deficits. Stabilization policy reactions may appear as a response to both inflationary tendencies and a menacing balance of payments deficit. In this stage of rapidly increasing prices and demand, mildly restraining measures will not be effective; it seems that only shock methods help, and perhaps even these are helpful only after the boom has, for various reasons, lost a part of its momentum.

One question is common to all countries: why does the policy response come so late in the cycle? According to the above sketch of a model, disequilibrium tendencies start during the first phase of rapid expansion of demand without much inflation. It could be argued that a restrictive policy – or perhaps less use of stimulating measures – should start so early that from the beginning the expansion is kept down to a rate that can be maintained. This means a less stimulating fiscal policy during the recession or—still better—milder recession or stagnation after the previous boom. One fundamental problem that can be raised is why the ceiling of expansion is so low, especially for the U.K. economy.

ACHIEVEMENTS OF STABILIZATION PROGRAMS

The achievements of stabilization policy – and the difficulties raised during the booms – must be judged against the background of the high ambitions as to the degree of full employment. However, the full employment in some countries seems to be more flexible than in the United Kingdom, where apparently there is less retardation in the growth of productivity during a boom. If the "revealed preference" of the responsible government authorities seems to be a more or less permanent excess demand pressure on the labor market, this type of disequilibrium should not be taken as only a welfare criterion and a good thing in itself for the majority of people; under certain policy conditions, it can be a favorable growth factor. The excess demand for labor in most skills and regions may imply good job opportunities, working in the direction of an adaptation of jobs to applicants, which will minimize obstacles to entrance into the active labor force. (In several countries, one visible result is a rapid rise in the participation rates of married women.) The unfavorable effects are excessive labor turnover and supply bottlenecks for rapidly expanding firms. These may, within certain limits, be outweighed by a fuller utilization of capacity and efficiency drives, necessitated by foreign competition on export and domestic markets. The longer-term danger from a more permanent high-pressure situation arises from wage inflation and negative effects on productivity resulting from the distorted allocation or resources in the direction of protected activities, such as building and services.

One of the most interesting stabilization policy problems of an economy with "overfull employment" conditions relates to labor mobility. It is self-evident that the excess demand for labor will be very unevenly distributed, concentrated in rapidly growing firms, sections, and regions; at the same time, there will be actual or potential deficit demand in other firms, sectors, and regions. Also, there will tend to be a concentration of excess demand for various types of skilled labor. The rapidly growing branches of activity and firms will have, to a large extent, to recruit their skilled and unskilled labor from the stagnating and declining sectors of the economy. In Sweden and some other countries an active labor market policy has become an important complement to the general stabilization policy, especially since 1959. It has aimed at raising the full-employment ceiling by mobilizing and activating the labor reserves (through extended labor exchange services, mobility grants, and vocational training schools).

A well known theory maintains that stabilization policies in an economy with very high ambitions as to full employment will have to take other forms than the old-fashioned Keynesian approach of general demand pull. In minor recessions, a general expansion of demand—with following risks of strong cumulative processes that, according to the post war experiences, are so difficult to control—should not be started. Instead, "differentiated point injection" of credits and subsidies should be introduced, and such measures should be combined with intensified efforts to mobilize labor and move it to expanding regions and branches of activity. This type of policy is directed toward the improved functioning of the labor market. Higher mobility of resources should help to prevent inflationary developments in the rapidly expanding branches and regions. At the same time, the pressures from a sufficiently rapid and general rise in wage cost should squeeze the profit margins of marginal firms and branches of activity in order to compel them to supply labor to the areas of expansion. There should be no concealed subsidies in the form of relatively slow wage increases in branches where there is stagnation or low growth.

There is a possibility that this type of active labor market policy — as a part of both stabilization and structural policies — may in the future imply and allow a somewhat lower ambition as to the degree of full employment. Here is an example of a conceivable interrelation between means and aims of policy. When the unemployed are quickly put to useful government work and sent, to an increasing extent, to vocational training schools with decent stipends (disguised unemployment of these kinds in Sweden have recently been double the revealed unemployment figures) and with good prospects for new employment, then gross unemployment figures above 1−2 per cent may again be tolerated. This would mean that not only a new name but also a new content and meaning would be given to the old calamity of becoming unemployed.

# COMMENT

ANGUS MADDISON
Twentieth Century Fund, Paris

My belief is that Lundberg, in his examination of the question of whether the business cycle is obsolete, places inadequate emphasis on three basic changes in the economy that make modern fluctuations different in character from the prewar cycles.

1. He defines the cycle in terms of deviations from the growth trend, and seems willing to treat decelerations in economic growth as if they were the same as absolute decreases in output. I believe the two are somewhat different phenomena. They are different in their impact on profits. If production does not fall, the problem of surplus capacity is felt much more mildly by the business community.

2. He says that the postwar price climate has been generally inflationary, but he does not stress this fact sufficiently. Most economies now have a downward price inflexibility, which is particularly important in sustaining profits. This situation contrasts strongly with 19th century experience, when price declines sometimes led to falling profits and were characterized as business-cycle downturns even in periods when output did not fall.

3. When postwar fluctuations are differentiated from those of prewar years, the new stability of financial institutions should be stressed. In the 19th century, many crises were accompanied by financial collapse; and in 1929 also, this was a major exacerbating factor. The new stability is due in large part to government action.

Largely because of these three characteristics, our economic system in postwar years has acquired the remarkable buoyancy with regard to profit expectations which Lundberg notes. In all Western European countries, the ratio of investment to GNP has been on a rising trend, as expectations of steady growth have become more deeply embedded in the minds of entrepreneurs.

This buoyancy of expectations has been reinforced by the fact that the supply potential of the economy has proved much more elastic than in the past. There are various reasons for this, which I do not want to examine here. But Shinohara's discussion[1] is of particular importance, as it shows that at least one economy (Japan) has adjusted to a lower trend in the supply potential without a major depression. Germany also has made this transition.

Government policy has obviously added greatly to the buoyancy of the economy and has been one of the main causes of rapid economic growth. Nevertheless, autonomous movements in the private sector are of major importance, so that policy has to be corrective as well as propulsive. But in a situation where government policy is continuously active, it is difficult to disentangle the rhythm of the private sector from that induced by governments. Governments keep fluctuations within a narrower range than would otherwise be normal; hence, government action is the proximate cause of most upswings and downswings. This has led some observers to speak of the "policy cycle" as the major source of instability in the postwar economic system.

There are several ways in which the government can accentuate or cause fluctuations in the economy:

1. Government policies may be destabilizing because of perverse technocratic advice. This has happened in Canada in the postwar period, but has been much less common than the perverse advice provided in prewar years, particularly in the 1929–1931 period.

2. Governments may make identification errors of three kinds: (a) the technocratic analysis may not be sophisticated enough to distinguish clearly the nature of the problem. This was probably true during the 1950's, when demand inflation was not distinguished clearly enough from wage inflation to avoid unnecessarily deflationary policies in the United Kingdom. (b) Analysis of the situation may be too slow. Improved statistical indicators and seasonal adjustments have made contributions to the efficacy of policy in this respect. (c) Whatever the degree of sophistication and however good the indicators, there will always be some residual ambiguity in the analysis of the state of the economy: in this area, good policy will depend on intelligent hunches. The aim of economic research and analysis should be to reduce the area of residual ambiguity to a minimum. A very important difficulty of this kind, which is mentioned by Lundberg, is the assessment of the short-term production and productivity potential.

3. The emphasis in government policy may be strongly biased in one direction because of political (not technocratic) weakness or conviction. This is what Lundberg calls the "revealed preference" of government policy. In most European countries, the postwar emphasis has been expansionist and somewhat

[1] Chapter 3.

inflationary. In the United States, the political emphasis in the 1950's was anti-inflationary almost to the point of perversity. In Germany, governmental attitudes were not very different from those in the United States, but the economy was saved from deflationary consequences by the competitiveness of exports, which tended to offset declines in the momentum of domestic demand.

Apart from destabilization, which may arise from government policy responses of the kind mentioned earlier, government action may be destabilizing because of instrumental lags. Lundberg's discussion shows how discretionary fiscal policy can be improved for dealing with fluctuations in private investment. In the fiscal field, there has been a steady improvement in the efficacy of policy and a fair consensus of professional opinion. However, Lundberg brings out the uncertainty that is often felt about the efficacy of monetary policy. In this field, there seems to be a genuine difficulty of communication between economists in different countries, particularly between economists in the United Kingdom and United States, and those in such countries as Germany, France, and Italy. There are wide differences in the institutional background of monetary policy in these countries—differences in the basic liquidity position of business, the dependence of business on credit, and the importance in the capital market of national debt. There are differences in the historical experience with inflation, which affect attitudes toward the "normal" level of interest rates and add a certain element of passion to the most academic discussion of monetary policy. There are also quite wide differences between U.S. and continental central bankers in their attitudes toward the legitimate range of monetary policy weapons. This is a field of policy analysis where more comparative empirical study is needed.

In discussing the international field, Lundberg might well have said more about the importance of new policy instruments which have greatly damped the international transmission of the cycle. The main developments have been the emergence of large-scale, organized international credit, much better mutual understanding between policymakers in different countries of their technical and political problems, and the observance of certain rules of good behavior in adjusting to payments problems. These rules prevent countries from channelling an excessive deflationary impact abroad by imposing import controls or other kinds of "beggar your neighbor" remedies. There are imperfections in these new international policy arrangements that should also be mentioned, for example, the virtual impossibility of changing exchange rates.

For the future, it seems likely that government policy will continue to be continuously active and will show further technical improvement. Some of the political obstacles to efficient policy have been reduced (particularly in the United States), but others will obviously remain. It will be increasingly difficult to distinguish between the rhythm of the private sector and the results of government policy. For this reason, the problems of applied economic policy can probably be divided into "conjuncture" economics and "growth" economics. The notion of the business cycle will probably fade away.

# VI  DISCUSSION AND DEBATE

# Chapter Sixteen

# SUMMARY OF THE DISCUSSION

M. BRONFENBRENNER

Carnegie-Mellon University, Pittsburgh

## I. Professor Gordon's Chapter (United States)

Illness prevented Professor Gordon from presenting his "keynote" paper; Professor Hickman summarized Gordon's argument under three main heads:

1. The alternation of higher with lower growth rates may itself constitute a cycle, provided such characteristics as pervasiveness, cumulation, and duration are maintained. What seems to be happening in the United States is not the obsolescence of the cycle but the replacement of the standard cycle of absolute quantities by a new cycle in growth rates.

2. There have been two main reasons for believing the cycle obsolete in all its forms. One is the duration of the post-1961 boom, and the other the usefulness of active stabilization policies — which, however, have not included price-level stability among the aims achieved. It is dangerous to generalize prematurely from what may be a special case.

3. Actually, the patterns of exogenous relations, parameters, and random shocks have not changed greatly since 1961, except for the conscious "policy" ones.

Dr. Moore and Professor Menshikov were the two formal discussants. Where they disagreed with Professor Gordon's discussion, they did so in the "conservative" direction. That is to say, they were less willing than Gordon to recognize, on the basis of a single observation (the post-1961 period), any shift from a traditional to a "growth" cycle. Neither supported any "obsolescence" thesis. Certain of Dr. Moore's main points may be summarized as follows:

1. The fear that the United States may be facing recession (in the Spring of 1967) itself implies that the cycle is not regarded as obsolete. The inflationary spurt and financial crisis of 1966 are also evidence along this line.

2. Many indicators still move up and down in the orthodox manner. Examples are profits, industrial investment, and the ratio of job vacancies to unemployment.

3. The "growth cycle" does not have the same policy implications as the traditional one. It may not even warrant active cycle policy. A lower growth rate may, for example, be more sustainable than a higher one, be more compatible with price-level stability, and be less productive of excess capacity.

4. Insofar as NBER indicators show changes in patterns, these changes are by no means all pointed toward greater stability. For example, consumer capital (including housing) is now more important than business capital, and (perhaps) more volatile in its supply, despite the greater stability of consumer incomes as a whole. (Saving ratios, in other words, are variable.) Labor participation rates, exports, and interest rates also seem to have become more volatile. Even policy was no more "correct" in 1965–1966 than it had been in 1959. Its error was merely in the opposite direction: the Eisenhower Administration put on the brakes too early in 1959; the Johnson Administration put them on too late in 1965–1966.

Professor Menshikov saw the cycle as only one aspect of an overall U.S. stability problem which includes inflation, balance of payments, hard-core unemployment, and regional imbalance. But, limiting himself to the cycle proper, he concentrated on such fluctuations as were clearly related neither to wars nor to random shocks, but to investment in plant and equipment (excluding housing and inventories). He found two major downturns (1947–1949, 1956–1958) each with minor "echoes" (1953–1954, 1960–1961), and claimed that similar results applied in the 1920's as well.

He went on to anticipate another downturn in 1967 or 1968. This will not, however, be of the magnitude of 1920–1921, to say nothing of 1929–1933, both of which embodied "panic" features based on ignorance. Little has happened to change the patterns of minor cycles, but there have been at least six major changes affecting major ones: scientific and technological advance; improved internal corporate planning; greater state intervention; a new balance of power between labor and capital; the rise of the "third world," replacing colonial empires; the importance of competitive coexistence with Socialist countries. But at least one of these, the rising power of organized labor, is, on many occasions, destabilizing and deflationary.

In the general discussion, a number of additional points were raised, pointing generally toward survival of the traditional cycle, probably in attenuated form:

1. The U.S. financial system and structure is not strong. The multitude of small, weak banks requires a stable interest rate structure, which could, however, be somewhat higher than it has been in the past. A reply was that monetary tightness at the 1966 level represented a peculiar policy aberration, not likely to be repeated by the Federal Reserve authorities.

2. The weakness of the U.S. balance of payments situation may possibly lead to tighter money and direct controls and emphasize a general shortage of world liquidity. There may be a wave of competitive currency depreciation, as in the 1930's. One participant argued that national economies have learned to live with considerable inflation, but the international economy has not. He doubted that international monetary reform could occur in time to remedy the defect without a major downturn.

3. The Kennedy-Johnson "New Economics" was a once-and-for-all shift in U.S. economic policy. It was "old hat" in much of Europe, where its effect had been to raise the general level of employment, but not to eliminate fluctuations around it. There is no reason to expect any different consequences in the United States.

4. Also (still on the topic of policy), the deflationary or contractionary gaps opened up by any significant recession are too large, and the multipliers too small, to permit of too much speed in recovery. One participant estimated the necessary reduction in current (1967) government spending (to alleviate the inflationary gap) at $17-18 billion, and the (alternative) necessary tax increase at $25-30 billion, both too large for practical policy. (These estimates were attacked later by other participants as being too high.)

5. One participant wondered about the consequences of an early end to the Vietnam war, and the "unleashing" of U.S. economic power on the rest of the world, including concealed subsidies to U.S. exports. His more general point was a lag in international behind national policies, rendering the latter ineffective.

6. Nothing had been said, as another participant pointed out, about the echo effects of waves of activity in investment goods, housing, and consumer durables. The speaker referred to these as "hog cycles," using an agricultural analogy, and saw no evidence that they would become increasingly damped.

7. A technical objection was made to the notion of a "growth cycle," related to the location of peaks and troughs. The rate of change of any regular oscillation has its peaks and troughs at points different from the original osciallation. In the simplest example (the sine curve), the displacement is 1/4 the length of the cycle. This difficulty is avoided with cycles are measured in deviation from trends of actual variables like outputs, or from trends of the potential values of these variables, rather than in growth rates proper.

## II  Dr. Daly's Chapter (Canada)

Dr. Daly, subdividing his treatment under the three heads of mechanism, institutions, and policy, was pessimistic on all three counts as regards any major modification of the traditional business cycle. His pessimism is characteristic of discussions of countries with a high dependence on foreign trade and a high sensitivity to external (exogenous) shocks.

Daly found the cyclical mechanism to be international in the Canadian case and, accordingly, persistent, at least until the present date. On the institutional side, he listed five important changes, all but one of which tended toward reduced cyclical amplitudes: greater worldwide stability, particularly in Canada's principal trading partners; greater importance of public expenditure within Canada itself; greater reliance on built-in stabilizers; decreased vulnerability of financial institutions; and (as a destabilizer) the greater importance of private residential construction.

Turning to discretionary policies, Daly found himself on the pessimistic side, when he compared Canadian experience with his reading of the consensus of the other country papers. In short cycles, Daly found the Canadian lags too long — longer than recessions themselves — for much mitigating effect. These lags were both "inside" (between the need for a policy change and its implementation by the authorities) and "outside" (between the taking of action and its effectiveness). For fiscal policy changes in particular, Daly found the main lag to be an inside one. As for long cycles, Daly applied to Canada a point which had come up in the U.S. discussion. The size of inflationary or deflationary gaps tends to be large, and the multipliers to be small. As a result, the required policy changes are usually too extensive for practical politics.

In his formal discussion, Professor Rosenbluth distinguished sharply between different types of cycles. He felt that the shorter (National Bureau) cycle had survived in Canada, but that the Kuznets cycle might well be obsolete, and that the major postwar Canadian movements might better be explained in terms of the 10-year (Juglar) cycle. In prewar Kuznets cycles, turning points in level and growth rate of any major indicator typically occurred within three years of one another; the postwar discrepancy was 11 years or more.

Rosenbluth also concentrated his comments upon the relations between U.S. and Canadian cycles. Canadian quantity series seem to have lower amplitude than the corresponding U.S. ones, and the differences are increasing. This suggests declining Canadian sensitivity, both from decreased trade dependence and from greater built-in flexibility. On the other hand, price and yield series do *not* show declining sensitivity — rather the reverse. In Rosenbluth's view, the transmission mechanism is not yet understood well enough to explain this anomaly.

Rosenbluth went on to criticize econometric cycle research and counter-cyclical policy in Canada. The numerous connections between the Canadian and U.S. economies are not represented adequately in these models. The correspondence between fluctuations in the two countries is due neither to similar lag structures nor similar shock patterns, but to the great variety of connecting links. These should be represented by exogenous variables in econometric models of the Canadian economy. On the policy side, Rosenbluth disagreed with Daly's view that discretionary policies were of little use against the short cycle.

One specific device against all disturbances, regardless of cyclical type, might be formula flexibility for tax rates, depreciation allowances, and transfer payments. Inside lags will fall, in Rosenbluth's view, by reason of technical progress, rendering economic technocracy more feasible.

The informal discussion was more general and less specifically country-oriented than had been the case with the previous paper. The lead-off participant made three principal points:

1. We can say very little about postwar changes in so long an oscillation as the Kuznets cycle. We should continue to concentrate on the 10-year Juglar cycle.

2. For policy, also, we should concentrate on persistent inflation and stagnation, rather than on short-term fluctuations. The desire to remedy each short recession produces primarily inflation.

3. Lag structures may be changing rapidly, since the planning process within individual concerns is shifting from the production of specific commodities to the production of a variable product mix. These shifts also lead to different price and investment behavior.

A second participant raised issues of interrelation between longer and shorter cycles, suggesting that the Conference title should have been "*Are* business *cycles* obsolete?" On the interrelations point, he wondered whether short cycles are by-products of lags within long ones, or whether the long cycle is more than a summation of short ones. He felt that lags were permanent, even in planned economies. Therefore, he believed that both long and short cycles will persist, at least in attenuated form. He found the *shortening* of the cycle an encouraging feature, since the amplitude of short cycles is generally small.

The third participant returned the focus to Canada. The main points of international interest in the Canadian cycle are its integration with that of the United States and the transmission mechanism between the two countries. He wondered why Daly had not said more about capital-market integration and exchange-rate variability. He suggested that investors in the two countries are often the same people, making parallel decisions, that Canadian imports are cycle-sensitive (a stabilizing factor), and that long-term capital flows from the United States have also been stabilizers. (Short-term flows, being interest-rate sensitive, are something else again. Later participants suspected that some long-term flows were also interest-rate sensitive.) Why, he wondered, was the Canadian recession of 1960–1961 more severe than the corresponding recession in the United States? Was this not a consequence of the Canadian resumption of fixed exchange rates? Why not, therefore, return to the fluctuating-rate system? (A subsequent answer was that Canada had not used its fluctuating rate for stabilization purposes, and had, on her own, made policy tighter than U.S. policy in 1960–1961.)

The next participant wondered whether U.S.–Canadian relations were comparable to interregional relations within the United States itself, and whether the political boundary was really important. He also suggested that, if long swings do not exist in North America, they do not exist anywhere.

The issue of seasonality then came up. The Canadian economy is strongly seasonal, and Daly had expected improved judgment (concerning short cycles) from improved seasonal indices. To this it was replied that firms in Scandinavian countries are slow to let official indices affect their internal planning methods. Other participants questioned the relevance of this Scandinavian experience for Canada.

Discussion shifted back to the general cycle problem. One participant warned against regarding inventory cycles as irremediable. There is danger of complacency about inventory cycles transmitting itself to fixed investment fluctuations, which he (the participant) wished to see damped down, perhaps by reducing the lag between corporate income and corporate tax payments. Another participant detected a certain tendency in the Canadian discussion to blame all fluctuations on the United States, and warned the Conference that cycles can occur in a system of interdependent economies of approximately equal size, in each of which the purely domestic cycle is heavily damped. The final participant warned against too much reliance on technocratic expertise. Ideal solutions are, he fears, impossible because each cycle is different, with both political and sociological problems interfering with cycle policy in the strict sense.

To close the session, Daly expressed his own views on certain of the points raised. On seasonality, he repeated his expectations of future improvements, both in Canada and elsewhere. The rationale for existing routines of seasonal adjustment had not, he felt, become clear until recently. Now that it had become clearer, he expected business to take greater account of it, and not change forecasts or plans on the basis of seasonal movements. Timing differences between traditional and growth cycles were, he thought, important only in such special cases as the excess capacity of the 1930's. He believed that inside and outside lags were not only important but additive, because reactions of different groups are involved. He agreed with several of the critics that the attention paid the short cycle was generally exaggerated, and that the Canadian models should be improved in their international aspects, to take more explicit account of developments in the United States.

## III. Professor Shinohara's Chapter (Japan)

Professor Shinohara's discussion was divided into three topics: the Juglar cycle, the inventory cycle, and contemporary Japanese policy on cycles and growth.

For the longer cycle, it is still too early to reach a judgment on its survival, but Shinohara tended, on balance, to doubt its demise. Judgment is difficult because contemporary Japan is making, for the first time in its modern history, the transition from a labor-surplus to a labor-shortage economy, and historical parallels are even less relevant than normally. Also, the current cycle may be unusually long, because it is accompanied by the wholesale introduction of foreign technology, capital, and managerial techniques. As evidence for the existence of a long cycle, Shinohara pointed to the persistence of low profits, high interfirm borrowing, frequent bankruptcies, and a high volume of dishonored bills well into the recovery period of short cycles.

When examining Japanese inventory cycles, Shinohara found that all the evidence points to their persistence in fairly traditional form. The duration of recessions is almost constant (10-12 months), but the duration of the upswing is increasing, especially at times when the fixed-investment cycle appears to be rising. The Japanese balance of payments appears to lead the inventory cycle by 12–18 months, with fiscal and monetary policy apparently endogenous and passive variables. Also, the inventory cycle for small firms seems to lead that for large ones; the same is true for the less marked fixed-investment cycle. To explain this dualism, Shinohara accepted a financial theory: stringency, in particular, affects small business before it affects large enterprises.

Shinohara believes that the cyclical passivity of Japanese economic policy has furthered the persistence of cyclical oscillations. Since 1960, two leading schools of policy have arisen in Japan: one (which includes Shinohara himself) favors a stable growth rate, and the other (associated with Dr. Osamu Shimomura) seeks a high growth rate at the risk of excess capacity and periodic instability. Commenting on the difference, Shinohara estimated the long-run marginal productivity of fixed invesment at 10 per cent, although the short-run figure is often higher (30 per cent). Shimomura implies, said Shinohara, that it is safe to base policy on the short-term figure, and ascribes short-term fluctuations entirely to domestic inventories. Shinohara himself takes the opposite view and believes that short-term fluctuations also involve some elements of fixed investment, not to mention substitution between holding inventories abroad and at home. (That is to say, Japanese firms accumulate inventories in Japan when the balance of payments permit their free import. They can often hold inventories abroad at other times, while awaiting relaxation of Japanese import controls.)

Professor Bronfenbrenner acted as formal discussant of the Japanese presentation. He was impressed by the distinctions between series for large and small business, with small business leading, and hoped that this Japanese innovation might be extended more widely. In particular, he associated these results with the argument that only under inflationary conditions can new small business obtain adequate credit facilities. He expressed his belief that it is valid for Japan, and that it may also lie back of much Latin American structuralism.

Bronfenbrenner called attention to the isolation, in the Shinohara discussion, of medium-term fixed investment cycles (measured in terms of deviations from trend) along with the starter inventory cycles. Whether this result is valid depends, he believes, on its sensitivity to the choice of trend lines. He noted that Shinohara had used lines of different slopes in the two Juglar cycles that he had isolated, and suggested that when there is insufficient reason for choosing one trend line rather than another, there is great risk of reliance on statistical artifacts, that is, deviations from mis-specified trends. (Shinohara later replied that he had not himself computed either the trends or the deviations from them.)

In cycle policy, Japan has become an example of monetary expansionism in the face of periodic balance of payments difficulties. On the fiscal side, under the influence of conservative U.S. bankers, Japan balanced its budget every year from 1950 to 1965. Growth, however, had permitted tax cuts almost every year. Perhaps it might be said that export expansion and monetary ease had compensated for the old-fashioned strictness of Japanese fiscal policy.

Bronfenbrenner closed with a methodological query. The Shinohara paper had made no mention of the multiplicity of detailed econometric models available in Japan. He wondered whether this might not illustrate some lack of contact between traditional cycle theorists and econometricians.

The initial participant raised three principal considerations:

1. Why should the growth potential of the Japanese economy (estimated by Shinohara at 8 per cent, against Shimomura's 10) be lower than in the previous decade? True, Japan's technology gap has been closed, and disguised unemployment has disappeared. But what about the demand-side stimulus of rising expectations?

2. Japan's imports seem more volatile than her exports, but Japan can perhaps afford to take balance of payments difficulties in stride, because export momentum is high and export prices are falling, relative to the export prices of her principal competitors. This discussant wonders whether Japan's export price level is not unusually flexible downward in recessions.

3. The volatility of the Japanese economy is increased in money terms by deflationary methods (inadequate prices for family labor, and also in the service sector). This feature has operated to increase the real growth rate, by minimizing unemployment.

A second participant expressed dissatisfaction with aspects of both Shinohara's and Bronfenbrenner's discussions. (a) He found nothing surprising about the persistence of the Juglar investment cycle in Japan. He believes that other countries, particularly the United States, have it also. (b) He found no adequate explanation of why Japan is different (from the West) or why it is now changing from the 1955–1965 decade. He expected the potential Japanese growth rate to continue very high. (c) He wished that more had been said about the interrelations of inventory and investment cycles, both in Japan and more generally. In his own view, the investment cycle leads the inventory cycle, because of the increase in output following the completion of investment projects. He felt that the Shinohara paper had suggested irregularity of the inventory cycle, but regularity of the investment cycle, and also that the latter was becoming more important because of technological change and excess capacity. (Planning in large corporations damps the inventory cycle at the same time that it increases excess capacity.) (d) He believed that U.S. data indicated differences between the cyclical behavior of prices and profits by firm size – similar to Shinohara's findings for Japan. (e) He felt that Japan had suffered a major financial crisis, particularly on the stock exchange, in 1965–1966, which might be the harbinger of a cyclical downturn.

The third participant's remarks were, for the most part, replies to this critique. (a) Such Japanese economists as Shigeto Tsuru have been warning since 1952 that passive fiscal policy would send Japan into a standard depression. It is an encouraging sign that deficit financing was adopted in 1965. (Shinohara later agreed with this view.) (b) Two sources of trouble for Japan are slowdowns in the world economy and overheating at home. Both cause difficulties for Japanese exports. (c) The duality between large and small firms may be expected to fade in Japan. Their wage rates are becoming similar, and the weak, small firms are being weeded out. (d) The rate of Japanese technical progress will slow down as the imitative aspect is reduced. (e) The 1965–1966 stock-market crisis in Japan should not be regarded as a sign of serious trouble. The stock market had been bailed out by public stabilization policies (easier money), just as the savings and loan associations in the United States (1966), and other financial institutions had been bailed out by central banks elsewhere.

The next participant objected on methodological grounds to the association of short cycles with inventories, longer ones with fixed investment, etc. He would have preferred that each type of cycle be associated with aggregate fluctuations. He felt that it was the interaction between more and less aggregated data that was most relevant.

A subsequent participant wondered whether Japan had not neglected, or at least postponed, opportunities for public investment. He believed that, in the future, there would be more such investment, which would hold Japanese economic activity closer to the Hicksian ceiling and would make Japanese fluctuations more like European ones. (Shinohara accepted this suggestion.)

## IV. Professor Matthews' Chapter (Great Britain)

The main focus of discussion of the postwar British trade cycle has been whether the cycle has been induced by public policy, and if so, why. Discussion of this so-called "political cycle" has led to some neglect of the underlying economic factors, in Professor Matthews' view.

"The" cycle has never been a clearcut phenomenon. In Britain at least, the postwar variety has been very different from either the pre-1914 or interwar experience. The fluctuations have been milder (at least milder than in the interwar period). They have been marked chiefly by changes in growth rates. The oscillations in real output and in employment are more marked than those in current-price gross domestic product (GDP); of the two, the output fluctuations are the larger, perhaps because, at a high level of overall activity, workers are kept on during minor slack periods. Cycles have become shorter, and inventory cycles have become prominent for the first time. Price perversity (rises in depressed periods) has also put in its appearance; Matthews suggested that this has represented lag effects from the preceding prosperity period, and a delayed adjustment to boom conditions.

Formerly exports had been an unstable, and the Government a stable, factor in British cycle history. The reverse is now the case. People claim the Government does it all, via "stop-and-go" monetary policy, whose alleged weaknesses have been taken to reflect on monetary policy as a whole. Inventories, imports, and consumer durable goods have become volatile elements under the influence of "stop-and-go." (Investment in plant and equipment has, to say the least, not been stabilized.) More important, there seems on the whole more similarity between successive British cycles than between British cycles and contemporaneous movements in neighboring continental countries or in North America.

Public policy in Britain does not seem to have been aimed at stabilization of the economy, but rather at adjusting the level of domestic activity to the exigencies of the balance of payments. The Government has not been immune to old-fashioned alternations of optimism and pessimism, directed particularly at the balance of payments. These have affected primarily monetary policy, the budget being relatively passive. Monetary policy, as has been said, has been dictated by the state of reserves as well as the level of current activity. Matthews added that perhaps the state of British reserves is related to the (mathematical) sum or integral of recent activity, rather than to activity as such.

Critics have claimed that, in addition to accentuating oscillations, British "stop-and-go" or "policy" cycles have slowed the rate of long-term growth as well. Matthews believes that such an effect is not proven; in fact, he sees no evidence of appreciable effects in this direction.

During earlier sessions, Professor Guitton had introduced the concept of a cycle *de bonne famille*. In his formal discussion of Matthews's presentation, Mr. Worswick elaborated upon this notion in applying it to the British case. A cycle *de bonne famille*, said Worswick, runs a well defined course and is largely endogenous in the sense that random shocks and international repercussions are unimportant. (A Schumpeterian cycle, dominated by innovational shocks, does not satisfy this requirement.)

The postwar British cycle, Worswick felt, has imitated many of the outward signs of normal good behavior, but has actually been managed at almost every stage. He said that British arrangements permit not only monetary but also fiscal interventions. The latter, traditionally concentrated in the April Budget, have increasingly become variable within the year, particularly on the tax side. This variability naturally increases the analyst's difficulty in distinguishing exogenous from endogenous movements.

As for the British record, Worswick agreed with Matthews's view of "stop-and-go." While better timing and less violence might have combined to iron out fluctuations to a greater extent, he was not sure that this alone would have sufficed to insure faster growth. Part of the difficulty, he thought, sprang from the paucity and delays of British data; he favored more quarterly series, and also commented that a GDP deflator was not an ideal price index number.

Worswick drew attention to the conflict between exports and the satisfaction of domestic demand, but pointed out that econometric analysis had shown that reducing British domestic demand did not lead to large increases in exports. Even more surprising was the failure of "demand pressure" to provide much explanation of the variability of British imports. His stress was mainly on how much was unknown, rather than on the substitution of any rival explanation based, for example, on prices or terms of trade.

Another unexplained aspect of the recent British record has been the behavior of manufacturing investment (plant and equipment) in 1965–1966. A downturn anticipated for the turn of the year did not materialize. How far, Worswick wondered as a result, can investment of this type be influenced by the British pattern of investment incentives, given the course of final demand?

The entire area of aggregate supply, Worswick thought, needed exploration. He mentioned particularly the labor market and the supply of manufactured exports, where preliminary explorations suggest price coefficients with the "wrong" signs.

Worswick closed by agreeing with two points of the main paper. One was methodological, the desirability of separating the study of pure cycles from that of cycle policy. The other was substantive, that postwar cycles were not, of themselves, responsible for the comparatively low growth rate of the postwar British economy.

The initial participant opened his presentation by agreeing with Matthews that postwar cycles seemed no milder than pre-1914 ones, suggesting that the interwar period and particularly the 1930's had been the abnormality. He himself leaned to a price-cost-profit explanation of the cycle, and welcomed Matthews' treatment of price movements, an often neglected aspect of oscillations. On the other hand, he could not accept Matthews's "lag" and "mildness" explanations of price perversity without adding that price administration by monopolistic concerns was part of the picture. As for the general inflationary trend of postwar prices, he felt that primary responsibility rested with governments which had abandoned the gold standard in favor of managed currencies.

It is an interesting phenomenon, the same participant felt, to have consumption of durables turn down before manufacturing investment, but it is not unique. The U.S. depression of 1957–1958 was foreshadowed by the disappointing 1956 automobile year; and a similar automobile year may be developing again for 1967.

As a methodological matter, this participant approved of abstracting as far as possible from government interventions, not only in Britain but quite generally. In the British case, the Government has become a recessional factor as a result of payments problems, but he declined to guess at what might have happened under a regime of world-wide shortage of sterling. He thought the theory of "policy cycles" especially valid when investment ceases to "work right," that is, when it lags instead of leading other indicators. The ordinary corrective mechanism for capitalist overexpansion is cyclical contraction, but it may be replaced by extraneous forces or by the Government acting as their "agent."

The second participant proposed to disagree with Matthews from the side of orthodoxy, but the differences were mainly in emphasis. He felt that "policy cycles" started in Britain at the beginning of upswings, when the Government encouraged consumption, inventory accumulation, and fixed investment simultaneously. The size of the push was often, he thought, excessive in view of the country's balance of payments. The Government could have improved matters by reducing the average level of demand pressure over the active cycle, but at the cost of lowering the average growth rate somewhat. This position he ascribed to Professor F. W. Paish, and felt himself more sympathetic with Paish than Matthews appeared to be.

Another minor difference between himself and Matthews, this participant continued, was in the treatment of exogenous factors. Matthews mentioned them at the start of each oscillation described in his paper, but were they not in large part endogenous effects of previous government policy measures? Along similar lines, Matthews might perhaps have said more about the errors in government forecasting. In this participant's view, it had been a failure of intelligence that permitted fluctuations to persist as they had. Errors of optimism have led several times to balance of payments crises, with international complications. The discussant mentioned inventory investment as a point of especial weakness, and included a plea for more and better econometric business cycle research.

Like the previous speaker, he felt that many features of the British experience were less unique than they may have appeared to Matthews. Two examples are the lag in postwar price cycles and the divergence between output and employment cycles. These are both quite common in the advanced countries of Western Europe.

The third participant divided his remarks under three heads. (a) On the perverse price cycle, he doubted the importance of price administration. Rather, he suggested, it might be well to look at wage lags and at the fall of labor productivity, consequent upon the attainment of full employment. Like Worswick, he had qualms about accepting the GDP deflator as a price index, because of the prevalance of secret rebates and other concessions. Also, price perversity may mitigate the cycle by reducing bankruptcies and their psychological effects. (b) On intercountry cyclical amplitude and growth rate comparisons: British cycles are milder than, for example, German, Swedish, or Japanese ones. But, given a political "floor" set in practice by stagnation at zero growth, a lower cycle amplitude means a slower growth rate. (c) On the lead of consumer-durable consumption: he wondered whether the true "leading series" might not be discretionary spending on nonessentials of all degrees of durability.

The fourth participant went further than any predecessor in criticizing directly the British Government's cycle policy. Pointing to the budgets of 1955 and 1964, he said that their errors involved more than poor forecasting or honest overoptimism. He suggested that they both were "political budgets" aimed at influencing elections. The 1966 budget may be another instance. He wished that the economy could be protected against political machinations of this sort.

Next, he felt constrained to raise the question of why the U.K. growth trend has been so low. In his opinion, this issue was relevant to the cycle, and he offered three interrelated explanations: (a) the economy is not internationally competitive; sterling is too high, and adequate devaluation might provoke U.S. retaliation. (b) The economy is illiquid; its international reserves are too low. (c) The burden of British foreign payments has been too high on capital account, meaning particularly the support of the sterling bloc and foreign military commitments. He would like to have seen Britain default on her World War II obligations in 1945. Rather than face these difficulties, he believed, Britain has turned to one short-term palliative after another, and the growth rate has suffered.

Others' remarks were briefer, sometimes taking the form of questions and suggestions for research. One participant, calling Britain "the most mysterious economy in Western Europe," wondered how the conventional picture of excess demand could be reconciled with the survival of inferior employment and regional imbalance, and with payments problems relating to capital rather than current account. Another felt that inventory adjustments might have reduced the effect of changes in British demand pressure upon British imports. The wish was repeated for more and better monthly and quarterly data, and also for the systematic computation of fiscal and export multipliers. Doubt was also expressed as to the usefulness of an amplitude measure which included duration, as Matthews' index does, and as to the reality of price perversity. (Prices adjust with a lag; the shorter the cycle, the more likely is some appearance of perversity.)

Professor Matthews closed by replying to certain of the criticisms.

1. He accepted, but minimized, the objections to the use of the GDP deflator as a price index. If it cannot be used, he said, the whole series of real or deflated GDP is suspect.

2. The British Government has been sensitive to forecasts of lagging domestic demand, and has looked for supports, through fiscal and monetary policy, to compensate for difficulties. It has not reacted in the same way to falling export demand. This makes it appear that exports are not on a par with other elements of aggregate demand, and that Britain underestimates the importance of its export sector.

3. The British Government has not only acted as a "cyclical agent" in the face of external imbalance, but has also been influenced in its reactions by political considerations. Its role in early upswings has replaced that played in other booms by such factors as good harvests, but it is true that some factors treated as exogenous (in his own discussion) actually depended on past decisions. Its forecasting errors were not only intellectual and political, but sometimes reflected "errors of sentiment." An example is 1964, when an influential assertion that the growth rate of labor productivity was increasing had a significant effect on British public opinion.

4. Even under continuous demand pressure, it takes many years to iron out regional imbalances. This is true in all countries. It is perhaps unusually important in Great Britain, which includes areas like Northern Ireland. (Northern Ireland is in many respects a separate country.)

## V. Mr. Dow's Chapter (France, Germany, and Italy)

This chapter, prepared in the National Accounts and Economic Forecasting Division of the Department of Economics and Statistics of OECD, is a progress report on a larger study. It comprises three separate essays on the three countries concerned [1], plus Mr. Dow's introductory summary.

Quite independently of, for example, Professor Gordon's discussion of the United States, the OECD group under Dow's direction had derived the concept of a growth cycle. Like Gordon on the United States, Dow concluded that the cycle was not obsolete in the OECD area, but that its character had changed. More clearly than other authors, moreover, Dow explored the special dating problems resulting from the substitution of a "growth" for a "conventional" cycle. The first chart in his summary illustrates the point with minimal resort to formal mathematics. Dow proposes to measure cyclical phases by indices of

[1] Writers primarily responsible for the three country studies were P. Gutmann (France), P. Schwanse (Germany), and Miss J. Sutherland (Italy).

slack in the utilization of capacity, without distinguishing explicitly between slack that is due to demand deficiency and slack caused by shortages of labor, raw materials, etc. If the "ceiling" and "floor" of a capacity utilization index (strictly speaking, of its logarithm) move in roughly parallel straight lines, and a sinusoidal curve is drawn between these lines, a derived curve representing the *rate of change* of capacity utilization reaches its peaks and troughs a quarter-cycle before the ratio of actual output to capacity output.

The three individual country papers were presented primarily as historical accounts (with statistical documentation) of upswings and downswings during the (roughly) 15-year interval between the Korean War and the conference out of which this book developed. Special efforts were made to measure the slackness of each economy at each period, but the measures used could not be made completely comparable between three countries with independent statistical offices. A second function of the three country studies was to accumulate data as raw materials for future econometric analysis of the separate economies and the OECD region as a whole. From cursory examination of preliminary data it is clear that, within the OECD area, the individual-country cycles are coordinated with each other, whatever may be true for the OECD countries combined and the rest of the world.

It appeared to Professor Spaventa, as formal discussant, that the major emphasis of Dow's presentation had been placed on forecasting, rather than on the analysis of cyclical behavior. This did not fit well with the nature of the overall concern of this book, and concealed a number of matters which might be relevant for forecasting as well. Turning to the criteria used to determine cyclical phases, Spaventa approved in principle of Dow's reliance upon indices of slack. Unfortunately, as different measures of productive potential were used for the three countries, the results were not comparable across national boundaries.

Spaventa was especially critical of the index of slack for Germany. This, he felt, was based on an inadequately defined concept of full-employment output. It turns out, in his view, that none of Dow's peaks corresponds to years of maximum growth, and only two of his troughs correspond to years of relative stagnation. For Italy, Spaventa noted a discrepancy between the dating in Dow's chapter and that obtainable from the standard Italian index of capacity utilization. (Minor troughs of February 1956 and January 1961 are both missed.)

Passing to problems of growth in general, Spaventa noted the omission of multiplier effects from the calculations of the relative contributions of different GNP components. He suggested an expansion of Dow's discussion to allow for differential multiplier effects.

On the four main components of demand (Investment, Consumption, Exports, and Imports), Spaventa felt that the treatments of the first three might be improved, and made more comparable as between countries, by an explicit

520     Summary of the Discussion

analysis of structural relations. (a) On investment, he felt that multiple-regression investment functions might have been fitted, allowance made for asymmetry as between upswings and downswings, and explicit attention paid to phenomena of capital-stock adjustment. (b) It seemed to him surprising that more satisfactory generalizations for consumption had not been reached for the OECD region. He suggested that incorporation of an income-distribution variable had already given promising results for Italy. (c) On the export side, Spaventa noted that relative price levels were mentioned only for France, and thought that indices of relative competitiveness (connected particularly with unit labor costs) might be introduced throughout.

Comparisons between the cyclical experiences of the three countries have not been made as easy (for the reader) as Spaventa believed they might have been. He felt that inclusion of comparative materials on the three countries' long-term economic structures and their changes would be relevant also for short-term forecasting. He could, however, draw two important "comparative conclusions:" (a) The most stable economic growth to date has been in Italy (although Spaventa doubted that this would persist). (b) The absence of coincidence between the three countries' cycles (except in 1958) suggests that the international transmission mechanism worked "in reverse," that is, to damp down individual country fluctuations.

The first participant criticized the Dow models as incomplete, from the forecasting viewpoint. On the other hand, he believed that this was, in general, the right sort of material to have assembled for the benefit of future analysis. A later participant expanded on this criticism to suggest that Dow seemed to be heading directly for the reduced form of his future forecasting model, whereas (in the participant's view) a detailed structural analysis might be more appropriate.

The second participant, after pointing out the importance of the OECD area for the generation and behavior of business fluctuations all over the world, praised the discussion's stress on investment as a dynamic factor, but wished that more attention had been paid to purchases of consumer durable goods (investment in consumers' capital) which is becoming increasingly important. Finally, he would have liked to find fuller accounts of stop-and-go fiscal and monetary policies in the OECD area.

"More disaggregation" was the watchword of the third participant. As particularly appropriate candidates for disaggregation, he mentioned corporate profits, inventory investment, new orders, contract awards, consumer credit, and capital stock or capacity.

An anomaly suggested by the next participant was the fact that all three individual-country series suggest a Juglar cycle which is invisible in OECD–wide series. As a partial explanation, he suggested that, while the individual-country cycles strengthened each other in 1958, subsequent developments were mere unsynchronized adjustments to slower growth rates.

The fifth participant began his observations by following the "disaggregation" line proposed by the third, suggesting the desirability for separating the series for automobiles from that for other consumer durables. (This is done in several U.S. models.) His main suggestion, however, was for more explicit examination of the cyclical effects of increasing Western European integration. His own surmise is that the linking of short-term capital markets, labor markets (via heavier migration), and rising trade-GNP ratios operate to damp cyclical oscillation. In addition, continental integration may weaken the ties of each of the countries concerned with the weaker British economy.

The final intervention was methodological. This participant felt that the paper had included elements of both "facts without theory" and "theory without facts." He felt that Dow's view came close to Hicks's, including a capacity concept; while the facts may eventually support some such theory, Dow's own study had not introduced capacity with adequate specificity.

Replying to his critics, Dow apologized for the preliminary nature of the OECD study. Time was lacking, he said, for econometric testing of the explicit OECD hypotheses. He agreed that expenditure on consumer durables could be fruitfully investigated, but questioned the usefulness of explaining consumption as a whole by consumers' disposable income, since the latter must then be investigated in its turn. Regarding exports, he said that relative-price elasticities are derived only with difficulty, and there is danger in overstressing unit labor costs as a determinant. The ratio of wages to the value of output is subject to cyclical influences because of complex output-employment relations; the ratio therefore needs to have its cyclical component removed before it can be used safely.

## VI.  Professor Gelting's Chapter (Scandinavia)

This discussion dealt with three small countries—Denmark, Norway, and Sweden—which are heavily involved in world trade. (Finland was omitted.) The three countries, however, are significantly different.

During the period reviewed, Swedish and Norwegian exports, but not Danish, have been cycle-sensitive. Nevertheless, total output has been more stable in Norway and Sweden than in Denmark. In Norway, the impact on domestic demand has been dampened by the shipping industry's low propensity to spend at home, and also by Norway's ability to borrow abroad. In Sweden, export fluctuations have been largely neutralized by parallel import fluctuations. (These were due in part to inventory investments with a high marginal import content.) The overall Swedish foreign balance has varied only slightly.

A high degree of stability in private fixed investment was achieved in Sweden, partly through a temporary investment tax, and partly through a system of blocked tax-exempt investment funds, from which releases are made at the discretion of the authorities.

The fluctuations in economic activity in Denmark have been due in large part to stop-and-go policies. These in turn were caused by failure to deal effectively with a weak balance of payments position. After 1958, conditions improved greatly, with rising industrial exports, substantial capital imports, and improved terms of trade. Unemployment fell from about 10 per cent in the 1950's to about 3 per cent in the 1960's. As a consequence of the predominant use of fiscal policy to control total demand, private consumption has fluctuated more widely in Denmark than in the two other Scandinavian countries.

Professor Rasmussen, as formal discussant, began by emphasizing the difficulty of treating the three countries together, although foreign trade is important for all of them. Fluctuations are largest in Denmark, where they cannot be easily ascribed to exports.

In Norway, exports—particularly of shipping services—fluctuate sharply, and investment appears to be largely exogenous. Saving is high, which provides a cushion. In Sweden, there seems to be more shortcircuiting of exports to imports *via* changes in inventories.

Denmark combines greater fluctuations in income with relative stability of exports. This suggests bad policy, but Rasmussen thought that the situation was difficult, because the supply-and-demand situation in Western Europe shifted in a manner unfavorable to Denmark by reducing the demand for her traditional exports. However, Denmark has been able to shift her own export structure toward manufactured exports and away from agriculture. This process has gone on steadily for 15 years, even in relatively depressed periods, and contrasts with the British failure to accomplish a similar shift towards a better export mix. As for the stop-and-go which Gelting mentioned, it has included both monetary and tax measures. Today, the nominal interest rate on safe bonds approaches 10 per cent, which makes Denmark a high-rate country. Boom conditions of the 1960's, Rasmussen agreed, resemble a Wicksell inflationary process, with investment in real capital an inflation hedge.

Rasmussen wished that more was known about the effectiveness of monetary policy. The effects of money were considered to be primarily on investment, operated not only through the interest rate, and varied from country to country. Perhaps a standardized set of flow-of-funds accounts, not yet available, will permit more to be said. Because of institutional differences, international comparisons will be difficult.

In closing his discussion, Rasmussen professed faith in the manageability of the stability problem in general. He agreed with Gelting that increased attention should be given to the problem of rational allocation. This raises the difficult problem of how to quantify or measure losses due to misallocations.

This last problem was discussed by several of the participants. Participants pointed to substantial losses from delaying the adoption of new techniques, maintaining balance of payments disequilibria, retaining too large a portion of the labor force in subsistence agriculture, and continuing widespread shortages of residential housing.

One participant, basing his remarks primarily on Sweden, interpreted Gelting as claiming that public investment had been a destabilizing factor, and dissented in part. While local government investment had fluctuated with the cycle, the central government had been a stabilizer. As to Wicksell inflationary processes, he felt that these had been more important in the 1950's than in the 1960's, because wages had risen faster relative to prices in the later period, and profit inflation had been reduced. Finally, commenting on the export performance of Swedish industry, he contrasted the position of many Swedish corporations, which export the major part of their output, and that of British export industries, which can shift supply to the home market if export demand should fall. In general, he doubted that parallelism between exports and imports could be explained (in Sweden) by the high import content of exports, because import content in iron ore and wood pulp is low. He laid more stress on a generally high marginal import propensity and import-income elasticity. He estimates the latter at 1.8 for Sweden. (Another participant suggested that the figure might be systematically higher in prosperity than in depression. Yet another wished for a separation of inventories and final purchases of imports, and, for inventories, a further division between inventories in export industries and inventories for domestic consumption.)

An enquiry was made specifically regarding Norway. Were not Norwegian fluctuations largely induced by the Suez crisis of 1956–1957, which caused a great oscillation in tanker freight earnings? The same participant also expressed surprise at the high unemployment percentages for Denmark, and wondered what full employment actually meant in the Scandinavian context.

The Scandinavian parallel movement between exports and the composite of exports less imports plus inventory accumulation does not hold universally, another participant stated, citing Swiss experience. He agreed that Scandinavia showed less tendency than Switzerland to maintain imports when exports fell.

A more general point, raised by another participant, was inspired by the expansion and diversification of Danish exports. One function of recessions, as he viewed cycle theory, was to accelerate structural changes of this kind, and he was glad to see it happening in Denmark. In general, however, he was pessimistic. In the first place, milder recessions were leading to greater complacency, and in the second place, administered pricing eliminated one source of readjustment pressure, and also gave the price indices some long-run upward bias. This participant concluded his intervention on a pessimistic note. There is not, or soon would not be, any important "natural" recovery features left in the system.

Professor Gelting closed the session by agreeing that the Suez crisis had been important in stimulating investment in Norway. On full employment, the Norwegian and Swedish records are better than the Danish, even in recent years. (Seasonal unemployment is important in Denmark.)

Much of Gelting's summary dealt with the parallel movements of exports, imports, and incomes. In Sweden, if we consider *changes* rather than levels of inventory, then export industries are important. Denmark's structural change was due, in the 1950's, largely to favorable industrial price-wage relationships. (Wage increases were restricted by a low overall level of activity, caused ultimately by stagnant agricultural exports.)

## VII.  Dr. Rothschild's Chapter (Austria and Switzerland)

These are two small countries in the heart of Europe, both dependent on foreign trade. Switzerland is the more advanced industrially; Austria has the more elaborate structure of controls. Switzerland, as a neutral, suffered no war damage in World War II, and recommenced normal development after the close of hostilities; Austrian conditions returned to normal only after a period of division, occupation, absorption of postwar unemployment, and repair of damaged facilities, lasting until approximately 1953.

"Growth cycles," measured in terms of deviations from trend, exist in both countries. Measurement is difficult, because of sensitivity to the choice of trends, and also because of trend shifts as between the 1940's and early 1950's on the one hand, and the late 1950's and 1960's on the other.

The cycles appear to be short. They do not generally coincide with those in other countries, nor with each other (1957–1958 was an exception). Cycle policy is not coordinated between the two countries; each country tends to rely on exports as a major means of avoiding the consequences of deflation. Switzerland is unusual in using its labor-absorption rate for foreign labor as well.

After this introduction, Dr. Rothschild passed to cycle history, beginning in 1957–1958. He called this recession "classical," although it worked out differently in the two countries. The Swiss recession was earlier, shorter, and sharper, with an actual decline in GDP. (This was a reaction from the boom and labor imputs of the previous year or two.) Both countries recovered with export-led booms in 1959–1960, including tourism as an export.

It is not easy to explain the sluggishness in the Austrian economy following 1962. Exports fell off, particularly those to Germany in 1962; unfavorable weather in 1962 and again in 1965 retarded agriculture and building. Also, Austria has developed some excess capacity in steel, and rising wages have reduced profit margins. A turn from internal to external finance found the capital markets poorly equipped for the change. There has been a shift in demand, to "modern" goods not produced in Austria, and political uncertainty has arisen regarding the country's relations with both the European Economic

Community (EEC) and the European Free Trade Area (EFTA). None of this, however, has been serious, because consumption and exports have held up well.

On the other hand, Rothschild ascribed the Swiss retardation in 1965 to deliberate policy. It was marked by direct controls on the immigration of foreign labor and on building activity, which Rothschild felt had been excessively stringent.

In general, exports and investment have played leading roles in both countries, as they also have done in the entire OECD area generally. Switzerland is interesting because of its intake of foreign labor, which is drawn largely into bottleneck industries. Both countries have been aided by the absence of balance of payments problems. Their exports have been structurally favored: tourism has boomed in both countries, and "special products," most notably timepieces and precision machinery, in Switzerland.

Since 1957, the instruments of cycle policy have become more similar in the two countries, although Austria has been traditionally more protectionist and Switzerland more given to free enterprise. There has been a considerable decline in ideology. Austria has attempted an incomes policy since 1957, but, at best, this policy has had only a delaying effect upon the general inflationary pressure.

Professor Niehans, as formal discussant, concentrated on additional material about Switzerland, despite the paucity of analysis and data for that country. He found little evidence of countercyclical policies there, in contrast to, for example, Great Britain. The money supply was dominated by balance of payments considerations, with attempts to maintain moderate and stable interest rates largely by moral suasion. On the fiscal side, there were built-in stabilizers only; Parliament, he felt, had been generally late in doing the wrong things, but Switzerland had not been significantly more or less stable than her neighbors.

Niehans believed there had been two Swiss Juglar cycles, 1948–1957 and 1957–1964, but the downturns had been shorter and less severe than in the past, and were indeed difficult to date precisely. They were in investment, security prices, interest rates, profits, and the rate of price increase. There were cycles in the absolute value of output, but only in 1958 was there any decline in real output. There was no unemployment cycle. Labor remained in short supply, while the number of foreign workers was altered.

Switzerland has experienced a number of exogenous shocks, beginning with the Korean War. For example, the restoration of convertibility (1958–1959) was a destabilizing influence because it increased capital inflows into Switzerland during boom periods, when the balance of payments might otherwise have been unfavorable. There was also a public-investment boom in the 1960's, concentrating on highways and hospitals. This was not consciously countercyclical, but it made the cycle look less classical by extending the boom. Niehans did not believe that controls on bank credit and private building had been effective in the same period.

Niehans went on to trace a "typical" Swiss cycle. It was set off, he felt, by random fluctuations on Swiss exports, as a result of foreign conditions, then magnified by multiplier and accelerator effects, plus monetary ease. Eventually inflation threatened a payments deficit, interest rates rose, and the rate of monetary growth declined. There was a reaction in private construction, and the favorable aspect of the accelerator had already run its course.

While Swiss oscillations have been smaller than in prewar years, stability does not seem to have increased since 1945. Niehans was skeptical for the future, saw difficulties ahead for the 1970's, and suggested the need for positive cycle policy in Switzerland.

Few other participants had much first-hand experience with either the Austrian or the Swiss economy, but discussion centered upon a number of issues more general in their application.

1. The 1952–1953 recession, which Rothschild had not considered a normal cycle in Austria, was in fact quite widespread in Western Europe, and its connection with the Korean War is doubtful. In fact, the fall in raw material prices after that war should have kept the boom going. The whole period needs further study. (In reply, others pointed to the U.S. postwar recession as causing a general squeeze on European exports and prices after the Korean War.)

2. Austria has a large nationalized sector. How has this, and similar sectors elsewhere in Europe, modified the course of the cycle, particularly in connection with trade with Eastern Europe? Replies from British and continental participants were that, in general, state-controlled sectors simply follow the cycle. Contracyclical policy is proposed, but has been difficult to apply in practice.

3. Large-country models do not apply in small countries, where the main problem is adjustment to pressure from outside. (This methodological point came up during a discussion which began with questions about Swiss statistical data. It was disputed by econometricians present.) Granted that models need not be uniform as between countries, and that more elements are exogenous in small countries than in large ones, the econometric approach is not ruled out. In fact, even the increased importance of exogenous factors can be reduced if one works with a network of several small countries. A second rebuttal also was made: What, in the economic sense, is a "small" country? The trade dependence of Great Britain is as high as that of Scandinavia. The problem may be satellitic dependence on a large economy (Canada, Ireland, and perhaps Austria are examples). Or it may be great dependence on a single commodity—but in this sense, Switzerland is not a "small country!" A final suggestion was that both Austria and Switzerland may be satellites of Western Europe as a whole.

3. After the 1949 devaluations, the Swiss franc was overvalued. This dampened total demand and inflation during the 1950's. By 1960, the rest of Europe had caught up, and Switzerland began importing others' inflation. Further, the effects of immigrant labor are complex. Directly, excess demands in

the labor market are reduced. At the same time, inducements are increased to invest in infrastructure and capital widening.

5. The vagaries of Swiss monetary policy, particularly its attempts to hold interest rates within bounds, led one participant to suggest that a constant monetary growth rate, as advocated by the Chicago School in the United States, might have produced a better record than was actually achieved.

Summarizing the discussion, Rothschild claimed that policies of both countries, while failing to avoid destabilizing influences from outside, had at least avoided making matters worse or curbing growth in the interest of disinflation. Nationalized industry in Austria had not been an important factor. As in Italy, it is run along commercial lines; also, it is concentrated in a few sectors (iron, steel, petroleum, and electricity). In these sectors, there has been some attempt to use trade with Eastern Europe as a stabilizer more intensively than is done in the private sector, but this issue had become political—Socialists generally favoring the policy, Conservatives opposing. Finally, Rothschild denied any intention to generate pessimism about either cycle policies or econometric models in small countries. He felt that relative freedom is obtainable by size (even with a large international sector); but that when this is lacking, structural diversification by commodities or regions can serve as well, as indeed it does in countries like Switzerland and Sweden.

## VIII. Dr. Rhomberg's Chapter (International Transmission)

Dr. Rhomberg limited his discussion to the transmission of cyclical disturbances from developed to developing countries, together with "echo effects" in the opposite direction. This global approach involves taking each set of countries as a uniform group, without regard for the special problems of individual countries. Another limitation was that of data, which, for the less developed countries (LDC's) in particular, had to be limited to annual observations.

Two channels of international transmission can be distinguished. The more conventional one operates through trade, with short lags. The other operates through capital movements, with longer lags.

In the period under review, the fluctuations in the developed countries were both mild, and except in 1958, largely unsynchronized. The LDC's benefited from this circumstance.

Using indices of industrial production to indicate the state of prosperity in developed countries, Rhomberg first considered LDC's exports to the developed countries. This is the most important transmission mechanism of business cycles, from the LDC's viewpoint. He found that the LDC's raw-material exports are influenced strongly, with a one-quarter lag (no lag in annual data). LDC's exports of manufactured products are a small element, but are affected in much the same way.

Capital exports to the LDC's are also affected by economic fluctuations in developed countries. Here much of the data are poor, but those available indicate a lag of one year (four to five quarters).

The characteristic LDC response mechanism has been to adjust their imports to their gross foreign exchange earnings. This effect is stretched out and diffused, depending upon the state of the LDC's reserves. The statistical evidence does not show any way in which the LDC's as a group have suffered greatly from these fluctuations in developed countries. Any "echo effect" back to the developed countries is so delayed and so long drawn out that the LDC's may be said for that very reason to have contributed to international stability.

In his discussion, Dr Meyer zu Schlochtern began by comparing Rhomberg's results for price elasticities with preliminary work done for a quarterly world-trade model being developed in the Organization for Economic Cooperation and Development (OECD). He found generally higher elasticities than did Rhomberg. This preliminary work also suggested a need to take account of competition between LDC's and developed countries like the United States, Canada, and (outside OECD) Australia, New Zealand, and the Socialist countries of Eastern Europe.

Meyer zu Schlochtern doubted that, once a downturn starts in the developed countries, the LDC's can continue to attract capital. The reason is that LDC's commodity exports seem, after allowance for lags, to be the most important determinant of advanced-country investment in the LDC's.

Much of Meyer zu Schlochtern's technical discussion suggested alternatives to certain of the Rhomberg equations. For example, he proposed an adjustment to LDC's export series to eliminate the cost of freight, insurance, and similar payments to developed countries; a more explicit use of lagged LDC's international reserves, partly as a dummy for changes in LDC's trade policies as determinants of LDC's imports; and a division of export series to separate quantum from price variations, since LDC's prices are more flexible than those of developed countries and move with shorter lags (or none at all). He also noted that LDC's terms of trade were correlated with LDC's international reserves. In testing several important functions it was unclear which is the relevant factor, reserves as a dummy for LDC's trade policies or LDC's export prices with their impacts on profits, investment, and therefore imports.

The first participant agreed that both contemporaneous and lagged values should be used together in estimating equations and criticized Rhomberg's choice of one or the other. He also agreed that price changes and terms of trade may be important, and suggested a possible expansion of the Rhomberg model to allow for the operation of export multipliers within the LDC's. As an historical matter, he disagreed with Meyer zu Schlochtern on the sensitivity of capital exports of developed countries to domestic business conditions in those countries. Great Britain, for example, had been studied by Lamfalussy.

5

5

5

According to this study, the British had for long periods continued to export capital during depressions. (Meyer zu Schlochtern, in rebuttal, doubted that the older data remain relevant.)

The second participant wished to have more attention paid to LDC's conditions (other than the state of international reserves) as determinants of their demand for imports. He had in mind their aggregate demand in general.

The third participant believed that it was important to consider irregularities between cycles, with special reference to the capital account. He felt that the relative marginal efficiencies of investment (m.e.i.) in the two groups of countries had varied as between cycles, and wondered whether irregularities had not been confused with lags.

A fourth participant was concerned largely with the meaning of published statistical series. Were prices really market prices, or did they reflect commodity agreements? How would the capital-movement series be affected by separating offical capital (including aid) from private capital? With regard to prices and price elasticities for manufactures, should not the processing of raw material be treated separately? (These criticisms were expanded by other participants, who feared that the entire LDC's series might be biased by inclusion of unrepresentative areas like Hong Kong, Puerto Rico, Mexico, and the oil countries, and wondered whether the Rhomberg results would hold for particular regions, such as Latin America.)

Why, wondered the fifth participant, should capital movements be made dependent on industrial production in the exporting countries? He thought that they were more responsive to individual commodity markets. The sixth participant raised the question of trends in the time series used by both Rhomberg and the OECD, and wondered whether they had been allowed for.

The seventh participant suspected that several of the larger LDC's, such as India, may affect the world economy by reason of their own autonomous shocks, and wondered whether subdivision of LDC's by size might not be worth while. He also professed himself unconvinced whether the slightness of the cyclical effects on the LDC's reflected primarily the mildness of postwar cycles. Some postwar change in the international transmission mechanism may also be involved.

The eighth participant was of the opinion that the LDC's would have merited a separate discussion, quite apart from the transmission mechanism. Such a discussion might have served more effectively than Rhomberg's as an antidote to those who, like Professor Myrdal and Dr. Prebisch, blame the developed countries for all the troubles of the LDC's. In his own view, the LDC's were largely responsible for their own difficulties; better output data would probably support his view. He repeated earlier pleas for disaggregation, in particular separation out of "satellites" among the LDC's. He suspected that now, in contrast to earlier years, LDC's were the staple producers of many goods, with stabilizing influence on LDC's exports. Finally, he raised questions about figures on capital movements. Do they include LDC's earnings of developed-country firms reinvested in the LDC's? Do they include short-term financing, particulary export credits?

The ninth participant made a plea for models larger than those presented by either Rhomberg or the OECD. Many single-country models exist; could they not be combined? In the developed-country series, industrial production is being overworked, as GNP is in some other studies. Also, data on population, income, domestic investment, and distribution are needed. It would be desirable to proceed by individual commodities, or at least by commodity groups, and to consider stockpiling and price changes separately. Capital movements should be related to profits and profit rates rather than to industrial production. Although he himself did not adopt the commodity-agreements approach of the United Nations Commission on Trade and Development (UNCTAD), he believed Rhomberg had gone too far in aggregating both all commodities and all LDC's.

In what way, wondered the tenth and final participant, were the LDC's different from such smaller advanced countries as Sweden and Switzerland? He would like to have seen transmission mechanisms compared, so as to bring out the *special* problems of the LDC's. In his view, one always finds "the rest of the world" to be a stabilizing force, so he is not surprised to find LDC's in this position.

Responding to this large body of criticism, Rhomberg concentrated on four points:

1. Restatement of his intended purpose: This involved use of NBER methodology to check transmission of cycles from developed countries (represented by their industrial production) to LDC's. He had not proposed to determine LDC's import functions, or to model their economies completely, but to determine what, in LDC's economies, corresponds to cycles in the developed countries.

2. Degree of aggregation: Rhomberg accepted the criticisms to a large degree. He said that he and his colleagues in the International Monetary Fund (IMF) were leaving this problem for the future, since they cannot do everything at once.

3. On LDC's response mechanism: In a previous IMF model, the LDC's were assumed to spend all their gross foreign exchange receipts. This was an oversimplification; the present work should lead to improvement in explaining LDC's imports. The IMF has also experimented with the inclusion of LDC's domestic factors, as suggested by several participants, but the results have not been statistically significant.

4. Capital exports with relation to cycles in developed countries: Rhomberg admitted that industrial production was not a good explanatory variable in general, but pointed out that its *changes* were a good proxy for cyclical

movements. He also admitted deficiencies in the statistics used, pointing to the large "errors and omissions" in trade and payments series as evidence of *net* deficiencies. (The *gross* deficiencies are even worse.) Nevertheless, despite the various criticisms, he stands by his basic results.

## IX.  Professor Nove's Chapter. (Socialist Countries)

There is no question that the socialist economies undergo economic fluctuations, or that these differ to some extent from the business cycles of capitalist economies. The issue is, how can these fluctuations best be understood? Professor Goldmann, in Czechoslovakia, has spoken of "pseudo-cycles;" both he and Professor Olivera in Argentina see socialist economies as subject to a compulsion to periodic overinvestment. This leads to overstrain on capacity, labor, and transport (Goldmann), or simply on people's patience (Olivera), which leads in turn to a period of relative retardation and declining growth. It is, however, impossible to define such pseudo-cycles with precision. The statistics are usually inadequate and sometimes misleading, as in the U.S.S.R. in the mid-1930's.

Another view of fluctuations in socialist economies is that they are simply reactions to such random shocks as a major rearmament program, a major policy change, or the death of a great leader like Stalin. Observers are trying to decide between and among these views.

Professor Nove turned his attention more explicitly to the U.S.S.R. The Soviet deceleration of 1933 seems to fit the Goldmann pattern, after the "great leap forward" of the first Five-Year Plan. A later example, as can be seen from the Bródy paper, is provided by Hungary, 1949–1953. In each country, there was first an acceleration associated with "social revolution from above," and a political atmosphere in which economic caution had become associated with right-wing deviationism.

On the other hand, the downturn in rates of growth, and probably living standards, in the U.S.S.R. between 1937 and 1940 does not fit any cyclical pattern, according to Nove. The period was marked by war preparation and great political purges. There was no overinvestment in Goldmann's sense, certainly not in the civilian sector.

The period after World War II is less clearcut. The postwar spurt looks like a cyclical boom. Military expansion, culminating in the Korean War, seems to have caused some braking of the economy in 1950–1952. The death of Stalin in 1953 coincided with the end of the Korean War, and was followed by a shift to consumption, and a decline in the importance of both fixed investment and forced saving. Nove finds no cyclical phenomena thereafter, but rather fluctuations and a declining trend of growth rates, which are explained largely by agricultural difficulties.

This is not to deny the presence in the U.S.S.R. of a propensity to overinvest, but merely to claim that it is continuous rather than cyclical. One reason for its continuity is the tendency of the Soviet fixed-investment enthusiasts to underestimate the costs of such investment and to perpetuate excess demand for capital goods.

Nove was unwilling to express an opinion on the probability that the post-Krushchev turn to "market Socialism" might produce cycles. He suggested (without having studied the Bródy paper or having seen the Goldmann paper) that fluctuations in other Eastern European countries might be more nearly cyclical than they were in the U.S.S.R., by reason of balance of payments problems. In closing, he reminded the conference on business cycles that even if the 1933 downturn in the U.S.S.R. was cyclical, it was far milder than the contemporaneous "crises" in the West, and could by no means have been avoided by following Western models.

The formal discussant of Nove's paper was Professor Levine, who, like Nove, had not studied the Bródy and Goldmann papers in detail. Levine's argument was highly statistical. The application of Western adjustments to official Soviet statistics would, he believed, have exposed cyclical oscillations not apparent in the official series. He feared that many official series were subject to "falsification from below," because of lower echelon officials' fear of admitting failures, and that this tendency was most widespread in slack periods. At a higher level of sophistication, Levine was concerned with Soviet errors in aggregation and in the construction of index numbers, and claimed that Western critics had improved Soviet series by reweighting them. Sometimes, too, series on civilian output can be adjusted to include military components.

Adjustments of this sort are more than minor. Professor Abram Bergson's modifications of the Soviet investment series largely eliminate the apparent recession of 1953. A more common effect is for disaggregated series to show offsetting perturbations which the aggregate series misses.

Levine referred next to Professor George Staller's comparative study of fluctuations during the 1950's in the Soviet bloc and the OECD member countries. Fluctuations of Soviet GNP were no less marked than those of France, Norway, and Sweden. In industrial output alone, however, the U.S.S.R. experienced the smallest fluctuations of any country studied, including the other socialist economies.

Why have fluctuations in the U.S.S.R. been so different from those of other economies, planned or unplanned? One reason suggested by Levine was that the constant pressure for growth eliminated, for example, acceleration effects, to a great extent. Whereas in the West overinvestment errors lead to excess capacity, in a Soviet context they are more likely to lead to bottlenecks, shortages, incomplete projects, and waste. Indeed, "shortage crises" in Eastern Europe are sometimes reported to result from overestimates of an economy's capacity to produce investment goods.

Levine criticized some Western students of socialist economies for looking at the wrong indicators. For example, Westerners should pay more attention to the growth of the productive capital stock than to total investment. (The variations are much smaller.) Also, it should be remembered that prices, wages, bank deposits, etc., have different meanings in the U.S.S.R. because of the pervasivness of controls and subsidies, and the setting of targets in physical rather than financial terms. It may be that planning currently gives plant managers greater roles in decision making than was true previously, but the practical significance of the anounced changes is not yet clear.

The U.S.S.R. has been under no compunction to produce salable goods either for domestic or foreign markets, and it has built on pre-1914 capital formation, especially in transport and urban facilities. Misallocation of resources and production of the wrong product mix has conceivably caused fluctuations in the growth of inventories, but it has not caused cycles.

Much of this may be changing, as living standards have risen and the "thin" wartime generation has lowered the average quality of labor. There is now need to pay attention to consumer tastes, since the original civil and military targets (of the late 1920's) were attained by the mid-1950's. The need for greater efficiency, and the subjection of output to market tests, may produce larger fluctuations in the future, although probably not cycles. A run-up of unsold inventory (1964–1965) was something new in Soviet experience, but was neither pervasive nor cumulative enough to produce a Western-type recession.

Discussion from the floor was postponed until after the presentation of Professor Bródy's paper, but Nove explained his reluctance to use Western recomputations of Soviet series. Many are just for a few benchmark years. Of the annual series available, he believes that the official Soviet ones are better than the recomputations, because they are based on more complete data. Also, he expressed doubts about "deflated" series, since Soviet prices are controlled and hardly suitable for deflation.

## X.   Professor Bródy's Chapter (Hungary)

As Professor Bródy was unable to attend the conference out of which this book developed, his discussion was presented by Richard Portes. Because there had been a delay in preparing an English translation of the original Hungarian text, Portes's presentation was unusually full.

The first main point which struck Portes in Bródy's discussion was one of dating. In dividing the entire 1924–1965 generation into appropriate periods, Bródy dates postwar developments from 1952, when *employment* reached its prewar level. The more customary opening date, both in Hungary and abroad, has been 1949, when *production* reached the prewar level. This change explains why Brody finds no postwar recessions in Hungary; he treats 1949–1952 as the final phase of reconstruction.

There have been fluctuations in the Hungarian growth rate, as Brody measures it. These are traceable to inventories and to fluctuations in the harvest, but they have not affected fixed investment. Minor fluctuations in fixed investment have been more pervasive; even shifts in the structure of investment, as between light and heavy industry, have had disruptive effects when managed imperfectly, and cycles in individual series can be found.

Bródy, however, does not make the Goldmann claim that occasional retrenchment is really necessary. Portes did not find any evidence of cumulative effects as per the multiplier-accelerator process. (If planning means anything, Portes argued, then it means the dethronement of such processes.) This was not to deny historical evidence in favor of the "pseudo-cycle" theory, either in Hungary or in the U.S.S.R. For example, Bródy thinks that a slowdown would have had to come in the Soviet Union in 1953–1954 even if Stalin had lived, and he finds a decline in real wages in Hungary in the early 1950's—sharp after 1952. But these points, important as they are, should be measured against the record of employment and output as a whole, which is one of steady growth. Prices are controlled; trade follows investment; the amplitude of fluctuations in investment, even of the cyclical sort, is narrow.

Another interesting feature of the Eastern European economies has been the synchronizing of their investment fluctuations, to a greater extent than is true for output. This is due in part to the increasing importance of trade relations; before 1956, Hungarian exports were in the neighborhood of 12–17 per cent of GNP, but in the mid-60's they have been 38–39 per cent. This is clearly a move away from autarchy. Investment fluctuations are small in countries that have the largest amounts of industrial and mineral resources, and large in the agricultural countries. East Germany and Poland are stable, like the Soviet Union; Czechoslovakia, Rumania, and Bulgaria, like Hungary, are less stable.

Have imports been stabilizing or destabilizing in Hungary? (Portes noted earlier Conference discussions of their functions in capitalist countries.) The record seems mixed. Hungarian imports were clearly stabilizing in 1959–1960, when they were financed partially by Soviet loans. They were destabilizing later, when consumer imports could not be financed readily.

Portes then considered the monetary aspects of the stabilization problem. It is not true that under Socialism money is just an accounting tool. Bródy has found monetary aspects in Hungary (1959–1960); they also existed in Czechoslovakia (1959–1961). In both countries, enterprises were allowed to retain funds primarily for decentralization. The results were somewhat chaotic, with industry bidding against the Plan for scarce resources. The problem was solved when the private bank accounts were blocked.

Professor Seton was the formal discussant of the Bródy paper. He simultaneously considered earlier Goldmann papers (the one prepared for this Conference not having arrived). If there is a cycle in a socialist economy, Seton began, it is *de mauvaise famille*—the economy pulsates, but hardly moves up and down. Under capitalism, pulsation is pervasive, affecting such aggregates as GNP and employment, and it has a cumulative aspect summarized in the multiplier-accelerator process. Each phase depends on the preceding ones, as in the theories of Wesley Mitchell; in particular, the downward movements are corrections for the excesses of the upward ones. Under Socialism, the growth rate may vary, and occasionally become negative (as in Poland), but what about pervasiveness, cumulation, self-propulsion, and self-reversal?

On pervasiveness, Seton observed that the record of Eastern Europe as a whole was not too good, but that of the U.S.S.R. was. He has extended Staller's results (through 1960) for an additional five years, and found the relative positions of three countries (U.S.S.R., Britain, Hungary) unaffected. On the side of savings, however, the use of a percentage of income (the saving ratio) rather than an aggregate makes the socialist countries look more stable.

On cumulation, Seton found fluctuating series in, for example, fixed investment, inventories, agricultural production, but he found no evidence of cumulative processes compounding the fluctuations to affect the rest of the economy.

There is a form of self-propulsion when plans are not fulfilled. This takes the form of ratchet effects—the frittering away of investment on a multiplicity of projects, new and old. In particular, there is concentration, and sometimes misallocation, on projects close to completion. This is more important for decentralized than for centralized economies. Seton suspects it is more important in the Soviet bloc countries, where decentralization is increasing, than in the U.S.S.R. itself, where the degree of decentralization fluctuates.

Seton suggested that a formal model of his theory can be found in the writings of Micheal Kalecki and Nicholas Kaldor. Suppose that investment *expenditures* determine income, while investment *completions* result from expenditures of the previous period. Also, "pipeline" investment expenditures depend, in accelerator fashion, upon the growth of income, lagged one period. The continuation of the three functions implied in this analysis can produce a cycle.

On self-reversal, Seton combined two views. According to Kalečki, downturn results from shortages of raw materials and foreign exchange. Goldmann sees upturns generated by the making and completion of long-term investment projects. Goldmann also speaks of "subjectivist" tendencies to excessive investment by individual managers, leading eventually to blanket moratoria on new starts. There are also sudden reversals of planning policy, based on such phenomena as overshooting and overheating. Seton wondered whether these changes should best be regarded as exogenous or endogenous.

Harking back to Shinohara's discussion of Japan, Seton argued that there were "Japanese cycles" (growth cycles) in the Soviet bloc countries, but only in investment in the U.S.S.R. Whereas Nove saw the difference as due to shifts in Soviet economic policy, Seton saw it as due to a different pattern of international trade, particularly the greater degree of exemption from raw material and exchange-reserve barriers. There is also a different propagation mechanism. In the socialist countries employment and industrial prices are kept fixed, at some cost to the efficiency of labor and usability of output, both of which fluctuate. The fluctuations brought about in the United States by the varying urgency of demand have socialist counterparts when the degree of rationality in public enterprises is permitted to vary with the degree of slack in the economy.

Soviet reformism was the next topic for discussion. Seton saw it as reducing inventory cycles, but, as a result of decentralization, increasing the urgency of propagation problems as a counterweight to the gains in efficiency that it was introducing. He professed inability to forecast the consequences of the reforms' effects operating through prices. Some price-setting powers (but not all) were being delegated to managers, said Seton, but "limit prices" or ceiling prices were still set centrally and were being eroded by inflation.

In general, Seton envisaged a long-term trend toward an increasing amplitude of fluctuations in socialist countries. There would be an increase in living standards in agricultural areas as a result of "internal emigration" from the frams and increased use of labor-saving devices in the cities. These would be balanced, of course, by an expansion in labor-intensive trade and service industries in the cities, but the new structure would be less amenable to centralized control and more consumer conscious. Rising consumer standards all round meant more discretionary income and required more sales pressure. New tricks (advertising, for example) would be required to "manage" consumer demand. There would be similar problems in the investment field, with "modernizing" investment playing the same discretionary role as luxury consumption. Seton expressed no doubts as to the over-all success of socialist countries in managing these problems, but he thought that imperfections of the management process would increase the magnitude of fluctuations.

Floor discussion of the Nove and Bródy papers was combined. Some initial questions were statistical, dealing with Western reconstruction of Soviet series. (It was agreed that fluctuations existed, but that their timing and their direction in such years as 1953 differed, depending on whether one used official of reconstructed series.) The main arguments against the Western revisions were that they were incomplete, being based on fragmentary data, and that there were too many conflicts among them. In rebuttal, the principal argument was that the "fragmentary" data available constituted an adequate and representative sample in physical units, so that Western series were better than Soviet originals even after allowance for the problems of price deflation. This interchange involved a half-dozen participants.

The initial nonstatistical point was raised by a cycle theorist, who recalled the Austrian analysis of pre-Keynesian days, particularly in Hayek's *Prices and Production*. In Hayek's model, there were cycles of both consumption and investment, but not of national income as a whole. Such analysis is now dormant in capitalist countries. But may it not be applicable in socialist countries?

The next participant opened with two methological observations. No series shows either neat cycles or complete smoothness. Also, the methodology of the NBER limits cycles to business firms. Therefore, if the NBER definitions are accepted, are cycles not ruled out tautologically in a country like the U.S.S.R.? This participant wondered whether, if Nove had applied the full range of NBER techniques (Burns and Mitchell, *Measuring Business Cycles*), he would not have found some cycles. In the Soviet record, he himself saw downswings of three to four years duration, which seemed pervasive, followed by sharp rises in investment and income. He was not persuaded by the *ad hoc* explanations heard at this conference session, and finds Goldmann's pseudo-cycle theory quite plausible.

The next participant objected to the view prevalent at this Conference, that the ironing out of fluctuations was an end in itself. The emergence of wider fluctuations might be an improvement, if associated with safe inventories rather than constant threats of shortage, or if associated with greater efficiency in production. D. H. Robertson and Joseph Schumpeter were cited as individual cycle theorists who had argued these points in the past.

The opinion of the next participant was that overinvestment in the smaller European countries arose from the great attractiveness of the Soviet model as a path to industrialization and modernization. There had possibly been a lag in recognizing its correlative disadvantages. Another reason for excessive investment is underestimation of its cost. Such underestimation is, to some extent, countervailed in large corporations—the too-high costs in *A* constituting windfall profits in *B*. Under Socialism, it is countervailed, if at all, by the partisans of light industry and consumption. Finally, this participant inquired, were there no annual or five-year cycles associated with the desire to show good records of plan fulfillment?

Consideration of international trade and coexistence with capitalist countries came up next. The participant who raised these issues assumed the persistence of Schumpeterian "innovational cycles" under Socialism. This results in one or another sector being built up too fast and too far. Many shocked lead-lag systems have solutions which propagate such shocks into cyclical oscillations. The initial overheating is made possible by imports, which export cycles to the capitalist world, as well as from country to country within the socialist sphere. As East-West trade grows, this participant forecast, this factor will increase in importance.

The next speaker returned to the NBER framework. In the first place, he said, the statistics indicate that "outmoded" Austrian theory remains alone in implying substantial fluctuations on the ratio of investment to consumption. Also, disagreeing with a previous participant, he said that NBER techniques find only extremely short (that is, random) upswings and downswings in both postwar Hungary and postwar U.S.S.R., at least until 1956. This is true of both GNP and agricultural production. There is some doubt about the growth rate of industrial production in the U.S.S.R., and there may be longer cycles there.

Eugene Slutsky's cycle theory was next recalled, as a middle ground combined exogenous and endogenous mechanisms. Slutsky showed, the conference was reminded, that any shockable, lead-lag system has a solution that may produce cyclical oscillations from a moving average of stochastic shocks. A multiplier-accelerator model of the type popularized by Paul Samuelson or Sir John Hicks is not needed; many other models will do. If Western cycles fit the Slutsky model, why not Eastern ones? There is no simple test which separates random from systematic components in time series. Furthermore, different sorts of systematic structures fit different societies, and no one has yet modeled a socialist society in any systematic way free of ideological considerations.

The final participant opened with the opinion that Nove's report proved the absence of business cycles in the U.S.S.R. So Soviet fluctuations, if any, are examples of a very different phenomenon. On statistics, he agreed with Nove about the superiority of official Soviet series over Western reformulations, especially for year-to-year comparisons. (On similar grounds, he decried socialist reformulations of Western statistical series.) He believed that Nove's summary of the Soviet record overlooked one fluctuation (1940) in both income and investment. This was connected with new territories, price increases, and a lengthened work-day; the latter can be traced to preparedness and to the "winter war" with Finland.

In the postwar Soviet experience, he continued, there was a falling tendency in the growth rate of industrial production until 1960, but since then it has been constant, at 8 per cent. With greater efficiency, it may rise to 10 or 12 per cent.

This participant found it noteworthy that the only paper suggesting obsolescence of the cycle dealt with the U.S.S.R. He has heard the view expressed, however, that cycles might re-emerge as a result of recent Soviet reforms. His own published views being to the contrary, he summarized them as pointing out that, along with decentralization and autonomy, a shift within centralization is taking place, and will erode arbitrary discretion by applying the methods of operations research and mathematical economics.

As for the other socialist countries, he believed that Goldmann was influenced unduly by the downturn of 1963 in Czechoslovakia. What Goldmann calls a pseudo-cycle is by no means inherent in the socialist system. This participant did not himself claim to understand what had happened in Czechoslovakia in 1963, but it may have been comparable to a fluctuation of the 1920's or 1930's in the U.S.S.R. If so, such perturbations have been eliminated in later stages of socialist development; in fact, their elimination is one of the purposes of Socialism.

Since neither Goldmann nor Brody could be present, Nove ended the discussion with another analysis of the Hungarian record. He found that the principal "crises" of postwar Hungary had been in 1953 and 1956. He associated them with the rise and fall of Matyas Rakosi, Hungary's closest approximation to Stalin. Subsequently, Hungary's dependence on trade has been rising—and not only trade within the Eastern bloc. There has also been substantial decentralization, which—disagreeing with some other participants—he regards as chaotic only when joined with an inadequate price system, and therefore as only a short-term problem. The post-1960 downturn is an example, having been brought on by the imposition of moratoria on fixed investment.

To illustrate his general point, Nove had recourse to a simple geometric model (Figure 16-1) developed by a Hungarian economist, Joszef Kornai. In this model, per capita consumption ($c$) is increased on the horizontal axis, and per capita investment ($i$) on the vertical one. All combinations lying within the point-set $I$ are feasible, but because of error, economists may believe some overlapping set, like $II$, to be feasible. The political leaders often hold out for an unfeasible point like $P$. In the long run, however, set $II$ tends to move to greater coincidence with set $I$, and the point $P$ moves to some other position $P'$ within the feasible set $I$.

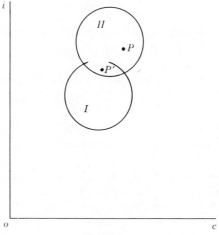

Fig. 16-1.

### XI. Dr. Goldmann's Chapter (Growth Rate and Inventory Fluctuations under Socialism)

This chapter was not delivered orally at the Conference, and became available to participants only after the Conference had adjourned. It was therefore not discussed explicitly.

### XII. Professors Evans and Klein's Chapter (Forecasting Model)

Professor Klein, in presenting this discussion, opened by relating it to the question of the obsolescence of the cycle. He has viewed models primarily as guides to policy for purposes of stabilizing the economy and rendering the business cycle obsolete, hopefully in the near future.

The particular model he presented has been developed at the Wharton School of the University of Pennsylvania. Three features of major interest are its forecasting ability, the multiplier attributes developed for short-run and long-run effects of both simple and complex policy changes, and its usefulness for historical simulations—applications in prior periods of policies alternative to those actually used. The authors are also planning expansion of these simulations to include random shocks.

Many such models of the U.S. economy have by now been developed. Klein wished particularly to compare the Wharton model with the larger one which he had assisted in preparing at the Brookings Institution under the auspices of the Social Science Research Council (SSRC). The Wharton model includes only ¼ as many equations as the SSRC—Brookings one, but the latter is based on outmoded national income accounts and is being updated. The size comparison led Klein to present his views on the disputed question of large versus small models (many versus few equations). He does not consider size as necessarily a virtue, but he has found that both business and government clients, as well as professional economists, often want more detailed information than the smaller models can provide. He anticipated that the SSRC-Brookings model would eventually become three times as large as the present published version.

Klein listed some historical simulations which had been run on the Brookings and Wharton model. His examples included the 1957–1958 recession, the 1961–1962 recovery, the 1964 income tax cut, and the 1965 excess-profits tax cut. On the Wharton model, Klein hoped to simulate a Vietnam ceasefire, and had already introduced a wide range of monetary policies, accelerated-depreciation schemes, and tax incentives for investment.

Neither of these models is perfect, but both are improvements over their predecessors, according to Professor Klein. They are mainly useful for short-term forecasting; they must be re-started periodically with new initial conditions for longer-term work. For example, a version starting in 1952 does not locate the 1957–1958 recession with any accuracy. Also, the models do better in real than in monetary terms.

In addition to improving on these weak areas and to other plans mentioned during his presentation, Klein suggested two topics for future research: application of the model to one or more statistically "average" cycles, and a study of the standard errors of the model's forecasting, including the covariances of errors in different equations.

Professor de Wolff, in his discussion, concentrated on technical issues, after pointing out that the Wharton model showed clearly that cycles were *not* yet obsolete. He stressed the dynamic character, not only of the model as a whole but of almost all of its behavioral equations. The lag structures go back as far as 40 to 60 quarters in the investment sectors, taking account not only of ordinary lags but of changes in dependent variables as well. Such dynamic systems cannot generally be solved by standard mathematical methods; solutions must be numerical. Computers permit the experimental study of the model by direct forecasts, but do not eliminate the need for normal statistical tests.

An important feature of the model, as de Wolff saw it, is its use of nonlinear equations. One simple cause of nonlinearity is the fact that some equations are in terms of physical volume, some in terms of prices, and still others in terms of their product, money value. There are also other important cases, for example, the equations for the production function and the adult male unemployment rate.

Evans and Klein use the Wharton index of capacity utilization, but the ratio of actual to full-capacity manufacturing output in their model implies that the degree of capacity utilization equals the employment rate in manufacturing. De Wolff wondered why Evans and Klein did not use separate capacity indicators for capital and labor. Also, the dependence of the manufactured goods price level on capacity utilization was found to be linear; de Wolff would have expected a curvilinear relation.

The wage-employment section of the Wharton model has interesting features. It includes two unemployment indicators, one for total unemployment and one for young males only. Wage-rate changes are explained by the differential between the two unemployment rates.

Monetary variables, including free reserves and rediscount rates, play a greater role in the Wharton model than in Klein's previous work. They seem to be important determinants of investment, although they operate with long lags.

De Wolff was impressed by the large number of exogenous variables in the Wharton model, some of which he thought should eventually be endogenized. In addition to dummy variables (seasons, etc.), there are "forward indicators" based on surveys and other expectations data. De Wolff wondered whether these really added enough to the accuracy of predictions to justify their use. (The problem is one of expectational *volatility*; in a model including policy changes, expectations are readily affected by such cases.) A third sort of exogenous variable relates to the rest of the world. This treatment is conventional, but de Wolff expressed doubts about it for large countries, where "rest of the world" indicators include feedbacks from past domestic changes. (Klein later corrected this statement as it relates to exports, which are in fact endogenous through relative prices.) Government expenditure and monetary variables might also be endogenized in part, de Wolff maintained, although they too are treated conventionally as exogenous.

The practical usefulness of econometric models depends upon the size of their errors. These can be of two types, errors in forecasting exogenous variables, controlled and otherwise, and errors in specifying the economic structure. In long-term forecasts a third source of error results from the cumulative effect of erratic shocks. (Cumulation is no problem in short-term forecasting, as the model is adapted to the actual situation in each previous period.)

The different types of error can be distinguished in *ex post* forecasts. In such forecasts, the exact values of the exogenous variables are available, the size of the shocks can be determined in each period, and hence their effects can be determined also. Evans and Klein make several experiments of this kind, for periods extending over eight and 48 quarters. The short-run (eight-quarter) results are quite satisfactory; errors increase with the length of the forecasting period, but less than proportionately. It is, however, difficult to get a correct impression of the model's performance. It is evidently more difficult to forecast a fluctuating variable than a relatively steady one, and insufficient numerical information has been provided about the variability of each variable.

The long-run forecasts are less encouraging. The trend is fairly well represented, and also certain minor fluctuations. The important cycle starting in 1959 has been missed almost entirely, although the 1962–1963 boom is quite clear. It is difficult to explain these results; no effort has been made to distinguish between the effects of mis-specifications and of erratic shocks.

Evans and Klein also report interesting experiments, simulating their model's reactions to policy alternatives. Sudden changes in policy parameters lead to short (six to eight quarters), heavily damped fluctuations not showing actual short-cycle characteristics. The question may be raised whether the model is really capable of explaining short-term fluctuations.

De Wolff's final suggestion was to study in greater detail the effects of errors of different kinds, in order to improve the quality and performance of the model.

A second formal discussion was presented by Dr. Steuer, who began by commenting on the rising popularity of econometric-model forecasts. These had been highly esoteric as recently as 1962, when an expository introduction by

Daniel B. Suits appeared in the *American Economic Review,* but now (1967) they are quite familiar. These models indicate that cycles are not yet obsolete, but may become so; they do not answer questions of responsibility for better performance. (Is it due to improved *policy* or merely to improved information?)

Passing to criticism, Steuer stated that most forecasting models placed too much weight on simple one-quarter lags. It would often have been better to distribute the lag effects over two or three quarters. Also, he would have preferred inclusion of a supply function for U.S. exports, and, like de Wolff, he thought that some public expenditures should be endogenized.

Steuer found considerable serial correlation of errors throughout the model, and questioned the concept of a "straightforward" multiplier. Too much depends, he opined, upon the method of financing public expenditures (by taxation, borrowing, or the printing press) for their multiplier to mean a great deal. He also doubted the applicability of normal statistical tests, since the regressions being tested are not a random sample of possible ones but a biased sample of only the best fitting ones.

The British Government, said Steuer, is waiting for improvements along these and other lines before making use of econometric models. Even after it uses them, it will probably do so only in conjunction with other methods. There is no question of exclusive reliance on econometric models.

The first five discussions from the floor raised technical questions. (a) How much is gained by disaggregation, both by sectors and variables? (b) Cannot some types of government expenditures be endogenized, with others left exogenous? As for the exogenous ones, is it not true that they are among the least accurately forecast elements of the entire model? (c) Policy intervention sometimes introduces ratchets, irreversibilities, and other nonlinear disturbances. How old can a model be, therefore, when a constant learning process is taking place? (The Dutch, while using old data, do not weight them equally.) (d) The international agencies have had trouble with erratic estimates. How are the related problems of preliminary estimates and data revisions handled at the Wharton School? (e) Apparently the long-run simulation does not track fixed investment well. Why is this?

The sixth participant raised several questions of economic analysis. In the Wharton model, as he interpreted it, consumption is affected by prior changes in income, in such ways that savings act like stock adjustment factors and fall to zero if income remains constant. The production functions seem to imply "Verdoorn's Law" of the dependence of man-hour productivity on the proportion of the labor force in secondary industry (manufacturing and mining). The wage-rate determination resembles the Phillips curve, which this participant believed to be unstable in the long run. If prices also depend on past wages, then do money and credit have any influence at all? Perhaps this weakness, if he interpreted the model correctly, helps to explain its poor performance in forecasting price levels. Another weakness on the monetary side, he believed, was using free reserves as a credit variable. This is in line with Federal Reserve practice, but actually reserve ratios and open-market operations have varying effects when used in different combinations, while leaving free reserves unaffected. Perhaps reserve ratios and open-market operations should have been used separately.

To answer one of Dr. Steuer's points, this participant concluded, it is not difficult to derive clear, unequivocal multipliers by assuming a single "standard" policy mix.

The next three participants also raised technical points. (a) Credit restrictions are important, and should have entered somehow into the Wharton model. Also, inventory investment was well as fixed capital investment may be affected by financial variables. (b) Quarterly models are supposed to be better than annual ones in that they predict turning points more precisely, and provide four times as many observations per year. Offsetting this, however, may be the fact that quarterly observations are less independent of each other than annual ones; thus, there may not be any net advantage from using them. (c) The Wharton model's wage relations do not fit well, Phillips curves are not reliable, and this participant found no theory of absolute wages.

The tenth participant raised an issue relative to *ex post* forecasting; that is, that errors tend to cumulate and become more serious over time. He did not understand why this effect was absent. The 11th and final participant expressed, unlike previous ones, satisfaction with both the Wharton model's "explanation" of 1957–1958 experience and its treatment of fixed investment. It struck him as almost uncanny that, starting in 1952–1953, the model had predicted the 1960–1961 recession with more accuracy than it had predicted the 1957–1958 one. He thought this might be evidence for the persistance of the 9–10 year Juglar cycle, a view that he had maintained throughout the Conference.

Replying to these criticisms and comments, Klein concentrated on two points, the wage-employment and capacity-utilization relationships. He agreed that the correlation was low in the wage-employment relation; the reason was that wage *changes* had been made the dependent variable. The correlation would have been higher if wage figures themselves had been used. It is important, in his view, to distinguish, in measuring unemployment, between more and less strategic sectors of the labor force. The strategic group is composed of males aged 25 to 35. The relationship between their unemployment rates was, as the discussion had brought out, purely empirical. He and Evans had modified the Phillips curve procedure by using a spread between the two rates—just as they had used the spread between long and short money rates—and did not think the weaknesses of the Phillips curve should be ascribed to their own model automatically.

On capacity utilization, Evans and Klein had constructed separate indices by industries, and found that the measures prepared from output data above agreed fairly well with those constructed from log-linear production functions, which were themselves related closely to industry employment rates. At both the industry and the national economy level, the employment rate has been a good forecaster of the Wharton capacity-utilization rate.

## XIII.  Professor Hickman's Chapter (Econometric Parameters)

If the cycle is to become obsolete, one of the projection-or-planning tools which will displace it is the econometric model. A number of promising econometric models, all basically of Keynesian persuasion, are in existence. Professor Hickman has sampled among the best of these, selecting 12 from 10 countries, compared certain of their parameters, and explored their cyclical properties.

The econometric models in Hickman's sample are of varying degrees of disaggregation. All have one or more endogenous consumption and import functions. All treat government spending and exports as determined exogenously (outside the models). All attempt endogenous investment functions. Some or all the functions are dynamic in that they involve lags. In some models these lags are discrete, with effects concentrated in single time periods; other models distribute lag effects over several periods. Hickman believes that most of them pay inadequate attention to effects which are dependent upon wealth, or upon the stock of productive capital.

In discussing the properties of his results, Hickman concentrated upon the multiplier effects of exogenous changes, as in exports and public spending. Most of the impact (first-period) multipliers he found small, as compared with textbook illustrations. In some cases, this result could be traced to leakages through imports; in others, to long consumption or investment lags. Other differences between models depended on what was treated as exogenous and what as endogenous, upon lag patterns generally, and upon the treatment of taxes, depreciation, and business saving.

Passing to longer-period dynamic multipliers, Hickman found the cyclical components heavily damped, except in one model (from Australia) which had omitted any import function. The theoretical implication of this result is that fluctuations, when they persist, are kept going by external shocks or by cyclical oscillations in the exogenous variables. If attention could be limited to unshocked models, then, the business cycle would indeed appear to be obsolescent if not obsolete.

These results were all derived from annual models. Hickman had also examined several quarterly ones, including two Japanese models of widely different character. Also, he pointed out, his two Canadian models yielded different multipliers. All the quarterly models were stable, in the sense that their oscillations were heavily damped.

Mr. OHerlihy acted as formal discussant, replacing Professor R. J. Ball, who was unable to attend. He professed himself initially astonished by the degree of stability indicated by Hickman's discussion. Of 12 annual models, 11 were stable (and the Australian exception later modified); all the quarterly models were stable. This surprised OHerlihy. He argued that large models imply high-order characteristic equations with many roots; why did only one model leave any explosive roots? As a possible explanation, OHerlihy suggested that a possible bias in the two-stage least-squares estimation procedure, used in most of the studies in Hickman's sample, had exaggerated the degree of stability.

Suppose that $\Phi$ and $\psi$ are linear functions of an endogenous variable $y$, while $F$ is a linear function of an exogenous variable $z$, and $E^{-1}$ is a one-period lag. There are two error or shock terms, $u$ and $v$, the first in an estimating equation and the other in the measurement of the exogenous variable $z$. (The $u$ term also involves allowances for omitted variables and for non-linearity in the functions $\Phi$, $\psi$, and $F$.) Then, a number of equations might be fitted, such as:

$$\Phi(y) + \Psi(E^{-1}y) + F(z) = u \quad \text{or} \quad \Phi(y) + \Psi(E^{-1}y) + F(z + v) = u.$$

OHerlihy interpreted a well known papar by Irma and Frank Adelman (on the cyclical properties of the Klein-Goldberger model) as deriving four-year cycles by shocking both equations and exogenous variables. Perhaps, he suggested, the models studied by Hickman had been biased toward stability because the estimated coefficients of lagged endogenous variables were biased downward by the two-stage least-squares procedure.

He suggested, as an alternative procedure, fitting the various models over subperiods and observing the variability of the coefficients. He also pointed out the difficulty of comparing models from different systems of equations, and expressed the belief that larger multipliers were general in less-developed countries.

The first participant added that there was great diversity in models between different countries, depending primarily, he thought, upon the degree of disaggregation. For the United States, for example, the Klein-Goldberger multipliers of 1.2–1.3, estimated in the early 1950's, were not considered too low. Larger and less aggregated models give values closer to 1.7 (between 2 and 3 under closed-economy assumptions). British, Dutch, and Japanese models are also in the neighborhood of 2. (The issue is important on the U.S. scene, in connection particularly with tax credits for investment.)

He next turned his attention to OHerlihy's proposition that the two-stage least-squares fitting method was biased toward stability. This, he said, was not correct. (Other econometricians present agreed.) If there is any bias in the Hickman results, it arises because the models were fitted to data assembled during a period when cycles were damped. One or more of the models might be made less damped, or even explosive, by nonlinearity, but the main point involved is the data. Contrary to OHerlihy, he himself believes that there is no evidence that econometric systems are unsuitable or explosive, except in special situations like hyper-inflation and social revolution. Neither did he feel that there was any significant difference between the two OHerlihy equation types represented above.

If he himself had any suggestion for improvement in Hickman's statistical procedure, it was that observed co-variances between the error terms should be taken into account more explicitly. A. L. Nayar had done this with the Brookings model in a limited way. The result was not only stable, but the *mean* stochastic path lay close to the nonstochastic solution, and both paths lay between limits set by (stable) movements of *extreme* stochastic paths.

The second participant was concerned with the international (import-export) aspects of the Hickman collection of models. He wondered of it might not make a difference to the values of multipliers whether constant or current prices were used. If there were fluctuating exchange rates, multiplicands might be affected too. He suggested repeating Hickman's experiments, using different price series.

The third participant sympathized with OHerlihy's surprise at the damped characteristics of the models. He wondered whether a particular specification— for example, implicit imposition of ceilings and floors—was responsible for some of the results. He suggested that the Hickman procedures be applied to explosive models (with explosions checked by ceilings and floors) to see whether the results would be the same as Hickman's.

The first participant intervened at this point to answer that exogenous ceilings and floors were unimportant, that good models generate their own ceilings endogenously, and that artificial generation of explosive models was not worth the trouble. In the specific case of fluctuations in the United States during the Great Depression, he found it difficult to simulate such results under modern conditions without assuming stupid policies. Tests of existing U.S. models imply stability even under 1929-type initial values and modern tax-transfer functions. To generate instability, one needs continued perverse shocks (that is, stupid policies).

The fourth participant, examining the Western European models particularly, felt that many of them are stable because of high import propensities. Also, he thought different conditions—specifically, different tax functions—might send some of them "over the line" into instability, and, in opposition to the first participant, he believed that it would be worth while to work with explosive models. He also believed that Hickman's results may have been due to the omission of potentially "explosive" elements from the mathematical models under study.

Three econometric interventions occurred at this point. One participant suggested re-application of models in "explosive" periods. Another introduced evidence that two-stage least squared fitting procedure did not eliminate the explosive character from explosive data. The third said that introduction of floors and ceilings into Dutch data had produced explosive oscillations only in prices, not in deflated series. He was, however, concerned about the sensitivity of measured consumption propensities to different concepts of "income" and "consumption," and thought that some of the differences between individual models with regard to consumption propensities and multipliers might be explained by differences in definition.

The next (eighth) participant added that, in addition to imports, exports might be not only endogenous factors but important stabilizers. In his own (small) country, he felt that export supply was an inverse function of domestic demand, so that exports tended to boom when the rest of the economy was depressed, and *vice versa*. He feared that the Hickman models might show synchronous cycles in exports and the domestic economy, concealing this adjustment factor.

The ninth participant, while agreeing that capitalist economies showed strong stabilizing tendencies, could not avoid feeling that these were overstated in the Hickman paper, so that some of the suggestions for further study were worth serious consideration. Also, he himself disagreed with the treatment of erratic shocks. Even when exogenous to individual capitalist countries, they are endogenous to the international capitalist world, and should be "endogenized" somehow. He also proposed that non-Keynesian as well as Keynesian specifications be used in econometric models, to see whether the results would hold up. Finally, on the statistical side, he noticed that some of the U.S. models omit the 1957–1958 recession. He believed that this omission of cyclical features made the system look more stable on paper than it was in fact.

The tenth and final participant commented particularly on the Canadian model used, which showed greater stability than Canadian economists had expected *ex ante*. He wondered whether the difference might be due to failure to consider the rise in the importance of the government, whose share of the national expenditure is now between 30 and 35 per cent. Also, he reported, Canadians working with the Canadian model had found stability, whether the starting position was one of full employment or of considerable slack. They had also introduced varying rates of price inflation into the model, and found that rapid rates of inflation decrease stability.

Replying to his discussant and the several participants, Hickman reiterated the cautions expressed in his paper concerning the adequacy of some of the models. He knew his multipliers were lower than anticipated, and also that many people had expected explosive results. Most of his models were in constant prices, so that monetary effects were not included. Most of them were fitted only to postwar data, but it is worth noting that the prewar models also were damped. He, too, had noticed that the presence or absence of capacity "ceilings" made little difference to stability properties. Finally, he found it encouraging that, despite the wide variety in his detailed results from model to model and from country to country, the values of the Keynesian multipliers were fairly uniform.

### XIV. Professor Verdoorn and Dr. Post's Chapter. (Policy-Estimation Model)

Professor Verdoorn presented this comparative study of the differences between the Dutch economy of the postwar and interwar periods, as simulated by the Central Planning Bureau's model. The purpose was to measure the differences between the interwar and the postwar cyclical fluctuations and to analyze the causes of the difference.

In broad outline, the Central Planning Bureau (CPB) model is an annual dynamic one. It is aimed primarily at short-term forecasting, and shows the effects of alternative policy measures. The coefficients having been estimated for the combined period 1923–1938 and 1940–1960, the same parameters are used for both periods in the present exercise, with the exception of weights in the definition equations.

The relevant structural differences between the two periods (1923–1938 and 1948–1960) involved: (a) the amplitudes and periods of fluctuations in individual exogenous variables; (b) the co-variance of exogenous variables; (c) changes in definitional equations, particularly the increasing weight of public spending and the increasing dependence on foreign trade; (d) differences in the initial data, particularly in the rate of unemployment (which appears to affect many other variables in a curvilinear fashion); and (e) differences in social institutions, especially the tax and social-insurance systems and the increase of "built-in stability" which they provide. However, since tax schedules vary widely over time, the prevailing average rates are taken as exogenous. Verdoorn suggested comparing the Verdoorn-Post summary of the difference between the two periods with that presented in the Gordon paper on U.S. experience.

How can the interwar and postwar cycle patterns be compared? Specifically, how could the response of the Dutch economy to the actual 1929 downturn and a hypothetical 1957 equivalent be compared? Verdoorn and Post began by measuring their variables as deviations from trend values. Fluctuations of exogenous variables were plotted as sine curves—the volume of world demand, the prices of both imports and competing exports, public expenditures, etc. The respective initial years, 1929 and 1957 (with exogenous variables at peaks), were chosen as the starting points for maximum cyclical impact. (Covariances between exogenous variables, as well as institutional differences between the two periods, were admittedly not considered adequately.) The external impulses (relative downturns) were taken as 1.4 standard deviations of the prewar period. This is comparable to the actual post-1929 downturn in relative magnitude.

It then appears that, without built-in stabilizers, the hypothetical maximum impact of an international downturn on the 1957 economy would have been comparable with that of 1929. There might have been a 12 per cent fall in consumption, in 1957, as compared with 11 per cent in 1929, and a $\frac{1}{3}$ fall in private investment.

A number of inferences can be drawn from this experiment of exercise, despite its admitted artificialities. The cycle has not yet vanished. Its period, and also the amplitude of fluctuations in such important variables as employment, have been reduced. But the reaction equations indicate that the Dutch economy was actually *more* vulnerable in 1957 than in 1929, because of its higher initial level, so that the shock of a second 1929 would have had greater effects in the later period in the absence of built-in stabilizers, and would have been extremely serious even with account taken of damping effects.

This is not to deny the increased importance and magnitude of built-in stabilizers in the Dutch economy, but rather to allow for the increased pressure upon them in the postwar economic situation with the postwar economic structure. Verdoorn therefore concluded on a pessimistic note: If the Netherlands should again face an international depression on the interwar scale, it would have difficulty in avoiding involvement without "beggar-my-neighbour" protectionism or without exchange-rate fluctuations.

The formal discussant, Professor Fox, distributed copies of the more technical aspects of his reactions to the Verdoorn-Post paper. His oral presentation was brief. He pointed out that changes in several policy instruments are correlated with each other in such fashion that 1957-style adjustment to a hypothetical 1929 might not be a reasonable adjustment, and adjustment to any set of actual data might be different from adjustment to a hypothetical sinusoid wave. He suggested, therefore, that the Verdoorn-Post experiment might usefully be repeated, using actual data, and also "reversed" by applying 1957 policies to 1929 data.

Another suggestion was that similar experiments be attempted for two or more countries simultaneously, as well as for the Netherlands alone. What would be the result if each country of the system had a conscious cycle policy based upon an econometric model, and if the international feedbacks were included in the several models? In this case, only errors and shocks would be really exogenous, and presumably the international record of econometric models would be somewhat better.

The initial participant pointed out that the basic CBP reaction equations (the first 13) had been kept the same in both periods, even as to their statistical coefficients, and that the most important difference between the two periods was in the weighting patterns of the definitional equations. This feature he considered somewhat less than realistic. He also would have liked to see the experiment repeated for other countries individually, and conjectured that similar results would be obtained for countries heavily dependent on foreign trade.

The second participant expanded on Fox's objections to the use of sinusoid waves rather than actual data. (Verdoorn, replying specifically to this criticism, defended the sinusoid only as a legitimate first approximation.)

After an introductory question, to assure himself that the Verdoorn-Post experiment showed greater vulnerability of the Netherlands in the postwar period (under a passive cyclical policy), the third participant raised a theoretical point about the relevance of Keynesian models. To him, it appeared the Keynesian theory was well adapted to low-pressure economies with considerable slack, but that it was less adequate for high-pressure economies at or near full employment.

The fourth participant wished to assure himself initially that the greater postwar vulnerability was due to fuller employment and greater proximity to capacity limitations or ceilings. (Verdoorn confirmed this point.) Then, he went on, could it perhaps be argued that recessions result from poor policy decisions rather than from the operation of the model, with its built-in stabilizer mechanism? Incidentally, he felt that the Netherlands' performance had improved since 1957. An answer came from a fifth participant. The main source of policy error, he thought, was politicians' reluctance to take technocrats' advice in time. This had led them to extreme measures at both peaks and troughs.

The sixth participant suggested that greater realism might be introduced into the Verdoorn-Post simulations by using tax *rates* rather than tax *revenues*. (Verdoorn agreed that the use of revenues tended to underestimate the degree of automatic stabilization in the Dutch system.)

The seventh participant wondered whether splitting the economy into public and private sectors, and then treating the second independently of the first, was fully justified, for the purposes of this experiment. The omission of covariance might have been another source of error. This participant also wanted a different definition of vulnerability, in terms of danger of a major depression, as distinguished from a mere recession. If possible, he wanted it in terms of parameters of individual equations of the CPB model. (This was difficult, interposed the fifth participant, for the curvilinear elements of the CPB model.)

The postwar working of the international monetary system was mentioned by the eighth and final participant as a reason for exogenous shocks being smaller in the postwar than in the interwar period. To the extent that it omitted this aspect, the Verdoorn-Post experiment may have exaggerated the postwar cyclical sensitivity of the Netherlands economy under all conditions. (This point was also accepted by Verdoorn, as a matter of political economy. Technically, however, it was quite irrelevant to the experiment.)

Since he had answered several criticisms from the floor, Professor Verdoorn limited his final remarks to a defense of the use of the sinusoid curve. Why, he had been asked, had he not used actual 1929–1938 data instead, for his standard disturbance? If he had done so, he felt, the results for 1929–1938 would have been too close to the actual record for that period, and less new information would have been gained. The reason is that the reaction equations were in large part derived from 1929–1938 data, as had been mentioned by the first participant.

## XV.  Professor Lundberg's Chapter (Stabilization Policies)

Professor Lundberg proposed to deal with policies to counteract economic instability in the large, and not merely cycles as defined technically. For example, he has considered the consequences of inflation, payments deficits, and overfull employment as falling within the purview of his discussion. At the same time, he reminded the Conference that stability was only one target of economic policy. Others include efficiency, growth, and distributional equity.

Lundberg believes that the three principal means of economic policy are monetary policy, fiscal policy, and labor-market policy. (Labor-market policy includes allocation of labor and investment, as well as wage-price regulations.) He realizes, however, that account must be taken of international differences as to policies approved and tabooed, and also as to the degree of fluctuation tolerated. Even neighboring countries may be different in these respects. For example, the Swedish Finance Ministry has become the main agent of cycle policy, whereas in Denmark, the Central Banks have taken over more independent authority.

In general, Lundberg suggested, Western Europe has experienced "policy cycles" with short recessions, in which expansionary changes come too soon and economies are permitted to overheat. On the other hand, when cooling-off policies are adapted, usually by reason of payments deficits, they are often too severe.

It is difficult to fit stabilization policies into any general formal model, econometric or otherwise. The models ordinarily treat policy as exogenous but, in fact, policy changes are at least partially determined by the course of the cycle, including the climate of opinion which that course generates. For example, in Sweden he suspects that a model, such as those examined earlier by Hickman, would have been explosive, because of steadily rising public expenditures, if policy changes had not entered implicitly. Stabilization policy in Sweden may be looked upon as an adjustment to avoid the explosive implications of a "policy-free" Swedish model. Lundberg admits that policy sometimes goes too far, so that an alternative model would be explosive for the short period, with oscillations damped over the long term.

Lundberg continued his criticism of econometric models by suggesting that both monetary and investment policy were difficult to fit into them. Monetary policy, he said, is often omitted from Keynesian models. Actually it is quite effective when firms can be squeezed, as in short-run inflationary situations. It does not work during recessions, for reasons which may be summarized as "pushing on a string." Also, it works with a variable lag structure, which may itself be shorter for large changes than small ones. No wonder, then, that it was hard to introduce monetary policy into these models. Lundberg also believes that econometric investment functions are hard to adjust for the Swedish investment tax, where corporate payments in boom periods are sterilized in government funds, to be spent when the Government believes it desirable, that is, in recessions. This tax changes the time-shape of investment, especially since its concrete application is a discretionary matter. He himself doubts the advisability of "modeling" it.

The last point of Lundberg's oral presentation was a plea for pinpoint rather than blunderbuss stabilization policy. Every recession is unevenly distributed, with its main burden falling on a relatively few industries and localities. Why stimulate the entire economy, running the risk of overheating some recession-free sectors, when intervention may be needed only in sectors affected directly? He realized that pin-point policies also tend to freeze the allocation of society's resources, but felt that, on balance, stabilization policies should be made less aggregative.

Mr. Maddison, in the formal discussion of the Lundberg presentation, dealt first with the obvious assumption that the cycle was not obsolete. He himself felt that this point needed further discussion. He wished that the presentation had made a sharper distinction between absolute downturns and mere decelerations, since the latter cause much less excess capacity and squeeze on profits. More might have been said about increased downward price rigidity, since many recessions had operated largely upon price variables. Also, he was of the opinion that financial structures were generally more stable than in prewar years, so that financial crises were of minor importance. (Japan in 1965 may have been an exception.)

Also important in Maddison's suspicion of obsolescence of the cycle was a certain buoyancy of the entire Western economic system (with the possible exception of the United States). This buoyancy provides an unexpected payoff for any successful short term policy, either public anti-recession policy or private investment policy. One reason why buoyancy has lasted so long has been a favorable supply situation, marked by a substantial amount of disguised unemployment, it is true—but Japan, at least, seems to have adjusted to the exhaustion of this source of labor.

Lundberg might also have expanded his references to the international economy and to international economic policy. Cycles have been damped, Maddison believes, by a greater volume of international credit, freer dealings of the consortium variety between leading countries, and "rules of the game" against exchange controls. He expressed a wish that debt moratoria and more frequent exchange rate movements had been included in the arsenal, and indicated fears of serious international liquidity problems in the near future.

What may be said about government policy, in this world of relatively insignificant cycles? It is hard to distinguish corrective from propulsive effects. It is easy to find cases where some government intervention has set off a recession; yet Maddison considered it a mistake to speak of "policy cycles" in Lundberg's sense. Actually, he has found few instances of really perverse advice, although there were many in 1929–1933.

Government have serious problems in determining their positions in whatever cycle still exists. Their analyses tend to be unsophisticated, involving, for example, repression of aggregate demand instead of direct controls. They also tend to be too slow, although the North American statistics are improving with regard to speed. They suffer from policy biases—either from weakness or conviction. In some countries, there is a great fear of unemployment; in others, the main concern is with price inflation.

A final difficulty with cycle policy, Maddison felt, has been an "instrumentality lag," that is, failure to utilize the best tools available. In his opinion, automatic or built-in stabilizers have not contributed greatly except in reducing lags; some such additional power as the Swedish investment tax is needed. On monetary policy, Maddison was skeptical, because he felt that the debt and other markets were so highly segmented that the effects of monetary policy were concentrated in the former. Additional room for improvement results from technocratic progress in research; perhaps the models will even reduce our political and ideological biases.

Eventually, it may become difficult to distinguish cyclical oscillations from explicit interventions. When this happens, economic dynamics will be divisible into "conjuncture economics" and "growth economics," hopefully better interrelated than they now are.

The first participant based his comments upon Dutch experience with the Central Planning Bureau (CPB) models as working tools for stabilization policy. He definitely did not feel that the models have solved all the problems of the Netherlands. They have improved the understanding and sophistication of Dutch economic discussion, but they have been hard to explain to the general public. The Netherlands has had good models and a powerful planning board, but politics have hindered acceptance of their advice. It may well be true, as Lundberg had suggested, that inclusion of government expenditures makes cyclical models explosive at times; at any rate, they are treated as exogenous variables in Holland. This participant had to admit that luck had played a large part in the apparent success of the applications of the Dutch variable investment-allowance scheme; the actual applications have been, in his view, timorous and inadequate. Yet, despite errors both in technical forecasting and in the use of the forecasters' advice, the Dutch view is that models are decidedly worth using as stabilization tools.

As a postscript, this participant agreed with Lundberg that economic slack tends to be concentrated in a few sectors when it first develops, and he favored the use of "scalpel" techniques on these precise sectors. In the Dutch context, this would mean varying the volume of building permits and the ease of credit for building construction.

The second participant made several points, with special reference to Italy. (a) Price inflexibility can work upwards as well as downwards, and is in any case more apparent than real. (b) The rules of the international game are not always so beneficient as Maddison believes. For example, their application within the EEC brought on a recession in Italy in 1963. (c) There may be an inverse relation between the efficiency of a government and its reliance on monetary policy. Italian use of monetary policy sometimes seems to be a poor substitute for control of the foreign short-term liabilities of the commercial banks. (d) The general working of stabilization policy in Italy has been disappointing, and may not improve in the future. The key problem in his opinion, is a lack of economic sophistication within the government.

The third participant raised, in the context of stabilization policy, a point which had been raised earlier in individual country papers: How different has the postwar situation been from earlier intervals of general stability? For example, there has been a succession of fairly mild cycles, but similar periods may be found before 1914. There has been a fortunate lack of synchronization in individual country oscillations, but synchronization may appear again. The discussant doubted that there has been any important change in price policy, arguing that price weakness was not apparent in many milder recessions before 1914. His basic point was that postwar stabilization policy has not yet been tested severely, and that it is too early to be sanguine about it.

The fourth participant concentrated his remarks on monetary policy, which he felt had been neglected in the stabilization-policy discussion. If it is to be effective, in his view, it must be based on differences between short and long rates of interest, which depend on methods of financing as well as on the amount of financing. He believes that monetary policy and interest rates operate in part through an adjustment effect on businessmen's desired capital stock. In this regard, its countercyclical effects may be much like those of the Swedish investment tax, probably concentrated upon construction.

The main objections to expansive monetary policy as a recovery measure are its effects on the balance of payments—causing a decline in international reserves—and to the size of the changes necessary to produce appreciable results. Also, even when successful, monetary policy has structural consequences which may be disliked, since some fields are more sharply affected than others.

The fifth participant raised two points. The first was a possible conflict between stabilization policy and long-run growth rates. He suspects that, if stabilization policy operates effectively against booms, some of the LDC's may be able to catch up with the industrial countries, but many others will not. His second point related to the investment tax, which he had himself proposed in Japan as an alternative to the existing cartel control of steel prices. The rise in the price of steel and the profits of steel producers during a boom acts like a private tax on Japanese investment, and vice versa during recessions.

The sixth participant inquired about the effectiveness of the Swedish system of direct controls. As is well known, both monetary and fiscal policy are aggregative, and he himself found in selectivity the main merit of direct controls. In particular, a great deal is heard in his country about the Swedish system of controlling investment, both geographically and by sectors, so as to maintain full employment with a minimun of forced migration and wage inflation. He has himself admired this system from afar, as have many of his countrymen. However, he wonders how it works in practice.

The seventh and last participant found it illogical to discuss stabilization policies in such general terms as many speakers had done. He felt that a number of the policies mentioned had other purposes as well. Also, he believed that much could be said for stabilizing such economic variables as the price level, the balance of payments, and income distribution. Stabilizing these, however, may create unemployment and end as destabilization for part of the population. How should such dilemmas be resolved?

Professor Lundberg opened his reply by discounting monetary policy, again in the context of econometric modelbuilding. In Sweden, monetary policy means largely credit rationing, and changes in the availability of credit are more important than changes in interest rates. He wondered how econometricians could adapt their models to deal with such situations of imbalance between supply and demand.

Lundberg admitted to concern about the allocation and growth implications of his country's economic policies. In Sweden, profits are drained off into government pension funds, leaving private firms dependent on government credits. Clearly, the Swedish Government has had no great interest in encouraging savings, which, from the distributional viewpoint, are made largely by the "wrong" people. But what about investment incentives? He wished it were possible to replace the investment tax with the more flexible steel price (mentioned by one participant), except for its distributional implications. The investment tax is clumsy in that it gives rise to speculation about the *timing* of changes in policy. It has increased the gap between short-term and long-term interest rates, but does not seem otherwise to have affected prices.

In the Swedish context, there may indeed have been some conflict between stabilization and growth. Probably investment and growth were both too low in the 1950's, but this mistake is not being repeated in the 1960's.

The last question Lundberg answered, again in a Swedish context, related to unemployment and the definition of full employment. Too low an unemployment rate means inefficient, high-cost labor. Even if it raises the measured growth rate, it does so at a high price in turnover and training expenses. Sweden's active labor-market policy tries to combine mobility with unemployment rates no higher than 2 or 2½ per cent; the Government pays the travel and retraining costs of workers who move or change jobs. The policy has proved very popular in Sweden, and the civil servants in charge leave wide powers in deciding on retraining, moving, and subsidization policies. They can even decide whether people or factories should be moved. Perhaps a still lower unemployment level could be arrived at, but only at a considerable cost in labor mobility.

## XVI. Suggestions for Further Research.

Following the presentation (by Professor Bronfenbrenner) of a draft of the present summary, Professor Hickman, as chairman of the final Conference session, requested suggestions for further research. The following ideas were presented.

*Professor Spaventa:* (a) The effect of the EEC upon the cyclical performances of the three major EEC countries of France, Germany, and Italy; (b) the influence of political factors on the imperfect synchronization of these countries' cycles in the past, and the outlook for future synchronization; (c) a detailed comparison of econometric models for these three countries, with possible explanation of the causes for any differences found; (d) the possible presence of a long cycle of investment in Western Europe, with peaks in 1963 (Germany) and 1966 (Italy) (Such a study should also consider the impact of this long cycle upon short-run stability.)

*Professor Menshikov:* (a) The cyclical behavior of the capitalist pricing mechanism; (b) the cyclical behavior of consumer durable goods industries, especially Western Europe and Japan; (c) the preparation of comparable series for major Western European countries, along the lines developed by the NBER for the United States. (A world-wide clearing house for important economic series relevant for the cycle might also be established.)

*Mr. Maddison:* (a) International transmission of cycles, with special reference to the importance of restored monetary convertibility and of European integration; (b) international comparison of monetary policy; (c) assembly of more and better historical series for cycle research; (d) a conference to study cyclical experience in less developed countries, particularly those of Latin America.

*Professor Matthews:* Forces determining the level of economic activity averaged over the cycle as a whole, and the reasons why this level has been high, by historical standards, in most countries since the War.

*Professor Rosenbluth:* Nontrade channels of international transmission, particularly capital movements and business expectations.

*Dr. Rothschild:* The dampening effects of trade liberalization on business fluctuations, and the extent to which this factor might be expected to continue in operation.

*Dr. Moore:* (a) Evaluation of short-term forecasts, particularly for Western Europe; (b) comparison and integration of the different results of alternative methods of measuring cyclical fluctuations.

*Dr. Daly:* International comparisons of output per worker, for purposes of welfare comparisons, aid programs, etc.

*Professor Fox:* Extension of modeling efforts, to include a large over-all model of the world economy.

*Professor Gelting:* The relation of activity levels, their changes, and the patterns of income distribution.

*Mr. Worswick:* International comparison of employment structures, and of the effect of changes in sectoral employment levels on manpower behavior, including labor supplies.

In addition, Professor Spaventa suggested that the Ford Foundation support the efforts of experts to coordinate modelbuilding efforts in individual countries. At the suggestion of several participants, it was agreed that conference members should keep Professor Hickman informed of important current work on econometric models in relation to stabilization and growth. This information should indicate the language in which each study has been published, or is being prepared.

# NAME INDEX

# SUBJECT INDEX

*Prepared by Toshihisa Toyoda

vii, 287–311, 330–331, 351–355, 531–533

Vacancies, unfilled, *see* Unemployment

Wages, 20–22, 124–126, 213–216, 217–219, 541, 544; *see also* Labor; Phillips curves; Prices; and Unemployment

Wicksellian process, 217–219, 223, 522–523